Above — K'ANG-HSI: GREEN HAWTHORN VASE

Metropolitan Museum of Art   See Text

Below — SUNG: CHUN YAO BULB BOWL.

Metropolitan Museum of Art   See Fig. 318

The Book of
Pottery and Porcelain

BY

WARREN E. COX

3000 illustrations. Pictures selected by the author. Lay-outs by A. M. Lounsbery

VOLUME I

CROWN PUBLISHERS

NEW YORK

This book is dedicated

to

ELIZABETH AND ETHLYN

who kept things going while I had the fun of doing it

INTRODUCTION

This book is both a history and a description of the processes of making pottery, stoneware, soft paste, faïence, "delft," porcelain and other wares together with criticisms of their various appeals and defects, both practically and artistically speaking, and suggestions as to methods for searching out such criticisms. It is intended for all craftsmen who would make things of fired clay, for collectors in any branch of ceramics who would like to widen their general outlook and knowledge, for students of art who are searching in the field of aesthetics for that which man calls beautiful, and finally for the layman who, I hope, will be caught by a little of that interest which already burns so brightly in many men.

Like all ancient arts of world-wide appeal, the art of ceramics or fired clay has grown about it much mossy bunk that demands a gentle scraping before one can get down to the real beauties that have made it appeal to all sorts of men through all sorts of ages. The very names which we must use for different kinds of fired clay vessels or figures, for the different processes with which they are made and for the colors applied to them are taken from half a dozen different languages because certain things were discovered or were famous in one place while others were famous in a far distant place and habit has associated these places with these things. We call the ox-blood color of certain K'ang Hsi period vases *"sang de boeuf"* because it was greatly appreciated in France during the 18th century and also because it was the fashion in England and America during the 18th century to think a French name added considerable class and distinction to anything. We also call it *"lang yao,"* *lang* being a Chinese name, perhaps of a viceroy of the times or perhaps of a family of potters. We are not certain which. And *yao* meaning simply ware. Thus we shall find words and names from France, Italy, China and many other places in such common use that we have to continue to use them to make ourselves understood.

Another thing is obvious at once and that is that few so-called authorities agree even on their definitions of such basic terms as *"soft paste"* or *"porcelain"*; the latter being derived from an Italian term used for a shell, that of the "purple-fish" or "Venus-shell" called also *"porcellana"* because "the curved shape of the upper surface resembles the curve of a pig's back,"—to quote from the Century Dictionary, because the Chinese ware brought to Venice earlier than the 15th century was thought to resemble this shell in texture. The term *"soft paste"* is properly applied to an imitation of porcelain which really was not at all like the original Chinese article either in composition or characteristics. Thus the often heard term *"soft paste porcelain"* is anomalous and contradictory to begin with. We need not now go into the various discussions concerning whether porcelain is necessarily translucent, whether it is porous, whether it must necessarily be white, etc., etc., for we are doing that towards the end of this book so that the reader, knowing how these terms came about, and how they were generally used, can make up his own mind in the end as to how they should be used. Meanwhile we shall leave the hair splitting of definitions to those who are interested in them. We shall try also to be consistent, though this we do not promise as it is almost an inhuman achievement save perhaps to lawyers, schoolmasters and successful businessmen. Most porcelain is translucent but we are certainly not going to throw out of this category some Ming wares which are so dense and thick as not to be. Those gentlemen who argue for translucence as a needed attribute answer that, if such porcelains were split to thin enough flakes, they would be translucent. We can only answer sadly that good authorities say that anything under God's heavens can, under these conditions, be called translucent. Gold, as an example, is quite a dense substance, yet gold leaf is quite translucent and of greenish hue.—But let us waste no more time with such nonsensical arguments. My warning is simply and solely that the reader must be tolerant with me because the words at my disposal are bound to fall far short of making everything perfectly clear. How can they help but do so, when they start out by being confused and far from clear themselves?—The man who has never held a piece of porcelain in his hand and looked at it could never understand what it is from a word description. The man who has never made a piece of porcelain can never really understand it either. All we really attempt, therefore, is to round up a few ideas which may be intriguing.

A lady came into my shop a while ago and asked me if I would show her my "best vase." There were three or four I thought of at once but finally brought out one and you should have seen her face fall. It wasn't a big vase and, aside from firing, I don't believe it could have taken the potter more than a few hours to have made it. It was not perfect. It wouldn't even make a very good vase for holding flowers. She asked me why I liked it and, knowing that she was an intelligent and understanding person, I undertook to tell her to the extent of about three hours of conversation, or perhaps we had better say oration. As the reader may imagine, my success was not of the best, accomplishing in her mind, very likely, a lowering of opinion of me rather than a raising of opinion of the vase. She was courteous but I notice she has not been back to ask about the second-best vase.

In the book, I shall probably not be one bit more successful in telling why I like this vase and dislike that one; such things are entirely personal and cannot very well be defined. Why does a man love one girl and pass another without a look? Is it associations? Is it his own endocrinal condition? Or is it, as the ancients contended, all in the stars? Certainly no one could tell by looking at him. And just as certainly he, himself, would be the very last to give a reasonable accounting. However, with half a chance he could tell you veritably a thousand reasons—none of which would be worth much to you. Therefore, as I consider the matter in cold blood, I don't believe one man or woman will ever turn collector or maker of potteries because of reading this book. I doubt if all these little words will make one reader love one vase the more or the less and I shall probably accomplish nothing more than a reduced opinion of myself. However, my kind publisher has given me the chance and, like the lover, I cannot resist putting down my thousand reasons for that which is largely reasonless.

There are some terribly dry parts of this book, not at all worth reading, and I don't have to tell you to skip them for you will anyhow, but let me tell you that I have saved you, the reader, an awful lot that is dryer yet, by making charts of much of this sort of material and by glossing over much scholarly proof of this or that point. I may add that my publisher has saved you more. Naturally I don't thank him now but probably will ten years from now.

As you probably know, all *"Introductions"* are written *after* a book is finished. It is only when the hull is launched that the leaks are discovered. And I am not the first to discover that one can get in apologies for shortcomings in the front of a book and get them read while after the reader has ploughed through some quarter to half a million words he gets into a state of semi-consciousness in which all the apologies in the world will do no good. However, they are not of much use anyhow so let us proceed.

Acknowledgments

Thanks should be extended to Charles Henry, through whom I met Jack Blitzer, who took me to lunch with Joseph Aronson, who brought Nat Wartels to my place, who in turn made this book possible. Many others have contributed, though in some cases without knowing it, such as those early instructors H. Kevorkian, the late Demottes both father and son, Matachia Miya, Oto Fukushima, the late Isaac Voron, the late Lee Van Ching and his son, L. Y. Lee as well as Quill Jones, the late Dr. Riefstahl and Dr. Berthold Laufer, and my instructors in painting Emil Carlsen and Harry Watrous both of whom have also passed away before their valued criticisms could be obtained. A very real debt is also owed to those great authorities who wrote articles for me in the 14th Edition of the Encyclopaedia Britannica and who, each in his own field, discussed various phases of aesthetics and also pots with a very young and not very well grounded "editor," who knew only just enough to trot to the best men available. These are too numerous to list but outstanding among them besides Dr. Laufer were R. L. Hobson, Percy Gardner, Bernard Rackham, Herbert Read, Ananda K. Coomaraswamy and H. R. H. Hall.

To the Metropolitan Museum of Art as a whole and to the staff individually a great debt is owed. To Evelyn B. Grier and her staff together with all those who aided in the selection of photographs to be used in illustration and for providing notes on color, period and sizes of the hundreds upon hundreds of objects too much thanks cannot be extended. Mr. Theodore Y. Hobby gave constant and unflagging help and advice in his kindness and enthusiasm for Far Eastern ceramics, a field in which he is leading authority. Mr. Alan Priest, Miss Josephine Hadley, Mr. James J. Rorimer, Miss Gisela M. A. Richter, Miss Christine Alexander, Mr. S. H. Han and Lt. Commander William Christopher Hayes were all very helpful in their kind assistance at various times over the past five years as was also the Vice-Director, Mr. Horace H. F. Jayne.

But the Metropolitan Museum was no more helpful than were many of the museums all over this country and such authorities as Mr. Howard Hollis of the Cleveland Museum of Art, Mr. James Marshall Plumer of Ann Arbor, Michigan, Mr. Charles Fabens Kelley of the Art Institute of Chicago, Miss Alice Wilson Frothingham of the Hispanic Society N. Y., Mr. Kojiro Tomita of the Boston Museum, the late Mr. John Lodge and also Mr. Carl W. Bishop of the Freer Gallery of Art, Washington, Mr. Langdon Warner of the Fogg Museum, Cambridge and Mr. Richard E. Fuller of the Seattle Museum should be especially thanked for their aid in both text matter and illustration.

Again the greatest of thanks must be given to many who are, although in the trade, among our really studious and serious scholars in their various fields, and who devoted much valuable time to consultation, help and advice, and to these I must express my gratitude. Such friends as Mr. C. Edward Wells, Mr. Walter Hochstadter, Mr. C. F. Yau, Mr. C. T. Loo, the late Mr. Zado Noorian, Mr. Benjamin Ginsburg, Mr. Quill Jones, Mr. Frank Stoner, Mr. Frederick Lunning, Mr. Howard Back, Baron van Haersolte, The Bluett Brothers, Mr. Morris S. Cuthbertson, Mr. Nasli Heeramaneck, Mr. Ralph M. Chait, Mr. Ellis Munroe, the late Mr. John Gibbons, Mr. H. Kevorkian and Mr. Lem Sec Tsang have been invaluable.

Finally among collectors again there are those who, not content with mere ownership, are serious students and who have helped me immeasurably and to whom I owe the fullest of appreciation for their assistance. These run into a great many but outstanding among them are the late Mrs. Christian R. Holmes, Mrs. Ogden K. Shannon, Jr., Mr. Delos Chappell, Mr. Benjamin d'Ancona, Mr. Fritz Low-Beer, the late Mr. Samuel T. Peters, the late Mr. Ernest Dane, the late Mr. Shepard K. DeForest, Mr. Nai-Chi Chang, Mr. Edgar Worch, Mrs. Charles Porter Wilson, Mr. Diedrich Abbes, Mr. K. M. Semon, Mrs. Louise Higgins, Miss Ethelyn C. Stewart, Mr. George Eumorfopoulos, Sir Percival David and Mrs. Warren E. Cox, from whose private collections I have in several cases illustrated a number of objects.

For technical advice throughout I have raised all questions to Mr. Walter Howat who has given me exact and practical advice. No one could be better equipped than he to assist in this field. However, Mr. Paul Freigang also lent aid in several matters of both technical and aesthetic consideration. To both of these friends I owe a debt of gratitude.

In conclusion undoubtedly the man who had most to do with this book, with the education of the author, with his opportunities with the Encyclopaedia Britannica and with the actual making of a large part of the Warren E. Cox Collection, is my good father, William J. Cox.

CONTENTS OF VOLUME ONE

LIST OF COLOR PLATES

DEFINITIONS

ALUMINA is CHINA CLAY or KAOLIN. It fires white and opaque and can withstand high temperatures. Bernard Leach says that some 10% to 40% is present in most bodies. It is this content which actually determines whether or not a ware is porcelain.

BALL CLAY is a plastic clay which stands high temperatures without wilting.

BASALT WARE is the name given to a certain ware of hard black quality by Wedgwood.

BELLEEK was made in Ireland and a similar ware made chiefly in Trenton, N. J., and called *Lenox* is made of pre-fused feldspar, flint and alkalis in a glassy mass, and is glazed with a very brilliant borosilicate of the alkalis lime, lead and zinc. The firing temperature is considerably below that of other types of so-called "porcelain," though the use of the term is incorrect.

Characteristics

1. It is highly translucent, even more than European soft paste as a rule.
2. It has a natural ivory color.
3. It is easily scratched.
4. It is decorated with gold or low-fired enamels, but recently slip in contrasting color to the body has come into use.

BISCUIT is unglazed porcelain. Unglazed pottery is usually referred to as TERRACOTTA.

BISQUE, *see* PORCELAIN.

BONE CHINA, *see* ENGLISH SOFT PASTE.

CHINA, *see* PORCELAIN.

CHINA CLAY is thought to be decomposed granite and is made up of silica and alumina and appears as a white amorphous powder. It is usually hydraulically mined. It is this clay that gives plasticity to the mixture before firing, but it is the nonfusible part of the mixture which the Chinese call *Kaolin*.

CHINA STONE, or *Petuntse*, as the Chinese call it, is mined and quarried like stone. It is sold in four grades:
1. "Hard purple" (white with purplish tinge and hard).
2. "Mild purple" (the same but softer).
3. "Dry white" or soft (a soft white rock).
4. "Buff" (similar but with slight yellow tinge).

Silica is about 80% in the colored varieties and 74% in the white. Alumina is about 18% in the white and 7% to 10% in the others. The china stone gives the body its translucency. Its function is that of flux. The Chinese say that Kaolin is the "bone" and Petuntse the "flesh" of porcelain. (Of course, this does not mean that it has any actual bone in its makeup in the Far East.) It is not always clear in the minds of students that china clay turns hard and china stone turns soft in the firing, exchanging characteristics as it were.

CHINESE SOFT PASTE is a porcelain to which has been added steatite (soap stone) or some similar substance which produces a softer ware fired at a lower temperature. Soft paste slip may also be added to a hard porcelain.

Characteristics

1. It is lighter in weight.
2. Its body can be scratched with a steel point.
3. It often has a slightly undulating surface.
4. It usually has a lower fired glaze, sometimes inclined to craze.

CLAY is a plastic substance composed largely of aluminum and silica and is simply decomposed rocks usually also containing some iron and also vegetable remains in its natural state.

CREAM WARE, *see* QUEEN'S WARE.

DELFT, *see* POTTERY.

EARTHENWARE is correctly used to name pottery whether glazed or unglazed in its more definite sense excluding all porcelains and stonewares. It is incorrectly used in the trade to designate a semivitreous or white ware sold to hotels and restaurants for heavy usage. Its composition is about 13% English ball clay, 13% feldspar, 25% English china clay, 10% North Carolina kaolin, 6% Florida kaolin and 33% flint and the firing is done at about 2,200° F. or pyrometric cone 8, the glost firing at 2,150° (cone 5) and the decorating at 1,350° (cone .017). The glaze is a boro-silicate of the alkalis, lime, lead and zinc in various compounds. The ware is similar to that made in Staffordshire, England, except that it is higher fired. Much of it is made in the U. S. at East Liverpool. Practically no underglaze decoration is used. This ware might more appropriately be called *white stoneware*.

ENAMELS are low fired colored glazes usually applied over harder glazes. When they are used over a biscuit the distinction between them and glazes becomes indefinite though generally speaking they are supposed to be less hard.

ENGLISH SOFT PASTE or BONE CHINA is a hybrid composition in which china clay is partly replaced by ashes of calcined bones. It should, of course, not really ever be called "china" for the Chinese never made any such ware, nor, in a sense, should it be called "soft paste" but habit has formed the two designations and they will probably continue to be used.

Characteristics

1. It is easily scratched but is not so soft as European soft paste.
2. It is more opaque than European soft paste yet it has some translucence.
3. It can be made nearly white.

ENGOBES are slips.

EUROPEAN SOFT PASTE was originally made in attempts to imitate real Chinese porcelain in such examples as "Medici porcelain," St. Cloud, Rouen, Chantilly, etc. Kaolin had not been discovered in the western hemisphere and the body was simply mixed with a frit or ground up glass in various proportions in an attempt to obtain translucency. The firing was done at very low temperatures, about those in which glass will melt.

Characteristics

1. It is easily scratched with a steel blade.
2. It is likely to warp in the kiln.
3. It is highly translucent.

4. It can be made nearly white but usually greenish or greyish by transmitted light.

The French term for it, and they were really chief makers of it, is *pâte tendre*.

FAÏENCE, *see* POTTERY.

FELDSPAR or FELSPAR is any one of several minerals, silicates of aluminum with potassium, sodium or calcium. It is usually white or pinkish and it melts at about 1200° to 1300° C. It loses its alkaline content through decomposition and then becomes china clay.

FLINT is the hard stone which we have all seen at times in the form of pebbles on a beach, but there are different flints and not all are useful to the potter. Some of the best come from France though there are many sources. They are calcined (heated), which turns them opaque and white and softens them so that they can be more readily crushed into powder which can be mixed with the clay. The ground flint when mixed with water appears a thin liquid paste of whitish or greyish color. It can withstand very high temperatures.

FLUX is a substance used to promote the melting of metals or minerals. It also causes overglaze colors to vitrify. Such materials as lead, borax or lime are so used.

FRIT is simply ground glass of various kinds and is composed of silica and alkaline salts.

GLOST FIRING is firing of the glaze often at a lower temperature than the body was fired, though many wares are fired only once.

GRÈS is the French term for stoneware.

HARD PASTE means PORCELAIN or CHINA as opposed to SOFT PASTE.

KAOLIN, *see* ALUMINA.

LEAD as galena or lead ore containing sulphide, red lead, white lead, litharge and massicot or lead monoxide of reddish or yellowish color, are all used as fluxing agents for low and medium temperatures. The metal fluxes at 326° C. It is, of course, highly poisonous and must be used with care.

LUSTRE is a thin metallic sheen applied usually over a tin glaze. It consists actually of finely divided metals of various sorts, and is fired at low, reducing atmospheres.

MAJOLICA or MAIOLICA, *see* POTTERY.

PARIAN WARE is a vitreous porcelain left

unglazed and composed of one part china-clay and two parts feldspar. It does not in the least resemble Parian marble from which the name is derived.

PÂTE-SUR-PÂTE is a French term for the process of building low relief decorations by repeated touches of a brush charged with thin slip. It is perhaps best known in some Minton wares.

PETUNTSE, *see* CHINA STONE.

PORCELAIN or CHINA are synonymous as true porcelain was found and developed in China and, though this country made other wares, it was porcelain to which Europeans referred when they used the term china. It is made of fusible silicates of alumina (called petuntse) and nonfusible silicates of alumina (called kaolin), called by the English "china stone" and "china clay."

Characteristics

1. It is not porous even when unglazed.
2. The body cannot be scratched with a steel knife.
3. It is naturally of a whitish color caused by the kaolin but the body may be stained many colors by mineral oxides.
4. It is generally more translucent than *pottery* or *stoneware* and less so than *"soft paste porcelain,"* though translucency is not an absolute test for some of the denser porcelains are not visibly translucent even in fairly thin flakes.
5. It is fired in saggers at first for about 24 hours at low temperature and then raised to about 1300° C. or in some cases to about 1450° C. for another 20 to 30 hours. Present day spark plug insulators, etc., are fired to 2650 to 3000° F. (cone 17 to 30).

Porcelain may be left unglazed and is then called *biscuit, bisque* or, in some cases by some English and American collectors particularly if it is of fine texture, *parian* ware.

Porcelain may also be originally fired with a glaze on it or may have a softer glaze added in a second firing and may also be decorated with enamels in a third firing as low as 700° to 800°.

POTTERY. 1. The term may be used inclusively to cover all types of baked wares, earthen, stone and porcelain. 2. It can also be applied to a factory in which any or all wares are made and fired. 3. More definitely it is used to name all classes of baked clay wares which are not stoneware or porcelain.

It is a slightly calcareous clay which when baked even at low temperatures hardens somewhat and has the following characteristics:

1. It is always porous.
2. It can be scratched with a knife or sometimes even with a hard wood stick.
3. It is opaque save in very thin flakes such as those ground for microscopy.
4. The color is usually reddish brown, yellow, brown or grey depending upon the content of the clay with which it was made and the temperature under which it was fired.
5. It may be sun baked.

Pottery is synonymous with *earthenware, red-ware, black-ware, primitive ware* and *terra cotta.*

When coated with glaze, which is usually of the lead type as pottery is frequently not fired at a high enough temperature to volatilize salt, it is called the same. When covered with a slip or when it has decorations on it in slip, it may be called *slip-ware.* When tin is mixed in the lead glaze so as to make it opaque to hide the body of the ware, it may be called *faïence, majolica* (or *maiolica*), or *delft* as the case may be depending chiefly upon the geographical location.

QUEEN'S WARE is plastic clay, freed as much as possible from iron so that it can be near white, but with some quartz and feldspar, and sometimes a little kaolin is added. It is fired in saggers but at fairly low temperatures. Is also called *"cream ware."* Was first made by Wedgwood.

SAGGERS are boxes of fire-clay into which objects to be fired are put for protection against direct contact with the flames. The word is spelled in various ways.

SALT GLAZED WARE is, as its name implies, a ware which is glazed by throwing salt into the kiln, which volatilizes at about 800° to 900° C. and deposits itself upon the surface of the ware as a glaze. These temperatures are higher than those at which many earthenwares are fired and, therefore, we usually find salt glaze on a stoneware or some type of porcelaneous ware.

Characteristics

1. The glaze can never deposit itself perfectly evenly and the surface is always slightly roughened.

2. The glaze is very thin and transparent so that all oddities of the biscuit show through it.

SHERDS or SHARDS are pieces of broken pottery and they are often ground and introduced into the body instead of grog or silica as a means of reducing shrinkage.

SLIP is simply a thin mixture of clay that is the consistency of thick cream. It is frequently identically the same composition as the body but thinned down with water.

SOFT PASTE, *see* EUROPEAN SOFT PASTE, CHINESE SOFT PASTE, ENGLISH SOFT PASTE.

STEATITE or TALC is a soft friable rock with slight plasticity and is used in glazes and bodies. It was thought the Far Eastern "Soft paste" was made with it but this is incorrect. It is a magnesium silicate, also known as SOAPSTONE, and is #1 on the Moh's scale. In glazes it makes viscous silicates with a long range of vitrification.

STONEWARE or GRÈS is a high fired and porcelaneous type of ware which differs from porcelain only in that its materials have been less well purified. It is fired usually without saggers at around 1190°.

Characteristics

1. Its natural color is ash-like or with higher temperatures red-brown.
2. It cannot be scratched readily with a steel point on the body.
3. It is nonporous even when unglazed.
4. A superior type called by the French "grès kaoliné" is really porcelain and the color of ivory.
5. It rings higher than soft paste.

TERRA COTTA, *see* POTTERY.

VITREOUS WARE in the present day designates a non-porous harder ware for hotels and restaurants. It is made of about 15% feldspar, 38% flint, 6% ball clay, 40% of china clay or kaolin and 1% of whiting and fired at 2,300° F. making a "stony" type of vitrification rather than a "glassy" type.

Thanks for assistance must be given Mr. Bernard Leach as much of the above material comes from his very excellent book, *A Potter's Book,* which is a fine and scientific handbook for practicing potters. Also to my friend Mr. Walter Howat who has been of constant help upon all technical questions in this book.

CHAPTER I

FUNDAMENTAL AESTHETIC APPEALS

CERAMICS, the art of making things in clay and baking them, is among the most ancient arts of man. Before man learned to chip stone (the paleolithic periods) he had learned to make clay cups. Young children instinctively love to make mud pies and from the mud pie to the mud cup is a short step. These first potteries have gone but the most ancient, as proven by the layers of earth from which they were dug, are so sophisticated in design that we can only conclude that thousands of years of practice must have preceded their making. Some are so good, in fact, that they have set styles of design which have lasted through many thousands of years.

Ceramics is not only one of the most ancient of arts but one of the most important. Here we meet with a strange misconception on the part of many; that the only works of fine art are those done in oil colors on canvas. The reason for this is that after the Renaissance, during which great craftsmen and great painters were honored equally, and great painters were proud to declare themselves craftsmen, the Gothic architecture with its slender columns and lack of wall space left no room for paintings. The Dark Ages provided few wealthy patrons for the painters. And even later when pictures became popular in the Low Countries, the rooms were small and wall space confined. Thus painting was no longer an applied art or a necessary art and it became a necessity for the painter to do "easel pictures," and to practice art for art's sake. Soon a defensive snobbery appeared and the term "fine art" began to imply that all other art was less fine because it served not art but utility. This is false reasoning but purposeless art became "fine" while all other art was classed as "minor." Even sculptors were excluded and one heard the reference, "Artists and sculptors," as though the latter were not also artists.

I believe that this condition is directly responsible for much misunderstanding and lack of appreciation of the arts. In the great periods no such distinction was made and, as I have written before, the Greeks did as fine things for a pediment as for a pedestal. The Egyptians, Romans, people of India and of China value a knife, a cup, a perfume vial or a carpet as much as a painting. Let us approach the study of this art, which is the very embodiment of form and color, without prejudice and see what ages of man have done with it.

To try to define beauty is like trying to stuff life itself into a box. We may like a thing one day and dislike it intensely the next, and the causes of our

1

likes and dislikes are subconscious and cannot be defined. Croce and others who have tried to define art, beauty, taste, etc., are attempting the impossible, for these are not single things around which we can draw a line and say that which lies within belongs and that which lies without does not. There is no one thing which is beauty; there are thousands of beauties and more are added every day. But I prefer a broader term and would suggest that we consider some of the unlimited number of *appeals* that men have enjoyed through ceramics.

. Man derives his happiness in life through the normal functioning of his body and is likely to associate the pleasant experiences of existence and of procreation with what he calls beautiful or appealing. Certain bowls make our mouths water for a fine soup, a stoneware tankard makes us think of cool beer, or a smooth surface and soft curves may consciously or unconsciously recall a beautiful woman's body. I am reminded of a circumspect lady who handed me a globular vase covered with a glaze called by the Chinese "ostrich egg" or "chicken skin" and saying, "Isn't it perfectly thrilling? Just hold it in your hands and feel it!" I sincerely hope she did not guess what went through my mind and the vase was no less beautiful for it.

The wise Chinese have a saying that the proper size for a tea-cup is that of a young girl's breast and they have a vase which is called "woman's form." Is there not an obvious amount of such appeal in a Rubens nude or a Franz Hals drinking scene? And perhaps in the ceramic arts it is less obvious, less conscious and, therefore, longer lasting and more intriguing.

Just as death is part of life, so the ancient potters made their wares also to serve in death or to help carry life over into the tomb and to some of these we owe our knowledge of past ages, of the aspirations of these men, of their hopes, their pleasures and their pursuits in peace and war. But it is interesting to note that the ceramic arts were never any aid to man in war. Weapons were made of wood, stone, brass, iron and many other substances, but pottery stands alone in being nondestructive.

First Developments

It is safe to say that the older appeals are the stronger. Man instinctively mistrusts that which is new and very little do any of us change from the habits of thought of our parents though we may strut and declare that we are original beings. Let us consider, therefore, the most primitive pots we know.

Certainly the first cups made were hand patted and took the place of leaves and shells. The first were sun baked and later it was found, probably when it was attempted to cook food in them, that they hardened with the fire.

Weaving is probably a less old art but still very ancient and where baskets were made an attempt may have been made to make them watertight by applying clay to the inside. Possibly again the basket was burned away and it was found that the clay had hardened. In any event many primitive potters have used mats to help them form clay vessels. Most of the earliest of such wares are more or less globular or pointed-bottom beakers, and man, having become used to the mat surface, imitated it consciously in many of the earliest known wares.

In Africa in one tribe the women make round pots by patting the clay over an original pot, allowing it to dry partly and then slipping the model out and pressing in the lip to form a narrower mouth. Perhaps a head or round stone was used for the first model.

Another primitive method is that of coiling a sort of rope of clay around and around on itself and finally scraping the inside and outside surface to flatten it. This is related to basket weaving again, of course, and it naturally led to cylindrical forms. In certain instances in America we will find that beautiful patterns were also developed. The scraper was a natural parent of the templet which later was not so beneficial, as it often took away all the impressions of the potter's hands.

The wheel may have come into being through making coiled vessels when it was found easy to place them on a stone so that they could be turned round and round. Later a stone wheel was made in truer form and a helper kept it turning, and then came the foot operated wheel of wood, the use of water power and of more modern means. However, the wheel itself is just about the same instrument as that used thousands of years ago. The power of electricity may have made the work easier, but the relationship of the speed and the action of the artist's hands in "throwing" a vessel is so delicately felt that some modern potters prefer the old foot wheel to power driven ones.

There are few more sensitive instruments than the potter's wheel and the clay can respond as sensitively to the potter's slightest touch as does the string of a violin or the brush of a Chinese painter. Every nervous tremor, every ghost of a touch is translated through the fingers into the imperishable clay which, if treated properly, will freeze it forever for the eyes of those who understand.

The mold is a much later method of making figures and also vase forms. It should never be used to make a round vase which can better be thrown on the wheel. Unfortunately for the art a mold is a cheap short cut and always is called into use when commercialism demands a quantity of pieces in one shape. When a sculptor does make use of a mold he should, of course, go over his work in detail removing suture marks, sharpening details and putting the hand of man freshly upon the work again. But at best this is repetition and his work will lack the first spontaneity. Moreover, casts should not be made from metal or wood or any other substance than clay or it will be obvious that they are not of clay structure or technique.

With these simple processes the potter makes his wares. There was a reason for everything he did and "modern art" creators would do well to consider some of the whys and wherefores before discarding them. As an instance, it was found at an early date in all places that a pot without a foot-rim would be easily broken when it was set down and therefore foot-rims came into general use. It was also found that if the throwing of a pot was not exactly true, the foot-rim could be slightly ground to make it stand straight. Different potters made these foot-rims in different ways and the collector can tell by the rim alone if a piece is likely to be of Near Eastern, of a certain period of Chinese potting, of Korean or Japanese workmanship.

Methods for handling a pottery vessel are interesting. A globular jar can be readily lifted only by using both hands or by grasping the lip-rim and therefore handles were found necessary or at least convenient. The simplest handle is the slightly curved projection to be held between thumb and hand on the Han period Chinese food bowls. Loop handles attached to the shoulder of a vessel and brought up to the neck or lip-rim are more structural, but all handles are easily broken. The bottle neck is easily grasped and when designed properly has strength through good structure. But it is dif-

FIG. 1. Rice bowls placed in the tomb for the use of the deceased. These are of heavy, red body and with green iridescent glaze of silver tone. Warren E. Cox Collection.

ficult to pour liquids into a neck small enough to be readily grasped and therefore flaring lip-rims were made to act as funnels. This flaring rim became a hazard in itself and was treated in various ways to avoid breakage. Another form is the al-berello developed first in Mesopotamia or Persia and this is simply a cylindrical jar with concave waist small enough to get a hold on. These jars could be stood on a shelf side by side and almost touching yet could be easily removed, as there is room to get one's fingers between them. Therefore, the form came to be used as an apothecary jar in Spain, Italy and elsewhere. A modification of the bottle

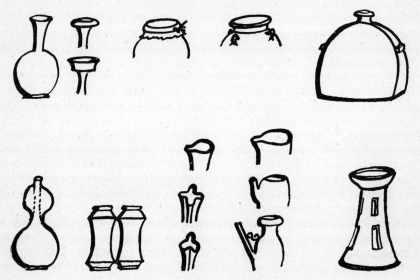

FIGS. 2–8. Elements of Form.

is the Chinese gourd shape with a bulging neck which holds more contents and yet permits an easy hold about the waist. Still another form that is well nigh universal is the pilgrim bottle, a circular flattened vessel with small mouth and often having loops for suspension. This form is undoubtedly derived from metal containers which were slung to a saddle or pack.

Pouring devices also dictate restrictions of form. At times the flaring lip of a bottle is pinched up in one place to make pouring from it easier. Some bottles, such as the small marbled clay T'ang one which I sold the Metropolitan Museum have the lips so pinched as to form quatrefoil or trefoil shapes. The pinching up of the lip was also used on cylindrical and globular pots and this became deeper until it was covered over and became a spout. But it should be remembered that all spouts are easily broken, if they are not made particularly sturdy and well supported.

Methods for covering also have developed many types of pottery covers, prominent rims over which a cloth or leather could be drawn and bound tightly, and various loops about the shoulder to help bind down covers. These should always be distinguished from "handles," as they are often called although they may be so small that one could not get the little finger through one. Covers also had to be so designed for pouring vessels that they would not fall off when the vessel was tipped.

Supporting collars, stands and legs were worked out so that vessels could be stood over fire. Thus we see large spool-like forms all over the world used to hold the pointed and round-bottomed vessels, tall reticulated hollow columns in Anau and Japan, and the well known three-legged "Ting" form of China.

THE USEFUL BEAUTIFUL

Early potters considered the practical reasons for forms and spent very little time on whimsy or endeavors to be different. It would seem, in fact, that the less the potter paid attention to artistic considerations the more pure, moving and enduring was his art. No vase form has ever lasted through the ages if it was not the result of such practical reasoning. What beauty then can lie in such things? How can appeals occur where there was not even the intention to create an appeal?

Michelangelo said that a piece of sculpture should be such that it could be rolled down hill without breaking. He did not follow out his theory but good potters did. We all dislike seeing things which look unstructural. The old broken-handled pitcher sits on the shelf so long that we get sick of it and throw it out. When we buy a new one, we look at it to see if the handle is more strongly made. It is not so much the losing of the pitcher but the pity that it was perfectly good except for that broken handle. Thus a piece of pottery should be so made that it at least appears to have good, sound structure.

You may say, "But surely everyone knows that!" Yet we will find that among the worst offenders in this respect are the so-called "classic" Greek vases which we have been taught to look upon as the greatest of ceramics.

I say that a work of art should be beautiful, satisfying and useful so long as it is recognizable and should meet the onslaught of time and usage with dignity, collapsing utterly rather than fall into the hideous wreckage of crippled distortion. It may be argued that if a thing is beautiful, what does anyone care how it will break? The answer is that one instinctively knows the weak points and subconsciously realizes what it will look like when broken. We cannot deny the appeal of structure.

The appeal of fragility is a corollary to the above. Certain works of art are like a "Prince Rupert's drop" or "glass tear" and will endure forever unless the careless hand destroys them and then they fly to pieces in utter destruction. Eggshell porcelain and Venetian glass are of this sort and it is astonishing how they have come down through the ages when handled by hands more roughly suited to the sword or knife than to their delicacy. An ear, a nose or a foot missing disgusts to the point of discard while the threat of utter demolishment seems to command respect and therein lies the appeal of fragility. Delicacy and fragility in some women may also influence our general judgment of these qualities in a work of art.

There is a human appeal in objects which show the hand of man in their manufacture or use. The arm of an old chair, the handle of a knife, a silver snuff box or an old walking stick recall love, respect and honor. They have served well and something of the character of those who have owned them has entered into them through the years. Of course our ceramic arts do not show such wear but they do bring out the character of the men who made them. In Japan tea-cups are made in what at first appear to be crazy shapes but when held properly they are found to fit the hand perfectly. To obliterate the form and even accidents which the potter put into a work is to sacrifice the human element for the purpose of gaining a cold perfection less appealing to the open mind of a true connoisseur.

There is also *tactile appeal* which is as important to some as visual appeal. As a young man I disliked oil paintings because they looked sticky like "molasses on sand paper" as I used to say. Later when I saw a Chinese gentleman lightly run his fingers over the old silk of a fine Sung painting, I found that there are others who understand this. So it is that some wares feel right in weight and form and some glazes are far more pleasant to the touch than others. Those potteries which can be handled gain great appeal and the real lover of such wares cannot be contented with looking at them. He must pick them up, turn them around, run his hand over the glaze, look at the foot, stand them on the table and frequently even then he keeps his hand on them turning them this way and that as he looks at them. One can easily tell how much a person likes a certain ware and how much he understands it by watching him handle it. And then there are those who can add to the value of a vase simply by the way they handle it. Such was Oto Fukishima, my first master.

Patination also has its appeal for we distrust the new. A soldier will work for days with saddle soap on his leather to make it look old. All boys will scuff their new shoes to take off the newness. Most men hate a new hat. The sculptor will patinate his bronze to make it fit better into the landscape, not for any purpose of faking age. The Chinese Taoists and Zen Buddhists have perhaps thought this out more clearly. They have a belief that one should live in the flow of the universe; should live naturally and to be rather than to seem. They say, I have heard, that a vase should be such that it might be put down in the woods and passed as a mushroom or some other natural growth.

Natural patination is the benediction of nature bestowed as a mark of honor which a fine work of art wears to prove its worthy age. Few of the weak survive to show it, as will, I fear, be proven by many of our modern creations. Upon no other work of man does nature place such brilliant and varicolored fire as upon the common pot of clay glazed with a bit of sand. It would seem that the original ordeal of flame which made it is recalled in the blaze of light.

But, it may be claimed, the potter had no knowledge of this, and that is true. However, a fundamentally poor pot, with glaze chipping off and ill made, would not wear its decorations any better than a war profiteer.

I delighted in reading in Lin Yutang's "The Importance of Living" about an old Chinese rule for the painting of rocks beneath pine trees. It seems that such rocks should be painted so that they will look very old and "stupid," old and solid and dull. Such rocks must wear their moss well and all the moss in the world would not help the brittleness of our sharp city stones. The artist then, although he has no part in making the patination itself, can, nevertheless, make an object which will wear it well, and perhaps a really fine vase can be built which is sturdy enough to last, so natural as to belong to nature itself and as stupid as an old rock under a pine tree.

"Modernists" say that ornamentation is out of place and unnecessary on a work of art and I am the first to agree that many vases are beautiful and most appealing in form, color and texture alone, but who could resist the ornamentation of clay? The vase is turned and smoothed. It has dried to a leather-like consistency and then perhaps been turned and polished. The least scratch can be made even with the fingernail. A clay of a different color and thinner consistency (slip) can be painted on or the vase may be dipped into the slip and have parts scratched away allowing the body to show through. Little patted or pinched up lumps of clay ("barbotine process") can be added to the surface. A glaze or glazes can be applied and decoration over or under these can be made in different colors. It is as hard for a potter to leave the surface of his vase alone as for a boy to resist marking a newly-made cement sidewalk.

An unornamented surface is as unknown as a perfect vacuum in nature. The smoothest pure white stone soon develops stains and cracks which slowly but surely bring it back to harmony with its surroundings in nature. The artificiality of plainness has been a recent cult in decoration and for a short time white rooms were attempted. But a white room is no more restful than a dead calm at sea which is so terrible an ordeal to man's momentum. It is the plainness of prison which punishes to the limits of endurance. What a world this would be if there were no shadows! And, if there are shadows, could they not be indelible and would they not then constitute design? Nature is forever making design before our eyes and we are simply resisting nature and becoming unnatural, if we think we can get along without it. An excellent example of such resistance to nature is the house designed by Frank Lloyd Wright for Edgar Kaufmann. It is built across a brook in a dense grove of trees and the architect made it in the character of great horizontal white slabs of concrete unrelieved save by plain areas of glass. It looks new.

It contradicts all that is about it. It is hard and tiring. It is a challenging place that the aborigines would look upon with fear and mistrust. It is the antithesis of Lin Yutang's "stupid rocks." But never mind, for nature will take care of all that in time although the process will not be a pleasant one.

Of course ornamentation and decoration can be carried too far and can become oppressive or disturbing. We may agree that much Italian majolica with its pictures of nude ladies writhing around among foliage and decorated with scrolls and grotesquerie have their faults. Many feel that perspective which makes a hole in a vase or plate is out of place. *In truth it is dangerous to go much beyond shadows in the decoration of a vase.* Shadows conform to the surface and fit well. Shadows are likely to have colors which contain something of the color of the vase. *Above all they help to define the form rather than distort it.*

Compare the decoration of a "Hawthorn" Chinese blue and white vase with that of a majolica plate. Then look at the beautiful brushwork on the Sung period Tz'u Chou wares. Finally turn to some of the Sultanabad bowls, and you will see what is meant by suitable design and how it is like shadows.

Size itself can be appealing or the opposite and size should be carefully considered in judging a vase or figure. Think of a pearl two feet in diameter. Who would want it? Thus a perfect "clair de lune" vase in its most delicate palest blue perfection would be unpleasant if it were a yard high. We expect a "sang de boeuf" or ox blood vase to be a good size, but who would want a peach bloom vase of the same size? Here we are considering an appeal most difficult to analyze but perhaps, if we use what Henri Bergson might call dream logic, we can make up our minds just about how big an object should be. I have heard people say that they were shocked and surprised when they first saw the Mona Lisa because it was so much smaller than they had expected. Can it be that the picture would have been more appealing had it been painted somewhat larger? Some vases gain power by being larger while others gain preciousness by being small. Of course purpose must be considered, but experiment with projecting things on the stereopticon screen leads to interesting results and size is a factor of appeal.

These are but a few considerations of appeal. Again I quote Lin Yutang, "There are so many kinds of beauty, beauty of quaintness, beauty of tenderness, of gracefulness—of majesty, of austerity, of ruggedness, of sheer strength and of a suggestion of the antique." He was referring to a pine tree, but all these beauties can be found in pottery and there are many more such as the beauty of stillness and there are vases as still as the moon, the beauty with which a vase can stand on tiptoe and slowly turn, the beauty of a jar which can hunch itself up as cosily as a cat, the beauty which suggests the comfort of a well-filled stomach and the beauty of a tall and graceful woman.

CHAPTER II

THE EARLIEST POTTERIES

NEOLITHIC AND EARLY BRONZE AGE POTTERIES

AFTER the days of Napoleon it was natural that Europeans should believe that the most ancient culture in the world was in Egypt and, of course, we do find one of the earliest cultures along the Nile, but it soon became apparent that the Danube, the Tigris and Euphrates, and the Yellow River valleys had their own very ancient cultures, while other areas challenged the antiquity of these.

In pre-dynastic Egypt as early as 4321 B.C., red and black pottery was made and decorated with some angular ornament and freely drawn human and animal motives. Sir Flinders Petrie found at Qua an even earlier ware of fine clay, thinly hand potted in true symmetry and containing iron ore which gave it a black polish resembling glaze. In neolithic times, it is claimed by A. J. Butler on good evidence, there were made, about 5500 B.C., votive tiles having a ribbed surface and blue-green glaze with inlaid hieroglyphics in color, and also examples of two colors of glazes blended. Also, still in the pre-dynastic times can be located two green glazed tiles, one with a figure of a Negro and some characters and one with a ram in relief, which were found at Abydos. It is established fairly certainly that it is to Egypt that we owe the first development of glaze and that naturalistic ornament is to be found there at an early date. (I dislike using the word *invented* because glaze, like many of the developments in ceramics, probably occurred more or less accidentally and may have been consciously used, lost and refound at different places in different times.)

Also at a very early date the Egyptians carved out bowls from rock and it was natural enough that later some pottery was made with mixed clays or painted to give an effect of the striations of rock. This technique we will find spread throughout the world and it led to "marbled" wares of many kinds.

At about 4000 B.C., it is thought, a conquering people from the North, possibly from Syria, brought the bronze age to Egypt and around 3500 to 3000 B.C. started the First Dynasty.

In Europe we know that in paleolithic times (that is generally speaking when man was able to make chipped stone implements but had not found out how to polish them smooth) very beautiful and sophisticated naturalistic animal drawing had been accomplished as is proven by the paintings of the Altamira caves and others. Yet no pottery has been identified with this culture though undoubtedly some must have been made. After the arctic

9

FIG. 9. Smooth buff ware tall pottery vase made in predynastic Egypt. Height 11½″. Metropolitan Museum of Art.

FIG. 10. Predynastic Egyptian double vase of red polished ware and white line decoration. Metropolitan Museum of Art.

FIG. 11. Vase of predynastic Egypt of the well made red polished ware with primitive decoration in white lines. Metropolitan Museum of Art.

FIG. 13. Predynastic Egyptian tall vase of smooth buff ware. Height about 14″. Metropolitan Museum of Art.
Note: This general form of tall jar with pointed bottom seems to have been made by most primitive potters the world over. It, the globular pot and the shallow bowl are the most fundamental forms in all potting.

FIG. 12. Predynastic Egyptian vase, suggesting a stone model but decorated with wavy lines suggestive of water design in weaving. Metropolitan Museum of Art.

FIG. 14. Black ware incised decorated bowl of predynastic Egypt having a good form and the well related design. Dia. 5¾″. Metropolitan Museum of Art.

10

conditions of this early stone age had modified, some men with the rest of the old quaternary fauna drifted north and various more or less isolated cultures developed. One of these, the "Kitchen Midden," located on the south shores of the Baltic Sea and in Southern Scandinavia, produced a primitive pottery with pointed bottom and rough decoration just below the rim. This form was developed in a number of places probably because it could be leaned against a rock or tree in country so uneven as to make a flat-bottomed or round-bottomed vessel difficult to place. It has been suggested that primitive man spent much of his time in making stones and sticks pointed and thus became what might be called point minded, but this seems to me doubtful.

Toward the end of mezzolithic times Europe began to feel influences from the South and East and among the most important advances were those in pottery. Mr. Miles Burkitt has pointed out, as I did, that it is impossible for man to leave alone the beautiful and so easily impressionable surface of unbaked clay. Thus, now we find red and also black wares (depending upon conditions of firing) which are incised, painted and sometimes first incised and then the incisions filled in with a white or colored clay inlay in contrast to the body. The designs of these wares are a series of deep zigzags running up and down about the body, and those in Central and Eastern Europe are better made and more vigorous and deeply incised than those in the western sections which are coarse and rough. Small ladles and cups were also made.

Probably between the Rhine and Elbe rivers there originated a culture identified by a type of beaker which the people buried with their dead. These beakers are also found in Holland, Denmark, Bohemia and even Britain. The graves contain little metal and that is supposed to have been imported. The theory has been advanced that these people came from the steppes of South Russia and it is admitted that the manner of burial is similar to that of the Russian kurgans (mounds). In Northern Germany cord-ornamented vessels are made with globular bodies and long cylindrical necks while possibly in Spain originated a similar vessel with wider body and widely expanding mouth decorated with bands of geometrical ornament. This latter is found also in Portugal, Sardinia, Sicily, Northern Italy and parts of France. In Bohemia are found both types, but the so-called "bell beakers" of Spanish type are not so good and there is a larger number of the Northern type. Either the former ware came from the Ukraine and was later developed in Spain, or the Bohemian ware shows a degeneration. We are not sure which.

In Greece during the early copper age the Thessalian peasants had been pushed from the East by South Russians and brought with them the painted pottery known as "Dhimini" ware, but before the bronze age this had deteriorated and its place was taken by a plain gray-black or red pottery decorated with light red and white. Finally all decoration ceased at about 2000 B.C. and "Minyan" ware, which was wheel-made of gray clay (sometimes burnt red), was either brought from Asia Minor or developed from the Thessalian plain pottery of earlier times. This plain ware lasted from about 2000 B.C. to 1625 B.C. when the Minoan influences of Crete became strong. (See Chapter III.)

EARLY POTTERY FROM THE BLACK EARTH REGION

1. Erösd; 2 and 4. Cucuteni; 3. Oltszem; 5–10. Government of Kiev.
Scale (Nos. 1–4) 1:6; (Nos. 5–10) 1:10

Note the S designs which have also been pressed into angular forms on the pot stand to upper right in the same way that they appear on Shang (1766–1154 b.c.) bronzes of China.

Note also the prominent "nose and two eye" design on # 6 and # 10 which also became a feature of Shang design.

Both may possibly have originated here in the "Black Earth Region."

Plate 1

Thus, to sum up the first Western European known potteries, they were either red or black, were 1.—decorated with incised or string-impressed designs, 2.—decorated with painted designs or 3.—left plain. The designs are all simple zigzags or bands with various hatched and line patterns; that is the sort that any child or primitive decorator would arrive at in a certain stage of development without any outside influence being necessary. Representations of animals or men were not used, either in freely drawn but naturalistic style, as in Egypt, or in compacted or conventionalized style.

Now coming to the "Black Earth Region" of Transylvania, Bukowina, Galicia, Bessarabia and the Ukraine as far east as Kiev we find the earliest wares of 3000 B.C. or older to be well-made bowls, pot-stands with slightly curved sides and flaring bases and jars having bottoms not pointed but so sharply rounded as to suggest it, stem-cups and, in Galicia, diamond-shaped jars

FIG. 15. Development of design of Pl. I, No. 1 by Dr. H. Frankfort in his "Studies in Early Potteries of the Near East."

having the upper half decorated as though they were made to set into a stand of some sort. They are decorated with black on red, or on a buff ware and parallel with them are plain wares which appear to be contemporary. The most obvious characteristic is the varied use of a horizontal S spiral or what is called a "pot hook" design. These at times are hooked end to end and at times are applied to the pot without regard to its structure. To quote Dr. H. Frankfort ("Studies in Early Potteries of the Near East II") "We see then that, underlying the peculiar designs in which pot-hook spirals, concentric circles, and animal representations are used, there appears persistently a framework of rectilinear bands. On some vessels these latter form the sole decoration." These would impress us at once as being remnants of earlier habitual designs. To continue, "Its correlative seems to be the use of black-painted designs on a polished surface, i.e., that technique which we have found to be characteristic of Cappadocia and the regions further east; and as at Anau I we find designs which may conceivably be a primitive stage of the 'Rautenstil,' there is the probability that the 'Rautenstil' is an aboriginal style of Eastern Asia Minor."

We will come to the Anau examples shortly, but here we find something quite different from anything in Western Europe or in Egypt. It is true that the reverse spiral is typical of the Halstadt Bronze Culture of Austria, but it was not found on potteries and this use of spirals is not so early. It is to be noted too that here we come for the first time to buff colored potteries, all the others being red or black, and also, for the first time in European wares, animals are mentioned.

This "Black Earth Area" northwest of the Black Sea is closely related to our next section of Syria, Mesopotamia and Persia where careful excavations tell us a clearer story.

Ur, near the mouth of the Euphrates, has attracted public attention due to the gold and precious stone objects found there, but the pottery is no less remarkable. Here many civilizations had built upon the crumbled ruins of foregoing civilizations and to give an idea of how these excavations are carried out let us see what Mr. C. Leonard Woolley, director of the joint expedition of the Pennsylvania University Museum and the British Museum,

FIG. 16. Animal Jug on Wheels which is of the Flood period found with jars with lumps of clay stamped with seals on top and dated by inscriptions to the first dynasty of *Ur* (3100 B.C.). Pennsylvania University Museum.

FIG. 17. Pottery of the Flood Period in Mesopotamia which is not wheel made and was found over 30 feet below the level which represented 3200 B.C. It is of whitish or greenish clay with designs in black, or of reddish clay with designs in chocolate brown. Note also the comb decoration in the bottom of one bowl. Pennsylvania University Museum.

FIG. 18. Figures of the period of the Flood —found in the graves with painted pots at *Ur*, these figurines are of white clay with Bitumen headdresses. Another was of green clay with black markings. They represent not human women but some goddess or demon and are about the only objects which were found to show religious significance. The square shoulders, prominence of breasts and general pose suggest some "goddess or demon" of our present age. Pennsylvania University Museum.

says about it. Starting at a level established as being of the date of about 3200 B.C. where were found clay seals for the tops of jars, tablets and the remarkable animal on wheels illustrated, they dug down *two levels* and found potteries painted in sealing-wax red and also in red, black and buff some of which had lead tumblers covering the tops. At the *fourth level* there were potteries quite unlike any of the others found. They were covered with a light slip and wiped off to make a crude sort of pattern. At the *fifth level* were pots of light clay decorated with bands of red paint. At the *sixth level* more three-colored sherds (broken pieces of pottery) were found of the

"Jemdet Nasr" type and then came a level of an entirely different type. At this *eighth level* the remarkable discovery of an intact pottery kiln was found with the last batch of pots stacked in it. Nearby was a clay potter's wheel with burnishers and other potter's tools. Here the pottery was of black on white and chocolate on pink of the "el Obied" type, after the later ones of plain red sometimes burnished and of plum-colored mat. Here was the end of the wheel-made wares and all below are hand patted. Then there was waterlaid sand about eleven feet thick and thirty feet down, but under that a layer of household rubbish and more pottery. In one place were lumps of clay burnt red and black and grooved. To quote, "In other words they were the remains of a reed hut plastered with clay which had stood and been burnt down before the Flood overwhelmed this part of the country."——This, I must intercede, is another way in which pottery could have been discovered.——But to go on, it was found that these people lived in brick houses also. And finally below this level came indications of sea plants, hard clay and other signs that this was the bottom of Mesopotamia below sea level. Mr. Woolley says that the civilization after the flood was the same as that before but feebler and degenerate and it died soon. The potteries are whitish and greenish decorated with designs in black, and also of reddish clay decorated with chocolate brown. Note the illustration which shows a pot with spout of this culture which seems to show a considerable sophistication and could only be the result of a number of generations of development.

In some of the graves female figurines were found, one of green clay with black markings and others of white clay with bitumen headdresses on their strange misshapen heads. They are nude and either have their hands on their hips or are holding a child. It is thought that these represent some goddess, for anyone who formed the bodies could have made the heads more lifelike, if he had so wished.

Other expeditions of the Pennsylvania University Museum have made discoveries at sites called Tepe Gawra and Tell Billa in the headwaters of the Tigris river. At the former place there are twenty strata and we know nothing of the origin of the "Painted Pottery People" who settled there before 5000 B.C. I show a boat-shaped bowl which is unique and decorated with alternating wave and fern patterns. (Upper right hand corner of plate.) A round bowl has an alternating panel design on the outside and is well potted. The globular jar with cross-hatched triangles about the shoulder is a more usual round bottomed early type, but the flattened pot with spout handle and alternating design about the upper surface is unique.

Billa VII & VI—From about 3000 B.C. to 1500 B.C. the two mounds have a parallel development, although the occupation of Billa did not begin until Gawra had already been covered up by fourteen meters of occupational débris. Here are, beginning with about 3200 B.C., goblet forms with painted bands having cross-hatched panels and rows of highly conventionalized birds and animals as well as plain pots wheel-turned and finished with a wash. They were first fired at about 1600° F and later up to 2000° F. They are similar to the Jemdet Nasr or first predynastic period of the south wares. The colors are purplish brown, black and red on buff, brown and gray. Later

TEPE GAWRA AND TELL BILLA SITES
At Head Waters of Tigris
Potteries found by the Joint Expedition to Persia of the University Mus.
and the Pennsylvania Mus. of Art of 1931

Potteries from Tepe Gawra in northern Iraq of the
al Obied period 4000 B.C.

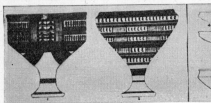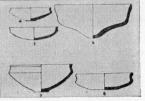

Rows of birds in silhouette, cross hatching, etc. Notice alternating areas in bands.
Painted designs become rare.

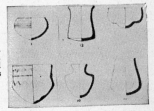

Tell Billa Potteries VII and VI 3200–2900 B.C.
Chalices in brown, black, and red on buff or grey.
Flat and pointed bases on bowls. Plain pieces finished
with a wash, early ones fixed at 1600° F., later ones
fixed at 2000° F.

Incising and relief become popular.

PLATE 2

TELL BILLA POTTERIES

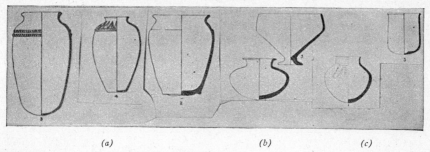

(a)   (b)   (c)

(a) Tell Billa Potteries V 2900–2700 B.C. Copper age begins and potteries become scarcer. Slips, red bands about shoulders, occasionally black paint spots. Note first foot rim on large pot in center. *(b)* Chalice has a lower foot. *(c)* Straight cup with round or flat bottom is characteristic.

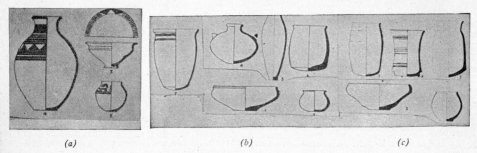

(a)   (b)   (c)

(a) Tell Billa Potteries IV Rustolian Period c. 1900 B.C. New shapes, better potting, flat or rimmed bottoms, well-defined lip-rims. Ribbing, knot handles perpendicularly pierced for suspension. Painting and incising. *(b)* Note alternating principle on rim of bowl and shoulder of pots. *(c)* Cream slips are frequent.

1   2   3

1. Tell Billa Potteries Stratum 3 Hurrian Period 1600–1400 B.C. New and distinctive shapes, small cups with button bases, bowls made into dishes or cups. Buff, grey or reddish. Cream slips and light red, dull black and white used in painting. Naturalistic designs confined to birds, goats, and fish. No humans or trees except as figurines with decoration. 2. Tell Billa Potteries Stratum 2 Middle Assyrian 1300–800 B.C. Red predominant. Bowls return. Button bases replaced by nipple type. Decoration almost disappears. 3. Tell Billa 1 Late Assyrian 800–700 B.C. Jugs, pitchers and amphoras appear. Post Assyrian. Glazes frequent, of a silvery sheen, bluish and greenish by accident. The pilgrim flask and slender bottle are new. Relief and incised ornamentation return.

PLATE 3

toward 2900 B.C. they become more elaborate in shape, greenish gray or buff, and painting gives way to incising and molding.

Billa V—Between 2900 and 2700 B.C. comes the copper age and the wares are mostly incised about the shoulder with touches of bitumen and red bands. There are no new shapes.

Billa IV—It is probable that the foregoing period had seen more interest in copper as a novelty than in the potteries. Ring bases are introduced and painting resumed with more angular shoulders and well made lip-rims. This is the Anatolian Period, and extends from around 1900 B.C.

FIG. 19. Iranian ewer from Siyalk of about 1000 B.C. with spout possibly also used as handle. Height about 10″. N. M. Heeramaneck Col.

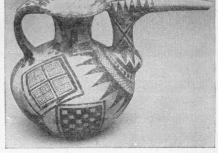

FIG. 20. Iranian unglazed pottery pitcher of buff clay with dark red decoration dating about 1100 to 1000 B.C. Height about 6″. Metropolitan Museum of Art.

Billa III—The Hurrian Period of 1600 to 1400 B.C. brings more new shapes and designs, a return to the lower 1600° F firing and much more painting along with Egyptian influences.

Billa II and I—Then we find the design entirely disappearing around 1300 B.C. in our middle and late Assyrian wares until in post-Assyrian times we come to the glazed Syro-Roman wares, etc.

A similar course is found at Damghan just south and east of the Caspian Sea, starting with angular stem cups and pointed-shaped bowls all painted in Hissar I around 3000 B.C., and then in Hissar II (2500 B.C.? to 2000 B.C.) going to nearly all plain wares which in Hissar III (1500 B.C. to 1200 B.C.) become more involved including vessels with hollow or deeply-grooved handle-spouts. These are not unlike the one we illustrate except that the loop handle was evidently a later addition and does not occur on those before 1200 B.C.

In the fertile valley between Askhabad and Merv just east of the southern tip of the Caspian Sea lies Anau where two sites have been found and the northern and earliest one is dated about 3900 B.C. to 3300 B.C. There the potteries are not wheel-made, have no handles and no incising and are painted with diamond cross hatched or solidly filled in bands and some with simple fern designs in bands. From the beginning at Anau there are light wares as well as red wares.

Again at Susa are most beautifully developed designs of animals and birds set in oddly shaped sections which, it has been suggested by Professor Meyers,

TEPE HISSAR "CASTLE HILL" EXCAVATIONS AT DAMGHAN

Potteries found by the Joint Expedition to Persia of the University Mus. and the Pennsylvania Mus. of Art of 1931.

HISSAR I (3000 B.C.)
Buff pottery painted with red, brown, or grey slips.

Note conventionalized leopard on first bowl. The ibex, gazelle, sheep and long horned cattle were known. Other designs are lines and chevrons. Jar second from end is very close to Han Chinese shape.

HISSAR II (2500–2000 B.C.)
Many shapes are identical with Hissar I. Grey wares, with some shapes further developed.

Base stands are eliminated, perpendicular rim disappears, base becomes less flat. Conical bowls are more rounded, all angular lines are eliminated. Spouts occur hollow topped and closed.

HISSAR III (1500–1200 B.C.)
Painted potteries survive as ritualistic objects. New forms had small loops for covers, no handles yet, spouts further developed.

Painted potteries continue for ritualistic use; common pottery for home use. Note pot stand, further developed spouts and bottles with applied necks.

PLATE 4

may have followed the shapes which cut out of leather could have been sewn together to make round forms. The masterful conventionalizing of the animals and birds shows northern nomadic influence, that is from a people who would have naturally worked in leather. In any event these are highly sophisticated and beautifully painted wares of somewhat later period.

FIG. 21. Persian dish said to date about 3000 B.C. with an interesting spotted cat on the rim, perhaps a cheetah judging by its long legs. Part of a similar figure remains on the opposite wall. Length 8½". Brown on light buff. Boston Museum of Fine Art.

FIG. 22. Persian jar said to date about 3000 B.C. which shows interesting associations with those from Ur in Iraq and from Assyrian examples. Note the alternating design. Height about 7". Boston Museum of Fine Arts.

There are many other sites waiting for the spade of the excavator, but these will help to give a general idea of what took place. Now moving on to India we find at Mohenjo Daro a common unpainted ware and around 2000 B.C. a painted ware at the Chanhu-daro site which shows definite Assyrian influence in its alternating bands of foliate, chevron, hatched and similar designs. These again have purplish black and red designs on a white or pinkish white slip, or on a definite red slip. At this site are also earlier potteries of the Harappa times, perhaps going back to about 5000 B.C., with very little difference except that the earlier wares have a little more detail and are more firmly painted, the plant forms being more naturalistic.

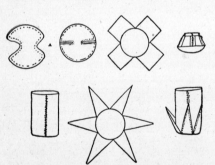

FIG. 23. An ingenious and probably true way in which the pointed designs and slotted circular ones on Susa pottery may have come about. It is suggested by Professor Meyers that these first occurred in sewn leather vessels.

In Eastern Baluchistan in the Zhob valley is the Tell Kaudeni site of early bronze age which is productive of similar wares, and so there are also sites in Turkestan, Sistan and Afghanistan, and we are led to believe that the Iranian Plateau, which is now desert, must once have been the center of a great culture.

In China, J. G. Andersson found at An-yang in Honan province and also in Kansu province further up the Yellow River, a largely wheel-made pottery having well-made loops and handles and of a hard baked red or brown color decorated with black, brown, purple, white and red designs. One of the first things that strikes the eye of the observer is that here again we have the well-defined horizontal S and concentric circular designs very similar indeed to those from the Black Earth Region. Perhaps at times a little more involved, perhaps applied with a better understanding of adaptation to the

FROM THE
ILLUSTRATED LONDON NEWS,
Nov. 21, 1936

FIG. 24. Indian painted potteries of the Jhukar culture (c2000 B.C.) and one, center right, of the earlier Harappa culture (c5000 B.C.).

FIG. 26. Harappa figurine showing appliques of breasts, necklace, eyes and headdress. (c. 5000 B.C.) found at Chanhudaro at Jhukar, near Larkana, in central Sind.

form of the pot, but having so many details in common that it is difficult to believe that there is not some definite connection between the two. These wares are supposed to date about 3200 B.C. to 2900 B.C. although Mr. Liang Ssŭ-Yung, in an excellent paper brought before the American Anthropological Association some years ago, says they are more likely between 2500 and 2000 B.C.

Alongside of this painted pottery there was a coarse, gray earthenware seemingly contemporary, but made without the wheel and often impressed with lines suggesting that they had been wrapped in mats or that strings had purposely been pressed into the moist clay to give this texture. Some of these are globular jars of the fundamental shape, but others are in the form the Chinese call a Li (or hollow-legged Ting), and this is a complicated form to make and most interesting. It is my theory that the earliest potters in China as elsewhere made pointed-bottomed beakers, and that, finding that three of these could be leaned together over a fire, some bright potter thousands of years ago, made up his mind that he would put the three together

POTTERY FROM SUSA I, IN THE LOUVRE
SCALE ABOUT 1:3

Note the beauty of the conventionalized antelope and running dogs on # 1, the long necked birds on the neck of # 4 and # 5 as well as the slotted circular treatments of the bowls and pointed treatments of the cups.

The points particularly occur on Shang bronzes of China.

PLATE 5

FIG. 27. An excellent example of the An-yang painted ware with black and red rope design. It is very thinly potted for its size. Note that cord from the two loops would pull sideways against the body and not upward so as to pull loops off when tying on a cover. Height 18½". Nasli Heeramaneck Collection.

FIG. 28. Neolithic jar from Kansu province in north western China, found by Andersson and said to date between 2000 and 3000 B.C. Note the reverse spiral which is a favorite design on these wares and is very similar to that on the pots from The Black Earth region. Height 15¼". Brooklyn Museum.

22

and give them a common mouth, thus making a Li. This theory is fully backed by Andersson and seems most logical.

The Chinese bronze Ting is of generally deep bowl form with three solid and untapered legs and usually having handles added above the rim. Thus Albert J. Koop is incorrect when he says in his "Early Chinese Bronzes" that, "It is generally accepted that the most ancient type is the Ting," for obviously our pottery Li form is closer to the three pointed pots leaned to-

Fig. 29. Chou period unglazed gray pottery jar with incised decoration of horizontal lines and impressed perpendicular lines. Height 9¼". Ex D. Abbes Collection.

Fig. 30. Unglazed pottery Li of the neolithic period, north China, Manchuria or Mongolia string impressed and showing prototype of many bronze vessels. The author thinks that this form was derived from the custom of leaning three pointed type vessels together over a fire. From the Palmer Collection, Art Institute, Chicago.

Fig. 31. Li, or hollow legged tripod, of gray ware from An Yang and certainly reflective of earlier wares. Length about 5¼". Ralph M. Chait Col.

Fig. 32. Two An Yang vessels of Li form and, though of Shang period and contemporary with the great bronzes, probably reflective of much earlier pottery forms. Gray ware. Heights about 4" and 5". Ralph M. Chait.

gether and, therefore, it came first. It is also interesting to note that the general conception, due to Mr. R. L. Hobson's writings, that most of the early pottery shapes copied bronze forms is not quite true, for here is a simple pottery form taken over by the bronzes.

From Hsi-yin come also wares painted much like those of An-yang or Yang Shao. There was little incising and the painted designs give the impression that they are made up of bands containing celts pierced for a cord.

I do not go so far as to suggest that this is the actual source of the design, though certainly the celt is a basic design the world over. In Mongolian and Manchurian sites the wares are more crude and the designs are made up of dots, short lines, diamonds, curves, loops, etc., but are different from the Chinese ones. There are also string-impressed wares there. Mr. Liang Ssŭ-Yung concludes that these wares are later.

In Japan in the Todoroki shell mound, the one of many which lies nearest Korea, are wares similar to the Manchurian, as we would expect, but no string-pressed wares. Ornamentation on many is done by pinching up and pressing with the fingernail. Incising and reticulation are both characteristic. The wares from Cambodia are astonishingly like those in Japan.

Mr. Liang Ssŭ-Yung comes to the conclusion that during the times of the Hsi-yin and Yang Shao cultures a painted pottery flourished on the base of a string pottery from Kansu to Fengtein in the Northeast. The string-impressed pottery, he thinks, came east and plain pottery from the south northward and met in Korea and Japan. At the end of neolithic times, the incised type with high stand and hollow foot appeared from around the northern borders of the Gobi Desert into Kingan and Yinshin and moved southward. He points out that it reached Anau (Culture III) near the Caspian about the same time. He does not venture to say that the relationship between China and Anau is solved.

However, Dr. Andersson has published a table with motives common to Honan and Anau I. Mr. Percival Yetts and Prof. L. Franz have endorsed and elaborated his views. Among these motives are the slanting oval. It may also be noted that Dr. Andersson found at Sha Ching on the Mongolian-Kansu border two sherds having rows of conventional birds much like those of Susa I and painted in red on a reddish ware. "Thus," to quote Dr. H. Frankfort again, "it seems that occasionally there appear in China, Armenia and Southwest Persia pot fabrics which present similarities in style of decoration as well as in technique."

Anyone acquainted with Chinese bronzes would agree that the design on the pot-stand #3 (Oltszem) shown on the plate of potteries from the Black Earth Region has much in common with the design of the background of some Shang period (1766–1123 B.C.) Chinese bronzes, and this is nothing but the "pot hook" or "horizontal S" or reverse spiral. Perhaps there is no direct connection, but *this motive does not come into use anywhere else in the world at any such early time.*

FIG. 33

Also near An-yang are found pieces of hard white pottery in sites associated also with black pottery usually accompanied by pieces of bone and ivory and which Mr. Yetts has dated about 1800 B.C. These are carved with the same designs seen on pre-Han bronzes. They are technically far ahead of any of the earlier wares we have discussed and on them occurs the horizontal S squeezed as it were into a rectangular form and made up of angles instead of curves. Other very refined potteries of black, hard ware, wheel-turned and thin have been found at Ch'êng Tzŭ Yai east of Tsinan, hence the name

Amazing jar of light pottery almost white of the Shang dynasty latter part probably about 14th to 12th century B.C. which shows bronze characteristics and may have even been a model for a bronze. Note V points and squared S patterns. Height about 14″. Freer Gallery of Art, Wash. Found at An-yang.

PLATE 6

Firmly potted dark grey ware of fine form and with rope handle design, Shang period from An Yang. Height 4". Ralph M. Chait Collection.

Grey pottery jar covered with a fine evenly impressed pattern suggestive of a basket weave. Note the reverse spiral appliques on shoulder which had become a basic motive. Late Chou. Height 13½". C. T. Loo & Co.

Black pottery jar of grey body with thin black slip incised, impressed and combed with basic designs. The form is that of Han potteries but without tall base or attached pot-stand. Early Western Chou. Height. 13½". C. T. Loo & Co.

Black pottery Hu with incised decoration and two relief Tao-tieh handles. This is of grey body covered with thin black slip. Said to be "Early Eastern Chou" though very much like the one called Han in the Eumorfopoulos Col. Height 13½". C. T. Loo & Co.

BLACK AND GREY POTTERIES OF SHANG AND CHOU DYNASTIES OF CHINA

PLATE 7

"Lung Shan" ware, and with them refined white wares showing technical proficiency.

In an interesting article in *Asia* (Jan. 1941), Mr. Sterling S. Beath writes of the black pottery as follows: "Some was found in a district near Lung Shan in Shantung and was called 'Lung Shan ware,' also this place is called Cheng-tzu-yai. Other sites are at Liang Cheng, Feng Huang Thai, Shang Ts'un and Wang She Jen Chuang, all in Shantung, also at Hou Kang, Honan province near An Yang and on the Kiangsu-Shantung border. The ware is found only in Eastern China. In the same sites there was gray impressed pottery which is probably later. In Chekiang near Hang Chou at Liang Chu and near the Chin Shan Lake there is more found, but with larger quantities of gray pottery."

He continues that the typical "black pottery" is shiny and glazed and that the body is at times less than a millimeter in thickness. Some of it is black outside and gray inside and this is later. It is wheel-made as a rule and wheel-burnished. (I do not think he means the ware is glazed, for it certainly is not; the term is synonomous with burnished.) He says the painted pottery is only found in the West from Honan to Kansu provinces. Then he says, "It seems possible that the Black Pottery People laid the foundation for Shang civilization," and points out a similarity between their pottery beakers and the bronze form "ku." He also speaks of "li" forms with hollow legs having been found, but no "ting" forms. Perhaps it was this culture, developed as a separate entity in Northeastern China and Manchuria, that provided the technique necessary for the making of the great Shang bronzes and very probably it was not until the design from the West met their skill that the An-yang white wares were made possible.

So used are we to the simple statement that the Shang bronzes occurred without known antecedents that we have almost come to the unconscious belief that there *were* no antecedents. As Mr. Alan Priest has so well put it, "It is as if we started mediaeval sculpture with Chartres and had no inkling of its antecedents, or suddenly came on the Baptistery doors of Florence and said this is the beginning." Of course, it is quite logical to state that man must have been able to make the beginnings of the bronze forms and the beginnings of bronze design in clay first, and a long time before he gained mastery of the more difficult medium. Thus it is likely that among potteries we find the pre-Shang roots of the great bronze art.

Dr. C. Hentze ("Mythes et Symboles lunaires") has, as Mr. Priest points out, interpreted much of the pantheon of the Wu tombs as moon worship and has shown a likeness in representation all the way from the Mediterranean to Central America. Mr. Priest goes on, "The thing which has permeated all Chinese thinking is the circle of perfection, the *t'ai chi*, divided into two component parts. These are the *yang* and the *yin*, light and darkness, male and female," etc. And what is this but our horizontal S in a circle? Allowing for natural differences is it not conceivable that from the Hallstadt Culture to Shantung there was a significance in this symbol, though this significance may have been differently interpreted in different places just as it is differently interpreted by different men today?

The *t'ao-t'ieh* seen on most Shang bronzes, miscalled an "ogre mask," is actually perhaps an owl, a buffalo head, a tiger and can, when divided perpendicularly, become the side view of dragons, cloud patterns and other things. This *t'ao-t'ieh* appears crudely indicated on a large painted pottery bowl from the Andersson finds, now in the Buffalo Museum. Mr. Priest says of the *t'ao-t'ieh*, "At first glance it is simply an elaborately conventionalized

FIG. 34. Large buff colored pottery bowl painted with black, two large eyes and a prominent nose on either side with conventional meaningless design between. Dia. about 15″. Philip Rosenbach Col., Buffalo Museum.
Note: Compare with jar # 10 on plate of Black Earth potteries.
Painted Pottery Bowl from Kansu in Northwestern China with T'ao T'ieh Face.

animal head. Look closer and you find it is an intricate composite of animal and bird forms." He shows that it is often a more or less conventionalized owl, a bird, one would immediately conclude, natural to associate with moon worship. We shall later trace the spread of the *t'ao-t'ieh* around the whole Pacific Ocean and on down to Peru where moon worship was the fundamental religion. The *t'ao-t'ieh* is not found on the early potteries of Western Asia or Eastern Europe, or, if it is, it is so highly conventionalized as to be hardly recognizable as in #6 and #10 of our plate showing the potteries of the Black Earth Region. Each has alternating prominent circles, possibly eyes, and perpendicular long areas, possibly a nose; but even, if the head itself is not recognizable, its component parts, the "pot hooks" and reverse spirals are certainly often seen.

One noticeable difference between the Western and Eastern Asian styles is that in the Western sections and particularly in Mesopotamia *bands of alternating design* form a prominent part of the designs. We shall take up this

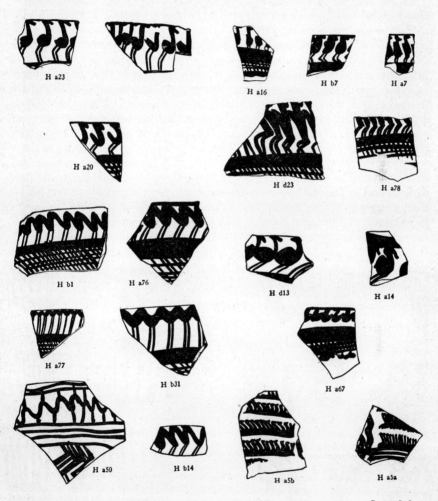

HISSAR I SHERDS—BIRD DESIGN AT VARIOUS STAGES OF CONVENTIONALIZATION. SCALE 1:3

FIG. 35. This plate is reproduced from The Museum Journal (Vol. XXIII, # 4, 1933) of the Hissar excavations of the Joint Expedition of the University Museum and the Pennsylvania Museum of Art. They are beautiful examples of what may be termed *degenerating conventionalization* brought about through repetition which grows more and more careless until unrecognizable.

This sort of conventionalization is quite different from that brought about in nomadic civilizations through having to compress a picture into a small given space. See # 1 on Hissar plate, and also # 1 on Susa plate.

method of design in the section on the potteries of Ashur, but it should be noted here that alternation plays an unimportant part in the earliest arts of China most of which are based rather upon a strictly symmetrical division of left and right with either a two front, or front and back section, *i.e.,* four quarters as are found in biological arrangements. Whether this was because study of life was closer to the Chinese and habits of weaving were closer to the Mesopotamians, we can only guess, but the difference is marked.

Finally it is obvious in the study of these early wares that *conventionaliza-tion was born and developed in the Northern and nomadic sections.* So far as I know this has not been pointed out, but it is simple to understand. The hunter-nomads lived exciting lives in which records of achievement, and magic demands for the bolstering of courage, were found desirable. They had little space on which to make such records and signs; they had to carry everything with them, and a piece of leather, the handle of a knife or later a small bronze buckle afforded the only areas available. Thus they had to compact their records into a sort of shorthand and this was the first source of conventional design. In the paleolithic cave paintings in Spain and Southern France, in Egyptian art and in that of India we find naturalism, for there was space in which to draw animals, birds and humans freely moving and as they are. The Greeks brought this naturalism to a high degree of per-fection. But in the northern sections where men were hunters or, later, herds-men, there was always a tendency to conventionalize or pack design into a given space. To be sure, there is no exact line of demarkation and we find each style penetrating the other but the separate influences are obvious.

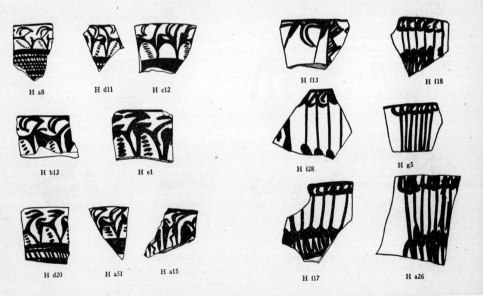

H a8   H d11   H c12   H f13   H f18

H b13   H e1   H f28   H g5

H d20   H a51   H a15   H f17   H a26

HISSAR I SHERDS—GAZELLE DESIGN AT VARIOUS STAGES OF CONVENTIONALIZATION. SCALE 1:3

FIG. 36. Another plate from The Museum Journal of the Pennsylvania University Museum similar to the preceding.

This type of conventionalism is quite different from that decadent, more and more careless, writing of a design until at times the whole meaning of it is lost. Here all vital qualities disappear and the subject matter is simply used because nothing else comes to mind. Even in early wares there are signs of such decadence as we can see in our first plate of the Tell Billa wares where the cup is decorated not only with cross-hatching, saw-tooth patterns, etc., but also with a row of birds that are not only hardly recognizable but also have lost all action and vitality, as again in the Hissar plate.

CHAPTER III

CRETE, EGYPT AND THE AEGEAN

ABOUT 3500 B.C. TO 1100 B.C.

HEINRICH SCHLIEMANN, a poor German boy, read Homer and became convinced that Troy really existed. After many years of hard struggle he set out amid jeers to find it and discovered not only the site of Troy but also that of Mycenae and Tiryns. These discoveries with others all pointed to Crete as a great center and later Sir Arthur Evans and Dr. Federigo Halbherr made their discoveries at Knossos, the home of King Minos of labyrinthian fame and of the Minotaur which Theseus and Ariadne slew. Crete lies midway between Egypt, Greece and Syria at the mouth of the Aegean Sea and became a crossroads of the ancient world.

Sir Arthur Evans divided the Minoan Culture into nine parts roughly paralleling the 1st Egyptian dynasty of 3500 or 3400 B.C. to the 20th dynasty of 1100 B.C. and also the first half of the Northern European bronze age and of the Hallstadt Culture as well as the Italian developments up to the Etruscan age.

The early development of Crete was due to Egyptian influences and Mesopotamian and Syrian influences through Egypt. In pre-dynastic Egypt we have noted that glaze was developed but also a crude, unglazed pottery was made and it deteriorated as the art of making stone vessels improved.

FIG. 37. Predynastic Egyptian bowl of the white line decorated ware showing a typical primitive border design on the shoulder and the reminiscent feeling of a basket origin. Dia. about 7". Metropolitan Museum of Art.

FIG. 38. Early Predynastic Egyptian pottery figure of reddish clay dating about 4000 to 3600 B.C. Metropolitan Museum of Art.

FIG. 39. Painted terracotta figure dating about 4000 to 3600 B.C. and found in Egypt. Metropolitan Museum of Art.

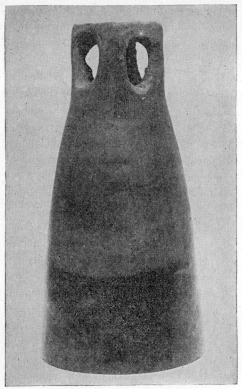

"Black topped" vase which, I am informed by Dr. William C. Hayes of the Metropolitan Museum of Art, was fired with the black part down in the ashes of the open fire, the upper part receiving more heat and less carbon deposit as it was inverted. This makes an interesting comment upon the black or gray wares and the red wares of China and other countries and shows how closely allied they were. Height 9". Metropolitan Museum of Art.

Predynastic Egyptian vase province unknown but certainly strongly reminiscent of the geometrical wares of Mesopotamia. Metropolitan Museum of Art.

Egyptian 12th dynasty of turquoise faïence with black decoration of lotus blossoms and buds conceived as though they were perhaps thought of as shadows cast upon the hippopotamus. Length 8". Metropolitan Museum of Art.

Flower vase of a form which we see used later in Persia, Mesopotamia and in the wares of Yüeh in China with spouts from the shoulder, though it undergoes many variations. This one is of the 12th dynasty Egypt and is of blue faïence with decoration in black. Height 3½". Metropolitan Museum of Art.

EGYPTIAN POTTERIES, PREDYNASTIC AND 12TH DYNASTY

PLATE 8

Vases have been found, like the one illustrated, with a row of ibex and flamingos which are strongly comparable with certain ones of upper Mesopotamia and their place of origin is unknown. Crude female figures with great avoirdupois about the hips are not unlike those of neolithic times in Europe and even of modern times among certain African natives. Some heavy oblate jars are direct copies of the stone ones. And finally a peculiar type of "black-topped vase" demonstrates to us at once the close relationship between black and red wares, for the part of these vases that rested in the fire is black and that above the fire is burnt to a deep red. Alternation is not marked but does occur. Simple chevron, diagonally hatched, fern, wavy line, and point designs are general.

EARLY MINOAN I (3500–3100 B.C.)

(Note:—I am using the dates given by Miss Gisela M. A. Richter, Litt.D. of the Metropolitan Museum, which are a little earlier than those given by E. J. Forsdyke, M.A., F.S.A. of the British Museum, but all of these are only approximate.)

In the early Minoan I period we find Crete also making stone vessels with more artistry than is shown in those of Egypt. The pottery is a rough reddish ware decorated with black slip in herring-bone, squares and various groups of parallel lines and dots. The same ware is also incised. The shapes are sturdy reflecting those of the stone vessels. Immediately we see reflected Mesopotamian influences in round-bodied stem cups and the trough spout used on ewers.

EARLY MINOAN II (3100–2600 B.C.)

This was the great time of Imhotep and Zoser in Egypt, of the Great Pyramids, and during it there was a well-potted, bright red and highly polished ware. In Crete rectangular paintings were done in brown or black and red on a buff ground and many varied and even fantastic shapes were imported from Syria, Mesopotamia and Egypt such as the trough-spouted ewers with handles added and tall inverted conical cups with loop handles, all undoubtedly influenced by the tenuous forms of metal now becoming popular.

EARLY MINOAN III (2600–2200 B.C.)

Pottery in Egypt developed along the line of perfection of the red ware, but after the 7th Dynasty invasion and civil war eliminated her influence and the Aegean Culture became predominant. "Vasiliki Ware" of red, covered unevenly with a black glaze and painted in white, came into use. The mottling of red and black was an attempt to reproduce the effect of stone. "Kamares Ware" (found in the Kamares Cave) with black ground decorated in bands of strongly stylized naturalistic motives in white, yellow and red, started and was carried through the next three periods until about 1600 B.C., becoming more and more naturalistic and decadent.

FIG. 40. Pre-historic Cretan vases dating from about 3000 to 1100 B.C. Of light buff unglazed clay. Heights from 5¾" to 11¼". Metropolitan Museum of Art.

FIG. 41. A group of Cretan stone vases dating before 2200 B.C. all said to be of steatite and measuring from about 3" to 6". Metropolitan Museum of Art.

FIG. 42. Early Minoan II cup with grooved spout dating between 2800 and about 2500 B.C. showing a sturdy and well made rim and an indented line about the foot-rim to set it off. Height 3¾". Metropolitan Museum of Art.

FIG. 43. Early Minoan III cup made between 2500 and 2200 B.C. with white on black design well suited to the intelligent and well potted form. Length 4½". Metropolitan Museum of Art.

FIG. 44. Cretan jug of about 2200–2000 B.C. of very light buff pottery unglazed. Height 3¼". Metropolitan Museum of Art.

FIG. 48. Jar from Knossos of the Middle Minoan II–III period (2000–1600 B.C.) with conventional poly-chrome decoration. The handles would suspend it in balance. Height about 5¼". Metropolitan Museum of Art.

FIG. 46. Lime-stone figure of Cynocephalus glazed, of the 12th dynasty Egyptian found at Sakkara.

FIG. 47. Middle Minoan II terra-cotta male figure of athletic appearance with what appears to be a knife in his belt. Ht. 6½".

FIG. 45. Pottery model of a house. Egyptian 12th dynasty. Length 12".

35

MIDDLE MINOAN I (2200–2000 B.C.)

The Middle Minoan period broadly corresponds with the Middle Kingdom or 9th to 12th Dynasties of Egypt during which the arts reached a crest of achievement. The potteries include scarabs in blue faience, small seated figures of males, many animals of glazed stone and pottery including the well-known hippopotamus in turquoise with black plant forms, like shadows, of lotus painted on it, which has been so admired at the Metropolitan Museum of Art. The stone vessels continued to be well made and the red ware became less frequent.

Crete was developing a large foreign trade and the wares became less thick and more like metal having also polychrome decoration. Relief sculpture was a natural result of the influence of metal work.

MIDDLE MINOAN II (2000–1800 B.C.)

In Egypt a general decline takes place between the 12th and 18th Dynasties and Crete is now dominant. The potter's wheel was developed and tended to simplify some of the over-playful shapes. For the first time there appear natural renderings of flowers and undersea plants, the octopus and similar forms. It is as though the Cretan artists had suddenly looked about and found that many things in their lives could supply pleasing design. I doubt that this was due to any outside influence for the designs are too local in subject and natural in treatment.

The wheel had the effect of developing a tendency toward the use of horizontal bands. The ware from the Kamares Cave seemed to reach its height and, in fact, Miss Richter is of the opinion that *all* of the vessels decorated in white, red and orange are of this period while the white-decorated wares were either Middle Minoan I or III such as those from Pachyammos.

Now, either through conquest or trade, or both, the culture at Mycenae, west of Athens near the tip of Greece, began to follow that of Crete in all arts but particularly in pottery. About this time the northern part of Greece was invaded by a people carrying bronze weapons and they brought with them "Minyan Ware" of red or light gray body and also another ware of mat, painted texture. These wares are common to the islands and to Mycenae but not to Crete and, therefore, are likely to have come from Western Asia. A small goblet from Lianokladi which has a horizontally ribbed column shows East Indian influence.

MIDDLE MINOAN III (1800–1600 B.C.)

During this period the Cretan influence was continuously growing. It seemed that by 1625 B.C. the overlords of this island held sway over all of the Aegean land areas.

Natural design developed on pottery in polychrome style and then gave way to a buff pottery decorated in a lustrous black. This brought the end of the Minyan Ware. Other wares show a sprinkling of white dots to imitate stone and a return, or feeble continuation, of the old designs of spirals and scrolls.

The most interesting development is shown by the "Snake Goddess" found at Knossos together with attendants and other objects. She stands about a foot high and is dressed in a six-flounced skirt with narrow waist and an open bodice showing very prominent breasts, entirely unveiled. The ware is light and treated with a polychrome glaze. Two remarkable reliefs are of a cow and a goat with nursing kid. These are of the highest quality of ceramic art, simple as an air from Beethoven and as sure in their beauty.

LATE MINOAN I (1600–1500 B.C.)

The Late Minoan period roughly parallels the New Kingdom of Egypt or the 18th to 20th dynasties. The potteries there were becoming over-ornate and in bad taste. Green scarabs replaced blue ones. Polychrome glazes fol-

FIG. 49. Middle Minoan III (1800–1600 B.C.) jug of very primitive form, probably for everyday use. Height 5½". Metropolitan Museum of Art.

FIG. 50. A Knossian faience figure of a snake-holding goddess with a pard on her headdress. (c. 1575 B.C.). Sir Arthur Evans.

FIG. 51. Cretan vase said to be from Knossos, Late Minoan I painted in brown on a buff body. Here, instead of the naturalism often spoken of in this period, we have pure, strong conventionalized design on a structural and beautiful form. (The neck and lip are repaired none too well.) Height about 12¼". Metropolitan Museum of Art.

lowing the development of glass were many shades of blue, violet, yellow, brown and green, but they slowly became less bright and generally decadent while the blue-glazed wares slowly became less good and returned to the turquoise color. This pale turquoise was used by the Greeks, but was soon given up.

Crete retained her position of supremacy, and naturalism continued less vigorously. The dark on light technique was used with red and white touches added, but soon the former and then the latter disappeared. This was also a period of renaissance at Mycenae and Thebes.

LATE MINOAN II (1500–1400 B.C.)

This was the approximate time of Tutenkhamun at Luxor. Greece is gaining dominance and the best that can be said about Cretan wares is that some were very large, of the so-called "Palace style."

A reconstruction of the famous "Harvester Vase" showing a procession of men singing and marching to the music of an Egyptian sistrum. Many are carrying "winnowing forks." The whole is in relief and shows some 26 figures. It was carved from steatite and shows the fine handling of relief by these very early artists. Late Minoan I or about 1600 to 1100 B.C. Height 7″. Metropolitan Museum of Art.

Late Minoan I pottery ewer found in Lower Egypt. Height 8⅝″. Brooklyn Museum.

Late Minoan I–II period vase but not from Crete; it was found in Mycenae, Greece, and has such strong Cretan feeling that it may show important trade relations at this time. Note the beautiful shape with naturalistic but wonderfully conventionalized design, due to northern influence either in Crete or Mycenae. Height about 24½″. Metropolitan Museum of Art.

This vase is called the "Boxer Vase" and is modeled in low relief with figures, some wearing visors and cheek-pieces, in fighting attitudes. The band second from the top shows not a "bull hunt" as it has been called but probably the bull-baitings indulged by the Cretans and possibly the source of the old Minotaur legend. Red terracotta. Height about 19½″. Late Minoan I (1600–1500 B.C.) Metropolitan Museum of Art.

LATE MINOAN I POTTERIES FROM CRETE

PLATE 9

FIG. 52. Terracotta figure of the late bronze age, Cypriote, dating about 1500–1200 B.C. with marbled effect obtained with slip painting. Height 3⅜". Cesnola Collection. Metropolitan Museum of Art.

FIG. 53. Four exceedingly primitive, though rather amusing figures from Mycenae of the Late Helladic Period III (1400–1100 B.C.) to be compared with Late Minoan III, which have similarities with figures from Ur. Heights about 2" to 4¼". Metropolitan Museum of Art.

FIG. 54. A none too well developed shape and unevenly potted basin dating c. 1400–1150 B.C. from Greece not at all up to Minoan standards. Dia. 15". Metropolitan Museum of Art.

FIG. 55. A rather ingenious ladle of Prehistoric Greek ware c. 1400 to 1150 B.C. or the Late Minoan III age of Crete. Length 9¼". Metropolitan Museum of Art.

FIGS. 56–57. Two cups with tall stems (Kylix). The one said to date about 1400–1150 B.C. and the other with an octopus design said to be from Mycenae and to date about 1350–1100 B.C. Heights about 7". Metropolitan Museum of Art.

FIG. 58. An early "Lekythos" or small ewer from the city of Sardis in Lydia, on the mainland of Asia Minor where the Greeks cut off access to the sea. The alternating wavy band decoration and form shows both Egyptian and Eastern influences. Height 8". Metropolitan Museum of Art.

FIG. 59. Egyptian 18th dynasty jar painted to imitate stone and with an inscription "One honored with Osiris—the official of Amun, Mery." Found at Gournah. Height about 8". Metropolitan Museum of Art.

LATE MINOAN III (1400–1100 B.C.)

An invasion at the end of this period destroyed the palace at Knossos and overran the island. The old Cretan stock which had settled in Greece now invaded Western Asia and Greece was also invaded from the north. The islands were troubled among themselves as the Egyptians have written and the end of the glory of Crete had come.

CHAPTER IV

GREECE

The Iron Age (1000 b.c. to a.d. 100)

WHEN CRETE lost power it was assumed by Mycenae, a city on the eastern part of the Peloponnesus, that tip of Greece which is almost an island, but soon the whole situation was to be changed by the use of iron as a weapon. Since 4000 b.c. Egypt had made beads of iron and a tool found at Khufu at Gizeh, inside the great pyramid, dates about 3100 b.c. Iron weapons had been found together with bronze ones dating about 1350 b.c. at the site of Hallstadt near Vienna, but these are thought to have been brought there perhaps by the Celts and possibly from the Caucasus Mountains. Jacques de Morgan is quite right when he says, "The Celts and the Dorians must have been the principal propagators of the iron industry," and it was the Danube Valley by which it entered Europe.

The Dark Ages of Greece (1100 to 700 b.c.)

The so-called "Achaeans" are thought to have invaded Greece from the north and this was very likely a Germanic tribe. It did not happen all at once but more as a slow infiltration, for the invaders are described as speaking Greek but also as being tall and blond. The Ionians, who had come from the Eastern Mediterranean shores, were short and dark. Some old authorities have said that three invasions took place from the north, the Ionian, Achaean and Dorian, but this is not correct for in Homer's time (*Odyssey* XIX.177) the Dorians were known only in Crete. This explains why most Dorian influences are in the southern part of Greece.

The Geometric Period (c. 1100–700 b.c.)

We have said that about 1625 b.c. the Minoan influences were strong in Greece and these brought Egyptian styles, somewhat translated, and then the more naturalistic styles of Crete itself.

FIG. 60. "The Warrior Vase" vessel of Late Minoan III period found at Mycenae and showing neither Cretan nor Greek types but bearded warriors with long noses which are probably representative of those from the Western Asian mainland. Height about 15″. Metropolitan Museum of Art.

41

A very well known example, the famous "Warrior Vase," found by Schliemann himself, gives us a good idea of the style around 1350–1100 B.C. The long-nosed and bearded warriors speak for themselves and the form is certainly derived from those of the Babylonian-Mesopotamian areas. Miss Richter says that the artist of this piece was afraid to break away from the fixed conventions, for he knew little of anatomy and nothing of perspective, and this may be partly true but I cannot help but feel he was trying for something else again and I find such touches as the curl which forms the back of the neck and ear in one stroke both amusing and clever.

FIG. 61. "Geometric period" (c. 1100–700 B.C.) "Dipylon" vessel, bowl derived from primitive cooking vessels. 9th to 8th century B.C. Height 9½". Metropolitan Museum of Art.

FIG. 62. A "Kantharos" or "Cantharus," a two handled drinking cup of the "Geometric style" dating between 750 and 700 B.C. from Athens showing that not all of these pieces were crowded with design. Height about 5". Metropolitan Museum of Art.

FIG. 63. A "Dipylon" bowl or "Skyphos" of the geometric period from Athens of the 10th–9th century B.C. Height 3¼". Metropolitan Museum of Art.

Now, as for the "Dipylon" vases found in the cemetery of that name near Athens, and others of the "Geometric Period" of 1100 to 700 B.C., we must declare at once that we like them for their design quality and rhythmical arrangements far more than do those who measure the excellence of all Greek art by its approach to perfect rendering of the natural, while, on the other hand, we dislike them for their slender, projecting and unstructural handles which have never been condemned by these same old-school Greek art worshippers. One might as well accuse Beethoven and Brahms of not

FIGS. 64–68. Elements of Design.

reproducing natural sounds as accuse the makers of these vases of not reproducing natural forms. Of course, they had no such intention whatsoever. We see at once, in the forms of the potteries, the old Western Asian influences and in the design, the alternating rhythms, the animal and bird forms strongly conventionalized, and other characteristics of this influence. Added to these are human and horse figures in the same feeling. Note the figures with long

Two "Dipylon" vases (so called because many were found in the Dipylon cemetery of Athens) of buff ware painted in brown glaze with typical "Geometrical period" decorations of horses and chariots, men and animals with three bustled dancing women on the neck of one. Heights about 25" and 28". Metropolitan Museum of Art.

An immense "Dipylon" of the typical geometric style from Greece and dating about 8th century. Height 39". Metropolitan Museum of Art.

DIPYLON VASES OF THE GEOMETRIC PERIOD: GREECE

Plate 10

legs, triangular torsos and rectangles formed of the arms, with circles in the
center for the heads, on the colossal "Dipylon" vase on stand. Note also the
soldiers with shields, below them. These later were used without the heads
and two legs as on the "Phaleron" jug found at Athens, now in the Metropolitan Museum. In other words the northern constructive conventionaliza-

FIG. 69. Cypriote animal on wheels with two vases of the early iron age which here was about 1200–1000 B.C. Height 8⅞".
Note: comparison should be made with the animal on wheels from Ur.

FIG. 70. A ship with helmsman of the Early Iron Age (or "Dark Ages") of Greece showing influence of the Northern invaders, about 1200 to 500 B.C. and probably made as a votive offering. Length 7½". Metropolitan Museum of Art.

FIG. 71. Early Iron Age terracotta group c. 1000–600 B.C. of a cart with two wheels on which is a woman and a boy playing a double flute. The prominent chins and noses are like those of the bronze centaur and man of the "Morgan group" and those on the "Dipylon vases." Height 4¼". Metropolitan Museum of Art.

FIG. 72. Early iron age pottery figure of a bearded man with a vase in either arm riding a horse. The same sort of pointed chin is often seen in figures of the "Geometric period." This piece dates about 1000 to 600 B.C. Height 5". Metropolitan Museum of Art.

FIG. 73. Terracotta head broken from a statue dating about 8th to 7th century B.C. and of the "Geometric" or "sub-Geometric" period. It shows definite early traces of Western Asian influences particularly in the treatment of the eyes. Height about 7¼". Metropolitan Museum of Art.

FIG. 74. Painted terracotta head found at the shrine of Athena Chalcioecus and said to be of the 8th century B.C. British Museum.

FIG. 75. M. E. L. Mallowan of the British Museum published this head-cup found at the Habur Region, north Syria. Yellowish clay painted in black, wheel-made with the modeling of the features done while the clay was still damp. Contemporary with Atchana-Billa-Hurrian ware about 1500 B.C. Height 5". British Museum.

tion is strong in these wares but, as was usual in each place we study, it soon descended to mere written conventionalization. However, while it lasted, these artists could catch the tense prancing of the chariot horses or the movement of dancers, as seen in the three bustled ladies on the neck of the larger of the "Dipylon" amphoras, as cleverly as any modern cartoonist.

On these potteries we find "Greek Key Fret" borders frequently used and always drawn with double lines diagonally hatched. It also appears at the same time in Northern Italy in Villanova bronzes and potteries and as there is no record of any connection between the two countries, it is likely that it was introduced from the North and descended from the Hallstadt and La Tène cultures, the double spirals having been pushed into a rectangular form so that it would fit into a band of parallel lines or into a square just as it was in China on the Shang bronzes of 1766–1122 B.C. Let us, therefore, call this a *rectangular maeander,* a *swastika* or a *squared spiral,* as the case may be, for the general forms belong to no country. (See "Design" *Encyclopaedia Britannica,* 14th edition, Vol. 7, p. 259.)

A group of crudely-modeled figurines roughly coincide with this period. A small ship seems to have many things in common with northern types and the prominent noses and chins (or beards) show Western Asian types. The wheels on the small cart and also on the animal from Cyprus recall those on the animal found at Ur. The painted terra-cotta head of the girl found at the shrine of Athena Chalciœcus of the 8th century, with sharp nose and staring large eyes, is similar to the Syrian one of about 1500 B.C. which shows a wonderful sense of humor on the part of the artist. In fact this innocent wench could well be the girl friend of the charming Syrian, found at Brak, although he is some 700 years older.

These heads and the vases of the period are all of buff or yellowish buff clay and are decorated in a warm black.

The "Oriental" Period
c. 700 to 550 b.c.

In the 9th century the Greek colonies on the shores of Asia Minor had brought closer the not exactly happy contact with Persia. By the 7th century the influence became predominant. Corinth became the great trade center and the Phoenicians brought much metal work and potteries there. The shapes were exotic and not well adapted to pottery in many instances. Red and white on black drawing was popular. Lions, antelopes and winged griffins or human-headed animals of Babylonian type along with the palmette, lotus and other designs from Egypt by way of Mesopotamia and Persia were similar to Hittite types. We see occasionally the variegated ware imitating stone and in general the design shows the well-known "horror vacui" or horror of vacant spaces which has been much discussed, but this is not always the case and some very beautiful results were obtained as in the Caeretan Hydria, or water jar, in the Louvre and the Cameran style jug, (Pl. 11—3) from the Metropolitan Museum.

Gradually the Oriental style became more free. The structural bands of the Geometrical style widened until they disappeared and the vase became

FIG. 76. An "ary-
ballos" (oil flask) of
"Proto-Corinthian"
or late geometric
style c. 750–700 B.C.
Height about 2".
Metropolitan Mu-
seum of Art.

FIG. 77. Three ewers or "Oinochoe" of 8th century and 7th century Proto-Corinthian period and one of Corinthian period about
625–600 B.C. The first two were found at Attica. All show the tenuous
form better suited to metal than pottery. Metropolitan Museum of Art.

FIG. 78. Early Corinthian "Pyxis" or toilet box typically painted in dark brown with red added
and incised lines for details, c. 600 B.C. and showing animals as well as mythical monsters. Height
about 5". Metropolitan Museum of Art.
  FIG. 79. A "Pyxis" or toilet box of Middle Corinthian style c. 575 B.C. Height 5". Metropolitan
Museum of Art.
  FIG. 80. Corinthian "Krater" c. 575 B.C. showing a Trojan scene of horsemen with shields
and spears as well as the expected animals. Height 16". Metropolitan Museum of Art.
  FIG. 81. "Black figured pottery" plate or "Pinax" of middle Corinthian style showing a poet
on his death-bed with a symbolic lyre, c. 575 B.C. Dia. 9". Metropolitan Museum of Art.

FIG. 82. An "Alabastron" or small ewer, Corinthian c. 625–600 B.C. with opposing lions looking
almost heraldic, and a parrot. Height 5". Metropolitan Museum of Art.
  FIG. 83. "Aryballos" with winged lion in red and black on tan ground of the Late Corinthian
style I c. 575–550 B.C. Height 2¼". Metropolitan Museum of Art.
  FIG. 84. An Eastern Greek hollow pottery duck, perhaps a vase as the hole is at the top of the
head, dating c. 530 B.C. The feathers of the breast are rendered much like the "scales" on some small
vases. The body is black with red decorations. Length 6⅝". Metropolitan Museum of Art.
  FIG. 85. A Proto-Corinthian "Lekythos," Greek of the 7th century B.C. with typical scale design
and petals of alternating colors about the shoulder. Height 4¼". Metropolitan Museum of Art.
  FIG. 86. Ewer from Sardis, Lydia, Asia Minor of about 600 B.C. of variegated black and tan to
represent stone. Height 6½". Metropolitan Museum of Art.

46

Early Athenian or "Proto-Attic" vase showing "Oriental" influence derived from Minoan and the "Geometric" vases. The Corinthian ware is, of course, more "Oriental." On one side is represented a combat between Herakles and the centaur Nessas and on the other a chariot with a woman in it. Note the animals about the neck. Height 42¾". 7th century B.C. Metropolitan Museum of Art.

An "Oinochoë" (wine jug) in the style transitional from proto-Corinthian to Corinthian with quite recognizable cats and rams about the body. c. 640 to 525 B.C. Height about 7". Metropolitan Museum of Art.

Jug of the Cameran style, "East Greek," of about 700–650 B.C. The decoration is in black, brown and red on a dull white ground. Height 14⅛". Metropolitan Museum of Art.

Jug showing transition between Proto-Corinthian and the typical Corinthian wares. There are winged animals with human heads of Assyrian origin, geese, lions and antelope probably of Egyptian origin, etc. Height 15¾". Metropolitan Museum of Art.

Probably due to an early Phoenician settlement in Corinth, the "Oriental style" consisting of monsters and very assyrian-like designs is found there on such examples as this "Pyxis" c. 625–600 B.C. Height about 7". Metropolitan Museum of Art.

A rather squat little "Hydria" from Corinth of about 575 to 550 B.C. with a black figure design of Herakles and a centaur. Height 7⅞". Metropolitan Museum of Art.

PROTO-CORINTHIAN AND CORINTHIAN VASES OF "ORIENTAL" STYLE

PLATE 11

FIG. 87. Terracotta two toned vase in the form of a right foot with sandal, c. 600–550 B.C. Greek. Height 2 5/16″, length 4⅛″. Metropolitan Museum of Art.

FIG. 88. Greek vase of the 6th century B.C. in the form of the head of the river god "Acheloos." Height 3¾″. Metropolitan Museum of Art.

FIG. 89. Lydian "Aryballos" in the form of a siren said to have been found at Sardis. It is of brownish clay. Length 4⅞″. Metropolitan Museum of Art.

FIG. 90. Terracotta funerary mask from Kameiros, Rhodes, of Greek workmanship late 6th century B.C. Note conventionalized hair design, almond shaped eyes, etc. Metropolitan Museum of Art.

FIG. 91. Fragment of a head from South Italy c. 560 B.C.? Note fleeting expression of resolute smile which is very alive. Larger than life size, the piece measures about 7½″. Terracotta. Metropolitan Museum of Art.

FIG. 92. A typical seated female figure of late 6th century B.C. probably from Western Sicily and likely a goddess. The stiff pose of this terracotta and its dwarfed proportions of the lower body do not spoil its life-like expression and quiet dignity. Height about 9″. Metropolitan Museum of Art.

FIG. 93. Terracotta figure of a seated goddess of the last quarter of the 6th century B.C. and said to have come from Tanagra. It is typical of the Archaic Period. Metropolitan Museum of Art.

FIG. 94. Late 6th century between 550 and 500 B.C. terracotta statuette of a woman with traces of the stiff early style with one arm straight down the side. Height 7¼″. Metropolitan Museum of Art.

FIG. 95. Terracotta figure of a maiden of the early 5th century and probably from Western Sicily. It still shows the archaic stiffness, though the features of the face are less conventional. Height nearly 10″. Metropolitan Museum of Art.

FIG. 96. Greek antifix, Gorgonion, said to have been found in Tarentum, of terracotta with traces of color originally applied, it is of the late 6th or early 5th century B. C. Width 10¼″. Metropolitan Museum of Art.

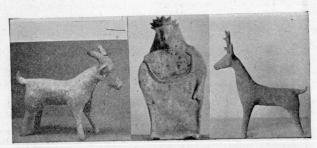 

FIG. 98. A stand with black figured design on top, a mask of Medusa from Athens of about 560 B.C. and signed *Kleitias* and *Ergotimas*. Note similarity of treatment to that of antefix in relief (above). Dia. 3½″. Metropolitan Museum of Art.

FIG. 97. Three terracotta figurines of the 6th century from Greece. The center is said to be a seated goddess and the animals are typical of the Western Asian influence. It will be remembered how prominent the goat figures in Assyrian art. Height 3½″ to about 10″. Metropolitan Museum of Art.

an open field on which anything could be painted. The painting became more naturalistic and separated into various local types.

CORINTHIAN AND OTHER WARES

From the 7th to 6th centuries a wider divergence took place. In the pottery center, Corinth, the wares were at first distinguished by simplicity and by distinctive miniature sizes. The clay was a smooth, pale yellow-buff and the design of black touched with red and white. Another ware has incised scales painted red and white. Still another ware, probably copied from Egypt, was of small figure vases, shells, animals, squatting men, birds, heads, etc., many having holes for suspension and were probably used for oils or unguents.

"IONIAN WARES"

The "Ionian wares" of Rhodes include vases in the forms of heads, especially with helmets, and are made of the buff pottery and also a black ware similar to "bucchero ware" of Italy. There are also large stoneware jars worked with plastic friezes from engraved cylinders. But the general type is covered with white "pipe clay" (we would suppose a refined slip) and this set off the designs well. Egyptian influence is great and the animals are generally better drawn than in the other oriental wares. A later continuation of these Ionian types will be found in the Etruscan wares of Italy.

In Boeotia and Cyrene the wares were similar although the latter had a reddish white slip, a bolder decoration and predominant black and white check and step patterns as well as the lotus, pomegranates, etc. This ware developed into some of those vases found around Sparta decorated in black silhouette with mythological or genre scenes. Other localities were similar with slight differences: we have Aeolic, Clazomenian, Milesian, Samian (which had drunken dancing figures, etc.) Rhodian, Delian, Melian, Corinthian, Chalcidian, Boeotian, Laconian and other sites both in Greece and Italy and finally Attic wares, the latter finally becoming the great "black figure" style wares which were traded to Etruria, Italy and all other parts. It takes much experience to compare and allocate all these wares, and the job is hardly worth the effort. The actual center of the manufacture is not known. Three of the pieces in the Metropolitan Museum are said to have come from Tarentum and two from Cyprus.

ATHENS AND THE BLACK-FIGURE WARES
c. 600 B.C.

To quote the Rev. Edward M. Walker, "In the Great Age the Greeks had learned to despise the Persian and the Persian to fear the Greek. In the 6th century it was the Persian who despised, and the Greek who feared." Thus the oriental styles were not particularly popular, while at the same time the Panhellenic festivals made athletic prowess and physical beauty much sought after. The beauty of well muscled men usually in the nude and of slender women usually lightly draped became the artist's ideal.

Fig. 99. This *"Skyphos"* (drinking cup with handles below the rim) is from Boeotia, Greece and shows a parody of the myth of Herakles hunting the Erymanthian boar. Metropolitan Museum of Art.

Fig. 100. 18th Dynasty Egyptian alabaster amphoras reflecting a type undoubtedly copied in pottery. Ex H. Kevorkian Collection.

Fig. 101. Amphora of red clay with a black slip. Shows in the form of the handles and lip rim as well as the general shape of the body a close resemblance to the alabaster vases of 18th dynasty Egypt. The addition of the base is a bad feature as it is frequently found broken. Height 16½". Athenian 5th century. Warren E. Cox Collection.

Fig. 102. Black figured "Amphora" from Capua decorated with a horseman on each side and having a good sturdy shape, well proportioned and usable. Greek c. 550–575 B.C. Height 14". Metropolitan Museum of Art.

Fig. 103. *"Amphora"* with less than usual distinction between neck and body but tapered foot. Athenian c. 525 B.C., "black figure style." The departure of a warrior on side not shown, and Dionysos and a satyr, Athena and Hermes shown. Height 23½". Metropolitan Museum of Art.

Figs. 104–105. Panathenaic amphorae, given filled with olive oil as prizes in the games held at Athens. Scenes are of horse racing, foot racing, a chariot race and the *"pankration,"* a mixture of boxing and wrestling, etc.

This shows Athena, as always shown fully armed, standing between two columns on which are cocks, symbols of strife. The writing says, "From the games at Athens."

The shape has been over weakened by stylization; the handles too small, the base over tapered, etc. Height 24". Metropolitan Museum of Art.

Attributed to the "Euphiletos Painter" and said to have been found in Etruria. It would date about the end of the 6th century or Archaic Period. Height 22". Metropolitan Museum of Art.

Fig. 106. "Krater (Stamnos)" from Athens, Greece, of the early 5th century with thin black glaze. Height 15½". Metropolitan Museum of Art.

Fig. 107. Toy *"Oinochoë"* "showing children imitating the spring festival of the ceremonial marriage of Dionysos, Athenian about 420 B.C. Many such small pieces have been found in children's graves. Height 2¾". Metropolitan Museum of Art.

Fig. 108. Late free style Athenian *"Bell Krater"* red-figure vase showing on one side three youths and on the other satyrs dancing. Attributed to Polion, c. 420 B.C. Height 10¼". Metropolitan Museum of Art.

Fig. 109. A red-figured *"Column Krater"* of the ripe archaic style showing a youth on one side and *Dionysos* on the other with effective restraint of other decoration. Athenian c. 500 B.C. Height 13½". Metropolitan Museum of Art.

To be sure the Egyptians had already started the fashion and though their attitudes were sometimes stiff and the anatomy not always correct, they could draw a man's arm to look hard as iron and a woman's torso and breast full of life and sexual beauty. There is at times a stupid hardness that goes with much training of the muscles and the athlete is not the sum total of human beauty. We, therefore, find at times a certain coldness in the art of the Greeks. It is as though they preferred a straight line to a curve.

Figures could not be fitted very well to the shoulders and neck of a vase form, therefore, some design was found necessary to fill such spaces and the Greeks did not invent ornament so much as refine such motives as ivy, lotus, palmette, laurel, the maeander and various ray and tongue patterns. Shapes were of less and less interest and so by the middle of the 6th century a comparatively few were formalized and used over and over again. Many of the old writers treat the Black-figure period as that cumulative time which lead to *"the greatest art of the ceramist ever known on this earth."* In this I distinctly disagree for some of the following reasons:

The *Amphora,* which had its beginnings in the round-bottomed Egyptian form, has two handles curving from the neck down to the shoulder. In sticking out of the neck they were never as graceful as were the T'ang, Chinese vases derived from them, on which the handles meet the lip-rim. The handles do not as a rule widen out where they touch the shoulder, thus they are not strong at this point and are often broken there. The excessive tapering, almost to a point, of the bottom necessitated a flat attached base which spoils the rhythm of the curves and is often broken because of bad structure.

The *Panathenaic Amphora,* a taller and more slender type, simply exaggerates these faults.

The *Hydria,* or water jar, is similar except that it has two usually useless small close horizontal handles on the lower shoulder and a long, slender and easily-broken perpendicular handle at the back.

The *Stamnos* is simply a more squatty hydria with the third handle left off, while the *Pelike* is like an amphora with a sagging, fat-bellied sack of a body.

The *Oenochoe* with its wide spout does not pour very well, although otherwise it is a fair ewer form.

The *Kelebe* or wine-mixing vessel is like a large, wide-mouthed amphora but has two lugs from the lip-rim from which drop double, straight handles to the shoulder. It has some dynamic strength of design but the same weak foot. It is sometimes called a *Column Krater.*

This may be said also of the *Bell Krater;* and the *Calyx Krater.*

The *Kalpis* is nothing but a Hydria on which the third handle joins the neck instead of the lip-rim and it is often stood on a high stand serving no particular purpose but inherited from those reticulated early ones which were used over fire.

The *Skyphos* or *Kotylē* is a clumsy, deep cup with two horizontal handles indicating a two-handled grip for drinking.

The *Kylix* in its very wide shallow form with foot stem and horizontal handles would seem to be a good example of our fragility challenge in ap-

FIG. 110. Greek (Attic) black figure *"Skyphos"* c. 550 B.C. but still showing the "Oriental influence" with its lion which does not occur in Greece and a crane. Height 3½". Metropolitan Museum of Art.

FIG. 111. Important signed piece of this period, a *"Kylix"* inscribed, *"Nikosthenes made me."* There are about 80 signed pieces known by this artist. Dia. 17½". Metropolitan Museum of Art.

peal. The other forms might lose an ear or other part while this actually looks as though it would break completely if broken at all.

Other cups are the *Kaythos,* like a teacup with loop handle twice its height and the *Kantharos* having two such unstructural loops sometimes further supported, as though the potter knew his mistake, by horizontal supports, and having a long stem to boot.

FIG. 112. An exceedingly interesting and really beautiful *"Aryballos"* has a clever device of crescents in four colors about the body and opposing crescents about the shoulder, while the lip shows a spirited battle between the pygmies and cranes with explanatory inscriptions. Height 2⅞". 6th century. Metropolitan Museum of Art.

FIG. 113. Athenian *"Aryballos"* in the form of a group of cockleshells with a black glazed mouth. Late 6th century. Height about 2". Metropolitan Museum of Art.

FIG. 114. Greek (Attic) *"Lekythos"* of black figured type with lion and deer c. 550 B.C. and showing remains of "Oriental influence." Height 7". Metropolitan Museum of Art.

The *Pyxis,* a small cylindrical box and cover, seems a satisfactory form.

The *Aryballos* originally meant bag or purse and is a small globular ewer for oil but was larger and used for carrying water to the bath. It is a good and well devised form.

The *Lekythos* is a tall and pleasant form of bottle with an extraneous handle, for the neck could as readily be grasped, and the same flat base as we have criticized on the Amphora.

The *Alabastron* came direct from Egypt and has usually a round bottom and two handles or loops, perhaps for tying on a cover.

Black figured Oinochoe with painting of Europa riding the Bull. Greek 6th century B.C. Height 8". Cleveland Museum of Art.

"Lekythos" of black figured Athenian ware c. 550 B.C. Height 6⅛". Metropolitan Museum of Art.

Athenian black figure vase c. 550 B.C. showing perhaps the height of this form in Greece, but with weak base flange and sharp edge at lip to chip and break. Height 17". W. R. Hearst Col. International Studio, Inc.

"BLACK FIGURE" VASES, GREECE

PLATE 12

The *Olpe* is a pitcher with a round mouth and no spout. At times it has a body like the unpleasant Pelike, but others are good in form as the one shown.

There are also the *Rhyton, Lebes, Askos, Hemikotylin* and others, which the reader may judge for himself, but perhaps one of the worst is the tall and involved *Loutrophoros.*

Fig. 115. Once in a while the Athenians of the 5th century made a fine pottery vessel without the usual over-decoration. Such an example is this *"Olpe"* of very perfect lines and proportions. Height 8". Metropolitan Museum of Art.

Fig. 116. A *"Pelike"* of the 6th century B.C., said to be from Ban. Distinguished from the amphora by having a less definite neck and more rounded bottom with wider foot. Height 10½". Metropolitan Museum of Art.

Fig. 117. A *"Psykter"* (wine cooler) of the early red figure style marked by formalized drapes, stiff action and eyes painted in profile faces as though seen in front view. Attributed to *Oltos,* Athenian, c. 520–510 B.C. Height 13". Metropolitan Museum of Art.

Fig. 118. A black figure "Loutrophoros" used by Athenian maidens to bring water for the bridal bath. They were also placed in the tombs of unmarried youths or maidens and libations were poured into them. In such cases they had no bottoms as with the specimen shown. The significance was that the marriage had taken place with Hades c. 500 B.C. Height 29½". Metropolitan Museum of Art.

Most of these forms had suffered very much from the influence of attenuated metal shapes and I believe that the Greeks were not truly pottery conscious; they merely used their ceramic vessels as objects on which to paint. This is further proven by the fact that they utterly ignored the beautiful glazes which they knew full well and had seen when brought from the Near East and Egypt. Thus those who study these vessels often think more of the painting than of the pot and the study really lies out of the scope of this book.

Only a few of the makers of the vases signed them but many of the painters did and we find that among the first of the black-figure artists were *Cleitias* and *Ergotimus.* Others are *Execias, Amasis* and *Nicosthenes;* the first had a style reminiscent of the Near Eastern designs and the second

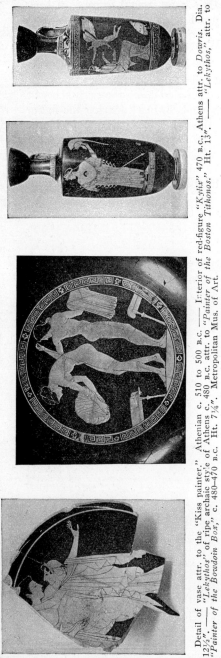

Detail of vase attr. to the "Kiss painter," Athenian c. 510 to 500 B.C. —— Interior of red-figure "Kylix" 470 B.C., Athens attr. to *Douris*. Dia. 12½". —— "Lekythos" of ripe archaic style of Athens c. 480 B.C. attr. to *"Painter of the Boston Tithonos."* Ht. 13". —— "Lekythos," attr. to *"Painter of the Bowdoin Box,"* c. 480-470 B.C. Ht. 7¼". Metropolitan Mus. of Art.

PLATE 13

RED FIGURE POTTERIES OF GREECE

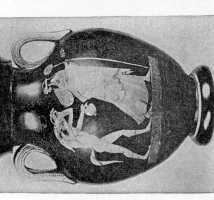

"Bell-Krater," c. 460-450 B.C. from Athens. Attr. to *"Villa Guilia Painter."* Ht. 14½". —— Early free style *"Amphora"* attr. to *"Painter of the Syracuse Pelike."* Athenian c. 470-460 B.C. Ht. 18". —— Early free style *"Stamnos"* c. 460-450 B.C. attr. to *"Villa Guilia Painter."* Ht. 13½". Metropolitan Mus. of Art.

drew in a formal and dignified manner. His name would suggest that he might have been Egyptian, or was at least of Egyptian heritage.

RED-FIGURE WARES

About 520 B.C. the style changed and instead of painting the figures in black on a buff yellow, light red or dark red ground, depending upon the locality, or a white slip ground, as was sometimes done, the artists began to reverse the process and paint the backgrounds in black leaving the figure the color of the ground, and then touch in the details with more black. Some artists used both styles. *Andocides* and *Pamphaios* were among these and belonged to the circle of *Epictetus* which quickly took up the style. Sometimes a yellow or brown color was added. These colors were made of an alkaline flux mixed with iron earth and are half way between a glaze and a slip.

Personal styles developed and we hear of the "Strong Red-figure Style" (*c.* 500–460 B.C.), the "Fine Red-figure Style" (*c.* 460–430 B.C.), the "Poly-

FIG. 119. Early red-figure style *"Kylix"* showing on the inside a youth running and on the outside revelers c. 510 B.C. Attributed to the *"Epeleios painter."* Dia. about 14½". Metropolitan Museum of Art.
FIG. 120. Miniature "Lekythos" from Greece of the 5th century. Height is about 2½". Metropolitan Museum of Art.
FIG. 121. Miniature "Lekythos" of Greek 5th century. The decoration is a rather startled looking owl. Height about 2½". Mrs. Warren E. Cox Collection.

FIG. 122. Athenian free style "Calyx Krater" c. 450–440 B.C. with two friezes, the above showing Nekyra, Heroes and Divinities, the lower the punishment of Tityas; contest of Zeus and Hermes against a giant. Height 15⅜". Metropolitan Museum of Art.

FIG. 123. A "Column Krater" early free style, 5th century attributed to "The Pig Painter." It shows a Satyr pursuing a Maenad on one side and a Satyr on the other. Height 17". Metropolitan Museum of Art.

An Athenian "Oinochoë," early free style red figured pottery c. 450 B.C. The painting is attributed to "The Manheim Painter" and shows three Amazons starting for battle. Height 13⅛". Metropolitan Museum of Art.

Red figure free style "Amphora" of about 440 B.C. with a warrior bidding farewell to his family on one side and a libation scene on the other. Attributed to the "Lykon Painter." Height 24⅛". Metropolitan Museum of Art.

A "Lekythos" and "Amphora" of the red figure style and attributed to the *"Painter of the Boston Phiale,"* the first showing the departure of a warrior and the second Herakles in the garden of the Hesperides. Heights 18" and 9½". Metropolitan Museum of Art. c. 460–420 B.C.

Athenian "Volute Krater" dating about 450 B.C. of the early free style attributed to the "Painter of the Shaggy Silenus." Height 25". Metropolitan Museum of Art.

Probably a *"Lebes gamikos"* (marriage-vase) the use for which is not known, this piece shows the bride during the *"Epaulia"* or day after the wedding when it was customary to bring her gifts. The whole is too crowded and confused. Height 22". c. 430–420 B.C. Metropolitan Museum of Art.

A Pelike of Greek Asia Minor of the 4th century B.C. showing "the florid style," in its form, and crowded design. Height 16¼". Metropolitan Museum of Art.

RED FIGURE PAINTERS OF GREECE

PLATE 14

gnotus Style" named after one artist (*c.* 460–445 B.C.), the "Pheidias Style" (445–430 B.C.), and the "Florid Style" (*c.* 430–400 B.C.). Among the best known artists were *Euthymides* who painted bacchanalian scenes without subdivisions of the pot surface, *Euphronius,* the famous kylix painter whose touch was exceedingly sensitive, *Sosias,* a pupil of his who developed a style strong and angular, restless but well composed, *Duris* whose style was something like that of *Euphronius,* and *Brygus,* the dramatic painter. *Hieron* was another but his anatomy was bad and his compositions less interesting. It was about this time that the artists learned to paint the face in three quarters. The effect of the sculpture of *Pheidias* was also felt, particularly by *Aristophanes* and *Erginus.*

White-Ground Wares

The white ground was usually used on lekythi, the inside of bowls and occasionally on pyxis and kraters. *Euphronius* and *Duris* signed typical bowls finished with white slip inside while the outside was treated with red-figure technique. The earlier lekythi are harder and slightly yellowish with figures in the black-figure style but later the white was less well fixed and whiter, with figures freely drawn in red, black or other colors. This technique necessitated a quick and sure fluency and might have developed something greater had it not been against the taste of the period. The best that can be

FIG. 124. "Aryballos," Greek c. 500 B.C. with all-over design of black palmettes on white ground. Height 5". Metropolitan Museum of Art.

FIG. 125. White "Lekythos" of the early type which show both red-figure and black-figure styles. This one shows Persus escaping with the head of Medusa while from the neck of Medusa springs the winged steed Pegasos. Greek c. 485–460 B.C. Height 10". Metropolitan Museum of Art.

FIG. 126. Plate of red figured Campanian ware with touches of white, of about 400 to 300 B.C. Dia. 8¾". Metropolitan Museum of Art.

Athenian *"Lekythos"* of black figured
type showing women working wool
about 550 B.C. Height 6½". Metropolitan Museum of Art.

Painting on white ground was heightened
by solid washes in various colors. *"Pyxis"*
showing Hermes leading the three goddesses
for the judgment of Paris, in black, brown,
purple and white. Height 6¼". Metropolitan
Museum of Art.

"Lekythos" side view of representation of Hermes conducting a man to
Charon's boat. The artist was too
lazy to continue the key-fret border
around under the handle. Greek latter
half of the 5th century. Height 11½".
Metropolitan Museum of Art.

Lekythos with white ground showing
mourning figures, Greek 6th century B.C.
Height 19½". The John Huntington Col.
Cleveland Museum of Art.

GREEK WHITE GROUND WARES

PLATE 15

said is that the figures were well placed and well drawn, though the weak outline can hardly be seen at a short distance and could hardly be said to form a proper vase decoration. The brush technique never reached the heights of that of Sung China as seen in the Tz'u Chou wares.

The placing of figures on all Greek vases was difficult. If they are too high the heads give a flattened effect due to the curve of the shoulder, and if they are lowered, they seem to sag about the bottom.

IV CENTURY GREEK POTTERY

By the 4th century B.C. Greece had come to the end of all true artistic achievement in ceramics. In the now prevalent "Florid Style" richly draped women toy with winged love-gods and other involved and saccharine subjects predominate. Poor craftsmanship and overcrowding of design are everywhere present. Blue, green, red and gold were added to the palette. These vases are called "Kertch Ware" and many were found in North Africa, and also in South Russia in the town after which they are named.

FIG. 127. Four terracotta figures from an Athenian grave showing actors of comic and tragic roles of the 4th century B.C. Hts. 4⅛" and 4¼". Metropolitan Museum of Art.

At the same time charming little figures were made and painted in pastel colors. The first of these found were in Tanagra and, therefore, the whole group has been given that name though they were made elsewhere in Boeotia, and in Greece, Asia Minor, the Crimea, in Rhodes, North Africa, Sicily and Italy. The Tanagra figures are distinguished by their simple grace and quiet charm. The Asiatic ones are more lively and the Italian less tasteful. In size they vary from 2 inches to 20 but about 7 or 8 inches in height is usual. They may have been temple offerings and some were buried with the dead but I think they were simply toys for grownups and served various purposes from that of a bachelor's etchings to decorations for the what-not, if the Greeks had such things. The subjects are varied and comprise youths, women and children of ordinary dress of the times, quite sexy girls of coy mien, some pensive ladies, actors, slaves and beggars. One amusing one at the Metropolitan Museum of Art is of Herakles with his finger in his mouth. Those of the Hellenistic period (*c. 325* to 200 B.C.) are of divinities such as Aphrodite and Dionysus with Erotes, satyrs, Sileni and Maenads with some hetaerae, warriors, etc.

FIG. 128. Modeled vase with figure of Silenus of the 4th to 3d century B.C. Greece. Height 4¼″. Metropolitan Museum of Art.

FIG. 129. Terracotta statuette representing Niké flying, of the III century or later. Height 9⅜″. Metropolitan Museum of Art.

FIG. 130. This tragic mask of the Hellenistic period is from Thebes, Greece. It is of terracotta. Height 6⅞″. Metropolitan Museum of Art.

Two out of every three that one sees are fakes, for the supply was quickly outrun by the demand. We can only suggest that fakes are likely to have a bit too much color left on them, to be a little busy and too detailed and also to lack true feeling. The sexy ones have always sold well so many fakes are of this nature. Most of the larger museums have collections of real ones and, much to their disgust, a fair number of fakes.

After the Tanagra ones, those from Myrina are valued highest. Here the subjects are from mythology as a rule, more nudes were tried with varying success and the figures are likely to have small heads and slender limbs.

Many of these figures were made in molds, usually of two pieces, and are naturally hollow. Holes were left in the backs so that a finger could press together the sutures from the inside and also so that the gasses could escape. The good ones were then worked over by the artist before firing, but less and less interest finally led to even leaving the suture marks on them.

Man seems always to come to a point when he likes to make little figures of himself, his wife, children and dog. They are inspired at first and get technically better as time goes on until the process of duplicating them with the mold is found, and then they die of their own cheapness. Verily, the preacher against idolaters should present them with the techniques and materials for making molds and all worship of the figures would soon cease!

OTHER MODELED AND RELIEF WARES

Metal had always been the inspiration and also the curse of Greek ceramics. Since the "Harvester Vase" of Crete the reproduction of repoussé had been

Left—Figure of 4th to 3d cent. B.C., Tanagra type. Height 9¼″. *Right*—Tanagra type figure of 4th to 3d cent. B.C. Height 12″. Metropolitan Museum of Art.

TANAGRA TYPE FIGURES

Left—Tanagra figure, 4th cent. B.C. Height 6½″. *Right*—Greek figure in terracotta of Tanagra type of 4th cent. B.C. Height 8¾″. Metropolitan Museum of Art.

PLATE 16

FIG. 131. Terracotta mask, which seems to have been a votive copy of an actual mask used in ritual dances in honor of the goddess Artemis Orthia, at whose shrine they were found in Sparta. c. 500 B.C. Photographs by the British School of Archaeology, Athens.

FIG. 132. Etruscan antefix probably of a Maenad from the roof of a temple. Though this is said to come from Italy it has strong Greek feeling and may have been brought from there. About 500 B.C. Height 16". Metropolitan Museum of Art.

FIG. 133. An almost portrait quality is seen in this Hellenistic "Aryballos" or oil jug. Height 2¾". Metropolitan Museum of Art.

FIG. 134. A "Kantharos" having a woman's face on either side and a red figure design attributed to Brygus, Athenian, about 490 to 480 B.C. Height 7". Metropolitan Museum of Art.

FIG. 135. "Rhyton" c. 475 to 450 B.C. from Athens of the "red figure" type. These vessels were used as drinking cups and some are pierced with a small hole for the liquid to spurt into the mouth of the drinker. Length 4¼". Metropolitan Museum of Art.

FIG. 136. A red-figure "Kantharos" (drinking-cup) of the free style having on one side a modeled head of a satyr and on the other that of a woman. Height 7¾". Metropolitan Museum of Art.

FIG. 137. Athenian red-figure "Askos" in the form of a lobster claw decorated with a mule. c. 460 B.C. Length 6½". Metropolitan Museum of Art.

FIG. 138. An "Askos" in the form of a rat made in South Italy 4th to 3d century B.C. It is of orangy buff color with black glazed decoration. Length 6⅞". Metropolitan Museum of Art.

sought. Now there was the added desire for ornate detail. *The art of the Greek had at best been a technical development rather than a spiritual one* and now the painted technique was as perfect as they could conceive it had any possibilities of ever being. Therefore, the artists could only turn to the more difficult technicalities of sculpture. Long since, all taste as to the *appropriateness* of the decoration for a vessel had been lost so there was nothing to hold them back from perpetrating the monstrous vases of "Kertch ware," the head vases and cups, odd rhytons in various forms and even the askos in the form of a lobster's claw.

CHAPTER V

ITALY

c. 1200 B.C. TO A.D. 100

IF GREECE started the trend toward the worst of bad taste, Italy carried it on to its ultimate conclusion. The Greek influence on Italian ceramics came when Grecian art had already deteriorated. But let us begin at the beginning in Italy.

If one were going to pick stepping stones, one might say that the stone age art was in Egypt and Crete, the bronze age in Greece and the iron age

FIG. 139. Cauldron stand of "Red ware" from Etruria c. 7th century B.C. Remarkably like those of prehistoric Japan showing how men's minds work alike in the solution of simple problems. Height 32″. Metropolitan Museum of Art.

FIG. 140. Bowl and stand of the first half of the 7th century B.C. found at Capena in Latium. Buff terracotta with black finish. Note the sgraffito decoration of animals much in the style of Western Asian metal work. Height 29″. Metropolitan Museum of Art.

FIG. 141. *"Oinochoë"* or pitcher of Italian *"bucchero"* ware with incised decoration showing Western Asian influence. Most of this ware is found in chamber tombs dating from the 7th to early 5th centuries B.C. 625–600 B.C. The red ware is earlier. Height 11″. Metropolitan Museum of Art.

FIG. 142. *"Bucchero"* *"Oinochoë"* with a frieze of animals and monsters incised and touched with purple and yellow, a sort of Italic imitation of Corinthian ware. Etruscan 625–600 B.C. Height 12¾″. Metropolitan Museum of Art.

in Italy. This country seemed destined to be the center of the metal industries. As early as the 12th or 11th century B.C. the "Villanovans," so called because the first finds of their wares were made at a little village of that name about 8 kilometers from Bologna, came from the north and probably from the Danube basin. They seemed to have had some connection with the Hallstadt Culture but were a different people because their burial customs were quite different. With them they brought an advanced bronze culture and also iron used as weapons. They also brought the conventionalized spiral, angular elements of design and the expected animal motifs.

Following this settlement came the Etruscans in about the 9th to 7th centuries and they grew ever stronger, at least in aesthetic influence, until about 500 B.C. Finally in 474 B.C. the Battle of Cumae started the series of disasters from which they never recovered. The Etruscans seem to have come by sea from some place in the Near East between Syria and the Hellespont. After their downfall we reach the Greek influence.

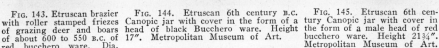

FIG. 143. Etruscan brazier with roller stamped friezes of grazing deer and boars of about 600 to 550 B.C. of red bucchero ware. Dia. 18¾". Metropolitan Museum of Art.

FIG. 144. Etruscan 6th century B.C. Canopic jar with cover in the form of a head of black Bucchero ware. Height 17". Metropolitan Museum of Art.

FIG. 145. Etruscan 6th century Canopic jar with cover in the form of a male head of red bucchero ware. Height 21¾". Metropolitan Museum of Art.

The Villanova pottery was based on a crude ware sometimes incised but never painted. When the Etruscans arrived there were, in the southern tip of the boot, wares painted in rectilinear patterns similar to those of Crete but showing no slightest connection; the people had simply reached the same stage of development. The Villanova pottery is crude and decorated with knobs, ribs and sometimes grotesque handles ending in crescents and horns. Other vases and probably earlier ones have globular bodies tapering some-what toward the foot and tall truncated conical necks taking half the height. The mouth is left fairly wide and prominent lip-rims are usual. They are found with bowls or helmets turned over the mouths. In the south, burial urns were also made in the form of little huts, probably representative of the deceased one's home.

As early as 900 B.C. decoration came into use with geometric designs very like those which came into Greece, and probably from the same source, but this was a crude red, brown or black pottery and the designs were incised rather than painted. The same maeanders, swastikas and simple borders were more crudely used. The wheel had not been discovered and the designs

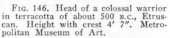

FIG. 147. Etruscan bucchero ware black cup on high foot dating about 610 to 560 B.C. Height 8½″. Metropolitan Museum of Art.

FIG. 148. Etruscan amphora c. 520 B.C. with cover which seems to have been made for it and a decoration of winged horses possibly of Assyrian inspiration originally. Height 15¼″. Metropolitan Museum of Art.

FIG. 146. Head of a colossal warrior in terracotta of about 500 B.C., Etruscan. Height with crest 4′ 7″. Metropolitan Museum of Art.

were in spots about the body with a few bands above and below as the tendency of the wheel to induce many band designs was lacking.

By the 8th century the Etruscan influence was dominant and we must not think of these people as simply an offshoot of Greek art for they brought ideas from the whole Mediterranean and even from Assyria. Their first homes were at Targuinii and Vetulonia, north of Rome on the western shore. They used winged monsters, tree designs and flower designs much like those of Mesopotamia. They were strong and warlike but could never organize sufficiently to stand against Rome. However, this independence is easy to see in their works of art. Take pause to study the great pottery warrior which I show from the Metropolitan Museum. Its size alone, some 8 feet, makes it a major problem, technically speaking. Yet it would be big and dangerous-appearing if it were only a quarter as big. Here we have an excellent example of appropriateness of size for it is just enough larger than a big man to give it the greatest strength. If it were still larger it would become a statue. As it is, it is a giant in smooth and powerful action. Ah, Italy, how very near you came to striking that clear note upon which your art would have gone up rather than down! But, alas, it was soon a business of copying the little Tanagra figures instead of creating such great pieces!

No trace of Greek influence can be found in the tombs of the 8th and 7th centuries. Trade was with the Phoenicians and the feeling was Egypto-Syrian. Toward the end of the 7th century came traces from Corinth and then by the beginning of the 6th century began the flood of Athenian painted wares. So many were found there that old collectors thought they were Etruscan vases and some even speak of them so today.

"Buchero" ware or the black type called "buchero nero" was made after

Etruscan figure standing 8 feet high of a warrior with black body, red armor and buff detailed designs. It shows strong Greek influence but a greater virility than is seen in most Greek works of art. It was made probably as a votive figure about 500 B.C. Metropolitan Museum of Art.

ETRUSCAN MONUMENTAL WARRIOR

PLATE 17

the Villanovan ideas. It is rarely wheel-made and usually molded or impressed. Small toothed wheels, cylindrical seals like the Egyptian and Babylonian ones, and various punches and stamps made possible an effect much like repoussé metal. Thus more and more mechanical means were employed, until finally the mold was brought into use. Some of this ware was red and both the black and red types were also treated with white and polychrome decoration which was poorly fired and is usually worn off. As the Greek influence gained it is easy to see how these wares grew into Hellenistic shapes such as those found at Cumae, Apulia, where finds were made at Gnathia, and in Campania at Cales, as well as in Etruria. Those from Etruria were not glazed and may have been gilded all over.

FIG. 149. Etruscan bucchero ware vase of black color dating from about 560 to 500 B.C. Height about 12″. Metropolitan Museum of Art.

FIG. 150. Etruscan amphora of black bucchero c. 6th century or before. Note the animals similar to those in Corinthian wares. Height 20″. Metropolitan Museum of Art.

FIG. 151. Etruscan "bucchero ware" pitcher or "Oinochoë" with Assyrian looking sphinxes in relief. c. 560–500 B.C. Height 12″. Metropolitan Museum of Art.

The Etruscans did not cremate as did the Villanovans and sarcophagi were made of terra-cotta shaped like a couch on which reclined the figure of a man and his wife in an easy and lifelike pose as though conversing. Some of the figures are quite heavy but others are slender and have an elfish smile which, with their almond-shaped and slightly upturned eyes, are typical

FIG. 152. Etruscan "bucchero ware" drinking cup or "Kantharos" with stippled decoration. c. 635–600 B.C. Height 12″. Metropolitan Museum of Art.

FIG. 153. Etruscan bucchero tray with pots and spoons c. 6th century B.C. The color is black or gray-black. Length about 22″. Metropolitan Museum of Art.

FIG. 154. Black bucchero ware "Krater," Etruscan of about 560 to 500 B.C. Height 16⅛″. Metropolitan Museum of Art.

It seems strange that at the same time that some Apulian wares were showing every sign of decadence others like this fine bell-shaped "Krater" could be made. 4th cent. B.C. Ht. 36½". Metropolitan Mus. of Art.

Apulian Hydria with thin black glaze or slip decorated with white and a dull, dirty yellow. The third handle is not visible. Ht. 16½". Warren E. Cox Coll.

Left: An involved "Krater," Apulian 4th cent. B.C. with a scene of offerings at a tomb, handles having masks and four small goose-head loops on the shoulder. Ht. 36". Metropolitan Mus. of Art.

Right: Apulian "Amphora" with red-figured decoration on one side of Bellerophon killing the Chimaera, and on the other of two youths. c. 350 B.C. Ht. 22". Metropolitan Mus. of Art.

APULIAN POTTERIES FROM ITALY

PLATE 18

Etruscan faces and give them a sprightly expression. The modeling is simple and good and these are real achievements for the 6th to 5th centuries.

In South Italy, from the earlier geometric wares "Peucetian" and later, came those flower motives called "Messapian." These wares, known as Apulian, Lucanian, Campanian and Paestumian, all have brown clays and are usually of bad and involved design. The last two are heavily ornate on one hand and mundane and stupid on the other. Here, of course, is another sign of decadence. How different the attitude of an artist who only does the side that shows (and overdoes that) from the true artist like the Chinese ones who make wonderful "secret designs" that do not show at all to the casual eye! The subject matter is just as uninteresting as the technique. It consists of unfelt mythological subjects, girls lounging in ornate grandeur among flowers, ribbons, pet animals and other sloppy ideas of design. In this, so-called, red-figure style we find also yellow, white and other colors dabbed on to enhance the effect.

The Hellenistic Period of the 3rd to the 1st century brought from Athens new ideas of perfume bottles of not heads, but whole busts, of women surrounded by scarves and swirls. Hannover has written, "These objects, with a jug in the form of Aphrodite and Adonis grouped together, are considered to be among the greatest treasures of the museums that possess them." (The Louvre, the Hermitage, the British Museum and the Berlin Museum)—But he does add, "—although they are in every way more curious than beautiful." But these fantasies are simple and compact as compared with the masterpieces from Canosa with gorgon masks, front halves of horses or centaurs plunging out of the sides and large statues or half statues of winged goddesses, cupids, ladies in distress and such, jumping out of them in the most surpris-

FIG. 155. "Oinochoë" from Apulia of the 4th century B.C. with a design of the chariot of Aurora. Height 16". Metropolitan Museum of Art.
FIG. 156. "Rhyton" with stag's head. At the lip is a painting of Eros with a bowl of fruit. 4th century B.C., Apulian. Length about 8". Metropolitan Museum of Art.
FIG. 157. "Amphora" of the 4th century, Apulian, said to be from Tarentum and having a scene of mourners at a tomb and of the dispute of Persephone and Aphrodite over Adonis. Height 42". Metropolitan Museum of Art.
FIG. 158. A very much degraded Olpe shaped pitcher of Roman make; buff pottery with green glaze. Decoration applied. Thought to date c. 1st century B.C. Height 7½". Metropolitan Museum of Art.

ing, fantastical and god-awful taste that man ever perpetrated. Here at last I am able to point out the *worst* that has ever been done in the art of potting.

The period was one of confusion. Realism had become the fanatical aim of artists (see the figure of Diadoumenos) and caricature and the grotesque became substitutes for sincere style. Invention replaced inspiration. Masks

FIG. 159. Roman vase with movable ring around the neck made of unglazed gray pottery and supposed to date between the 1st and 4th century A.D. Height 14¾". Metropolitan Museum of Art.

FIG. 160. Roman lamp of the sort given as New Year's presents. This one is of red clay and shows Victory in relief holding a shield inscribed with a New Year's wish. 1st century A.D. Length 4½". Height 1". Metropolitan Museum of Art.

FIG. 161. Roman vase of the 1st century B.C. of unglazed gray pottery with scratched and applied design. Height 9¼". Metropolitan Museum of Art.

FIG. 162. Mask of a satyr's head late Greek, made of terracotta. Height 9". Metropolitan Museum of Art.

FIG. 163. Hellenistic period (3d to 1st century B.C.) jug in the form of a sleeping youth. Height 7½". Metropolitan Museum of Art.

FIG. 164. Terracotta Roman "rattle" or hollow pig with glass inlays. Length 3½". Metropolitan Museum of Art.

FIG. 165. Graeco-Egyptian of the Roman period figure of a camel with four large jars attached to the saddle, found at Ephesos. Height 4¼". Metropolitan Museum of Art.

FIG. 166. Terracotta figure of Eros riding a lion found at Tarentum and said to be of the 3d century B.C. or the beginning of the Hellenistic period. Height 6¾". Metropolitan Museum of Art.

and antefixes reflected the trend. In some parts simple and even crude work was done but it was not good. It was the old story of the combination of too many undigestible influences. On top of that and beyond all the usual bad results was the terrible result of the everlasting urge of realism that the Greeks were responsible for.

CHAPTER VI

HAN CHINA

206 B.C–A.D. 220

GENERALLY speaking, the known history of China begins with the Han dynasty. What went before that is divided into four periods, Hsia, Shang, Chou, Ch'in.

The *Hsia* period (2205–1766 B.C.) is purely legendary but when one reads H. G. Creel's book "The Birth of China" he is likely to be amazed at the amount we know about the *Shang* period (1766–1122 B.C.) and also at the state of culture that did exist even in those ancient times.

The *Chou* period (1122–249 B.C.) is the longest in Chinese history and we know that the rulers came from the North West and settled in Honan on the Yellow River. This was on the same caravan route that Anau and Samarkand touched in the West. The period was one of high attainments. During it Confucius, Mencius and Lao Tzŭ devised their great philosophies. But the state finally was divided and overcome by the rulers of *Ch'in* (249–207 B.C.) a land lying west along the Wei River. This was a short period but during it China enthroned its first emperor who set up a central govern-

FIG. 167. Rubbing from a tile found at Loyang in the tombs. It shows a street scene with an old man followed by a Confucian scholar with his bamboo book and two women. Length 6 feet. Royal Ontario Mus., Toronto.

ment, the Great Wall was built, standard weights and measures were instituted, and the territory was extended to Fukien and Kwangtung provinces south and east on the coast. It was this same first emperor, nevertheless, who despite his enlightenment had all the existing books burnt.

The *Han* period is counted as from 206 B.C. to 220 A.D. after a period of civil war and Liu Pang carried his territory well into what is now Sin-Kiang

73

province, halfway to the Caspian Sea, making contact with the Hellenistic world. A Chinese embassy reached the Persian Gulf and the Romans traded iron and silk with them. Meanwhile, from India came Buddhism, bringing a new system of thought, more Hellenistic designs carried there by Alexander the Great, etc.

We do have a very few potteries which can be called pre-Shang or Shang and of these the most notable is the crude gray ware described in Chap. II.

FIG. 168. Front and back rubbings from a Loyang 3d cent. tile with stamped designs. Royal Ontario Mus., Toronto.
FIG. 169. Loyang tomb-tile of hard grey pottery with impressed border and incised design of geese, dogs and stags. Late Han or first part of 3d cent. Royal Ontario Mus., Toronto.

During the Chou and Ch'in period this gray ware seemed to continue with its string-impressed design (though the pointed wares we know seem to have stopped). Such gray wares have been found in Chinese Turkestan and Szechwan province. So far as we know, the hard white pottery with fret patterns carved in it or stamped, which was found on the site of the Yin emperors' tombs (1401–1122 B.C.) at Hsiao-tun in Honan, also ceased.

HAN WARES, 206 B.C.–A.D. 220

If one looks at the chart of Hissar I potteries, the #5 form is identical to many of the early Han wine jar forms. It was derived from the old original primitive pointed pot which had to be set into a ring stand which was made separately for a time and then sometimes made attached to the pot. This had become a bronze form in China, called a *"Hu"* but it did not appear until late Chou times, or about 500 B.C., some 2000–2500 years after the Hissar I potteries and it was not until Han times that it was frequently used. Thus Hobson is right when he says that this, among other Han pottery forms, was copied from bronzes, but he neglected to go far enough back to find that they in turn had been copied from potteries.

FIG. 170. A primitive form of Han pottery vase very much like one form of the Hissar I jars and probably arrived at in the same way though very likely the one was not influenced at all by the other. Ht. 17″. Warren E. Cox Coll.

FIG. 171. A further advanced pottery form in which the foot has widened to become more a part of the body and the lip-rim takes on a cup shape. Ht. 16″. Warren E. Cox Coll.

FIG. 172.

A large part of Hu wares are unglazed gray, reddish or dark brown painted with designs in unfired or lightly fired pigments and molded or stamped appliqués. Only occasionally was a fine black dressing applied and polished, not unlike the finish of some American Indian potteries. Many of the painted designs are of dragons or animals, some show the floral motives or key fret bands of Hellenistic wares, but a large number have the sharp points that we described in the Susa potteries and the "pot hook" reverse spirals found on those of the "Black Earth Region." On these the bands are wide and the spirals are no longer angular as on the early bronzes but curved again almost exactly like the originals, flowing in a free and interlacing movement.

With these indications of a Western Asian heritage we are not surprised to find that at this time a simple alkaline glaze, transparent and varying from yellowish to brown, and in many shades of green due to the addition of copper, was introduced probably through association with the so-called Syro-Roman two-handled jars which have a closely allied glaze allowing for local differences in materials. These latter we know to have been found at widely different places (see last figure on Tepe Gawra Chart) and some are likely to have found their way to China through trade. They are contemporary and earlier than the Han period.

This was the first glaze used in China. It appears on a rather soft reddish

Hollow tile of grey pottery with stamped decoration made by applying several blocks over and over. Han dynasty. Length 41½″. The Cleveland Mus. of Art.

Grey pottery tiles said to have come from a tomb near Hsianfu and to be of the Han dynasty. Lengths 10¾″ to 12¼″. The Cleveland Mus. of Art.

HAN DYNASTY TILES (206 B.C.–A.D. 220)

PLATE 19

FIG. 173. Hu shaped vase having two t'ao-t'ieh head and loop handles in relief, of red pottery with dressing of brownish black clay polished and lightly incised. Ht. 16¼". Eumorfopoulos Coll. #80. Late Chou or Chin; not Han.

FIG. 174. Han pottery Hu showing very prominent use of the pot-hook and also the points (about the neck) which we have spoken of as probably originating in the Black Earth Region and at Susa. Ht. 21". Mus. of Fine Arts, Boston.

FIG. 175. Han pottery wine jar of usual reddish color covered with a white slip and showing traces of painting. The precision of potting and the fact that the loop handle is made free rather than in relief would possibly indicate that this piece was of early origin. Russell Tyson Coll. (Art Institute of Chicago).

and fairly heavy body and was often streaked and mottled purposely. Like its Near Eastern prototype, it takes a beautiful iridescence from burial, which is more often silver but at times golden and full of fire. The Chinese potters were quick to see the advantages of relief decoration in catching and holding this glaze for a rich effect and we have a type known as "Western Han"

FIG. 176. Han dynasty painted pottery vase of dark buff gray ware with traces of white, red, and green. This type originally had a shallow pyramidal cover, but seldom the loops for ring handles. Perhaps metal ones were affixed to these. Ht. 23". Fuller Coll. Seattle Art Mus.

FIG. 177. "Syro-Roman" vase said by the museum to date between 100 B.C. and 100 A.D. but possibly a little later. The glaze is a deep green and has considerable iridescence from burial. Ht. about 11". Metropolitan Mus. of Art.

FIG. 178. Two miniature Han vases, one a reproduction of a typical wine jar even to the three spurs on the bottom, and the other a flattened bottle. Both pieces stand about four inches high, while the average wine jar is 14 inches to 18 inches in height and the granary urns the same.

These miniature pieces are rarer than the full sized ones and their particular use has not been discovered. Warren E. Cox Coll.

which always has a band, about the shoulder, of imaginary and actual animals, dragons, tigers, men riding great galloping lizards or dinosaurs while shooting bows and arrows or hurling spears and such. Some of these were also made in a mold but during the period, strangely, did not seem to lose their vitality thereby.

FIG. 180. Pair of strong wine jars with nine sided bases and curved bronze-form bodies of reddish buff clay with traces of light green glaze and some iridescence. A comb incised wave band is used about the body and lip rim. The rings are omitted from the loops of the usual Tao Tieh design. Note: These two jars are much like # 11 Plate 3 the Eumorfopoulos Coll. which Hobson calls "Late Han" but I think they may be looked upon as perhaps even later. Ht. 16¼". Warren E. Cox Coll.

FIG. 179. A remarkable wine jar with cover made to fit it. This is unusual for most of these are found simply with material tied over the top or a bowl inverted over it. The ware is the usual red pottery with iridescent green glaze. Ht. 18½". The Cleveland Mus. of Art.

FIG. 181. Shensi province or "Western Han" wine jar with relief band of the "Flying gallop." Dark red-brown, covered with a thick and very rich green glaze part of which is smeared over the bottom. Ex Thomas B. Clark Coll. Warren E. Cox Coll.

FIG. 182. Most Han wine jars are fired upside down so that the drips of glaze are at the lip rim, but this very strong example with its high relief handles and three wedge-shaped spurs was fired right side up. Ht. 18". Warren E. Cox Coll.

FIG. 183. Two Han wine jars showing contrast in sizes. The smaller is 3 inches high and the larger 15 inches. The shapes are much alike as are also the bodies of red clay and the glazes. Mrs. Ogden K. Shannon. Warren E. Cox Coll.

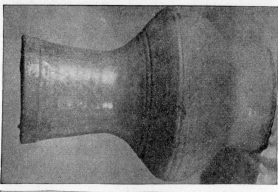

Han vase of beautifully slender form with rhythmical lines and also having its three spurs. It is of red clay with silvery pale green iridescent sheen. Ht. 16½". Warren E. Cox Coll.

Han vase such as usually contain wine in the tombs. Rarely examples are found with faceted bases, always octagonal. Possibly these represent stone plinths supporting bronze vessels which had round bottoms. This piece is of red clay with a bright apple green glaze showing large areas of silver iridescence. Ht. 16½". Warren E. Cox Coll.

The most powerful and dynamically designed Han dynasty vase or wine jar the writer has ever seen with fine high relief loop handles. The clay is of dark red and the glaze of a very dark green with blotches of iridescence. Best known example with the octagonal faceted base. Ht. 17¾". Warren E. Cox Coll. Note t'ao-t'ieh heads holding loops.

Red pottery vase covered with green glaze corroded to a silver iridescence through burial. The form is the primitive Hu with well defined foot which in some earlier forms in the Near East were pot-stands. Ht. 14½". Warren E. Cox Coll.

HAN DYNASTY WINE JARS

PLATE 20

The simple vase form described was used as a wine jar and may or may not have had the plinth base attached but all have wide and strong lip-rims about which were tied thongs, probably, to keep the covers on. Rarely a specimen is found with cover intact so we know that covers were used but no provision was made for seating them and in fact a peculiarity of most of these vases is that they were fired upside down so that the lip-rim often has irregular drops of glaze projecting from it.

It was the custom in Han times to bury a personage surrounded by pottery images of everyone and everything which he treasured in life. It had been the custom to bury the whole household alive in earlier days but Confucius had put a stop to this. He was even opposed to the inclusion of pottery images for fear of a relapse to the older custom, but because of it we know more about life in China 2000 years ago than we do about many intervening periods. How they dressed, how the women did their hair, what were their amusements, what food they ate and how it was prepared, their musical instruments, tools and weapons, the architecture of the times, the dance steps, the legends and even the humor is all becoming more and more clear as excavations proceed. Not many years ago, in our present generation, this was all found. For it was when the first railroads were cut through that grave mounds were opened against the religious laws of the country.

FIG. 184. Detail of Western Han jar c. 100–200 from Shensi showing men on horse-back shooting bows and arrows at tigers. Olive brown with golden iridescence. Ht. 13″. Warren E. Cox Coll.

FIG. 185. Flat foot of Han wine jar which was cut off the wheel with a cord, forming what the Japanese call an "ito-kiri" mark not usual in Han jars. Warren E. Cox Coll.

There are many forms of the "wine jars" but all have oblate bodies and strong concave tapering necks on which are the strong rims. They vary in size from 3 inches to 2 feet or more. It seems the finer ones have a hollowed plinth from the bottom up while most are made with the hollow of the vase extending down into the plinth. The glaze is sometimes thinly applied and almost mat while at other times it did not associate well with the body and had a tendency to chip off, a trouble carried well into T'ang times. The forms are from slender and graceful to the most dynamic and powerful to be found in all the art of potting. Some are fired right side up and are then stood on three or more "spurs" or small triangular pieces which adhered, due to the glaze, to the bottom. The t'ao-t'ieh head is used on the shoulder, usually one applied on either side, with a loop from the beak or mouth which holds a ring handle. In the earlier specimens the rings were made separately and stuck on with the glaze but later the whole handle was cast in the form of the vase in shallower and shallower relief and weaker design. Many are wheel-turned vessels and well defined grooves were usually left about the widest part of the body and at points above and below—such as where the neck joins the body, perhaps reminiscent of the bronzes which were joined at these points. The later "Western Han" vases and also the late Han porcelaneous vases have poorly formed bases or none at all and this may be taken into consideration in dating them for the tendency was toward a rounded softness in the following period, perhaps brought about by southern influences.

FIGS. 186–188. Two Han period granary urns, one of a slender shape and light green iridescence and the other more sturdy and showing an indication of a tile roof at the top. The feet of both represent bears for some reason as yet unknown. It is thought that these silos were set upon feet and floored so as to keep the rats out, but little credence need be given the idea, for the same feet appear on the "hill jars." Warren E. Cox Coll.

Granary urns in the form of a farmer's silo are less numerous than the wine jars and, as these do not occur in bronze, they must have been taken directly from architectural structures. They are usually nearly cylindrical or a little wider toward the top. They stand on three feet of the form of seated bears, perhaps some magical defense against marauders or vermin, and the tops are often made to simulate tile roofs. I have never seen a cover on one of these vessels and the lip-rim is not well defined enough to tie onto so we must assume that they were left open in the tomb. They are found filled with rice and other grains. The same variation is found in them from graceful to strong forms and from well potted early ones to more casual later ones.

"Hill Jars" are shorter cylindrical vessels also set upon three bear feet, usually having a band of relief decoration consisting of waves and strange animals about the body and always surmounted by a cover modeled in the form of a mountain with dashing waves about it. These jars are called "*po shan lu*" by the Chinese or "braziers of the vast mountain," representing the "Isles of the Blest." The great Wu Ti (140–86 B.C.) of the house of Han was a Taoist as were also his successors. The Emperor Shih Huang Ti of the 3rd century B.C. is said to have sent an expedition to find these islands. It was in command of a magician who appropriately took with him a group of young men and beautiful maidens, but in spite of all these precautions, contrary winds drove them back.

FIG. 189. Han dynasty or later gray pottery covered "Ting" copied from a bronze form. Courtesy of the Palmer Coll., The Art Institute of Chicago.

"Hill Censers" have similar covers set upon cups having slender stems and wide shallow saucers attached. Some are pierced as though for incense and some are not. This form also occurs in bronze.

FIG. 190. Watch tower of usual red Han pottery with green glaze and a well of buff pottery with green glaze. Hts. 29" and 19½". Eumorfopoulos Coll. # 48 and # 49.

FIG. 191. A glazed pottery "house," as the Art Institute calls it, which is probably a watch tower with indications of machicolations, a tile roof, etc., and interestingly set upon bear feet such as are also used on the hill jars and the granary urns. Buckingham Coll., Courtesy of the Art Institute, Chicago.

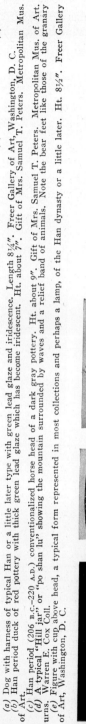

(a) (b) (c) (d) (e)

(f) (g) (h) (i) (j)

(a) Dog with harness of typical Han or a little later type with green lead glaze and iridescence. Length 8¼". Freer Gallery of Art, Washington, D. C.
(b) Han period duck of red pottery with thick green lead glaze which has become iridescent. Ht. about 7". Gift of Mrs. Samuel T. Peters. Metropolitan Mus. of Art.
(c) Han period (206 B.C.–220 A.D.) conventionalized horse head of a dark gray pottery. Ht. about 9". Gift of Mrs. Samuel T. Peters. Metropolitan Mus. of Art.
(d) A typical "Hill jar," or "po shan lu" showing the mountain surrounded by waves and a relief band of animals. Note the bear feet like those of the granary urns. Warren E. Cox Coll.
(e) Figure with cup above head, a typical form represented in most collections and perhaps a lamp, of the Han dynasty or a little later. Ht. 8½". Freer Gallery of Art, Washington, D. C.

(f) "Incense burner" (Po-Shan-Lu) of red pottery with a green glaze showing considerable iridescence. The cover is not pierced and is probably therefore, simply a symbol made to be placed in a tomb. Ht. 7½". Warren E. Cox Coll.
(g) Han pottery object called a "lamp" but may be the lower part of a "hill incense burner" or a pot-stand. Usual red body and green iridescent glaze. Ht. 6". Warren E. Cox Coll.
(h) Han "alms box" with a pottery bell so suspended inside that the dropped coin makes it ring and the figure bob. About the rim of the bell are round coins with square holes in relief. Length about 12". Gift of Robert E. Tod to Metropolitan Mus. of Art.
(i) Han pig-sty of buff clay with dark olive glaze showing some iridescence from burial. The incline and corner platform to the left is rather a characteristic suggestive construction. Length 8¼". Warren E. Cox Coll.
(j) Han ladle (or Tou) in the form of a rectangular bowl with flat bottom and dragon-headed handle. Similar to Eumo. Coll., Vol. I, # 53 and of red pottery with green glaze incrusted with iridescence and earth from burial. Length 8". Mrs. Charles Porter Wilson.

HAN DYNASTY POTTERY OBJECTS

PLATE 21

The Ting, it will be remembered, was derived from the Li and became a bronze form. Now we find pottery examples showing every sign of having been in turn copied from bronze ones. Some have lip-rims for covers and others have not.

Among the architectural forms are tall stage towers called "hunting towers" by the Chinese and made by setting one structure upon another, each with its balcony and rail, and the top one having a wide, projecting tile roof. It has been said that the Chinese shot birds from such towers and frequently they have bird finials or birds about the rails for decoration. Another form seems to be a barn set upon bear feet and with small windows set high up. The remarkable group from the Hoyt Collection in the Museum of Fine Arts in Boston shows a whole country house probably much as they were built. Then there is the goat yard, in Boston, with a little figure wearing a pointed

FIG. 192. A glazed Han pottery "pavilion" which is undoubtedly the upper part of a structure similar to the watch tower from the Freer Gallery and showing a similar bird finial and tile roof. The latter is interesting as it shows the decorative modeling at the ends of the tiles. The timber supports for the roof at each corner are also interesting. Buckingham Coll., Courtesy of the Art Institute, Chicago.

FIG. 193. An interesting glazed figure of the Han dynasty showing distinct semitic characteristics with high bridged nose and beard. The purpose for which these were put in the tombs is unknown. A number of later type seem to represent merchants and some have packs on their backs. Ralph M. Chait Coll.

cap and playing on a piccolo under his small private shed at the back, and my own porker in a pen provided with an inclined approach to a platform for feeding him and also for toilet facilities.

There are many animals and birds, chiefly domestic but not invariably, and all spirited and characteristic in modeling.

Furniture was provided, including chairs and tables laden with food and pot-stands incorrectly called "oil lamps," deep cups set upon a plain or human-figure base, but one of the most ingenious pieces of furniture that I have seen is a small chest set on human rather than bear feet and studded all over, but having a slot just above the lock in front and a figure suspended above it. When a coin is inserted there is a clink and the figure bows. This is probably the earliest mechanical bank known. It is in the Metropolitan.

The human figures are usually fairly natural and quite active. There are soldiers, dancing girls, servants, concubines and members of the household. Of course all sorts of people did the modeling and some are very fine while others are childlike.

Added to these things were stoves, well heads and a number of different types of eating bowls, buckets, dishes, etc.

Generally speaking the Han people were great and powerful potters so long as they stuck to their simple vase forms; their representative work is more curious and interesting than imbued with any aesthetic appeal.

SOUTHERN HAN WARES

Definite separation of northern and southern types of Han pottery is difficult due to lack of archaeological data but in general we know the southern wares to be more rounded and soft in form. Globular jars of true pottery forms often lack the horizontal ridges or have them only faintly indicated.

FIG. 194. Southern Han ovoid jar without horizontal grooves or ridges such as were copied on the northern ones from bronze examples. Ht. 9½". Warren E. Cox Coll.

FIG. 195. Late Han employment of the old texture representing mat marks. This vase has also imprints of a seal, perhaps the owner's.

FIG. 196. Ewer of softened Chinese wine jar form with loop handle seen in various places, and an elephant spout closely resembling a North Chinese t'ao-t'ieh head. Found at Thanh-hoa.

In northern Annam Prof. O. Janse made extensive excavations and found potteries reflecting both Chinese and Indonesian wares. I think his contribution from the field of great value, but do not agree with many of his deductions. For instance, in the ewer shown, he sees Indonesian influence in the elephant-head spout and loop handle at the top. We know that the elephant head appears as one modification of the t'ao-t'ieh head on early bronzes from An Yang and that elephant or mastodon forms have been frozen in the ice of Siberia, while the loop handle occurs in the ewer found at Ur and other very early and not necessarily southern sites. He also shows a vessel which looks like a spittoon, jumps to the conclusion that it is a spittoon, and states that it is a vessel "employed above all by people who chew betel-nut" and then goes on to state that the Chinese are not a betel chewing people, which

Mortuary model of a house: "Rectangular enclosure with gate and spirit walls in south, main hall in north, kitchen in east and storehouse in west. Mortar and grist mill; seven figures and saddle horse. Clay: buff, washed with white clay, traces of black trim. Ornamental rockery painted in black on main spirit wall. Ht. 17″, plan about 32″ by 36″. Hoyt Coll. Mus. of Fine Arts, Boston.

Han pottery barn yard with goats and the goatherd in a small shed in the background playing a pipe. Length about 8″. Boston Mus. of Fine Arts.

HAN DYNASTY POTTERY HOUSE AND GOAT YARD

PLATE 22

Fig. 197. Unique South China Han Dynasty pottery jar and cover with red body and green, glossy glaze which was crackled before burial and makes the iridescence appear like confetti. Ht. 8″. Ex Warren E. Cox Coll. Cleveland Mus. of Art.

Fig. 198. A vessel not necessarily a spittoon as Prof. Janse concludes but with a rim for tying down a cover. (See chart of Hissar II potteries.)

Fig. 199. Han jar from Annam of the usual Chinese shape except that it is softer and more rounded in form, lacks the t'ao-t'ieh and ring handles and has loops on the shoulder and slots in the base.

Fig. 200. Southern Han wine jar (hu) of hard red body with a transparent amber finely crackled thin glaze over it. Type found at Chang-sha, Nan yang, etc., and probably extends well into the 6th cent. or possibly even T'ang. Ht. 13¾″. Warren E. Cox Coll.

Fig. 201. An Annam incense burner with bird top which does recall certain East Indian brass and bronze treatments.

Fig. 202. The use of the cock-head suggests a connection with Yüeh.

Fig. 203. Pot-stand incorrectly called a "lamp" by Professor Janse. It bears a close relationship to Silla and earlier Korean ones and also those of Japan.

Fig. 204. A *Ting* formed vessel with one horizontal handle added instead of the usual two perpendicular loops. This is undoubtedly a Chinese form derived from the *Li*. (See neolithic section.)

Fig. 205. A typical eating bowl quite similar to Han examples but called a "saucepan" by Prof. Janse. Such forms are used in China to-day.

Fig. 206. Iron cook stove of late Han or 3d cent. type with writing in style of period. Found in the same grave with one of the porcelaneous vases in Shen-si province. Field Mus., Chicago.

is all a little fast as reasoning. Furthermore he calls the pot-stand a lamp. However, the wares are interesting. The reticulated pot-stand and globular vessel show a technique close to that of Korea and Japan. The smooth, rounded shapes are distinctive. But most interesting is the Ting found at Qui-giap, Han-loc in Thanh-hoa province with rooster head spout much like those found on vessels from Chiu yen of the Yüeh ware.

THE FIRST PORCELAIN

FIG. 207. Actual vase of earliest type porcelain. The body is of greyish buff and appears to contain iron while the glaze is yellowish-green, vitrified and covers only the upper part of the jar. The bottom is flat and shows spur marks. Ht. 6⅝". Field Mus., Chicago.

Through a vessel found on an iron cook stove in Shensi province and dated thereby, it was discovered by the late Dr. Berthold Laufer, assisted by the analysis made by Mr. H. W. Nichols, that the Chinese made a much harder ware than the pottery, and that this ware contained kaolin and was a true porcelain. The body is a gray porous substance coated with a white engobe covered with a transparent greenish-yellow glaze which is inclined to run unevenly over the shoulder and thin out toward the bottom. Frequently it was so badly chemically fitted to the body that it chips off in large areas. An unexplained feature of these wares is that none of them ever have the typical cylindrical bases that are found on the pottery vases and many do not even have base rims of any sort. They look as though they were meant to stand upon pot-stands but so far as I know no stand of this ware has ever been found. The loss of the bases would also indicate a later development around A.D. 200 or a little later.

It has only been some fifty years or a bit more that these early wares have been known. They were first discovered when railroads were permitted to cut straight across country and in grading, opened several grave mounds. It had been against the laws of the country and the religious laws to excavate such mounds before, but when the wares came to light and it was found that they brought high prices, the Chinese began to do some digging of their own and recently a large number of pieces have been exported.

However the 2nd World War put a stop to that and it is very unlikely that any such amount of wares will ever be found and shipped again. Of course, to the porcelain lover or perfectionist these wares may seem crude but to the collector who can look with an open eye they have superb form and are fine pieces of craftsmanship.

Fig. 208. Porcelaneous pottery vase of grey ware covered partly with brown slip and a glaze over that of light green variable color. The weight is great, being nearly six pounds. This piece has both loops with rings in relief and free loop handles, a treatment not found on pottery examples. Ht. 14″. Field Mus., Chicago.

Fig. 209. Han porcelaneous vase of typical type with yellowish-olive thin glaze on upper part. Ht. 13″. Warren E. Cox–Mrs. Gibson L. Douglass Coll.

Fig. 210. Han porcelaneous jar of *lei* shape. Buff gray ware with lower part covered with brown-red slip, upper part and inside of bottom with greenish-yellow glaze. Decoration is combed wave type, handles cast in animal-head design. Ht. 10¼″. Field Mus., Chicago.

CHAPTER VII

"SIX DYNASTIES"
(A.D. 220–587)

AND SUI PERIODS
(A.D. 581–617)

OF CHINA

DECADENT WEAKNESS of the ruling family permitted the Han period to break up into three parts sometimes called the "Three Kingdoms," the *Wei* in the north, the *Wu* in the central part and the *Shu* in the west. The last was ruled by descendants of the Hans. The civil wars made opportunity for invasions by people from the north where much of the territory north of the Yangtze was taken. Thus we may list the *Western Chin* (A.D. 265–317), *Eastern Chin* (A.D. 317–420), *Liu Sung* (A.D. 420–479), *Northern Wei* (A.D. 386–636), —— the longest and most dominant period, —— then the *Ch'i* (A.D. 479–502), *Liang* (A.D. 502–557) and the *Ch'en* (A.D. 557–589) which, considering the two Chin dynasties as one, are called *"The Six Dynasties."*

This was a period of chaotic conditions, but during it much transpired that indirectly affected our art of ceramics. Liu Pei (later called Kuan Ti, the god of war) and his two aids Chang Fei and Kuan Yü along with Chu-ko Liang, the strategist and inventor of war machines, made history and are often portrayed. The conquering Tartars, Tibetans and "Hsiung Nu" or barbarians to the North West brought many strange things and new beliefs. Buddhism gained power. It was a formative period.

Horses had been known in Han times but not so generally and we now see attempts to model them, with uneven results. Camels were at times strange in anatomy but often more alive and full of nasty camel character than those which followed in the T'ang period. Dogs are not often seen but the superb bitch and pup shown illustrates how wonderfully the great black and brindle dogs which ran with the horses in the hunt and in war could be caught in character. All the woodenness of the Han dogs had gone out. Some more or less imaginary animals, like the curled and snarling cat-like one shown, were made repeatedly, as though they had some well known significance. The beginning of the development of "Earth Spirits" from animistic forms to the human "Lokapala" was made, as can be seen in the very interesting two illustrated. And human figures show a great divergence

90

FIG. 211. Horse of Northern Wei. Black and olive pottery coated with white slip and painted in red and green. Ht. 8¾". The Cleveland Mus. of Art.

FIG. 212. One of two very crude but spirited camels probably of Wei or even earlier origin. The pottery is buff in color. Ht. 10½". Fuller Coll., Seattle Art Mus.

and variety in technique. There are little silly ones dancing around like dwarfs and gnomes, stupid soldiers on horseback so clothed as to hide the faults of anatomy, strange symmetrical doll-like forms like inverted beakers with heads stuck on, and also some beautifully expressive sculptures. A certain elfish smile is rather significant. The group of small dancers, musicians

FIG. 213. Wei period (221–265 A.D.). One of the "Three Kingdoms" curled catlike animal of gray pottery covered with a white slip. Dia. about 10". Gift of Robert E. Tod. Metropolitan Mus. of Art.

FIG. 214. Two early transitional forms of the "Earth spirits" partly animistic and partly human demon-like forms, of grey clay without sign of polychrome coloring. Hts. 7" and 8". Eric Mansfield.

and attendants (from the Metropolitan Museum of Art) are beautifully conceived and masterful in the portrayal of movement. Other standing figures of women show a great dignity and strength of character in these wives of fighters and farmers and herdsmen, a great dignity and restrained charm.

FIG. 215. Grey, pottery unglazed, box-like object without a bottom, said by Hobson to be a well head (see similar example in the Eumorfopoulos Coll. #100). He calls that one "3d or 4th cent." but it is quite likely that this piece was made during the Han period (206 B.C.–A.D. 220). Length 9¾", width 6½", ht. 5". Fuller Coll. Seattle Art Mus.

FIGS. 216–220. Nine small figures of the Wei period, (6th cent.), of dancers, servants and a musician in buff pottery showing traces of polychrome decoration. Ht. about 4". Metropolitan Mus. of Art.

These are not the pretty ladies usually portrayed in T'ang times but staunch supporters of the household.

One of the most interesting and often occurring animal forms is the Triceratops-like form illustrated. Mr. Hobson describes it as "remotely resembling a rhinoceros." That it definitely is not a rhinoceros is convincingly proven by Dr. Laufer in his "Anthropological Series" (Vol. XIII, No. 2 Publication 177, page 158) where he states, "There can be no doubt of two points,—first, that the ancient Chinese, from the very beginning of their history, were acquainted with two species of rhinoceros, the single-horned and two-horned ones, distinguished as 'Se' and 'Si'; and, second, that the former is identical with the present *Rhinoceros indicus unicornis* (as proven above all by the linguistic relationship of the word Se with Tibetan Bse and Lepcha Sa), and the latter with the present *Rhinoceros sumatrensis*." In the same treatise we find that the Chinese used rhinoceros hide for armor and at very early dates drew perfectly recognizable likenesses of them.

FIG. 221. Sui or Early T'ang figure of groom. Ochre-colored clay with traces of polychrome. Expression strangely like that of Mussolini. Ralph Chait Coll.

FIG. 222. Typical Six Dynasties conventionalized woman with bell shaped skirt. Grey clay with brown, red and white pigments. Ht. 14". L. R. Mintz.

FIG. 223. Wei merchant traveler in reddish unglazed ware with Eastern Mediterranean type face. Ht. 12½". C. T. Loo & Co.

Now the form we are considering is not at all like a rhinoceros in several features: 1.—It invariably has three large horns. 2.—It always has prominent lumps (usually five in number) on the back ridge. 3.—It has a smooth hide not plaquetted as is the rhinoceros hide. 4.—It always has indications of an armored jowl. Certainly a people who knew the rhinoceros could not have made all these points as errors in construction! and repeated them many times! And finally, 5.—It has a very large and prominent tail which is entirely uncharacteristic of the rhinoceros.

Northern Wei figure of grey ware covered with white and then red slip except for face and hands which show light pink traces. This remarkably modeled bearded figure with the tremendously vigorous hand and tall shield with relief lion's head is unique and appears to be a Tartar or North Russian type, certainly not Mongolian. The shield has a Roman lion mask. Ht. 12½″. Warren E. Cox Coll.

Six Dynasty figure of dignified woman. Lifelike face but little anatomical modeling. Upturned toes to shoes usually associated with T'ang costume, yet of very heavy potting. Dark grey, almost black, with traces of white, red and pale green. Ht. 15¾″. Warren E. Cox Coll.

Right: Gray pottery woman of 5th or 6th cent. showing typical treatment of skirt but more detailed treatment of face than usual. Ht. about 10″. Metropolitan Mus. of Art.

SIX DYNASTY FIGURES

PLATE 23

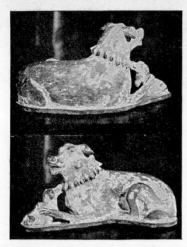

Wei or Six Dynasty bitch and pup of gray clay with traces of white and red encrusted with buff earth. Typical of modeling of period, sometimes lacking in true anatomical detail but imbued with life. Length 9". Warren E. Cox Coll.

Grey terracotta figure of tiger dressed with white pigment. Wei period. Ht. 8½". C. T. Loo & Co.

Left: Camel of gray pottery. Wei (one of "Three Kingdoms") period (A. D. 221–265) or earlier. *Right:* Northern Wei dragon-like animal with a head already beginning to be somewhat ornate.

Pair of painted Six Dynasty horses. Nickerson Coll., Art Institute, Chicago. Length 31".

SIX DYNASTIES POTTERY ANIMALS

PLATE 24

Dr. Laufer goes further and tells of the finding of rhinoceri in Miocene or Pliocene deposits (6 to 12 million years ago) in Europe, India and Northern China, the latter by A. R. Wallace, and of two found between the Yenisei and Lena Rivers frozen and quite recognizable with their hairy coats and two horns, "The skin being smooth and without the characteristic folds of the now living species." But here we have two horns again!

Mr. Roy Chapman Andrews states (*Ency. Brit.* 14th edition, Vol. 15, page 713), "Four days after starting it was found that the main trail between Kalgan, China and Urga, the capital of Mongolia, which had been traversed by several geologists, runs directly through the rich fossil beds—one of Oligocene and one of Eocene, of the age of mammals, and one *Cretaceous*, of the age of reptiles." Mr. Andrews found the dinosaur eggs in this section. But here his finds were of the protoceratops, a small dinosaur similar to our animal but without horns.

I then had a talk with the eminent Dr. Barnum Brown and found that the triceratops, or three-horned dinosaurs had only been found in the northern part of North America to date but he stressed the point that field research had not been able to "scratch the surface" on the Asiatic side of the

FIG. 224. The finest of the Chinese reconstructions from Triceratops remains that I have found. Note the power of modeling. Length 12½″. Warren E. Cox Coll.

Bering Straits and such negative results are not to be taken too seriously. He pointed out that the buffalo and early elephant types are identical on both sides and also stated that migrations of men had not only been from Asia to America but also in the opposite direction.

Mr. Andrews further states, in reference to the dinosaur eggs, "Three had broken out of a small sandstone ledge and lay exposed," and later he says, "The skeleton of a small dinosaur was found, lying 4 inches above the eggs in loose sediment on top of the rock."

With this evidence I present the, so far as I know, new theory that *these animal forms are actual reconstructions made by the Chinese from dinosaur bones found along the caravan routes of Mongolia.* The alignment of the horns is easily explained by the fact that skulls of triceratops when found are

Triceratops-like form of animal found in Mongolia or Alaska. Grey clay with white slip and red under the encrusted earth. Length 12″. Detroit Institute of Arts.

A Six-dynasty "Ting" having handles showing Hellenistic design. Red ware with green glaze having some iridescence. Dia. 7″. Warren E. Cox Coll.

Jar c. 2nd to 4th cent. One of earliest of this type later developed by Yüeh, Lung ch'üan and southern Kuan kilns. The figures include a dog, dragon, guardians of a portal and front view of flying bird. Ht. 12″. Warren E. Cox Coll.

T'ang or earlier gray stoneware pilgrim bottle with olive brown glaze. This type with grape and phoenix design (and sometimes Bacchanalian figures) shows very strong Roman influence. Ht. 8″. Metropolitan Mus. of Art.

SIX DYNASTIES OBJECTS

Plate 25

almost always crushed flat. All other points could be observed from the skeletons *en situ,* these bones were often not greatly disturbed and they were right along the caravan route.

This puts a different light on our ideas of the source of the t'ao-t'ieh, "thunder monster," and dragon forms, the original sources of which were much less imaginary than may have been supposed. It is known that the legend of a meteorite will live in the memories of a people for centuries. Add to such legends the finding of actual bones of dinosaurs much larger than those of any living animal and it is easy to see how the well founded belief in a fiery dragon descending from the heavens could take hold of the minds of a people and become part of their religion and a source of many of their art motives.

Vase forms like the Han wine jars, but showing decadence in the use of lower relief and softer forms, continued and I am convinced that many which are now called Han will, when we learn more, be placed at somewhat later dates. As for the "proto-porcelain" which I described under the Han

FIG. 225. Smaller vase of type found in Shensi province. Typically heavily potted with border about shoulder which Reinach has named "the flying gallop" but which occurs on bronzes only of a later epoch.

Larger vase probably Six Dynasties or later T'ang dynasty. More thinly potted, has even and thinner, greener glaze and the body is more brown than the reddish Han type. Though these vases are later copies of Han ones, they are more rare and costly. Warren E. Cox Coll.

FIG. 226. T'ang or Sui dynasty flask with circular body, concave neck and broad tapering lip-rim, set upon a flaring base. The clay is of reddish buff and the glaze brownish green. Ht. 9". Buckingham Coll., The Art Institute of Chicago.

period, some of it belongs in that period but most of it was made around A.D. 300 or later. I placed it in the earlier period because it began then. The style seemed to tend toward the use of a gray ware rather than red, perhaps because the clay was not so well fired or so well protected from smoke in firing, but it is entirely wrong for dealers to make up their minds that all gray wares are Wei while all red wares are Han. Glaze seemed not so generally popular as the use of painted slips much like those of the Han period and in some cases hardly distinguishable at all, but it is not reasonable to assume that glaze was entirely discontinued and we actually find improvements in it.

Glaze was used on new types of wares. The flattened bottles or "pilgrim bottles" of red ware covered with a green or brown glaze and decorated with relief designs very similar to those of Han or slightly later bronze mirrors and showing strong Hellenistic influences in grape motives and dancing figures such as existed from about 3rd century B.C. to 4th century A.D. in the Western World, are undoubtedly earlier than T'ang although the form does continue into the later period. We find it represented hanging to the saddles of T'ang camels and rarely even in the T'ang streaked yellow and green glazes on a white ware. (See my example.)

Another red stone-ware, usually globular jars, decorated with various scallops, applied rosettes, etc. and covered with a dark brown glaze seems to have all the characteristics of a pre-T'ang ware and is so called by Hobson

FIG. 227. Pottery jar with cover, grey body coated with thin greyish glaze, foot not glazed. About body are Zodiac figures in high relief. Said to be Wei. Ht. 14". C. T. Loo & Co.

FIG. 228. Pottery jar and cover of red ware with mottled olive brown glaze, called Sung or earlier by museum but actually of pre-T'ang times. Ht. 10½". Hoyt Coll. Mus. of Fine Arts, Boston.

FIG. 229. Vase and cover on stand of the Six Dynasty period (A.D. 386–589) of buff gray pottery decorated in white and red slip. Ht. about 19". Metropolitan Mus. of Art.

in the Eumorfopoulos Collection (see #159) on the authority of an association between that piece and one published by Prof. F. Sarre and attributed to the Sassanian period (3rd to 7th century A.D.). The one illustrated from the Boston Museum is incorrectly called "Sung or earlier." These are not to be confused with the similar looking globular jars of brown ware with brown glaze of Ming and later times which come from Indo-China and South China although their general look and perhaps even their province is the same.

A rarer type is represented by the brown-gray jar shown herewith. It is decorated with the pinched-up or very crudely modeled decoration consisting of a portal with guards with arms akimbo on either side, a dragon, a running figure, a horse (head missing), dog, etc. including an amazing bird flying directly head-on toward the spectator. The glaze is of very thin "tea-dust" type sunk into the body so that it is mat in texture and brown in color. This appears to be a prototype to the tall pale celadon mortuary jars of the T'ang period. Its cover is missing.

That Yüeh ware was made before the T'ang period we now have full evidence. Yüeh is the name of an ancient district now called Shao-hsing in Chekiang province and we shall speak of the three Shang-lin-hu kiln sites in

Yüeh yao writer's water vessel made in an ingenious manner. Body is a vase, neck of which potter cut off and applied near bottom to form animal's mouth, adding legs, nose, eyes, ears and handle-like a tail afterwards. Typical light grey-green glaze. Length 4″. Warren E. Cox Coll.

Rare Chiu-yen Yüeh box with grey-green glaze and evenly spaced iron-brown spots. A prototype of the Lung-ch'üan ware called "tobi seji" by the Japanese. That it was considered an important work even in Yüeh days is proven by beautifully fitting and very thin rim of cover. Bottom is slightly concave and fired on spurs. c. 6th cent. Dia. 3⅞″. K. M. Semon Coll.

Ewer from Chiu-yen kiln, made c. 2nd to 4th cent. Finely modeled rooster-head spout and dragon-head handle, incising on the shoulder and typical two squared loops make this an interesting piece. Ht. 15″. Fuller Coll., Seattle Mus.

Small Yüeh yao jar with stamped design and applied heads with ring handles. The glaze is the usual frosty grey green. Ht. about 4″. Judge Edgar Bromberger Coll. Brooklyn Mus.

Important Yüeh yao jar probably from the Chiu-yen or "nine rocks" site. The glaze is mat olive green of greyish tint. Ht. about 11½″. Nasli Heeramaneck Coll.

SIX DYNASTIES YÜEH WARES
FROM CHIU-YEN (NINE ROCKS) SITE

PLATE 26

the T'ang section for the wares from there are of that period, but the late Mr. A. D. Brankston has published (*The Burlington Magazine,* 1938, December issue) another site called the Chiu-yen (Nine rocks) section near Shao-hsing where a type of Yüeh ware was also made at earlier times. The basin from the Sir Percival David Collection corresponds exactly with bronzes dated A.D. 101, 132 and 194. The small jar from the Judge Edgar Bromberger Collection with its cross-hatched pattern and t'ao-t'ieh heads is like,

FIG. 230. Small Six Dynasty Yüeh jar from the Chiu-yen site. Glassy, crackled glaze is characteristic of the heavier sort of these wares. K. M. Semon Coll.

FIG. 231. This jar shows small figure of Buddha applied to shoulder on either side. K. M. Semon Coll.

FIG. 232. Jar with doubled loop handles, which came into use on T'ang wares. Ht. 7". Warren E. Cox Coll.

 *Right:* Yüeh, Chiu-yen, basin which A. D. Brankston placed as between 1st and 3d cent. A.D. Dia. 12¾". Sir Percival David, Bt.

Writer's coupe of frog form similar to one illustrated by Brankston belonging to Mr. P'an Hsi and inscribed Kê-erh meaning "guest child" and, therefore, said to be of 5th cent. A.D. Length 3½". Miss Grandin Baldwin.

FIG. 234. Ewer c. 7th cent. or before having typical Six Dynasty glaze of mat olive but similar to T'ang examples set on separate stands. Form is from the Near East. Ht. 14¾". Warren E. Cox Coll. C. T. Loo.

FIG. 235. Six Dynasty jar of grey ware with olive green glaze finely crackled. Note the double loops on the shoulder which originated in Han times. Ht. 9½". John Platt— Warren E. Cox Coll.

FIG. 233. Chiu-yen Yüeh ewer with cock spout. A small circular or star-shaped tool was used to press down clay around spout, places of attachment of loops and handle. Usual grey ware with olive green glaze. Ht. 8". K. M. Semon Coll.

in many details, several in the Historical Museum, Peking, which were made in Chê-ho-chên, Honan province and were found in a tomb dated A.D. 99. Finally the ewer corresponds in all details, the cock spout, the tapered handle, the squared loops (probably for suspending it to make pouring easier) and the hard gray ware covered with transparent green glaze, with the one owned by Sir Herbert Ingram and placed by Brankston in the 2nd to 4th century. It will be noted that this piece also has incised points on the shoulder, and, what other known specimens lack, the fine dragon at the top of the handle so often seen in later T'ang amphoras. (See Pl. 26)

Another hard gray stoneware dressed with a very thin brown slip or burnt brown where exposed is covered about two thirds of the way down with a rusty olive green glaze almost identical to the early Yüeh glaze. It will be noted that the stopping of the glaze part way down first puts in appearance on these jars and the one with pinched-modeled figures, and this is quite definitely a Near Eastern technique used much earlier in Western Asia. It is also to be noted that the characteristic double loops, three of which are set on the shoulder, correspond with those of the Han example shown and were used to tie on a cover. (Fig. 235)

Finally the two ewers, one without handle but with trefoil lip and one with handle and spout, the one having a buff body and the other gray again, have the same sort of mat olive green glaze heavier and darker than we expect in T'ang times. The one without handle corresponds to those of the

Fig. 236. Six Dynasty painted pottery house with what appear to be tile roofs beamed walls and sliding doors. Buckingham Coll., The Art Institute of Chicago.

T'ang period which were stood upon tall pot-stands and was probably so equipped.

The architectural potteries include a further development of the detail of forms, such as beam ends, and of structural details. One seemingly new trick was the making of loose sliding doors set in grooves. The polychrome painting in blue, green, red, white and black seemed to be favored for these as for the large jars but here structure governs the designs rather than the traditional and merely decorative pot hooks and scrolls.

It is obvious that our information is fragmentary concerning this period of some 400 years and it offers a fascinating field for future collectors, but a word of warning must be inserted. In a period in which the styles varied so much and in which the potteries offer no great technical obstacles the forger finds a happy playground and it is conservative to estimate that out of all the Wei and T'ang pieces on the market not one third are correct. Some are cast from old pieces and some are made whole by the Japanese and modern Chinese.

CHAPTER VIII

T'ANG PERIOD OF CHINA

A.D. 618–906

WE NOW enter upon one of the great periods of world art. One thinks of T'ang, Sung and Ming in the Far East as one thinks of Egypt, Greece and the Renaissance in the West, though they are not, of course, contemporary, and are quite unlike in styles. The first represents *simple beauty* and perfected craftsmanship, the second the *pinnacle of the classic* and the third the *ornate but not yet too decadent flowering*. Actually the T'ang period was much influenced by Hellenistic art but so strongly burnt the flame that no amount of smoke could serve to dull its light.

The Northern Wei lost power to the southern Liang dynasty with its capital at Nanking (A.D. 502–557) and Buddhism came strongly there by sea through the straits of Malacca. The art which represented this religion

Fig. 237. Globular jar of polished black pottery with incised peonies much in technique of rare Han examples but having design more like that of Sung. In London exhibition of 1935–6 it was given the attribution: "Probably T'ang." Ht. 9½". D. Abbes Coll. Mrs. Margot Holmes Coll.

FIG. 238. T'ang coupe and cover of white pottery with a very thin, light, straw-colored glaze. Ht. 4½". Metropolitan Mus. of Art.

FIG. 239. T'ang white pottery cup with transparent white glaze. Well proportioned and thinly potted. Ht. 2¾". Fuller Coll. Seattle Art Mus.

was not much affected by that of Gandhara but rather that of the Maurya dynasty of the 3rd century B.C. With it came the great winged lions and also the fluted column. In 589 China was again united for a short period until 618. This is loosely known as the Sui period (A.D. 581–617) and may be thought of so far as we are concerned as a continuation of the Six Dynasties.

The territory of the first great T'ang emperors after their conquests extended into Tibet and Turkestan and intercourse with the West was exten-

Superb pilgrim bottle of the T'ang period showing strong classic influence in the carved low relief foliate design. It is of white ware with straw colored thin glaze. Ht. 13″. Gift of Mrs. H. O. Havemeyer. Metropolitan Mus. of Art.

Pedestal of red ware covered with a buff and green glaze somewhat iridescent from burial. This piece shows some Hellenistic influence. T'ang. Ht. about 12″. Metropolitan Mus. of Art.

Rare small T'ang pilgrim bottle similar to the larger brown glazed Six Dynasty ones. It is of light buff body with mottled green and amber glazes inclined to chip off as is usually the case with T'ang glazes. Ht. 5¼″. Warren E. Cox Coll.

T'ang coupe of white pottery with light straw colored glaze showing very strong resemblance to Roman ones which are often found with green lead glaze. Ht. about 4″. Gift of Mrs. Samuel T. Peters. Metropolitan Mus. of Art.

T'ANG DYNASTY WARES
SHOWING GREEK AND ROMAN INFLUENCE

PLATE 27

sive. It was during this time that Wu Tao-tzŭ, the greatest of Chinese painters, lived. Wood block printing was extensively developed. Much of the classic literature and poetry was written, and the famous Li Tai Po lived, who, like our Poe, drank heavily and wrote well.

Ever since the conquest of Alexander the Great into India and the formation of Greco-Bactrian states north west of India, communications between China and Western Asia had been continuous. The drapery of all Buddhistic figures is really Greek as are also the features of many and the poses. An examination of many T'ang potteries will disclose Greek origins or at least Western Asian ones. Portraiture in the figures is not at first frequent just as it was not in Greece but during the T'ang period a revolt against this

FIG. 240. T'ang candlestick of hard white ware with greenish white glaze. Ht. 11¾". Cleveland Mus. of Art.

principle occurred just as in Rome, although the portraits were pretty much confined to pottery rather than wood, stone, or bronze. Most early T'ang paintings were of a religious nature and symmetrical in design as well as conventional in treatment. Only during the later part of the period did masterful landscape and animal painting commence. The Chinese were close observers of distance and could render aerial perspective better than many western artists but they were more interested in design, in catching the struggle of a tree branch against the prevailing wind, in the movement of the wind at the moment of painting, that the water (and there is usually water) be flowing or rippling or full of water life and spirit. In other words the transition from the static qualities of Buddhistic art were cast aside during this time and an interest in movement and life was assumed which has not been lost since.

The technique of potting had been improved and we find T'ang wares usually whiter in body and varying from soft to porcelaneous, though some are also buff, light gray, and reddish. Thus the mere color of the body is no final criterion of period. It was generally thinner in the smaller pieces especially. The old lightly fired pigments, red, black, white and rarely blue and green were continued, though sparingly. The most usual glaze is transparent and straw colored, thinly applied but finely crackled and likely to chip off because it was not well associated with the biscuit. The Chinese did not learn how to govern crackle until the end of the Sung period and some T'ang glazes are not crackled at all though this is rare and was only luck. This glaze is simply a refined type of the old alkaline lead glaze of Han times and the same greens, browns, amber tones, etc. were used a little more purified and brighter. Quite rarely cobalt was added to make a blue but no manganese was ever consciously employed and it occurs only by accident in some of the browns, some of which have a purple cast. This is strange for the blue was undoubtedly learned from the Near East where the purple also had been used for thousands of years. Many splashed, dripped and running effects were employed, perhaps because the glaze tended to act that way and the Chinese made use of its characteristics rather than tried to curb them. However, that the glazes could be controlled by the use of incised outlines may be seen by the beautiful pillow illustrated. It is interesting to note that glaze had first been employed in the Near East because the wares were porous and were thus aided in being liquid-tight, here it became a style to let the glaze just splash over the edge and come part way down on the body. In China the Han wares were denser and did not need glaze inside but the association with bronze made the potters glaze the outside down to the bottom carefully so as to imitate metal. We see the first Near Eastern stopping of the glaze short of the foot-rim in the Six Dynasties times and now it becomes prevalent.

At Samarra, half way between Baghdad and Ashur, on the Tigris River were found sherds of stoneware and true porcelain with feldspathic glaze of high fire, and corresponding with Chinese wares. This site is definitely dated as of the 9th century. The glazes were yellowish white, closely crackled and a green mottled transparent type. Others were sea green (or "celadon"), pure white, ivory, chocolate brown verging on black and of mat texture, watery green, gray and finally a group of transmutation glazes of brown splashed with frothy gray with bluish and whitish tinges. Of the latter it is not easy to distinguish between the T'ang and Sung wares and reliance must be placed mostly on the style of the foot.

It is typical of the T'ang foot that it was flat bottomed and beveled before firing, but the disadvantages of such a bottom were discovered and some T'ang wares have simple foot-rims. Thus we cannot depend too much on this characteristic.

Continuation of the animals and human forms of Han times and Six Dynasties times was, of course, to be expected and others were added while here again we find them ranging in sculptural qualities and beauty or appeal all the way from childlike attempts to masterpieces. This was natural for some tombs were of great importance while others were for minor officials or family heads. The movement and action of the Six Dynasties is usually preserved and forms come closer to nature with greater details. Horses seem to vary from Arabian types to heavy fellows almost like Percherons, but they were rare and costly animals in China and were all used for saddle purposes while carts were drawn by oxen. In different sections there were different styles but so little is known of the tomb sources of many that no clear plan of these sources has yet been laid out, though Dr. Laufer did take some steps in this direction.

He states generally that horses from Honan are: 1.—more realistic, 2.—more lifelike, 3.—always harnessed, 4.—in various poses with turns of the neck, 5.—have grace of motion, 6.—have narrower chests, 7.—the hair of the mane hangs straight downward, 8.—carry riders of which the women are bet-

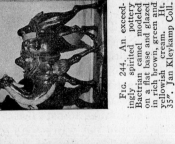

FIG. 244. An exceedingly spirited pottery Bactrian camel modeled on a flat base and glazed in rich brown, green and yellowish cream. Ht. 35". Jan Kleykamp Coll.

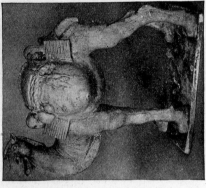

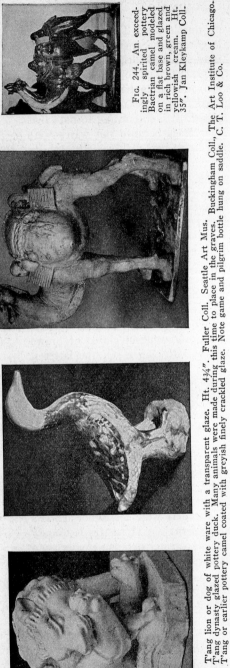

FIG. 241. T'ang lion or dog of white ware with a transparent glaze. Ht. 4¾". Fuller Coll. Seattle Art Mus.
FIG. 242. T'ang dynasty glazed pottery duck. Many animals were made during this time to place in the graves. Buckingham Coll. The Art Institute of Chicago.
FIG. 243. T'ang or earlier pottery camel coated with greyish finely crackled glaze. Note game and pilgrim bottle hung on saddle. C. T. Loo & Co.

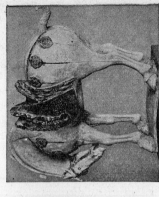

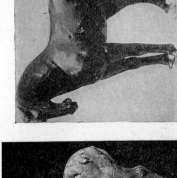

FIG. 245. T'ang unglazed pottery horse with faint traces of color on a cream white ware. Ht. 16½". Fuller Coll. Seattle Art Mus.
FIG. 246. T'ang horse with yellowish brown glaze and green glazed trappings. The saddle is left in biscuit. Ht. 21". Warren E. Cox Coll.
FIG. 247. T'ang horse, bactrian type, made of almost white ware covered with a rich brown glaze. This animal, though heavy, is spirited and shows certain points of possible Arabian strain. Ht. 22". Gift of Mrs. Edward S. Harkness. Metropolitan Mus. of Art.
FIG. 248. T'ang pottery horse with light straw colored glaze and green and yellow trappings and saddle. Length about 30" or a little more. Boston Mus. of Fine Arts.

T'ang bullock cart. The wheels are unique in that spaces between spokes are carved open. The two figures are of identical red pottery and white slip. Length about 20". Mrs. Charles Porter Wilson.

T'ang pottery lion chewing his leg. The glazes on these pieces are usually yellow of a brownish tone and clear grass green, though rarely blue was used. Ht. 7½". Freer Gallery of Art, Washington.

T'ang hound not unlike a present day greyhound but with fuller tail hair. Ears not so long nor hairy as Afghan hound's. The ware is white and the thin glaze is cream and green. Ht. about 9". Metropolitan Mus. of Art.

T'ang pottery pillow decorated with beautifully drawn design of two ducks in yellow and white against a green ground. Length about 14". Judge Edgar Bromberger Coll. Brooklyn Mus.

T'ANG POTTERY ANIMALS

PLATE 28

ter seated than the men of Shansi province, 9.—have ears pricked up, 10.—necks elegantly curved, 11.—the manes are either upright or fall to the right side, 12.—when they have riders stirrups are always represented.

Those from Shensi province he says are: 1.—usually a bare horse, 2.—sober and mechanical, 3.—massive dimensions, 4.—not well modeled harness, 5.—strong build, 6.—broader chests, 7.—curly manes combed and parted to the sides, 8.—men riders wore a pompom on the front of their round hats, and 9.—they were poor riders. He shows one with left foot pressed forward and right foot backward and the hands too near the horse's neck and seem-

FIG. 249. T'ang figure of lady dancing. K. M. Semon Coll.

FIG. 251. T'ang figure which is not Chinese and looks semitic in type. The large head also suggests that this may have been a dwarf. Ht. 5". Warren E. Cox Coll.

FIG. 252. T'ang merchant portrayed, as was the custom, clutching his money-bag. The glazes are of green, brownish-yellow and almost black on a whitish ware. Ht. 14¾". Fuller Coll. Seattle Art Mus.

FIG. 253. Pair of T'ang pottery ladies in spotted green, yellow and straw colored glazes, the heads as usual left in biscuit. The tall slender proportions give dignity and charm. Ht. 14". Ex Warren E. Cox Coll. Courtesy of Mrs. Alvin Thalheimer.

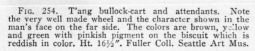

FIG. 254. T'ang bullock-cart and attendants. Note the very well made wheel and the character shown in the man's face on the far side. The colors are brown, yellow and green with pinkish pigment on the biscuit which is reddish in color. Ht. 16½". Fuller Coll. Seattle Art Mus.

Fig. 250. Two T'ang unglazed figures of ladies quite similar to the pair in the Eumorfopoulos Coll. # 181 and # 182 of pinkish white pottery decorated in gold, black, red and green pigment. Ht. 15¼". Fuller Coll. Seattle Art Mus.

ingly moving. He says, "Whoever has observed Chinese riding will have witnessed such performances; and in this case the potter must be granted all credit for his power of observation." Finally there is one type of rider which seems to be seizing the bridles with the left hand while his right is pressing against his chest.

All of these horses are made on thin rectangular bases and are potted hollow inside with an opening in the belly. The tails are usually made sepa-

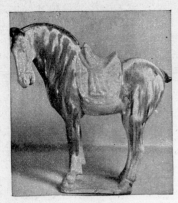

Famous T'ang period horse of buff ware with glaze of straw color with blue mottlings. The saddle shows traces of original red pigment. I know of only three "blue horses." Length and ht. 11½". Ex Warren E. Cox Coll., Mr. Delos Chappell.

Fine large Honan horse of T'ang period with brown body and green and yellow as well as straw colored glazes. Ht. about 36". Nasli Heermaneck Coll.

T'ang female rider perhaps representing a polo player on large Bactrian running horse of reddish clay with white slip. Length 14". Mrs. Charles Porter Wilson.

Arabian type horse. Light buff clay with straw colored transparent finely crackled glaze. Mane of yellow brown, hooves and saddle-blanket of green glaze, saddle is unglazed and shows traces of iron red. Length 21". Warren E. Cox Coll.

T'ang horse of Arabian type with fine trappings, of light buff colored ware and showing faint traces of red and other colors as well as gold. Ht. 15½". Ex D. Abbes Coll.

T'ang horse of rather heavy body and slender legs. A brocade cover seems to have been thrown over the saddle. The horse is of buff pottery with a transparent glaze and there is some green and yellow. Ht. 22½". Fuller Coll. Seattle Art Mus.

T'ANG POTTERY HORSES

PLATE 29

rately and sometimes glazed on and sometimes just stuck in a hole left for the purpose. Slots occur in the mane ridges and it is possible that real hair may have been used for both tails and manes though none has been recorded. Some are glazed and some left in the biscuit and more or less painted. The glazed ones may have a plain straw-colored glaze or may be treated with splashes of green or amber or very rarely blue. Others have a body color of brown, straw or amber with saddles in biscuit and harness in various other of the colors mentioned.

Although T'ang painting and the sculptures in wood, stone and bronze are largely religious and also symmetrical in the early T'ang times, these pottery figures being intended for tomb use are not, although we do have animistic demons, "Earth Spirits" (which Hobson says are properly so named "T'u Kuai" when they have human faces only), and the tall symmetrical dignified

Fig. 255. Group of T'ang pottery figures of dancers of buff ware decorated with white and dark red pigment. Ht. 8". C. T. Loo & Co.

figures often holding a "kuei" (or symbol of authority representative of a sort of jade scepter) in their two hands clasped before them. These have variously been designated as legendary or mythological personages, or, on the other hand, possibly contemporary dignitaries. I am inclined to the former belief because they are always perfectly symmetrical in pose. However, the large preponderance of figures represent entertainers, musicians, lovely ladies, soldiers, boxers, etc. and a group which it is difficult to understand such as merchants, curly-haired Western Asian types which might have been slaves, and other characters which it is hard to imagine could have been thought necessary for the happiness of the deceased. The treatment of glazes or pigments on figures is much like that described for the horses and other potteries. The faces and hands are often left in biscuit, probably because the glaze tended to cover the delicate modeling, but sometimes a thin straw-colored glaze was used and at times darker colors to show the character of the skin color.

The Lokapala is an interesting form. It represents a guardian of one of the quarters of the Buddhistic Heaven. This figure originated in the Civaitic worship of India and spread to Tibet, Turkestan, China and Japan. Dr. Berthold Laufer (Chinese Clay Figures, Part I, Field Museum, Chicago) says

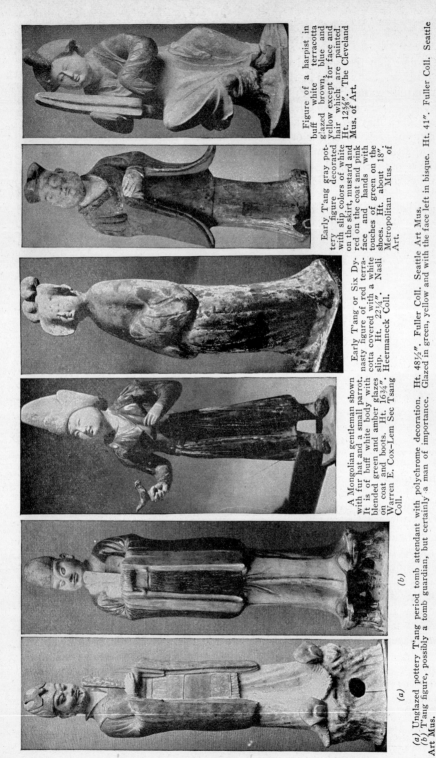

Figure of a harpist in buff white terracotta glazed brown, blue and yellow except for face and hair which are painted. Ht. 12⅝". The Cleveland Mus. of Art.

Early T'ang gray pottery figure decorated with slip colors of white on the skirt, mustard and red on the coat and pink face and hands with touches of green on the shoes. Ht. about 18". Metropolitan Mus. of Art.

Early T'ang or Six Dynasty figure of red terracotta covered with a white slip. Ht. 22¼". Nasli Heermaneck Coll.

A Mongolian gentleman shown with fur hat and a small parrot. It is of buff white body with blended green and amber glazes on coat and boots. Ht. 16¾". Warren E. Cox—Lem See Tsang Coll.

(a) Unglazed pottery T'ang period tomb attendant with polychrome decoration. Ht. 48½". Fuller Coll. Seattle Art Mus.
(b) T'ang figure, possibly a tomb guardian, but certainly a man of importance. Glazed in green, yellow and with the face left in bisque. Ht. 41". Fuller Coll. Seattle Art Mus.

(a)

(b)

T'ANG POTTERY HUMAN FIGURES

PLATE 30

Two figures from Shen-si and Ho-nan having horns still but human faces of a bull-like type, the first having a hole in the right hand probably for holding a weapon. They also have armor and a plumed head-dress. One is standing on a demon. These were developed from *Yama* as triumphant warriors. Hts. 18″ and 12″. Field Mus., Chicago.

Left: This figure, according to Berthold Laufer is "*Yama*," God of Death, standing on a body of a sow. His head is that of a bull and he has three-clawed hands and feet. The head is surrounded by flames. From Shen-si province, T'ang period. Traces of red pigment, the eyeballs being black. Ht. 23½″. Field Mus., Chicago.

Center: Further development from animistic to human forms of guardians. This figure, from Shensi Province, shows Yama standing on a bull. Ht. 25″. Field Mus., Chicago.

(a)	*(b)*	*(c)*	*(d)*

(a) Glazed T'ang figure from Honan with flame from the head similar to above and a winged animal body but distinctly human face. Buckingham Coll. The Art Institute of Chicago.

(b) The human warrior in full armor standing on a demon represents the Triumphant God of Death. It is all glazed in green, blue and brown save the head. Ht. 21″. Shen-si. Field Mus., Chicago.

(c) Shen-si figure of the God of Death standing on a reclining bull, unglazed clay. T'ang period. Ht. 26½″. Field Mus., Chicago. Note that the figure has now become passive except for the facial expression.

(d) Honan tomb guardian lacking all trace of the demon expression. Note dragon repoussé metal shoulder plates and helmet and skirt of leather with padding in the helmet and a knitted sweater under the armor. Ht. 23½″. Warren E. Cox Coll.

T'ANG POTTERY FIGURES OF LOKAPALA
ZOOMORPHIC TO ANTHROPOMORPHIC

Plate 31

Fig. 256. Ovoidal pot on three legs of light buff clay with yellow and buff glazes on blue glazed ground. This blue color, rarely found, was evidently developed during this period. Ht. 4¾". Ex D. Abbes Coll.

Fig. 257. The rare blue glaze covers this sturdy formed jar which is probably after a bronze form. Ht. about 6". Freer Gallery of Art, Wash.

the variations may be classed under Dharmapāla (protectors of the dead) or as Yama (the God of Death). He proves his case clearly that they originated as zoomorphic and developed into anthropomorphic types. It is not necessary here to go into the full series and I have, therefore, picked a few representative high spots. A study of the sequence of illustrations will show the development.

Vase forms are largely much simplified. The globular jar seems to have

Fig. 258. Typical T'ang jar of warm white clay and decorated with a design of green, yellow and transparent colorless glaze finely crackled. Ht. 7". The Buckingham Coll., The Art Institute of Chicago.

Fig. 259. T'ang period jar of pinkish-buff ware with iridescent green glaze. The decoration is of appliqués with slight incising on shoulder. Ht. 4½". Warren E. Cox Coll.

One of pair of unique deep green vases on mustard yellow bases. The green glaze has brilliant silver iridescence in large areas. Ht. 10½". Ex Warren E. Cox Coll. Courtesy of Mrs. Alvin Thalheimer.

7th cent. "Kalása" or "vase for holding amrta (ambrosia); symbol of Maitreya, Man-la, Padmapani, Amitayus, Kubera, Usnīsavijaya, Vasudhara and Cunda." (The Iconography of Tibetan Lamaism by A. K. Gordon.) Ht. 16". Base is restoration. Warren E. Cox Coll.

Amphora showing Hellenistic influence in general form and in shoulder ornamentation. White pottery with light grayish-green crackled glaze covering the upper two thirds. The handles have been changed to dragon forms by the Chinese. Ht. 18". Warren E. Cox Coll.

T'ang vase of usual white body and cream glaze finely crackled but also showing suggestions of "tear drops" similar to those found on Ting yao. Ht. 6". Ex D. Abbes Coll.

Vase of light buff white pottery with thin finely crackled cream glaze down to near foot. Ht. 10".

T'ang period vase of white ware covered with a rather rough white glaze and having yellow green in the foliated mouth. The crude striping about the foot is done with dark brown. This shape was developed and simplified into better proportions in the Sung period. Ht. about 11". Metropolitan Mus. of Art.

A beautiful T'ang period small bottle of simple and growing form more classic than almost anything the Greeks ever did. The glazes which run down over it are yellow, brown and green. Ht. 7¾". Fuller Coll. Seattle Art Mus.

Ewer and stand of light buff pottery and green glaze almost entirely covered with silver iridescence. The tall, tapering neck and the gracefulness of the body make it one of the most beautiful specimens known. Applied relief ornaments show this technique to perfection. Ht. 37½". Freer Gallery, Washington, D. C.

Jar of the same period and ware but having a glaze with a slight greenish tinge. Ht. 5¾". Ex D. Abbes Coll.

T'ANG POTTERY VASE FORMS

PLATE 32

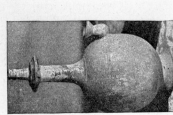

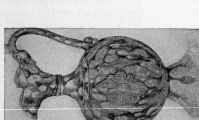

Left to Right: Ewer with characteristics of Greek oenochoë and certain Near Eastern metal forms, of pinkish buff clay with amber and green glaze. Ht. 10½". Eumorfopoulos Coll. # 330.—Ewer after Near Eastern form with relief designs of a bowman on one side and a fênghuang (sacred bird) on the other. The glazes are straw, amber, green and blue. Ht. 11½". Warren E. Cox Coll.—Pottery ewer with saucer of yellowish buff body with partly iridescent green glaze. After bronze form characteristics of which originated in Near East. Ht. 15½". Cleveland Mus. of Art.—T'ang vessel used for drinking water as Ananda Coomaraswamy has pointed out. Filled from side and spout squirted water into mouth just as a Frenchman uses a wine-skin. Hts. 7" and 8¼". John Platt–Warren E. Cox Coll.—T'ang or perhaps a little later "Marbled" or "Wood Grain" vase made by mixing dark gray and buff clays and glazing over with a transparent brown glaze. Though shape suggests T'ang origin, fragments were found by Sir Aurel Stein in Sung and Yüan sites. Buckingham Coll., Art Institute of Chicago.

T'ang pieces of "marbled ware" with light and dark clays and glazed with transparent brown. Distinct East Indian influence. Bottle ht. 7". Ex Warren E. Cox Coll.

Incense burner of brown and light buff clays covered with straw colored transparent glaze splashed with green. Supported by lions rampant with hind legs braced against rim of stand. Dia. 6". Warren E. Cox Coll.

T'ang "marbled vase," form from Han bronze. Unglazed. Ht. 8¼". Warren E. Cox Coll.

Late T'ang or Sung grey marbleized porcelaneous stoneware with transparent glaze. Dia. 6½". Fuller Coll. Seattle Art Mus.

T'ANG EWERS AND MARBLED WARES
PLATE 33

been most frequently used and collections show a great number of these all with different glaze patterns consisting of spots, streaks, cross hatching and chevrons. They are frequently found with covers to match and probably all had them, though usually no rim was provided, the cover being held in place simply by a rim, usually unglazed, on the bottom of it. At times this form was fitted with three claw feet, making it a "ting." Infrequently the form might have loops on the shoulder and even a spout in short cylindrical form and also a few are found with small round and leaf-shaped low relief appliqués. Some of the thinnest and best potted jars of this shape were treated simply with near-white glaze and these are usually somewhat larger, being nearly a foot in height rather than 8″ or 9″. In fact it is noticeable that many of the finest vase forms and ewer forms were treated with plain light cream glaze depending upon the beauty of form alone. Other simple forms, but perhaps more bronze-like, such as the ewers with tall and sometimes ribbed necks, that stood upon pot-stands, are covered with green glaze and are unornamented except for occasional appliques.

The old marble-cake or imitation stone technique was introduced and evidently used quite extensively. Probably the earlier ones, and possibly these are even of the Six Dynasties period, were unglazed and of sturdy form recalling Han bronze forms, although ewers and bowls were also done in this heavy ware. An interesting gourd bottle also of very heavy and thick ware is treated simply with glazes rather than the clays. But as the period de-

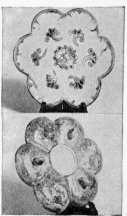

velops these marbled wares became thin and beautifully potted while the Chinese, not contented with making haphazard patterns, devised means of doing circles, rings and such, of the mottled clays, set off by plain areas. A beautiful example of this is shown in the small bottle having strong Indian influence which we illustrate from the Metropolitan Museum of Art.

Ewers after Near Eastern metal forms and occasional vases such as the unique rectangular pair shown (Pl. 32), were often cast complete in molds but they lost no strength thereby and in fact often represent the strongest shapes in T'ang pottery.

Finally we see the beginning of real decorative technique as it appears on plates, small wrist rests for writers, occasional boxes, etc. The artist in most instances resorts to incising the outline and then freely applying his glazes within these bounds, but he also uses what might be called his blending technique as may be seen around the edges of the six-lobed dish shown and in the dappling and rim painting of the

FIG. 260. T'ang plate on three small spiral legs. Front iridescent straw color with green rim, design in green, deep blue and dark amber. Back in mottled, iridescent, amber tones. Dia. 8⅝″. Warren E. Cox Coll.

beautiful spotted dish from the Eumorfopoulos Collection.

Although the Chinese poets wrote appreciatively of some wares, there is little real data concerning famous kiln sites and it is generally true that American and European collectors know as much about the wares as the

Chinese themselves. In the *Book of Tea,* which describes the fact that this beverage had become popular, two wares of outstanding merit are mentioned —*Yüeh Chou Yao* and *Hsing Chou Yao.* (The first two words refer to the location and the last means simply ware.) Yüeh Chou was near Hangchow

FIG. 261. T'ang pottery pillow with incised decoration and glazes of green and yellow on straw color. Length 14″. Warren E. Cox Coll.

FIG. 262. Small T'ang pottery object called a pillow by museum but actually a wrist rest for painter or writer. Length 4″. Boston Mus. of Fine Arts.

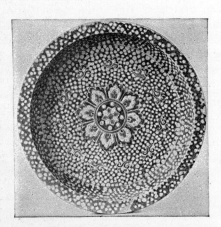

FIG. 263. Dish with rounded sides and flat rim, flat base and three elephant-tusk supports of soft white ware with straw colored glaze and design in brown and green. Dia. 15″. Eumorfopoulos Coll. #403.

FIG. 264. Shallow T'ang bowl with flat bottom and rounded sides decorated with incised and painted design in green and amber on cream. Finely crackled glaze. Dia. 9¼″. K. M. Semon Coll.

in Chekiang province and Hsing Chou was in the southern part of the same province. It is said that Yüeh Yao was valued because it made the tea look green; and Hsing Yao, because it made the tea look red, being itself white. Yüeh Yao is described as being the blue of distant hills or "Ts'ui," the color of kingfisher wings or that of certain jades. The Hsing Yao was supposed to be white as snow. Both were also used for "musical cups" by Ku Tao-yüan. Other wares were said to have been made in *Ting Chou* in

An exceedingly beautifully proportioned Yüeh yao vase with cover having the usual dense but sandy gray body burnt reddish brown where exposed and covered with a transparent olive green crackled glaze. This piece shows a distinctly classic tradition. Ht. 14¾". Warren E. Cox Coll.

Yüeh wine jar beautifully made of grey body with the usual transparent, olive-green, crackled glaze. Note below that the potter signed the piece with his thumb-print on the bottom. Such pieces always are glazed underneath while the Lung-ch'üan ones are not. Ht. 16". Warren E. Cox Coll.

Yüeh vase of pale greenish grey color and fine form from Shang-lin-hu site. Cover missing. Ht. 11⅞". K. M. Semon Coll.

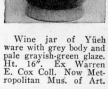

Yüeh yao Sung period bowl beautifully carved in a low relief design of dragons among waves. The ware is a dense gray stoneware and the glaze the typical olive gray green of pale tone. Dia. about 9". Metropolitan Mus. of Art.

Wine jar of Yüeh ware with grey body and pale grayish-green glaze. Ht. 16". Ex Warren E. Cox Coll. Now Metropolitan Mus. of Art.

YÜEH WARES FROM THE SHANG-LIN-HU SITES

PLATE 34

FIG. 265. Yüeh yao vase with deep inverted lotus petal cover modeled in relief, and hexagonal knob. The lightly incised large flowers are bifurcated in each case by one of the five ridges from the "spouts" which are not round as is usually the case but seven sided. The glaze is light grayish green. Ht. about 10". From the K. M. Semon Coll.

FIG. 266. The small jar is rarer than the typical taller funerary jars and the potting is thinner. It is of dense gray clay burnt reddish brown where exposed and the glaze is the same as that on the others. Ht. 8". Warren E. Cox Coll.

FIG. 267. Yüeh yao vase of fine style with interesting applied ornaments of flying birds on the shoulder. Later these jars were made with spouts and then the style developed into the placing of dragons, animals, etc., about the shoulder, chiefly at Lungch'üan and the Southern Kuan yao site. Nasli Heeramaneck Coll.

Shensie province, *Wu Chou* in Chekiang, *Yo Chou* in Hunan, *Shou Chou* in Anhwei and *Hung Chou* in Kiangsi. The poet Tu Fu also mentions *Ta-yi* in Szechwan which was also white as snow and would ring like jade when

FIG. 268. Yüeh yao tea or wine pot of the incised type, specimens of which were found also at Samarra, Persia and Fostat, Egypt. Others have relief decoration as well as the incised. Ht. 5". The Metropolitan Mus. of Art.

FIG. 269. Yüeh yao bowl-stand showing interesting incised petal decoration. Nasli Heeramaneck Coll.

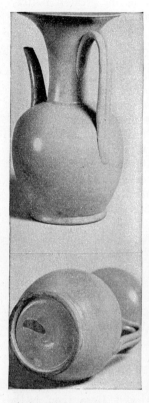

A beautiful ewer from the "nine rocks kiln site" of Yüeh yao with the usual grey body and dull, mat, grey-green glaze. Note the way the handle follows the lines of the neck and body and how nicely it would fit the hand for pouring. Ht. about 7½". T'ang period. Yamanaka & Co.

Yüeh wine-jar of grey stoneware, burnt orange where exposed and covered inside and out with a pale yellow-green glaze. This piece, though it leaned in firing, shows rare curved spouts about the shoulder and a beautifully designed cover the knob of which was actually set in a hole to make it secure. Ht. 14". Warren E. Cox Coll.

Yüeh dish with incised decoration, light olive green glaze and an incised mark under the glaze under the foot meaning "Bamboo," which might have been the mark of some potter or of some certain kiln. Note typical smooth and well turned foot-rim with marks from the supports. Dia. 6". Mr. K. M. Semon.

DETAILS OF YÜEH WARES FROM THE SHANG-LIN-HU SITES

PLATE 35

struck. The wares from Yo Chou were "Ch'ing" (green?) (or "natural color") and yellow, and those from Hung Chou brownish "like coarse cloth" or "Ho" or yellowish black making the tea appear black. This latter ware was made not far from Ching-tê Chên, later famed as the greatest pottery center in the world, and it is probable that it was from here that some of the wares found at Samarra were sent.

The allocating of most of these wares is pure speculation and personal opinion to date, but the Chinese descriptions should be taken quite seriously, contrary to the opinion sometimes expressed by the late R. L. Hobson, for when we do find a kiln site, we are often made to feel foolish because the descriptions have fitted so perfectly. Thus much has recently been learned about Yüeh Yao and we find that it has been more or less under our noses for some time, all unrecognized. Probably Mr. Yuzo Matsumura was the first to recognize the mounds of kiln wasters and he published an article in *Oriental Ceramics,* a Japanese periodical in 1936. Hobson and Sir Percival David had identified two fine bowls in the latter's collection through sherds sent them by Dr. Nakao. In 1937 Mr. J. M. Plumer visited three kiln sites at Shang-lin-hu and described them in detail and Mr. A. D. Brankston followed him in the same year. They found the natives still using the precious wares as building materials and the clay for making bricks. Previously Dr. Manzo Nakao had visited the neighboring site of Yü Yao Hsien to the east and nearer the seacoast and had found the very similar ware which Sir Percival says, in an article in the January, 1929, issue of *Eastern Art,* was believed by the editor of the *T'ao lu* to be the actual ware described by the ancients as Pi-sê Yao, or "secret color ware." Thus we have now sorted out the Shang-lin-hu kilns, the Chiu-yen kilns and the Yü Yao kilns all of which made Yüeh Yao.

Sir Percival quotes the collated literary allusions brought together by the author of the T'ao Shuo as translated by Dr. Bushell after warning, "Translation at its best can only be like the reverse side of a brocade—the threads are there, but the subtility of color and design is lost." Here, then, is the list:

1.—Lu Kuei-mêng, a T'ang poet, uses these terms:
"The misty scenery of late autumn appears when Yüeh kilns are thrown open;
"The thousand peaks have been despoiled of their color for the decoration of the bowls."
2.—Ku K'uang, also contemporary, says:
"The cups of Yüeh-chou paste like jade."
3.—Mêng Chung refers to them:
"Yüeh-chou cups like molded lotus leaves."
4.—Hsü Yin in a verse composed to accompany some teacups made for presentation to the Emperor says:
"Like bright moons, cunningly carved and dyed with spring water;
"Like curling disks of thinnest ice, filled with green clouds;
"Like ancient moss-eaten bronze mirrors, lying upon the mat;
"Like tender lotus leaves, full of dewdrops, floating on the riverside!"

And it would be difficult to better describe these beautiful wares! Here is what Mr. Plumer says he found: "Specimens of the ware are all but totally lacking in museums or private collections, though unidentified pieces doubtless exist. A hard, light grey porcelaneous stoneware was found at them all" (He refers to the three Shang-lin-hu kiln sites.) "with a thin, transparent glaze, the color effect covering a rather limited range of greens, yet including numerous gradations. The idea came to me that we might almost call it 'subtile color' rather than 'secret color' ware. Greyish-greens and olive greens predominated; a light bluish green was sometimes in evidence, and occasionally a brownish-yellow, lacking any greenish tinge. Discoloration in the form of small accidental Chün-like blue and purple splotches was sometimes found."

He goes on to say that there were bowls, saucers, vases, pots for tea and wine, tiny cosmetic boxes, flower-pot stands, etc. including a type of "mortuary jar" usually having spouts about the shoulder. The technique was that of incising, also low relief modeling and low relief appliques molded and applied, with infrequent use of the comb and also of reticulation. Some were crude and some recalled Mêng Chung's words, "like tender lotus leaves." And one was incised under the foot before firing, with a date corresponding to our A.D. 978.

Brankston says others have been found with the date A.D. 987 but he did not produce them. He also warns against clever imitations so dated.

As we look at these wares could the Chinese descriptions have been better? And yet *after* we learned about them I found I had about a dozen in my collection which had never been thought of except as "Northern Sung Celadon," and I must confess that I have made lamps out of a few just as fine as the one I sold the Metropolitan Museum in 1937. Thus the collector often says to himself, "If I had only known! If I had only had the eyes with which to see!"

In the 11th century these Yüeh kilns met the strong competition from the Lung-ch'üan kilns in the southern part of the province and near the capital Ch'u Chou which also later became a great ceramic center. Many of the Yüeh shapes were made with modifications at Lung-ch'üan but the wares there had a beautiful glaze quality (the finest "celadon" wares, so called) and it was probably this, rather than finer potting which made them more popular. (Actually Lung-ch'üan potting is always more crude.)

It is agreed that the Shang-lin-hu kilns did not operate any earlier than the 7th century although those of Chiu-yen were probably, to quote Brankston, "nearer to Han than T'ang in date."

Another ware which we find usually in the form of very high wine jars with a row of 12 figures about the shoulder and a dragon coiled around the tall slender neck on which are also appliqués of birds, stags, cloud scrolls, etc., sometimes with the "pearl of purity," a disc standing off perpendicular to the surface, is similar to Yüeh yao but cruder and rougher in potting and thicker. This ware gives every indication of being pre-Sung but, so far as I know, the kiln site has not been found. Just as was the case with the Yüeh yao many pieces have come on the market and the value has been proportionately low, but some day we shall find the source of this ware and

FIG. 270. Jar and cover incorrectly called "a mortuary jar" and thought to be Yüeh ware by Dr. Laufer. Actually it came from a different kiln-site not yet found and was used for wine, perhaps in some ceremony. Ht. about 15″. Ex Warren E. Cox Coll.

FIG. 272. T'ang wine jar (cover missing) of grey ware with thin grey-green glaze and of the usual form with twelve immortals about the shoulder, a dragon, fêng huang or sacred bird, etc., including a "pearl of purity" standing off the neck. Ht. 30″. Warren E. Cox Coll.

FIG. 271. Two T'ang ewers of white ware, the one glazed with mat brown and the other with cream, crackled glaze. Hts. 7″ and 7½″. The dark one C. T. Loo Coll. The light one Warren E. Cox Coll.

it will then become important to the museums. The range of color and the texture of the glazes are so close to those of Yüeh yao that it is likely that the kilns are somewhere near that great center in northern Chekiang.

Perhaps from Hung Chou may come the first of the brown glazed wares although many of these were made in Honan and elsewhere by Sung times. In any event the transition seems to be from the thin olive-green glazes to thin, and therefore mat, greenish brown and finally, in T'ang times, to an even mat brown or "tea dust" type glaze. The ewer shown, similar to that in the Eumorfopoulos Collection #430, has all the characteristics of T'ang ware; a white body, flat beveled foot, the cylindrical spout, etc. It is interesting to note in passing that the white glazed ewer is very similar in shape and technique and is undoubtedly of the same period. Another brown glazed example with typical T'ang neck and lip-rim, with the double loops inherited from Han times and with the same flat beveled foot has also splashes of the Chün-like blue mentioned in connection with the Yüeh ware by Plumer. These are evenly spaced about the shoulder and, therefore, certainly intentional. The effect is not unlike that produced in the "Kian Temmokus" of the Sung period and this seems to be one of the earliest of the "transmutation glazes." Mr. Walter Hochstadter says these were made in Yu Chou and are the first Chün type.

There is a quantity of white wares which, far from being able to allocate in certain kiln sites, we are not sure as to whether they are late T'ang or early Sung. A good example is the globular ewer mentioned above which we are fairly certain is of the T'ang period because of the flat foot. However, some of the wares found at Samarra did have foot-rims and, therefore, we must assume that during T'ang times they were at least occasionally used in some places. Often the glaze of these wares is not pure white but has a very slight yellowish tinge, and this glaze at times shows only a slight tendency to crackle where it runs thicker.

Ewer of almost white stoneware with olive green glaze of "tea dust" texture. Six dynasties. Ht. 9½". John Platt– Warren E. Cox Coll.

Early Lung-ch'üan vase perhaps even of T'ang period. The base is nearly flat and the ware is grey. Ht. 8". Warren E. Cox Coll.

T'ang jar of white stoneware with "tea-dust" brown glaze with large patches on the shoulder symmetrically arranged of pale blue. The foot is flat and the double loops are a T'ang or earlier characteristic. Ht. 9¼". Warren E. Cox Coll. Note: Many of these wares are found about northern Honan and may have been made at Yu chou, being a sort of prototype of the Chün wares.

CHAPTER IX

THE FIVE DYNASTIES

A.D. 906–960

AFTER THE T'ang period China split into various warring states certain of which gained ascendency for short periods of time. The periods are generally called 1.—Later Liang, 2.—Later T'ang, 3.—Later Tsin, 4.—Later Han and 5.—Later Chou, but these do not particularly interest us as the potteries were simply transitional between T'ang and Sung.

As short a time ago as 1926 Mr. Hobson in writing the Eumorfopoulos Catalogue said that the period was only mentioned in Chinese annals for two kinds of ware both of which were "somewhat mysterious," and yet one of the wares was Yüeh which seems perfectly reasonable to us of today and which I have just described in some detail.

The other ware was "Ch'ai yao" and Ch'ai was the family name of the Emperor Shih Tsung of the posterior Chou, or last period, who ruled at K'ai-fêng Fu between 954 and 959, in northeastern Honan just about where the Yellow River divides into its north and south outlets. It is said that the potters of Chêng chou about 60 miles south of the capital were able to make this ware colored "blue as the sky after rain." Hobson jumps to the conclusion that they made it "only four or five years," which I think is foolish first of all because potters cannot perfect an imperial ware in so short a time and secondly because there is no indication that they stopped. Just as several of the Yüeh kilns made wares for many years and were taken under imperial patronage for a comparatively short time, so could it have been with the kilns of Chêng chou.

The *Ko ku yao lun,* a book I shall speak of in the first part of the next chapter, says Ch'ai yao was rich, refined, unctuous and with crackled lines. It also states that in many cases there was yellow clay on the foot of the ware. The more poetical Master Kao in his book the *Tsun shêng pa chien* and also the author Ku Ying-t'ai of the *Po wu yao lan* state that the ware was as blue as the sky, brilliant as a mirror, thin as paper and resonant as a musical stone.

Hobson suggests, and we quite agree with him, that among the wares which have been given the broad name of *ying ch'ing* there are some that answer all of these characteristics. The bodies of these are white but burn a yellowish buff where exposed. They are thin, translucent, ring when struck and of the pale sky-blue. Some are of a remarkable delicacy of potting particularly when the age in which they were made is taken into consideration. The Chinese have always lauded their finer wares highly and this quite

128

justly. On the other hand modern collectors who now praise the delicacy and charm of a fine Yüeh yao vase could not see anything in it five or ten years ago. I think that the kilns made much more than we suppose and that right before our eyes there are probably Ch'ai wares to be seen.

"Earth worm marks" in a Chün yao glaze at just about normal size.

Typical "crab's claw" crackle as it appears on a Lung-ch'üan "kinuta" of finest quality. Full scale.

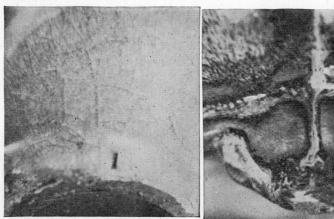

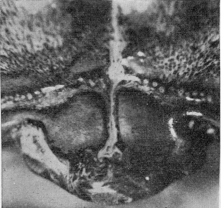

Crackle and flow of glaze on what Hobson calls "Kuan type Chün yao." The crackle is like the "ice crackle" of Southern Kuan but the ware is far heavier.

Foot of a Chün yao bowl showing how glaze runs in mixed blues and purples. About full size.

LUNG-CH'ÜAN AND CHÜN GLAZES

CHAPTER X

THE SUNG DYNASTY

A.D. 960–1280

THE STATEMENT that during the Sung period, "The reins of government were more securely held over a unified, though diminished China," is false for during this time there was internal conflict, intrigue and constant threats from the North which finally ended in conquest and flight. General Chao Kuang-yin (called T'ai-tsu) attacked the Khitan Tartars to the Northeast and they reacted by taking some territory while to the Northwest the kingdom of Hsia fought both sides. In the reign of Hwei-tsung (1101–1126) the terrible mistake was made of persuading the Chin or Nuchih Tartars to help against the Khitan Tartars which they did and then promptly took over all the territory north of the Yangtze River forcing the Sung rulers to move their capital to Nanking and then in 1127 to Hang Chou. Close on the heels of the Chins came the Mongols under the great Jenghiz Khan in 1214 and his son Ogodai was left heir to the whole northern section at his death in 1227. Another alliance was made between the Mongols and the Chinese to fight the Chins and the promise was made that Honan would remain to the Chinese but a quarrel led to the Mongolian conquest south until the last Sung emperor cast himself into the sea in despair and Kublai Khan became emperor of all China and much more in 1280.

Strangely the art of Sung China is not martial but rather poetic and transcendental, not lacking in strength but with the strength of the willow which bends before the storm that breaks the oak; having the strength of the foil rather than that of the broad-sword. It was so close to nature that it did not seem so much to copy nature as to be a very part of it. This art was not so much due to any one group or to patronage as it was lived by almost everyone. I think that critics often try to explain a great flowering of art by some glibly caught phase of history which the artists of the day, perhaps living more apart than might be supposed, had never heard of. A tree shows no interest if one of its branches is broken off; it goes right on growing and eventually the open space fills in. So it is that war simply does not affect some people.

Another very vital fact must be understood before one can understand Sung art and that is that the Far Easterner can be a tough fighter and at the same time a sensitive soul. The good fencer holds his foil cupped in his hand gently as though he were holding a bird, not to let it get away but not to crush it. An old Chinese saying goes, "He who knows the cherry blossom bough can best handle the sword." We men of America suffer more than any

others from a masculine-complex; we feel that a real man should enjoy base-
ball, whisky and poker rather than fencing, wine and art. A real man is not
supposed to take his women too seriously at least in talk with his com-
panions. Before World War I it was considered sissy to wear a wrist watch
or carry a cane until expedience and necessity dictated the use of both.
This manly swagger seems childish to the Chinese for the Chinese man knows
his own qualities of courage and in his country life is held cheaply. Thus it
was possible for many artists in the troublous Sung times to think philo-
sophically and spend time searching for little beauties of nature without any
idea of having to prove themselves worthy or masculine.

One thing the wars did was to shut off to some degree the foreign influences which had poured into China ever since Han times. A chance was
provided to search the inner soul and to develop what was undoubtedly the
most clear strain of purely *Chinese* art that the country ever knew either
before or after. We materialists can perhaps grasp the greatness of the times
through the reports of Marco Polo who visited the country in 1280 in which
he tells of the city of Hang Chou with its many canals bridged, it is said, by
12,000 stone bridges, its hundreds, literally, of hot water baths, its many
markets, the great lake covered with pleasure boats and the fine streets
thronged with busy people. He tells of the good lives of the merchants and
of the craftsmen, and speaks of the fact that no person carried arms, a
wondrous thing to an Italian of that day. Little did the roll of distant thunder disturb them and they made life merry and productive, and among their
products was pottery valued quite as highly as jade or bronze. The wares as
we know them were no longer always laid away in tombs. Wooden, paper and
clay figures long ago fallen to dust in many places were used for this purpose,
much that we have is the precious inheritance of ancient families and the
wasters cast aside at the kilns. Thus when one looks at a Sung vase one
often sees the purest Chinese taste, expressed by an inspired artist of a great
age and cherished and held dear for well-nigh a thousand years by generation
after generation of sensibly sensitive people. But even the wasters from these
great kilns, often as perfect as the day they were potted, carry to us the
inspiration of the artists as studio sketches sometimes show a freshness not
always preserved in a finished painting.

The Chinese themselves have always loved the wares of Sung and we can
turn to their books for much of our information. Of these the best known
are:—

1.—The *Cho Keng Lu* (1368) a miscellany on art.
2.—The *Ko Ku Yao Lun* (1387) (2nd edition 1459)
3.—The *Album of Hsiang Yüan-p'ien* (1561)
4.—The *Tsung Shêng Pa Chien* (1591)
5.—The *Ch'ing Pi Ts'ang* (1595)
6.—The *Po Wu Yao Lan* (1621–1627)
7.—The *T'ao Shuo* (1774) which incorporates the information given in the
     former works and others.
8.—The *Ching-tê Chên T'ao Lu* (1815) which also covers much of the same
     ground, and which has to do with the famous potteries at Ching-tê

Chêng in the Ch'ang-nan district east of Po Yang Lake in Kiangsi province, given its name by Ching Tê (1004–1007) and which in the 18th century was commanded by the Emperor Yung Chêng to make reproductions of Sung wares for which purpose specimens were sent down from the Imperial Palace Collection.

We read of the wares of Ju (pronounced Ru), Kuan, Ko, Lung-ch'üan, Chün, Chien, Ting and Tz'ŭ Chou but these were only a few of the best known factory products and many others copied the famous wares and also made wares of their own. It should also be stressed that none of these kilns started at the beginning of the Sung period and stopped at the end of the period. Also the beautiful wares of Lung-ch'üan were carried on with slight differences at the capital of Chekiang province, Chü-chou, and these together with the Ting and Tz'ŭ Chou were sent to the ends of the earth and copied by potters in Japan, the Near East and Europe.

In general the bodies are now high-fired and porcelaneous though the change was not an abrupt one. This body clay usually contained iron so that it was white, grey or buff where protected but often burnt reddish-brown where exposed due to iron oxide. It was usually well refined and smooth to the touch though some of the buff bodies are rough and some of the more vitreous ones gritty as in certain Ying Ching wares which are also translucent.

The glazes are frequently of one color or combinations of two colors ranging from palest blue or green to deep blue or to brown and even black. There is no doubt but that the Sung Chinese collectors preferred the restraint and simplicity of single colors rather than dramatic decorations of color as we find in Chün wares for instance and later in Ming wares. T'ang glazes were soft lead types, thinly applied and minutely crackled much like those of the later Ming period but Sung glazes are hard, feldspathic types which are either not crackled at all or are definitely and boldly so, at first by accident but soon by direct intent as in Ko ware. A few of the terms used by Chinese critics are "tzŭ jun" (rich and unctuous), "hsi ni" (fine and glossy), and "jung" (lustrous). So beautiful are these glazes that, though the whole world has tried, and the Chinese of later days tried, they have never been truly copied. Mr. W. Burton has explained this as follows: "The Chinese method of firing naturally produced glazes in which the oxide of iron and copper were present in the lowest state of oxidization; and this is the explanation of the seeming paradox that the green glazes, known to us as celadon, and the copper-red glazes, were amongst the earliest productions of the Chinese porcelain makers, while in Europe they have been among the latest secrets to be acquired." Thus it is perhaps so that this was another natural development rather than abrupt invention but this takes nothing away from the glory of these artists who made so much of what they had in hand. The same general principles of potting were probably used in all the kilns and the same glaze due to differences in local clays and other materials might turn out green, grey, lavender or turquoise blended with red.

One of the difficulties in reading the Chinese descriptions is their seeming lack of a definite meaning for the terms used for the colors. Thus the word "ch'ing" which annoyed Hobson to the point of distraction might refer to a blue, a sea-green of celadon, a pale bluish shade of clair de lune, grey, brown and even black. The Chinese dictionaries define it as the "color of nature," and this seems to me a perfectly understandable qualification. Our own Western terminology is vague and most misleading and few of us designate a color by its three elements. We speak of a leaf green which may include hundreds of different hues and various values of each and various qualifications of each. The Chinese mean by ch'ing a color of nature rather than an artificial appearing color such perhaps as the horrible green seen on cheap Japanese toys. Perhaps they are not so interested in the actual hue as in its quality just as they think of the *consistency* of shark-fins or of bird's nest soup as much as of the taste. We Westerners pay less attention to consistency unless the steak is too tough to chew. But there are certain colors which we see more often in the world about us and which are pleasant therefore, like the colors of vegetable dyes so qualified as to be soft and pleasing. Later chemistry produced colors which, like the sound of the klaxon horn, had never been on this earth before and which are most unpleasantly shrill and hurtful and which have to be qualified to be tolerated. These colors are not ch'ing.

There are great varieties in the weights of Sung wares from paper thin to well-nigh an inch in thickness, but they are all of a heavy feeling for the thickness used and the glazes always adhere perfectly though at times they were not applied evenly over the whole surface and there may be small areas where they round down to the body when melted in the kiln.

Ju Yao & Ying Ch'ing

Our knowledge of Ju yao is scanty. We do know that Hsü Ching visited Korea in 1125 and wrote that Korean pottery was "like the modern Ju and the ancient Yüeh wares." Other contemporary writers wrote that it was of ch'ing color. Furthermore it was written that the potters at Ju Chou south of the Yellow River in central Honan province were ordered to supply their ch'ing ware to the Imperial Court in place of the wares of Ting Chou because flaws occurred in the Ting yao. Whether the potters were actually moved to the court in K'ai-fêng Fu is debatable. The *Cho kêng lu* quotes a 13th century writer, Yeh Chih, as saying that the Ju potters were chosen because they were better than those at T'ang and Teng (in southern Honan) and Yao (in Shensi) where the wares were similar. So much is fairly strong evidence.

As second rate evidence we have the *Ko ku yao lun* stating that the glaze was "tan ch'ing" or pale ch'ing. Kao Lien says in the *Tsung shêng pa chien,* "Ju ware I have actually seen. In color it is egg white 'luan po' the glaze is transparent and thick like massed lard." This "luan po" could refer to ducks' eggs which are usual in China and are pale bluish or greenish. Hsiang Yüan-p'ien illustrates three pieces, two of which are described as of "yü lan" (sky blue) and one as of "fên ch'ing" (pale ch'ing) and the glaze is crackled. Finally the 19th century imitations were made of the "blue like the sky after rain" which was also the description of Ch'ai yao which it was

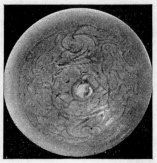

FIG. 273. Ying Ch'ing Sung dish of white porcelain with clear pale blue transparent glaze of considerable brilliancy. Dia. 5¾". Mrs. Charles Porter Wilson. Warren E. Cox Coll.

FIG. 274. Ying Ch'ing bowl of white porcelain covered with a clear pale blue transparent glaze slightly crackled. The dynamic whirling design has been scratched into the body with a sharp instrument with flattened tip. Sung. Dia. 6½". Ex Warren E. Cox Coll. Now K. M. Semon Coll.

FIG. 275. Incised Ying Ch'ing type bowl showing "happy boys" among flowers, a favorite design for a certain type of fairly heavy ware with glossy glaze. Dia. about 7½". K. M. Semon Coll.

said was made in Chêng Chou in the same district. None of the early writers gives any description of the body.

One of the world's greatest collectors and students, the late Mr. George Eumorfopoulos has advanced the theory on this evidence that Ju yao may be searched for among the wares which we now arbitrarily label Ying Ch'ing. His points are all well taken and particularly it does seem impossible that

FIG. 276. Ying Ch'ing bowl of rather heavy porcelaneous ware and having a somewhat gritty foot burnt light brown. The design of a swimming duck is swiftly incised as is also the outside petal motif. The glaze is clear light blue. Dia. 6½". Sung Period. Warren E. Cox Coll.

FIG. 277. Ying Ch'ing type incense burner with three legs, two handles on shoulders and two added loose ring handles. The ware is white and porcelaneous and the glaze a very bright pale blue. It is perhaps of late Sung period. Ht. 6". Metropolitan Mus. of Art.

FIG. 278. One of pair of Ying Ch'ing type incense burners of white and porcelaneous ware with very brilliant pale blue glassy glaze. The period is late Sung. Ht. 9". Metropolitan Mus. of Art.

any such group of wares showing such beauty and subtility could have gone unnoticed by the ancient Chinese writers. Thus they must have been described under Ch'ai, Ju, Kuan or Ko wares and we are fairly certain that they were neither of the last two. Moreover the testimony concerning Korean wares is to the point for in that country we do find many of the Ying Ch'ing types of ware either imported or perhaps made there by Chinese potters. I am inclined to give greater credence to this theory than to the later one expressed by R. L. Hobson in the Sir Percival David Catalogue (1934).

FIG. 279. Cup-holder of early Korai period Korean ware having a green glaze with crackle on a white body browned where exposed and fired on seven spurs. Dia. 7". John Platt, Warren E. Cox Coll.

FIG. 280. The upper bowl is rather heavy in potting and has an imperfect glaze pitted and having, "numerous pin holes and shallow depressions," as Hobson says. The foot-rim is glazed and it was fired on three spurs. Dia. 5".
  The cup-holder is similar and even more heavy in potting. Dia. 6½".
  Both of these are termed Ju ware by Hobson, I think arbitrarily for they appear to be rather ordinary Korean wares of heavy potting and not at all of imperial quality. Sir Percival David Coll.

FIG. 281. Oval "brush-washer" of the Sir Percival David Coll., called Ju ware by Hobson. There are two sesamum flowers incised in the bottom. I think it a Korean piece not very well made. Note the poor spacing of the spur marks, fire crack in glaze of bottom and irregular shape. Length 5½".

Hobson thought that Ju yao would have been compared with the "common Korean wares" or the celadon type but I see no reason why a rare ware should not be compared with another rare ware in the mind of a traveller and the Ying Ch'ing wares found in Korea are not so very rare at that. He more or less takes the word of a poet of the Ch'ien Lung (1736–96) period or perhaps that of the emperor poet himself that two rather heavy dishes (#B100 Eumo. Cat.) (Pl. II David Cat.) may be Ju yao though they certainly do not rival Ting yao in potting, and only by a long stretch of imagination could be thought to resemble the clear sky color. The only slightest resemblance these have to Korean wares is that they are glazed over the foot rim and fired on five spurs. They certainly do not represent any general type of ware, being odd and not very fine pieces. Having established in his own mind that these are possibly Ju yao, he includes a cup-holder in the

"Ying Ch'ing" type vase of white porcelain, burnt brown where exposed, and covered with a clear, pale blue crackled, transparent glaze which is silvery iridescent on one side on which it probably rested in burial. Ht. 9″. Sung Dynasty. John Platt–Warren E. Cox Coll.

Ying Ch'ing type jar with cover of buff clay and finely crackled glaze showing pale blue toward bottom shading up to buff probably due to over firing. Ht. 9½″. Warren E. Cox Coll.

Ewer reported found near Kinkiang, of the Sung period, and of the so called Ying Ch'ing type though it is paler and more buff than blue. The form is a Near Eastern one and the potting excellent. Ht. about 9″. Metropolitan Mus. of Art.

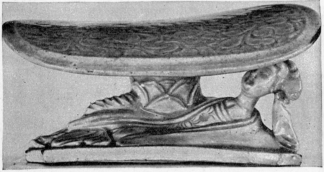

A beautiful small pillow of Sung period ware which we call Ying Ch'ing. It is heavily potted and porcelaneous. The glaze is pale blue. Metropolitan Mus. of Art.

Ying Ch'ing type ewer of rather rough pottery with a pale blue glaze discolored red-brown by earth in which it was buried. The potting is thin and well done. Ht. 7⅛″. John Platt–Warren E. Cox Coll.

YING CH'ING WARES OF SUNG DYNASTY

PLATE 36

Sir Percival David Catalogue which is typically Korean and quite like ours in the John Platt Collection Fig. 279 as may be seen by comparison, and neither of these, though they are very fine potting, can actually rival the Ting yao in thinness of potting or perfection. (Fig. 280)

It must be remembered that the *Tsung shêng pa chien* was written in 1591, the latter part of the Ming period and that Ming writers frequently used the phrase that we have had translated "like massed lard." This may have an entirely different connotation than we give it, that is, it may not mean a thick glaze at all but rather a soft, unctuous quality which certain of the Ying Ch'ing wares do have to a marked degree. Moreover, it seems obvious to me that the Ying Ch'ing thinner wares are even thinner and more truly potted than the Ting ware while none of the other Sung potteries even including Yüeh, which is perhaps next in thinness, can rival these two. (Note the three delicate small bowls which are well-nigh paper thin.) Thus I feel we must still grant Mr. Eumorfopoulos the more sound theory.

Ying Ch'ing porcelain has a hard, white vitreous body and the glaze is full of bubbles which give it a soft effect. This glaze is of palest blue show-

FIGS. 282–283. Three Ying Ch'ing bowls of exceedingly delicate and true potting with thin foot rims and very thin lip rims certainly finer than any Ting yao specimens. The ware is a white porcelain and the glazes all palest blue. Dias. 3½″ to 6″. John Platt–Warren E. Cox Coll.

ing darker where it runs thicker. The blue was made by the slightest possible addition of cobalt as can be proven by tiny specks to be seen in some pieces. The glaze sometimes crazes though often it does not. The lip-rims are usually glazed and the bottom is often not glazed sometimes showing the marks of a ring on which it was fired. The body turns brown where exposed. Rarely the Ting technique was copied and the bowls were fired with the lip-rims for support and the bottoms glazed. They were then mounted

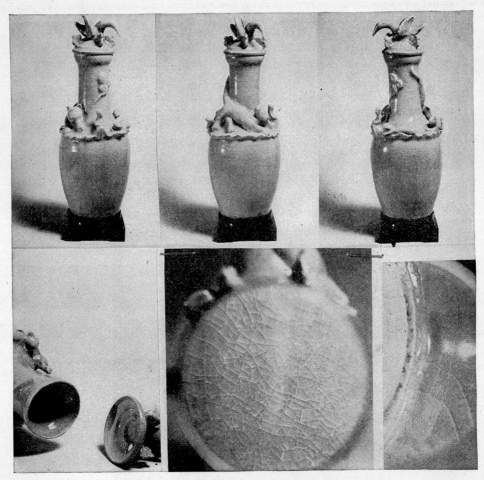

Superb specimen of the rare Southern Kuan yao from "below the Suburban Altar" site. The only large and perfect piece known. It is of grey "wu-ni yao" beautifully potted and more thin than the finest Lung Ch'üan "kinuta" type ware. The glaze is of grey-blue shading to olive-brown and has the "ice crackle" with long curved "crab's claw" crackle. The form is traditional, inherited from T'ang mortuary jars and found with modifications in Yüeh, Lung Ch'üan and other wares but the beautiful proportions with the long neck, stalking tiger and "Feng-Huang" bird show the work of a master potter as technically can also be seen in the fine finish of the inside of the cover. Ht. 13⅜". Ralph Chait–Warren E. Cox Coll.

SOUTHERN KUAN WINE JAR FROM "BELOW THE SUBURBAN ALTAR" SITE

PLATE 37

with a metal rim. This may have been during the times that rivalry was set up between the two kilns. The decoration consists of incising, modeling, molding, appliqué and even reticulation but all was conservatively used and in good taste until the Ming period. The designs are of ducks, boys among flowers, "happy boys," fishes, etc., and seem to be similar to those of Northern Sung celadons. Beautiful vase forms reflect those of Tz'u Chou and tall ewers called "hu p'ing" are of Near Eastern and probably metal origin. The *Ko ku yao lun* tells us that these were introduced first by the Mongols in the Yüan period (A.D. 1280–1368) but we know this to be untrue for we have proven conclusively that Near Eastern relationship was very strong and continuous in Tang and earlier times.

The quality and thickness of these wares varies more than any other and this is, of course, explained by the various sources. South and east of Ching-tê chên alone there were five sites: Nan shan, Hu-tien, Hsiang-hu, Fu-tien-ts'un, and Wang-ts'un where it was made in pre-Ming times according to Brankston.

KUAN YAO

Kuan yao literally means simply "imperial ware," but the term was used by the early Chinese writers to designate that which was made in the Im-

Fig. 284. Pair of Lung-ch'üan jars of Kuan (Imperial) type thinner in potting even than the "kinuta" type. One is olive-green and almost without crackle. The other is pale grey-green with a prominent "crab's claw" crackle. Note the thin foot-rims. Ht. 9¼". Warren E. Cox Coll.

perial Factory near the capital of Honan, K'ai-fêng or K'ai-fêng Fu. This ware was called Ta Kuan by later writers. It was supposed to have been made during the Ta Kuan (1107) and Chêng Ho reigns (1111–1117) and the factory was established by the Emperor Hui Tsung but in 1127 when the court fled the potters were taken along to Hang Chou where two kilns were set up, one under Shao Ch'êng-chang in the Imperial precincts at Hsien Nei Ssŭ near the Surveyor's Office, and one, "Below the Suburban Altar." The wares from K'ai-fêng Fu have not been definitely identified but those from both southern sites have. Both were said to imitate the Ta Kuan shapes but were less well potted due to difficulties in the handling of the new materials. The first or, "Surveyor's Office site," made "Nei yao" or Palace ware. Meanwhile at Yü-hang Hsien, near Hang Chou, still another ware was made imitating Kuan yao, and shortly after the Lung-ch'üan kilns also made a "Kuan yao." (Figs. 284 & 285)

Early descriptions say that Ta Kuan yao was "fên ch'ing" (pale blue), "ta lü" (deep green), "yüeh pai" (moon white), and finally, *Ch'ing t'ai fên hung,*" (ch'ing with a tinge of pale red). It had a large crackle called "crab's

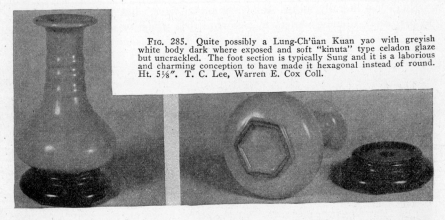

FIG. 285. Quite possibly a Lung-Ch'üan Kuan yao with greyish white body dark where exposed and soft "kinuta" type celadon glaze but uncrackled. The foot section is typically Sung and it is a laborious and charming conception to have made it hexagonal instead of round. Ht. 5⅛". T. C. Lee, Warren E. Cox Coll.

claw" and a finer "fish roe" one. There is no word of the body color of the original ware but the second was said to be "tzŭ" (dark brown or purple) which caused a "brown mouth and iron foot." And finally it was stated by Hobson that, "yellow, black, red and purple (or brown) forms of great beauty," appeared on the surface and took the forms of natural objects such as, "butterflies, birds, fishes, unicorns, leopards and the like." This is translated from the *Tsung Sheng pa chien* (1591) and Ko ware is included in the description. The *Ch'ing pi Ts'ang* (1595) by Chang Ying-wên speaks of, "ice crackle with lines as red as eel's blood," and of, "plum blossom crackle with lines ink colored." This might apply to crackles stained from oxidation of the body or artificially colored by soaking in dye.

Here we get into one of those common difficulties in making translations. Hobson, jumping to the conclusion that, "ch'ing t'ai fên hung," meant, *"splashes* of red on blue color," built a whole theory to the effect that certain

 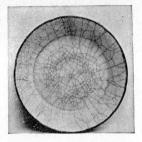 

FIG. 286. For imperial potting one would search far before
finding a finer specimen than
this jar of blackish stoneware
with brownish-grey glaze and
black (probably stained) crackle.
It is, I believe incorrectly, called
Ko by Hobson but may well be
Ta Kuan. Ht. 3.9". Eumor-
fopoulos Coll. # B64.

FIG. 287. "Küan yao plate"
of black ware with gray-blue
glaze having brown crackle. It
is thinly potted and mounted
with a metal rim. Dia. about 7".
Metropolitan Mus. of Art.

FIG. 288. "Küan yao" beg-
ging bowl of the Sung period
of dark stoneware with black
rim and blue-green or green-
blue glaze and dark brown
crackle. Dia. about 5". Metropolitan Mus. of Art.

of the more refined and thin (though still fairly heavy) Chün wares, with
their brown or olive green edges, dark bodies, blue and often crackled glazes
and red splashes, were Southern Kuan ware. On the other hand the translation should really be, "a bluish or greenish color *tinged with* red," which any
person, used to mixing color, would agree would produce browns, lavender,
dull green fawn and vinaceous or cinnamon colors depending on the proportions. The point is important as we shall see.

The *Ko ku yao lun* (1387) said the ware was, "fine and unctuous, the
color ch'ing with a flush of pale red *and varying*," according to Hobson's own
translation. It also says specimens with black body are called "wu-ni yao,"
which I take to be an inference that there may have been other kinds. It
further states that Kuan yao made at Lung-ch'üan has no crackle. We know
that crackle was not under control there until the very end of Sung or even
later times though it did occur slightly at times. This type is quite possibly
represented by our small bottle with hexagonal foot. (Fig. 285)

The *Cho Keng Lu* (1368) states, "Southern Kuan is of fine clay with
translucent color and brilliant right through." This is quoting Yeh-chih. The
meaning may be that the ware is translucent or that the color (or glaze) is
translucent as seems to be the case.

Our present day findings are beginning to make this ware quite certain.
Dr. Menzo Nakao found shreds in the Surveyor's Office site including dark
bodied wares, a greyish white bodied "kinuta" type "celadon" probably
from Lung-ch'üan, a crackled "celadon" and others with a thinner and more
bubbly glaze; at least four types. Mr. Karlbeck, Dr. Burchard and Peter
Boode found others of great variety both in color and glaze which are in the
British Museum. It is upon these that some sort of classification has been
attempted though many of the wares at first called Ko are more likely to
be Kuan and vice versa. Perhaps the most sensible way to approach the
matter is to assume that certainly *the Imperial Ta Kuan and Southern Kuan
wares would have been better potted than the more ordinary Ko ware,* all
of Mr. Hobson's bubble theories to the contrary, and, if we apply this simple

FIG. 289. Southern Kuan vase (neck cut) from the Suburban Altar site. Thin grey ware burnt brown, with lavender-brown transparent glaze crackled typically. Note ogival plan. Ht. 4". Benjamin d'Ancona Coll.

FIG. 290. Sung bowl of black stoneware thinly potted, the foot having a narrow and shallow rim and six black spur marks. The glaze is of greenish oyster gray with black crazing, broader on the outside and denser on the inside. Called Kwan yao. Dia. about 4". Metropolitan Mus. of Art.

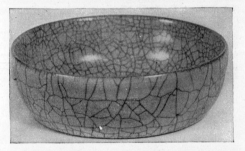

rule certainly the Eumorfopoulos example #B64 (Our Fig. 286) would belong in the Kuan category as it is a superb piece of potting.

Just before World War II a few dozen small and mostly broken pieces of an exceedingly thin and beautifully potted ware came onto the American market and it was stated that they had been found "below the Suburban Altar." The pieces were said to have come from a dealer named Chow of the Rue Bron Gros, French Concession, Shanghai. The body is invariably dark grey or brown and the glaze is bubbly and transparent so that you can, "see right through it," and prominently crackled with what may well be described as an "ice crackle." The colors of no two are alike and vary even on a single piece. The range is through soft blues and greens to buff, lavender and reddish browns perhaps best described as near the colors of moth wings and all consisting of "ch'ing tinged with red." So thinly potted is it that it compares with the thinner Ying-Ching. It makes Pai-Ting Yao feel heavy. Lung-ch'üan even of the "kinuta" type is crude and heavy by comparison. Thus master potters must have made it. The forms are often derived from bronze shapes but made in ogival plan at times with the suture marks so exaggerated as to become actual flanges. Other forms are simple potters' forms but with great charm and beauty of proportion.

Just recently Mr. Ralph M. Chait and I acquired the finest specimen of this ware which has ever been seen (Pl. 37), and which I illustrate in detail. This piece clears up one interesting point. It had worried collectors that although the ware was exactly as described in every detail the reference to

Early Lung-Ch'üan jar and cover having a dragon, chicken and reclining figure about the shoulder and the "Feng-Huang" bird on the cover. Note the similarity of the form to the Southern Kuan ware example but the much finer potting of the latter. Early Sung. Ht. 13″. Warren E. Cox Coll.

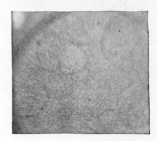

Two interesting examples, the one of Southern Kuan (the darker) and the other of Lung-Ch'üan ware, showing how closely the former took up the designs of the older kilns, and how much better the potting was. Late Sung. Hts. 3″. Warren E. Cox—John Platt Coll. The Kuan example is from C. T. Loo.

EARLY LUNG-CH'ÜAN WINE JAR PROTOTYPE OF A
SOUTHERN KUAN FORM

PLATE 38

various animals appearing on the surface as quoted from the *Tsung shêng pa chien* could not be explained. Some had suggested that one with imagination could envision animal forms in the crackle but this stretched the imagination altogether too far. In our jar this final question is settled. The animals appear *not painted,* as Hobson assumed in working out his Chün type theory, but beautifully *sculptured* in the round and covered with the glaze so they appear in color. They include a tiger, a dog and two human figures. The cover is surmounted with a most beautiful bird with half opened wings.

FIG. 291. Brush-washer (hsi) of water-chestnut flower (ling hua) shape called "Ko ware" by Hobson. It must be admitted that the potting is heavy but the glaze of buff, bluish and brown at edges, with its "ice crackle" is much like that of the Southern Kuan ware from below the Suburban Altar site. Dia. 7.35". Sir Percival David Coll.

FIG. 292. Southern Kuan incense burner from below the Suburban Altar of thin brown-grey ware covered with a transparent deep green-blue glaze. Ht. 3". N. M. Heeramaneck Coll.

It so happened that I had an early Lung-ch'üan jar (Pl. 38) in my collection which is a likely prototype and represents an ancient, traditional form dating at least from the second century A.D. (See brown jar Pl. 25, Fig. 3), but in this Southern Kuan example the form reaches its greatest beauty. The color of the body of this jar is dark grey and the glaze is gray-blue shading to buff and greenish-buff. The thinness of the lip and cover rims speaks for itself. So far as we know, no comparative example is in existence, and when it is placed near one of the Lung-ch'üan jars of similar form but with squat bodies, short necks, flattened covers and heavy potting, its aristocratic beauty stands out clearly. (See Pl. 40 for late example.)

Ko Yao

Ko yao (or the "Elder Brother's ware") is invariably associated with Kuan yao in the ancient Chinese texts which in most cases make no distinction between them. It was supposed to have been made by the elder brother Chang in the latter part of the Southern Sung period (A.D. 1127–1280) in the lung-ch'üan district in Ch'u Chou Fu (Chekiang province) at a place called Lin-t'ien. The other brother made a celadon very much like Lung-ch'üan yao and treated under that section.

The story has been doubted but there was some potter who made this ware and he may have had a brother. It is immaterial and the story persists. The dark clay from Phoenix Hill at Hang Chou was imported and this

LATE SUNG TO EARLY MING: LUNG-CH'UAN TEMPLE VASE.

This is one of the finest examples of the Lung-ch'uan glaze known. Neck is cut.
Ht. 18¼ inches·   Ex. S. K. de Forest Coll. Warren E. Cox Collection   See Plate 45

FIG. 293. "Ko yao" writer's coupe with grey body which burns brown about the foot and mouth, and a translucent gray glaze filled with just visible bubbles and crackled in brown and black. Yung Chêng period (960–1280 A.D.). Width 3½". Judge Edgar Bromberger Coll. Brooklyn Mus.

FIG. 294. "Ko yao" Sung period bowl of dark gray stoneware and having a greenish gray glaze with black crackle and dark gray lip rim. Dia. about 6". Metropolitan Mus. of Art. Comparison should be made of the crackles.

made the "brown mouth and iron foot" similar to Hang Chou Kuan yao (see preceding section). Crackle was purposely developed in Ko yao and Hsieh Min of the Yung Chêng period (A.D. 1722–1736) said "Ko glaze on an iron body of two kinds—mi sê (millet-colored) and fên ch'ing both copied from ancient specimens sent from the Palace," in the descriptions of the wares he was ordered to copy. The least good color according to the older critics was hui sê or ash-colored, but the poet Ku Liu describes a Ko yao

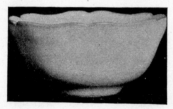

FIG. 296. Termed "Kuan yao" by the museum but doesn't fit requirements, is heavily potted, has light body, etc. Possibly Ko. Sung. Freer Gallery of Art. Washington, D. C.

FIG. 295. Bottle called "Kuan type" by the museum, of black body and bluish-grey glaze which is crackled. The heavy and none too sure potting makes it difficult to suppose this a real imperial ware. Sung. Ht. 8½". Metropolitan Mus. of Art.

FIG. 298. Ovoid vase with black stoneware body and thick opaque glaze of pale bluish-grey with irregular crackle of the "crab's claw" type. "Ko type." Ht. 10.75". Eumorfopoulos Coll. # B60.

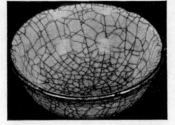

FIG. 297. "Ko ware" bowl, said to be Sung. Grey-green with a definite crackle and also a fainter one. The glaze full of quite perceptible bubbles. Dia. 4¾". Gift of Mrs. Thos. D. Stimson. Seattle Art Mus.

A typical Ko vase of grey stoneware with opaque gray-buff glaze having strong black and lighter brown crackle. Inside the lip is engraved a poem by Ch'ien Lung:
"Despite the hundred-fold crackle lines, its surface is smooth to the touch.
"This, the ware of Ch'u-chou, was the work of the talented Elder Brother.
"When one has once discovered the worth of undecorated wares,
"The elaborate products of Hsüan and Ch'êng will be less esteemed."
Ht. 5.9". Sir Percival David Coll.

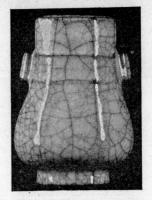

"Ko yao," Sung vase after a bronze form, having a dark body and bluish gray glaze filled with small bubbles but not having the "brown mouth" often found in such wares. Ht. about 4". Freer Gallery of Art, Washington.

Small vase called "Kuan yao" by the museum but so proportionately heavy and comparatively crude that I should say it was "Ko yao" if of either type. Ht. 4". Freer Gallery of Art. Washington, D. C. Is also called "Sung" but may be later.

"Ko ware" fairly heavy incense-vase (hsiang lu) or leys jar (Cha-tou) of dark brown stoneware with brown crackled pale green glaze. The lip-rim is copper. Dia. 4.6". Imperial Coll., Peking. Cf. Eumor-fopoulos Coll. # B64. Sir Percival David Coll.

Wide necked bottle on flaring foot in which there are two rectangular holes. Thinly potted dark ware covered with a pale gray green glaze, similar to that of Lung Ch'üan yao, which is irregularly crackled with what may be called a "crab's claw" crackle. Called Ko yao. Sung period. Gift of Mrs. Samuel T. Peters. Metropolitan Mus. of Art.

Ko ware bulb-bowl (shui hsien p'ên) of blackish brown ware burnt red-brown where exposed and covered with a slightly greenish buff-grey glaze crackled in black and brown probably stained. Sung. Dia. 7". Sir Percival David Coll.

Lung Ch'üan Sung period bulb bowl of white porcelain with rich and translucent green glaze. Dia. about 6½". Gift of Mrs. Samuel T. Peters. Metropolitan Mus. of Art. Note similarity of form to the Ko one above, which tends to bolster the theory of the Brothers Chang.

KO WARE OF THE SUNG DYNASTY

PLATE 39

ink-stone as lü (green) as the waves in spring. This may have been poetic license or perhaps he simply got mixed up. In any event, as has been explained, the glazes of these wares may vary considerably in color and should be judged chiefly by their texture. The *Ch'ing pi ts'ang,* a book not on our list and of doubtful authority, speaks of crackle varying from "the crab's claw of Kuan yao to the fish-roe of Ko yao, which was less beautiful," but this general description of a small crackle is not borne out by other authorities. However, it is true that the small privately owned kiln did perhaps make a ware less good than the Imperially patronized Kuan yao. The old reports also speak of "touches," "splashes," or "tinges" of warm contrasting color (see preceding discussion) and I believe these to be similar to those in Kuan yao. The Hobson theory that Kuan might have been a kind of Chün yao type ware should also receive its fatal blow when the ancient writers associate Kuan and Ko so closely together. Certainly we cannot admit Ko yao into this same category of Chün-like wares.

Perhaps here a word should be said about crackle in general. It is caused by a different rate of expansion and contraction under heat and cold of the body and the glaze. Thus a tension is set up which results in a cracking of the weaker part, the glaze. This is not usually sufficient to crack the glaze off the body. The *T'ao lu* (1815) says that the potters of Yung-ho Chên during the Sung dynasty used a special clay called "hua shih" in the glaze and it may be that they added some ingredient to make a wider divergence between the rates of expansion and contraction. However, this was no invention and again was a simple adaptation of a phenomenon which occurred by accident. Another method said to have been used was to heat the piece in the sun and then plunge it into cold water. This might *aid* to develop a crackle but it could hardly *cause* a crackle if the tension was not already present. It must be explained that the crackle does not take place entirely in the kiln as the piece is cooling off. I have heard a modern piece of porcelain sitting on my desk days after it was made suddenly begin to snap and crack and have watched the crackle developing further on it.

Ko yao was greatly copied from the time of its origin and the collector therefore must be careful. But although it is rare, and beautiful, pieces can be had for a price running from a few hundred dollars up, we need hardly go to the lengths of at least one old Chinese eunuch who, it is reported in the *Pi chuang so yü,* had a man thrown into prison simply because he was jealous of the ownership of a piece of Ko yao "about two inches in height."

CH'ING TZ'U (GREEN PORCELAIN)
LUNG-CH'ÜAN YAO, CH'U-CHOU YAO AND OTHER "CELADONS"

I have already used the word "celadon" a number of times in reference to such wares as Yüeh yao, Kuan yao, Ko yao, etc. It further applies to Lung-ch'üan yao, Ch'ü-chou yao, some Northern Honan wares, some Korean wares and imitations made both in the Far East and Near East as well as Europe. Stretching its meaning to cover cheap green oil lamps, as some department stores have recently, is wrong for they have nothing whatsoever to do with the original Far Eastern ware which has been so popular in nearly every country in the world for over 500 years. We are not sure of the origin of the word. Some say it was derived from the name Saladin but the best known theory is that it came from France where a play featured a shepherd who wore the then new and popular color in the 17th century.

 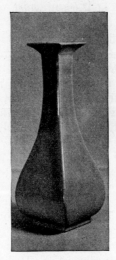 

FIG. 299. Early Sung Lung-ch'üan bottle. Grey clay burnt red where exposed and covered with transparent crackled glaze shading from buff to olive green. Ht. 9¾". Warren E. Cox Coll.

FIG. 300. Lung-ch'üan square bottle c. A.D. 1100 with grey body burnt red where exposed and transparent pale green crackled glaze. Ht. 9¾". K. M. Semon Coll.

FIG. 301. Pair of important Sung vases of Lung Ch'üan yao which are very close to the shape of the T'ang period mortuary jars. White and porcelaneous; foot-rims show brown where exposed. Glaze of soft yellowish green color without crazing. c. after A.D. 1127. Ht. 31". Formerly Warren E. Cox Coll.

Chinese "celadon" of various types has been found extensively in the Near East in Persia and Egypt where it is called "martabani" from the port of Martaban on the coast of Pegu from which the wares were shipped, we know at least from the 9th century on. They are in the form of bowls, jardinieres, vases, bases for hubble pipes, etc., and were thought to make harmless any poison that might be poured into them. In China these wares are known as "ch'ing tz'u" (green porcelain) and in Japan as "seiji."

The body of Lung-ch'üan yao the best known site is a hard, high-fired porcelain varying from light grey (not so deep as that of Yüeh yao) to pure white. It is likely that the whiter wares are later and were due to better perfected methods of refining the clay. There is one type in particular made by the younger Chang, it is related, which shows white where the glaze runs thin and is generally more refined than the ordinary Lung-ch'üan wares. (Pl. 46) This was toward the end of the Sung period. The bodies all contain a large amount of iron and therefore burn a yellowish or reddish brown where exposed but they are so light that no "brown lip" occurs.

As the finds at Samarra prove, the Lung-ch'üan factory must have started well before the 9th century in T'ang times. I show an example which has a flat almost rimless foot and a form which might well be T'ang and from

Left: Early Lung-ch'üan wine jar. Grey ware burnt red where exposed and covered with rich, transparent, green, crackled glaze. Ht. 14″. Warren E. Cox Coll.
Center: Lung-ch'üan jar after Yüeh type but heavier. Glossy olive green glaze, full of bubbles. Ht. 10½″. Early Sung. Warren E. Cox Coll.
Right: Lung Ch'uan yao jar and cover. Reflects some characteristics of Yüeh yao, but is much heavier and glaze is more glossy, transparent and thicker. Ht. 10½″. Warren E. Cox Coll.

Right: Lung Ch'üan vase of late Sung to early Ming period, of heavy white porcelain with rich, beautiful green glaze without crackle. Ht. 8″. Metropolitan Mus. of Art.

Two wine-jars, smaller from Lung-ch'üan with white body burnt brown where exposed and covered with transparent olive-green glaze except under foot. Note perfunctory potting of cover.
Taller jar from Imperial Yüeh kilns at Shang-lin-hu. Of grey body burnt brown where exposed, covered with similar transparent olive glaze even under foot. Thin, deep lip on cover shows greater care taken in potting. Hts. 11″ and 13½″. Warren E. Cox Coll.

DEVELOPMENT OF LUNG-CH'ÜAN WINE JARS

PLATE 40

Jar called "Northern Celadon" in Percival David Catalogue but which is Yüeh or Lung-ch'üan (I have not examined it) inscribed as follows:

"On the 15th day of the intercalary 9th month of the 3d year of the Yüan Fêng period (Oct. 30th 1080 A.D.), I have baked this first class urn in the hope that it may hold fragrant wine for thousands and myriads of years; that after a hundred years, it may be handed down to my descendants; that I may have a thousand sons and ten thousand grandsons; that they may have wealth and occupy high positions in the government continually: that they may live long and enjoy good fortune and unlimited happiness; and that the world may be at peace." Ht. 14.8". Sir Percival David Coll.

Early Lung-ch'üan jar and cover of gray ware with crackled olive green glaze. On cover, protected with glaze, is inscription, "chu shih pa lang ch'ien nien chiu ku tzu," or "Chu the 18th thousand-year-wine store made." The last word may also be rendered "chih." Thus this jar along with Sir Percival David one illustrated prove that these were made to contain wine.

Possibly spouts having holes that do not enter main compartment were to hold flowers.

Yüeh examples are lighter in potting and have glaze on bottom which this has not.

Thanks must be given to Mr. Nai-Chi Chang, chairman of the translations committee of the Chinese Art Society of America, to Mr. C. F. Yau and Mr. Hsuge K. Pao as well as Mr. Shinzo Shirae for working out this translation. Ht. 12¾". Warren E. Cox Coll.

UNIQUE WINE JARS WITH INSCRIPTIONS PROVING USE

PLATE 41

this kiln. Other early examples such as the one illustrated clearly show the influence of the Yüeh yao jars with covers and we are led to believe that this factory took away the trade from the Yüeh kilns. In this type the glaze is glassy and crackled but thinner and very different from the much later Ch'ü-chou types largely of Ming and Ching periods. It also shows, on close examination, roughened frosty spots like the beginning of iridescence from action of the soil in which it was buried. Still others which are perhaps even

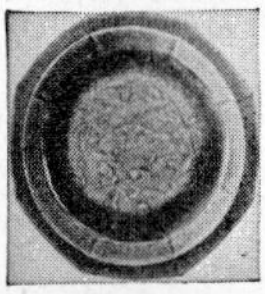

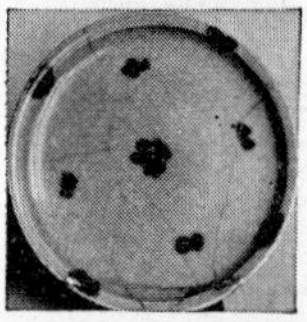

Fig. 302. Chekiang celadon dish (p'an) of greyish porcelain with pale emerald-green transparent glaze crackled. On base is wide unglazed ring burnt reddish brown, enclosing disc of glaze beneath which is incised mark "ta sung nien tsao" (made in great Sung period). Dia. 14.8". Sir Percival David Coll.

Fig. 303. A pao pie (leopard skin) Lung-ch'üan or, as Japs say, "tobi seiji" (buckwheat celadon) of light grey-green with spots of brown caused by iron. Sometimes these have silvery sheen. Ht. 10¾". Sir Percival David Coll. ♯ LV.

Fig. 304. Lung-ch'üan bottle of pale green with silvery-brown iridescent spots evenly spaced. In 1931 a similar piece brought some $45,000 in a Japanese auction. Ht. 10¾". Eumorfopoulos Coll.

Fig. 305. "Celadon" dish of Lung Ch'uan ware spotted by iron. Dia. 6½". Metropolitan Mus. of Art.

earlier are almost exact imitations of Yüeh jars with the spouts around the shoulder, incised decoration, etc., but the ware is a little heavier and the glaze more glassy. (Pl. 40, 41) These early wares are all definitely green without any bluish and little greyish cast. The crackle on them is never stained and appears to be entirely accidental.

In Sung times it appears that the glaze was constantly improved along with the potting until at the end of the period it reached its apex when it declined under Mongol influence, as did all wares of the time, through the Yüan into Ming times. The *T'ao lu* tells us that at the beginning of Ming times the Lung-ch'üan kilns were moved to Li-shui Hsien in Ch'u-chou Fu and that the ware was known as Ch'u yao but this must not be taken to mean that Lung-ch'üan kilns did not continue to operate or that the Ch'ü-chou kilns only started at that time. As a matter of fact we have dated Sung Ch'ü-chou wares as well as Lung-ch'üan ones bearing Ming dates. It is exceedingly difficult, therefore, to distinguish between the two wares or between Sung and Ming wares from either. The *T'ao lu* says simply that the Ming wares were not so good and that they were more grey and had a ring of brown unglazed under the base on which the pieces were fired but this

FIG. 306. Lung-ch'üan late Sung bottle or "hsien wên (string-lined) p'ing," of greyish porcelain with clear green "kinuta" glaze glossy and uncrackled. Ht. 12½". Sir Percival David Coll.
FIG. 307. Lung-ch'üan bulb-bowl of white porcelain with grey-green transparent glaze. Dia. 7". Sir Percival David Coll.
FIG. 308. Lung-ch'üan dish in form of lotus leaf with fire crack possibly intentional as it occurs just where leaf would split and such a piece is easy to fire. Glaze of deep, rich green. Dia. c. 5". Ethelyn C. Stewart Coll.
FIG. 309. Lung-ch'üan dish with relief three clawed dragon in biscuit fired brown with soft grey-green glaze. Under bottom is a raised seal mark: "Kien Chung, Tsing Kwoh of the Hwei Tsung reign" (or A.D. 1101). Dia. c. 4". T. C. Lee Coll. Warren E. Cox Coll. Mrs. L. G. Sheafer.

has all been discredited by Mr. Hobson and others. Generally speaking the Lung-ch'üan wares have a more creamy and unctuous and less glassy glaze while they are also thinner in potting, though this is not always the case as may be seen by the large vase illustrated. As a rule, the Sung examples are less ornate in both factories and less heavy for the ornate taste was that of the Mongols and the greater weight came with the increased export trade, but this again is open to exception.

FIG. 310. Rare small dish with sharp, beautifully molded design of birds and clouds in unglazed relief. Ware is white but burnt red-brown where exposed. Glaze clear pale green. Dia. c. 6". Formerly John Platt–Warren E. Cox Coll., (Boston Mus.)

FIG. 311. Incense burner (ting) of "Chang, Lung-ch'üan ware." Grey-white porcelain with green glaze. Known in Japan as "hakama-goshi koro" (skirt-shaped incense-burner). Dia. 5.3". Sir Percival David Coll.

FIG. 312. Pair of Lung Ch'üan yao vases which leaned together in the kiln during process of firing and glaze stuck them at body and rim. Unique and interesting example of difficulties confronting ancient potters. Ht. 6". John Platt Coll.

FIG. 313. Sung period Lung Ch'üan dish with bluish green glaze and two fishes in relief left unglazed. Clay red-dish brown where left exposed. Dia. 5". Mrs. Charles Porter Wilson.

Modern celadon glaze is made by adding a small amount of iron to a clear glaze and sometimes the least bit of cobalt to make the color bluer. In Chinese wares the same coloring agents were used and in the beginning at any rate may have been simply due to the iron content of the materials used for glaze. The color was developed to imitate jade and is described as "ts-'ui pi" jade green. The late Mr. Shepard de Forest, one of our greater collectors of the ware, went so far as to state that he thought the brown clouding, far from being an accident of the kiln, was welcomed by the Chinese potters because it is like that in the "skin of jade"; the outer covering which has become further oxidized and also in clouded areas inside a piece of jade of the "fiet-sui" or jewel type. The word "fiet-sui" not only designates this type of jade but also has the literal meaning of "green brown" which seems also to bear out his theory. In any event although the Chinese writers of earliest days never wrote disparagingly of the brown areas sometimes seen in Lung-ch'üan yao they certainly did point out that the red and purple splotches of Chün yao were not desirable.

Much more definite than the clouding referred to above are actual spots of dark brown with roughened surface which probably occurred accidentally at first, but which, due to their careful placing, force us to believe they were entirely intentional later on. They are never large, being about the size of a five cent piece and of irregular form. These are undoubtedly due to the introduction of iron in the body or glaze and occur very rarely on some of the finest pieces. The Japanese have named this particular kind "tobi seiji" meaning literally "buckwheat celadon" and prize it very highly some pieces having fetched close to $50,000 at auction. These may have been made at Lung-ch'üan or some other kiln site. The Chinese call them "pao-pie" or leopard-skin celadon. (Figs. 303–305)

The bluer wares some of which were thought to have been made by Chang the younger and some of which were probably not are also loved by the Japanese who have called them "kinuta" meaning "mallet" from a celebrated vase of mallet shape preserved in one of the old temples. (Pl. 42) The actual "kinuta" vases may be seen in our illustrations of the one from the Freer Gallery of Art and in the Nai-Chi Chang collection formerly in my own collection, and that of Mrs. Charles Porter Wilson and it will be noted that the better ones have delicately modeled fish or bird's head handles. A heavier type has handles in the form of seals or are perhaps less detailed fish. The kinuta type, however, includes wares with the same glaze and of various shapes.

In decoration the potters made use of incising, appliqués and modeling for the glaze was transparent enough to show up the first and hung richly in deeper thickness over the latter two techniques. A variation was developed in which the design was left in unglazed relief so that it burnt reddish brown and the background was glazed giving a beautiful contrast. Small dishes were generally so treated but the figure illustrated of the seated Kuan Yin in bisque on a rocky grotto and with her feet in waves is so far as I know the only Lung-ch'üan example of a figure so treated during the Sung period. (Pl. 43) Later rocky grottoes were made, which we will touch upon in the

Lung-ch'üan "Kinuta" with delicate fish handles. Irregular crackle probably intentional. Ht. 11½". Warren E. Cox Coll. Nai-Chi Chang Coll.
　Late Sung or perhaps later Lung Ch'üan bottle of fine form. These more ornate pieces probably made to suit Mongol taste. Ht. 13½". Warren E. Cox Coll.
　Late Sung or early Ming bottle with glaze more glassy than that of usual Lung Ch'üan yao but very beautiful in shape. Ht. c. 10". Warren E. Cox Coll.

 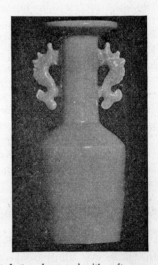

Pair of small "Kinuta" vases of white ware showing gray at foot and covered with soft gray-green clear glaze. Handles seem to represent foreparts of flying birds. Sung period. Ht. 6¾". Mrs. Charles Porter Wilson–Warren E. Cox Coll. Nai-chi Chang Coll.
　"Kinuta" (Japanese term) or club-shaped vase of Sung dynasty Lung Ch'üan yao. White porcelaneous ware covered with bright grey green glaze without crazing. Ht. 10". Freer Gallery of Art, Washington, D. C.

LUNG-CH'ÜAN "KINUTA" AND BOTTLE-FORMED VASES

Plate 42

Ming section, although the body and glaze of those too would tend to suggest Lung-ch'üan rather than Ch'ü-chou as their source. The dishes or shallow bowls usually have fish, dragons or birds and clouds for decoration although some are known with floral treatment. (Pl. 44 & Figs. 309–313)

Large jardinieres and "temple vases," some of which at least we know by inscriptions were offered to the temples, began to come into use toward the end of the Sung period. They were heavily made and often decorated with either carved or cast appliqué floral decorations. (Pl. 45) One interesting feature is that the bottoms were often made separately and, in the vases, the bodies of which were made in upper and lower sections, placed in the open foot before the upper half of the body was put on and stuck into position with the glaze alone. In the large example shown, which incidentally has the finest color I know, this bottom disc has slipped and attached itself at a slant. Collectors give the general period of late Sung to these but many of them are of the Ming period I am convinced.

Another classic Chinese vase form which was made in celadon and other wares such as Ting yao and Ko yao, is the "tsu ts'ung" or symbol of the deity Earth. In this case the form is taken from ancient jades which were, when first found, thought to be wheel hubs or axle supports, a theory entirely confuted by Dr. Berthold Laufer (see "Jade" page 125) in his criticism of the *Ku yü t'u p'u*. The form represents that of a cylinder thrust lengthwise through a square vase and projecting above and below (see Pl. 46). A pottery one of the Han period has the inscription "grain vessel." A jade one in the *Fang-shih mo p'u* published by Fang Yü-lu in 1588 has three characters "shih ts'ao p'ing" meaning "vase for plant shih" which is a species of Achillea the stalks of which were used for divination. In any event this is a most sturdy and beautiful form and the eight divisions on each corner, perhaps representing the eight divisions of the earth, take the glaze in a beautiful soft and undulating manner.

Other Celadon Kilns

Besides the two mentioned there were other kilns in Chekiang province such as the ones at Chin-ts'un and Li-shui the wares of which have not been segregated to date and, of course, the one at Liu-t'ien run by the younger Chang brother. In the Northern Sung days before A.D. 1127 there were a number of kilns in Honan near the capital Kai-fêng and in other northern provinces. For years the Yüeh yao was included in this group but there are a number of wares quite as thinly potted and with beautiful incised and molded decoration which have a more transparent and bubbly sort of glaze and which are in design closely associated with the Ying ch'ing and Korean wares which may be allotted to these kilns. The ewers often show Near Eastern influences and some of these wares were found at Samarra and along the overland route in Chinese Turkestan, Kharakhoto, etc. At Ch'ên-liu, southeast of Kai-fêng Fu, was one of the most important of these kilns.

It must also be remembered that the kilns at Ching-te Chên operated from early times. Here also a celadon ware was made distinguished by its white body which in more recent times was dressed on the exposed parts with earth

Beautiful and unique Lung-ch'üan figure (unglazed and burnt brown terra cotta color) seated
on a glazed rocky throne with waves below. Probably made c. A.D. 1050 to 1127. Ht. 12″. Lem
Sec Tsang–Warren E. Cox Coll.

LUNG CH'ÜAN BISQUE FIGURE OF KUAN YIN

PLATE 43

Heavenly shrine with Buddha in the center and Kuan-yin above while adoring disciples stand to either side. At the bottom is a tortoise and snake as though on a seal while toward the top is a lotus flower and above that a lichen-scroll. The figures are in bisque burnt brown. The objects, including also the halo about Buddha's head, and a bird and vase to either side of Kuan-yin are brown but seemingly glazed with a transparent colorless glaze. The rest is in typical Lung-ch'üan green glaze of good quality. Late Sung to Early Ming Period. Ht. 13½". Warren E. Cox Coll.

BUDDHISTIC HEAVENLY SHRINE OF LUNG CH'ÜAN WARE

PLATE 44

Lung-ch'üan amphoras of similar materials and potting. One has straight foot-rim; the other a bevelled one more associated with Ming wares. Late Sung and Early Ming. Hts. 12½" and 17¼". Mrs. Charles Porter Wilson.

Two Sung Lung-ch'üan bowls with straight, narrow foot-rims and frosty line where glaze meets body. Dias. 8½" and 9⅛". John Platt–Warren E. Cox Coll.

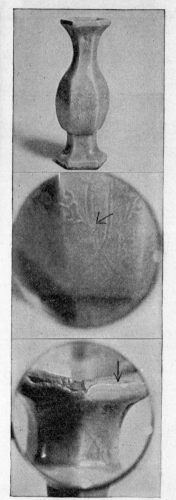

Lung-ch'üan amphora (neck cut) with finest glaze to be seen on such wares. This perfection of glaze, appliqué design, heavy, bevelled foot-rim all would indicate Ming rather than Sung origin. No frosty line appears on these pieces where glaze meets body clay. Note bottom saucer dropped in and stuck with glaze. Ht. 18½". Warren E. Cox Coll.

One of pair of small Lung-ch'üan vases rare in that they have a slip-trailed decoration. (Note enlarged detail showing where it smudged on lower left part of body.) Enlargement of foot-rim shows typical frosty white line on glaze where it meets body-clay, due to corrosion in burial. Usually present on Sung period Lung-ch'üan wares and is sure sign of authenticity as I have never seen it on any Ming or later example. Ht. 6". K. M. Semon Coll. Note: This also appears on Southern Kuan wares.

LUNG CH'ÜAN VASES SHOWING FOOT-RIMS
PLATE 45

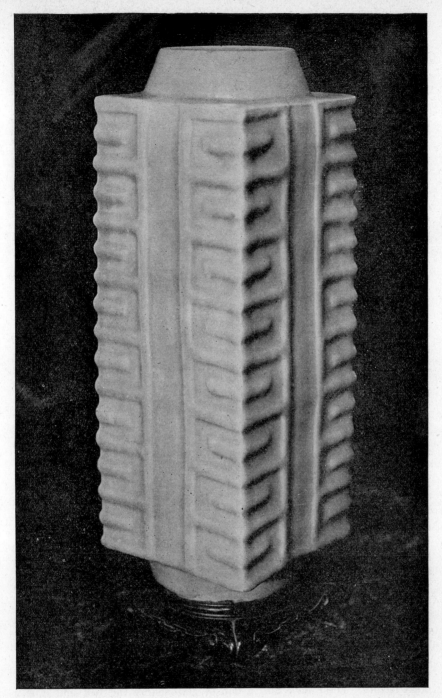

Lung-ch'üan late Sung vase in form of jade "ts'ung" or ritual vessel used in worship of earth and intended to hold divining rods. Of greyish porcelain with rich and glossy green glaze having brown clouds and showing white through it on ridges. (Of type supposedly made by Chang the Younger.) The only comparative one in size and quality is that of the Sir Percival David Coll. Ht. 16¼". Warren E. Cox Coll.

LUNG CH'ÜAN "TS'UNG" OR SYMBOL OF EARTH

PLATE 46

Fig. 314. Lung Ch'uan large jar of thinly potted white porcelain covered with clear green glaze and showing iron red brown foot where exposed. Ht. 10½". Warren E. Cox Coll.

Fig. 315. Chü Chou large jar of white ware with frosty green glaze of rich color and light and dark brown crackle. Foot and lip rims, unglazed, show red brown. Probably late Sung. Ht. 10". Warren E. Cox Coll.

containing iron to simulate the wares made of iron containing clay. Ching-tê Chêng also used a coarse yellowish clay. In Kwangtung not far from Canton a ware was made with reddish brown body.

The factory at Ch'ên-liu mentioned above made the well known "tung yao" or "Eastern ware" which the *Ko ku yao lun* describes as "pale green with fine crackle and in many cases with brown mouth and iron foot." It is, we are told, "similar to Kuan yao but lacks the red tinge and the material is coarse and wanting in fineness and lustre while at the present day it is not often seen." (1387) We find that there was a light and dark Tung yao imitated in Yung Chêng times. A poem by Chang-lei of the 11th century compares the glaze with green jade (pi yü). For some unknown reason Mr. Hobson in the Eumorfopoulos Catalogue jumps to the conclusion that the ware must be, "a superior kind of Northern Celadon," and indicates two bowls, "conspicuous for the beauty of their celadon glaze, but not obviously referable to the Lung-ch'üan type; and these may be regarded as possible specimens of true Tung yao." The #B202 is very much like the two bowls I show herewith (Pl. 45) and I can only say that in these the potting is actually better than even the "kinuta" type Lung-ch'üan yao and the glaze of a deep and most lustrous green. They are heavier than most wares assigned to the Kuan type but no less well made and certainly not of a "coarse" texture as the fine paste and beautifully potted foot-rims will testify.

Deep bowls of heavy potting and often having impressed designs inside, of figures standing and on horse-back and characters (jên) benevolence, (shou) longevity and (fu) happiness were dug up at Showchow in Anhwei province and are probably of local manufacture. They are of a white ware which burns brown where exposed and are covered including the lip and also the foot-rim with a thick, frosty, crackled glaze often of an olive green but at times, as in the small plain bowl illustrated, with a bright pea-green color of great beauty. These have also a dab of glaze under the foot and it is a mystery how they were fired for there are no spur marks and no regular ring under the foot. Some of these may be pre-Ming, but their weight would seem to indicate a Ming feeling.

Left: "Northern Sung Celadon" bowl with incised decoration and crackled olive green glaze. Nasli Heeramaneck Coll.

Center: Sung Honan celadon bowl. Dense gray stoneware with impressed and carved design of "Happy boys and chrysanthemums." Dia. 6". Gift of Sadajiro Yamanaka. Metropolitan Mus. of Art.

Right: "Northern Sung Celadon" bowl from Honan. Grey body burnt brown where exposed and covered with a vetiver green or tea green semi-mat glaze. Design carved in relief, not incised or impressed. Dia. 8". Warren E. Cox–John Platt Coll.

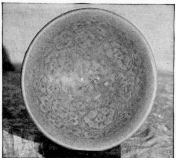

"Northern Sung Celadon" bowl. Grey body and watery grey green glaze with many large bubbles. Dia. 4¾". Warren E. Cox Coll.

Bowl of dense gray ware thinly potted with carved design under transparent olive green crackled glaze. Type found in northern provinces. Dia. 5". D. Abbes Coll.

Center: Northern Sung celadon bowl dating about A.D. 1200. Grey burnt to tan and glaze very light olive green full of bubbles and roughly applied. Dia. 6¾". Warren E. Cox Coll.

Left: Sung celadon bowl from Honan province with gray body and olive brown transparent glaze over an incised design. The potting is refined and well done. Dia. 5¾". Warren E. Cox Coll.

Center: "Northern Sung Celadon" bottle probably before 1127. Well potted grey porcelain body burnt brown where exposed around foot-rim and in scraped out symbols, which are seven in number and not all so clear as two shown. Glaze olive green filled with tiny bubbles. Ht. 7¼". Warren E. Cox Coll.

Right: Sung period Honan celadon coupe of light gray stoneware with olive green glaze filled with tiny bubbles and quite transparent where it runs thin. Ht. c. 5". Metropolitan Mus. of Art.

"NORTHERN SUNG CELADON" WARES FROM DIFFERENT KILNS

PLATE 47

FIG. 316. Small ewer from Northern Honan, possibly Yu Chou. Buff grey stoneware body, "tea-dust" greenish brown glaze and splashes of blue produced by copper added to glaze. Loops and handle repaired. T'ang period and perhaps a prototype of Chün wares. Ht. 6½". Warren E. Cox Coll.

FIG. 317. Flower pot from Chün Chou. Gray stoneware body covered with light blue glaze turning to olive green at edges and on ridges where thin. These plain blue Chün wares were valued highly by the Chinese. Sung. Ht. c. 8". Metropolitan Mus. of Art.

FIG. 318. Bulb bowl made in Chün Chou. Gray stone ware covered with pale blue and blue and purple glazes. Sung. Dia. c. 7½". Metropolitan Mus. of Art.

FIG. 319. Chun yao porcelain flower pot dish, having purple glaze flecked with grey and marked #7 under base. 2½" by 8⅛". Gift of Mrs. Thos. D. Stimson. Seattle Art Mus.

In Sawankhalok, Siam, a heavy ware was made also possibly in Sung times. It is heavily potted of a greyish-white porcelaneous ware reddish brown where exposed and covered with a transparent glassy glaze often tinged with blue. The plates often have rings on the bottom where they were supported in the kiln, much as have the crude blue and white ones from the same section.

In Persia a ware with beautiful celadon glaze was made which can be distinguished simply by the porous and sandy body.

Finally there were many Japanese factories which made celadons and which we shall treat under that section and then some of the modern Japanese and Chinese factories have made exceedingly close copies, so close in fact that the collector must be careful.

CHÜN YAO

There are not so many kinds of Chün wares as there are celadons but at least five or six can be distinguished. The first was made in the early part of the Sung period not at Chün Chou as has often been said, but at Chün-t'ai (Chün terrace) in a place which is now Yü-chow in central Honan province and it continued well into the Ming period, for we learn from the T'ao kung *pu hui k'ao* that in Hsüan Tê and Chia Ching reigns vases and wine jars were supplied the court.

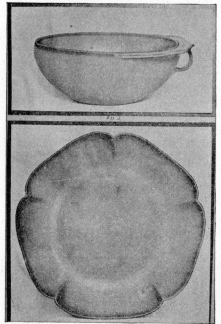

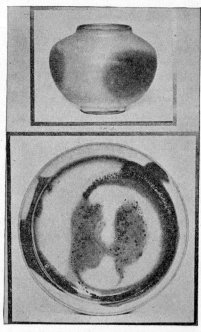

FIG. 320. Plates # 24 and # 25, Vol. II of the Eumorfopoulos Coll. showing four typical shapes of thinner and finer wares which Hobson surmised were of Kuan type although they were made at Chün chou, the place now known as Yu chou. Dish and bowl with ogee-edged flange are pale lavender blue grey. Dia. of foliated dish 10″, of plain mottled dish 7½″, of bowl 7″ and ht. of jar 3½″.

"Celadon" vase from Siam. Crudely potted light gray body burnt red-brown where exposed, covered with glassy transparent glaze faintly crackled. Ht. 5″. John Platt—Warren E. Cox Coll.

FIG. 321. Plate # 27, Vol. II, of the Eumorfopoulos Coll. showing various shapes of "Kuan Chün." Hts. 2″ to 4″.

This ware is heavy grey stoneware burnt brown where exposed and sometimes particularly under the base and at the lip-rim showing brown, under the very thin parts of the glaze, or olive, where it is a little thicker. Chinese numerals 1 to 10 are carved on the bottom before glazing on this type and the *Po wu yao lan* tells us it is the best. The glaze slips from the upper edges where it is very thin down to thick pools in the bottom of the bowls and hangs in heavy ridges and even drops about projections or near the bottom. In this particular sort it is not crackled but shows Y and L shaped marks called by the Chinese "earthworm" marks which were caused by a crackle or

uneven flowing together of the glaze which has not quite melted together, leaving no surface depression but little denser lines in which there are fewer bubbles than in the surrounding parts. The general color seems to be olive green in which there is an opaque pale blue occurring in the tiny bubbles with which the glaze is filled and which, having burst on the surface, cause pores which are called by the Chinese "ant tracks." Sometimes this whole glaze is infused with plum color or red but still preserves the olive at the thinnest places. At other times the warm colors run in streaks and mottlings in the blue which yet again may become quite definite patches or splotches sometimes taking on the vague forms of animals and birds or even of Chinese characters as may be seen in the pillow illustrated. (Fig. 324)

This ware is confined almost entirely to bulb bowls, small jardinieres or flower pots with saucers and similar useful objects of heavy potting. The forms, though heavy, are accurate and well designed and well made.

FIG. 322. A wonderful Chün bottle of grey stoneware burnt brown where exposed, and covered with blue and purple to plum clouds. Glaze under the base. Ht. 11½". Sir Percival David Coll.

Associated with this ware and probably from the same factory is the rougher type which the *Po wu yao lan* calls "coarse and thick and not beautiful." This is of buff sandy ware roughly finished at bottom with a foot-rim often deeper on the center edge than on the outer edge and a shallow cone unglazed under the foot. This same style is sometimes of grey ware burnt brown and with a glaze inside the foot. In both of these the colors are essentially the same but the glaze itself is more like thick glass and crackled. These never have the numerals and the glaze usually stops short of the base. It has been a silly collector's habit to call these all Yüan in period but they are certainly contemporary with the first described type and show many characteristics which would indicate that they are even earlier. Among these is the lack of scroll feet and other such involved forms, for they are all very simple and beautifully proportioned bowls, nearly globular vases, etc. (Pl. 48)

What even Hobson himself admitted may be an entirely arbitrary division

Sung dynasty Chün yao bowl of greyish white stoneware burnt brown where exposed and covered with a thick, blue, crackled, translucent glaze which runs thin and shows olive green at the lip. Dia. 5¾". Warren E. Cox Coll.

Small Chün yao vessel with three legs after a bronze form, of porcelaneous ware with a blue glaze and purple clouding. Ht. 2⅜". Ex D. Abbes Coll.

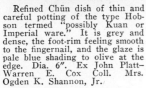

Refined Chün dish of thin and careful potting of the type Hobson termed "possibly Kuan or Imperial ware." It is grey and dense, the foot-rim feeling smooth to the fingernail, and the glaze is pale blue shading to olive at the edge. Dia. 6". Ex John Platt—Warren E. Cox Coll. Mrs. Ogden K. Shannon, Jr.

Wide mouthed jar, Eumorfopoulos Col. # B80. "Grey porcelaneous ware, brown on the raw edges. Warm lavender glaze irregularly crazed and with splashes of purple shading to crimson. A wash of glaze under the foot. Kuan Chün," says Hobson. Ht. 4.9".

Rare Green Chün jar of dense grey stoneware which Hobson called "Chün ware of Kuan type," covered with a transparent, bubbly olive green glaze much like that of some Yüeh and Lung-ch'üan pieces. Ht. 5". John Platt—Warren E. Cox Coll. Note: The Chinese texts mention "crab-shell green" and also "parrot-green" which was a favorite color of Chün, yet few examples exist in western countries.

Left: Chün yao flower pot of grey ware with pale blue and lavender glaze. It has five drainage holes in the bottom and the incised numeral ssŭ (four) under the streaky brown glaze on the bottom. Ht. 8¼". Eumorfopoulos Coll. # C1.

Center: A Cha-tou (leys jar), possibly an incense burner of grey ware with white slip and transparent glaze of yellowish tone where thick. Sung period, said to have come from Yu Chou. Ht. 4". Baron C. T. von Seidlitz Coll.

Right: "Kuan Chün. Emorfopoulos Coll. # B78. Bubbly lavender glaze shading to pale brown at the mouth and splashed with plum-purple patches which break into grey and crimson." Hobson. Dia. 7.6".

"KUAN CHÜN" AND CHÜN WARES

PLATE 48

is probably simply a finer ware of the same kilns which is thinner in potting, has regular and narrow foot-rims and a perfectly controlled glaze that stops just short of the foot and is evenly applied under the foot. These too are not numbered but include many more delicately potted pieces than the first group such as small jars with covers, small "ting" (three legged incense burners), large foliated bowls, etc. The colors are essentially like the others again although one which I illustrate is of an even olive green similar to Yüeh yao celadon. They again are fairly evenly crackled and do not show "earthworm" marks. In the Küan yao section I have explained why I do not think these can possibly be maintained in that category and I believe them to have been made from early to late Sung times and perhaps even into Ming, for the shapes range from simple and beautiful ones to somewhat involved and unstructural forms.

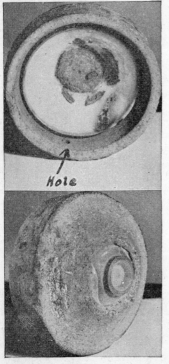

Hole

Fig. 324. Southern Chün type pillow of late Sung or Yüan period (1127–1368 A.D.) of buff stoneware covered with a slightly opaque blue glaze and having a large character drawn on it in purple-red. This confutes the earlier theories to the effect that the color was due "to inequalities of heat in firing." The marks are actually made by the introduction of iron oxide in the body of the ware before glazing. Length about 11". Gift of Mrs. Samuel T. Peters. Metropolitan Mus. of Art.

Fig. 325. Small Southern Chün yao bowl ground down to show the introduction of iron in the body to produce the purple markings in the glaze on both outside and inside. When one surface only is to be marked the iron is pressed into the body under the glaze. Dia. 3½". T. C. Lee–Warren E. Cox Coll.

Fig. 323. Collapsed sagger with Chün bowl in it. Note the small hole at the side wall for transmission of gases. Also note that purple mark is far to the right of this hole. It has been said that the purple was due to inequalities of heat but it is obvious that such variations would be hard to make inside a sagger. Actually they are produced by iron particles in the body of the ware. Dia. 9". T. C. Lee–Warren E. Cox Coll.

These, then, are the three original Chün wares. Hseih Min lists the colors as "mei kuei tzŭ" (rose purple), "hai t'ang hung" (cherry-apple red), "ch'ieh hua tzŭ" (aubergine purple), "mei tzŭ ch'ing" (plum-bloom green), "lü kan ma fei" (donkey's liver and horse's lung), —— probably in derision —— "shên tzŭ" (deep purple), "mi sê" (millet color), "t'ien lan" (sky blue), "yao pien" (furnace tranmutation), etc. (I am using the Bushell-Hobson translation.) One thing was made clear and that is that the *Cho kêng lu* and the *Ko ku yao lun* do not even deign to mention these wares and even in Ming times the *Ch'ing pi ts'ang* says, "The best is uniform in color and has the numerals underneath. The mixed colors are not worth collecting." During the Yung Chêng period four kinds had to be sent for outside the Palace Collection for reproduction. Thus it was not until taste in China had become decadent that the ware was taken note of and it took our Western hemisphere millionaires to boost the demand because the color so appealed to their child-like instincts. The plain colors which the ancient collectors thought worth while were, "cinnabar red, parrot green and dark aubergine purple along with the 'ch'ing' or pale blue." A white ware was also made at Yu-Chou. (Pl. 48)

The numerals mentioned have been proven to indicate simply sizes although much nonsense was talked in the earlier days of our century about their indicating various qualities, etc. Numerals and poems cut in the glaze are of course of fairly recent date and mean nothing.

Mr. Hobson has written (*Chinese Pottery and Porcelain* page 118) (1915), "How far the old Chün effects were due to opalescence it is impossible to say, but we know that all of them can be obtained, whether turquoise, green, crimson, or lavender grey, by that 'Protean medium,' oxide of copper, according as it is exposed in the firing to an oxidizing or reducing atmosphere, conditions which could be regulated by the introduction of air on the one hand, or wood smoke on the other, at the right moment into the kiln." Through this passage the general impression has gained footing that the Chün splotches are accidental or uncontrolled. Perhaps they were at first but, as I have said, the potters soon became sufficiently proficient to be able to write characters on pieces. Now Chün wares were fired in individual saggers of heavy clay either set slightly apart so air could enter and escape or having a small hole to one side. How then in the world could a potter vary the conditions of his kiln so as to produce a given symmetry of splotches or even to write a character?—Obviously the explanation is not correct.

Through the offices of my friend Mr. T. C. Lee a small Chün "bubble bowl" was sent to me from China which had been examined by the Acadamei Sinica. This had been so broken as to expose a cross section at a point where the purple mark occurred and we found upon analysis of a small dark place in the body at this point that it is iron in an oxidized state. The placing of slight iron filings in the body made the purple mark *on both sides*. It is possible that simply pressing them into the clay on one side would affect that surface only. In any event we must come to the conclusion that this slight use of iron so affects the copper glaze as to make the irregular marks in it.

"Soft Chün yao" or, as the Chinese call it, "Ma-chün" was supposed to have been originated by a potter named "Ma" who worked in the late Sung period. It has a buff earthy body and a glaze more waxy and less glossy than Chün yao. It is a pale lavender blue or a deep peacock blue and seems not to run or slip so much as the Chün glaze. There is always a crackle and the splotches are usually of crimson color. These pieces are rare and have a beauty of their own in some ways more appealing than the original wares.

Finally there were imitations made at Yi-hsing and in Kwangtung during late Ming times and even down to the present, while at Chêng-tê Ching really beautiful copies were made in the 18th century but with white porcelain bodies as a rule. This rule was not always followed, however, and the ones with stoneware bodies are even more deceptive. Just recently I have seen pieces

FIG. 326. "Soft Chün yao" gallipot of buff stoneware covered with an opaque and porous blue glaze. These are usually called Yüan but I believe them to have been made from 1127 A.D. to well into the Ming dynasty. Gift of Mrs. H. O. Havemeyer. Ht. 9". Metropolitan Mus. of Art.

FIG. 327. Soft Chün small vase which shows a prominent crackle and opaque quality of the glaze. Ht. 5¾". Ming or later. Warren E. Cox Coll.

FIG. 328. Double gourd of "soft Chün" ware made of reddish buff stoneware covered with a thick glaze of lavender-blue and splashed in front with dull purple. Ming. Ht. 7½". Sir Percival David Coll.

FIG. 329. Green Chün ware jar with the rough, sandy buff foot of the "soft Chün type," Southern Sung. The glaze is thick, crackled and full of large bubbles many of which have burst on the surface. Ht. about 5". K. M. Semon Coll.

of the 20th century made at Yü-chow which are very close to the old wares indeed and these were of the type of shallow dishes having the olive green to brown glaze underneath and all characteristics very close to the old wares. In Japan the wares of Hagi, Akahada and Seto include similar glazes and some streaky Cantonese wares are similar and are called "Fat-shan Chün."

FIG. 330. Honan Tsung Sê tz'ŭ jar of rough and porous light buff stoneware covered with a lustrous blue-black glaze shading to tan at lip and lighter and more bluish about lower half. Sung period. Ht. 6½". Warren E. Cox Coll.

TSUNG SÊ TZ'Ü
DARK BROWN COLORED POTTERY

It is recommended that we cease to use the name "Honan Temmoku" for these wares as they were made elsewhere and it is anomalous to use a Japanese word for a Chinese ware. "Chien yao" is also too narrow a term and can only properly be applied to the wares from certain sites in northern Fukien. I, therefore, at the suggestion of Mr. C. F. Yau have adopted the term TSUNG SÊ TZ'Ü meaning "palm leaf brown colored pottery" or "dark brown colored pottery." The word Tsung according to Giles derives from the brown leaves of the palm used in China for the making of brooms. Various other suggestions seem less good. Mr. Hochstadter says that he has used "Hei Sung tz'ŭ" successfully in asking for the wares in China but this literally means "black Sung pottery." A common term is Tzŭ chin tz'ŭ meaning "lustrous brown pottery," but this also has the implication of "purple brown," which is not always the case. Let us then adopt TSUNG SÊ TZ'ŭ as a more reasonable term generally covering all brown potteries wherever made and at whatever time.

The possibility has been pointed out that the thin mat brown glaze developed from the olive mat glazes of the Six Dynasties and we have illustrated an ewer which is likely of this period and another of the T'ang period having the brown glaze. As most of these glazes look like ground up brown or greenish brown tea-dust, I shall use this term to describe them. A sort of intermediate type may be called chocolate and then we finally come to the glossy or treacly glazes which I do not believe developed until toward the latter part of the Sung dynasty. No kiln had an exclusive use of these earlier glazes. They are about as natural and simple to come by as the old alkaline glazes of the Han period. Once our colored maid was dusting my collection and made the remark that they looked just like her old "mammy's salt pot." This is about true for they do not differ much from our Early American kitchen wares save in the fine techniques.

Mr. Hobson gives them the arbitrary name of "Honan Temmokus" and then proceeds to say at once that they also come from Chihli, Shantung, Shansi, Shensi, Anhwei and Kiangsu but he might have added all the other provinces that made pots, with perfect safety, for certainly the use of brown glaze was as universal as that of the green or celadon types, or for that matter the cream or Ting and Tz'u Chou types, these three being easiest to make and most pleasant for general use.

The word "Temmoku" is foreign and also narrow in its true application as is also the Chinese name "Chien yao" and neither should be used for this entire classification. There is an old Japanese tradition that their pirates used to swoop down on the Fukien province coast to loot and kidnap and that tea-bowls were demanded as ransom. In 1888 Hippisley published the information that these bowls came from "the department of Chien-chou, the present district of Chien-yang in the department of Chien-ning, Fukien province." That is in the most northern part. Pelliot is reported to have located the kiln site in the T'ien-mu Shan in Che-kiang. And recently Mr. Plumer has published further kiln sites. Hetherington says, "There was a mountain in the neighborhood of the place of manufacture called T'ien-mu Shan or the 'Eye of Heaven' mountain. In Japanese T'ien-mu Shan becomes Temmoku-zan. The name Temmoku is now applied to all tea-bowls with hare's fur marking whether made in Chien-yang or not." Now the term has unfortunately been broadened to include all brown wares as has also Chien yao with no better reason. I propose that these be called simply "Brown Wares" or, if we must have a Chinese term let us adopt "Tsung Sê tz'ŭ" (dark brown ware), even though this was not used by the ancient Chinese writers. One could so ask for them in China today and be understood.

Plumer went to the little villages of Hou-ching, Ta-lu and T'ieh-tun on the left bank of the Chien Ch'i river just north of Kien-ning in the northern part of the Fukien province, and found three large piles of sherds. At Shui-chi there was an open cut where the natives had mined their bowls for years. In Hou-ching a pig was eating from a sagger. There were only bowls varying from a few inches to a foot or more in diameter; no vases. They all had a grey body almost black and reddish where exposed and the glazes were typical

FIG. 331. Four Tsung Sê tz'ŭ tea-bowls. The top is an "oil spot" with grey body and black glaze silver spotted. The two on either side are of the Kian-fu, Kian-si province, type with greyish bodies and brownish black glazes with yellowish and buff floral and leaf motives. The bottom is said to have been found in Tz'u Chou and has a brownish black glaze with white slip and glazed rim. Dias. 5½" to 8". C. T. Loo & Co.

Chien yao type which we will describe. Mr. Plumer believes the kilns to have started in late T'ang times and to have run into Ming.

The *T'ao shuo* quotes a supposedly 10th century work, "In Fukien are made tea-bowls with ornamental markings like the mottling and spots on a partridge (chê ku pan). The tea-testing parties prize them." We need not quote the other books but they all speak of this Chien yao in the early texts. In the Ming period little was said but in Japan, due to the development of the tea ceremony (cha no yu) Chien yao came into great favor. These bowls are properly called Chien yao or, in Japanese, Temmoku.

The real ones have a rough stoneware body of very dark brown best described as reddish-black. It is open grained and earthy in feel. The glaze is of blue-black streaked and mottled with brown which appears to have forced its way up through the glaze making "hare's fur" or "partridge marking" effects. Rare specimens have small silver spots all over called by the Chinese "oil spots."

Mr. Hetherington quotes William Burton in explanation of these markings, "The glistening appearance as well as the fine striation both arise from

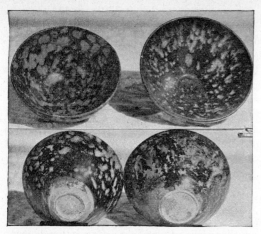

Two bowls of the so called "Kian Temmoku" type made of the typical greyish white ware and having the dull brown glaze and pale blue spots. This type would certainly appear to be earlier than those with ornate but skillfully handled designs in them. Dia. 4½". John Platt Coll. Warren E. Cox Coll. Note later type in lower right corner.

Honan tea-bowl (wan) of white porcelaneous ware dressed with brown-black where it is exposed and having a thick, black glaze showing silver "oil spots" so prized in Japan where it is called "yu teki temmoku." Dia. 3½". Sung. Sir Percival David Coll.

Three Chien yao or "Temmoku" tea-bowls showing "hare's fur" markings, the irregular drips of glaze near the bottom and the heavy dark rough body. Dias. 4½". Warren E. Cox Coll.

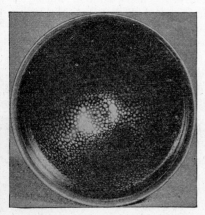

Honan tea-bowl reported to have a dark body, black glaze and showing the silver, "oil-spots." Dia. about 3". N. M. Heeramaneck Coll.

"Kian temmoku" bowl of the ware reported to have come from central Kiangsi. It is a rather crude gray stoneware with transmutation glaze of brown, yellow and bluish gray. Dia. 5½". Gift of Mrs. Thos. D. Stimson. Seattle Art Mus.

CHUNG TZE TEA BOWLS OF CHIEN, KIAN AND NORTHERN HONAN TYPES

PLATE 49

the fact that microscopically thin plates of artificial mica crystals segregate from the cooling glaze, while it is still somewhat fluid, and arrange themselves with their long axes parallel to the lines of flow of the glaze, thus producing the effect." He goes on to say that the "hare's fur" ones are Phlogopite glazes or those containing a considerable amount of iron called Biotite while the silvery spotted ones are either Phlogopite or Muscovite.

Usually the glaze slips so that the lip-rim is actually exposed and at times the Chinese added a silver rim but not, as was the case with Ting yao, because the piece was fired on its rim. A heavy irregular ridge of glaze forms near the bottom and there is a thick pool inside. No vases occur in this ware.

"KIAN WARE" OR CHI CHOU YAO

Through hearsay alone, but which has never been confuted, Hobson gave the name of Kian Temmoku to another class of ware consisting of bowls and

FIG. 332. Vase called "Honan Temmoku" by the museum but actually quite like the so called "Kian Temmoku" bowls in its rather soft buff body, glossy blue black glaze and small brown and blue spots. Probably Yüan or Ming. Ht. 13". Gift of Mrs. Samuel T. Peters. Metropolitan Mus. of Art.

occasional vases. It is said that they are found near the old kiln sites at Yung-ho Chên in the department of Kian or Chi-an Fu in south central Kiangsi province. We hear that the bowls are found by dragging the river at this place and Hobson points out that it is likely that this would then be the "Chi Chou Yao" spoken of in the *Ko ku yao lun* and described as being brown (tzŭ), like that of Ting Chou but thick and coarse and "not worth much money." There is also a white ware, and a crackled ware like Ko yao was also made here, and during the Sung period there were five kilns of which that run by the Shu family was the best. This is the place where it was reported that when the Sung minister passed all the wares in the kilns turned to jade and the potters fearing that this portent might reach the ears of the Emperor fled to Chêng-tê Ching.

Actually there is a considerable divergence in technique and taste shown in the wares so lumped together, some being perhaps over refined and too ornate while others are exceedingly crude, but this may be due to the long time the kilns were working.

Probably fairly early are the bowls two of which are shown with rudimentary foot-rims and of thick and none too sure potting, covered with a mat brown glaze having splotches of pale blue both outside and in. The body is buff and gritty but more so on one than on the other. Perhaps a little later is the vase with the same glaze and technique of potting but on a slightly more refined body long called "Honan Temmoku" by the museum but certainly of this classification. And then toward the end of the Sung period and later we came to the bowls which have leaves, birds, etc., actually roughly drawn in them in dark brown against the blue and brown flecked ground. Perhaps the earlier ones of this type had the designs so roughly indicated that they seemed like natural accidents and one can imagine what a stir they must have caused in Japan. Some again show light decorations against dark brown glaze.

"KOREAN RED TEMMOKU" OR "RED TING?"

Almost certainly from Chihli province comes a fine white ware often as thinly and beautifully potted as Ting yao. It is covered either in part or all over (except for the foot rim on some, or the whole base on others) with a soft, mat, brownish red glaze which is amazingly absorptive and which often

FIG. 333. Light buff ware bowl with dull reddish brown glaze very similar to a sherd found in Samarra. This piece was found in Korea and is given a Korean attribution by the museum. Dia. 6". Metropolitan Mus. of Art.

FIG. 334. Brown glazed bowl with well made light buff body. The glaze is washed in so as to leave an exposed area in the bottom. The foot rim is a strong argument that these wares are Chinese. Dia. 5¼". Warren E. Cox Coll.

FIG. 335. Bowl given "Korai Korean" attribution at the museum as are all of their similar wares, but more likely Chinese in origin. Dia. 7¼". Metropolitan Mus. of Art.

runs very thin (though it is all thinly applied) at the lip, and there has olive green tinges. Sometimes where it is a little thick it takes on the blue-black and glossy look of other glazes of the sort and even shows the "partridge breast" effect. In two bowls illustrated the thin glaze is used outside and the thick inside with drips running down the outside. When moisture is applied to these bowls they take it up almost as fast as blotting paper. Another beautiful treatment is like tortoise shell as can be seen on the outside of the finest specimen (Pl. 50) and this bowl is remarkable in another way, for just faintly traceable inside can be seen a charming floral design. I am told that this design was originally in gold and that slight traces of the metal itself can be seen on two specimens in the Rioke Museum in Seoul, Korea. This was reported by Sir Percival David who said he had seen no other specimens similar. Whether the gold was fired on or not he did not say.

The Metropolitan Museum and others have for years labeled these pieces "Korean" simply because a number have been found in that country although Bernard Rackham as far back as 1918 in the Catalogue of the Le Blond Collection put them in the doubtful category. They were called "kakigusuri" by the Japanese who attributed them to the T'ang period. Since our more detailed study of Sung ceramics there can be no slightest doubt but that they are of Sung period and made in China. It has been guessed that they might be the famous "red Ting" ware spoken of by ancient writers and, in truth, some of the pieces such as the bowl just described might be, but recently Mr.

Walter Hochstadter has said that he heard on good authority in China that they come from Ching-ho Hsien east of Tz'u Chou in Chihli province. There the matter will have to rest until excavations give us clearer evidence.

FIG. 336. Wine ewer of red glazed light buff ware often found in Korea but probably made in China. Ht. 7″. Metropolitan Mus. of Art.

FIG. 337. White bodied vase with terracotta red glaze called by the museum "T'zu Chou type," but which is often found in Korean tombs. Ht. 7½″. Gift of Mrs. Samuel T. Peters. Metropolitan Mus. of Art.

FIG. 338. Vase called by museum "Korai Ting" and having a mottled red-brown glaze running to olive at lip where it is thin. It is more likely the "Red Ting" of tradition. Ht. 7¼″. Metropolitan Mus. of Art.

TSUNG SÊ TZ'Ŭ, TZ'U CHOU YAO
BROWN POTTERY INCISED

The Tsung Sê tz'ŭ (Brown Pottery) found in the general district of Tz'u Chou in Chihli province has a similar glaze more brown than red and with a silvery sheen by reflected light. The body is buff and heavy but well potted

FIG. 339. Jar of the Tz'u Chou type although none of these may have actually been made there but just as likely in Chihli or Shansi as in Honan. Ht. 8″. Ex Warren E. Cox Coll.

FIG. 340. Tsung Sê tz'ŭ vase possibly from Tz'u Chou, of buff-gray ware with dull, middle Sung type glaze of chocolate brown incised through and into body. Ht. 14″. The Cleveland Mus. of Art. Dikran G. Kelekian Coll.

FIG. 341. Bowl possibly made at Tz'u Chou during the Sung period. The body is buff-grey and the glaze olive brown. Dia. 13¼″. Mus. of Fine Arts, Boston.

Three finely potted examples with red glaze shaded at the lip-rims with olive green. The one on the right has a beautiful mottling of the back and the tracery of flowers which were in gold inside. Dias. about 4½" and 3¼". John Platt–Warren E. Cox Coll. Note: The kiln-site of these pieces are unknown and they vary considerably but the white body and thin potting makes it possible that some were made at Ting Chou and that they may be the "red Ting ware," mentioned in the old texts.

Jar of the "Kian Temmoku" from south western Kiang-si province of the same ware as the early type tea-bowls with rough body and streaked brown glaze. Early Sung. Note numeral five incised before firing. Ht. 10½". Warren E. Cox Coll.

Two conical bowls such as are used for drinking tea in summertime, with glossy black glaze touched with red-brown inside and having the light red-brown glaze outside. The ware is greyish white. Dia. 5¾". John Platt–Warren E. Cox Coll.

TSUNG SÊ TZ'U (DARK BROWN WARES)

FROM KIANG FU, CHING-HO HSIEN AND POSSIBLY TING CHOU

PLATE 50

Early Sung vase of the type made in northern Honan, Shansi and Chihli provinces. It has a brown body and olive green-brown "tea-dust" type glaze. The foot-rim is crude and low. (c. 960–1000 A.D.) Ht. 10½". Warren E. Cox Coll.

The mat glaze on this piece would indicate that it was of fairly early Sung period (c. 1100 A.D.) even though the design is florid and somewhat decadent. Ht. 12½". Ex Warren E. Cox Coll. C. T. Loo Coll.

Early Sung (c. 1000–1100 A.D.) Tz'u Chou vase with brown body and incised "tea dust type" brown glaze. Ht. 14½". Metropolitan Mus. of Art.

The more refined grey stoneware body and more glossy, better perfected glaze would indicate that this piece is of middle Sung period (c. 1100 to 1127 A.D.). Surely it shows no Mongol influence in the design. Ht. 11¾". Warren E. Cox Coll.

TSUNG SÊ WARES OF TZ'U CHOU TYPE

Plate 51

Tsung Sê jar of the Tz'u Chou type with deep buff body and the typical mat brown glaze of Early Sung to possibly T'ang origin. The foot is very slightly concave. The neck is cut. Ht. 16". Warren E. Cox Coll.

One of the earliest Sung types of brown globular jars dating about 1000 to 1100 A.D. It has a brown body and greenish, tea-dust type glaze simply incised. Probably made in Shansi province. Ht. 13½". Warren E. Cox Coll.

Late Sung globular jar with buff body and brown somewhat mat glaze without greenish ting. The ornate design has all the flamboyance of the art of the Mongols or Mings, therefore it was made surely after 1127 A.D. when the conquest began. Ht. 13". Warren E. Cox Coll.

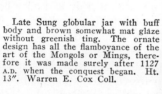

Vase of Tz'u Chou type with buff body and mat brown glaze. The broad, low foot-rim places this as probably Sung and the glaze as of the early part of this dynasty. Ht. about 14". Diedrich Abbes Coll.

Tz'u Chou wine jar of light buff body covered with a mat brown glaze of typical late Sung type and incised with a very beautiful design of lotus blossoms and leaves. Ht. 9¾". Ex Samuel T. Peters Coll. Warren E. Cox Coll.

TSUNG SÊ INCISED JARS T'ANG TO LATE SUNG PERIOD

PLATE 52

and very much like that of the light glazed wares from Tz'u Chou and Chü-lü Hsien. The glaze is evidently applied all over and reaching down nearly to the foot, and then the design is scratched out with a sharp point which often cuts even into the body, and finally the background is scraped away on some pieces.

Although we give these the general name of T'zu Chou wares and though the body clay is quite similar to proven Tz'u Chou examples we must admit at once that the slightly bulging cylindrical forms, angular shoulders and rather flat everted lip-rims do not occur in the light glazed wares. Perhaps this was due to the personal taste of some one potter or perhaps they come from some nearby kiln.

Nearer to the usual Tz'u Chou form of tapered melon shape with everted lip-rim are several which I illustrate. The first has a nearly white body and chocolate brown glaze while the second is of a buff grey very hard stoneware with glossy brown glaze having a very slight greenish tinge where it is thickest. Certainly these must come from different kilns as undoubtedly yet again does the shorter one of buff ware with a distinctly olive glaze and the large globular one with a sort of oatmeal body and olive brown glaze. All of these are of Sung shapes but widely different materials. Let us tentatively place them in Chihli and Shansi provinces and it is fair to associate them with the Tz'u Chou type in general. Of these incised glaze wares the only ones which I should assign to Honan are the heavy globular large jars similar to the one shown but with more treacly glossy almost black glazes which we shall touch upon in the Yüan and Ming sections.

Smaller examples with the same rough body heavily potted and covered with a blue-black glaze running to brown streaks or sometimes brown with thick blue black areas running over them are also likely from Honan and of late Sung or later periods. These are set apart also by their uneven and poor potting, wobbly lip-rims, etc. They are not quite so rough as the Kian wares but exhibit more careless craftsmanship. Perhaps a few are of the Sung period but even this is doubtful. None of these have painted or incised designs. (See Ming Section.)

Returning to the more northerly provinces, there is one type of wide mouthed globular jar with perpendicular arrangements of ridges and two small loops from lip to shoulder which Mr. Hochstadter says have been found at Ch'ing-ho Hsien. The shape is certainly one of that region but these show none of the usual staining from submersion that the light wares do. Perhaps that is due to the denser glaze. Again there is the grey stoneware olive green tea-dust glazed pear shaped bottle with flying phoenix decoration in near black which he claims was found near Ho-chou in Shansi province and which is truly and beautifully potted. This is just a little heavier than the beautiful buff ware bottles with glossy brown glaze having a silvery sheen and silver birds or brown ones painted on them which I think may very well be actual Tz'u Chou pieces. Their shapes are among the most graceful and well proportioned of all ceramic wares, and the counterparts in the same body but with cream slip and brown decoration are of the same size and shape. Others with buff and buff-grey bodies are covered with glazes ranging from the

Vase with wheel marks about the body. Buff stoneware covered with a dull "tea-dust" type of glaze which I believe was used on the earlier type. Probably early Sung. Shansi province. Ht. 14½". Ex Warren E. Cox Coll. Walter Hochstadter Coll.

"Honan temmoku" jar of hard, smooth grey stoneware covered with a blue black glaze having streaks of light brown. Late Sung to Early Ming (c. 1127 to 1400 A.D.). Ht. 8". **Warren E. Cox Coll.**

Late Sung or early Ming jar carefully designed with rounded shoulder so that they would roll and not break when knocked over, and a small neck with wide mouth and heavy lip which is easy to grasp. Dark brown stoneware with dull brownish black glaze. Ht. 11". Warren E. Cox Coll.

Buff stoneware vase covered with a dull chocolate colored glaze, unlike earlier examples which have a slightly greenish tinge. The everted lip has degenerated into a simple cylindrical mouth with a bulge. Late Sung or even later. Ht. 14". Warren E. Cox Coll.

"Honan temmoku" jar. Buff grey body over which is a thin dressing of brown slip, and a thick black iridescent glaze showing light brown at lip-rim and on handle loops. Sung period. Ht. 8". Warren E. Cox Coll.

Jar of typical Sung shape attributed to Ch'ing-ho Hsien. Grey stoneware, glossy blue-black glaze streaked with brown. Ht. 9". Ex Warren E. Cox Coll. Walter Hochstadter Coll.

Jar possibly from Honan but having a grey stoneware body heavily made and a black glaze of plum tone showing iridescence. Sung period. Ht. 6¾". Ex Warren E. Cox Coll. Mrs. Ogden K. Shannon, Jr.

Flower pot with five holes in the bottom. Brown stoneware covered with black glaze running in brown and bluish streaks. Ming period. "Honan Temmoku." Ht. 8½". Warren E. Cox Coll.

TSUNG SÊ UNDECORATED WARES EARLY SUNG TO MING

PLATE 53

tea-dust to the glossy type and are of typical Tz'u Chou shape (an elongated tapering melon form) but have somewhat modified lip treatments and for decoration only more or less prominent helical grooves executed in turning. These again are beautiful examples of potting in which is caught the very touch and movement of the potter's hand. They must certainly be from southern Chihli or eastern Shansi if not from Tz'u Chou itself.

FIG. 342. Tz'u Chou bottle of beautiful form, of light buff stoneware with glossy varicolored brown glaze and painted with flying birds in iron lustre. Late Sung (1100–1127 A.D.). Ht. 11½". Warren E. Cox Coll.
FIG. 343. Ching-ho Hsien jar of almost white ware with mat black glaze having iron-rust spots evenly distributed. Ht. 5". Warren E. Cox Coll.
FIG. 344. Grey stoneware jar treated with white slip, brown decoration and yellowish transparent glaze. Dr. Oscar Rücker-Embden called it Tz'u Chou which it probably is. Ht. 9¾".
FIG. 345. The close similarity in shape and design treatment of the Tsung Sê tz'ŭ globular jars to the Tz'u Chou one shown would seem to indicate that they too were made in Tz'u Chou. Buff-grey stoneware, greenish "tea-dust" type glaze which I associate with early Sung wares. Ht. 14". Warren E. Cox Coll.

Another closely associated group and very likely from the same source consists of globular jars with small mouths having modified everted lip-rims and made from light buff to dark brown clay. These too have tea-dust to glossy glazes and painted bird or floral designs.

Finally there are many odd wares which have body clays ranging from white to dark red-brown or hard grey stoneware and glazes of plain, rich, lustrous, iridescent black, of rich brown, of mottled and even of the "tobi seiji" technique which we have seen in the celadons, which we cannot place at all but which have characteristic shapes of the Sung period and techniques of Sung potting. These indicate many kilns some of which we hope will be found in the future.

The appeal of these wares is not at once apparent but for flower containers against a light background there is a beauty in them which grows upon one. They have always commanded fairly high prices and have not missed the attentions of imitators in Japan and elsewhere. Others of the Tsung Sê tz'ŭ yao group will be described under the Yuan and Ming sections.

TING YAO

Hirth (*Ancient Chinese Porcelain*, op. cit., p. 4) discovered a passage in the *T'ang pên ts'ao* (pharmacopoeia of T'ang dynasty) compiled about A.D. 650 which mentions "pai tz'ŭ" or "white ware" made at Ting Chou and it is likely that some of the pieces found at Samarra came from this site in central

Amphora made in Ching-ho Hsien north east of Tz'u Chou dating before 1108. Greyish white, black glaze with splashes of iron rust some of which are on the foot and the unglazed body inside the mouth showing they were applied by hand and were not glazed accidentals. Ht. 11″. Warren E. Cox–Mrs. C. P. Wilson Coll.

"Tz'u Chou" bottle of hard grey stoneware with brown glossy glaze and a design of flying bird quite typical in silvery lustre. Late Sung period (1100–1127 A.D.). Ht. 12″. Ex Warren E. Cox Coll.

Two "Tz'u Chou" jars of the usual well potted buff-grey or brown stoneware. The one on the left has a greenish "tea-dust" glaze with black design and is earlier than the other which has a glossy blue-black glaze and design in iron-lustre-brown. Hts. 8½″ and 7″. Warren E. Cox Coll. Note: The close similarity in the body materials, the development of the glazes and the flying bird designs, almost always seen, make it fairly certain that these globular jars and the pear shaped vases were both made in the same place and that is very likely Tz'u Chou.

Chung Tze jar with light buff body and rich glaze like tortoise-shell with decoration in golden lustre. Probably Late Sung origin unknown. Ht. 7¼″. Ex Warren E. Cox Coll.

Bottle of buff stoneware with "tea dust" type of glaze and birds painted on it in black said to have come from Shan-si province. Sung period. Ht. 10½″. Ex Walter Hochstadter Coll. Warren E. Cox Coll.

Two jars of almost white body, heavily potted and with broad foot-rims. Blue-black glaze with iron-brown spots at even intervals. Probably late Sung to Early Ming, province unknown, possibly Honan. Hts. 12″. Warren E. Cox Coll.

CHUNG TZE DECORATED WARES

PLATE 54

western Chihli province just southwest of Peking. The place is now called
Chên-ting Fu. In the *Ko ku yao lun* we find that the best wares were made
during the years A.D. 1111 to 1125, therefore the ware must have improved
after the royal patronage was taken from it because of flaws in the glaze and
given to the Ju Chou potters. In 1127 when the court fled the potters went
along and settled near Chêng-tê Ching where they made "nan ting" or
Southern Ting supposedly almost undistinguishable from the former product.
Actually identified pieces have not been established by western collectors.
That some of the potters remained is proven by the Administrative Annals

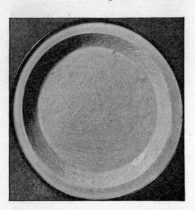

FIG. 346. One of a pair of pai-ting dishes
with molded design of mandarin ducks,
symbols of marital fidelity. Note that the
lip-rim has been left unglazed though the
flat rim would not permit its having been
fired upside down. Dia. 4". N. M.
Heeramaneck Coll.

FIG. 347. Ting yao bowl of the Sung period
with a graceful design of lotus incised on the
outside which is less often seen than decoration on the inside. Dia. 6½". Ex D. Abbes
Coll.

FIG. 348. Rare black Ting yao bowl with
typical cream white glaze inside showing spur
marks, an unglazed rim and the outside coated
with a brown-black teadust type glaze of
considerable richness. Dia. 8½". Ex John
Platt–Warren E. Cox Coll. Judge Edgar
Bromberger Coll., Brooklyn Mus.

of the Ming Dynasty which states that wine jars were supplied the court in
the Hsüan Tê period (1426–1435) and again in 1553 and 1563. There is also
a mold in the B.M. which bears the "nien hao" or honorific title of the
Emperor Ta Ting (the actual date corresponds with A.D. 1189) of the Chin
Tartar dynasty.

The *Ko ku yao lun* gives the earliest description mentioning the "lei hên"
or tear-stains which are slightly straw colored places usually on the outside
of the bowls where the glaze runs thicker and were regarded as a sign of
genuineness. It also mentions "hua hua," engraved decoration, "yin hua"
impressed decoration and "hsiu hua" which can only mean painted designs
although we have never seen any of these. The wares in order of their importance are "fên ting" or flour ting, "pai ting" or white ting and "t'u ting"
or earthy ting which had a yellower glaze. The Chinese writers also speak
of "tzŭ ting" which would be brown or purple, "huang ting" or red ting "like
carved red jade," purple ting and black ting. The *T'ao shuo* mentions Ting

FIG. 349. Group of Ting ware of Sung period including a rare and beautiful small dipper and a heavy pure white bowl in the center of upper shelf. John Platt–Warren E. Cox Coll. C. T. Loo & Co.

yao "mottled like hare's fur." Of these wares we are certain of the first three classifications and the black Ting yao which is surely the type of bowl with black outside and creamy glaze inside or on rare occasions black all over. These are of the same ware and identical style of potting and some of them have a slight indication of the "hare's fur" markings. But of the purple which

FIG. 350. One of pair of stem cups stated on good authority to be Sung although the shape would certainly be more expected in the Ming period, of creamy white porcelaneous ware with cream glaze. Ht. 4". Ex D. Abbes Coll.

FIG. 351. Ting yao "cup stand" or cup attached to stand of what appears to have been a pure white ware but now somewhat stained brownish. Ht. about 3½". Gift of Mrs. Samuel T. Peters. Metropolitan Mus. of Art.

FIG. 352. Ting yao bowl rather heavily potted but of clear white color and with a freely and beautifully incised design of lotus flowers. Foot is glazed, lip rim left unglazed and mounted with a silver rim. Dia. 8". Gift of Mrs. Samuel T. Peters. Metropolitan Mus. of Art.

appears in Hsiang Yüan-p'ien's *Album* none has appeared and we are inclined to believe that he relied on a misconception of the ancient texts. And of red Ting yao there is nothing except the very fine white bodied Tsung Sê tz'ŭ yao often called "Korean" and mentioned previously. This probably is not the

Pai-ting bowl with center medallion only decorated with incised design of two fish among waves. Has original silver rim. John Platt–Warren E. Cox Coll. Dia. 8¼".

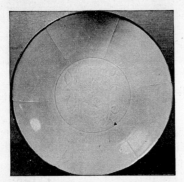

Typical bowl from Ting Chou with incised floral design and sharply raised radial lines to give it a floral form. Dia. 7½". N. M. Heeramaneck Coll.

Fine dish with low relief design made over a mold. Sung dynasty. Dia. 8⅜". Metropolitan Mus. of Art.

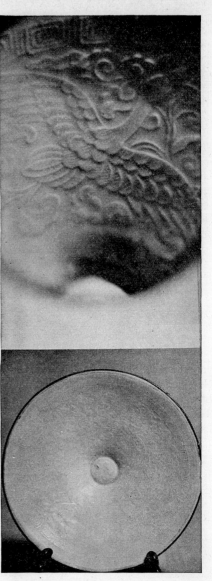

Fine Pai Ting shallow bowl with small foot. This is the type made by patting the clay over a mound on which was the engraved design so that in reverse it appears on the bowl in low relief. Note the fine drawing in the flying goose. Dia. 6½". Has original metal rim. John Platt–Warren E. Cox Coll. This is perhaps the finest known to Western collectors.

T'ING WARES INCISED AND MOLDED

PLATE 55

ware (though it is fully as delicate) because the method of potting is different, the foot ring being left unglazed and the bowls being fired right side up.

Ting yao is of white or slightly greyish, dense porcelaneous ware usually high fired enough to ring but not always. It is slightly translucent and is covered with a more or less transparent glaze of pure white or light ivory tone usually not crackled in the fên and pai classes but with crackle in the t'u ting. It has always been written that the bowls were fired upside down on the lip-rims to keep them from wilting and distorting their shapes during firing. Here we come to an interesting modern finding. Mrs. Ogden K. Shannon Jr. of Fort Worth, Texas, brought in the observation that the running of the tear-stains was usually *toward the bottom* and not away from it as we should expect, if the above statement is correct. Upon examination of many bowls her observation was found to be true, though amazingly enough hundreds upon hundreds of collectors had never raised the question. There seemed no reason to the thing. The bowls simply could not have been fired right-side up for there was so sign of spur marks or other support and the foot-rims were covered with glaze which surely would have stuck had they

FIG. 353. Sung period Ting yao vase of bronze form. The ware is nearly white and the glaze an impure white. Ht. about 8". Gift of Mrs. Samuel T. Peters. Metropolitan Mus. of Art.

FIG. 354. Sung period Tu Ting pilgrim bottle. Form similar to those which showed Roman influence in the T'ang period but with simplified design. Light buff, glaze brownish, purplish and gray due to staining during firing. Ht. about 8". Gift of Mrs. Samuel T. Peters. Metropolitan Mus. of Art.

rested upon the foot-rim. In a general discussion I brought the problem to the attention of Mr. Walter Hochstadter and, after considerable deliberation, he suddenly hit upon the only reasonable solution:—The bowls were fired standing upright on edge, probably in a rack of some sort into which the unglazed edge could be slipped. Upon more careful examination it was found that the glaze does not *all* run toward the foot-rim, though it appears to, for the heaviest accumulation is at that point of stoppage; it does run

Tu Ting (earth Ting) covered with cream colored glossy glaze having brown crackle. Foot and bottom both glazed, rim being unglazed and bound with metal rim. Dia. 6½". John Platt–Warren E. Cox Coll.

Left to Right: Unique Ting yao jar with typical white glaze showing "tear stains" and forming a large globule of greenish brown where it runs thick inside of bottom. The body is white and porous and left exposed at bottom. Ht. 4½". Warren E. Cox Coll.—Greyish white vase probably made at Ting chou, heavily potted, covered with white slip over incised design. Transparent glaze inclined to darken into "tear stains" where thick and even into a green-brown drop as shown just below the shoulder. Ht. 12⅜". Warren E. Cox Coll.—Sung period Ting yao bottle of pure white or pai ting ware. Note that the potter has purposely left the marks of his templet with which he shaped it. Ht. 11". Ex Warren E. Cox Coll. C. T. Loo Coll.

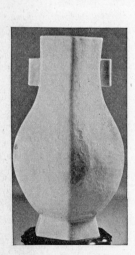

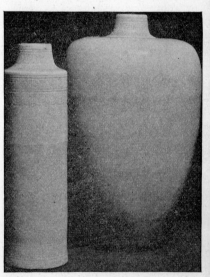

Left: Tu Ting vase of the Sung period. Thinly potted buff gray porcelaneous ware covered with a creamy glaze. The design of four clawed dragons on front and back is in relief from the mold while the sides are decorated with incised clouds. It is of the bronze form called Hu and hexagonal in plan. Ht. 12¾". Ex Samuel T. Peters Coll. Ex Warren E. Cox Coll.—Baron C. T. von Seidlitz.

Center: Sung period Tu Ting gourd shaped bottle of buff ware with glossy, finely crackled glaze over an incised design. Note the typical horizontal ridges where the sections are joined together. Ht. 12". Metropolitan Mus. of Art.

Right: Two Tu ting vases with incised design under a soft creamy and glossy glaze which is mottled with lavender about the shoulder of the larger piece. Hts. 8¾" and 9¾". Warren E. Cox Coll.

PAI TING AND TU TING WARES SUNG DYNASTY

PLATE 56

away on one side opposed to that side where the tear stains show most markedly. Our thanks to two enthusiastic and most observant collectors!

It was the custom to cover the unglazed lip-rim with a copper or silver rim but these are often missing or have been replaced by modern ones usually of heavier construction. When replaced the collector should beware of hidden chips in the rim.

The impressed ornamentation was done by means of a mold in the form of a mound carved with the low relief design. The clay for the bowl was pressed down over this and when partially dry shaved off with a knife to the proper thinness. A detail of this beautiful work is illustrated. (Pl. 55) The incising was swiftly done with a sharp instrument and was in outline only. Collectors have a mistaken idea that the incised pieces are more to be desired than the impressed, for only one of a kind was made. However there are no duplicates of the impressed ware known, there was nothing careless in their execution and they appear in the very finest quality of pieces. This is once when the use of the mold shows not the slightest decadence.

Besides the bowls vases were made in ancient bronze forms and occasionally in the most beautiful slender pear shaped forms such as the one illustrated. Some of these are of the true fên and pai quality. Most of the t'u ting ware consists of vases, some also of sensitive and beautiful form, and all well potted though just slightly heavier and lower fired than the others. The body may appear slightly greyish or ivory where exposed. In the Eumorfopoulos Collection is a bowl #188 with the mark under the bottom "ta sung hsi ning ni en tsao" or "made in the Hsi period of the great Sung dynasty" (A.D. 1068–1077). (See Burton & Hobson *Marks on Pottery and Porcelain.*) Therefore these are definitely of the Sung period although some of the more ornate and involved forms may be later or at least after A.D. 1127 when the Tartar taste would have had effect. Due to impurities which may or may not have been accidental in the body clay, many of these wares of a basic ivory tone have cloudings of subtle rosy and lavender tints that enhance their beauty. Some were molded in low relief while others have "secret design" decoration delicately incised so as often to be hardly visible under the quite transparent glaze. (Pl. 56)

So far as I know there were no wares made at Ting Chou with a slip while those at T'zu Chou being of darker clay were always dressed with a slip, therefore it seems confusing to me to include, as Hobson does in his descriptions, slip treated wares under the heading of Ting yao. Let us make this arbitrary division and call the light bodied wares Ting type and the dark bodied, slip dressed ones Tz'u Chou type.

Besides the Southern Sung Ting yao made at Chêng-tê Ching a great many other places copied this ware more or less accurately but never approaching the original in conception or technique. Hsiang yao is described by the old writers as being rich and lustrous with "crab's claw" crackle and valued when fine but not when it was coarse and yellow. This was probably made at Hsiang-shan in Chekiang near Ning-po south of Hang-chow Bay. Fêng-yang had a substitute at Su Chou in Anhwei but it was inferior. In Ssŭ-chou in the same province there was a "bargain lover's" Ting yao and at Hsüan Chou another. Brinkley speaks of a ware "Nyo-fu" which has an earthy looking body and is very light in weight. We have seen an example of this with poorly impressed design and a pitted glaze having slight hardly perceptible Ying-ching bluish cast. At the "White Earth Village" Pai-t'u Chên near Hsiao Hsien in northwestern Kiangsu or southern Shangtung a ware was noted "very thin, white and lustrous, beautiful in form and craft," and here were some thirty kilns employing hundreds of potters. Actually sherds found there are greyish, slip covered and with a warm creamy crackled glaze, probably not of the type described at all. We illustrate an interesting vase reported to have been found at Hsiang-hu Shih southeast of Chêng-tê Ching in Kiangsi province which is well potted from a white clay that is slightly pinkish where exposed perhaps due to the earth in which it was buried. The glaze is glossy white with irregular places of crackle. The foot is roughly potted not unlike the Kian Tzǔ Chin wares, but it grows thinner higher up and the lip-rim is thin and well potted.

Hobson states that the *T'ao shuo* speaks of four factories in Shansi under the heading of Hsi yao. They are P'ing-yang Fu in the southern part, Ho Chou also in that part, Yu-tzǔ Hsien in the T'ai-yüan prefecture in the north and P'ing-ting Chou in the west. These probably all date from T'ang times and the Ho Chou was supposed to be the best ware of "fine, rich material, the body unctuous and thin, the colour usually white." The poorest was from Yu-tzǔ Hsien, "a coarse pottery."

Many other kilns are recorded and many wares have been found which do not seem to fit any of the descriptions. It is a field upon which many books will be written in future years as the evidence piles up.

Tz'u Chou Yao

Always loved and cherished by the Chinese people and crystallizing into one medium perhaps the best of the taste of this purest and most Chinese of all periods was the T'zu Chou type pottery embodying at once the greatest mastery of form with the uttermost perfection of restrained decoration. In the *Ko ku yao lun*, later quoted by the *T'ao lu* almost verbatim, it is said that "The good kinds are like the Ting ware, but without tear stains. Some specimens have engraved ornament (hua hua), while others are painted (hsiu hua). For even the plain ones the price is higher than that of Ting ware." When Mr. Hobson gives this passage he notes that, "None of them, however, can be said seriously to challenge the Ting ware." And here I beg to differ for reasons we shall state as we go along. The one is a very perfect and beautiful ware within a narrow scope; the other shows more breadth of conception, greater mastery of technique, a human quality closer to the hand of the potter, a natural quality full of the Taoist or Zen Buddhist spirit, moods of power, of delicate beauty, of humor and of many other human emotions.

The most important center of manufacture was Tz'u Chou now in southern Chihli but formerly included in northern Honan. The place was called Fu-yang but the name was changed in the Sui dynasty (A.D. 589–617) because of the "tz'u" stone found there and according to Chinese authorities it was a pottery center even at that time. This may be true for there were

Three Tz'u Chou type vases with blue glaze. Larger of brown stoneware with white and brown slip under deep sapphire blue, crackled glaze. Flat foot, swift drawing and shape indicate that it is Sung.—The smaller one beside it has typical S form of early Ming, deep foot-rim and glaze, though deep, is not so fine as first. It is also not crackled.—The other example is typical later Ming with paler blue glaze, crowded design and double foot-rim. Hts. 17½″, 9½″, and 10″.—Largest vase Warren E. Cox Coll. Others Ex Warren E. Cox Coll. Note: Blue glazed Ts'u Chou wares are rare and all are inclined to have the glaze chip away from the body.

BLUE GLAZED T'ZU CHOU TYPE JARS OF SUNG AND MING

PLATE 57

pieces of the ware in the 9th century site of Samarra and old Chinese writing records finding it in T'ang tombs. The K'ang Hsi encyclopaedia notes that wine jars were furnished the Court in Hsüan tê and Chia Ching Ming times, and the *T'ao lu* mentions the continued existence of the factories there in the 18th century. Thus there must have been a tremendous and varied output.

In general the body of this ware is described as putty colored or buff-grey

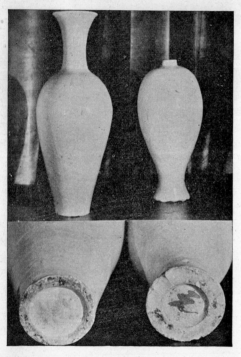

Fig. 355. Two early Sung Tz'u Chou type vases both having buff stoneware body, white slip somewhat imperfectly applied and transparent glaze. The larger is slightly yellowish. Note completely different methods of potting of bases which indicate different kilns. Hts. 21¼″ and 15¼″. Warren E. Cox Coll. and Warren E. Cox–John Platt Coll.

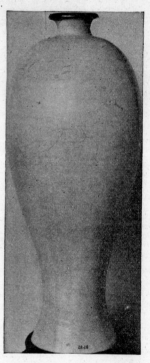

Fig. 356. A simple and fine form of a Tz'u Chou vase called by the Chinese "Woman form." A number of the undecorated wares have dark brown tea dust type glaze at lip-rim and in mouth. Metropolitan Mus. of Art.

and the Sung period ones are dense and smooth to the touch. The later Ming period ones are inclined to be either sandy buff or harder porcelain. Some of the wares from other kilns are also buff but less gritty during the Sung period. Over this ware and usually down to near the foot or right to the foot a slip was applied probably by dipping. This slip is nothing but a refined white or cream colored clay brought to the consistency of cream. It was used to fill the small imperfections in the body and to make a light ground. The decoration then consists either of cutting lines or removing areas of this slip so that the grey body color shows through, or of painting the design on it

FIG. 357. Superbly classic form and rich cream-white glaze make this an outstanding example of Tz'u Chou art. Buff stoneware, lip and inside treated with a mat brown glaze. Note "wheel-marks" use of the drips of slip to give interest to an otherwise plain surface. Ht. 13". Ex Warren E. Cox Coll. Delos Chappell Coll.

FIG. 358. Tz'u chou type vase. Gray stoneware covered with creamy slip and transparent glaze making it eggshell color. The design is incised in the slip and rubbed in with brown pigment under the glaze to give an inlayed effect not unlike what the Japanese call "mishima" in Korean celadon wares. Note the way the stems enclose the flowers and also the vigorous spiral drawing of the lotus petals at the bottom. Ht. 16¾". Ex Samuel T. Peters Coll. Warren E. Cox Coll.

FIG. 359. Tz'u Chou type vase found at Chü-lu Hsien and dating before 1108 A.D. Buff gray covered with a slip and incised with a beautiful all over design of flowers toned to old ivory through action of the soil. Ht. about 11". Metropolitan Mus. of Art.

FIG. 360. Tz'u Chou buff body covered with white slip painted in dark brown over the finely crackled glaze. Russell Tyson Coll. Courtesy of The Art Institute of Chicago.

FIG. 361. Three typical Chu-lu Hsien vases. Early Sung type buff stoneware. White slip and cream glaze showing crackle and stains due to inundation in A.D. 1108. Hts. 10" to 11". Warren E. Cox Coll.

FIG. 362. Chü-lu Hsien ewer showing Near Eastern influence in shape. Grey stoneware covered to near bottom with white slip, having colorless transparent glaze finely crackled and slightly stained from burial. Ht. 11½". Ex D. Abbes Coll.

191

Left: Rare dated Tz'u Chou type vase. Characters about neck read, right to left or clockwise: "Great Sung Kia T'ai three made," and as Kia T'ai took throne in 1201, this would indicate the year 1203. Body buff, glaze straw colored and not crackled and design in black. From southern kiln site perhaps near Hang Chou. Ht. 7". Ex Warren E. Cox Coll. Metropolitan Mus. of Art.

Right: Wine jar designed to be rolled on side for pouring. Body yellowish buff, decoration brown and glaze yellow tinted and transparent without crackle. Characters are a *chiang ch'en tsze* or "flute lyric." Finest of the type ever to come to western hemisphere. See text for translation of poem made by Mr. Nai-Chi Chang and Mr. C. F. Yau. Ht. 14¾". Ex Tonying & Co. Warren E. Cox Coll.

RARE T'SU CHOU VASES WITH INSCRIPTIONS

PLATE 58

in dark brown or black over which the transparent glaze is applied. Many variations were developed which we can note as we proceed, and many of the vases were made simply with the slip and glaze without decoration. The glaze is usually slightly straw color and sometimes finely crackled and sometimes not. By adding copper or cobalt a rich green or light blue could be obtained and toward the end of the period a deep sapphire blue was made which continued into Ming times in the well known gallipots on which are painted figures under a blue glaze. The finest of these prototypes is illustrated herewith along with an early Ming example and a typical later Ming example. It may be Late Sung to Early Ming.

  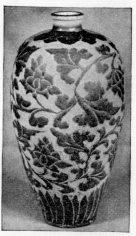

FIG. 363. Vase from Chü-lu Hsien, similar to one at Metropolitan Mus. but with more dynamic, stylized design. Ht. 8¾". Freer Gallery of Art, Washington.

FIG. 364. Vase reported found at Chü-lu Hsien. Grey stoneware with usual black and white slip decoration and incised lines. Form similar to those in Tz'u Chou, but somewhat wider. Ht. c. 11". Metropolitan Mus. of Art.

FIG. 365. Vase probably from Ch'ing-ho Hsien. Yellow-brown glaze typical of that place painted into incised design over white slip and transparent glaze. Ht. 13". Metropolitan Mus. of Art.

Other sections which produced this beautiful Tz'u Chou yao have been traced. Just northeast in Chihli province is Chü-lü Hsien only about 70 miles from Tz'u Chou where we know that an inundation occurred in 1108. Here are found wares of a soft, creamy feeling which have been stained a reddish brown in some places and this stain has accented the crackle of the glaze pleasantly. The body clay is buff here but also dense and smooth. The foot-rim is usually a little heavier than that of the Tz'u Chou wares. Gallipots usually have flaring horizontal lip-rims rather than everted ones. Large ovoidal bowls are typical as are also small amphora shaped vases on conical bases and with widely flaring lip-rims. Many of what appear to be the earlier wares have T'ang characteristics and are plain. Incising of the body was practiced and later incised designs were filled in with a black glaze with details scratched in it while the background was filled in with white. The style of the design was vigorous and smart as may be seen by the illustrations.

Just a bit further along the river is the site of Ch'ing-ho Hsien where a

Rare type vase. Buff-grey ware with white slip, black decoration and over-all green glaze. Ht. 12". Benjamin d'Ancona Coll.

Incised vase. Soft ivory brown stained color with beautiful design. Ht. 13". Ex Warren E. Cox Coll.

Bowl said to have been found at Chü-lu Hsien. Gray ware with incised black and white design of slips. Ht. c. 6". Metropolitan Mus. of Art.

Fish-bowl of buff stoneware with white slip and cream glaze showing brown irregular crackle. Five spur marks inside. Dia. 9½". Warren E. Cox Coll.

Buff pottery vase with black decoration and filled-in white slip. Ht. 19½". Ex C. T. Loo & Co. Mr. Hsieh's Coll.

SUNG T'SU CHOU TYPE WARES FROM CHÜ-LU HSIEN

PLATE 59

similar ware was made but instead of the black glaze a greenish brown glaze was employed in a similar manner and also painted on over the glaze quite thickly. Sir Percival David has said that on the whole the Ch'ing-ho Hsien wares are potted better and are more choice than the Chü-lü Hsien ones. The body clay here is a bit more grey and seemingly denser.

Still other sections produced similar wares in abundance for they were very popular, and slowly we are gaining ground in the identification of certain types. Thus in Shansi province to the west at Ping yang Fu just south of Ho Chou a type was made which is crude in technique, quite possibly intentionally to produce a natural or close to earth feeling, but which are often beautiful in form as may be seen in the example shown herewith.

At Wei Hsien in Shantung province were found some Tz'u Chou type painted wares in a Sung tomb and some of these had the light blue glaze.

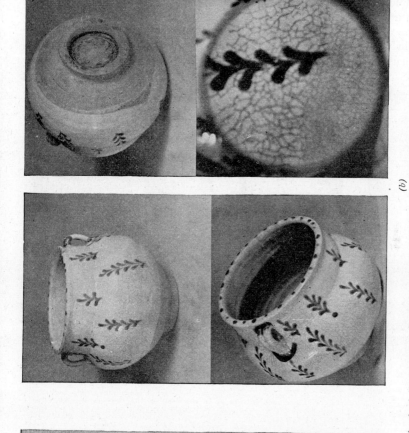

(a)

(b)

(a) Ching-ho Hsien or Chü-lu Hsien bowl of T'ang period. Buff stoneware with straw colored slip and glaze, decorated with peculiar green-brown transparent glaze. Chinese had written that these kilns were in operation in T'ang times but this is the only example which has come to light. Note flat bottom and heavy potting. Dia. 6⅞". Warren E. Cox Coll.

(b) Ching-ho Hsien jar of buff-grey stoneware with white slip and creamy, crackled glaze decorated in greenish brown transparent enamel with delicate sloping design of leaf-stems. Ht. c. 7". Given Metropolitan Mus. by Mrs. Wilfred H. Wolfs, Mr. John Platt's daughter, in his memory.

T'ANG AND SUNG WARES FROM CHING-HO HSIEN

PLATE 60

Hobson seems to decide out of hand that these were made at Po Shan Hsien where he says kilns have been in operation "time out of mind," but this is doubtful for the only wares we have which can definitely be attributed to Po Shan are quite different. Laufer described some of the Wei Hsien pieces as having a light reddish or reddish buff body which was often completely dipped in white slip as though to hide it. The glaze is also a little more glassy than that of the Tz'u Chou Yao and where painted decorations occur

Fig. 368. Pilgrim bottle which was made at Po-shan according to its inscription. Buff-grey with white slip, painted in black under a transparent glaze. Note the slanting keyfret border and the rather close decoration of cloud scrolls about it. Ht. 16½". Eumorfopoulos Coll. # C299.

Fig. 367. Two vases possibly from Po-shan. The vase on the left with script decoration is of gritty buff clay with black specks though the glaze is of a creamy sort over white slip more usually associated with Tz'u Chou. Base is more crudely potted, without glaze under it.
    The vase on the right is of gritty buff clay, lighter in weight, glaze is transparent and of light straw color over white slip. Both have the typical "tea dust" type brown glaze around the lower parts. Sung period. Ht. 13". Warren E. Cox and John Platt Colls.

Fig. 366. Vase made in Shansi province probably at Ping Yang Fu or Ho chou, of gray stone ware, incised and then covered all over with white slip and a transparent glaze showing crackle in some areas. The background of the design is then covered with a brownish black glaze. Ht. 15¾". Ex Samuel T. Peters Coll. Warren E. Cox Coll.

they are nearly black but being underglaze are not as strong a black as the Chü-lü Hsien color. Another type found at Wei Hsien is buff to brown rough ware heavily potted in melon shaped vases with small mouths and slightly flaring heavy lip-rims. There are usually three or four small loops on the shoulder as though for tying on a covering. The lower third and under the foot, but leaving the rim exposed, is covered with a tea-dust mat type of brown glaze. The upper third is covered with a white slip on which are very summarily painted flying birds and plant or flower forms and rarely four characters in the same brown under a yellowish transparent uncrackled glaze. Hobson again assigns these to Po Shan but the attribution is now somewhat doubtful. Judging by our findings of the dull mat glaze of brown on T'ang wares and its displacement by the glossy blue-black brown flecked glaze during Sung times, I think it fair to assume that these Wei Hsien pieces are of the first part of the Sung period.

It is interesting to note that aside from the beautiful deep sapphire glaze the technique and the form of the large blue vase shown are not unlike these vases. To be sure the potting is thinner and the ware darker brown. Also the piece has a flat bottom rather than the low board foot-rim but these changes might have been due to an endeavor to make a superfine pot. Of course the painting is much finer also but it is in the same dark brown glaze with a wide band of brown at the bottom and I assign this piece to northern Shantung, tentatively at least.

At Po Shan Hsien there was a cream ware with black decoration as is proven by the well known pilgrim bottle in the Eumorfopoulos Collection #C299 on the shoulder of which is an inscription "yang kao chiu," "lamb wine," and also "po shan ho chia tsao" "made by the Ho family at Po Shan." This is a pilgrim bottle with buff-grey stoneware body dense and hard, covered with a white slip and cream colored transparent glaze not at all like the above described ware, the breezy willow landscape on it being far more skillful than the broad painting on any of the part-brown part-cream pots. This is also called "Yüan?" by Hobson probably because the design fills the space rather fully but the ware is certainly Sung in craftsmanship and I am certain that in these northern sections the decadence due to the Mongolian conquest was felt first or that is immediately after 1127 in any event. We show a small jar (with mouth cut) which seems to be of a similar if not identical ware in the paragraph on humor because of the painting of the rabbit on it, and this again is typically Sung in all respects. A disconcerting pot #295 in the Eumorfopoulos Collection has a very similar key fret border (though more cautiously rendered) to the one on the Po Shan pilgrim bottle and a rather curlicue style of decorative painting quite similar. It too is described as of grey porcelaneous stoneware with white slip and cream glaze with black painting and remains of brown glaze inside and it is dated "chêng t'ung shih i nein wu yüeh ch'u i jih" or "the first day of the fifth month of the eleventh year of Chêng T'ung" (A.D. 1446). Does it make the pilgrim bottle Ming in period or did the style persist?

To add evidence, the flower on this jar is almost identical to that on a pear shaped vase I recently acquired which again has all of what we have known as Sung characteristics. We know these designs were copied but were they done so well four or five hundred years afterwards? I am still of the opinion that the pilgrim flask and the bottle are Sung, but this gives an idea of the difficulties in dating these wares.

A similar problem is posed by the "ku hsiang" (or Old Hsiang) pillows. A number of these are known containing the above words in inscriptions and some of them the potter's mark containing his name, "Chang." Hsiang, Mr.

FIG. 369. Tz'u Chou bottle which in its sort of curlicue linear technique suggests it may be "Ku Hsiang" or "Old Hsiang." Ht. 9¾". Warren E. Cox Coll.

FIG. 370. "Old Hsiang" type pillow of typical character and having an inscription in the border reading, "Made by the idler of the bank of the Chang." On the bottom is a bell shaped stamped mark reading, "Mr. Wang Shou-ming." Sung, and probably made at Tz'u Chou. Length 16¾". Eumorfopoulos Col. # C310.

Hobson found, is the name of the old prefecture now Chan-tê Fu in which Tz'ǔ Chou is located. Judging by the style of the potter's mark and also by the fact that there came a number of these on the market at once, Mr. Hobson came to the conclusion that they were of the 17th century. However, subsequent comparisons have led us to place them back into the Sung period and certainly from the Tz'ǔ Chou kilns. They have the typical buff-grey stoneware body and cream slip with transparent glaze. The painting in underglaze black consists of landscapes with animals and figures in economical and direct Sung style. These are set off in ogival medallions set upon rather closely decorated grounds of clouds, rock and wave and such all-over patterns.

FIG. 371. "Ku Hsiang" type jar of grey stoneware made without foot-rim, as are most of these large jars, and covered with white slip and transparent glaze under which is a vigorous drawing of a dragon on one side and a Fêng-huang bird on the other. Ht. 17". Warren E. Cox Coll.

FIG. 372. Tz'u Chou type jar with the usual cream glaze over a white slip and brown decoration of a dragon and bird. Several very similar ones in shape and decoration are glazed with the turquoise color. Ht. 10⅞". The Cleveland Mus. of Art. The Dikran G. Kelekian Coll.

A remarkable jar illustrated herewith has similar characteristics and one of the finest drawings of a dragon I have ever seen on one side with a Fêng-huang on the other. Both are tearing their way through tattered clouds in an ogival medallion while a band about the shoulder has a fine rock and wave pattern. The ware is typically Sung Tz'u Chou with a pinkish stain on one side. The dragon style is reminiscent of the paintings by Ch'ên Jung in the Boston Museum and these are dated A.D. 1244 and our potter may have seen such pictures.

Probably also from the main center come the slip incised wares with almost white transparent glaze sometimes crackled but pure and clear. We show a bowl stand and a vase having bands of foliage, coins, ducks and

Fig. 373. Large painted Tz'u Chou wine jar with flying cranes and a poem reading, "Keep the cover on and you keep the fragrance inside. Remove the cover and the fragrance greets your nostrils. Keep the cover off and a beautiful golden glow comes over your countenance." Ht. 24½". Sung Dynasty. Warren E. Cox Coll.

Fig. 374. Tz'u Chou type jar of Sung period made of buff stoneware with carved white slip and transparent glaze. Ht. 4". Note: This is almost identical to # C404 Emorfopoulos Coll. Warren E. Cox Coll.

Fig. 375. Tz'u Chou vase of gray stoneware covered with white slip which is then incised with the design and glazed over with a transparent glaze. This piece, though noble in size and proportions, is roughly handled and of a gray tone due to the impure glaze running unevenly. Sung period. Ht. 20". Gift of Mrs. Samuel T. Peters. Metropolitan Mus. of Art.

lotus petals of this type. Of the same ware is the larger Samuel T. Peters incised vase from the Metropolitan Museum of Art, and again the partly painted and partly incised vase which I think is the greatest one known.

This example shows a simple mastery of brush work beyond any other known. The petals of the lotus are nearly an inch in width and the pigment has been applied so that it hangs thickly at the bottom of each petal. Yet so wonderfully did the painter handle his brush that the pigment had just about been used up at the end of each stroke, giving a shaded effect. On close examination it will be seen that the petals actually seem to grow out of the stem.

Above: An amazing similarity in style and treatment leads us to believe this vase was made by the same master. The same characters are incised in the same style. The form is similar. But most of all the brilliant and feeling brush work is so alike that only some great master could have done both.

The bodies of both are of gray stoneware and the slip and glaze give a brown or old ivory color. Ht. 14½". Warren E. Cox Coll.

Left: The finest Tz'u Chou vase I have seen, interesting because it combines the incised-through-slip technique with masterful brush work and fine form. The vigorous characters mean "snow," "moon," "wind," and "flower" and constitute a sort of short poem perhaps painting a landscape of snow-flowers being blown by the wind in the light of the moon. Ht. 14". Warren E. Cox Coll.

T'ZU CHOU MASTERPIECE

PLATE 61

In the incising too, partly done with a stylus and partly with a comb, the fluid and yet dynamic writing of the characters makes the incising of most other vases seem mere child's play. The characters used mean "snow," "moon," "wind," and "flower"; a sort of poem or impression of a landscape but also expressive of the seasons, and of such duality of the universe as "wind" movement and "moon" quiet, of "flower" life and of "snow" death.

Tz'u Chou type pil'ow with carved s'ip decoration under a transparent glaze. The color is buff to cream white. Ht. 4¾". Fuller Coll. Seattle Art Mus.

Tz'u Chou type pillow of grey stoneware with white slip beautifully incised and covered with a greenish straw colored crackled glaze. It is said to have come from Shansi province and is of the Sung period. Length 9¾". Warren E. Cox Coll.

Left: One of a near pair of Sung period tz'u Chou type vases with carved slip under a transparent glaze. This was purchased from Lee van Ching the famous Chinese collector in 1927. An almost identical one was bought in 1941. Ht. 14". Warren E. Cox Coll.

Right: Cup stand with incised band about the wide lip. It will be noted that a comb was used in doing the background of the cloud scrolls. Sung period. Ht. 6". Warren E. Cox Coll.

T'ZU CHOU TYPE INCISED SLIP WARES

FROM T'ZU CHOU, CHÜ-LU HSIEN AND SHANSI PROVINCE

PLATE 62

This vase was surely made by one of the greatest potters that ever lived, and amazingly I recently found another lesser work by the same hand as can be judged without a doubt by the brush work and also by the script.

In Shansi, mainly at Ho Chou a grey ware was made with the usually white slip incised with a free and charming manner and covered with a yellowish-greenish closely crackled distinctive glaze. Two excellent examples of this are the vase #C390 in the Eumorfopoulos Collection and the pillow from my own. The ware is rare and beautiful equaling that of Tz'u Chou. This attribution is given through the research of Walter Hochstadter and several pieces have been traced to the neighborhood. Of course it may be that they were actually made in one of the other three large kilns of the province, but unless otherwise proven let us assume that they came of Ho Chou, the largest and most central.

In Kiangsu a grey ware was made and also a red ware which Mr. Hochstadter says was made in Tan-yang Yu in northwestern Honan just southwest of Chang-tê. I show an excellent example of this ware with red body dipped, foot-rim, base and all in white slip which has been incised in a sort of checkerboard pattern and with a band of the same key fret we saw on the Po Shan pilgrim bottle, and with the body exposed by incising carefully covered by a painted-in grey slip to hide the red color that might have been very effective. One other small jar has plain white slip and glaze outside and grey on the inside. Where the slip goes over the bottom of these and is not covered with glaze it is inclined to crack and curl up and comes off easily when picked.

Note should be made that most of the sherds found by Sir Aurel Stein in Turkestan and at Kharakhoto are of yellowish buff body. This is all the information we have to date on the kiln sites and it is just as difficult to date these wares. Style is the best criterion and style is difficult to define. Some of these wares are aristocrats of slender and tall form, thinly potted, true and beautiful in conception. They are likely always to be Sung. Other Sung pieces are peasant wares squat and of the soil, heavily potted and without pretense. They may at first be confused with the fatter bellies of the Ming period which are also heavily potted but the feeling is quite different between the two.

I have criticized perhaps severely the Greek forms. Their parallels and derivations can be found in these Sung wares and a glance at the accompanying illustration will make my point clear. I show an Apulian vase which in simple proportions has perhaps reached the height of the Mediterranean art. See how useless the little handles at the sides are, note that the neck has grown so thick that it cannot be used to grip in one hand, note that by trying to taper the bottom overmuch a rounded almost pot belly is obtained and an added pan-cake base made necessary and see how the sharp edged lip-rim is nicked. Now compare the Chü-lü Hsien and Tz'u Chou vases which are like trim athletes and turn back to the other forms. The "wheat sheaf" and slender pear shaped bottles, the melon shaped jars and globular ones all have simplicity and firmness such as no Near Easterner or European can achieve. There was a self-discipline in the Chinese heart that tells its story here.

FIG. 376. Reddish brown jar treated all over with a white slip which is carved and filled with a grey slip under a transparent glaze. Walter Hochstadter claims this ware is made in Tan-yang yu in north western Honan near the Shansi border. Ht. 6″. Warren E. Cox Coll.

FIG. 377. Chü-lu Hsien vase of gray stoneware decorated with a white slip and finely crackled glaze turned cloudy brownish from the inundation in 1108 before which it was made. Ht. 7½″. Warren E. Cox Coll.

FIG. 378. Vase of beautiful form and having spirited bamboo design. The body is buff stoneware, the slip and glaze are cream in color and the decoration is in a warm grey almost black. Tz'u chou Sung. Ht. 15¾″. Warren E. Cox Coll.

FIG. 380. Fine simple forms with beautiful tints to the glazes. Note the delicately formed full throat of the bottle, the sturdy quality of the "wheat sheaf" vase. Hts. 8″ and 9″. Warren E. Cox Coll.

Apulian amphora (see text, p. 202).

FIG. 379. Late Sung ware made at Yu chou in central Honan. Body is of thickly potted gray stoneware not unlike that of some Chün types, covered with white slip and creamy glaze inclined to show faint greenish yellow, and crackle where it runs thick. Ht. 8¾″. Ex Samuel T. Peters Coll. Warren E. Cox Coll. Baron C. G. von Seidlitz Coll.

Finally the superb example of both useful and decorative form is again developed from the amphora in the example shown which I recently acquired from the Peters collection. This piece was made at Yu Chou, where the Chün wares were made. It has a similar hard, grey stoneware body but is covered with a white slip and thick, glossy, creamy glaze which turns yellowish and crackles where it runs thick. This ware is very rare and always beautiful in form.

The painting on these vases is truly like shadows cast across them and adds to the meaning of the forms, becoming an integral part of them. The old saying was that a leaf touched with the brush twice dies, and the Chinese brush has, therefore, to be large enough to carry all the pigment necessary for one stroke however long it may be. The brushes are not trimmed but made rather of tapered hair of mink, sable, mouse whiskers and such. Mr. L. Y. Lee

FIG. 381. A beautiful example of Sung Tz'u Chou yao with white flower on one side and dark on the other. The wide band about the shoulder is vigorous and interesting. It is all painted in brown under a glossy glaze. Ht. 13¾". Warren E. Cox Coll.

has told me that children are made to practice painting and writing with the water cup balanced on the quarter inch end of the bamboo handle, the brush perfectly perpendicular. Thus a spiral can begin thin and end up wide, or it can begin wide and taper. Thus a leaf can be made in any given direction and a swift writing of the design becomes possible. An ancient master is said to have condemned his student's work many times without seeming reason because in painting the long tapering lily leaf bent down toward the earth he had not put into it the upward pull of "sky longing" which all green things have. Old men are palsied and beginners need wrist rests but the artists held their brushes far up the handle and moved them freely. What a vehicle! Compared with this the violin bow resting upon the strings is a heavy and crude instrument. No effort was made here toward the careful and painstaking drawing in truest possible anatomy of cavorting or posed human figures with heads and shoulders bent over a vase form. Here instead is caught the fleeting mood, the instant beauty of the still, full blown lotus flower lifting proudly to the heavens, of the fragile willow and bamboo bent before the wind, of the instantaneous flash of the wings of a flying bird, of a child playing with a kite, of an old man observing the flight of a bat the symbol of happiness, of the twitch of a rabbit's nose or of the forgetful pause of a rambling professor. Here we have dragons and waves that thunder, and peace, and the observance of a single leaf. The artist is exuberant and in love with the world about him.

Fig. 382. Sung period Tz'u Chou vase of typical buff grey stoneware covered with white slip down to within about an inch from base, painted with black which is freely handled and scratched out for the veins in the leaves at shoulder, and then covered with a straw colored transparent glaze. Ht. 11¼". Formerly Mrs. Charles Porter Wilson Coll. now the Warren E. Cox Coll.

Fig. 383. Tz'u Chou small jar with neck cut but showing a humorous and life-like painting of a rabbit, a crane and a "happy boy" in three medallions about the body and a beautiful floral band about the top. Ht. 6". Sung period. Warren E. Cox Coll.

Fig. 384. Sung Tz'u Chou bowl of buff grey ware covered with white slip and transparent glaze allowed to run down unevenly on the outside. Beautifully painted picture of a philosopher observing the flight of a bat, the emblem of happiness, and holding a book in his hand. Dia. 6". Mrs. Charles Porter Wilson.

Fig. 385. Tz'u Chou type jar with buff stoneware body, white slip and transparent glaze, of rare molded type, having four heads about the shoulder. The eyes and cheeks are touched with brown accents. Ht. 6". Sung period. L. G. Sheafer Coll. Formerly Warren E. Cox.

Fig. 386. Tz'u Chou jar showing two medallions with sages and one with a black flower. Note the half forgetful pose of the sage and conventionalization of verdure, clouds and rocks. Ht. 12". Warren E. Cox Coll.

Fig. 387. Tz'u Chou Sung Dynasty water vessel for a writer's table. Buff ware with white slip and transparent, glossy, crackled glaze decorated on slip with black and tan painting of great charm. Ht. 3¾". Warren E. Cox Coll.

Fig. 388. Amusing pillow said to have come from Chü-lü Hsien with design of a baby and duckling. Length about 10". Nasli Heeramaneck Coll.

Fig. 389. Tz'u Chou pillow of the Sung period humorously showing a boy riding a bamboo hobby horse. The painting is black on cream. Length about 10". Nasli Heeramaneck Coll.

205

Fig. 390. Small figure of a child showing an almost Disney-like humor. Length 2¼". Warren E. Cox Coll.
Fig. 391. Small dog probably made in northern Honan. Buff ware with light greenish brown glaze. Length 1⅜". Warren E. Cox Coll.
Fig. 392. Tz'u Chou pillow with writing meaning, "Wise men agree that when you have nothing to do go early to bed." The color is soft cream and the writing in brown. Length 9¾". Warren E. Cox Coll.

Humor is not lacking. I illustrate a few examples, the philosopher and the rabbit, a jar with jolly masks that peer out between flowers arranged in it, a Walt Disney child on hands and knees, a most sensitive and bashful soul with his umbrella over his shoulder, a yellow pup of "coon-dog" indeterminate breed with ribs showing and a playful and expectant flap of the ears and finally a small horse that is everything that a T'ang horse is not, being large of head and small of rump, narrow of chest, fat of belly and short of leg. Certainly no artist could better poke fun at the great T'ang animals! The superb bowl showing a philosopher's studies interrupted by a bat (fu) symbol of happiness, and the babies on the pillows and vase, playing horse, posing with a fat duck and flying a kite are other unmistakable examples of light humor.

THREE COLOR TZ'U CHOU WARES

Toward the end of the Sung period and into the early Ming these figures were made of a grey clay covered with the usual white slip and transparent somewhat glossy glaze. Black outlines of the details were painted underglaze and often also overglaze on the faces particularly. Bowls and dishes usually have no outlines or if they do, they are in the iron red. The bowls are usually of buff rather than grey ware. This pigment red which is nothing but ground up iron oxide or more properly hydro ferrous oxide 2 Fe_2O_3 3 H_2O (rust) was applied to the glaze and after firing became ferric oxide Fe_2O_3 the brown of the one being changed to the red of the other, by driving out the water in the heat of the kiln. It had been used a little in T'ang times or earlier but here it appears for the first time on a glaze. The potters did not succeed in fixing it perfectly at first and we frequently find it partly rubbed off but shortly they learned to handle it better. Added to the old green and yellow or amber of the T'ang glazes now used as enamels on the cream glaze it became a new medium of overglaze decoration very rarely applied to vases and usually seen on small bowls and figures.

Of the figures the *Liang ch'i man chih* of the early 13th century says, "In Kung Hsien (in the Honan Fu) there are porcelain (tz'ŭ) images called by

Late Sung incense burner of buff stoneware covered with creamy slip and transparent glaze and decorated in yellow, green, brown (outlines) and pale iron-red. Largest and finest specimen of this ware I know. Ht. 7¼". Ex Warren E. Cox Coll. Mr. Delos Chappell.

A boy with portrait-like quality, of rare "Three color" Sung Tz'u Chou ware with yellow, green and iron red decoration. Ht. 5¾". Warren E. Cox Coll.

Two Tz'u Chou figures possibly made at different kilns but both of Sung period and showing masterful characterization of both dog and gentleman. Ht. 8". Warren E. Cox Coll. Yamanaka & Co.

Two figures with yellow and green enamel and iron red decorations. The little lady has much the same expression as has the Metropolitan Mus. one and the man a most polite and unctuous look. Hts. 7" and 7¼". Ralph M. Chait Coll.

Figure of grey clay covered with white slip and painted with iron red, green enamel and black. Ht. c. 6". Metropolitan Mus. of Art.

Small horse, the opposite in all features of the great Bactrian or Near Eastern breeds so celebrated by T'ang potters. Animals in this ware are rare and humor of this makes it a valuable example. Ht. 4". Mrs. Warren E. Cox.

T'ZU CHOU "THREE COLORED" FIGURES OF LATE SUNG PERIOD

PLATE 63

the name of Lu Hung-chien. If you buy ten tea vessels you can take one image. Hung-chien was a trader who dealt in tea—unprofitably, for he could not refrain from brewing his stock. Hung-chien formerly was very fond of tea, and it brought him to ruin." This is Hobson's translation and he adds, "Possibly the images of Hung-chien, which were given away with tea vessels, were made at Tz'u Chou or Hsü Chou." I do not place entire confidence in this, our only report of the times and it occurs to me that again the meaning might have been that, if you were collecting you might find ten vessels to one figure. The proportion is even greater today.

Left: Three bowls of late Sung period Tz'u Chou. Buff body covered on the inside and down to near bottom with white slip and transparent finely crackled glaze. Decorated with low fired iron red and green and yellow enamels. Note that red is considerably worn as usual. Dias. 6¼″ and 6″. John Platt–Warren E. Cox Coll.

Right: Sung period Tz'u Chou bowl of "three color" type but having deeper and stronger red and more sophisticated design. Dia. 7″. Warren E. Cox Coll.

Tz'u Chou type bowl with grey-buff stoneware body, white slip and creamy transparent glaze decorated with iron red, green and yellow enamel. Red is of a deep color which would indicate this bowl is of Ming, rather than Sung period. Dia. 3½″. Seattle Art Mus.

T'ZU CHOU "THREE COLOR" BOWLS OF LATE SUNG AND MING DYNASTIES

PLATE 64

Another late Sung technique for vases was the application of actual leaves to the body after which the piece was dipped in slip, the leaves plucked off so that the body was exposed where they had been and then as usual glazed and fired. Hobson calls one of these in the Eumorfopoulos Collection Ming with a question mark and it is a rather heavy and clumsy one. However, the typical grey stoneware body and all other characteristics of the one illus-

FIG. 393. Figures of Tz'u Chou type with muddy yellow and green enamels and iron red decoration on cream glaze. These figures rare and almost never unbroken. Made in molds and show some decadent features but are amusing and portrait-like character studies. 6″ to 10″. Late Sung. Miss Ethelyn McKinney the smaller and center figures and Mrs. L. G. Sheafer the standing dignitary. Ex Warren E. Cox Coll.

FIG. 394. Tz'u Chou figure of rare "three color" type. Buff and slightly gritty ware, covered with white slip and transparent glaze minutely crackled and decorated with iron red and yellow, green and black enamels. Sung. Ht. c. 10″. Gift of Mrs. Samuel T. Peters. Metropolitan Mus. of Art.

trated have convinced me that it is Sung. The tall and very beautiful vase is made in the same manner but cut-out patterns, perhaps of paper, have been used instead of the leaves. When the leaf or pattern is plucked up it causes the edge of the slip to come up slightly to a sharp edge quite different from that of an incised pattern. It should be noted how beautifully the potter of the tall vase has used his various bands of biscuit, biscuit with glaze, drips of slip, a plain band of slip and glaze and then the two with pattern.

Besides the lustrous brown wares or Tsung Sê tz'ŭ, as we have decided to call them, are certain ones which combine this glaze with the Tz'u Chou technique. Fairly frequently we see tea-bowls with a dull mat brown set off by a white slip and glazed edge. The beautiful bowl from Mrs. Charles Porter Wilson's collection has the outside in dull brown glaze as has also the brush holder shown. Both of these are of buff ware the holder being lighter,

FIG. 395. Vase of smooth grey stoneware covered with white slip which has been dipped over leaves stuck on the surface and then plucked off. Vase then glazed with transparent glaze showing yellowish and lavender tinted stains and fine crackle where thick. Sung. Ht. 8". Warren E. Cox Coll.

FIG. 396. Brush holder of Tz'u Chou type ware. Brown glaze at foot. Slip and brown painted treatment on upper part. Body of rough, buff stoneware. Sung. Ht. 10". Warren E. Cox Coll.

FIG. 397. Tz'u Chou type vase with design made by using paper cutouts. Smooth grey stoneware body. Slip and glaze have pinkish brown stains particularly in central band. Late Sung to Early Ming. Ht. 13¾". Warren E. Cox Coll.

and possibly of Ming date though the bowl has painting in perfect Sung taste.

Finally on Plate 58 I am able to show two unique and wonderful examples of Tz'u Chou type ware. One is a small jar with free, beautiful, feathery foliage design and about the shoulder an inscription reading in a clockwise direction, "Great Sung Kia T'ai three made," and as Kia T'ai ascended the throne in 1201, probably indicates the year 1203. According to Sir Percival David's theory this should indicate a Chinese workman as the Mongol or Tartars begin their writing in the upper left hand corner and write downwards in columns moving toward the right while the Chinese begin in the upper right, moving downwards and toward the left. Therefore, it is likely that this piece was not made in the north, which at the time was in the hands of the Nuchih Tartars, but perhaps near Hang Chou and for imperial use. Certainly this is one of the earliest *nien hao* marks known, and I am delighted that the piece has passed from my hands to the Metropolitan Museum of Art.

The other example is a globular wine jar of nearly 15 inches in height and able to contain some three and a half gallons. At first glance it may appear a clumsy shape necessitating two hands to lift it but it is a well known Chinese shape often seen in Tsung Sê and Tz'u Chou wares in various sizes. The everted lip-rim is, of course, designed so that a leather or cloth cover can readily be tied on, but why the shape? I am proud to say that it occurred to me and I have seen no reason given for it elsewhere: —Such a jar can be rolled over easily, though very heavy even when partly filled, and one can pour into a small cup from it while it would be almost impossible to *lift* a pot containing three gallons and pour steadily from it. Hence we find once again the practical good sense behind the Chinese pottery forms.

The jar is of yellow-buff stoneware, covered with a white slip on which the design is painted in brown and over which there is a thin, yellowish glaze showing no tendency to crackle. I think it likely to have been made in some southern Sung kiln not yet located as I guess the other small jar (see above) to have been, though Walter Hochstadter is of the opinion that this type of globular jar comes from Shansi. The potter used his thumb to finish the inside of the foot-rim and the whole has a sturdy handmade look about it. Around the shoulder is a beautifully designed lotus border about four inches in width and the whole remainder of the body is covered with the characters of a poem which, through the kind labors of Mr. Nai-Chi Chang and finally of Mr. C. F. Yau together with Mr. Hsuge K. Pao, was translated into English form. It is entitled a

FIG. 398. Sung period bowl of Tz'u Chou type. Rounded form with cylindrical foot and wide, perpendicular slightly concave rim treated with white slip and transparent glaze inside and brown "tea dust" type glaze outside unevenly applied below rim. Body is buff and sandy. Brushed design inside of brown-black and swiftly executed with a whirling feeling. Dia. 7". Mrs. Charles Porter Wilson.

"Chiang Ch'eng Tzu," or "Flute Lyric" which Mr. Chang explains was a form composed to be sung or chanted to the accompaniment of a flute as certain Greek poems were composed for lyre music, but Mr. Yau also says it may have been the poetic name of the composer. Thus let us think of the following words as though associated with the cool, wavering notes of the Chinese flute:

CHIANG CH'ENG TZU
(A Flute Lyric)

Despite the cold, she eagerly seeks the prunus blossom amid the snow.
Still she ponders—
From whence comes the subtile fragrance?
But soon the wafting perfume guides her to the blooming branch beyond the
    Bamboo Grove
And here she meditates in the chilly twilight, until the moon arises
Casting its varied shadows
Around the Tower of the Winds (Feng T'ai).
With slender fingers she breaks the jade-like blossom and brings it home
Where its enchanting fragrance permeates the draperies and screens
Reminding her that Spring is now returning.
She sways with the rhythm of the flute coming from the tower top
And all is tranquil.
Ever we cherish this sweet isolation that induces our poetry to song.
Shall we linger a moment longer?
Then let us partake of the golden cup.

The beauty of the Tz'u Chou type pottery is, therefore, not only compounded of the beauty of fine forms, of rich and lovely textures and subtilely thrilling colors; of the superbly masterful painting but also of words. Is it any wonder that the Chinese for ages have loved it and can I be blamed for ranking it among the highest arts of the life of mankind? Greatest of the ceramic arts it stands alone.

SUNG BLUE AND WHITE WARES

Generally speaking it is agreed that blue and white wares did not originate until the end of the Sung or beginning of the Yüan period and even this is doubtful so far as records go being based on a vague reference in the T'ao lu, and yet some pieces are so nearly Sung in taste that we are inclined to believe that it will eventually be proven the underglaze blue painting was attempted by some of the Sung factories. I submit two bowls, one of a buff ware with creamy crackled glaze stained café au lait and under which there is a soft lavender grey blue design of conventionalized flower and foliage scrolls. The one side of this bowl has been fired brown and the blue has disappeared. The other small bowl is of a white porcelaneous ware covered with a sort of bismuth-paste white glaze also slightly café inside and decorated with an underglaze blackish lavender blue with very smart bird and flower design. There is a floral medallion inside and a character (undistinguishable) under the bottom. These two last point to Ming characteristics but the handling of the blue seems to be experimental and not entirely satisfactory from a technical viewpoint. Both of these look life early experiments in underglaze blue decoration

FIG. 399. Possibly late Sung bowl with decoration in impure blue. Dia. 4″. Mr. B. d'Ancona.

FIG. 400. Bowl with buff body and white slip decorated in greyish-lavender-blue under greenish-white crackled glaze burnt brown on one side. Probably late Sung. Dia. 5¾″. John Platt–Warren E. Cox Coll.

and may possibly be Sung. Finally a dated ewer is again not clear to the naked eye but may give us evidence under ultra-violet examination. (See the illustration.)

KWANGTUNG SUNG WARE

At the ancient kilns in Kwangtung province, south China, there were made wares far thinner than the usual Yüan and Ming or later types and with even more beautiful, softly blended glazes. These are undoubtedly Sung. Mr. Hochstadter says that all of these have light bodies and that later wares have dark bodies or are more coarse in potting. Of course some Chün and "Celadon" copies are early but most are of 18th century or later.

FIG. 401. Pilgrim bottle of Kwangtung ware, hard brown and thin, covered with café-au-lait glaze streaked with brown and blue in beautiful tones. Sung. Ht. 8″. Mr. B. d'Ancona.

CHAPTER XI

KOREAN POTTERIES AND PORCELAINS

THE influences of Sung China naturally spread also to Korea. The love of nature expressed by the Zen Buddhists and Taoists, the well digested Hellenistic forms from India and the wonderful craftsmanship of the Sung artists were bound to have their effect.

We know little more about Korean history than that it was a chaotic land beset by Tartar hordes to the north and island invaders from the east. About the middle of Han times there were the "Three Kingdoms":—1.—The Shiragi

FIG. 403. Silla dynasty (A.D. 632–936) Korean jar and cover turned on wheel and decorated with stamped design. Handle stuck on. Mr. Hobson gives this type dating of 9th cent., while the type following early Japanese potteries he calls 5th cent. Slate gray. Ht. 7½". Freer Gallery of Art, Washington.

FIG. 402. Silla cooking bowl with hollow foot and pierced outer frame holding it at rim. Ware is gray with thin brownish primitive glaze. Ht. 4". Warren E. Cox Coll.

(Japanese) or Silla (Chinese) in the south founded about 57 B.C., 2.—The Kokuri or Koriö (Jap.) or Kao-li (Chin.) in the center c. 37 B.C. and 3—The Kudara (Jap.) or Po-chi (Chin.) in the north c. 18 B.C. They continued until about A.D. 632 or the beginning of T'ang China in A.D. 618 when the southern dynasty, the Silla gained dominance.

The monk Shuntao (Jap.) or Tat'ung (Chin.) is supposed to have come in 372 from China to the Kokuri court and it was the old story of missionary followed by soldier, followed by tax collector and in time by the artist, and great artists must have come for the great bronzes and frescoes are of very high art, the latter being as fine as those of Ellora and Ajunta caves in India. Much of the sculpture is also great. Then in T'ang times the calendar, many laws, clothes and customs were of T'ang taste. This Silla dynasty lasted from A.D. 632 to 936 although the Korai had already taken hold in the north in A.D. 918.

The Silla pottery does not compare with T'ang wares probably because potters are craftsmen at heart and it takes time to have them settle and to translate the beauties about them. The single sculptor or painter may do

214

several works of art and the critics call it a great era of art. Pottery more closely expresses what *all* the people know and feel. In any event the ware was unglazed or had a colorless glaze that appeared to emanate from the body itself. It was of reddish or grey tones. The wheel had been introduced and pieces found at Taiku and Fusan in the extreme south are like those in tombs in Japan. The subtility of line was not entirely missing and for decoration there was reticulation, incising, stamped designs and very occasional pinched-up technique. Tiles and architectural grotesques were made and some have a green Han type glaze.

The Korai period started between (A.D. 918 and 946 as one counts the conquest and lasted until A.D. 1392 or into the beginning of Ming times, roughly paralleling the Sung period. The capital was at Song-do and the country took its present name of Korea. We hear that late in the 11th century the courts interchanged ambassadors after the Sungs had saved the Koreans from Khitan

FIG. 404. Silla dynasty pottery bowl and cover called "sacrificial vessel" by museum. Gray clay partly incised, partly stamped with pattern of various bands arranged horizontally. Ht. 8¾". Freer Gallery of Art, Washington.

Tartar invasion in 1016 and there was peace for about 200 years until at the end of the 12th century the Mongols invaded and the king fled to an island called Kokwato in 1232.

Most Korean wares are found in tombs rather than at kiln sites and were not "Imperial wares" in any sense so they were not very much affected but by 1280 the Chinese government fell and then Korea simply became a vassal state to Khublai Khan and finally was invaded and sacked by the Japanese who had never been invaded by the Mongols. Thus we visualize a very unhappy time for artists.

The Yi or Ri dynasty was started by Yi Taijo or Litan in 1392 and paid homage to the Ming emperors again for a few hundred years of comparative peace but in 1592 Hideyoshi started his "conquest of the world," by sending 300,000 troops to Korea. China aided the Koreans with 60,000 men and there were six years of strife. The capital which had been moved to Seoul was raided and art and artists were carried off to Japan. In 1598 Hideyoshi died but Korea never recovered from the hate of the islanders. This country has ever been between the devil (the Tartars) and the deep blue sea (the Japs). Undoubtedly its present capital "Chōsen" meaning "Morning Calm" is now filled with boiling hate and takes joy in the war between her ancient enemies. Yet strange are the ways of this world, for it was through Korea that Japan was brought Buddhism, that religion which has meant so much in peace and beauty.

The Korean wares are found (what the Japs have left) in Kaijo, on the island of Kowato, Keisho, Zenra, Chūsei and rarely in the district of Kōkai, in Kōgen, Kanyakō and Heian. Many other objects were placed in the tombs such as jewels, seals, ewers of metal, bronze mirrors, knives, boxes, glass beads, hawk bells and other valuable or useful things. The *Ko ku yao lun* says of Korean ware, "It is of pale green color and resembles Lung Ch'üan ware. Some are covered with white sprays of flowers, but this kind is not worth much money." This is, of course, either ignorance or a bit of local bias, for the wares are most economically decorated and not "covered" with flowers and the quality was high. Other authorities compared it more favorably with Yüeh yao, Pai ting yao, and even Ju yao and Pi-se yao. But here we do not have to rely so much on the Chinese writings.

My good friend and fellow collector, the late John Platt, many of whose things I now have to sell after they spent some fifteen years on loan at the Metropolitan Museum, wrote in the Burlington Magazine in 1912, "We may infer that the perfectly formed specimens, with thin body and uniform glaze, of the color of Ju-Chou porcelain, were in all probability made about 1100 A.D.; the heavier undecorated pieces with fine, soft, wax-like glaze and thick tomb oxidation being of earlier date."

He continues, "Our study of a great number of specimens leads to the assumption that the earliest Korean porcelain was undecorated, and that it had a hard grey proto-porcelain body, which invariably showed the iron color where exposed to the heat of the kiln and not covered with the glaze. The glaze was of a very soft uncrackled texture, the best color being either green or blue, both of them generally merging into a soft grey.

"There is also evidence that the pieces of a single color, with engraved scroll work and modelling in low relief, were of an early date, having been made before A.D. 1125.

"But by far the greatest number of pieces taken from the tombs has 'mishima' decorations and is of varying thickness and quality. Most of these wares were undoubtedly made between the years A.D. 1100 and 1392; the heavier ones with harder and more glass-like glaze being made probably between the years 1250 and 1392, as during this period the art was said to be on the decline."

The word "Mishima" is a Japanese term said to have derived from the semblance of the designs to the columns of characters in an almanac compiled in Mishima a town in Japan, or from the small islands called Mi shima (Three islands) now Koybunto which had a harbor at which ships may have stopped between Japan and Korea. Mr. Platt was speaking only of the celadon wares and not the white and other types found, of course.

Dr. Nakao has drawn up a similar outline of the wares and it may be well to compare them:

1.—Heavy undecorated wax-like glazed wares showing oxidation. Platt says before 1100. Dr. Nakao does not distinguish them.

2.—Thin well made wares with carved decoration only and "Ju-Chou glaze" no crackle and apt to lose shape in firing. Platt says about 1100 and modeled ones before 1125. Dr. Nakao says from 1050 to 1170 and the BEST PERIOD.

Left: Excellent example of earliest type of Korai pottery. Well potted, decorated with vigorous carved lotus petal design on outside. Glaze blue gray green and has only few lines of wandering crazing. Dia. 6¾″. John Platt–Warren E. Cox Coll.

Center: Bowl of olive green color with well designed but ornate "mishima" decoration and crudely made foot showing four sand supports. Dia. 6½″. John Platt–Warren E. Cox Coll.

Right: Large fish bowl probably of 2nd period or c. 1200 of Korai era. Fired evidently with circular support like some Ming period celadons of Chinese, rather than usual three spurs. Dia. 10¼″. John Platt–Warren E. Cox Coll.

Left: Fine simple bowl of first and best period according to Dr. Nakao dating between about A.D. 1050 and 1170. Gray-white clay which turns brown where exposed and glaze is thin bluish gray green uncrackled. Slight radial lines on outside and indentations at lip with delicate line incised around about ¾″ below lip inside. Dia. 8¼″. John Platt–Warren E. Cox Coll.

Center: Bowl with tasteful "mishima" design and partly green, partly olive glaze, fairly thin and well potted, dating c. 1280. Dia. 7½″. John Platt–Warren E. Cox Coll.

Right: Bowl probably dating c. 1300 or in the 3rd period of Dr. Nakao (A.D. 1274–1350) or our period of 1250–1392. No spur marks and rough foot-rim. Dia. 7½″. John Platt–Warren E. Cox Coll.

KORAI BOWLS OF THE FIVE PERIODS

PLATE 65

Rare stem-cup of 3rd Korai period or later with fair potting and well designed all-over inlayed pattern. At least as early as Sung Dynasty Ting ware. Ht. 3½". John Platt–Warren E. Cox Coll.

(c)

Korai cup and saucer of c. 1250 or earlier with inlayed flowers in white and black under transparent crackled glaze. The repair at the lip is of gold lacquer done in Japan. Potting not so fine as cup with incised decoration only. Dia. of saucer 6¼". John Platt–Warren E. Cox Coll.

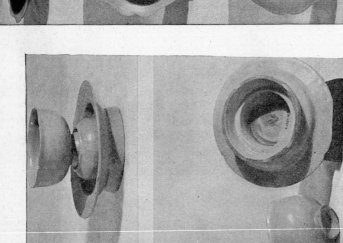

(b)

(a)

KORAI CUPS AND CUP STANDS

PLATE 66

(a) Finest wine cup I have seen of Korean ware of early Korai period. Delicately potted and has wax-like gray green glaze. Delicately incised flowers in six sections of outside of cup and on rim of saucer with inverted lotus petals also on saucer base. Dia. 6". John Platt–Warren E. Cox Coll.

(b) Cup with stand attached dating between c. 1050 and 1170 according to Dr. Nakao. Grayish white ware with glossy blue gray green glaze. Foot with covered rim and four spur marks would almost certainly designate this piece as Korean. Beautifully incised. Edges cut to form six-petal flower pattern. Dia. 5¾". John Platt–Warren E. Cox Coll.

(c) Cup and saucer of crude, thick potting. Inlayed and incised decoration. c. 1300 or Dr. Nakao's 3rd period. (A.D. 1274–1350). Ht. 5". John Platt–Warren E. Cox Coll.

Left: Wine pot of sturdy form with fine pouring spout and handle which fits hand. Covered with smooth gray green glaze having little crazing which was unintentional. Agrees in quality with those of Dr. Nakao's first period of about 1050 to 1170. Ht. 9½". Warren E. Cox Coll.
Right: Excellent specimen of gourd shaped ewer with twisted handle and slight incised design. c. 1200 or earlier. Ht. 14". Freer Gallery of Art, Washington.

Wine ewer of interesting form indicating turtle on lotus blossom, with dragon head. Twisted rope-like handle. Between 1250 and 1392, that is Yuan to Early Ming. Mus. of Fine Arts, Boston.

Wine ewer with ornately modeled cover finial and some inlay. Glassy glaze and heavy, insecure potting place. c. 1250 to 1392. Ht. 9". Metropolitan Mus. of Art.

KORAI EWERS

PLATE 67

Korai period, made c. 1280 to 1300, inlayed or "Mishima" set of boxes for the toilet or for condiments. This is the only complete one I know. Dia. 7⅝". The Cleveland Mus. of Art.

KORAI SET OF BOXES

PLATE 68

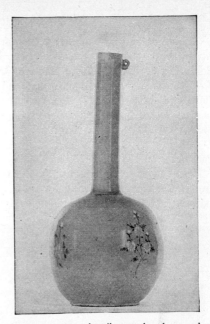

Left: Bottle with usual hexagonal tall neck and loop near top, heavily potted and covered with rich crackled blue gray green glaze. Early Korai. Ht. 13½". Warren E. Cox Coll.
Right: Heavily potted bottle with incised and also inlayed design called by Japanese "mishima" and usual loop near top perhaps for securing a stopper which is missing. c. between 1200 and 1250. Ht. about 13¼". Freer Gallery of Art, Washington.

Korai period bottle dating between 1280 and 1300 with "mishima" in-layed decoration. Ht. about 13". Mus. of Fine Arts, Boston.

Unique bottle with "mishima" design and reticulated body having rich crackled glaze somewhat thicker than usual. According to Dr. Nakao, not later than c. 1300. Only pieces in China with such carved bodies are of Ming pe-riod, 1368–1644. Per-haps special technique originated in Korea. Ht. 10½". Warren E. Cox Coll.

KORAI BOTTLES

PLATE 69

3.—Thinnest and best quality "Mishima" type wares without crowded decoration. Platt says 1100 to 1392. Dr. Nakao says "First inlays," stamping molding, etc. and tribute to Emperor between 1170 and 1274.

4.—Heavier wares with more crowded inlays and glaze "like glass." Mr. Platt says 1250 to 1392. Dr. Nakao says that the Tz'u Chou types, with painted design in underglaze black and often coarse, were between 1274 and 1350.

5.—Finally Dr. Nakao says that inferior, dull and cement-like brown wares were between 1350 and 1392.

It will be seen that essentially the two are in entire agreement Mr. Platt, probably correctly, allowing for a bit more overlapping of types. With this material in hand it is not difficult to date our specimens fairly accurately but

Early (1st period) Korai vase dating according to Dr. Nakao between A.D. 1050 and 1100. Thin gray-white ware with bluish gray green glaze uncrackled because thinly applied. Ht. c. 12½". Metropolitan Mus. of Art.	Graceful typical-shaped gallipot of light gray green with "mishima" decoration and dating c. 1280 or earlier. Ht. 11½". John Platt–Warren E. Cox Coll.	Large "mishima" decorated jar dating c. 1300 and showing both combed incising (around shoulder) and free hand incising filled with white slip and covered with transparent green glaze over brown body. Ht. 15". Warren E. Cox Coll.

Right: Two gallipots labeled 15th to 16th cent. in museum but probably better allocated in latter part of 13th cent., one without inlay or "mishima" decoration perhaps being a little earlier. Hts. about 12". Metropolitan Mus. of Art.

Two bottles, one of early Korai period c. 1100 (with cup mouth) and other of last part of period, according to Dr. Nakao, 1350 to 1392. Hts. 8¼" and 9½". Warren E. Cox Coll. and John Platt–Warren E. Cox Coll.

KORAI VASES

PLATE 70

when it comes to making clear distinctions between the places of manufacture we are met with an unsolved problem and, in fact, several wares are likely to have been made almost alike in China and Korea.

Mr. Bernard Rackham in his catalogue of the Le Blond Collection in the Victoria and Albert Museum (1918) makes three divisions:—1.—Wares undoubtedly made in Korea, 2.—Wares probably Chinese imports, 3.—Wares which we are sure are Chinese.

In the first category Mr. Rackham places:

1.—Pure white porcelain with translucent body of granular fracture; soft translucent, readily scratched bluish or aquamarine tinged glaze full of tiny bubbles; crackled exceptionally and occasionally showing slight brownish tone where body is exposed. In the form of small boxes, flat dishes, cups and other small objects, these pieces have incised foliage, combing, pressing and modeled slip or relief from mold. One small box in the collection has the name Ch'ên Shih-i, in relief on the bottom. As it was in the mold we may infer that it is the maker's name. It is the only possibly signed piece we know.

Another group of small objects are of the same glaze but coarser in body and with sandy bottoms. These are said to be toys but I am wary of the toy theory unless it includes toys for grownups. There are so many other reasons for making miniatures other than the fitting of the hand of a child, such as the making of small testers and the universal novelty appeal of "cute little things." This is another of our appeals which artists should take account of in passing.

Another class similar to these two is probably later and with greyish glaze and even coarser body.

All of these are more vitreous than

FIG. 405. 1st period (according to Dr. Nakao) dish of gray white ware with bluish gray green glaze with slight tendency to crackle in one place, having the thin covered foot rim and three spur marks. Dia. 7". Ex Warren E. Cox Coll. N. M. Heeramaneck.

Ting yao and more closely associated with the "Ying ching" or "Ju types."

2.—Porcelaneous celadons with hard, dense body having a slightly violet tinge and burnt reddish brown where exposed; covered with a thick semi-transparent greyish-greenish-bluish glaze varying in translucency and resembling jade in texture. This ware varies to grey and greenish-brown and has a soft satiny feeling. The bases are covered with glaze, even the foot rims, and show three clean spur marks rather than three piles of sand as do the coarser

FIG. 406. Cup with handles of crude
Ting yao imitation, heavily potted and
having imperfect and glassy glaze.
Ricio or Yi period (1392–1910) probably made in the late 17th cent. Dia.
4½″. Metropolitan Mus. of Art.

FIG. 407. Korai vase of white porcelain with glassy glaze quite different
from its T'ang prototype. Ht. 5⅛″.
Metropolitan Mus. of Art.

wares. Mr. Rackham does not mention crackle but the examples he shows all have a transparent crackle of "ice type" while only a few in the Platt-Cox collection are without it. Note should be made that the heavier type has usually a more translucent glaze while the slightly later very thin type rival-ing Ting yao in weight has a more satiny glaze, applied thinner and usually without crackle. The two finest examples I know of this ware are shown, the bowl of Ting-like form, the cup and saucer. (Pl. 66a & Pl. 65, lower left.) Mrs. Langdon Warner states, "Korean pottery glaze is watery, transparent, vitreous, seldom greasy, and though brilliant in color is neither opaque nor jade-like." Perhaps she had not seen this type for they are undisputably Korean, not watery, not vitreous nor transparent in glaze and not brilliant in color though they are distinctly soft and jade-like.

Mrs. Warner moreover states, "The collector who enters the field today must content himself with mediocre examples or else pay exorbitantly for the occasional good piece that is offered for sale." I have heard from the Warners that they bought a number of pieces "for a song in Korea," but in general these best pieces bring no more than comparative Ting examples and about as many hundreds as Chün wares bring in thousands. Therefore the collector should not be discouraged.

Our illustrations will speak for the subtile and lovely shapes of the refined wares. A characteristic which the bowls share with Ting ones is the very slight indentation of the edge dividing it into six sections which are further set off by very slightly indented lines from the outside making a floral form. Melon shaped gallipots have a cup shaped lip-rim of modified T'ang form. Pear shaped bottles are slender and graceful and a distinctive type has a globular body and tall slender neck of hexagonal tubular form. Ewers express Near Eastern forms in metal but are well modified to suit pottery technique. Bottles with spouts at top and small open mouthed spouts at the side for filling are after bronze forms said to have been ritualistic but originated for quite practical drinking without touching the vessel to one's lips.

Small ewers of melon form are typical and of them Mr. Rackham says, "By a strange singularity, tea-drinking, though practiced from early times in China and Japan, was unknown in ancient Corea; the vessels which might

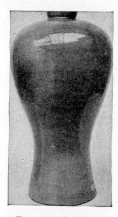

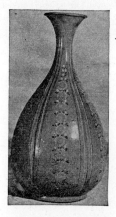

Fig. 408. Gallipot with incised design and gray green crackled glaze quite similar to the one in the Eumorfopoulos Coll. which Mr. Hobson dates about 1200 or in Dr. Nakao's 2nd period. Metropolitan Mus. of Art.

Fig. 409. Graceful bottle, notable for the adaptation by the Koreans of the delicate floral design alternating with grooves and lines setting them off. 3rd Dr. Nakao period and may be dated about 1280 to 1300. Ht. 13″. Warren E. Cox Coll.

Fig. 410. Ewer of gourd shape with rather irregularly potted spout and handle. The cover and handle have small loops for attachment by a cord. The glaze is of light gray green and uncrazed. This is probably of the first period, dating about 1150, of the Korai times.

be mistaken for tea-pots were used for pouring out wine, and the small bowls and cups for drinking it." Emil Hannover, R. L. Hobson and S. C. Bosch Reitz seem to agree while Mrs. Warner says, "But the Koreans of the Korai period are known to have been great tea-drinkers, and it is safe to assume that many of these (referring to the ewers) are tea-pots. Bronze and stone tea-pots of the same period have been found." I have no doubt but that all

Fig. 411. Wine pot in the form of an eggplant which is a favorite one in Korea. This piece, which has been on loan at the Metropolitan Mus. of Art for many years, is full of simple charm. Ht. 6″. John Platt–Warren E. Cox Coll.

Fig. 412. Group of small flattened bottles probably used for oil or other precious lquids and dating around 1280 or in Dr. Nakao's tentative 3rd period. John Platt–Warren E. Cox Coll.

of these authorities have ample reason for such definite statements. We can only wish that they had given reasons and more definite evidence where such contradiction occurs. The .tall ewers are, of course, descendants of bronze forms of the Near East, but as to whether or not the melon shaped ones are is a question and I have never seen the stone ones mentioned. I see no reason why the melon and gourd shaped ones are not designed after the fruits and vegetables for the potters even went to the trouble to place a stem on the cover in many instances.

We have said that the Koreans were masters of carving and modeling but it is strangely true that when they attempted brush decorations they

FIG. 413. Mishima type ewer showing Western Asian influence. The design has been impressed with small tools and then inlayed a good deal as was done with the Henry II or "Orieon" ware of France. This piece was made about 1280 to 1300. Ht. 11″. (Spout repaired). Warren E. Cox Coll.

FIG. 414. A rather well painted Korai vase after the Tz'u Chou style and dating between 1300 and 1350. The glaze is greenish brown. Ht. 10½″. Warren E. Cox Coll.

FIG. 415. Late Korai period vase with decoration inspired by the Tz'u Chou Chinese type but losing all the spirit and beauty of the original brush work. The glaze is brownish green. Ht. 9¾″. Warren E. Cox Coll.

were clumsy. Perhaps this is because the painted wares were done in the decadent period toward the end of the Korai period, but it is often the case that good carvers and etchers are poor at handling the far more facile medium of the brush. This may be because they cannot lean on the brush and a better control of the nerves is necessary. Perhaps it is because of a different speed of thinking; the carvers being slower and more methodical. In any event the Koreans were great carvers and even when they wanted a painted effect they devised the means of getting it through carving known to the Japanese as "mishima." The technique is very simple and quite ancient for we find it practiced in neolithic times elsewhere but the Koreans brought it to a fine degree of perfection. It is simplicity itself for it consists of nothing more than incising the design with a sharp instrument and then, after the clay is dry and fairly hard, of rubbing into the incisions, white or black clay, over which the glaze is then applied. It is a sort of simple inlay and let me say here that it is not "inlayed jade" as some super salesmen have declared.

The designs consist chiefly of small well spaced floral sprays, flying birds among cloud scrolls and sometimes trees or grasses. A Near Eastern influence, due to the fact that the Northern Caravan Route terminated not far from where Korea joins the mainland, is sometimes prominent as in the beautiful tile from the Boston Museum laid out much as a Persian rug would be.

Ting yao was found in large quantities in Korea and although it has been stated that all of this ware was imported we are inclined to doubt it for there are also several Ting types not readily traceable to known Chinese sources and we do know that Chinese potters worked in Korea. The habits of a potter are hard to change. Mr. Rackham quotes Mr. Bosch Reitz, "The record of Hsü Ching, already cited, refers not only to green ware or celadon as being made in Korea, but also to bowls, cups, platters and other vessels, all closely copying the style and make of Ting ware." "This statement," says Mr. Rackham, "taken with the large quantities of white ware found, is good evidence in favor of a Korean manufacture, although it is not easy to differentiate the indigenous from the imported specimens." Many collectors are inclined to believe that any ware with a regular foot unglazed and well potted, instead of the usual foot on many of the celadon wares; shallow, glazed over and with three spur marks, cannot be Korean yet an examination of the fine little cup and saucer and of some of the bowls which have typical Korai celadon glaze of the best sort will show them to be comparable with many of the better Chinese wares.

FIG. 416. Inlayed plaque variously described as a "rug design to be shipped to the Near East to copy," a "writing board," etc., but showing certainly a strong Near Eastern influence. Length 12½". Ex John Platt–Warren E. Cox Coll. Boston Mus.

Moreover Ting technique has many things in common with Korai such as: 1.—the indentation of edges, 2.—the use of carved petals on the outside, 3.—incised and low relief molded design, 4.—the glazing of the foot-rim and 5.—the making of a very thin ware.

Much of the "Northern Sung celadon" in the form of bowls large and small with molded all-over floral design is also found in Korean tombs and it presents much the same problem. However, these are slowly being located in definite places in China and we can now definitely recognize the Yüeh, early Lung Ch'üan, and some of the Honan wares so that these are eliminated. It is also true that they do not so closely approximate the other Korean techniques of potting as do the Ting wares.

The marbled pottery wares with transparent glazes are recognized as T'ang Chinese and there are comparatively so few found in Korea that there is no doubt but that they are imported.

Some of the type of Tz'u Chou wares such as were found at Wei Hsien and attributed to Po Shan Hsien are undoubtedly of Shantung make and logically enough would be carried the short distance to Korea. The Japanese have called this ware "Yegōrai" meaning "painted Korean" but this was simply

Fig. 417. Bottle of the latter part of the Korai period made probably between 1350 and 1392 or in Dr. Nakao's last period. Ht. 11½″. Metropolitan Mus. of Art.

Fig. 418. Gourd shaped ewer of ornate and badly involved design with celadon glaze and red outlines to the petals. The conception of the frog for the loop on the handle is an amusing feature. Ht. 12″. Freer Gallery of Art, Washington.

Fig. 419. Very crudely potted and with a poor glaze, this vase dates in the Richo period, about the middle of the 18th cent. Ht. 11¾″. Metropolitan Mus. of Art.

because they had not traced them back to their place of manufacture much as we speak of "Coromandel screens" and as the Italians speak of "maiolica" or "Majorca pottery" simply because these things were shipped from those sources.

Nothing of importance was made after the first Japanese conquest. Some wares copied "Imari" such as was made at Arita in Hizen province, Japan.

Fig. 420. Korean bowl of the 17th cent. and seemingly somewhat influenced by some Japanese wares though not to be compared exactly with any of them. Dia. 6¾″. Metropolitan Mus. of Art.

Fig. 421. Drinking vessel similar to the earlier examples in general form but far more crudely potted and having a brown green glaze. Ht. 12″. John Platt– Warren E. Cox Coll.

Fig. 422. Jar with blue and red underglaze decoration made probably about 1700 to 1800. The ground color is pale greenish buff, the glaze glassy and crackled. Ht. 15″. Metropolitan Mus. of Art.

During the 17th and 18th centuries a coarse white porcelain of heavy appearance was made and sometimes painted in more or less spirited decorations of a dull underglaze blue of muddy and greenish tone. Some of this ware was influenced by late Ming characteristics. A dark underglaze brown developed into a rusty red and a fiery crimson. Overglaze colors particularly green enamel with underglaze blue and also rather poor copies of "five color" wares were made, and some reticulation but in bad taste was practiced.

Modern pottery in imitation of the old "mishima" ware was imported to America up to about fifteen years ago by The Japanese Fan Co. It began as crude but fairly tasteful and fairly close copies of the old but was soon "improved" by the addition of red blotches and then was discontinued.

CHAPTER XII

JAPANESE POTTERIES AND PORCELAINS

EVEN before the war there was a wide divergence of opinion in the West concerning Japan, her people and her art: some were enthusiastic while others find everything Japanese anathema. I recently talked with a lady of significant culture and she told me that she had always longed to live in Japan, but after she had seen the country and gone on to China she decided that she preferred the latter. "In spite of all the smells and dirt, there is something *real* about China," she said. That others have felt differently was proven by Fenellosa, Freer, Binyon and Havemeyer to mention only a few. Let us try to clear our minds of all prejudices concerning California, the Philippines and the war and remember that the artists are not like the business men, the soldiers or the politicians. Let us see what they have had to offer.

The earliest people on the islands were the Ainus who were not unlike European prehistoric people so far as we can determine by the shell mounds. These people were driven north by invasions of people from Korea, who may have originated in central Asia, and by the Polynesians. Even later invasions from Korea left records in the dolmens dating from about 300 B.C. to A.D. 700 where are found potteries not unlike that of the Silla period, not yet glazed but well modeled figures of men in armor, horses, boats, etc. all showing influences of China and Siberia. It was these invaders who brought the use of iron. These northern as well as the southern influences both came from the south simply because it is there that the Korean peninsula most closely approaches the islands. As could be expected this caused a confusion of influences and that confusion of traits which persists in all Japanese and can be seen clearly in their art.

Perhaps the dominant characteristic of Japanese art is the love of nature. No other people have been able to build their houses to blend so well with the landscape. No other people have written poetry which so expresses the moods of nature of the sea and land. Only the Chinese of Sung times ever surpassed them in painting landscapes, but where the Chinese go to the mountains and look at them the Japanese bring their mountains into their gardens and live with them.

NARA OR TEMPYO, HEIAN AND KAMAKURA PERIODS
(A.D. 710–794) (A.D. 794–897) (A.D. 1185–1336)

Pottery did not develop except from outside sources and even in the Suiko and Hakuho periods (A.D. 552–710) there was a yearning for Chinese ways and many Chinese settled in Japan. Buddhism did not become at once popular but increased as time went on and received a stimulus from Shotoku Taishi and the Chinese writings. By 710 the T'ang influence was strong, the language was worked out with Chinese script and dress, architecture, the calendar and customs all were as nearly Chinese as possible. The Shoso-in, a wonderful storehouse has actually been kept from that time to this and contains much of general interest but little pottery and that of the mottled T'ang type. Mr. Langdon Warner says, "preserving every jot of their teacher's skill, they lent to continental shapes and styles something that we shall, as soon as the eighth century reaches its second decade, recognize as peculiarly Japanese."

Mr. Warner points out that the volcanic structure of the rock of Japan made it impossible for them to carve colossal rock sculptures so they made the DAIBUTSU-DEN the largest bronze figure ever seen and housed it in a temple. Here we find another point of interest, for the Japanese are masters of *scale* and from this great Buddha down to the smallest netsuki in ivory (button for holding the cord of an inro in the belt) or the little animals in Dōhachi yaki (yaki means ware as yao does in Chinese) things are scaled so that they may appeal to our child-like instincts or so that they cause awe and wonder. This conscious struggle for significant scale does not please some Westerners. A friend of mine once said that in Japan everything was too big or too little. Towels are either little shreds good for nothing or so big you cannot handle them and cups are either thimbles or soup bowls. It is strange but in the Sung Chinese art we never think of scale and this shows that it is far better.

Nothing of interest so far as pottery goes occurred in the Jogan or Early Heian period (A.D. 794–897) or in the Fujiwara or Late Heian (A.D. 897–1185) and we may pass over this time except to note that taste became ornate with a fondness for gilding, Buddhism became involved and to quote Warner, "The very names of the gods became legion and each was different from the others in attitude and attributes." 1000-armed Kwannons were made and other feats of amazing patience. It was a time of *vulgar appeal of number*. If one god is good, a hundred are better. If two arms are good, why not a thousand? But the Japanese corrected this attitude in their tea ceremony as we shall see.

The Kamakura period (A.D. 1185–1336) began to feel the Sung culture of China. In 1223 the priest Dōyen is said to have taken Kato Shirazaemon to China to study the work of Sung potters and after a while he opened a kiln in Seto, Owari province and made a thin ware of purplish-black body glazed in brown with a brilliant black overglaze applied unevenly over it. Other glazes were "ko-Seto" (old Seto) which is yellowish or reddish in tone over a gray body and also a little later black, yellow brown and chocolate. But these are exceedingly rare.

Zen Buddhism, the sect for the individualist and self-reliant, has no scriptures and teaches that one should not heed the words of others but learn to know one's self and try to find out where one fits into both the spiritual and physical worlds. It encouraged portrait painting of its priests and also the type of pottery which is a part of nature. A jar should look as though it were growing rather than simply to have a picture of a growing plant on it. But still there was little in ceramics to interest us.

The Mongolian invasion stopped at the coast because of a typhoon which sunk the Mongolian boats.

Ashikaga Period (a.d. 1392–1568)

Now, a hundred years after the Sung period was through and done with, its influence became dominant in Japan and Sung paintings and ceramics were easy to obtain for they were not exciting enough for the Ming Chinese people. The Ashikaga period is looked upon as a sort of Sung Renaissance.

In order to understand the aesthetics of this time it is necessary to grasp the significance of the Tea Ceremony in Japan. This again was started in China by "Tea testing competitions" which were of ancient practice. A game was played and still is played in which the Chien yao tea-bowls were bet against each other in the following manner:—All were filled then drained and the bowl to hold the remaining moisture the longest time or the shortest time as decided upon won the others. This may sound silly until we find out that some of these bowls brought the equivalent of as much as $40,000 each and perhaps it is no more silly than watching a little ball skip around a roulette wheel. This, however, had another element involved, namely, the judgment of the bowls, for who would bet a very fine one against a mediocre one? And thus it was that much aesthetic and critical ability was developed and what started out to be a mere gambling game became one of the most powerful influences in the art of Japan.

By the time of the Ashikaga period the old Chinese game had changed to the Tea Ceremony. In this ceremony the tea is powdered and is highly selected and cured. Sometimes it is the brilliant green of "apple green porcelain" or of jade. It is kept in a small jar with ivory cover and small ivory spoon of just such a size. (I give the names of most of these implements below the illustration of the ceremony equipment.) This tea is very expensive. There are never more than a few guests, perhaps four at most, and they are served individually by the host who then washes the tea-bowl carefully and prepares another. Only a tiny amount of tea is used and hot water is placed in the bowl and the mixture frothed up with a small piece of bamboo split at the end so that it looks like a shaving brush. The guest often compliments the host on the tea-bowl and then drinks his tea in three and a half sips, making the proper noise of enjoyment and showing the proper expression of delight. The water is kept to just the temperature so that it makes a noise like wind through the pine trees as it simmers over a charcoal fire. A pottery jar of about eight or nine inches in height and provided with a lacquer cover receives the water with which the bowl is washed out.

The room is just two and a half mats square or about nine feet and ostentation and rank are cast aside in it. One enters not through the house but from the garden after carefully washing at a special pool arranged for that purpose. The door is so low that one has to enter on hands and knees. Everything must be simple and the idea is to show the best of taste with cheap materials. This is not entirely adhered to for I have heard of a single piece of

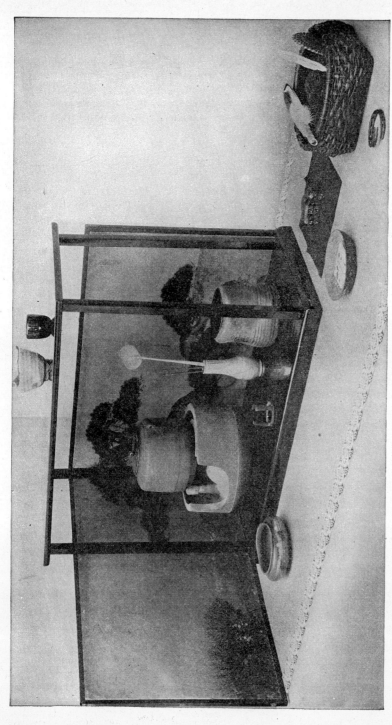

Japanese tea ceremony equipment including a "tea screen," the charcoal stove and iron kettle, a vase with iron chop sticks to handle the charcoal and the bamboo dipper for the hot water, the large jar into which the bowl is washed, etc. Metropolitan Mus. of Art.

JAPANESE TEA CEREMONY EQUIPMENT

PLATE 71

driftwood bringing hundreds of dollars, if it was just what was wanted. The only ornamentation is a simple arrangement of a painting and a few flowers or some object of art on the little platform which is raised about six inches from the floor and called the "takanoma." This is made for the one occasion only and great care is taken. Girls spend half their lives learning flower arranging in Japan and are not considered expert until they have spent years at it.

The Tea Ceremony was started after a time of internal strife and the originator, or that is he who made a cult of it, did so for the purpose of getting men's minds off of worldly advancement, ambition and ostentation. Its very essence, therefore, is economy and this great appeal in art the Japanese came to understand as no other people. The story is told of the man who first brought the morning glory to Japan. The mysterious and wonderful vine was talked of far and wide. Its beautiful flowers which appeared only in the early dawn, which were clear blue on bright days and purple toned when the humidity was high seemed impossible and a great prince of state traveled a long distance to come to see them. When he arrived the gardener's grounds were bare; all the flower beds were empty and strewn with white sand. It was an insult, a personal affront, unforgiveable! Perhaps the gardener did not know that the prince was friendly with the local governor and could have his head chopped off! But, as a samurai should be, the prince was punctilious and when he was received for the Tea Ceremony decided that he would go through with it first.

He washed his face in the cold springwater, sat a few moments which were supposed to be devoted to the enjoyment of the garden and were not, and removing his shoes, entered the softly lighted tea room. No picture hung in the "takanoma" (the little alcove with raised floor) but there stood a slender vase with one beautiful morning glory blossom, a few leaves and a curling tendril. After such an understanding of the appeal of economy in art the Japanese of culture did not go on with that cloying appeal of mere numbers like the 1,000 arms on a Buddha, until in the 18th century commerce made it popular again.

In the Momoyama period (A.D. 1568–1615) the great conqueror Hideyoshi took Korea and brought from there potters who were, shall we be kind enough to say, "under Imperial patronage" in Japan. The great hunger for good taste was about to be satisfied. The longing for culture could be fulfilled but, alas, the Mings of China were setting another standard and the inclination was to force more and more labor into a work of art. Craftsmen were but slaves to a ruling class which demanded more and ever more and thus all taste was lost. Only here and there among the Zen Buddhists do we find traces of appreciation of the Ashikaga art and the art of Sung China. And finally came the blight of western influence which we shall describe in the late 17th, 18th and early 19th centuries in China, of factory work, mass production and commerce.

JAPANESE POTTERY

The study of Japanese pottery is full of confusion for different wares may be called by the same name or one ware may be called by the name of the city in which it was made, the province, the place where it was extensively sold, the name of some "tea-master" who recommended it, or any one of the often many names of the potter who made it. In Hizen, Nagato and Tosa provinces the wares were not signed. Many adherents of the Tea Ceremony were amateurs who made their own pieces. Great artists in other fields occasionally made a pot while on the other hand great paintings were copied by the potter on his ware and given the original artist's signature as tribute. When commercialism started many intended forgeries resulted. It would take a volume many times this size to sort out much of this but I shall simply

FIG. 423. Raku water jar of 3rd generation. Coarse red clay covered with yellowish glaze, dating about 1600. Said to be by Do-niu or Nonko. Ht. 6¾". Metropolitan Mus. of Art.

FIG. 424. Shino flower vase named from the tea-master or *chajin* Shino Sōshin who dictated the style, it is said, near the end of the 15th cent. This piece dates 18th cent. Ht. 9¾". Colman Coll. Metropolitan Mus. of Art.

FIG. 425. "Oribe ware" tea-bowl from Narumi near Seto in Owari province. Dating about 1780. Dia. 4¾". Havemeyer Coll. Metropolitan Mus. of Art.

touch upon the most famous wares and cover some of the others in the following charts giving full warning that the collector can only depend upon his understanding and taste plus a large amount of technical knowledge in order to collect these wares. Marks mean little or nothing.

The earliest Seto ware of the Kamakura period, about the 13th century, was symmetrical and wheel made. It was a close copy of the Tsung Sê tz'ŭ (or according to Hobson the "Honan Temmoku") wares, and consist of small bottles, jars and cups. In the Ashikaga period (A.D. 1392–1568) the potters were no longer content with the simple irregularities of glaze and began to scorn the wheel, making wares entirely by hand and not even trying to make them straight. This was a new thought about pottery; the endeavor to return to the primitive without improvement; the natural making of a piece of pottery in the easiest and simplest way. Of course it is an artificial attitude and we see altogether too much of it in our present day "modern art," the decadent sophisticate who tries to be the simple primitive. However, many wares resulted such as Shino-yaki, Oribe, Karatsu, Bizen, Hagi-yaki, Raku-yaki, Dohatchi-yaki, Chōsa-yaki, and early Satsuma and all were undecorated or only slightly and crudely decorated with dabs of the brush or finger, depending chiefly upon the irregular running of the glazes, splashes and splotches. It has been suggested that the appeal of asymmetry might have started from some Korai pieces which were not perfectly fired or had wilted in the kiln but, in any event, the appeal of the impression of the human hand fitted into the Zen Buddhistic philosophy of personal expression. Some potters used the wheel just a little. Some dispensed with a foot-rim or even a flat bottom. Many indented or pressed their wares between the palms when in the "leather state," partly dry before firing.

Asymmetry once discovered was found also to be true in many instances in nature and the flower arrangements, the arrangement of furniture and of the tray for eating all followed asymmetrical patterns quite the opposite of the Chinese symmetrical arrangements. We find precedent for this in Suṅg bird and flower painting but all Buddhistic art is symmetrical in China. It was a step forward and a great contribution which, if started in China, nevertheless should be largely credited to Japan. The little American newlywed will invariably try her best to make her room "balance," will put pairs of vases on the mantlepiece and buy pairs of lamps. Hundreds of American living rooms have a pair of lamps either side of a sofa and directly opposite another pair on either side of the fireplace. Symmetry is stiff, formal and uninteresting while asymmetry gives motion and life to an arrangement and it can regain a certain balance so as not to be disturbing. The dance has been described as a successive loss of one's balance and the regaining of it. Asymmetrical arrangements may be, like the dance, pleasant or unpleasant.

KENZAN

Some things which look like just nothing on first sight slowly impress themselves on us in time as the very soul and essence of an expressive art stripped of every last unnecessary and hampering detail. Such is the art of Kenzan, one of the greatest potters of Japan and one of the greatest artists

FIG. 426. Small jar of Japanese Musashi pottery by Kenzan.

FIG. 427. Kyoto ware writer's box, from Yamashiro province (1690–1741 A.D.) attributed to Kenzan. Length about 10". Bequest of H. O. Havemeyer. Metropolitan Mus. of Art.

FIG. 428. Incense burner of Japanese Musashi pottery by Kenzan from Tōkyō. Freer Gallery of Art, Washington, D. C.

FIG. 429. Fire-pot of Japanese Musashi pottery by Kenzan, Tokyo. Flowers of this sort were also designed by his brother, Korin, who used them on wood block prints. Freer Gallery of Art, Washington, D. C.

the world has known. He was typically also called Ogata Shinshō, Sanshō, Shinzaburō, Shoko, Suiseidō, Shisui, Reikai, Tōin and other names. He was the younger brother of Korin, one of the greatest lacquer artists and painters that ever lived. Kenzan lived between A.D. 1661 and 1742 and was not only a potter but a poet, painter and master of the Tea Ceremony. As he enjoyed a fair sized surface on which to work, he made chiefly the "hiire" (brazier), the "kōgō" (incense box), the "sara" (tray), the "chawan" (tea-bowl), desk screens, writer's boxes and such things. Flowers, landscapes, occasional figures, birds and trees were his subjects and they were rendered with the fewest possible brush strokes in a few simple colors. He was never a static

FIG. 430. Dish of Japanese Musashi pottery by Kenzan, Tôkyô. Freer Gallery of Art, Washington, D. C.

FIG. 431. *Ogata Shinsho* or *Kenzan* pottery tray of the province of *Musashi* Japan 18th cent. This is c. 1720. Ht. 1½", length 9¾". Metropolitan Mus. of Art.

FIG. 432. Incense-box of Japanese Musashi pottery by Kenzan, Tokyo. Freer Gallery of Art, Washington, D. C.

artist and his styles varied. Many followed his various styles in all sincerity and unfortunately many in later years made outright fakes. The Japanese love his work and there are many enthusiastic collectors of it the world around, but many of the things even "in the style of" Kenzan are in our largest museums and are beautiful works of art.

FIG. 433. Fire-pot of Musashi pottery by Kenzan, showing his simple and direct brush work. Freer Gallery of Art, Washington, D. C.

FIG. 434. Screen for writer's desk from *Musashi* province, 18th cent. attributed to Kenzan. Ht. 10¼". Length 15¾". Metropolitan Mus. of Art.

FIG. 435. Bowl signed by Kenzan and dating about 1840. Decorated only with the face of Uzume modeled in low relief. Dia. 14½". Metropolitan Mus. of Art.

"MISHIMA" AND OTHER KOREAN WARES

As early as A.D. 1200 glazed pottery was made at the town of Karatsu in Hizen province and to the Japanese "karatsumono" (things from Karatsu) is an old term meaning pottery. Here imitations of "Korean" potteries and stonewares were made, many of which were black bodied like Chien yao and probably were not Korean at all. Some of these were intentionally of irregular shape and had splotches and daubs of different glazes. These are called "Chosen Karatsu."

There was also "e-Karatsu" (painted ware touched with swift strokes), "kenjō Karatsu" (presentation ware) and "mishima Karatsu" (inlayed ware) said to have been made as early as 1530 and in production by 1592 after the return of Hideyoshi. At Yatsushiro more naturalistic designs were also made in "mishima" ware with flying birds, etc. The earlier wares are more geometric.

Interesting pottery tray with a painting signed by *Korin* and a poem signed by *Kenzan*. Length 8½". Morse Coll. # 4035. Boston Mus. of Fine Arts.

Kenzan jar, Kyoto ware province of Yamashiro with crackled buff glaze decorated in dark brown and gray. Ht. 4". Metropolitan Mus. of Art.

Two trays, the iris painted in green and brown, the bracken in vivid green, brown and blue and both bearing the signature of Kenzan. Dimensions 9¾" by 9½". Fuller Coll. Seattle Art Mus.

JAPANESE POTTERIES IN KENZAN STYLE

PLATE 72

Fig. 437. 17th cent. Bizen tea-jar. Ht. 1⅞". Metropolitan Mus. of Art.

Fig. 436. Bizen figure of a "Shishi" dating about 1800. Ht. 8". Macy Coll. Metropolitan Mus. of Art.

Fig. 438. Bronze-like bottle made in Imbe, Bizen province during the 18th cent. Ht. 6". Colman Coll. Metropolitan Mus. of Art.

BIZEN WARES

At Bizen a ware was made much like the Yi-hsing yao (described in the Ming Dynasty) or what is loosely called "Chinese bucchero" from a clay that burned smooth and hard at times looking like bronze, or again "aka" (red)

Fig. 440. 18th cent. figure of Shoki seated on waves about a rock, of hard pottery with metallic sheen of brown. Ht. 12¾". Freer Gallery of Art, Washington.

Fig. 441. Bizen 18th cent. incense burner of Kinko sitting on a carp. Ht. 9¾". Metropolitan Mus. of Art.

Fig. 439. Bizen 18th cent. glazed or partly glazed pottery incense burner showing excellence of modeling which was often associated with this place. Ht. 8½". Fuller Coll. Seattle Art Mus.

or "ao" steely blue. This unglazed ware was modeled into vases, animals, incense burners of fantastic shapes and plates. More recently bricks and drain pipes were made there. The amount of detail possible to achieve led to ornate and tasteless naturalism. Here again we find a too easy medium leading to mere virtuosity.

At best we can give in a book of this scope a general idea of the types of potteries made and, as we have tried to do, a method of approach to further study. The following chart will serve as a rough outline on which to build:

Left to Right: A symmetrical wine bottle of Seto ware from Owari province of 18th cent. Ht. 8". Colman Coll. Metropolitan Mus. of Art.—Owari province Seto ware "oil-bottle." According to museum of "Shino ware," named after *chajin* Shino. 17th–18th cent. Ht. 9½". Freer Gallery of Art, Washington.—19th cent. Shino square bottle, Owari province. Ht. 8½". Colman Coll. Metropolitan Mus. of Art.—Owari ware saki bottle signed "Shun-Tai" dating from 19th cent. Ht. 9". Metropolitan Mus. of Art.

Left to Right: "Ki-Seto" (yellow Seto) vase from Owari province, showing influence of Ming "three color" ware. Ht. 13⅜".—Owari province Seto ware called "Shino-yaki" after *chajin* Shino who is supposed to have set the style. Ht. 13½".—Owari province flower vase called "Akatsu" by museum. Ht. 9½". Freer Gallery of Art, Washington.—Brown crackle glazed bottle with exaggerated neck. 17th cent. Seto ware from Owari province. Ht. 11½". Colman Coll. Metropolitan Mus. of Art.

Left: Water jar from Narumi near Seto in Owari province, of the Oribe type following the traditions of Furuta Shigeyoshi. Ht. 5". Warren E. Cox Coll. *Center:* 18th cent. Shino type, Owari tea-jar. Ht. 3¾". Warren E. Cox Coll. *Right: Chawan* or tea bowl of *"Ki-seto"* from Owari province of brownish greenish ware with incised decoration in some ways resembling the heavy "celadons" found at *Showchow in Anwei* province, China. 18th cent. Ht. 3". Metropolitan Mus. of Art.

OWARI PROVINCE POTTERIES

PLATE 73

"Ko-seto" or old Seto
bowl of the type # 3.
Dia. 5½". Metropolitan
Mus. of Art.

Seto late 18th cent. glazed pottery dish painted in black and
blue. Dia. 9½". Fuller Coll.
Seattle Art. Mus.

"Chōsen Karatsu" bowl
from Hizen province of the
18th cent. This is of the
"hakeme" type and the
inlayed design makes it
possible also to call it
"mishima." Dia. 9¾".
Colman Coll. Metropolitan
Mus. of Art.

(a)   (b)   (c)   (d)

(a) "Shigaraki" (Omi province) oil dish c. 1770. Such dishes were placed under hanging oil
lamps to catch the drip. Dia. 8½". Metropolitan Mus. of Art.
(b) "Ye-Karatsu" or "E-Karatsu" water jar painted in brownish black after the Tz'u Chou
style. Ht. 6¼". Freer Gallery of Art, Washington.
(c) Asymmetrical bottle of Imbe ware, Bizen province, with a metallic sheen over it. Late 17th
or early 18th cent. Ht. 7½". Freer Gallery of Art, Washington.
(d) 19th cent. (c. 1820) Takatori group comprising Kanyan and Jittoku. Ht. 8". Macy Coll.
Metropolitan Mus. of Art.

Left: Takatori, (Chikuzen province) water jar for the tea-ceremony. Dark reddish-brown clay
and a splashed glaze. 18th cent. Ht. 7¼". Colman Coll. Metropolitan Mus. of Art.
Center: Kōda ware bottle (Yatsushiro) of gray clay with white decoration. Ht. 9". Freer
Gallery of Art, Washington.
Right: A Kōda (Yatsushiro) water jar from Higo province. Ht. 6½". Freer Gallery of Art,
Washington.

JAPANESE POTTERIES

PLATE 74

Rikei type bowl from Hagi in Nagato province showing the strong brush work called "*hakeme*" Korean style. Dia. 5¾". Freer Gallery of Art, Washington.

Left: Late 19th cent. Yatsushiro vase. Ht. 8½". Macy Coll. Metropolitan Mus. of Art.
Right: 19th-cent. Kutani vase, crude in manufacture but with spirited writing. Ht. 16½". Freer Gallery of Art, Washington.

Shidoro type water jar of 19th cent. Ht. 5½". Colman Coll. Metropolitan Mus. of Art.

Tea-jar with ivory cover. Japanese Awaji ware attributed to Mimpei, first generation, c. 1830. Freer Gallery of Art, Washington.

Center: From Rakuzan, this bottle, given date c. 1835. Izumo province. Ht. 9¾". Freer Gallery of Art, Washington.

Jar into which water is poured after washing tea cup. Kyoto ware, Yamashiro province, attr. to Koyetsu. Glaze red and green. c. 1620. H. O. Havemeyer Bequest. Metropolitan Mus. of Art.

Raku-yaki tea-bowl marked "Banjen" 1790, of 9th generation. Dia. 3½". Mus. of Fine Arts, Boston.

Center: "Onohara" saki bottle. Probably a Tachikui piece, date, 1750. Ht. 9½". Freer Gallery of Art, Washington.

JAPANESE POTTERIES

PLATE 75

Left: A tobacco box said to be of Raku ware dating 1840. Macy Coll. Metropolitan Mus. of Art.
Center: Awata (Yamashiro province) tea-jar by Ninsei (Nonomura Seibei) c. 1660. Dark body with thick metallic brown-black and dull white glaze. Ht. 3″. Metropolitan Mus. of Art.
Right: Vase from Awata (18th cent.) probably by Takahashi Dōhachi, who was a bamboo carver too. Perhaps it reflects a slender bamboo feeling. Ht. 11½″. Colman Coll. Metropolitan Mus. of Art.

Left: Awata saki bottle of the 18th cent. Ht. 8¾″. Metropolitan Mus. of Art.
Center: Awata, kettle and stove perhaps made by the Hōzan family. Late 18th cent. Macy Coll. Metropolitan Mus. of Art.
Right: "Daikoku, god of luck" figure of so called "Kyōtō ware" but actually from Kiyomizu, Yamashiro province. Ht. 8″. Metropolitan Mus. of Art.

Awata, bowl made about 1800. Dia. 11¾″. Metropolitan Mus. of Art.

Left: Kyoto (Yamashiro province) tea-jar supposed to have been decorated by "Zengoro Hozen" but certainly very strongly like the design of a late Sung or Early Ming Lung-ch'üan "celadon." Ht. 5½″. Metropolitan Mus. of Art.
Right: Awata, incense burner of the old Taoist symbol of a child on a water-buffalo. c. 1720. Metropolitan Mus. of Art.

JAPANESE POTTERIES

PLATE 76

Musashi province statue of Manzai dancer probably by Kōren, Tōkyō c. 1825. Ht. 18½". Freer Gallery of Art, Washington.

Bowl from Kishū province, copy of Chinese *san ts'ai* or three color type with cloisonnes. 19th cent. Dia. 4¼". Macy Coll. Metropolitan Mus. of Art.

Satsuma tea-jar of the late 19th cent. far better than most of the time and place. Ht. 2½". Freer Gallery of Art, Washington.

Saki bottle from Kiyomizu, (Yamashiro province). Buff body, faun colored finely crackled glaze, decorated with underglaze blue of grayish tone. c. 1750. Havemeyer Coll. Metropolitan Mus. of Art.

A *cha wan* or tea bowl of black Satsuma pottery from the island of Kyūshū c. 1680. Dia. 4⅛". Metropolitan Mus. of Art.

Kiyomizu (Yamashiro province) saki bottle. Faun color with irregular stains and underglaze decoration in gray-blue. c. 1750. Ht. 7". Havemeyer Coll. Metropolitan Mus. of Art.

Soma ewer c. 1840 from Iwaki province with greenish gray buff ground and colored glazes on the relief decoration. Ht. 9¾". Macy Coll. Metropolitan Mus. of Art.

Satsuma vase said to be of Korean form and covered with a dark brown glaze. Ht. 12½". Freer Gallery of Art, Washington.

Satsuma flower vase of the type called "*mishima*" by the Japanese. Inlayed in imitation of the Korean wares. Some of this ware was made by actually Korean potters who settled there. Ht. 9½". Freer Gallery of Art, Washington.

Yamashiro charcoal fire bowl by Dōhachi. Possibly by Dōhachi II the most famous member of the family, the one who practiced first this entirely Japanese style. Dia. about 12". Freer Gallery of Art, Washington.

Dish by Miura Kenya which has much the feeling of the art of Kenzan. Length 6½". Freer Gallery of Art, Washington.

Finely crack'ed cream ware of the Boku Heii type. This Satsuma water jar is good in form and well decorated after the Tz'u Chou style of the Ming period. Ht. 6". Freer Gallery of Art, Washington.

JAPANESE POTTERIES

PLATE 77

IDENTIFICATION CHART OF JAPANESE POTTERIES

OWARI PROVINCE

Town	Chajin or "Tea-man"	Artist	Description of wares
Town not known for certain—for first ware. The town of *Seto* was center for later types.	The priest *Dōyen* set out for China in 1223 and took "Tōshirō I" with him, to learn Chinese potting.	*Katō Shirozaemon* was a potter called "Tōshirō I." Did not sign his work.	*First type.*—Clay brought from China was purplish brown and finely washed, potting done with very thin walls and foot smooth and flat or "*hon-itokiri*" that is with lines swinging clockwise around to the right from the thread with which the piece is separated from the wheel. A first glaze of brown was applied evenly and a black glossy second glaze was poured over showing streaks and spots. "*Old Seto*" or "*ko-Seto*" grey body of yellowish or reddish tone, coarsely and more heavily potted. This clay was first from Seto and with Japanese glaze. It has a reddish-brown underglaze and black brilliant overglaze. *Variations.*—Two more variations are: a.—with light spots strewn over the brown primary glaze and b.—with the reverse.
Also *Seto*		*Toshiro II*, no signature on pieces.	*Unglazed type:*—Brinckmann has called attention to a piece in the Hamburg Museum, a "chaire" or small tea-ceremony jar of age-darkened pale grey, body with a chestnut brown glaze inside only (see Hannover—Pottery & Porcelain of the Far East Fig. 350). This piece has relief decoration, and Hannover suggests that it may be one of those made from "clay from strange parts" such as Tōshirō is said to have tried such as from Asahi in Mino. Brinkley says have a similar body to "ko-Seto" and a brilliant, thick and not very transparent glaze. From them Hannover says descended the thin and transparent, pale yellow glazes, crackled and sometimes shaded with blue of the 16th century called "yellow Seto" or "ki-Seto. (See Ki-Seto from Freer Gallery c. 1630 vase.) The piece illustrated certainly shows Ming Chinese influence strongly though the earlier bowls do not.
Seto		*Toshiro III*. Did not sign his work.	Tōshirō III is said to have made a new glaze of golden color called "*kin-kwa-zan.*" Hannover states that no examples from these masters are known in the Western hemisphere, though later pieces of similar style are well known.
Seto	"chajin" *Shino Sōshin*.	This style set by the tea-master was followed by many artists.	*Shino-yaki* was ordered to be made in Seto near the last of the 15th century by the tea-master Shino Sōshin and lasted to the end of the 19th century. It is thick, and coarse, of irregular shapes and high-fired with bubbly and large crackled only slightly fluid glaze decorated in blue, brown or iron oxide with very brief painting of a few strokes only.

IDENTIFICATION CHART OF JAPANESE POTTERIES—*Continued*

Town	Chajin or "Tea-man"	Artist	Description of wares
Narumi near Seto	*Furuta Shigeyoshi* commonly called "*Oribe*" founded a school in 1585.	Many artists.	*Oribe-yaki* as a style was set by Oribe when he ordered 66 tea-jars of strange shapes a few of which were very roughly painted with cranes, plum blossom, etc. in dark brown, moss-green and other colored glazes.
Nagoya		*Chin Gempin* was a Chinese potter who did sign his wares.	*Gempin-yaki* is grey stoneware with a soft crackled glaze with brief decorations of figures, cranes and bushes, flowers etc. in blue and black. These were made in the 16th century.
(See Marks, Japanese)			
Tokoname		Various artists.	A coarse, red and unglazed earthenware decorated with cord marks and also incised designs of trees, birds, etc. Near end of 15th century was making a glazed ware which more recently was decorated with dragons, clouds, scrolls, etc. stamped on.
Nagoya		*Oki Toyosuke* 19th century potter.	One sort of earthenware with white glaze opaque and crackled and decorated with "Raku-like green spots", according to Hannover. Another with black or dark green lacquer and designs in gold, silver and colors.
Inaki near Nagoya			"*Inuyama-yaki*" has a grey, stoneware body with thick, opaque glaze of Shino type but more even and is decorated with trees and leaves in brown, vivid green and red. The name comes from a castle nearby. Imitations bear a spurious Kenzan signature. (See Hannover, Fig. 347.)
			HIZEN PROVINCE
Karatsu		Corean potters brought to Japan by Hideyoshi's officers.	"*Oku-Kōrai*" or "old Corean" ware was probably of typical Corean type including the "mishima" or inlayed type and others. In fact the collector can differentiate these only by surmise from the clay; an odd piece of Corean ware is likely to have been made in Japan. "*Chōsen Karatsu*" is a later ware for the name Chōsen was given to Corea during the revolution of Yi Taijo.—Some are of blue-black clay with glaze which looks like cast iron, and others are smeared with streaks of white or olive green over a brown, green or black glaze. This is called "*hakeme*" or brush streaked. "*Mishima Karatsu*" previously mentioned and above under oku-Kōrai. "*E-Karatsu*" means painted Karatsu ware which is usually swiftly touched with black or brown in a rude manner. "*Kenjō-Karatsu*" is similar to the above but finer having been made for the prince of Hizen for a "presentation ware." This is of a fine yellowish or brownish clay with transparent crackle glaze and generally has *mishima* work on it.

Hizen	*Goroshichi* may be a purely legendary potter but according to Ninagawa he is supposed to have worked somewhere in Hizen c. 1530.	*"Goroshichi"* is used to designate all large tea bowls, but also a special type are supposed to be like the ones he did (if he existed) and they are large, of brownish clay with white crackled glaze and decorated in a not very good blue.

BIZEN PROVINCE

Imbe	Many Kyōto artists over a long period of time not definitely established as yet. In 1400 a large kiln 120 feet by 15 feet is reported built. Firing lasted 60 days and cooling the same length of time. A short while ago *Mimura Mosaburo* tried to revive the industry but failed.	*Bizen* ware or *Bizen-yaki* fires dark grey on the inside and brown or bronze colored on the outside. It is not glazed but has a glossy look and sometimes it appears to have a brown glaze or black glaze over it. Nearly all bear a stamped mark—circle, rectangle or rhomb with numerals in it. Figures, vases, tea-ceremony vessels (after the 16th century), were made but the best are of the 18th century, technically speaking, at any rate. *"Aka-Bizen-yaki"* is the common red Bizen ware and *"Ao-Bizen-yaki"* is steel blue. Bizen plates were made in the Meiji period (1868–1912) for European use in competition with Chinese *Yi-hsing yao* or so called *"buccaro."* (See Chinese and Roman sections.)

SETTSU PROVINCE

Sanda		*Sanda-Seiji* is a celadon porcelain and is further mentioned in the porcelain chart.
Kosobe	*Igarashi Shimpei* c. 1800 studied in Kyōto and made imitations of Ninsei and Raku. *Shinzō* his successor took his ideas from Takatori, Karatsu and also Corea. In the third generation the shop followed Rokubei. *Komatsuya Tasuke* was an amateur potter who worked at times for the 4th generation.	*Kosobe-yaki* is a stoneware with a hard and sandy body ranging from dark grey to buff or reddish white. The glaze is pearly grey, reddish grey-yellow, or white. The sketchy decoration is in black or brown. It is hardly recognizable from other wares except for being stamped *KOSOBE* and sometimes *TAINEN* the art name of *Komatsuya Tasuke*.

ŌMI PROVINCE

Shigaraki in the *Nagano* district.	There was a very ancient pottery made here. Beginning the 16th century. *Rikyū* lived at the close of the 16th century. *Sotan* c. 1630. *Enshū* c. 1650 prince of Tōtōmi and a famous chajin.	*"Fōō Shigaraki"* ware is grey clay turned reddish in firing and has a reddish-brown or brown primary glaze with an olive or grey green glaze running down irregularly and sometimes with small pieces of unfused quartz in it. *"Rikyū Shigaraki"* is a grey crackled stoneware. *"Sotan Shigaraki"* a variety like the others and various. *"Enshū Shigaraki"* also similar. All are perhaps distinguished by a certain feeling of rough and irregular shape and surface.

chajin Fōō.

IDENTIFICATION CHART OF JAPANESE POTTERIES—Continued

Town	Chajin or "Tea-man"	Artist	Description of wares
Zeze, a district on the Lake Biwa.		Only from c. 1650 to c. 1700.	Chaki (articles for the tea-ceremony) resemble old Seto and not inferior to Takatori masterpieces. The body is dark grey and fine. The glazes are golden brown, brownish-red and purple.
		CHIKUZEN PROVINCE	
Takatori n.e. of Hizen.	Enshū c. 1650 also liked this ware.	Originally by two Coreans carried from that country by Hideyoshi's generals: Shinkurō and Hachizō. Shinkurō dies c. 1825 and (as we find in Hannover) Hachizō is thought to have gone to Enshū although this would seem to make him about 175 years old! Brinkley says that there are three kilns only one of which is now copying the old wares but not very well.	Chaki for the tea-ceremony. Ko Takatori (old Takatori) is dull brown, yellow or black spotted in glaze. Enshū Takatori-yaki was produced by Hachizō, his son and also by Igarashi Jizaemon, a potter from Karatsu experienced in Seto glazing. Wheel thrown shapes and golden Autumn brown glazes. Morse says, "The usual form is cylindrical, slightly tapering below, often with two ears or knobs on the shoulder. The thread-mark (itokiri) is right handed and finely cut. Other forms occur, some short and wide, others globular; the double gourd form is not unusual. The clay is very fine, usually a grey-drab, though sometimes a light or dark brown or fawn. The glaze is rich, dark-brown often subdued in lustre. All shades of brown are seen, such as olive-brown, golden-brown, purplish-brown etc. Sometimes a light fawn glaze appears. A splash of fawn overglaze is usually seen on one side." Hannover continues, "The only tea-jars with which those of Takatori can be confused are those of Buzen and Zeze in certain of their forms. In order to procure fresh material, the pottery works were repeatedly shifted from place to place. According to Brinkley, it should therefore be possible to determine the approximate age of Takatori ware from the clay. In the earliest period (1600–1660) it is said to have been light grey, then (1660–1700) nearly white, and in the third period (1700–1800) reddish and at times purple tone." The glazes are usually grey or greyish-yellow with touches of green, brown or blue.
		BUZEN AND HIGO PROVINCES	
Agano in Buzen.	Enshū influence also.	1602 founded by Sonkai who called himself Agano Kizō and died in 1646, when the Prince of Buzen was given charge of Higo province Kizō established himself at Yatsushiro. His son remained in Agano. There are still endeavors in this town to imitate old wares.	Sonkai's first work was like the Corean of coarse clay, and with black glazes. Under Enshū's influence he made things more like Takatori. Some later wares are of reddish clay with a purplish brown or brownish-yellow glaze with texture like melon skin. In Yatsushiro, Kizō resumed his Corean style and made partly hakeme and partly mishima ware with white or rarely black inlay but always more loosely and less formalized than the Corean, some are "unkaku-de" or cranes flying among clouds. In Agano c. 1820–30 large bowls were made very light in weight of yellow clay with transparent glaze or harder fired white. Some have poured over them "robin's egg" or other colored glaze sometimes alternating from the center radially with a rich brown glaze.
Yatsushiro in Higo			

BUZEN AND HIGO PROVINCE

Yatsushiro in *Higo,* and *Kōda* a town nearby.

These towns have also revived the old wares but they lack the "soft and mild sheen."

Yatsushiro-yaki or *Kōda-yaki* has a cold grey clay which does not offer the same contrast with the white that the old clay does, which was reddish. Larger pieces are always modern.

In the old ware the inlay is restrained to white, only rarely is black or blue used. The glaze is yellowish-grey or olive-brown-grey or greyish coffee-colored.

Larger pieces such as vases are always modern.

NAGATO AND IZUMO PROVINCES

Hagi in *Nagato.*

Rikei a Corean adopted the name *Kōraizaemon.*

Hagi-yaki is developed from the Corean stoneware called *Ido-yaki* has a grey crackled glaze clouded with salmon.

Rikei also produced Corean *hakeme* with its powerful brush strokes in grey and later in pale green and light lavender-blue or on grey and yellowish-white grounds.

Oni-Hagi was made by *Gombei* and it means "demon Hagi."

Rakuzan in *Izumo.*

Gombei was a pupil of the master *Kōraizaemon* and was summoned to *Rakuzan* in c. 1675.

Matsumoto and *Fukagawa* also in *Nagato.*

Matsumoto-yaki and *Fukagawa-yaki* Morse says cannot be distinguished except occasionally from those of *Hagi.*

Hagi's late reproductions are not of interest except perhaps a *mishima* similar to *Yatsushiro-yaki.*

KAGA PROVINCE

Ōhi (See *Kutani* porcelain also in *Kaga.*)

A member of the Raku family came in 1683,—Haji Chōzaemon. (See *Yamashiro* province.)

Brown glazed ware like *Raku* sometimes brownish-red in the early 15th century but similar to Raku since 1683, has a reddish-yellow, honey or amber colored glaze and bears the mark Ōhi stamped—

ISE PROVINCE

Banko

Mostly from 1868 and made in great quantities all over *Ise,* especially at *Yokkaichi.*

Usually tea-pots, flower-vases, etc. usually of thin walls and shaped by hand showing finger marks or molded and bearing sprays in relief or flowers in enamel colors on the unglazed grey ground, but sometimes made of "marbled clays" of different colors.

Kuwana? Yedo?

Old Banko-yaki perhaps made by "*Gozaemon*" who was a wealthy amateur potter whose real name was *Numanami* but there is some doubt about this.

By 1878 there were 21 potters from Ise showing at the Paris International Exposition.

Old Banko appears in many forms many of which copy Karatsu, Shino, ki-Seto, Raku, Kōda and some Satsuma wares, so closely that they would be indistinguishable save for the mark.

Town	Artist	Chajin or "Tea-man"	Description of wares

YAMATO PROVINCE

Town	Artist	Chajin or "Tea-man"	Description of wares
Akahada-yama, a mountain province.	Derived from an older kiln which was reorganized in 1761 by the prince of Kōriyama with potters from Kyōto.	The prince was a *chajin* and painted some articles.	Marked or it would be hard to tell from Takatori, Hagi or Kyōto wares save that it is perhaps a bit more sandy in body. 2nd period ware have brown or reddish yellow glazes, not bright, with designs painted over in enamels delicately. Some are in low relief with designs such as Fuji. Others had white crackled glazes, monochromes and flambé. Still another type have dull gold ground on which are painted flowers and ornaments sometimes also laid on in pipe-clay or paste.

AWAJI ISLAND

Iga	c. 1830 a Kyōto potter named *Ogata Shuhei*.	Kashū Mimpei was a rich *chajin* also called *Toyonosuke*.	*Awaji-yaki* has a yellow glaze similar to Imperial Chinese and also a deep green similar to Chinese apple green and later a greyish-white and a black. Later still tortoise-shell effects were obtained. Also understood gold and silver.
	His nephew *Sampei* kept up with his son and a pupil.		*Ogata Shuhei's* own ware is of pale grey, has a dense and hard body and the glaze has a yellow crackle (small) and resembles Awata ware (see below). This is rare.
Sumoto	Also a new kiln at Sumoto was established in 1883.		The nephew and the Sumoto wares are of earthenware like Kyōto with a yellow crackled glaze decorated in enamels and gold.

IZUMI PROVINCE

Minato	It is amusing to know that it was here that the potter's wheel was said to have been invented *in the 18th century by Gyōgi-bosatsu*, a priest.		An early ware has grey, purple or blue glaze, and there are also unglazed pieces, all with a light body similar to Raku.
	Also *Dōroku* called *Kichibei* and brother of the 3d *Raku* started a kiln in 1655 and adopted *Yakei* a Kyōto potter. 8 generations lasted to 1861.		Most of the generations used the name *Kichiemon*, and do even to-day. They made a light Raku-like ware with a colorless and transparent glaze and an opaque, mat, dark yellow glaze over it. The family used also a green glaze, as well as white, yellow and green combined.

IGA PROVINCE

Marubashira		Enshū was the *chajin*.	Stone-ware like that of the nearby Ōmi province in the town of *Shigaraki* though not quite. so reddish. Usually of rough and crude shape and undecorated.

TŌTŌMI PROVINCE

Shidoro	Enshū	c. 1670–1730. Also later activity in kiln.	Shidoro-yaki is quite simple in form and undecorated but has autumn yellows and browns, rich brown-black, alternating with yellow- or red-browns covering a darker glaze as with a net.

IZUMO PROVINCE

Fujina		Gombei went to Rakuzan c. 1675 for 18 years and about 1750 to Fujina.	The wares attributed to him look like Hagi-yaki being very primitive and sometimes with a granulated glaze. From Fujina come wares with yellow or flambé glazes.

TAMBA PROVINCE

Originally in Onohara but c. 1650 moved to Tachikui.			Tamba-yaki is said to "combine the beauty of Takatori-yaki," with the simplicity of Shidoro-yaki," with the simplicity of Seto-yaki and the solidity of Shidoro-yaki," by the Japanese collectors. It is a hard fired ware of reddish body with chocolate, mahogany and bluish-black glaze and at times with splashes of yellow. To Tachikui are also attributed saki bottles with colored liquid glazes also unglazed ones in grey with a crane or flower painted in white or brown.

YAMASHIRO PROVINCE

Kyōto or also called Yamashiro but also Awata Iwakura Mizoro Kiyomizu		2nd half of the 16th century many Seto potters came to the city of Kyōto. Also the Corean, Ameya or Masakichi came perhaps c. 1525 or a bit later. His sister continued work. Ameya's son Chōjirō who died sometime between 1592 and 1610 was given a golden seal by Hideyoshi, with the character Raku meaning "contentment." The family is still working and using the same seal. Also Honnami Kōetsu and his son Kūchū made Raku-yaki.	The Corean style was used in the capital before elsewhere, perhaps 50 years before. After Ameya's death his widow as a lay sister or "ama" carried on making Ama-yaki. Raku-yaki is of coarse clay and lightly fired, is of grey or light brown and shaped by hand into thick walled bowls with carved or scraped surfaces. First it was black glazed, then red was added, then, still later a green glaze was used and finally a straw-yellow and even white. The glaze may be thin and porous or thick and glossy and often covers the foot. This ware does not transmit heat readily and is valued for tea-drinking. It is usually not decorated but sometimes has a lightly sketched design in a contrasting colored glaze or even gold. The firing only lasts a few hours and the pieces are taken from the kiln with tongs the marks of which are to be often seen. Such pieces are called "hasami-yaki" or "tong-ware." There were many copyists and also forgeries so the oldest looking piece may be quite new.

Note:—Hannover says truly, "The value of Raku ware can hardly be fully appreciated by Europeans, as it depends to a great extent on refinements connected with the enjoyment of tea, such as only the Japanese chajin can thoroughly relish." We can hardly agree with Mr. Hannover's modest statement, however, for we cannot help but enjoy these wares so honestly made to show attributes we have already discussed.

Town	Chajin or "Tea-man"	Artist	Description of wares
Kyōto		Ninsei was a painter and amateur potter from about 1630 to 1640. The Japanese say of him that he could turn out anything but porcelain or celadon. Note:—Many imitations exist, and some bear his mark. But these are among the most costly rarities.	Ninsei-yaki at first was like Takatori, Seto, Shigaraki or Chinese and Corean models. Now it is interesting to note that at this early period the search for the secrets of potting was going on and he, Ninsei, had to get his ideas surreptitiously from the potters of Arita, who were masters of enamels. His stoneware is of red or yellowish clay and is dense, smooth and hard fired. His crackles formed a circular mesh of yellow or fish-belly-grey color, and quite regular. Among his monochromes is a metallic black over a grass green, to give it life. Over such grounds he painted flowers or ornamental patterns in gold, silver, red and other enamels with economy.
Kyōto Iriya in the Musashi province.		Kenzan or Ogata Shinshō or (see text) 1661-1742. Kenzan spent his old age in Iriya.	He made all sorts of chaki or tea-ceremony potteries except the little jars for holding the powdered tea which are called chaire. He painted usually the haire or braziers, the kōgō or incense-box, the sara or tray and less often the chawan or tea-bowl. The older he became, the bolder was his brush work, on pieces called Iriya-Kenzan. So many were the types of rough and swiftly painted wares that he made and so many many more are the imitations by such men as Dōhachi, Kenzan, Sandai, Kenya, Makuzu, and many others right up to the present day, that competent distinction can hardly be made. Some have considered Brinckman, who depends upon Ninagawa, as the best authority but I have heard Japanese collectors laugh at his attempts. Perhaps this is more a problem for the study of the styles of Kenzan's painting than the actual technical aspects of his potting. The illustrations will give the reader some notion at least.
Iwakura and later at Awata.		Kinkōzan family.	A crackled yellow or grey Awata export ware with bright coloring and shiny enamels in scratchy designs but originally the ware was not unlike a sort of thin Kenzan type of design.
Was first in Ōmi but came to Kyōto Awata		Taizan family:—Takahashi Tōkurō was the founder coming to Kyōto c. 1680 and later to Awata in 1711. The early generation called themselves Yohei.	A blue glazed ware was made for the Imperial Household. Export wares in modern times with red or blue glaze or with colored decoration on a mat yellow glaze.
Awata		Hōzan family after the 18th century and even to to-day, though not in Awata.	Blue underglaze ware with a finely crackled thick glaze over a yellow or white slip which is sometimes even laid on in relief.

Kiyomizu near Kyōto.

Seibei Yahyō c. 1700 who was also called Evisei.

Ebisei-yaki is not unlike *Ninsei-yaki.*

He imitated Chinese Lung Ch'üan yao and also Ming painting in red, green and go.d.

Eisen was a pupil of *Evisei* and he founded the first true porcelain factory in Kyōto.

His work shows great technique in enamels and a certain artistic, though over sweet taste in application. He followed *Maruyama Okyo's* realistic ideas and also *Gekkei* or *Goshun* and even at times had these masters decorate his wares. His monochromes are famous and sometimes he worked in decoration in reserve and often in underglaze blue.

Robukei was still another pupil (1738–99). He was of the Kotō family which continued through *Rokubei II, Shichibei,* and *Shorin Rokubei.*

Avata

Takahashi Dōhachi was a pupil of Eisen (1740–1840) and he carved bamboo as well as making pottery.

He did porcelain, earthenware and stoneware, and different from the Chinese styles; more of the *Shijō* or realistic school and some speed and directness.

Gojōzaka near Kiyomizu.

His son Dōhachi II came in 1811 to *Gojōzaka.*

Momoyama

Dōhachi III in 1842 moved to Momoyama.

Dōhachi IV was recently president of the Kyōto Potters.

Aoki Mokubei (1767–1833) was another pupil of *Eisen.*

Porcelain and stoneware of some considerable variation and no great importance.

Kitei.

Followed Dōhachi and also made porcelain.

Then the *Yosobei,* the *Zōroku* or *Ōtani, Hiaku ju,* etc. families began to make porcelain and the conditions were not unlike those which held sway in Europe.

Kyōto

Moderns.
Seifū Yohei is the third of a family. The 1st died 1861. The 2nd in 1878. His art name is *Baikei.*

Baikei makes porcelain, pottery and stoneware specializing in celadon and blanc de Chine, also underglaze blue porcelain and blue and red.
His work suffers from the same fussy over ornate quality which is prevalent in Japan to-day.

In 1870 he moved to *Ōta* near *Yokohama,* in *Musashi* province.

Miyagawa Kōzan has the art name of *Makuzu.*

Imitations of Satsuma ware, they are earthenware with high relief and naturally colored birds, fishes, flowers etc. These are terrible, but later he made copies of many of the K'ang Hsi and Yung Chêng periods. He also made forgeries of Ninsei ware.

Thus we see that in the 18th and 19th centuries the Japanese were not behind in the merry game of copying and stealing designs and technical "dope" from every hand, but it is not necessary to go further into the iniquitous practices.

253

IDENTIFICATION CHART OF JAPANESE POTTERIES—*Continued*

Town	Chajin or "Tea-man"	Artist	Description of wares
Asaki (Uji) in *Yamashiro* province.	*Zōroku* 17th century.		Yellowish-white or greyish-yellow glazes.
MUSASHI PROVINCE			
Tōkyō also *Irya* and *Imado*.		*Kenzan* settled at *Irya* in his old age and died in 1743, at 81.	See Kyōto.
		The *Hanshichi* family worked for several generations in *Imado*.	*Imado-yaki* in the first generation is unglazed *chaki* (tea-ceremony wares), in the 2nd a sort of *Raku* ware.
		Haritsu or *Ritsuō* was a pupil of *Kōrin* and *Kenzan*.	He made flowers, insects etc. of low fired *Raku-yaki* to inlay in his lacquer of gold etc.
Asakusa north of *Tōkyō*		*Miura Kenya* came from *Kyōto* (c. 1830–1840).	He too fired at low temperatures a sort of *Raku* ware in flowers and insects to use in inlaying similar to that of *Haritsu*. (See just above.)
Tōkyō		*Hattori Tsuna* is a woman called *Kōren*, worked in the last part of the 19th century.	Plastic figures modeled in an unglazed ware resembling wood in appearance.
IWAKI PROVINCE			
Iwaki		The artist *Kanō Naonobu* once visited *Iwaki* province and did the design or model of the horse. He died in 1650.	"*Sōma-yaki*" named from the house of *Sōma* have, as a rule only one design, that of a *tethered horse*. The ware is of coarse, grey stone-ware with a thin, transparent glaze of brown-speckled, or pin-holed type or at times with various colors or a sort of transmutation type,—or it may be without glaze. The decoration is painted with a few strokes in black or blue, brown or white or infrequently in gold. It is also rarely incised or in relief having been moulded and applied. A type with granulated glaze but same designs is of the late 18th century.

254

Satsuma also *Nawashirogawa* near *Kagoshima*.	Late ware not over fifty years old is terrible, ornate and over detailed export ware on a finely crackled, glassy, cream colored ground, in all colored enamels and gold, made only for the Japanese conception of European taste. Much of this ware does not even come from Satsuma.
	Chaki were made by the Koreans of fine, brown stoneware with greenish or golden brown fluid glazes. The earlier Koreans made a dark colored stoneware.
	"White Satsuma" is very finely made and without decoration but covered with an ivory colored very finely crackled glaze. (See also below.)
	Korean potters settled here in the 15th century and made dark Korean wares. In the last of the 16th century a prince of *Satsuma* brought from Korea 17 potters who soon scattered.
Nawashirogawa is where the clay was found. They worked at *Tadeno*.	*Boku Heii*, one of them, found a fine clay from which he made a finely crackled cream ware and with *Kanyu* from c. 1640 made "white Satsuma" which is fine and good.

ŌSUMI PROVINCE

Chōsa or *Chūsa* in *Ōsumi* province still subject to the prince of *Satsuma*.	Both here and at *Nawashirogawa* (see above) monochromes with finely crackled glaze such as apple greens, straw yellow, black and gold dusted black were made. Also rough wares with fluid glazes in two or more layers including *jakatsu-gusuri* (dragon-scale glaze) which is speckled with milky white, and highly prized in Japan.
Hōchu another of the 17 potters (see above) came from *Korea*.	*Mishima* wares were also made inlayed with white and dark clays like the Korean ones. But the above are both very rare indeed and seldom seen in the West.
	Satsuma nishikide (Satsuma Brocade) design was first made in *Chōsa*.
Kōno Sōnemon by royal command, added gold to the muffle colors at the end of the 18th century.	*Kinrande* (gold brocade) style is, though bad, not so overladen as the later wares. They used a dry, iron red, bluish green enamel, a glossy blue, a soft purple, black, a yellow and the gold was subdued mat relief. Few are ever seen in the West.
	"*Old Satsuma*" is even later than this ware and has already become ornate and offensive. It used the dragon and phoenix but never human figures.
Imitations were made about 1860 with dragons, the phoenix and figures. The peacock followed.	*Imitations* introduced the human figures, peacock, and even faked antique stains; the red is thinner, and it is less dry, the blue less pure and more muddy,—the purple, black and yellow are seldom seen,—but pink is added from c. 1830 and later a mat black and dull brown. There are many old and undecorated pieces which have modern painting on them.
Arita, Ōsaka Ōta, Tōkyō and *Kōbe*.	

JAPANESE PORCELAINS

Some Japanese pottery was original in conception; most Japanese porcelain is imitative and not particularly attractive even to the Japanese themselves. A man of taste there would far prefer a Sung Tz'u Chou or piece of Korai pottery or stoneware first and secondly an old "chawan" of rough shape. Thirdly he would like a piece of Chinese porcelain and only after that the porcelain of his own country. It is true to state that it was largely export ware, but, as was the style in Europe in the 18th century, some princes gave porcelain royal patronage and some things of real beauty were made.

In the Japanese word "yaki" they include pottery, stoneware and porcelain, making no distinction but their porcelain is a true, hard porcelain much like that of the Chinese. Luckily enough the chief source of materials, Mountain Izumi-yama, provides both kaolin and petuntse already mixed by nature, but the material is difficult to handle for it is inclined to wilt in the kiln and must be given a light firing first and then a higher one.

In earlier days the underglaze blue was imported from China and specimens with the right "gosu" are always of antique make. Later a thinner, more purple and less pure blue was used. At Hizen bowls were made resembling Ming ones and supposedly by a potter named Goroshichi in the late 16th or early 17th century. The blue of these is poor and the painting flabby rather than direct and primitive. These were not porcelain but other potters such as Shonzui made porcelain ones which were widely copied. Arita porcelain also from Hizen province, and "Hirado" made for Prince Hirado's own use were decorated with delicate underglaze blue and the latter was of fine milky white quality. The motives were landscapes, children at play, etc.

The enamel colors were also much like those of China and in the so-called "Imari" ware we have a chance to compare them. There are these obvious differences between the Chinese and Japanese:

1.—The Chinese porcelain is thinner and denser in body and the glaze has a greenish tinge while the Japanese has a coarser and more sandy body with a glaze of greyish tint and of what Emil Hannover calls a "muslin" texture.

2.—The Chinese iron-red is thin and coral colored; the Japanese is opaque, thick and Indian-red.

3.—The Japanese wares were fired on spurs which will never be found on Chinese.

4.—The Japanese yellow is greyish and yet lighter than the Chinese impure Ming yellows.

5.—The Japanese green enamel is bluish as compared with K'ang Hsi greens.

Imari is in Hizen province and about 1650 Sakaida Kakiemon and Toshima Tokuzaemon decided to go to China to study but got only to Nagasaki where they met a Chinese potter who helped them. The result is the ware known as "Kakiemon" which was copied so extensively in Meissen and elsewhere in Europe. It is a refined type of Imari ware painted in iron-red, blue-green, light blue, violet and greyish-yellow and rarely with gold added and rather thin but tasteful designs. Other "Imari" had "nishikide" (brocade) patterns taken from actual brocades and distasteful to the

Left: Typical censer with *nishikide* or brocade pattern made at Arita and shipped from *Imari* during 18th cent. Ht. 7″. Macy Coll. Metropolitan Mus. of Art.

Center: Arita (Imari) porcelain from *Hizen* province, by *Kakiemon.* This style was often copied in Meissen and other European factories and some are difficult to tell from originals. Dia. 9⅝″. Metropolitan Mus. of Art.

Right: Hizen province 17th to 18th cent. dish by Kakiemon painted in blue under transparent glaze, with enamels of various colors. Dia. 12½″. Mus. of Fine Arts, Boston.

Late 17th-cent. Arita blue and white porcelain bottle with nicely graded crackle shading down from shoulder. Ht. 14¼″. Lent by Mrs. Russell Robb. Mus. of Fine Arts, Boston.

Many wares made for *Prince Nabe-shima* resembled those of *Kakiemon.* This vase a good example. Ht. 9⅞″. Metropolitan Mus. of Art.

IMARI WARES, PARTICULARLY THOSE OF KAKIEMON

PLATE 78

Japanese themselves. This "Imari" ware was made in Arita, the name coming from the port from which it was shipped. At Arita also was made a finer ware decorated in lilac blue, reddish-brown, purple, black and pale-yellow up to about 1830 but chiefly for home consumption, after which time it lost its quality, and finally ended up in the "Nagasaki vases" with exaggerated

FIG. 442. Japanese "Imari ware" of 18th cent. in imitation of so-called "Lowestoft" ware made around Canton for western trade. Dia. 11¾". Boston Mus. of Fine Arts.

FIG. 443. Ko-Kutani dish from *Kaga* province in northwestern Japan. Technically crude porcelain but considered artistically superior, including underglaze blue, of poor quality, red, yellow, green, gold and silver. Dia. 10". Freer Gallery of Art, Washington.

FIG. 444. Late 18th or early 19th cent. Kutani ware from Kaga province, of Imari style, probably made by Honda Teikichi. Dia. 14½". Smith Coll. Metropolitan Mus. of Art.

flaring mouths and decorated in cold lacquer. Arita is also known for pierced ware, low relief ware, celadon with enamel colors and old and new blue and white ware, there having been about forty factories all told.

Another of the early sites was Kutanimura in Kaga province which from about 1650 had used a local porcelain earth. From here Prince Maeda sent Gotō Saijirō to Hizen to study. The ware is decorated in deep green glaze with purple, yellow and a soft greenish prussian blue called "ao (green) Kutani." The enamels of Arita were also used but the green and red were

FIG. 445. Satsuma vase c. 1800. Finely crackled buff colored glaze. Decorated in low-fired enamels. Ht. about 9½". Macy Coll. Metropolitan Mus. of Art.

FIG. 446. Arita porcelain vase of "Imari" type from province of Hizen. Decorated in underglazed blue and iron red, etc. Ht. 8⅜". Metropolitan Mus. of Art.

FIG. 447. Hizen province white "*Hirado*" porcelain vase decorated in underglaze blue of purplish cast. Typical shape. 1740. Ht. 10½". Metropolitan Mus. of Art.

FIG. 448. Hirado bottle, made between 1830 and 1843 by Furukawa in Tempō period. Less delicately painted than early wares under patronage of Prince Matsura. Ht. 10¼". Lent by Mrs. Russell Robb. Mus. of Fine Arts, Boston.

supplemented by purple, yellow, overglaze blue, gold and silver. It is the most impure porcelain of all Japan, and the enamel colors thick. Some look like attempts to get celadon effects but the green is bright and unpleasant. "Ko-Kutani" (old Kutani) is covered with a close pattern in red with medallions reserved and containing small compositions of ornaments in yellow, green, purple and red. Underglaze blue gave them difficulties and is rarely, and always badly, used.

Another "five colored" ware was "Eiraku" with its "kinrande" type decoration in gold, which in this case is on a red ground first applied solidly.

Not all of the enamels were employed on porcelains. Ninsei, one of the most famous potters, used various enamels on black or grey or cream grounds with some taste and artistry. Other similar wares came from Iwaki and Yamashiro but those from various places and known as "Satsuma" are perhaps the best known and the worst of taste. The real Satsuma ware was first of Korean influence and consists of a closely crackled white ware with ivory glaze, a "white Satsuma" of close hard paste almost microscopically crackled and of ivory color, an apple green, a straw yellow, a pure black, a gold dusted black and also a crude looking ware with several glazes including the famous "dragon-scale glaze" or "jakatsugusuri."

These are types reaching up to the 18th and 19th centuries and few of which interest us at all artistically speaking, but we must bear in mind that during this time decadence had set in over the entire world and the Chinese and European potters were showing little better taste.

The following chart, on pages 260–267, will give some slight aid in identifying Japanese Porcelains.

Other towns mentioned by Brinkley are in part as follows:

Higo (from 1791) similar to *Arita,* still producing.

Izumo (from 1873) poor blue and white.

Iwami (from 1860) similar coarse blue and white.

Iyo (from 1796) same.

Nagato (from 1846) ivory colored porcelain and other wares.

Kotō province of *Ōmi* (from 1830 to 1860) blue painting, enamel painting, and red and gold.

Himeji province of *Harima* (from early 17th cent. to 1868) blue and white and celadon.

Meppo-dani province of *Kishū*—celadon with relief decoration under glaze and stamped *"Zuishi,"* the name of a grass of similar green.

Aizu or *Wakamatsu* modern porcelain blue and white.

Ōta province of *Musashi* (from 1879) *Miyagawa Kōzan* who called himself *Makuzu* made copies of Chinese wares.

Koishikawa a suburb of *Tōkyō* (from c. 1900) blue and white, and pale red Chinese imitations.

Tōkyō (from 1863) European exports of wares looking as though they were painted in oil colors, some with gold spotted grounds.

This charming little dish made c. 1750. From Ōkōchi. Length 5½". Macy Coll. Metropolitan Mus. of Art.

Porcelain covered dish made by *chajin, Kashū Mimpei* in *Iga* on Island of *Awaji* c. 1830–1840. Greyish white with transparent glaze. Dia. 7". Mus. of Fine Arts, Boston.

Mokubei bowl, Kyōtō, Yamashiro province dating about 1785, decorated in red, yellow, green, and aubergine enamels with gold. Dia. 9". Metropolitan Mus. of Art.

Late 18th- or early 19th-cent. Kutani jar with cover, from Kaga province. Slightly greenish toned in glaze decorated with landscape in purple, yellow, green and black with borders in red. Ht. 8½". Mus. of Fine Arts, Boston.

Ko Kutani wine bottle from Kaga province, 17th cent. Greyish white painted in red, yellow, green, aubergine and black enamels. Ht. 9½". Gift of Marshall H. Gould. Mus. of Fine Arts, Boston.

Left: "Sanda ware," Japanese vase of porcelain with clear "celadon" glaze. Mark "Kotō" incised under glaze on base. Ht. 11½". Morse Coll. Mus. of Fine Arts, Boston.

JAPANESE PORCELAIN

PLATE 79

Geisha girl playing samsen in *Kaga* province ware dating c. 1870. Ht. c. 12". Macy Coll. Metropolitan Mus. of Art.

Satsuma figures c. 1800 or later showing life-like modeling and soft naturalistic coloring. Ht. of rider about 7". Belonging to Mrs. Frederick Fish.

Teapot from Kyoto, 1790, potted by Kentei. Decorated by Ogata Shūhei in enamels. Ht. 4¼". Metropolitan Mus. of Art.

Porcelain water-pot from *Bishu, Owari* province, made by *Hansuki,* c. 1820. Ht. 7¾". Smith Coll. Metropolitan Mus. of Art.

JAPANESE PORCELAIN

PLATE 80

IDENTIFICATION CHART OF JAPANESE PORCELAINS

HIZEN PROVINCE

Town and Province	Chajin or "Tea-ceremony Master."	Artist	Description of wares
North west corner of the island of *Kiûshû* in *Hizen* province.		*Gorodayû Go Shonzui* went to Ching-tê Chên in the start of the 16th century and brought back porcelain art to Japan. Some examples bear his name and some a Ming mark, if attributions are correct.	A fine porcelain decorated in Japanese style with birds, trees, flowers etc. in underglaze blue. There are many imitations the best from China, which in turn imitated the imitator, and from a factory in Japan started for that purpose (1825–40).
Arita in *Hizen* province.		The Korean potter *Risampei* c. 1605 discovered an already mixed porcelain clay containing both *kaolin* and *petuntse* in mountain *Izumiyama* and started a kiln in *Arita*.	The early Arita porcelain was also blue and white (See Hannover p. 210 Guide to the Pottery and Porcelain of the Far East). Hobson says that green and red enamels were used in the earliest Arita porcelain. (See Guide to the Pottery and Porcelain of the Far East, British Museum, 1924, P. 146.) However so few really proven examples exist in the Western Hemisphere that statements concerning them include considerable speculation.
Imari in *Hizen* province.		*Sakaida Kakiemon* and *Toshima Tokuzaemon* c. 1650 started for China but met a Chinese in *Nagasaki* who showed them how to paint in enamels over the glaze.	Kakiemon porcelain called by the French the *"première qualité coloriée de Japan"* was painted in iron-red, blue-green, light blue, violet, greyish-yellow and rarely with gold. It competed with some Chinese wares in export trade.
Arita and other places also produced similar ware in Japan.			It is not always easy to tell the Chinese wares from these, therefore the following points should be noted:—
			1.—Japanese added flower-baskets or *hanakago* and simpler colored landscapes often only underglaze blue, iron red and gold.
			2.—"Old Imari" is the more fully colored type.
			3.—Huge quantities came from both Japan and China.
			4.—The designs cannot differentiate them for China copied Japan as Japan copied China.
			5.—The Chinese ware is thinner and denser and has a greenish tinge.
			6.—The Japanese is more sandy, coarser, and has a greyish tint with "muslin" surface.
			7.—The Japanese underglaze blue is muddy and darker than the Chinese.
			8.—The iron-red of the Chinese is clear and coral color; that of the Japanese is Indian red, thicker and opaque.
			9.—There are spur marks on the Japanese dishes which never occur on the Chinese ones.
			10.—The Japanese dishes are undulating to the touch while the Chinese are perfectly potted.
			11.—On vases the Chinese allowed the wheel marks while the Japanese did not.

262

All of which is technically interesting in that it shows us another sidelight upon the differing mental processes of the two people, but hardly necessary as Japanese on the whole certainly did not appreciate the wares and they are truly more expressive of European taste, particularly that of August the Strong, than of the Far East, though they were made there.

Arita

A finer ware was made at Arita for Japanese taste from c. 1750 to c. 1830.

It was decorated in lilac-blue, reddish-brown, purple, black and pale yellow.

It also slowly descended to the depths of decadence of the so called "Nagasaki vases" decorated in red and gold and cold lacquer colors and of monstrous shapes.

Recently old *Arita* has been revived but with a poor red and blue.

Other wares made in *Arita* are perforated and relief decorated as well as celadon types decorated in enamels and gold.

"*Arita* egg-shell" occurs in underglaze blue decoration and a more modern ware with figures of women and warriors in gold, red, blue and sometimes with a fine net work over them called *ajirogumi*.

Many of the blue decorated type are marked:— *Zōshun-tei Miho sei* meaning "Made by *Miho* in the *Zōshun* pavilion. (See 321—2 Hannover) *Miho* only worked from about 1825 onward.

The *Fukagawa* family worked in *Arita* from c. 1650, and there were about 40 factories in this province all told.

Some of these are *Koransha* and *Seijisha* which was founded by *Tsuji* and are still working.

Mikōchi also in Hizen province.

Nagasaki

Kameyama in 1803 made wares near *Nagasaki*.

Sakaida Shibanosuke was founded by *Sakaida Kakiemon* (1615—53).

These were blue and white wares cleverly painted but with a less deep blue and of cruder potting than good *Arita* ware.

Ōkōchi eight miles from *Arita*.

In 1660 *Prince Nabeshima* founded a kiln with *Korean* potters.

No marks are found, but many have a comb-like pattern *kushide* around the foot, but this is also found on *Kaga* porcelain and modern forgeries. (Hannover Fig. 321—7.)

Protection ceased in 1868 and its importance as well.

The wares made were purely Japanese taste. It is whiter, cleaner and more lustrous than *Arita* porcelain. The enamel decorations resemble *Kakiemon's*. Gold was used moderately as was also underglaze blue which is sometimes omitted. New enamel is lilac-purple, and the iron-red is more orange and lighter. Another kind is painted in a fine but pale underglaze blue. Red and blue were also combined.

A finely crackled celadon "*seiji*" porcelain was also made. The paste is either white or red stoneware-like material.

A later ware is a coarse crackled brown or celadon glazed stoneware ornamented in red and gold.

263

IDENTIFICATION CHART OF JAPANESE PORCELAINS—*Continued*

Town and Province	*Chajin* or "Tea-ceremony Master,"	Artist	Description of wares
Mikōchi in *Hizen* province, (see also above) on the island of *Hirado*.		In 1650 some Koreans started a factory but porcelain was not made until 1712 after the ingredients were found on *Amakusa* island. In 1750 *Matsura*, prince of *Hirado* became patron. Between 1750 and 1830 it was the finest porcelain in Japan. The fine work ceased in 1868, but it has been revived. It is rarely marked, though those with the name of the potter belong to the *Tempō* period (1830–43).	"*Hirado porcelain*" is largely plastic and usually of small objects and was only made for the prince himself; its sale being strictly forbidden. It is even cleaner and more brilliant than *Nebeshima*. Decorated usually in underglaze blue, it sometimes had added a pale brownish tone imported from China. The painting is miniature in delicacy and often shows Chinese children playing under a fir tree called *karako*. This is, of course, a well known Ming design. The number of children seems to indicate the class of the ware there being seven boys in the best, five in the second and three in the third. Freely, modeled fish, dragons, and figures were also made and colored in blue, red-brown or black. Very delicate perforated wares were also made.
		A smaller factory existed as an independent venture.	This place made egg-shell decorated in a fine brilliant blue underglaze color.
Kyōto	*Chajin Eisen.*	In the 18th century porcelain was produced by *Eisen.* The mark was his name painted in red or stamped.	Imitations of Chinese celadon and Ming porcelain in green, red and gold.
		Aoki Mokubei (1767–1833) was a pupil of *Eisen.* He also marked with his name which has often been copied on modern forgeries. *Ogata Kichisaburō* or *Shūhei* signed as another individual.	He imitated blue and white, enamelled porcelain, celadon or a ware called *Kōchi-yaki* imported from China, a semi-porcelain decorated with brilliant enamels of purple, yellow, green and bronze.
			He did coral red glaze with decoration in gold or enamels painted over it.
		Nishimura Zengorō died in 1855. He was also called *Zengorō Ryōzen* or simply *Ryōzen*, but later he adopted the name *Eiraku* meaning Yung Lo, after the Ming Emperor and then *Kahin Shiryū* which means "scion of *Kahin*" *Kahin* being the name of a mythological ceramic product.	Coral red glaze was one of his best achievements, and it was this that gained for him his last two names from the prince of *Kishū*. His *Eirakukinrande* or "Yung Lo gold brocade pattern" and his *akaji-kingwa* or "gold pattern on red ground" are considered in Japan among the most precious. He made, too, celadon porcelain, blue and white and copies of *Kōchi-yaki* which he called after his kiln name *Kairaku-en* and also *Oniwa-yaki* or "Royal Park ware", as he had been asked to place his kiln in the grounds of the prince's palace near Wakayama. The blue he obtained in the medallions in his red glaze is almost as bright as any known.

264

Kaseyama near Nara in Yamashiro province. Omuro Ōtsu on Lake Biwa	He worked a while at Kaseyama and then became an instructor at Settsu and in the same year 1840 he started a kiln at Omuro to copy Ninsei pottery. Later in 1850 he moved to Ōtsu and changed his name to Butsu-yu. Wazen one of his sons took the style to Kaga province in 1857.	Here he made akaji-kingawa (see above). Very similar to the above. Both also made "three colored" ware in glazes of three or more colors painted within raised outlines after the Chinese ware. Eiraku's wares have been copied in Otoko-yama (1847–66) and Ota (1874——) in Kishū province.
Kyōto	Rokubei Seisai was a son of the famous Rokubei in the early 19th century. Mashimizu Jūtarō with the art name of Zōroku (1849–78). Seifu III. Yohei (1861–).	Blue and white signed with his father's name in a hexagon. Celadon and other wares. Blue and white and red and gold wares.

There are, of course, still many potters in Kyōto but they are of little real account so far as we can judge in later exhibitions.

KAGA PROVINCE

Enuma	Prince Maeda sent Gotō Saijirō to Hizen to get secrets. Made from the latter part of the 17th century to about 1750 and called Old Kutani. Old Kutani was seldom if ever marked by the potter but at times bore the inscription:—Dai Nihon Kutani tsukuru, "Made at Kutani in Great Japan."	Deep green glaze predominant with purple, yellow and a soft greenish blue made ao- (green) Kutani ware. The glazes were used in close patterns or washed over designs in black on the biscuit (manganese). Arita porcelain was also copied without green and red but with purple, yellow, overglaze blue, gold and silver. Old Kutani porcelain is technically the worst in Japan but among the most valuable and artistic. It has also a typical opaque red-brown or brown-red. The designs are of landscapes, flowers and simple bird and flower ones of the Kano school. Seldom there are Chinese children at play called "kara-ko." Ko Kutani (a special sort of old Kutani) has a close ground of red pattern with medallions in reserve having designs in yellow, green, purple and red. Underglaze blue is much less used than in Arita. That with blue only is rare and poor in quality. The ware is gray or brownish and the glaze too is grayish and often crackled. It is only rarely a true porcelain.

IDENTIFICATION CHART OF JAPANESE PORCELAINS—*Continued*

Town and Province	*Chajin* or "Tea-ceremony Master."	Artist	Description of wares
Wakasugi		*Honda Teikichi* came from Hizen with three other potters, and worked until 1822.	The ware was a sort of Imari style.
		In 1832 *Hashimoto Yasubei* re-opened the same shop and Yujiro won fame.	*Akae Yujiro-aka-e* means "painted only in red," but he worked in the other enamels.
		From 1830 *Matsumoto Kikusaburō* in work with *Aōda Genemon*, occupied the same place but moved in 1850 to 1867 to *Komatsu*, in the *Nomi* district where 200 workmen were employed.	They reproduced the old Kutani.
			Old Kutani was also reproduced here.
Enuma continued		Meanwhile *Yoshidaya Denemon* (1809–1840) at *Kutani* and later at *Yamashiro-mura* also copied old Kutani. "*Hachiroe ware*" which was continued by *Zengorō Wazen*, the son of the great *Eiraku*, was first made by *Iidaya Hachiroemon* about 1840.	Old Kutani designs.
			This style uses red for outlines and also ground color. Wazen used underglaze blue for the inside of some bowls and red on the outside painted over in gold. It is usually marked *Kutani ni oite Eiraku tsukuru* "made by Eiraku at Kutani."
		The revolution of 1868 stopped all endeavors but in 1885 some 2,700 workers were making true porcelain.	These again were copies of Old Kutani and of Eiraku styles. Various other porcelains from different parts of Japan were sent there to be decorated.
		About 1850 the potters in *Kaga* province began to mark their work with painted marks, in red, black, green enamel or gold, the last two more seldom.	The modern Kaga province wares are very inferior export wares of no value.

OWARI PROVINCE

Seto

Porcelain began to be made only in the 19th century when *Katō Tamikichi* in 1807 returned from *Hizen* and was backed by Prince of Owari.

The best period was between 1830 and 1860 when such artists as *Kawamoto Jihei*, the modeller, and the potter *Kawamoto Hansuke* were working there.

Seto-mono became the term meaning porcelain in parts of Japan.

Sometsuke was the earliest and was underglaze blue of Japanese cobalt until 1832. Later European blue was used for the export wares.

They made famous large vases, painted plaques, etc. One type had raised designs on white with blue grounds. Enamels were more recent as a rule though *Michihei* did use them as early as c. 1835.

Other techniques were used and even imitation cloisonné was made.

Maruyama-yaki or copies of old Chinese tea ceremony wares were also made, and the *Nabeshima* style was copied.

Seto ware was also sent to Tōkyō to be decorated, though this should not be confused with "*Seto-suke-yaki*" which is a coarse ware made in *Yedo (Tōkyō)* before 1860.

MINO PROVINCE

Tajimi-mura

Kato *Gosuke* was one distinguished artist.

Wares were influenced by both *Seto* and *Kutani*. Most of the pieces are smaller than *Seto* ones. Many eggshell blue and white pieces were made with delicate designs of flowers, landscapes etc. *Gosuke's* wares were of this sort and were protected by fine basket work from *Suruga*.

Modern "*Tajimi* porcelain" is white with floral designs in high relief.

Kaga style porcelain has been made since 1878.

SETTSU PROVINCE

Sanda

Merchant, *Kanda Sobei* erected 12 kilns and obtained men from Kyōto and Hizen.

Blue and white wares and a vivid green celadon "*Sanda seiji*" of unpleasant quality was made and is today.

CHAPTER XIII

POTTERIES OF PERSIA, WESTERN ASIA AND EGYPT

Historical Background

Persia is a large country equalling in size Greece, Bulgaria, Albania, Yugo-Slavia, Rumania, Austria, Hungary, Czecho-Slovakia, Germany and half of Poland. It was a center of travel East and West as well as North and South. When we add to Iran the other countries of Iraq, Syria and Turkey we have a country as large as Europe and touching the Aegean culture on the west and that of Asia on the east. This territory is loosely called the Near East.

The people are of Indo-European origin. It was called Ariana (the land of the Arians) hence the Middle-Persian Eran and modern name Iran. South Russian names are largely Iranian and we suppose that migrations took place, before our history begins, from the North into Eastern Iran and down the Indus valley as well as west as far as the borders of the Semitic world.

The first historical records of any country tell of invasions from the North simply because the histories were written by the stay-at-homes in the South. These agriculturalists were easy meat for the hunters of the north who were always called savages but they were not necessarily racially different and were mentally more alert being hunters. Their minds were no less keen and active, in fact quite the contrary. Joseph Strzygowski, in "The Northern Stream of Art from Ireland to China, and the Southern Movement," says "On the European side we have the Celts, Germans and Slavs, together with all those races which burst out of Asia and penetrated to the West of Europe in all the first millennium, namely, the Huns, Avars, Magyars and, later, the Mongols. These peoples, all of them nomads of the North, were bearers of Asiatic ideas of art to Europe in historic times; but they must have been preceded by similar movements long before the Christian era during the Bronze Age and the La Tène period."

Horses, which became the subject of much western art and of the Han through T'ang period of China, were introduced into Babylonia, Egypt and Greece about 1700 B.C. as war instruments by the Medes, Persians, Hyrcanians, Bactrians and Sogdians in various conquests.

And so we may imagine a seething to and fro of the northern nomads with every now and then a sally southward for conquest which nevertheless always brought a new spirit and life to the arts of the southern peoples. Such was the condition when in 715 B.C. the Assyrians led by Sargon penetrated into the mountains to the east and subdued a few Medean tribes. In 612 B.C. the Medeans and Babylonians conquered not only the Assyrians but also the territories of Persia, Armenia and Cappadocia south of the Black Sea.

King Cyrus and the Achaemenid Empire (558 to 330 b.c.)

About 558 B.C. King Cyrus revolted and overthrew Astyages, the Medean king. He called himself "King of the Persians," and by 550 B.C. had founded the Persian Empire but had lost in the process the allegiance of Babylonia, Egypt, Lydia and Sparta which were in 546 B.C. beaten and finally brought into line along with all the Greek littoral towns, Cilicia, the whole Chaldean Empire, Syria and Palestine. Then the great Cyrus turned to the east and fought the Dahae Scyths and Massagetae until he finally died in 528 B.C.

His son took Egypt, Cyprus and the other islands off the coast of Asia Minor. This then was one of those great amalgamations which bring together many different arts.

One of the greatest factors in this conquest was the expert use of the short bow from horse back. In Turkestan even to-day I understand that riders can gallop full tilt past a post and leave several arrows sticking into it while White Russian cavalry could not do so well with army automatics. Many ancient legends tell of achievements with this bow. Perhaps the best known is that of Bahram Gur, the Sassanian king (A.D. 420–438) and

Fig. 449. Persian tile of lustred pottery probably from Kashan of about 1300 A.D. portraying Bahram Gur and Azadeh on a camel. Length about 13". Metropolitan Mus. of Art.

Azadeh, often pictured on ceramics. It seems the king saw two gazelles, an old male and a young female and asked "the moon of his delight" which he should kill. Azadeh answered, as the passage of Firdusi's "Shahnameh" is translated by Dr. R. Meyer Riefstahl.

" 'Oh lion,
A man does not fight gazelles.
But transform this female with thine arrow into a male,
And change the male into a female,
Then goad on the dromedary (on which they are usually portrayed)
And when a gazelle runs away from thee,
Hurl the dart of thy crossbow, (short bow)
So that she bends her ears along her shoulder.
The dart shall tickle her ear without hurting her

And she shall raise her foot toward her shoulder,
Then thou shalt pierce her head, foot and shoulder,
And then I will call thee the light of the world.' "

Nothing daunted, Bahram shouted and, when the gazelles ran, he used a double tipped arrow to shoot the horns off the head of the male, thus making it a female. He then planted two arrows in the head of the female appearing like horns and quickly touched the tip of the ear with another so that she raised her foot to scratch it when he sewed together the foot, ear and head. Azadeh, moved to pity and with the contrary whim of a woman, told him he was inhuman and had the nature of an evil spirit at which the kindly gentleman

"——stretched out his hand,
He threw her from the saddle to the ground
And bade his dromedary
Trample the girl with the face like a moon.
He covered her breast, her hand and her lute with blood.
He said:
'Oh, senseless lute-player,
Why didst thou try to trick me?
If I had missed my shot, my family would have been covered with shame!'
Azadeh died under the hoofs of the dromedary
And Bahram never again took a woman with him
When he went out to hunt."

You may draw what lessons from this tale you wish but in any event it is often illustrated.

DARIUS THE GREAT (521–485 B.C.)

Six noble Persians helped the young Darius to kill a usurper in 521 and take the throne. The colonies revolted and Medea, Sagartia and Margiana rose with kings of their own while Babylonia had two revolts and Susiana three. With a small army made up of Persians and Medes he finally brought order and then subdued the nations of the Armenian and Pontic mountains bringing the Persian rule to the Caucasus. Though an ardent Zoroasteran he permitted the Jews to build the Temple of Jerusalem and he himself built temples in Memphis, Edfu and the Great Oasis in Egypt.

GREEK WARS

In 512 he started a series of unfortunate wars with the swift Scythians. Then came the revolt of Egypt, inevitable war with the Greeks, the defeat of Marathon in 490 and the death of Darius in 485 B.C. Soon the Athenian fleet met the Perso-Phoenician armada at Salamis and added further defeat. Persia neither wanted the Greek coastal cities nor could she let them go. A way out seemed possible in the formation of a league against Sparta. Then in 387 Greece had to join the Persians again renouncing all claim to Asiatic possessions and even proclaiming Persian suzerainty over her but this was due to Greek weakness rather than Persian strength and although the Persian Empire reached its greatest geographical extent by 338 B.C. it was rotten at the core.

ALEXANDER THE GREAT AND THE FALL OF THE PERSIAN EMPIRE

Philip of Macedon was trying to liberate the Greek coastal cities of Asia Minor when he was assassinated and his young son Alexander, later known as Alexander the Great, took his place with a keen mind for both war and organization. In five years he had the situation well in hand. In 331 the victory of Gaugamela took place and shortly after Darius III was assassinated being the last of the twelve Achaemenid Dynasty kings. Alexander adopted the dress and ceremonial of the Persian kings and in 330 drafted 30,000 young Persians and trained them in Macedonian war technique. In 324 he held a great marriage feast at which all of his superior officers and about 10,000 more Macedonians were wedded to Persian wives. He then disbanded his veterans and used Persians in his army. Persia then was again a great melting pot where many of already mixed race were mixed again just as they were in North Europe, in the "Celtic basin" and about the Mediterranean, and we see Hellenistic influences brought into India from where they were later spread to China.

THE SELUCIDS (319–190 B.C.)

Alexander died in 323 B.C. leaving no heir. Most of the wives of the mass marriage had been discarded but one general or "Diadochi" kept his and, making Babylon his headquarters, struck at the strategic moment and took the whole of Iran except Northern Medea and the frontiers of the Indus river. He founded Selucia on the Tigris river and a circle of Greek towns about Medea one of which was Rhages, Rai or Rhagae about which we will hear much to do with potteries later. It was now an Hellenic city.

THE PARTHIAN EMPIRE OR ARSACIDS (C. 250 B.C.–A.D. 224)

Meanwhile Justin Arsaces, chief of the Parni tribe of the Dahan Scythians who came from the steppe east of the Caspian Sea, with the help of his brother Tiridates, founded the Parthian kingdom in 248 B.C. It was during the same times that Rome was threatening and the Selucid Empire was finally shattered by Rome to which it paid tribute in 190. The Parthians were much overrated by early historians and actually owed their gains to Roman interference in Asia Minor. During the years between 159 and 139 B.C. the Scythians of further east, called Yue-chi by Chinese, and true nomads living chiefly from the loot of the caravans between Han China and the Romans, took first Sogdiana and then Bactria. The Parthians were always between the slowly encroaching Romans and the lashing attacks of their cousin Scyths. In the period between about 147 B.C. and A.D. 77 there were two and sometimes three kings ruling at once and in 113 to 117 Trajan reduced Armenia, Babylonia and Mesopotamia to imperial provinces. In 162 Marcus Aurelius and Aelius Verus attacked Armenia and Osroene and in 164 Avidius

Cassius finally destroyed Selucia and Hellenism was no more heard of east of the Euphrates. Ardashir I (Artaxerxes) now started his career by killing his neighbors in Medea, then his brothers and so started a conquest in A.D. 212 finally ending up in 224 with the finish of the Parthians and the beginning of the famous Sassanian Empire.

THE SASSANIAN EMPIRE (A.D. 224–633 OR 226–251)

When Selucia was destroyed by the Romans and Hellenism in the Near East with it, the culture of the Aramaic section began to take its place. Palestine, Damascus and Mesopotamia, the old section through which Persians had travelled to Egypt was now influenced culturally by the fast growing power of Christianity. At the same time the vitality of Persia continued the Zoroasterian beliefs, and at this time Vologaeses III collected the Avesta. The new Persia was more like the old original Achaemenid period than the intervening Arsacid period. It recovered from its illness and at the same time Rome was having distracting troubles, and finally when the Goths defeated Decius in 251 the whole empire collapsed. Now the Persian empire was not much enlarged and the old title "King of Kings" could hardly apply, but there was a growing strength.

CHRISTIANITY VERSUS ZOROASTERIANISM

Armenia had become Christian under the Romans and what had started out as a fight between the Romans and Persians now became not only a national duel but a religious duel. To quote Edward Meyer, "The time was come when, in the western and eastern worlds alike, the religious question was for large masses of people the most important question in life, and the diffusion of their own creed and the suppression of all others the highest and holiest of tasks." But the opponents could not clinch, for Rome was harried by the Goths and Persia by the Scyths, yet about 390 Armenia was divided and by A.D. 430 the Persians had removed all trace of the Arsaces' kings who had taken refuge there.

Chosroes II raided Syria, Antioch in 611, Damascus in 613, Jerusalem in 614 and Egypt in 619 but in 623 Heraclius, the Roman, repaid him with interest and finally Chosroes was killed by his son and chaos reigned. Wars had now weakened both Rome and Persia softening them and preparing them for the conquest by Islam, that other great weapon of religion which had been forged in Arabia.

ISLAMIC PERSIA (A.D. 633–1235)

The Arabs had devised a heaven which promised fountains running with wine and beautiful damosels of willing nature and the key was sure for those who died fighting the unbelievers. The Arabs were toughened by desert and sea. They entered Persia in A.D. 633, the fate of the Sassanians was decided in 637 and by 650 they occupied every province of the country north to the Oxus and Balkh. Zoroasterianism disappeared. For about 150 years Persia was governed by Muhammedan caliphs in Medina and Bagdad who wished only to destroy its nationality and religion and to grow rich on the spoils. Turkish officers were favored to do the work and they held sway until Isma'il b.Ahmad, the Samanid stepped in.

THE SAMANIDS (A.D. 900–1229)

The Samanids were the first important non-Arabic Persian dynasty since the fall of the Sassanian kings. The Arabs had not harmed art for, although they had no art of their own, they had like other nomads a hunger for that of the peoples they conquered. Finally in 999 the last of the Sassanids were cleaned out by the Ilek-Khans of Turkestan.

GHAZNEVIDS AND SELJUKS

Alptagin, a slave of Mansur I, ran away to Afghanistan where he founded a semi-independent group, the first of the Ghaznevids. The Seljuks were another band of nomads from Turkestan who settled in Transoxiana and in the 11th century crossed the Oxus river which flows north west into the Sea of Aral from what is now northern Afghanistan, and plundered eastern Persia making Merv their capital in 1040. Three of their leaders took Balkh, Jorjan, Tabristan, Khwarizm, Hamadan, Rhages, Isfahan and finally Bagdad in 1055 thus introducing once again the northern animistic art and a new blood. The Syrian dynasty of the Seljuks came into contact with the Crusades and ended in three generations. In 1172–1199 Tukush and later in 1199–1220 Ala ed-din Mohammed subdued Khorasan, Rhages, Isfahan, practically all of Persia, Bokhara, Samarkand and Otrar finally reaching Ghazni where he was stopped by Jenghiz Khan.

MONGOLS (A.D. 1220–1335)

It is reported that Jenghiz Khan wished only to trade in the West, but the unfortunate killing of a camel train in Otrar and later of his envoy sent to Mohammed Shah led to war. It was planned carefully and the army was of Chinese and Mongols trained for the march. Juchi, the oldest son moved south into the old trade route while the main body continued westward. Chepé Noyon was already in Turkestan. Across the "Roof of the World" they moved and some starved, some fell and never arose, wagons and horses were left behind and the cold was killing but by Spring they had reached Lake Balkash and approached the frontiers of Islam. Soon the Turks learned a costly lesson from the ragged fur-clad hordes and Mohammed was pushed from pillar to post until he finally took refuge on an island in the Caspian Sea where he died. As the cities fell the useless were put to death, the women taken for the amusement of the troops and able bodied men beaten into slaves, chained like animals, and fed with the dogs. The system was thorough and every living thing and every object was used if possible, or destroyed if it was not of use to the horde.

Chepé Noyon and Subotai drove north into Russia and turned west to the Dnieper meeting a hastily assembled Russian army and annihilating it. They were about to enter Europe when Jenghiz Khan recalled them some 2,000 miles and they returned loaded with treasure having taken two divisions on a march across 90° of longitude in less than two years and having made careful note of the resources of the country and captured many men of learning. Subotai liked the "black earth" region of South Russia and years later he returned from the other side of the world to overrun Moscow and crossed the Dnieper to invade Europe. A generation later Marco Polo was to visit Kubhlai Khan the grandson of Jenghiz in the grandeur of Yüan China (A.D. 1280–1368).

THE ASSASSINS

Persia had been divided after the death of Jenghiz, 1272, by two of Jenghiz Khan's sons Jagatai and Tului. Hulagu was the son of the latter and he set himself to rid the world of the Assassin stronghold called "Alamut" or "Eagle's Nest." Hasan, the "Old Man of the Mountains" had organized a secret society of believers in the Muhammedan heaven who were fed hashish derived from hemp to boost them on this earth. Young men were allowed to live for a time in a sort of artificial heaven where they disported themselves with wine, women and hashish until suddenly they were commanded to fulfill a mission of death. The system should not be hard for us to understand for our own gangsters operate on a similar basis. One of the first victims was Hasan's former friend, one of the Seljuks, whose son also met the same fate. After Hasan died a separate branch was started in Syria and in Persia the last ruler of the Assassins was Rukn ad-Din whom Hulagu captured. The story is that he sent him to the other ruler Mangu who in true gangster style immediately put him to death sending word to Hulagu to do away with his competitive followers. Hulagu, the true Mongol, was nothing loath and promptly liquidated about 12,000 of them.

The Mongol rule now stretched from the dominions of Jagati on the north to Egypt in the south and from the Byzantine Empire on the west to China in the east.

TIMUR OR TAMERLANE (A.D. 1336–1405)

In the Northeast was bred another conqueror, Timur of the "green city" Shahr-i-Sabz or Kesh just 50 miles south of Samarkand. He was scholarly and so poor a military type in the beginning that he had trouble holding Transoxiana. However, later he took Balkh (in what is now Afghanistan). He then turned to the north west to the Caspian and later crossed the Volga. In the south he took all of Persia. After he was 60 in 1398 this energetic gentleman was "informed of commotions and civil wars of India," and went down to stop them, crossing the Indus River and sacking Delhi. It is said by Clavijo that ninety elephants worked one quarry in carrying stones for Timur for a mosque at Samarkand. Later he also took Bagdad, Aleppo and Damascus, beating the Turks at Angora. His final holdings were from the Volga to the Irtish and from the Hellespont to the Ganges.

Timur died in 1405. By 1447 the Timurid dynasty ceased to hold sway over Persia and here we leave what might be called the arena of the Near East. Other things happened there and will happen there but the world turned over and Europe took the stage as the most important center. Of course the conquest of Islam crossed Egypt and spread along North Africa jumping to Spain and nearly half way up into France but that we shall trace later.

THE STORY OF GLAZE

We know that glaze was used on stone and potteries very early in Egypt. We have also very early records in Mesopotamia (now Irak) and Persia (now Iran) but we do not know where the first conscious use of it came into being. Certainly it appears so suddenly and so late in China that it must have been an imported art. Not until the Han period 206 B.C. to A.D. 220 is there any real glaze there.

In the Near East we have found wonderful and brilliant blues that never were made elsewhere. Lustre made to imitate metal and actually made of metallic oxides blazed forth all unforeseen with its iridescence as beautiful as that created by nature on some glazes and seemed to catch the very fire of the kiln and preserve its smoldering lights for ever. These wares appeal not with sensitive forms or colors but with the royal pagan beauty of the wares of kings, and shahs, of caliphs and khans. They have the blazing of hot skies and ominous sunsets as well as the blue black cobalt of nights with stars too many and too large. They are vessels which held precious wines and poisons. They are bizarre, voluptuous, fantastic and as defiant of the laws of nature as were the devils who handled them and broke so many thousands of them in passions of love, lust or cruelty. Some escaped the trembling hands of slaves who lost their lives therefore and others were crushed by the rough shod march of conquest. Anything may be found among them except the firm and disciplined simplicity which only the artist of the Far East has ever mastered. From Arabia to the frozen steppes, from India to Greece, from Egypt to Samarkand, from China to the coast of Spain the pendulum swung and in the center of it all was Persia, Iran, land of kings.

EARLY DEVELOPMENTS

Whether glazed pottery was first made in Egypt or in the land of the Tigris and Euphrates called Mesopotamia we do not know. Its development was probably almost parallel for, as we know, the countries were often under one rule. One reason that the Greeks did not make use of glaze is that they were inclined to draw pictures on their vases and the glazes were not readily controlled. Perhaps for this reason we find many tiles in the earliest wares of the Near East for they could be fired flat and there was less likelihood that the design would be ruined by running glaze. As early as the III Dynasty in Egypt tiles were made and they have been found also in Mesopotamia of even date. Some claim that there are earlier records from Syria.

Butler tells us that at Tell el Yahudia in the palace of Rameses III dating about 1200 B.C. and in Tell el Amarna (about 1370 B.C.) tiles were found showing variety of color, modeling and flat inlay. Walter Andrae tells us that at Ashur on the Tigris were found many tiles and several pot sherds placed about 1300 and showing distinct traces of glaze. Emil Hannover speaks of a fragment of a vase on which the name of King Mena is inlayed in violet glaze, which he, therefore, reasons must belong to a period of about 3300 B.C. but this sort of evidence does not prove any place of origin nor any definite date, and my opinion is that glaze may have been found and lost in a number of places before it came into general use.

EGYPTIAN GLAZED POTTERY

Tiles and bricks with one face glazed seem to show the earliest conscious efforts to make glazes in Egypt as elsewhere, though some accidental salt glazes did occur early in bowls. In the VI Dynasty (about 2550–2350 B.C.) a dark blue was added and in the XIII Dynasty (2000–1788 B.C.) a light blue

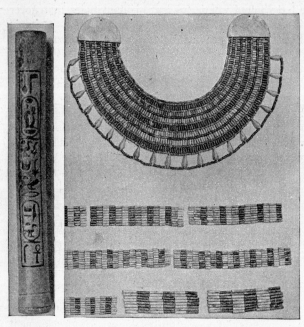

FIG. 452. Fragment of a sistrum of green faïence of Saitic origin showing Isis. Ht. 5¼". Metropolitan Mus. of Art.

FIG. 450. Kohl tube of blue faïence made during the reign of Amenhotep III of the 18th dynasty. Ht. 5½". Metropolitan Mus. of Art.
FIG. 451. Egyptian 12th Dynasty collar, anklets and bracelets of faïence of various colors found in the Cemetery of King Amen-em-het. Metropolitan Mus. of Art.

and soft manganese black were added but it was in the XVIII Dynasty (1540–1350 B.C.) that the greatest development of the art of ceramics took place. Beautifully formed "lotus cups" and other graceful forms were devised. Added to the earliest copper oxide blues and greens obtained by the addition of iron were manganese purples from bluish to violet, chrome yellows and oranges, iron reds, brighter greens and a glaze which through the addition of tin was milk white. Pieces of inlay for architectural purposes, small scarabs, beads, vases, bowls and "ushabti" figures shaped like mummies and supposed to aid or protect the dead were also made. These "ushabti" sometimes hold in their hands, with arms crossed, a basket and a hoe. They

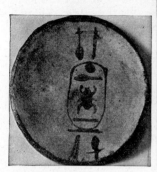

FIG. 455. Heavy cup of faïence inscribed with the name of Ramses the Great made during the 19th dynasty. Ht. 4″. Metropolitan Mus. of Art.

FIG. 453. Dish of blue faïence with black rim and cartouche of Thut-mose II, from Thebes, Egypt. Dia. 3⅛″. Metropolitan Mus. of Art.

FIG. 454. Figure of Horus made during the late dynastic times. Blue faïence. Ht. 3″. Metropolitan Mus. of Art.

have also, on the bottom, an inscription from the VI Chapter of the Book of the Dead. Others represent *Hathor* with the head of a cow (the Egyptian Aphrodite), *Thoth* with the head of an ibis, *Amen* with human head and a crown of plumes, *Pasht* with the head of a lion, *Bast* with the head of a cat, *Isis* with *Horus* and finally *Nephthys*. Until the XXVI Dynasty hundreds of

FIG. 456. Fragment of a vase of pale blue faïence, Ptolemaic Egyptian. Ht. 1⅛″. Metropolitan Mus. of Art.

FIG. 457. Egyptian Early Roman period (about 1st cent. A.D.) faïence ram feeding. Metropolitan Mus. of Art.

FIG. 458. Miniature pylon of blue faïence, Ptolemaic Period, Egypt. Ht. 3½″. Metropolitan Mus. of Art.

figures were placed in tombs with scarabs which are faithful images of the "dung beetle" or "tumblebug" (Scaraebus sacer) which lays its eggs in a ball of dung and then pushes it up a mound with its hind feet and allows it to roll down several times probably to pack it harder. We uncertainly have come to the conclusion that the Egyptians associated it in some way with rebirth and that the small globe was compared to the sun. The beetle was sacred to the sun-god. It was mummified at Heliopolis, many figures of it were placed about the bodies and a large figure with outspread wings was placed over the heart. Many were pierced longitudinally so that they could be worn on cords. A large group of stone ones bear royal names but the pottery ones never do unless made for tourist trade.

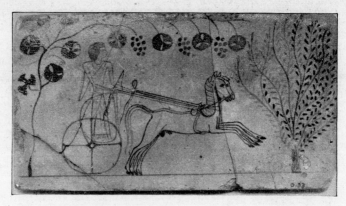

18th dynasty blue faïence tile with finely drawn charioteer and plant forms
in black. This is quite static in feeling but charming decoration. Length
6¼". Metropolitan Mus. of Art.

Egyptian Late Dynastic period about 500 to 350 B.C. polychrome faïence inlays for a wooden
shrine. Not only the drawing but the soft colors of these are very beautiful. Metropolitan Mus.
of Art.

EGYPTIAN TILE AND FAÏENCE INLAYS
PLATE 81

21st dynasty pectoral of Entui-ny in blue faïence. Ht. 3¾". Metropolitan Mus. of Art.

19th or 20th dynasty (1350–1090 B.C.) faïence cup of graceful shape with a lotus stem and base and relief figures in two bands about the body. Ht. 5¾". Metropolitan Mus. of Art.

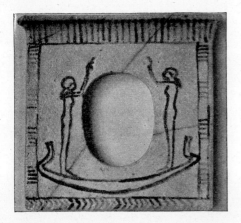

Pectoral of blue faïence. 20th to 26th dynasty. Ht. 4¾". Metropolitan Mus. of Art.

26th dynasty two handled amphora of light colored faïence. Ht. 6". Metropolitan Mus. of Art.

EGYPTIAN 19TH TO 26TH DYNASTY FAÏENCE

PLATE 82

21st dynasty Ushabtis of the High Priest of Amun-Pay-nudem. Blue faience. Ht. 6⅜″. Metropolitan Mus. of Art.

Figure of Isis of faience of the 26th to 30th dynasty. Ht. 5″. Metropolitan Mus. of Art.

Shawabti of King Seti I in deep blue faience made at Thebes. Ht. 11¾″. Metropolitan Mus. of Art.

19th dynasty "Shawabti" of Pa-ser in blue faience of rich color but with details somewhat blurred. Ht. 5¾″. Metropolitan Mus. of Art.

Ushabti of glazed steatite (soap stone) from Thebes, 18th dynasty. Metropolitan Mus. of Art.

EGYPTIAN USHABTIS AND FIGURES OF DIVINITIES

PLATE 83

Most amazing is the sameness of Egyptian pottery from the beginning of the Middle Kingdom, the IX Dynasty right through to the 17th century A.D. Even in the Roman and Arab epochs little change is seen. As an example the bowl in the British Museum, having portraits of Constantine and Fausta is located in the 4th century yet in its color, blended blue on the back and manganese inside, and technique it is no different from the Islamic wares of centuries later.

FIG. 461. Egyptian faïence tragic mask in turquoise color of the Early Roman Period about 1st cent. A.D. From the Carnarvon Coll. Metropolitan Mus. of Art.

FIG. 459. Blue faïence figure of the Ptolemaic period, Egypt. Ht. 2¾". Metropolitan Mus. of Art.
FIG. 460. Fragment of a vase of faïence of the Ptolemaic period. Metropolitan Mus. of Art.

NAUCRATITE POTTERY

At the "Potter's Gate" near the extensive kilns in Naucratis was found many pieces. This was not only the most important town of the Greek colony in Egypt from the middle of the 7th to the middle of the 6th centuries B.C. but also a shipping port for wares from Athens, Corinth, Miletus, Samos, Lesbos, Clazomenae and Cyrene. Three pieces only were also said to have been found from Phoenicia or Assyria, but this is not hard to understand when we remember that in 612 B.C. the Medeans and Babylonians were fighting and probably had little time for pottery exports to Egypt. Egypt was on the outskirts of the Near Eastern civilizations and was less disturbed. When conquered, Egypt could draw back into herself up the Nile like a sea-worm and on the other hand there was little incentive for her to reach out beyond her own fertile valley. This accounts for her slow development, her uninspired but basically sound art. She was unwhipped by the constant raids of the nomads and her artists saw little to shock them into new endeavors.

The local Naucratite ware was of soft creamy ground on which was polychrome decoration. The inside was usually black with lotus designs of red and white. The designs were of lions, stags, lotus borders and buds, dancing figures, winged griffins, human headed birds and various other animals and birds, all drawn as well and as life-like as possible but without the compacting of them into given spaces or what we know as conventionalism. It is likely that we find here ancient ideas from the Tigris and Euphrates plus contemporary observation.

ALEXANDRIAN POTTERY

Rhacotis, for centuries a pottery center, had new kilns built in 310 to 230 B.C. for Greek potters, and there is an unbroken succession of dated pieces from 271 to 239 B.C. Most of these potteries are not glazed but enamels were used as were also the application of both silver and gold. In the Alexandrian Museum is a skyphos of blue enamel with horizontal band of olive leaves, a design often seen later. Another fragment with portrait of Arsinoe or Berenice is from an Oenochoe and has traces of gold leaf on it.

At this time there was considerable warlike activity in Asia Minor, Spain, Etruria and Magna Graecia, therefore the Egyptian kilns were probably by far the most active. Prof. Griffith found at Tell el Amarna 150 houses in every one of which were molds for making small ornaments, and from Meroe to Wadi Ghâzai there were many kilns.

COPTIC POTTERY

Most Coptic pottery is crude and badly decorated, made only for common use. One fine example is in the Metropolitan Museum and has been assigned to the 8th or 7th century by Dimand and 6th century by Butler. In the Monastery of Epiphanius at Qurnah were found some typical Egyptian and small Arretine ware bowls interesting because they are glazed on the inside only with the lip-rim covered. Lamps have been found that cover the transition between classical and mediaeval, including Roman forms and those with deeper bodies, more open spouts, higher handles and a definite rim around the oil hole. The later ones have a higher neck and lengthened spout like those found at Fostât.

FIG. 462. Babylonian 6th cent. B.C. panel of enameled bricks from the "Procession Street." The colors are white, tan, blue and green. Length 7 feet 5½ inches. Metropolitan Mus. of Art.

MESOPOTAMIAN GLAZED POTTERIES

From the 9th to the 6th centuries B.C. were placed in the temple of Saragon's citadel, Khorsabad, figures of bulls, lions, eagles and trees wonderfully designed in glazed brick, of various colors. There were also glazed bricks in the archivolt of the town gate, and the walls and floor tiles of the palace of the Assyrian Kings at Calah, now in the city of Nimrud or Kalakh, were also decorated with colored glazes. Unfortunately some of the glazed bricks from Babylon were lost by the excavations forever in the Tigris but the few known give us an idea of the splendor that must have enshrouded this city. From Susa excavated by the French, from the royal citadel of the Akhaemenes dating about 500 B.C. came the parts of the relief of the "Immortals" and the famous "Frieze of Archers" which we hope is still in the Louvre. The colors used are bright yellow, yellow brown, white and soft olive green, now of course tempered by time but with beauty undiminished. With anatomy the artists who made these were fully acquainted but the dignity of feeling and organization of design raises them to a rating with the greatest of fine arts. Only fragments were found of Nebuchadnezzar II's gigantic frieze from the "Procession Street" and the walls of the Ishtar Gate and the Throne Room in Babylon of his time but the Germans have made remarkable restorations of them.

Ashur

The Deutsche Orient-Gesellschaft's excavations at Ashur have taken us still further back for they reach from the fall of the Assyrian Empire in 606 B.C. back to the 13th century B.C. In the Temple of Ashur were found bricks stamped as made for the Temple of Adad and they must be earlier than the time of Tiglath-Pileser I of the 12th century B.C. for he alone we know restored that temple. Still older are the potteries from Kar-Tukulki-Enurta on the left bank of the Tigris opposite Ashur for they are fully matured and show a well-developed style, already stiff and altered from the original craftsmanship of prehistoric vase painting of Susa from which they are directly descended. Patterns are of the palm, pomegranate and only later about 1500 B.C. does the lotus appear from Egypt for it grows on the Nile and not on the Tigris and Euphrates. But the most startling characteristic of the Ashur pieces is the strong predominance of alternation in design.

Alternation in Design

Here is another principle of art appeal. In nature the alternation of leaves up a stem or that of two sizes of petals on a flower or that of the effect of calyx and petals at the back of a flower is about all one finds. In the stripes of animals to be sure it occurs in simple form but not often. Alternation implies an abrupt cutting off of one state for another which is in turn severed for a reintroduction of the first or for the introduction of still a third. Nature is largely continuous so this is to a great degree an invention of man. An alternating border may have two or any number of separate blocks unrelated but recurring at stated intervals. There may be a connecting flow but this is unnecessary and simply acts as a softening of the effect. Alternation undoubtedly grew out of the art of weaving and is essential to it. These are the simple facts but the true artist is seldom contented with static alternation of 1-2-1-2 type or even of 1-2-3-1-2-3 type, or the ascending and descending type 1-2-3-2-1-2-3 type, and he may develop constantly varied types such as the enclosing of three dots in a box and four dots in the next but always arranged differently or he may develop growing alternation which introduces a simple pair or more of subjects and makes them ever more complicated always retaining the given forms in some certain rhythm until a crescendo is reached as in a rhapsody. He often imposes rhythm upon rhythm as 1-2-3-5-2-1-2-4-3-2-1-5-2-3-2-4 etc., in which our ascending and descending rhythm has a simple alternation imposed on its every fourth beat.

There is a strange liking for alternation in Mesopotamia and Persia which is lacking in the art of the Far East. It is probably due to the constant invasions of nomadic peoples to whom the weaving of unbreakable baskets and also rugs or other fabrics to protect them against the cold are very important arts. Therefore, we have here another perfectly reasonable explanation of why the Northern and nomadic art was responsible for the development of conventionalization. Those people of the warmer climates made pottery for they did not have to move and carry it with them. In Mesopotamia and Persia we find the two arts meeting to the benefit of ceramic design.

But to return to the potteries of Ashur and to quote Mr. Andrae, "Originally the fruit-bearing turioniferous palm, and probably the rosette, and the he-goats, represented symbolically the cult of the goddess Ishtar; but later palmettos and pairs of facing goats generally on their knees, became simple ornaments with no deeper meaning." This would imply a long development and beginning decadence. Mr. Andrae gives the following list of characteristics peculiar to the Assyrian pottery:

1.—Hardness of curves shown in the palm leaves and tree of life.
2.—Preference for the compact, heavy and almost cumbrous with an apparently willful avoidance of all delicacy and lightness.
3.—The interlacing of patterns and filling of ornaments with other forms such as the leaves with many colored geometrical figures or other plant forms. This, he says is carried for 3,000 years down to the patterns of Islamic carpets and printed cottons.
4.—The pomegranate is probably an Assyrian invention, he thinks, while the palm, which is not indigenous was developed in another form.
5.—The use of the chevron is at its height in the 9th century and was lost by the 7th.

Finally tin glaze is thought to have been consciously discovered and made use of in about 1100 B.C. and through its ability to cover a colored surface and make a clear ground on which to paint decorations, brought about the use of glazed bricks in greater numbers. The colors used were much the same as those used in Egypt though this does not imply that they came from there. The colors were well used and did not run into each other, which implies high technical ability.

ORTHOSTATS AND PROBABLE ORIGIN OF THE CLOUD MOTIF

Large bricks measuring more than 45 inches by a foot and 4 or 5 inches thick were used to protect the lower parts of the walls from blows or damp and are called orthostats. They were usually unglazed but the kings had theirs beautifully decorated. One was found which was dated by its inscription (890–884 B.C.) while a much earlier one shows the god Ashur flying above a charioteer and drawing his bow while about him is a nimbus shown by double yellow rings and to either side is a design of clouds like bags holding dots to

FIG. 464. Tin enamel faced bricks, many having the following inscription stamped on the upper surface:
"Tiglath-Pileser,
The Great King, The Mighty King, the King of All, the King of the Assyrians,
Belonging to the 'Kigal' of the bulls
Of the Gate of Adad's Temple."
(Tiglath-Pileser reigned in 1120–1100 B.C.) Found at Ashur. The colors are turquoise and green ground, white cufic characters and yellow and orange designs with brown outlines. The tiles had been reassembled about 300 years after they were made. Length 5' 9". From *Coloured Ceramics from Ashur* by Walter Andrae.

FIG. 463. Brick orthostat with colored enamel painting of Ashur, the chief national god, receiving an Assyrian noble. He is either thanking or petitioning against a plague of locusts (see one above his head). Above the god's head are symbols of the three other chief gods,—the sun (Shamash), the moon (Sin) and Venus (Ishtar). On his head he has the crown with horns, feather trimming and the eight-rayed disk supported by a lily as in the relief in Malthai, which is well known. Ht. 22", width 10¾". From *Coloured Ceramics from Ashur* by Walter Andrae.

represent drops of rain. It may be that these are the first of that motive which became so prominent in later Chinese design. I know of nothing in China as early.

ASHUR POTTERY VESSELS

Most of the pottery vessels belong to the two last centuries of the Assyrian Empire and almost exclusively to the reign of Sargon ("The legitimate King") who assumed the name of the famous king of Babylon who ruled some 2,000 years before. He lasted from 722 B.C. to 705 B.C. and his conquests included,

FIG. 465. A flat truncated conical "bucket shaped vase" the sherds represented as lying out flat, the biggest and most beautiful one found in Ashur. Note the pair of double handles or loops near the top. The ground is sky-blue. The other colors are mustard yellow and white. Note the alternation of coloring of the flowers and the upper borders. Ht. about 16½". From *Coloured Ceramics from Ashur* by Walter Andrae.

Jar, light buff and sandy clay. Greenish-blue, light grey (which was dark blue), yellow and black outlines. Ht. 14".

Vase with pointed panels in blue, grey and yellow (grey having been dark blue probably), and rare treatment of kneeling goat and flower in wide band about the body. Ht. 14½".

Oblate vase with wide mouth and small base of late Assyrian period having interesting check-ered arch design around lotus blossoms and buds arranged in symmetrical panels. Green which was once more blue, white, yellow and brown. Ht. 8⅝".

Possibly from temple of Anu and Adad. Late or post-Assyrian date. Light blue, yellow, dark blue, black outlines and white. Shape typical. Ht. 11⅝".

ALL PHOTOGRAPHS FROM *Coloured Ceramics From Ashur*, BY WALTER ANDRAE

ASSYRIAN (ASHUR) POTTERY VESSELS

PLATE 84

Egypt, Damascus, Palestine and the Philistines, as well as eastern Armenia, the Hitites and Moschi 717 B.C. It is said he sent a statue of himself to Cyprus. Probably the empire's fall was a signal for looting of the temple and the vases were broken then or subsequently in handling.

Mr. Andrae makes three classifications:—1.—buckets, 2.—pots, 3.—bottles. The first are all about the same shape though they vary in size, and some have handles. The bottles are close to the prehistoric forms of many countries. The pots are wide-mouthed forms without the appendages which ruined the forms of many Greek vases. They were probably used for daily life, for burial and also for ceremonies. The colors are warm golden yellow, light wine-yellow, ivory, blue (said by Andrae to have faded from the original depth, but very pleasing) and dark violet. The designs are in bands which seem to be suspended on the sides from above rather than supported from below. This is unique.

FIGURES FROM ASHUR

Fragments of figures include a horse head, a torso and the body of some small fat animal which might have been on wheels like the one found at Ur. All show fine craftsmanship and the horse head is as good as most found on

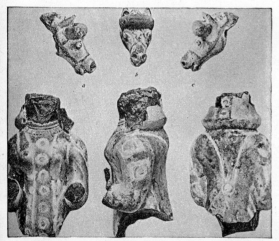

FIG. 466. Polychromed horse's head said to be from the figure of a mounted man. Ht. 2¾". Part of a figure of a woman in the position, with hands raised before her, of prayer. Ht. 4¾". The probable height of the figure was 9½". From *Coloured Ceramics from Ashur* by Walter Andrae.

FIG. 467. A few knob-plates of Neo-Assyrian times restored from fragments. The circular ones 20" in dia. The square 15" on a side. From *Coloured Ceramics from Ashur* by Walter Andrae.

T'ang Chinese specimens 1,200 to 1,400 years later. These are covered with white and decorated with the same colors as were used on the vases. They may have been small household gods though I think to pin this theory of so serious use on every ancient object is not to allow for simple human reactions.

KNOBS AND KNOB PLATES

The walls were ornamented with plaster painting and the orthostats while inner walls were almost covered with pottery and besides that the upper parts had crenelles and friezes of polychrome bricks and having unglazed or polychrome enameled knobs stuck into them, called by the Assyrians "zigat." These knobs were also found in Nineveh and Calah but were thought to be vases. In Babylon they were cones with inscriptions on the shaft or head. Mr. Andrae says they are established as being in use in the third millennium B.C. and thinks they were put in as "key stones" on the completion of the building just as little inscribed barrels, prisms and tablets were put in as "foundation stones."

FIG. 468. Possibly restorations by Dr. Herzfeld of an enamelled knobplate from Ashur of King Ashurnazirpal III. Inscription about the base of the knob, PALACE OF ASHUR-NAZIRPAL, KING OF ALL, KING OF ASSYRIA, SON OF TUKULTI-ENURTA, KING OF ALL, KING OF ASSYRIA. Shows that even to the words there is a sort of alternation. Width and ht. 14½". The knob extends 5". From *Coloured Ceramics from Ashur* by Walter Andrae.

FIG. 469. Knobs found in a heap of rubbish in the Old Palace in Ashur. Middle 9th cent. B.C. Such objects were thought to be vases when first found. Greatest length 7½". From *Coloured Ceramics from Ashur* by Walter Andrae.

They are not phallic and derived from pegs. Later ones in Assyria have larger and flatter heads. As bases for these pegs there were found concave square and round plates which Mr. Andrae thinks were alternated. In the 9th century the round ones are larger and this has cast some doubt on his assumption but I see no reason why it should. Some were under the crenellation while others seem to have been placed at about the height of a man. I cannot help but wonder if they did not serve as pegs on which to hang clothing, etc., or if they did not support cords of some sort perhaps for wall hangings.

Such, then, was the general state of the great ceramic art of Assyria during the Sargonid period when she was at the height of her culture. The forms were sound and strong. The designs were alive and full of the rhythm of alternation. The colors were masterfully handled and there is a sureness which seems to grow out of stone carving (at which they were also masters) which disciplines the brush into a secure and definite handling. There are no fancy flourishes here, none of the later Persian sweetness, and yet there is a ferociousness, almost cruelty, in the movement which is entirely lacking from the Egyptian things. These potteries have come a long way up from those we found in the 12th layer at the bottom under the sand of Mesopotamia. They have reached their peak. Now follows the Babylonian and Medean conquest and turmoil with later King Cyrus of Persia.

ACHAEMENID EMPIRE POTTERY (558–330 B.C.)

This was not a productive time in Persia but it was during the Achaemenid Empire that the "Frieze of Archers" was made and important finds have been made in Susa. The main stream of art came from Assyria and such things as the great winged lions with human heads (Propylaeum at Persepolis) and animals were well drawn but with less power in Persia. The tall slender fluted column with Indian feeling was now developed. The modeling of animals was carried from extreme conventionalism as in Luristan to the purely naturalistic of the South. But perhaps most significant is the discarding of the old Semitic modesty concerning the human body. Finally King Cyrus, as also at a later time King Darius, will be found often portrayed as are George Washington and Abraham Lincoln in the United States.

GLAZED POTTERY NOTES OF THESE TIMES

The glazes used in Egypt and the Near East are composed of silicic acid or simple quartz sand combined with some medium which helps it to fuse at a lower temperature, called a "flux." It is this flux which determines the type of glaze. The palette of colors could not be broadened because the glaze we are discussing was alkaline and would be acted upon by the most diluted acids. It is this which also explains how they easily became iridescent. An interesting point is that the silicates of lime and soda with a little alumina used in the Near East would not stick to ordinary potter's clay but only to a body similar to itself and made of siliceous sand. Such a body is not plastic and had to be mixed with a potter's clay in order to be made so. Therefore it is clear why the beautiful effects accomplished in Persia to Egypt were not obtained elsewhere, for it would be difficult to find all the ingredients; proper sand, clay and the oxides with which to color the glazes all in one place.

Glazes containing lead oxide were used in both sections as far back as Ptolemaic times and, though the Romans with their Greek heritage used little glaze, the pottery that succeeded theirs in Western Europe and Byzantium was generally glazed with a substance rich in lead. These glazes are more or less transparent and showed the texture of the body but the sometimes unpleasant imperfections were hidden by dipping the piece first in a "slip" or what the French call "engobe" and then glazing over that. It will be remembered what a wonderful use the Chinese made of slip treatments in the Sung period. Similar and earlier treatments though less beautiful are found in what is known as "Gabri ware" in the Near East.

Tin glaze is quite as early as lead glaze and probably originated in Assyria. The tiles or glazed bricks found at Nimroud, Khorsabad and Nineveh as well as the famous wall pictures at Susa were stanniferous. This takes such glazes back to at least 500 B.C. In the buildings of Muhammed I at Brusa the tin glaze was decorated with low-fired enamels easily melted in the "muffled kiln." This is all definitely Assyrian for in Egypt even up to and after the Islamic times the older alkaline glazes persisted.

FIG. 470. Roman terracotta or unglazed pottery bowl on foot with four handles painted in slip to imitate marble like those of Egypt and Crete of far earlier date. 1st cent. A.D. Ht. 3¾". Metropolitan Mus. of Art.

PTOLEMAIC EGYPTIAN POTTERIES
(End of 4th century to 1st century and Roman Period)

The Egyptians had always tried to imitate the veining of their marble vessels by mixing potter's clay and we see similar effects done in Crete. By the time the idea reached China not only the body clays but slips and even glazes were so mixed. Then the idea was reflected back from T'ang China (A.D. 618–906) to Samarra. Of course the technique persisted simply because it was pleasing and not with any conscious idea of imitating stone. In the XXVI Dynasty ushabtis were made with a mixture of sand and turquoise glaze all through the body and shortly after bowls were made which look as though they had been carved from dark blue veined onyx.

ASSYRIAN AS WELL AS GREEK INFLUENCES IN EGYPT

The conquest of Egypt by Cambyses in the Achaemenid period during the 6th century had little influence on Assyria but brought designs from there to

FIG. 471. Egypto-Roman vases, first two said to be of 2nd or 3d cent. and having green-blue glaze. Lower two of 1st cent. and glazed in deep manganese blue with turquoise inside and green relief decoration. From *Islamic Pottery* by A. J. Butler Coll. of Eton Mus.

FIG. 472. Heavy pottery vase with swan handles crudely and unevenly potted and covered with green glaze. Found in Greece and thought to date c. 100 B.C. to A.D. 100. Ht. 5". Metropolitan Mus. of Art.

Egypt and tended to a refinement in potting. The art of making portrait figures started about 500 B.C. and continued until in 200 B.C. the casting process cheapened and destroyed it.

Jars with globular bodies and wide necks had been made for many centuries and the one with cover of about 800 B.C. is little different in general potting from the more graceful example of the 1st or 2nd century B.C. from the Kelekian Collection save that the handles of the latter are joined to the body with a leaf-like spread probably Hellenistic in origin. Another without handles but with horizontal bands of decoration reminiscent of the "Oriental Period" of Greek vases but rendered in beautiful light and dark turquoise is also of the 2nd or 1st century B.C. The one at the Metropolitan Museum has been badly restored but the two published by Butler from the Eton Museum show the real shape with flaring foot of more or less weak classic form and flaring mouth. Of the same period of Egypto-Roman potteries are the jars with more angular shoulders and squared handles. These are usually covered with dark blue glaze on which are modeled plant forms in low relief and picked out in turquoise. A piece with green glaze but showing similar characteristics was found in Greece. It has swan handles and a weaker form.

SYRO-ROMAN POTTERIES

A type of jar thought to have been made in Syria from about the 3d or 2nd centuries to about A.D. 100 shows certain similarities of form including the angular shoulder and double handle although in these the two parts of the handles are sometimes twisted to give a braided appearance. They are about 12 to 14 inches high as a rule, are of sandy body and covered with a green glaze of alkaline type turned, through action of the soil, to beautiful iridescence at times. They inherit the unstructural Greek foot but are otherwise sturdily made and powerful in proportion. At times appliqués in low relief were added but this was a development toward the end of their period and not at all unlike the relief decorations found on typical Roman cups of the day both from the continent and the islands such as Cyprus. It has been suggested that this type of vase is the sort which was sent to China and thus introduced the glaze of the Han period. I do not know of any having been found there although examples have come from all over the Near East, yet similarities in form and the very similar glaze point to this as a reasonable theory. In any event these vases are stronger than those of Rome and the Chinese are stronger than these.

IRIDESCENCE

Collectors of Near Eastern wares and those from Han China pay greater prices for pieces showing fine iridescence. This is entirely an accident of nature and the potters never had any slightest idea that their wares were to be so beautified. Iridescence is not color nor any sort of pigment but refraction of light and may be thought of as caused by millions of tiny prisms making "rainbows." These prisms are simply the irregularities caused by the rotting away of the glaze due to chemical action in the soil in which the potteries were buried, and every color from deep violet to brilliant red can be found

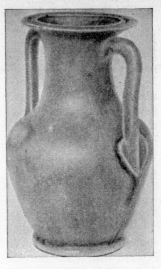

Egyptian covered vase with rich, deep turquoise glaze over usual buff pottery dating c. 800 B.C. Ht. 6½". Eton Mus.

Beautiful Egypto-Roman vase with glaze of mottled pale green and turquoise dating c. 1st or 2nd cent. Ht. 8¾". Ex Kelekian Coll., Victoria and Albert Mus.

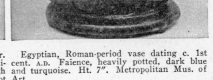

Egyptian vase, light and dark turquoise color. Middle Ptolemaic period (200–100 B.C.) showing similarity in design to Oriental Period Greek vases, though latter are not carried out in glaze and relief. Foot and neck are repairs. Metropolitan Mus. of Art.

Egyptian, Roman-period vase dating c. 1st cent. A.D. Faïence, heavily potted, dark blue and turquoise. Ht. 7". Metropolitan Mus. of Art.

JARS SHOWING GREEK AND ROMAN INFLUENCES IN EGYPT

Plate 85

"Syro-Roman" vase, excavated at Bagdad. Light buff clay with glaze which varies from blue to green and with brown areas, also iridescence from burial. Ht. 13¼". Warren E. Cox Coll. Ex Demotte Coll.

Roman or "Syro-Roman" vase with unusual appliqués about neck and fine iridescence due to burial. Ht. 14⅛". Metropolitan Mus. of Art.

Left: Roman vase dating about 1st cent. B.C. Much like that called Syro-Roman because much of it was found in Syria. Beautiful iridescence from burial. Ht. 9½". Metropolitan Mus. of Art.

Roman cup with pressed design in relief, from Cyprus 100 B.C. to A.D. 100. Ht. c. 2½". Metropolitan Mus. of Art.

Right: Roman buff pottery cup with two ring handles, decorated with moulded relief design under greenish glaze dating c. 100 B.C. to A.D. 100. Ht. 2¾". Metropolitan Mus. of Art.

SYRO-ROMAN POTTERIES

PLATE 86

in all sorts of combinations. Far more beautiful than the color of a peacock's tail or that of a South American butterfly are these subtle sheens of ever-changing light.

I have in my collection from the Kevorkian Collection an ewer of the 12th to 13th century found at Sultanabad which is covered with a silvery lavender colored iridescence. When it is wet the moisture fills all the little interstices between the tiny prisms and makes an even surface. Then it can be seen that the glaze is of deep blue and that it has a design in black painted on it. When the piece dries again this disappears under the sheen of silver and lavender again. Many pieces do not respond so quickly because their

FIG. 473. This ewer shown first dry and then partly wet so that the black of the design shows clearly on the blue ground. When dry the whole is a lavender, silver color. Sultanabad Persian piece of 12th to 13th cent. Ht. 9¾". Ex Kevorkian Coll. Warren E. Cox Coll.

iridescence is deeper but all will show the original color underneath if soaked in water for some time. I do not advise doing this to repaired pieces for they will fall apart and never under any conditions should a rag be touched to such a surface for it will only rub in dirt and dull the effect. The piece should be wet with clear water and allowed to dry of its own accord.

PARTHIAN AND SASSANIAN WARES (190 B.C.–A.D. 224 AND A.D. 224 TO 633 OR 175–226 AND 226–651 ACCORDING TO DIMAND)

Of the Parthian wares little is known and in truth probably the art of pottery was in an absorptive period rather than productive. We have said

FIG. 475. Dark green glazed earthenware vase, Parthian 1st to 2nd cent. A.D. Ht. 13½". Metropolitan Mus. of Art.

FIG. 474. Sassanian pottery jar, 2nd to 6th cent. More powerful shape than usually seen. Glaze olive green with silver iridescence. Ht. about 22". Nasli Heeramaneck Coll.

FIG. 476. Sassanian, Mesopotamian, large jar of unglazed earthenware. Buff colored clay with impressed design, irregular and crude. 3rd to 4th cent. found at Takrit, Iraq. Ht. 16¾". Metropolitan Mus. of Art.

that the nomadic influences are usually inspirational and this is true but their inventions take some time to digest and they are seldom seen at once. This period was also one of decline both in Rome and in the Near East and during it the great religious wars were starting. If the Parthians won their power chiefly through the weakness of Rome, their pottery also shows a rather weak character. The Sassanians continued a relief technique and some show a "barbotine" or slip treatment in their wares. They also decorated the unglazed water jars with impressions from seals possibly after the Parthian influence. Sassanian metal work was superb and many of the potteries were influenced by this craft. Sassanian and early Islamic pieces have been found at Kufa, Takrit, Samarra, Ganaur and Bagdad.

ISLAMIC POTTERY

From the days of late Rome to Islamic times there is little identified Sassanian pottery and the "Parthian," "Syro-Roman" and a few Egyptian continuations are all we have though excavations in Constantinople may bring to light the Byzantine sequence.

"GABRI" TYPES

The "Gabri" (or "Guebri") ware was so-called because its enthusiastic discoverers believed it to have been made by the fire-worshiping Pre-Islamic peoples before 633 but it is now agreed that most of these wares are actually of the 8th to 10th century. The body of these wares is usually reddish and they are coated with a white slip over which is a yellowish or green transparent lead glaze sometimes given green, yellow or purplish brown areas. The usual type has the slip cut away to form designs in contrast with the body color, a technique expertly handled in Sung Chinese Tz'u Chou type wares. Here, however, the designs are bold and show northern animal and bird forms, floral scrolls and figures often within geometrical diapers. The wares have been excavated chiefly in Northern Persia at Zendjan, Rhages, Hamadan, Susa, Kermanshah and in Amul just south of the Caspian where yellow and an ocherous red were added, with very rare examples of white

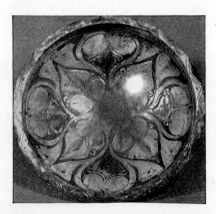

FIG. 477. Hamadan-Zenjan bowl. Reddish brown ware with thick white slip incised and covered with yellowish white glaze having splashes of green. 9th to 10th cent. Dia. about 15". Nasli Heeramaneck Coll.

FIG. 478. Bowl from Samarkand in Western Turkestan. Samanid period, 10th cent. Glazed pottery with cream glaze and design in olive green, red-brown, and black. Dia. 10¾". Metropolitan Mus. of Art.

Bowl of brown pottery with white slip and lead glaze showing green at rim but otherwise colorless and transparent. Located near Amul or Rei (Rhages). c. 8th to 9th cent. Dia. 13″. Dikran G. Kelekian.

Bowl, 9th cent. Green glaze over carved slip decoration on brown ground. Found at Zendjan, Persia and shows Sassanian influence. Note filling in of rump with circular design. Dia. 7¾″. Dikran K. Kelekian Coll.

Left: Reddish pottery bowl of conical form with low concave base having white slip and scratched out design under green transparent glaze. Slip and glaze cover only part of exterior. Note spur marks inside. Zendjan type, so-called because many were found there, though there is no proof of their manufacture there. 10th to 12th cent. Eumorfopoulos Coll. # F356.

Center: "Gabri type" green incised tile for top of stove or for outlet plaque for running water. Nasli Heeramaneck Coll.

Right: "Gabri" type slip-covered sgraffito pottery. Red-brown ware with lead glaze having streaks of purplish-brown. Found at Hamadan or Zendjan. 10th to 11th cent. Dia. 8¾″. Metropolitan Mus. of Art.

INCISED SLIP WARES OF SO-CALLED "GABRI TYPE"
PLATE 87

painted on a ground of black slip. A red ware of the Samanid period (A.D. 819–1004) painted with colored slips is found as far east as Samarkand, in Western Turkestan.

The Amol potteries are similar with polychrome decoration on white slip of Kufic writing and medallions in orange-red, aubergine, olive-green and white.

T'ANG TYPE SAMARRA WARE

Professors Sarre and Herzfeld made systematic excavations at Samarra on the Tigris (where the Affasid Caliph Matasim lived between 836 and 883 when he left for Bagdad), and found a distinctive close grained buff ware with opaque greyish white tin glaze painted at times with lustre of golden brown, green or blood red tones, or at times with dark cobalt blue with now and then touches of green and dark manganese brown. This lustre was both monochrome and polychrome. Another ware is thin and reddish buff with designs in relief under a green glaze and much like Roman wares. The buff ware is also treated with white, yellow and green monochrome glazes, and

Fig. 480. Samarra bowl. White reserved in red lustre. 9th cent. Mesopotamian. Dia. 6¾". Metropolitan Mus. of Art.

Fig. 479. Samarra dish. Conventionalized character is undoubtedly Arabic, in brown lustre. 9th cent. Dia. 2¼". Metropolitan Mus. of Art.
Fig. 481. Samarra bowl. Incised yellow and green glazes of T'ang type. Dia. about 11½". Nasli Heeramaneck Coll.

also with splashed and mottled treatments very much like those used in T'ang China (A.D. 618 to 906) which they copied without a doubt. There is also an unglazed pottery; water jars with stamped, molded or applied decorations of Kufic writing (angular Arabic letters) arabesques and animals; designs which became more elaborate later in the 11th and 12th centuries.

RAKKA WARES

In Mesopotamia on the Euphrates about 100 miles east of Aleppo is Rakka which was important between the 8th and 15th centuries. It was the home of Caliph Harun Al-Rashid (A.D. 786–809) with his magnificent following, but most of the pottery is of the 12th century. Much of the ware found there is probably not of local manufacture but some types are more plentiful than elsewhere. The body of these is gritty and easily crumbled. It is of a nearly white color. It is often covered with a transparent greenish white or green glaze which becomes opaque when colored blue of deep turquoise hue. Kiln sites yield a white ware of the 11th to 12th century with engraved designs under a clear glaze frequently splashed with blue. Very similar examples come from Rhages with the added colors of yellow, green and purple. Among other decorations are used Naskhi characters (round Arabic letters).

Chatfield Pier's book shows a bowl which is dated 831 and it is painted with a black design under a pale blue glaze, which is characteristic. Other vases and bowls have painting in both black and blue and this is typical of Syrian and Egyptian wares of the 13th to 15th centuries. Thus they are known as Syro-Egyptian. Many are decorated with a brown lustre often with added turquoise and blue touches and in some cases over bold relief and these reach back to the 10th or 11th centuries or earlier. (See following discussion of lustre.) The glaze is transparent and greenish. The various decorations are often confined in compartments. At "Rusapha," Syria, near

Left: Bowl, Samarra type, 9th cent. Dia. 10″. Eumorfopoulos Coll. # F377.
Center: Bowl found at Nishapur. Probably 9th cent. Design incised, with green and brown on cream ground. Nasli Heeramaneck Coll.
Right: Samanid (c. 10th cent.) deep conical bowl found at Nishapur. Salmon, rose and white. Dia. 7¼″. Dikran G. Kelekian.

Left: "Rhages" bowl. 10th cent. Aubergine on cream ground. Boston Mus. of Fine Arts.
Center: 9th–10th cent. bowl found at Amol. Umber, sienna and olive green on cream ground. Nasli Heeramaneck Coll.
Right: Amol bowl. 9th–10th cent. Raw umber, sienna and olive green. Nasli Heeramaneck Coll.

Samarra jug. Black on cream ground. Dia. c. 12″. Nasli Heeramaneck Coll.

Center: 9th cent. Persian jar from Susa. Glaze transparent and crackled. Decoration in green and dark blue. Ht. 8″. Metropolitan Mus. of Art.
Right: Early Rakka vase. Sandy ware with greyish green pale toned design in reserve on black ground. Brilliant silvery iridescence. Ht. 7″. Dikran K. Kelekian Coll.

9TH–10TH CENT. WARES FROM NISHAPUR, AMOL, SAMARRA, SUSA, AND RAKKA

PLATE 88

Vase, typical Western Asian. Writing around shoulder in relief. Turquoise glaze. Ht. about 10". Freer Gallery of Art, Washington.

12th cent. mosquelamp-shaped vase which may or may not have actually been intended for use as lamp. Pierced neck supports former possibility. Ht. 6¾". Metropolitan Mus. of Art.

Mesopotamian jar of 12th cent. Rare because of inscription about body. Ht. 19⅞". Metropolitan Mus. of Art.

Mesopotamian jar with relief decoration and iridescence from burial. Reconstructed. Ht. 15¾". Metropolitan Mus. of Art.

Rare type ewer with one handle and narrow mouth. Light buff clay with deep turquoise blue glaze and golden iridescence. Ht. 21". Warren E. Cox Coll.

Syrian or Mesopotamian vase. 14th cent. Crowded design in blue and black under grayish glaze. Ht. 12¾". Metropolitan Mus. of Art.

RAKKA POTTERIES (12TH–13TH CENT.)
PLATE 89

Rakka are found similar lustred wares of deeper colors, red, gold, etc., over purplish-blue and colorless glazes.

Some of the most powerful heavy pottery comes also from this site and is likely to be found to reach back earlier than its present dating of 12th to 13th centuries. Certainly it is reminiscent of the Sassanian and Parthian wares. This is usually covered with a turquoise glaze turned brightly iridescent through burial.

Left: Stem sweetmeat dish of Rakka or Rhages ware. Light blue arabic writing in cups under transparent aquamarine tinted glaze largely covered with golden iridescence. 13th cent. or older. Dia. 11½". Warren E. Cox Coll.
Right: Rakka 11th to 12th cent. plate of deep turquoise with spirited black design of bird drawn with great verve. Dia. 14". Ht. 3¾". Dikran G. Kelekian.

Right: Syria or Mesopotamia bowls of 12th–13th cent. with charming and spirited decorations. Black on light ground, deep turquoise glaze. Dias. 3¾" and 4½". Metropolitan Mus. of Art.

Vases of 13th cent. having crude but graceful form and simple design in black under transparent turquoise glaze. Iridescent. Ht. 10¼". Warren E. Cox Coll.

RAKKA POTTERIES (12TH–13TH CENT.)

PLATE 90

RHAGES WARES

The Mongols sacked Rhages in 1220 but it was not abandoned until the 17th century. It was a great trade center in the 12th and early 13th centuries and probably only to a small extent a pottery center for few wasters are found there. Most of the wares are the typical sandy white body finer and thinner after the 12th century and the glaze is usually creamy and opaque frequently decorated with a light golden brown lustre, typical of Persia. Many of the wares are decorated in relief or are actually modelled or molded

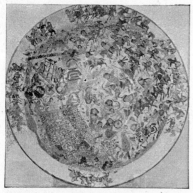

Largest and one of finest Rhages polychrome plates known. On front, battle scene between Iranians and Turanians. On back (except for center inside foot-rim), continuous hunting scene. 13th cent. Dia. 19". Dikran G. Kelekian.

One of finest Rhages 13th cent. bowls. Deep blue wall inside, with white ground center and beautiful polychrome decoration. Dia. 6¾". Dikran G. Kelekian.

Jug probably after metal design. Relief decoration in gold and blue, green and tan slips. 13th cent. Ht. 7¾". Metropolitan Mus. of Art.

Ewer with reticulated outer wall in turquoise-blue, black and lapis-blue. 13th cent. Ht. 8¾". Dikran G. Kelekian.

Persian 13th cent. vase with enamel decorations of horsemen, seated figures, in polychrome. Ht. 7½". Metropolitan Mus. of Art.

PAINTED WARES FOUND AT RHAGES

PLATE 91

in the round sometimes pierced and covered with a white, turquoise or cobalt blue glaze. Some of these are further enhanced by touches of leaf gold and enamel colors, and finally there is a whole class of the so-called "Minai" technique which is carefully painted from miniature sources with pictures in enamel and gold over white or pale blue grounds. The enamels include cobalt, turquoise, manganese purple, red, green, brown and black and colors mixed with white. They are all mat except the blue and adhere well to the

Bowl with purplish-blue glaze and incised decoration. Persian 12th–13th cent. Dia. 12½". Metropolitan Mus. of Art.

"Lakabi" Persian dish, probably 12th cent. Cream ground and harpy in purplish-blue, aubergine and yellow. Dia. 12¼". Metropolitan Mus. of Art.

Small dish found at Rhages (or Rei), 11th to 12th cent. Cream white ground and three fish in cobalt blue, turquoise and aubergine. Dia. 8⅞". Dikran G. Kelekian.

Persian 12th cent. bowl. Creamy-white with incised decoration glazed deep blue, turquoise green and manganese. Dia. 16". The Cleveland Mus. of Art.

EARLY SELJUK RHAGES INCISED WARES

PLATE 92

ground. Such enamels are also found on unglazed water jugs of porous body often molded in relief and are found all over the Near East. Frequently the lustre ware has lines or touches of blue. Most of these wares were made between the 12th and early 14th century. Great prices have attached to the miniature decorated wares which do not merit them from an artistic viewpoint but which are full of human interest and tell us much of the life of the times.

From various sources comes an early Seljuk ware forming a link between the "Gabri" and 13th century wares. It has incised outlines of the decoration

Rhages bottle with typical fluted cup mouth to aid in pouring into it and fine relief design about shoulder. Commonly covered with cobalt or turquoise blue but some have aubergine glaze. Transparent and crackled. This is turquoise. 12th to 13th cent. Ht. 9″. Boston Mus. of Fine Arts.

Ewer in form of seated lion cub found at Sarah (Persia). Ht. 7¼″. 13th cent. Dikran G. Kelekian.

Cylindrical jar of white sandy ware with turquoise glaze. Said to be from "Rayy" by mus. Hobson shows one in Eumorfopoulos Coll. and calls it Sultanabad 13th or 14th cent. Ht. about 13¼″. Boston Mus. of Fine Arts.

Typical Rhages vase. Light sandy pottery with deep blue glaze. Ht. about 12″. 13th cent. Boston Mus. of Fine Arts.

Persian ewer, 13th cent. Cock's head mouth and conventionalized tail for handle. Light buff and blue glaze on whitish sandy ware. Ht. 10½″. Metropolitan Mus. of Art.

"Rhages" type light buff ware with turquoise glaze. 13th to 14th cent. Ht. 10¾″. Metropolitan Mus. of Art.

POTTERIES FOUND AT RHAGES AND SARAH

PLATE 93

13th–cent. tile with turquoise ground and dark blue writing of "Rhages" type. Length 12¼". Metropolitan Mus. of Art.

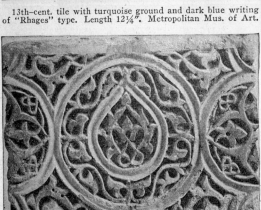

Glazed tile of 14th to 15th cent. Length 15¼". Metropolitan Mus. of Art.

"Rhages" 13th–cent. tile. Conventionalized writing covered with bright turquoise glaze touched with red lines. Length 14". Metropolitan Mus. of Art.

Iranian or Persian wall tile. Beginning of 14th cent. Relief letters and birds show Chinese influence. Sandy light buff, glaze cobalt. 15¾" × 14½". Metropolitan Mus. of Art.

Turquoise blue glazed light buff pottery tile from Persia. 13th to 14th cent. Length 13½". Metropolitan Mus. of Art.

PERSIAN POTTERY TILES

PLATE 94

filled in with turquoise, cobalt and purple under a transparent glaze and often on a white ground. The bold birds and figures suggest the 12th century.

SULTANABAD WARES

From the ruins of Sultanabad in Kazvin come lustre wares without the added blue, relief wares under green, blue or turquoise and also wares painted in blue, green and brown under a clear glaze. Others are painted in black with frequent touches of cobalt with turquoise, cobalt or creamy transparent glazes. This is the most characteristic and often the design of foliage, birds or human figures is in relief against a painted background having spirals or dots in deeper tone. The designs are strongly Chinese in character and pure Chinese motives are seen in the dragons and fêng-huang birds, probably indicating that the wares are to be dated after the Mongolian conquest or late 13th century.

FIG. 482. Rare and beautiful mosque lamp inscribed with statement that maker is Ibn al Ghaibi from Tabriz. Second half of 14th cent. Decoration blue and white on black. Ht. 13". Metropolitan Mus. of Art.

Many other sites have been found such as those at Khar, where many Rhages wares were found, and Nishapur the source of white ware decorated with highly styled and very beautiful black designs, black and red designs and even one 9th century bowl of buff clay with light slip upon which was drawn a horseman with straight sword in black outline. There are filled-in black areas on the horse and elsewhere on which is painted a bright yellow pigment which is also carried around the ground leaving the design in black and buff. Over this was placed a transparent glaze having splashes of green. The entire background is covered with birds, flowers and the word *"barakeh"* (blessing) in tiny *Kufi* letters and the body of the horse is filled with the yellow scrolls showing the typical horror vacui of much Iranian art. The design was taken from that of a Sassanian silver dish but lacks all the movement and vigor of such pieces. At Nishapur was also found a bowl of the type ascribed to Samarkand of the time of the Samanids having interlacing scrolls with writing about the rim reading "Blessing, prosperity, good will, peace and happiness to you," the whole in dull red and black. But there will undoubtedly be many more sites found and we must wait for the deductions from them before more closely allocating the various wares.

LUSTRE

Lustre ware is pottery that has a brightly shining metallic overglaze that has become iridescent. The art of lustre consists of the special technique of so handling the metallic overglaze that it will become lustrous.

The somewhat biased Dr. A. J. Butler feels a grievance because Dr. Sarre and Dr. Herzfeld believe that "The art of lustre-painting arose in Mesopotamia and thence spread to Syria, Egypt and Spain, and eastward to Persia." This is thought to be of the 9th century. We need not go into

Sultanabad vase having black design painted under transparent glaze. Late 13th cent. Ht. 8½″. Warren E. Cox Coll.

Type found at Rhages but more extensively at Sultanabad. Sandy light buff body with turquoise glaze over which is black left open to show writing and decoration through in turquoise. One of finest examples known. Ht. 11″. Warren E. Cox Coll.

Sultanabad deep dish of glazed pottery with underglaze decoration of black, green and white. 14th cent. Dia. 7⅛″. Metropolitan Mus. of Art.

Jars, called *albarellos* by Spanish who adopted it for lustre apothecary jars and transmitted it to Italy. From Rhages. 13th cent. Hts. 6″ and 11″. Warren E. Cox Coll.

Right: Jar of great importance. Deep blue-green glaze and black underglaze decoration. Ht. 28″. Dikran G. Kelekian.

POTTERIES FOUND AT SULTANABAD

PLATE 95

the well-known and unsound arguments of Dr. Butler save to list them:—
1.—He quotes a letter from Hadrian who was traveling in Alexandria in A.D. 130 and sent a present of *"calices allassontes versicolors"* which he translates as "challices color-changing" but which anyone can well imagine might mean polychrome, and which certainly does not definitely indicate lustre ware.
2.—He claims Egyptian origin for many lustre wares found at Fostat which agree in body and glaze (being white) with Mesopotamian examples but not with any known Egyptian ware which has a red body as a rule.
3.—He claims that a Persian, Nâsir-i-Khusrau while in Egypt in 1035 to 1043 saw "bûqalimûn," a ware which "changes its color according to the time of day,"—that this was lustre, that Nâsir did not recognize it at once,

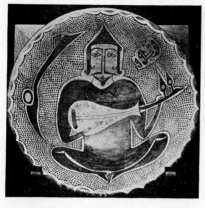

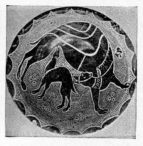

Large flat plate in light
and dark lustre. Many fragments of this sort found in
Samarra (complete pieces
rare). Said to have come
from Rhages and to be of
10th cent. Dia. 15⅛".
Dikran G. Kelekian.

Persian lustre bowl of greyish
pottery with reddish yellow design. 9th to 10th cent. Dia. c.
9". The Louvre.

Bowl described by the museum as "West Asian, 9th to 10th cent., Samarran type." Interesting design in
lustre. Dia. 14¼". Freer Gallery of Art, Washington.

Fine example of ware found at Fostat, dating
11th to 12th cent. Lustre heavy and brilliant
of varying copper color. Dia. 10". Dikran K.
Kelekian Coll.

Lustre bowl found at Fostat (old Cairo) of
Fatmid period (11th to 12th cent.). Rare,
for fragments only usually found. Dia. 9⅞".
Dikran K. Kelekian Coll.

EARLY LUSTRE FOUND IN PERSIA AND EGYPT

PLATE 96

and, therefore, that there was no lustre in Persia at this time. It is rather
obvious I believe that Nâsir may possibly not have known the right people.
I have heard of people even of culture having been in London and not going
to see Mr. Eumorfopoulos when he was living at 7 Chelsea Embankment.

4.—Nâsir-i-Khusrau went to Rakka and Rhages and did not report on the
kilns, thus Dr. Butler declares flatly that there was no lustre there either
of local manufacture or imported from elsewhere in Persia or Mesopotamia.

5.—He admits that some of the pieces from Samarra are of the 9th century
but contends that they were not made there and particularly one being in
a tripod form is certain to have come from Egypt because, to quote a Herr

Gallois, "The tripod is very rare in Eastern ceramics, while it is common in Coptic bronze-work." One would recall the ancient Ting form in ancient Chinese bronzes and wonder.

6.—He argues against the well-founded theory that metallic lustre was applied with the idea of imitating more or less actual metal, though this would seem the most natural thing in the world to do.

7.—He then says, "The truth is clear—that Nâsir was not speaking of lustre ware in general, and the kind of lustre which impressed him as novel was exclusively the brilliant counterchanging lustre." Consequently we are likely to assume that all the foregoing arguments were just kidding and that it was "counterchanging lustre" that was being written about all the time!

Of course this is all so much nonsense and I give it simply because there are still those who take this man Butler seriously even though R. L. Hobson of the B.M., Miss Alice W. Frothingham of the Hispanic Society of America and others have taken care to expose him. The real fact is that in using metallic substances in thin glazes and to paint on glazes would be sure to lead to lustrous effects which might be found pleasing and tried for again. Of two pieces fired in the same kiln and treated exactly alike one may be brightly iridescent while the other shows a plain metallic sheen. Lustre was probably found and lost by dozens of potters and invented in several places as an intended result after it had happened accidentally in perhaps many other places. It is likely that glaze perhaps did originate consciously in Egypt and that much design also came from there but it does not follow that lustre technique was also an Egyptian invention.

DATED PERSIAN LUSTRE

Dr. Ernst Kuhnel has brought together a very interesting study of actual dated examples. The earliest piece is a jar in the B.M. with broad and sure design on a light ground and also reserve design on a lustre ground, and it is marked 575 A.H. which would be A.D. 1179. (Pl. 97, top.)

The next is a bowl we show from the Chicago Art Institute and which shows a more delicate technique. It is dated 587 A.H. or A.D. 1191. (Fig. 485)

Next comes the dish from the Havemeyer Collection and that from the Eumorfopoulos Collection which we show and both of which are dated 607 A.H. or A.D. 1210. Both have a ground filled with delicate spirals and the first is perhaps finer in painting but the latter superior in the lovely treatment of scalloped rise to the rim, and the interesting and typical use of the row of faces to make pattern. (Pl. 97, center left)

The next one dated 608 A.H. or A.D. 1211 is more crude but has an interesting treatment of the birds and leaves of the background in that they are so nearly alike as to make even texture. This bowl is in the Pennsylvania University Museum, Philadelphia and it is possibly from the same atelier as the Boston Museum one which is not dated. I would also place the remarkable figure of an antelope with vase on its back, in the Seattle Museum, at about this same time and place. (Pl. 97, lower right; Pl. 99, upper left.)

The next dated piece known is in the Kelekian Collection and was made in 1227, after the Mongolian Conquest of 1220 it will be noted. It is, as we

Broken jar which is the earliest dated lustred piece known (575 A.H. or 1179 A.D.) and which shows a broad treatment quite unlike the minute drawing at the beginning of the 13th cent. Note also that the decoration is partly reserved. British Mus.

Below Left: Dish found at Rhages of sandy white ware covered with a creamy glaze and decorated in brown lustre having ruby reflections. The design is reserved and plants and scrolls etched out. The inscription reads —"Made by Saygid Shamr al-din al-Husaini in the month Tumada II in the year 607" (or 1210 A.D.). The illustration is of King Khosrau discovering the Princess Shirin bathing. Eumorfopoulos Coll. # F403.

Below Right: Lustre bowl found at Sultanabad and dated 624 A.H. (or 1227 A.D.) with grey ground and blue, green and brown lustre. There are two borders of Arabic inscription, one inside and one outside which bears the date. Dia. 7¾". Dikran K. Kelekian.

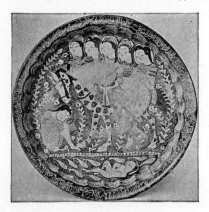

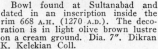

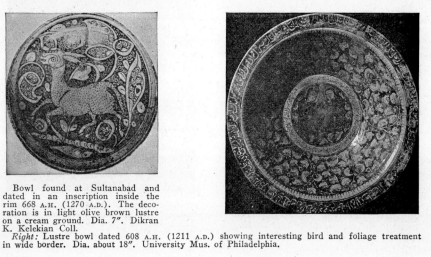

Bowl found at Sultanabad and dated in an inscription inside the rim 668 A.H. (1270 A.D.). The decoration is in light olive brown lustre on a cream ground. Dia. 7". Dikran K. Kelekian Coll.

Right: Lustre bowl dated 608 A.H. (1211 A.D.) showing interesting bird and foliage treatment in wide border. Dia. about 18". University Mus. of Philadelphia.

DATED PERSIAN LUSTRE

PLATE 97

would expect, quite different. Dr. Kuhnel says, "The former brown and gold metal tones have given way to a cobalt blue and turquoise and the drawing has become decidedly more scant and summary. Furthermore, it is said to have been found in Sultanabad, which for a long time, but perhaps wrongly, has been considered the home of a large number of Persian faiences, especially those of the Ilkhani." (Pl. 97, center right)

FIG. 483. Late 12th cent. lustre bowl of characteristic style. Dia. 18½". N. M. Heeramaneck Coll.

FIG. 484. Rhages bowl of the late 12th or early 13th cent. with brown lustre on white glaze having a fine crackle. Dia. 19¼". Sears Memorial. Boston Mus. of Fine Arts.

FIG. 485. Rhages lustre bowl dated 1191 A.D. and typical of this period. Dia. 15". Logan–Patten–Ryerson Coll. The Art Institute of Chicago.

FIG. 486. Early 13th cent. lustre plate of brown lustre and with direct but less detailed drawing. Dia. 16". N. M. Heeramaneck Coll.

A jump of 43 years now takes us to the next known piece which is also in the Kelekian Collection and dated 668 A.H. or A.D. 1270 in which the technique is similar but shows decadence.

An entirely different ware was made in the Safvid period under Shah Abbâs I, showing strong Far Eastern influence, but the only dated piece is marked 1084 A.H. or A.D. 1673.

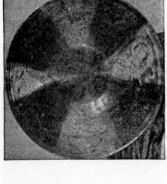

Center: Rhages type bowl of almost white clay covered with tin glaze and having sectors of cobalt blue, turquoise and white outlined in lustre and with lustre spots, a suggested arabesque design, and figures on the white. The outside is coated with cobalt and has lustred writing. Similar to Eumorfopoulos Coll. # F406. Dia. 7". Warren E. Cox Coll.

Right: Two lustred 13th cent. pieces both having a brown lustre on a transparent greenish white ground and the larger plate having crossed marks of dark blue and turquoise showing iridescence from burial. Dias. 8½" and 4¼". Warren E. Cox Coll.

Bowl said to have been found at Samarcand, extreme north eastern Persia, and to be of the 11th cent. Freer Gallery of Art, Washington.

Left: "Rhages" lustred pottery bowl of the 13th cent. Dia. 8⅞". Metropolitan Mus. of Art.

PERSIAN LUSTRED BOWLS—11TH TO 13TH CENTURY

PLATE 98

Center: Vase of the Rakka, Mesopotamian, type with pale aquamarine glaze and dark copper brownish lustre design. 12th cent. Ht. 8½". Metropolitan Mus. of Art.

Right: Persian lustred ewer found at Rhages and believed to be of the 13th cent. The lustre is of a golden brown quality. Ht. 8¾". Metropolitan Mus. of Art.

"Rhages" lustred pottery animal with whitish glaze and brown lustre, of the first half of the 13th cent. This is one of the best specimens I have seen. Ht. 17½". Fuller Coll. Seattle Art Mus.

Center: Rakka greenish glazed pottery jug with underglaze blue and dark lustre decoration. 12th cent. Ht. 6". Metropolitan Mus. of Art.

Right: Pilgrim bottle from Veramin, but perhaps not made there, made during the 13th cent. The lustre is pale and golden and considerably worn. Ht. 14½". Metropolitan Mus. of Art.

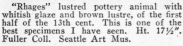

Lustre "Veramin" pottery tazza, Persian about 1300 (Compare style with dated bowls.) having a rather dark toned brown lustre. Dia. about 8¼". Metropolitan Mus. of Art.

Left: "Rhages" ewer of late 12th to early 13th cent. with brown lustre decoration on greenish cream white. Note alternation of panels in rhythm of 1 2 2, 1 2 2 and also the use of conventionalized arabic script. Ht. 10½". Metropolitan Mus. of Art.

Right: "Rhages" 13th cent. lustre sweet meat dish of the general form of a lotus pod made hollow with a hole in the bottom for air escape in firing. Decorated with brown lustre on cream. Alternating cups have portraits and the rims of all show alternating bold and delicate designs. Dia. about 9¾". Metropolitan Mus. of Art.

PERSIAN LUSTRED WARES—12TH TO 13TH CENTURY

PLATE 99

LUSTRED TILES

We have tiles through the 14th century and one in the B.M. is dated 810 A.H. or A.D. 1407 while the earliest known is dated 600 A.H. or A.D. 1203 and has a design of four seated figures. (See Herz Bey Catalogue #50, page 240 from Musee Arabe, Cairo.) This is about 25 years later than the first dated vessel but there is no doubt but that the lustred tiles are among the first wares made. They are rectangular or star-and-cross tiles with the dates on the stars. The technique is much like that of the vessels but less well executed. The Mongols did not have much influence on the traditions and the Seljuk designs are much like the earlier ones.

From Veramin come a large number of tiles of both sorts with typical purely floral designs and Dr. Kuhnel points out that they must have worked about two years on the sanctuary Imâmzâdeh Yahya for there are tiles dated 1262, 1263 and 1264 with the mihrab completed during the following year.

A series thought to have come from Damghan in 1267 have not only lustre on white ground but sparing touches of turquoise blue. In these the animals are drawn in their most mature form. A tile now at Breslau shows that there was an increased use of cobalt blue next to white as early as 1240.

The Sultanabad center must have been important about 1271 as is shown by the style of a dated tile in the Berlin Museum which is strongly Mongolian, while another shows a loosening up of the tight arabesques by 1283. There are many showing relief in the similar style and one dated as late as 1407 in Timurid style.

LUSTRED MIHRABS

A mihrab is made up of one or more tiles with a border of inscription sometimes added and is used instead of a deep niche to indicate the "Qibla" wall

FIG. 487. Persian early 14th cent. Mihrab arch with mosque lamp suspended and the usual writing in gold lustre and blue. Metropolitan Mus. of Art.

FIG. 488. Mihrab of faïence mosaic or tin glazed pottery pieces set in plaster. This piece came from the Midrasah Imami, Isfahan which was built in A.H. 755 or 1354 A.D. Ht. 11' 3", width 7' 6". The colors are cobalt, turquoise, white, golden yellow and dark green. Metropolitan Mus. of Art.

FIG. 489. Mihrab of lustred tiles probably made in Kashan about the beginning of the 14th cent. Ht. 43". Metropolitan Mus. of Art.

Small star tile found at Rhages but quite possibly not made there. Buff clay with cream glaze containing tin and has brown lustre inscription. Dia. 4". 12th to 13th cent. Metropolitan Mus. of Art.

Star tile with tin enamel and lustre decoration found at Veramin and dated 663 A.H. which would be 1265 A.D. Dia. 15". Metropolitan Mus. of Art.

Kashan star tile with lustred decoration of the first half of the 13th cent. Dia. 12⅜". Metropolitan Mus. of Art.

A "Veramin type" tile with copper lustre on a white ground and blue outlines. 13th cent. Dia. 7¾". Metropolitan Mus. of Art.

Kashan wall tile with the writing in blue and the ground design in brown lustre, dated 707 A.H. or 1309 A.D. Length about 14¼". Metropolitan Mus. of Art.

Kashan corner tiles (2) from a prayer niche with lustre decoration of the second half of the 13th cent. The lustre is gold with dark blue and turquoise. Relief parts in cobalt. Ht. 17¼". Metropolitan Mus. of Art.

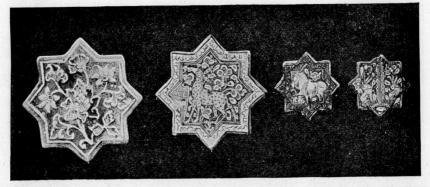

Persian tiles 13th cent. "Veramin" and 14th cent. "Sultanabad." Dias. about 8½" and 3½". Metropolitan Mus. of Art.

PERSIAN LUSTRED TILES

PLATE 100

This beautiful Mihrab is dated 661 A.H. (1264 A.D.) and came from the mosque in Veramin about 10 miles from Teheran. It was brought by Mostofi el Mamalich and sold to H. Kevorkian. On exhibition at the Pennsylvania University Mus., Philadelphia.

PERSIAN LUSTRED MIHRAB

PLATE 101

of a mosque or other holy building. It consists of a variously formed arch
with sometimes a suspended mosque lamp. The inside of the arch is also
filled with script, which is usually in relief and at times touched with blue
to make it legible against the background of arabesques. Large mihrabs often
have more than one arch set one within another, and supported with columns.

The earliest mihrab known is in the Berlin Museum and came through
H. Kevorkian from the Median mosque in Kashan. It is 2.84 meters high
(about 9 feet) and bears the name of the potter, Hasan ibn'Arabshâh and
the date 622 A.H. or A.D. 1225. It is generally assumed that while Rhages
was making vessels and tiles, Kashan was making mihrabs. The second, still
in the possession of H. Kevorkian, is also probably from there and bears
the date 661 A.H. or A.D. 1264 though it was found in the mosque in Veramin
or about ten miles from Teheran. They look very much alike in style. It is
possible that the star and cross tiles found near the Veramin one and the
mihrab itself were not made in Kashan. The 14th century ones show little
difference in style or writing but are perhaps less imposing.

Thus by comparisons of the dated pieces we reach the conclusion that the
earlier pieces except those at Rakka are of light gold as a rule and that later
this changes to a more bronze or copper tone. Hannover states that blue was
found on the border of the oldest known tiles dated 1217 but we see by
Kuhnel that there are at least four earlier and he does not speak of blue
being used until 1240 on tiles, although he does mention a bowl having lustre
and turquoise as early as 1213. One amusing thing is that the potters thought
so little of the writing which they copied over and over that it finally became
unreadable design only.

POTTERY MOSAIC

The tomb-mosque of Khudabanda Khan dating about 1316 shows an early
method of covering the cupolas and minarets with slabs of blue glazed pottery,
with white ones used now and then, but this system could only be employed
on rectilinear or geometrical patterns. Later curved lines were achieved by
sawing out pieces of various shapes from slabs of faïence and finally by the
15th century even the backgrounds were so covered. A large color range also
had been achieved including transparent cobalt-blue, black, green, yellow
and brown with opaque white and turquoise, and all had brilliance and
depth. The masterpiece of this technique is in the Blue Mosque at Tabriz
(1437 to 1468) but it was also used in the Green Mosque at Brusa, at
Konieh and in Constantinople in the Chinili Kiosk (Faïence Pavilion) while
to the east it spread to Samarkand and finally by the 17th century to India
and later to North Africa and Spain.

LATER PERSIAN TILES

Tiles of the Shah Abbas period 1590 are of similar technique to the Brusa
tiles with tin glaze and muffle-painting in designs very much like those of
carpets. The tiles no longer made a complete design in themselves but were
part of a larger scheme. At the same time tiles used on civil buildings
showed contemporary life (though those in the mosques never have figures,

That a considerable amount of good taste and excellent craftsmanship remained even in the late 18th cent. in Persia is shown by this wonderful set of tiles measuring 14" × 7" and consisting of 198 matched tiles in many colors. Ex Quill Jones Coll.

SET OF 18TH CENTURY PERSIAN TILES

PLATE 102

of course). Either miniatures or fabrics may have inspired these. They are often strong in yellow while red hardly occurs before the 18th century and strangely even later it was the custom to leave out one of the primary colors. Perhaps the intention was to establish a mood of color harmony. Still later came the use of cobalt blue and white only.

FIG. 490. Wall panel of assembled tiles showing merchants in the royal grounds. 17th cent. The colors are blue, black, and yellow. Length 78″. Ht. 40″. Metropolitan Mus. of Art.

In the late Safawidian times tiles were made with transparent or semi-transparent glaze of hunting scenes, amatory groups, etc., and these were copied in more glassy glazes with even worse taste. By the end of the 18th century the poor copies of famille rose Chinese designs are not worth consideration.

LATER "SOFT PORCELAIN" WARES

Few examples exist between the 14th and 17th centuries when the ware became "soft porcelain" of white body or buff covered with slip used with a creamy transparent glaze. Some wares were treated with blue outside and white inside. The lustre varies from greenish to ruby red and is brilliant. The shapes are somewhat simpler than the early ones. The kiln sites have not been established save that Ispahan the capital of Shah Abbas I (1587–1628) was important. Concerning the style it can be noted that reserve was not used, the use of animals or birds with trees or plant forms is usual and the technique is naturalistic rather than conventional. Chinese influence was strong and Chinese marks sometimes were copied. Such wares are of the Shah Abbas period but died out during the 17th century and only poor imitations have been attempted since.

This same soft paste which is somewhat harder than the European type was also decorated with underglaze blue and black, and overglaze colors sparingly used. It was even treated with the *pate sur pate* technique as may be seen in the example from the Metropolitan Museum.

Another very similar ware is that called "Gombroon" or "Gombrun" from the name of the port from which it was shipped in South Persia. The decoration consists of incisions through the body which are filled with glaze like the Chinese ware which the French term "grain de riz" (grain of rice). Sparse painting in blue and black underglaze colors is also used. Like all such wares it is inclined to distort in firing.

Left: Early 17th cent. ewer of soft porcelain ware with dark lustre decoration. Ht. 5". Metropolitan Mus. of Art.
Center: Porcelaneous ware though not high fired, with decoration of black and blue underglaze on a white ground. 17th cent. Ht. 17¼". Metropolitan Mus. of Art.
Right: Pottery base for a nargile or waterpipe with greenish glaze decorated with sage green and black. 1700 to 1750 A.D. Ht. 10¼". Metropolitan Mus. of Art.

Left: "Gombrun" semi-porcelain bottle of early 18th cent. Incised tracery and white glaze of glossy sheen somewhat pitted on the upper neck. Ht. about 13". Metropolitan Mus. of Art.
Center: Lustre ewer with spout to one side and strainer and spout to the front. The lustre is pale gold with red and green reflections. The dragon and flower design is filled in with a purplish underglaze blue. Ht. 11". Quill Jones Coll.
Right: Persian porcelaneous ware of the early 17th cent. with a design of birds and clouds. Ht. about 12½". Metropolitan Mus. of Art.

Left: 18th cent. semi-porcelain tazza of "Gombrun" ware, decorated in blue and black on white and the body incised all the way through in a pattern with the glaze filling the incisions, a technique like that of the "rice grain" bowls of China and probably derived from that source. Dia. 6½". Metropolitan Mus. of Art.
Right: Two bowls of the "Gombrun" ware of the 18th cent., one having black underglaze design and both having the usual incisions through the rim. They are glossy and of light ivory tone. Dias. about 7⅛". Moore Coll. Metropolitan Mus. of Art.

PERSIAN 17TH TO 18TH CENTURY WARES

PLATE 103

OTHER 17TH AND 18TH CENTURY POTTERIES

A large class of heavy potteries called by the trade incorrectly "Kashan" or "Kubatcha" where many were found come from unknown potteries of small towns of the Caucasus mountains, Syria and all the way through Persia. Mr. K. Kelekian has brought to attention 4 pieces actually dated 15th century although most of them are of the late 16th and 17th centuries. The body is of the same gritty quality that we always find in the Near East but it is often

FIG. 491. "Gombrun" bowl with an amusing riot of pagodas all over the center and sort of lambrequin border in underglaze black and blue. Dia. 10¼". 18th cent. Metropolitan Mus. of Art.

FIG. 492. Kubatcha turquoise plate with design in black painted underglaze. Dia. 13". Persia 17th cent. Fuller Coll. Seattle Art Mus.

stained brown by oil used in them and frequently on the vases the stain has penetrated through the body giving a not unpleasing mottled ivory to brown effect. These are largely painted by farmers who were instinctive artists or by other primitive and untutored painters using the same old traditional designs of flowers, fish, animals, etc., with now and then a Chinese motive such as high hills, peculiar pagodas and even stranger human figures. One type has aubergine added and is usually a bit more refined but given to allover patterns rather than pictorial designs. Crackle was not intentional but occurs on some pieces. Others of the same sort are painted in black or blue under a deep turquoise glaze. Still others have decoration in yellow, brown, blue, green, black, and bolus red though these are often later than the Safavid period (1507–1736). The simple directness of conception has made these wares popular and they have been badly copied by weak imitators the designs showing more flowery feeling, having relief treatment or added colors and imitation staining.

This completes the Near Eastern wares except for the tin glazed enamelled wares from Turkey or Damascus. This group will be taken up under the section on European enamelled wares.

The illustrations show a group of typical Near Eastern pottery forms and it will be seen at once that many of these followed metal in their slender

FIG. 493. Plate found at Koubatcha in Daghestan and dated 873 A.H. (or 1480 A.D.) made by a Persian artist. Turquoise decorated in deep blue. This piece gave first direct evidence of the period of the wares found in this place. Dia. 14¼″. Dikran K. Kelekian Coll.

FIG. 494. Plate said to have come from Kubatcha. May have been made in Daghestan. Turquoise glaze with reserved design against a black ground partly scratched out. 15th cent. Dia. 14″. Metropolitan Mus. of Art.

FIG. 495. "Kubatcha" glazed pottery jar which may or may not have been made there. Brown stained cream glaze slightly greenish in tint and decorated with black and blue underglaze colors. Ht. 8″. Metropolitan Mus. of Art.

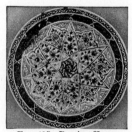

FIG. 496. "Kashan" bowl showing conception of Chinese landscape in the center and with glaze-filled piercing in the side design. Creamy white with blue and black design and some greenish tinge. Dia. about 10″. Ex Warren E. Cox Coll. Mrs. Bernard Jolis.

FIG. 497. Persian Kerman pottery plate with underglaze blue and black decoration, of the 17th to 18th cent. Dia. about 18″. Metropolitan Mus. of Art.

FIG. 498. "Kashan" jar of pottery with greenish cream ground stained brown and blue and black underglaze decoration. Ht. 8¼″. Metropolitan Mus. of Art.

FIG. 499. "Kashan" or "Kubatcha" peasant potteries showing the Chinese influence in the drawing of pagodas and high hills. 17th to 18th cent. Jar ht. 9″. Warren E. Cox Coll.

FIG. 500. Kutahia plate dated 1719 A.D. Decorated in clear yellow, black, deep blue, green, turquoise and red with the Armenian Saint Sergius on horseback carrying off a Greek woman. Signed with potter's name. Dia. 6″. Dikran K. Kelekian Coll.

handles, involved and not always structural (in pottery at least) shapes, in the relief which imitates the repoussé and finally, of course, in the use of actual metallic lustre. The fact that there was a great pottery tradition also must never be lost sight of and some beautiful and suitable forms were made ranging all the way from the most solid and sturdy to those of graceful delicacy. Nowhere else was the ewer so varied and at times so charming. The albarello or apothecary jar of concave cylindrical form was certainly invented in the Near East and became tremendously popular in Spain, Italy and spread through the whole world. The bowls of inverted conical form with delicately flaring sides curving only slightly from the straight are of great beauty. If these potters were not so disciplined as the Chinese, they nevertheless showed delicacy and a strength of their own more colored by emotion but not lacking in power.

CHAPTER XIV

EUROPEAN POTTERY

(FROM LATE ROME THROUGH SPANISH AND ITALIAN LUSTRE WARES)

THE OLD wars were simple struggles for territorial rights and were fought over geographical boundaries. We have seen that religion was a growing power, as in the spread of Buddhism in the Far East, and though it had profound indirect results upon art the effects were not like those of conquest. Now at the beginning of the Christian era there came into use the fanatical manipulation of *religion as a weapon* which, like flood or fire often destroyed aggressor and defender alike. There had, of course, been wars brought about by medicine men of the most ancient tribes and by priests of the higher developed civilizations, but never before had such huge masses of men thrown away their lives simply because they were sure that they believed in the true god while the poor benighted enemy believed in none at all or the wrong one. It was found possible to overthrow the strongest ruler by outlining a code of laws of supposed moral value, by promising a heaven and by exorcising the masses to be good. Their goodness often grew in enthusiasm to the zeal of a crusade against all who did not believe as they did.

Rome had become all powerful but just as the Greeks had become involved in wars with Persia, so Rome made the mistake of diverting power to Byzantium, now Constantinople. This city had, since it was founded in 657 B.C. by the Greeks, been a bone of contention and had been destroyed by Darius Hystaspes, recolonized in 479 B.C. by the Spartans, then became Athenian, Spartan and Athenian again. It was besieged by the Macedonians and, it is interesting to note, was saved from a surprise attack by a flash of moonlight wherefore the Byzantines stamped a crescent on their coins, a device adopted by the Turks and kept to this day. Later the Rodians and then Goths attacked it. In about A.D. 288 Constantine the Great was born and after having been sent to Byzantium as a hostage returned with that city well in mind so that when his father died and he was declared head of his army he became a Christian and the head of the Roman Christian Empire and took the city calling it "New Rome." It was the capital of the Roman Empire of the East from about A.D. 330 to 1453 when it was taken by the Ottoman Turks.

Meanwhile Rome itself in the 5th century lost its western territories to Teuton invasion and in 486 its Gaulish territories to the Franks and was threatened by the expansion of the Slavs and Saracens in the 7th century. Suddenly the forces of Islam arose and swept Persia to the Oxus, Syria and

Egypt, Alexandria falling in A.D. 643, and Carthage in A.D. 698, and finally extended to Spain which was absorbed by A.D. 714. Thus Rome was girt about on three sides by Islam while on the North her ancient enemies were always ready to strike. Little of the old power was regained while Byzantium became the greatest city in the world up to that fateful date 1204 when the Crusaders delivered it to Venice which sucked it dry until it was taken by the Turks.

The Muhammedans had swept much of the world with their holy wars and Jerusalem was in the hands of the unbelievers. The pestilence had scourged Europe in the 10th and 11th centuries and finally the Church had preached penitentiary pilgrimages. There was also, of course, the promise of rich loot in the Near East. Therefore, not holy knights in shining armor, but adventurers, fugitives, tramps, villains, bankrupts, camp followers, hucksters and the like made up the Crusades. In 1096 the "People's Crusade" started and killed some 10,000 Jews, won the complete dislike of the Greeks in Constantinople and were finished up by the Hungarians, Bulgarians and Seljuks. The "Crusade of the Princes" reached Constantinople in 1097 about 150,000 strong. Alexius Comnenus had appealed to Rome for aid in his fight against the East and one can imagine his chagrin at being beset by this motley mob. We need not go into detail but the Franks had control of the caravan routes from Persia to Egypt and from Damascus to the Red Sea until the "Jihad" or counter crusade was started and Nureddin took Damascus in 1154 and opened the way for the Atabegs who finally were fatal to the Franks.

In order to gain some understanding as to what all this meant to art and the ceramic arts particularly let us see the description given by Mr. Ernest Barker in the 14th edition of the Encyclopaedia Britannica of the life of these Franks, these Crusaders: "They returned from the field of hard fighting to divans with frescoed walls and floor mosaic, Persian rugs and embroidered silk hangings. Their houses, at any rate those in the towns, had thus the characteristics of Moorish villas; and in them they lived the Moorish life. Their sideboards were covered with the copper and silver work of Eastern smiths and the confectioneries of Damascus. They dressed in flowing robes of silk, and their women wore oriental gauzes covered with sequins. Into these divans where figures of this kind moved to music of Saracen instruments, there entered an inevitable voluptuousness and corruption of manners. The hardships of war and excesses of peace shortened the lives of the men. While the men died, the women, living in comparative indolence, lived longer lives. They became regents to their young children; and the experience of all mediaeval minorities reiterates the lesson—'woe to the land where the king is a child and the regent a woman.'" Thus as Crusade upon Crusade took place, as Barker puts it, "Native Franks with commercial intercourse and diplomatic negotiations could not feel the urge to make a dash for the 'infidels' as the newcomers wished." The 2nd Crusade burned itself out by 1150, the 3rd and 4th by 1202–1204 and the 5th and 6th by 1229.

Meanwhile, the weapon had been forged and crusades became nothing more or less than a game of politics just as they have been ever since. The French barons launched a small crusade of their own against the heretics of

Southern France whom they exploited quite successfully. When Frederick II after several trials did get off on the 6th Crusade the papal soldiers of the church invaded his territories. And so it went. But though they wrought a great deal of unhappiness in this world the Crusades did develop the first ideas of colonization in Europe, they developed the first "chartered companies" which began as charitable groups, developed into military organizations and then became commercial companies owning banks, territories and navies for their protection, they brought about a spirit of toleration which, in a sense, made the Renaissance possible, and finally above all they discovered the East to Europe. Lemons, melons, maize, cotton, muslin, damask, lilac and purple, powder, mirrors and even the rosary itself were introduced through these contacts.

Thus we shall see that as Islam brought the *art of lustre* to Spain where it spread to Italy, so the Crusades brought the *art of tin glazed, enamel decorated pottery,* along with Chinese designs and those of Turkey and Damascus, to Italy where it spread throughout Europe. These two brilliant and colorful arts were emplanted upon the modeling and molding arts which had become so decadent in the Hellenistic world and the three: LUSTRE, ENAMEL DECORATION and RELIEF DECORATION were the basis of all the ceramic arts that followed. We shall take them up in the order named tracing each to the beginning of the 18th century.

BACKGROUND OF EARLIEST SPANISH POTTERY

The center of production of ceramics seemed to move ever westward and just as it was in Greece and then Italy so it came in time to that third large peninsula, Spain. But let us begin with the earliest days there:—The rock paintings show us that there was a fairly even paleolithic and neolithic culture over the entire peninsula. We have spoken of the bell-shaped crude pottery called "campaniform" and during this aeneolithic or Late New Stone Age period there are indications of North African contacts and affinities between Spain and the Baleric Islands, Sardinia and Sicily from about 3000 to 2500 B.C. After this time a period of retrogression set in and there are no reflections from Crete. It is true that spasmodic trading was done with the Greeks, but this so-called "Almeria Culture" lasted without influence up to the time of Christ when it was absorbed by the Roman culture. The indigenous people were entirely submerged about the 6th century by the Celtic invasion of the iron age (that same wave which swept over Greece and Italy), except for the Basques who retreated into the mountains. By 70 B.C. the southern districts were Roman.

In A.D. 406–407 the barbarians burst the Rhine frontier and flooded Gaul and Spain. The potteries were Roman but did not reach the point of decadence that they did elsewhere perhaps simply because the Spanish people were too primitive to have reached this bypass.

By 712 Musa b.Nosair the Arab had completed the conquest of Spain and by 732 the North African troops had reached Poitiers, France where they were turned back by the Austrasian Franks, but this Muhammedan conquest was made up of Syrians and Berbers as well as Arabs and there was no govern-

Late New Stone Age pottery from *El Acébuchal* of polished uneven brownish black with chalk white incised design. Ht. 4¾". Hispanic Society of America.

Bowl of brick red glazed pottery of the bucchero type, Gallo-Roman of late 1st cent. or early 2nd. Dia. 3¾". Found at Carmona. Hispanic Society of America.

Left: Amphora used for wine by the Romans. Pitch-lined light yellow, sandy clay. Found near Sevilla. The Hispanic Society of America.

Center: A Pre-Roman pottery cinerary urn from *La Cruz del Negro* of unglazed soft tan clay with reddish-orange and brown circles, thought to date about 500 B.C. Ht. about 13¾". Hispanic Society of America.

Right: Cinerary urn found at *Mérida*. Cream unglazed pottery with incised design. It appears to have been done with a comb. Roman period. Ht. about 6½". Hispanic Society of America.

Gandul bowl of taupe-gray glazed Roman pottery. Ht. 2¾". Hispanic Society of America.

Right: Gallo-Roman flask or pilgrim bottle of brick red lead glazed pottery of the 1st cent. A.D. Ht. 7". Hispanic Society of America.

ROMAN AND EARLY SPANISH POTTERIES

Plate 104

ment or organization. In 750 there was the plague followed by drought and famine. During the 9th and 10th centuries the Norse pirates raided the coast. Christianity was tolerated and gained a new foothold. In 1037 or thereabouts Fernando I established a kingdom in Castile. Another invasion of Berbers took place in 1120 and it was not until 1212 that the king of Castile organized a crusade against the Almohades which overthrew them and from that time onward Muhammedan Spain was under the control of the Christians. Finally the marriage of Ferdinand of Aragon to Isabella of Castile brought comparative order.

Meanwhile much was accomplished:—Vasco da Gama reached India in 1498, Columbus had found the New World, Cortes had conquered Mexico and by 1535 Pizarro had conquered Peru. Toward the end of the 16th century took place the golden age of literature boiled up from this cauldron of racial and religious hatreds. It was in 1502 that the Muhammedans were expelled, and even converted Muhammedans were sent out in 1610, and with them went most of the true culture that had been the heritage of Spain. Ferdinand had entered a war with Italy in 1497 which proved the might of Spain but also wasted much of it.

Charles V (of Hapsburg) had been educated in Flanders and could not even speak the Spanish language. His only interest in the country was what he could get out of it. His son Philip II (1556–1598) was much the same and the vices and elegance of the court were at the expense of the country. The Reformation had taken place and Philip's Absolutist tendencies were feared by the Netherlands. Finally he became involved with the religious wars with England and the defeat of the famous Armada of 1588 resulted in tumbling his attempts to rule all western Europe. Meanwhile Drake in 1587 swept the West Indies and burnt a number of Spanish ships in the harbor of Cadiz.

The decline had long been due and now it was felt. The war with the Netherlands made shipping unsafe. An attempt to send troops through France ended in a war with that country. In 1640 Portugal separated without a blow being struck. The revolt of Naples and of the Catalans followed. Charles II was an imbecile and the government was directed by his mother and her successive favorites (1665–1700). By the 18th century there is nothing left of interest. Like a multi-colored gleam from one of her beautiful Hispano-Moresque plaques Spain flared and was gone but she preserved and developed one of the greatest of ceramic arts.

HISPANO-MORESQUE POTTERY

From the 8th to the beginning of the 12th centuries the Arab culture under the caliphate of the Ommiads at Cordova was high. They were overcome by the Almoravide who brought a different culture with them but all Moorish tribes were confined to Granada in the southeast part on the coast after the crusade of 1212. In 1566 the Moorish writing, dress and style of decoration were prohibited until 1610 when these people were put out for good.

Our potteries are therefore easily divided into two groups:—
1.—Those *before 1566* with *pure oriental style*.

2.—Those between *1566 and 1700* which show *Italian Renaissance style,* and almost continuous decadence.

Tiles similar to those in Persia were made but used only along the lower part of the walls. The earliest are from the Alhambra and were sawed or molded into symmetrical convex polygonal shapes meant to be set in mosaic designs of geometrical nature. These were colored black, white, greyish-blue, green and brown.

FIG. 501: *"De cuerda seca"* architectural finial with yellow peak, stripes in green, yellow and black and horizontal arrow band of green and white with touches of yellow. Late 15th or early 16th cent. probably at Toledo. Ht. 20½". Hispanic Society of America.

"Cuerda seca" technique is a labor-saving device. Instead of having to lay each piece of mosaic carefully, larger square tiles were made in molds having very slight relief designs in outline, which produced slightly depressed outlines in the tile. These were filled with a greasy manganese medium which formed compartments in which lead and tin enamels of blue, green, brown, black and white were filled. At first the manganese had simply been painted on and later a cloisonné effect was produced by the use of wooden molds which left the outlines in slight relief, on which manganese was also applied. These tiles were cheap, and in Spain when they wanted to say a person was poor they would say "non ava casa azulejos" or "His house has no tiles." However some have spirited and pleasant designs reminiscent of Near Eastern ones. These tiles along with finials, etc., were made at Puente del Arzobispo and in Andalucia before the 15th century. Those for the palaces of the Dukes of Alba and Medinaceli were made in Sevilla in the late 15th and early 16th centuries. The Toledan ones are probably a little later. A water pitcher formed like the bust of a woman and an aguamanil of a crouching animal that looks like a sheep are at Sèvres while in Valencia and Sevilla are also a vase, a large bowl and an albarello.

Tiles made like those described above, with the pattern sunk but a little more so and without the manganese outline, were called "de cuenca." Only the very oldest are of Moresque mosaic, the others being of foliage, palmettes and flowers. These were made in Toledo in central Spain and Sevilla and Triana in the south.

Terracotta tiles of the 14th and 15th centuries are found in Aragon and have some decoration in slightly fired black, brown and occasionally red.

From Valencia of the 15th century are a type that is not Moorish but almost exactly taken from the Italians. These are square or lozenge forms so proportioned that the square can be fitted into the center and four of the others about it making an octagon. The earliest have Gothic designs in blue but early in the 16th century when Spain wanted nothing to do with Martin Luther or the Reformation, they changed the designs to Italian

14th cent. dish from Paterna of tin enameled earthenware, white ground, with green and manganese design. Dia. about 11½". Metropolitan Mus. of Art.

Bowl of cream-colored clay with white slip and lead glaze over blue decoration. Dia. 9½". Hispanic Soc. of Am.

Left: "*Cucrda seca*" or "*Puente del Arzobispo*" plate probably made at Sevilla. Rabbit yellow-brown with blue tail. Rim green and foliage blue, yellow, green and black on white ground. Dia. 8⅞". Hispanic Soc. of Am.

Left: Vase made at Teruel. Red clay with tin enamel decorated in manganese purple and green. Three shields about the body have (1) triple-tower, (2) green basket, and (3) initials AT in Gothic letters. Ht. 15¾". Hispanic Soc. of Am.

Right: Late 15th or early 16th cent. jar. Light buff colored ware with green glaze. Sevilla. Ht. about 14½". Hispanic Soc. of Am.

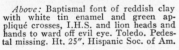

Above: Baptismal font of reddish clay with white tin enamel and green appliqué crosses, I.H.S. and lion heads and hands to ward off evil eye. Toledo. Pedestal missing. Ht. 25". Hispanic Soc. of Am.

Right: Glazed earthenware deep dish. Dia. 21½". From Teruel. Metropolitan Mus. of Art.

SPANISH 15TH CENTURY WARES

PLATE 105

ones. They were said to be floor tiles and in the latter part of the century the output was increased and many were also made in Portugal.

From the latter part of the 16th century Talavera de la Reyna (or Reina) was the center of all earthenware production decorated with tin glaze of soft opaque cream color containing small black specks and with decoration having manganese outlines and a purplish grey-blue both sunk in the glaze

Right: 17th cent. plate of buff ware covered with peachy-white ground, design outlined in aubergine, and filled in with deep blue and orange-red hatching. Dia. 10". Warren E. Cox Coll.

Left: Talavera de la Reina plate designated "Valencia?" by museum but typical in technique and substance. Dia. c. 10". Gift of Miss Theodore Lyman. Mus. of Fine Arts, Boston.
Center: Plate perhaps earlier than typical 17th cent. type which is usually badly overcrowded in design. Near Eastern influence. Brown body and glaze with decoration in yellow, brown and green. Mus. of Fine Arts, Boston.

 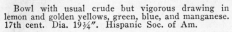 

Bowl with usual crude but vigorous drawing in lemon and golden yellows, green, blue, and manganese. 17th cent. Dia. 19¾". Hispanic Soc. of Am.

Jar decorated in violet-blue, green, lemon, golden-yellow and orange. 17th cent. Ht. 21". Hispanic Soc. of Am.

TALAVERA DE LA REINA POTTERY
PLATE 106

and an orange-red on the surface probably fired at lower temperature. This was not unlike the rare Paterna ware of the 14th century. Paterna was a small town not far from the capital of Valencia. In it was made a ware *par excellence* with tin enamel and design in manganese purplish-black and green which predated the early lustre ware and finally gave way to it. The beautiful plate from the Metropolitan Museum is a fine example. In the 16th century copies of this ware were made at Teruel, and continued down to

Left: This albarello has band about neck of conventionalized Naskhi writing, also wide band of *alafia* characters about middle. Blue and gold on tin glaze. Valencia. 15th cent. Hispanic Soc. of Am.

Center: Jar said to have been made in late 14th or early 15th cent. Ht. 13⅛". Metropolitan Mus. of Art.

Right: Albarello with device of double crown about middle. Tin glaze with gold and blue decoration. 15th cent. from Valencia. Ht. 12". Hispanic Soc. of Am.

Left: 15th cent. from Valencia with flowers in blue and lustre having copper and lavender reflections. Ht. 12". Hispanic Soc. of Am.

Center: From *Talavera de la Reina* bearing coat of arms of Order of Our Lady of Mercy in shades of grayish blue on white tin enamel over buff pottery. 17th cent. Ht. about 12". Hispanic Soc. of Am.

Right: Possibly 17th cent. Decorated with blue, yellow, orange and manganese purple on white tin enamel, from Sevilla (Triana). Ht. 7½". Hispanic Soc. of Am.

SPANISH ALBARELLOS

PLATE 107

modern times, but the Talavera de la Reyna ones are of Italian influence with conventional floral scrolls, birds and the like. Very soon, however, by the 17th century the style became more ornate and detailed showing the sloppy pictorial inclinations of the Italian majolica.

HISPANO-MORESQUE LUSTRE WARE

Lustre was not unknown in Europe as early as the 12th century. Examples are found in the walls of buildings in Italy and France of the Romanesque period. An account by El Idrisi, an Arabian geographer, says that in the 12th century lustred faïence was made at Calatayud in Aragon. In the 13th century it was made in Andalusia and shipped from Malaga but we have not one single piece which can be authenticated as before the 14th century. A. J. Butler claims a 10th or 11th century gold lustre was found at Madinah al Zahrah, by Cordova, on the site of the Muslim city but goes on to say that this has not been proven of Spanish manufacture.

In 1492 the Moorish king, Boabdil, was driven by Ferdinand and Isabella from the Alhambra, his palace at Granada, back to Africa and some 200 years later a large vase was found of amphora form with strange wing-like handles so broad as to be useless for lifting it and seemingly over styled. This Alhambra vase and six others were supposed to have come from the grounds of the palace. One is, so far as we know, still there. Another is in the Hermitage. The neck of one is in the Hispanic Society of America, etc. I have examined none of these except the latter piece and it is of terracotta colored clay with blue and white glazes and pale golden lustre. The vase in the National Museum in Stockholm is 4 feet 5 inches high and has a band of arabic inscription above which is an open field with gazelles reserved in cream and golden lustre on a blue ground. The rest of the body and handles are covered with compartments with arabesques and inscriptions in the same colors and the neck is not unlike ours here. The others have arabesques and writing but not the gazelles. The dates of these are not entirely agreed upon but it is supposed that they are late 14th or early 15th century. The technique is similar to that of a much discussed wall tile with an inscription supposed to refer to Yusuf I, II or III depending on which authority you believe.

Since there is considerable confusion concerning these vases I quote an excerpt from a letter to me by Alice Wilson Frothingham which clears up the matter in good shape, "As for the 'Alhambra' vases, that name, of course, leads to much confusion, since all of them were not found at the Alhambra. Actually excavated from the grounds of the Palace in the 17th century were two vases and the fragments of a third. One of these vases is the example, until recently in the *Hall of the Two Sisters* and now installed in the *Museo de Arte Arabe, Palacio de Carlos V,* also in the Alhambra. It was in this new location in 1940, and to the best of my knowledge is still there. The second vase, a few years previous to 1837, had been broken, but not before detailed drawings of it had been made. In 1869, the collar of this vase was in the home of Rafael Contreras y Muñoz, architect in charge of conserving and restoring the Alhambra. Later, the collar and fragments of the body found their way into the art

Right: Neck of late 14th–early 15th cent. vase. Reddish body with blue and white glazes and golden lustre. Ht. 17". Hispanic Soc. of Am.

"Tinaja" with globular body and short neck. On the shoulder are useless handles with which it would be very difficult to lift such a jar. Ware is coarse red clay. Museum says design is incised but I think it is impressed. Probably made in Andalucia toward end of 15th cent. Ht. c. *2'.* Mus. of Fine Arts, Boston.

Left: One of several vases of "Alhambra type" but found at Salar. Probably made at Malaga. In Hermitage, St. Petersburg. Lustre of darker and heavier color. Probably early 15th cent. Ht. c. 4'.

Center: Pale golden lustred vase made at Manises. Perfectly functional form for it pours very well when three fingers are inserted into handle. May be derived from a form which predated even the "Alhambra vase" on theory that handles are useless on these huge pieces and were maintained simply through habit. Ht. 15". Warren E. Cox Coll.

Right: Drawing of one of two actual "Alhambra vases" said to have been found filled with gold pieces in 16th cent. in vault under the Comares tower, Granada. Reddish body with blue and white glazes and golden lustre. 14th to early 15th cent. Ht. about 4' 3". Muses Espanol de Antiguedades, Madrid.

"ALHAMBRA TYPE" POTTERIES

PLATE 108

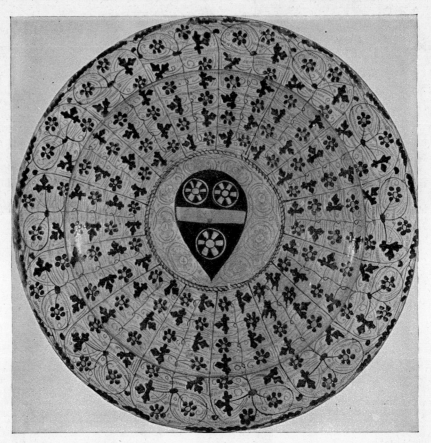

Fig. 502. Hispano-moresque plate of 15th cent. said to have come from Malaga. Decorated with blue and gold lustre. Dia. 18¾". Ex W. R. Hearst Coll. International Stud.o Coll.

market; the collar was purchased for the Hispanic Society in 1913 from a Persian art dealer.

"All the other vases which are similar to these two in shape and design, but which have come from different sites, should I suppose be distinguished by another term, but they have become known popularly as 'Alhambra' or 'Alhambra type' vases. The Leningrad vase came from Salar, a town near Granada. I do not know from where the Stockholm vase was excavated, but it appears to have been manufactured at Málaga. According to Ferrandis, it belonged to Queen Louise, sister of Frederick the Great; it was transferred from the castle at Drottningholm to the National Museum at Stockholm in 1866."

Hannover who usually displays good taste waxes enthusiastic over the Alhambra vase calling it, "one of the immortal works of ancient craftsmanship." We are, however, privileged to differ and to look upon these vases as monstrous and degenerate forms which imply a more sound and practical prototype. A reproduction of such a prototype I think I have found. This

Deep dish with white enamel glaze and decorations of blue and gold "*alafia*" reflecting red and blue green. Reverse has eagle, fern leaves and scrolls also in gold. Valencia, 15th cent. Dia. 19". Ht. 2¾". Hispanic Soc. of Am.

Large bowl of early 15th cent. from Valencia probably at Manises in imitation of Malaga model. Decorated with blue and gold of coppery tint with red and blue "*reflejos.*" Four small loops from lower to upper surface of rim. Dia. c. 18". Ht. 5½". Hispanic Soc. of Am.

Plateau with outward flaring brim and near center another brim. Pinkish tan clay with white enamel and blue roses surrounded by green-gold lustre leaves having opalescent "*reflejos.*" Two holes in foot-rim for hanging. Dia. 16¾". 15th cent. From Valencia. Hispanic Soc. of Am.

Plate c. A.D. 1450–1500 from Valencia with coat of arms probably for Tedali family of Florence. Brim pierced by two holes. Dia. c. 17½". Hispanic Soc. of Am.

SPANISH LUSTRE PLATES

PLATE 109

15th to 16th cent. Valencia semipherical bowl with four ears. Usual type called *"escudelles ab orelles"* or bowls with ears, have two only. Handles are concave both top and bottom for easy grip. Lustre yellowish gold and faded. Dia. tip to tip 12″. Hispanic Soc. of Am.

15th or 16th cent. plate painted in pale gold lustre. Note use of patterns to break plain area of body of bull and rabbit and leaping wolf. Dia. 16⅛″. Nasli Heeramaneck Coll.

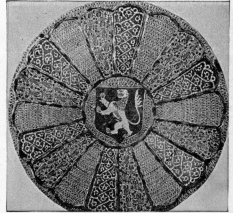

15th or 16th cent. Valencia plate with rampant lion outlined in blue and gold lustre. Details yellowish brown metallic color. Dia. 18½″. Hispanic Soc. of Am.

15th to 16th cent. Valencia plate with wide rim of wheel pattern in relief, sectors having triple alternation effectively used. Gold is reddish brown and reflects mother-of-pearl tints. Dia. 17¾″. Hispanic Soc. of Am.

SPANISH LUSTRE PLATES

PLATE 110

vase is of a type of lustre dating from the 17th century and made at Manises so it cannot be an original but it was undoubtedly copied from some now nonexistent one which is perfectly beautiful in proportion and the handles of which we find are, in this size, well fitted to the hand, structural and of great beauty. One need only insert three fingers in the notches to find that it pours as well as the best of ewers. It is my theory that the large vases were a debased and pretentious development of this charming form which must have existed in normal size in early 14th century examples which have all been destroyed.

A beautiful bowl in the Sarre Collection, Berlin is of this ware and has similar decorations. The inside is divided into eight segments showing the effective use of continuously changing alternating designs (see section on

An *"orza."* Clay pinkish tan, glaze known as stanniferous, as it has tin in it. Lustre is gold. Spot of green under one handle. Valencia 15th–16th cent.   Ht. 10½″. Hispanic Soc. of Am.

Ewer of pinkish tan clay with white tin enamel and gold lustre which reflects purple. 16th cent. from Valencia. Hispanic Soc. of Am.

Vase, early 16th cent. from Valencia. Base and lip of ormolu added later. Pinkish tan clay with white enamel and gold-brown lustre reflecting lavender.   Ht. 19½″. Hispanic Soc. of Am.

Right: One of a pair of covered vases bearing the arms of Camillo Borghese, who reigned as Pope Paul V 1605–1621. Two shields with between them busts of men wearing morions with chin pieces and plumed crests. Pinkish tan clay with tin enamel and copper colored lustre, from Valencia. Ht. 19½″. Hispanic Soc. of Am.

Left: Pharmacy jar or *"botijos"* of early 16th cent. Valencia. Lustre of yellow-gold. Ht. 8⅜″. Hispanic Soc. of Am.
Center: Blue glazed vase with delicately painted horizontal bands of bright copper lustre. This type once believed made in Caltagirone, Sicily by Moors and was called "Siculo-Arab ware," but what evidence there is points more truly to Manises as its real source. Ht. 10¼″. 17th cent. (?) Hispanic Soc. of Am.

SPANISH LUSTRE VESSELS

PLATE 111

Ashur). On the bottom is a mark construed as meaning "Málaga" thus confirming the general location of Granada as a source and the possibility that they were all made in Málaga. In 1487 Málaga passed into the hands of the Christians and it would be reasonable to suppose that the pottery either ceased or commenced to change. There is also some possibility that the ware was actually made at Granada in a royal manufactory.

VALENCIA LUSTRE WARES

Several writers have made an error in stating that the family of Manises in the town of the same name made a later lustre ware. This was due to the misconception concerning the evidence of Eximenes at first supposed to date 1499 and found actually to date 1383. The wares were undoubtedly similar to those of Málaga and in fact are referred to in general by the name of "Obra dorada de Málaga." In Manises the ware was evidently made chiefly

FIG. 503. Tazza from Valencia, 16th cent., decorated in coppery gold. Sacred monogram IHS placed in square medallion inside. Raised gadroons painted in designs in alternating rhythm 1,2,3,–1,2,–1,2,3, except where they do not come out right. Dia. 12½". Ht. 8½". Hispanic Soc. of Am.

FIG. 504. "Orza" or globular vase. Fluted neck and four loop handles. Decoration yellow gold color with mother-of-pearl tints. Vertical gold stripes inside neck. 15th or 16th cent. Valencia. Ht. 8¾". Hispanic Soc. of Am.

FIG. 505. Late 18th–early 19th cent. barber's basin or "bacia" made at Manises. Potter's initials are on bottom As. Rim pierced so it could be hung on wall. Yellow, grey-green, lavender, blue and deep cobalt blue. Dia. about 18". Hispanic Soc. of Am.

for the Buyl or Boil family who were overlords levying taxes and occasionally making sales.

Other locations are Paterna in Valencia where we have already said an enamelled ware was made in the 14th century and those near the Valencia center:—Mislata, in 1484 Gesarte, in 1507 Calatayud and 1589 Muel which is also in Aragon. Blue and white wares were also made in this section.

DATING OF SPANISH LUSTRE WARE

Our evidence is still too vague to make it possible to assign certain pieces to definite kiln sites and the best we can do is classify them in more or less definite categories so far as dates go. Generally speaking the following facts will help the student:

1.—Those pieces showing pure Moorish style are likely to be earlier. This style is marked by arabesques, the "tree of life," palm motives, animals

Deep dish of *"Brasero"* shape showing interesting use of radial alternating design on inside and of three fish on bottom outside. Probably Valencia, 15th to 16th cent. Dia. 18½", depth 2". Ex W. R. Hearst Coll. International Studio, Inc.

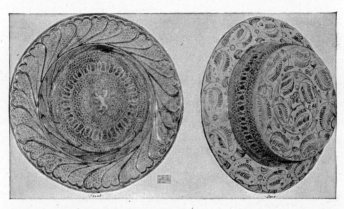

Hispano-moresque plate shaped like *"Brasero"* or Spanish hat. Decorated inside with gold lustre and blue, outside with lustre only in feathery leaf design. 15th–16th cent. Dia. 19¼", depth 4⅝". Ex W. R. Hearst Coll. International Studio, Inc.

SPANISH LUSTRE PLATES, FRONT AND BACK

PLATE 112

showing Western Asian style and Arabic inscriptions such as the word "alafia" (blessing) repeated in formalized characters.

2.—Rare instances of Spanish inscriptions misspelt would be by Moorish craftsmen and therefore early.

3.—Vice versa, Moorish or Arabic inscriptions misspelt are by Spanish Christian craftsmen and would be later, as are also such highly conventionalized inscriptions as to be not legible.

4.—Often the centers of the plates bear the coats of arms of the Buyl family, of the king or queen of Aragon or of other Valencian or Italian families and these aid greatly in dating.

5.—Emil Hannover proves neatly the correctness of the date of one type

Lustre plates, one with soldier of the reign of Philippe II–late 16th to early 17th cent. Dia. 13¾″.
Other with turbaned head has probably portrait of Sultan Suliman II (1520–1566). Dia. 13½″.
Below are backs of these two plates which show verve and spontaneity typical of fine examples.
Dikran G. Kelekian Coll.

PLATE 113

of alberello or apothecary vase decorated with blue and lustred foliage for
one was painted in the foreground of a picture by Hugo van der Goes in the
famous altar-piece of Portinari which is definitely dated between 1474 and
1477.

The greatest number of pieces are dependent upon style. We no longer
believe that the blue color was used only after 1500 and in fact it may have
even predated the lustre itself. The Moors or Moriscoes were driven out in
1609–1610 and took with them the secret of the pale gold lustre. After this
time the lustre is copper colored and becomes ever more heavy. Earlier in

the 15th century there were animals in blue against a lustred ground of spirals. From 1450 the heraldic designs were made for export to Italy and are set among Gothic diapers and foliage. Some alternate the flowers in blue with the leaves in lustre. By the middle of the 15th century alternation has descended from the use of large panels to small details and soon the principle is lost. By the 17th century we see no trace of it. In the earliest wares and up to the 16th century the spirals form a separate background in another plane behind the design but later they become more heavy until they clutter up the main design. Another motive is the "chain mail" so called because it resembles meshes. Hannover says there is no known origin for this but it must surely descend from the "scale" patterns of the Damascus and Turkish wares.

The backs of the plates were more freely and broadly painted with lustre and here we can tell more about the artist for no imitator can get the same swift feeling in his strokes as can a man who has done hundreds in his own way.

A word may be said about shapes:—The wide shallow conical plates with concave, narrow bottom and small raised center, and also the flat plates with straight sides and flat rims are of the 15th and 16th century types while the more ornate raised center ones with a trough around and a wide rim having a shallow second trough around are of the 17th century. The alberello was brought direct from Persia and Mesopotamia. Other of the shapes will be found on comparison to resemble more or less Near Eastern prototypes, but all have a scale and boldness seen only in the early Assyrian wares

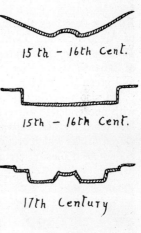

15 th – 16th Cent.

15th – 16th Cent.

17th Century

Fig. 506.

before. Both modeled and pictorial designs were well modified to the general forms and aid rather than detract from them with the only exception perhaps the late wares from Talavera de la Reyna which are strongly Italian.

CHAPTER XV

NEAR EASTERN AND EUROPEAN TIN SLIP AND TIN GLAZED WARES

NORTH AFRICAN POTTERY

BUTLER describes the finding of kiln sites at a place on the western border of Algeria called "Tilimsân" or "Tlemcen" which M. Bel believes to date 10th century. The wares are said to be similar to those found at Madînah al Zaharah except that they all consist of the enameled type with manganese and green decoration.

He also describes bricks enameled only on three quarters of the surface with one end left untreated. These were found at the Fortress of the Bani Hammâd, further eastward. At Qalàh were found both partially and wholly glazed bricks which are white, yellow and brown as well as green. M. Marçais is quoted as placing certain tiles, also found there, as before those of Koniah

FIG. 507. Drinking vessel or "cántaros" with filling spout and squirting spout which delivers a thin stream of liquid into mouth when held above head at right angle. Brick red with polished design. Generally left unglazed so evaporation on outside kept them cool. Modern but an old form.

FIG. 508. Jar and cover from North Africa and made at Meknès, 16th to 17th cent. Ht. 19½". Warren E. Cox Coll.

FIG. 509. North African faïence plate from Meknès. Difficult to date but design similar to those of Paterna. Wider range of colors which include manganese brown, blue, turquoise and yellow, indicate perhaps the 16th to 17th cent. Dia. 14½". Warren E. Cox Coll.

or "presumably not later than A.D. 1150." One of these was not believed to have been made on the spot as the drawing of a leopard is much finer than the other animals portrayed. This may or may not be a good reason. Good artists occur in poor kilns just as poor artists occur in good kilns but less frequently.

It is obvious from these and other finds that all the wares were of

Egyptian or Western Asian inheritance and that nothing of interest was indigenous. The one plate from my own collection closely resembles Paterna ware but has added colors.

TURKISH ENAMELED WARES

Tin had been used for many centuries to make a white, opaque glaze over an impure, buff or reddish body. We have traced the one great art of *lustre* which was almost entirely developed on this beautiful white surface. Now let us go back to the Near East again and pick up the thread of the other art of ENAMEL DECORATION. Finally we shall see how they unite in Italy, how the use of color supplants that of metallic lustre and how both arts are, though debased, spread throughout the whole of Europe.

The development of tin glaze was certainly directly brought about by the constant attempts to get an effect something like that of the beautiful porcelain which was being made in China. By the 16th century or the Chêng Tê reign

FIG. 510. Pottery globe for suspension as a weight made in Damascus, 16th cent. Silicious tin glaze with enamel decorations. Dia. about 10″. Metropolitan Mus. of Art.

FIG. 511. Well potted and decorated faïence bowl from Turkey 17th cent. Usual blue, green and red colors. Ht. 9″. British Mus.

FIG. 512. Turkish enamel decorated tin glazed earthenware mosque-lamp shaped vase. Ht. 11¾″. Metropolitan Mus. of Art.

of the Ming dynasty in China (1506–1521) the "Muhammedan blue" had long been used, had run short and a new supply was acquired. We learn that "hui hui wen" or "Muhammedan scrolls" were a popular sort of design borrowed from the Near East and adapted to Chinese taste. It is of this period that we find the writer's equipment with Arabic writings and quotations from the Koran, on them. By the following reign, that of Chia Ching (1522–1566) such things had not only become popular for Muhammedans in China but a considerable export business was under way and objects like the bases for hubble pipes and the rose water sprinkler I illustrate in that section are extensively found in the Near East. We must also note that the art of "five color" enamel decoration on white porcelain had by now become highly developed on China which did not need the tin glaze or a slip treatment because the bodies of the wares were naturally so white.

If the Chinese borrowed Near Eastern designs, the compliment was returned and how closely the process went on can readily be seen by comparing

FIG. 513. Ming, Chia Ching bowl with greenish white glaze and floral design inside and out of liver colored underglaze. Dia. 14″. Metropolitan Mus. of Art.

FIG. 514. Turkish dish of blue on white ware dating 16th to 17th cent. and very similar in decoration to the Chia Ching bowl shown. Dia. 11⅜″. James J. Rorimer Coll.

FIG. 515. Turkish blue on white plate of the 16th to 17th cent. with strong Chinese influence shown in the drawing. Dia. 15″. James J. Rorimer Coll.

the first blue and white dish I am illustrating from the wonderful sequence belonging to James J. Rorimer to the liver and white bowl shown among the Chia Ching wares. It is not much of a stretch of imagination to say that one might serve for the saucer of the other, if the colors had been the same, yet the one was made at Ching-tê Chêng while the other was made in Turkey. Another bowl with blue on white decoration and having a pomegranate design could also, technique aside, be of earlier Ming make. Mr. Rorimer conservatively places these as 16th–17th century and 17th century but I think it quite reasonable to call them both 16th century and undoubtedly made from contemporary Chinese originals as models.

At first glance there seems to be a definite break between the enameled wares of Damascus and Turkey and those of the 12th to 13th century of

FIG. 516. Turkish glazed earthenware with blue, green and red design. Note the scale ground copied extensively in European wares of later date. Dia. 13½″. Metropolitan Mus. of Art. Gift of James J. Rorimer.

FIG. 517. Turkish plate of the general appearance of a "Kubatcha" type. Note design of reversible landscape. Glossy, crackled glaze. Dia. 12½″. James J. Rorimer Coll.

FIG. 518. "Damascus type" plate probably made in Turkey, 16th cent. symmetrical design extending to edge shows strong East Indian influence rather than Chinese. Dia. 12⅛″. James J. Rorimer Coll. Metropolitan Mus. of Art.

Persia and Mesopotamia. Yet near Damascus there are kiln sites where large amounts of the so-called "Syro-Egyptian" ware was found. It is painted in blue and black under a clear glaze and was made up to the 14th century. Tiles have also been found nearby with delicate Persian scroll designs in black under a blue glaze and of a style which seems to indicate the 15th century. Butler shows one from Broussa and another from Turkey which is green with gold decoration. All of these are symmetrical. The tin glaze may have been first used at Ashur, for a vase found there and of about 1300 B.C. has tin in the glaze. But it must have been the renewed Chinese contact that was responsible for this art.

The ware itself is of sandy, whitish body and all the better pieces are also dressed with a fine white slip often containing tin. Upon this is painted the design in black outlines which are filled in with brilliant blue, turquoise, green, and, if the ware be Turkish, a thick red, or, if the ware be from Damascus, a soft manganese purple, and over all is a thin glassy glaze. In these wares of Turkey and Damascus the tin was not at first used in the glaze but in the slip, if at all, and the colors are actually, technically *underglaze* colors. This may seem strange when we know that in China to date there had been developed only an underglaze blue and a very uncertain underglaze red, but the answer lies in the difference of temperature. The one ware was a high fired porcelain reaching 2200° F. or more while the other had a feldspathic glaze which melted at so low a temperature that the heat did not harm the colors used underneath it.

Another distinction between the two types is that the Damascus plates have the design reaching to the edge while the Turkish ones have the rim treated with separate motives, very often Chinese "rock and wave," "cloud scroll" or the slanting key frets such as we have seen on Tz'u Chou type Sung wares. But this is not always to be counted on for a large Syrian, Damascus one in the V. Everit Macy Collection of the 17th century has the separate border treatment.

It will be remembered that the "Kubatcha" ware described in the last section and dating from the 15th century is technically very similar. The Chinese influence is probably from the time of Shah Abbas I (1587–1628)

FIG. 519. A very simple and beautiful asymmetrically designed Turkish plate of the 16th to 17th cent. Dia. 12⅛". Coll. of Mrs. James J. Rorimer. Metropolitan Mus. of Art.

FIG. 520. Turkish pottery plate with tin glaze and enamel decoration including red. These are usually about 14" in dia. Boston Mus. of Fine Arts.

FIG. 521. A rare Turkish plate with animal decoration in the center and a petal formed edge. Decorated in blue, turquoise, green and red on white ground. 16th to 17th cent. Dia. 12⅝". James J. Rorimer Coll.

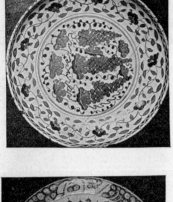

Left to Right: Turkish plate 16th to 17th cent. with symmetrical quatrefoil design. Dia. 12". James J. Rorimer Coll.—16th to 17th cent. dish decorated in dark and light blue on white ground and showing strong Chinese characteristics. Dia. 11⅞". James J. Rorimer Coll.—Plate 16th to 17th cent. Decorated with blue on white with a conventional design of Chinese derivation. Dia. 12½". James J. Rorimer Coll.—Plate reminiscent of the bronze mirror designs of Roman origin with clusters of grapes on them. 17th cent. Dia. 13¾". James J. Rorimer Coll.

Left to Right: Plate with simple design which is so beautiful in the earlier ones during the transition from the symmetrical to the asymmetrical. Dia. 11¼". James J. Rorimer Coll.—Plate with symmetrical design in usual colors. Dia. 12⅞". James J. Rorimer Coll.—Plate with typical asymmetrical design and cloud scroll border in usual colors of blue, green and red on white ground. Dia. 13⅝". James J. Rorimer Coll.—Plate of 16th to 17th cent. showing the later trend toward over crowding of decoration in red, green, gold, blue and black on white ground. Dia. 11". James J. Rorimer Coll.

TURKISH ENAMELED PLATES: 16TH TO 17TH CENTURIES

PLATE 114

for it is known that he imported Chinese potters and great quantities of Ming wares. But the Turkish wares also were influenced strongly by Persian craftsmen and we see little of the loose Caucasian feeling but rather formal flowers at first symmetrically arranged. It is conceded that the Damascus, Syrian, ones came first and the symmetrical flowers are very likely of East Indian, via Persia, origin. It would seem that during the latter part of the 16th and early part of the 17th centuries the Chinese style also brought about the asymmetrical arrangement of the flowers as on the Turkish plates. Possibly it was the Chinese who also helped with the red color. The fact that the red was very difficult to handle is testified to by many Chinese examples in which it has become liver color or suffered other catastrophes. It is furthermore shown by the fact that when imitations of Turkish wares were made at Candiana near Padua in the 17th century, the Italians were unable to produce the red. This then seemed to need first hand supervision to learn.

The elements of decoration were now: 1.—Natural flowers, 2.—Ornamental imaginative flowers, 3.—Persian scroll stems, 4.—Geometric designs and arabesques, 5.—Animals and birds, 6.—Human figures and 7.—Sailing

FIG. 522. Turkish mug of 16th to 17th cent. with the usual colored enamel decoration. This type is probably earlier than those with colored ground. Ht. 8¾". James J. Rorimer Coll.

FIG. 523. Turkish mug of early 17th cent. with enamel ground of green, blue and white borders at top and bottom. Red, blue and white design of animals. Ht. 7⅝". Metropolitan Mus. of Art.

FIG. 524. Jug of Turkish pottery of early 17th cent. Decorated in white, blue and red on an emerald green ground The glaze contains tin as well as some of the enamels. Ht. 8⅜". Metropolitan Mus. of Art.

ships. The last two are most rare and perhaps least pleasing. The animals are also not so well drawn as they are on the earlier Persian wares. But the drawing of the flowers is sure and beautiful. The ground was usually left white as possible but sometimes a green ground, as in the mug with animals, or the jug with ships would be used on a scale pattern, as may be seen in one of the plates, given by Mr. Rorimer to the Metropolitan Museum of Art.

The shapes are rather sturdy jugs and mugs, plates, rarely mosque lamps and even more rarely stem-bowls with covers. Marks do not occur as a rule, except for the false Chinese characters that we do see on some Persian wares, but in the Godman Collection there is a small jug which has an Armenian inscription stating that it was made by "Abraham of Kutaia" in the 16th century. The wares from Kutaia, Demitoka, Lindus and Nicaea are hardly distinguishable from one another and they all deteriorated in the 18th and 19th centuries so that they do not interest us.

ITALIAN MAJOLICA

Even by the time of the fall of the Roman Empire nothing had been developed in Italy except the old red or black pottery. A somewhat new technique applied to it was discovered at the Forum in Rome. It is of coarse, red clay with "sgraffito" design and a yellowish, transparent glaze sometimes stained a vivid green with copper oxide. This carried on the technique of the T'ang Chinese, the "Gubri" or "Gabri" wares and some of those of Rhages or Rakka, Persia but the designs are generally more crowded and ornate and less spirited. "Mezza-majolica" or "half majolica" was a step forward being covered with a white slip which was incised and painted with colors and was closer to the prototypes. The earliest of this type is said to date about the 12th century or earlier. The technique continued so long as the fusible colors tended to flow together.

As we have said, tin glaze came from the Near East but, though the technique had been known, tin was as costly as gold and very little was used. It was first employed as a tin ash mixed with the slip to make that creamy

FIG. 525. Stem-cup of mezza-majolica found in Cyprus, dating 9th to 11th cent. This Italian ware is decorated in green and treacle-brown on cream ground showing similarity to T'ang Chinese wares. Ht. 4¾". Metropolitan Mus. of Art.

FIG. 526. Italian (Ferrara) dish with incised decoration and brown and green glazes on tan. 14th to 15th cent. Dia. 9¾". James J. Rorimer Coll.

FIG. 527. Italian tazza of the *sgraffito* majolica ware dating about 1500 and, in a way, carrying on the technique of T'ang and "gabri" Persian wares having similar transparent yellow and green lead glazes. Ht. 2¼". Dia. 9¾". Mortimer L. Schiff Coll. Metropolitan Mus. of Art.

clay white and opaque. About a hundred years before the sgraffito wares were made in Italy tin enamel, that is a lead-silica glaze with tin added, had been introduced but actual use was not made of it until about 1500, although the mezza-majolica sometimes had a sparing touch of it here and there. The introduction had come through Spain, and the early wares were made at La Fratta, Citta di Castello, where the ware called "alla Castellana" was

Sgraffito decorated pottery bowl from Italy (Lombardy?) late 15 cent. Dia. 7". Ht. 3". Ex Count Bracciforte Piccenza Coll. James J. Rorimer Coll. Metropolitan Mus. of Art.

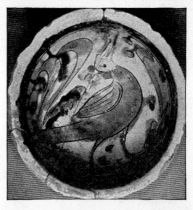

Bowl with sgraffito design swiftly executed and with dabbed spots of colored glaze on a cream white ground, attributed to Ferrara and of the late 14th or early 15th cent. Dia. 5½". Ht. 2¼". James J. Rorimer Coll. Metropolitan Mus. of Art.

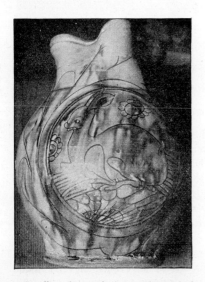

Sgraffito decorated jug with spirited design attributed to Ferrara c. 1400–1450. Apparent is a strong Persian and Chinese influence and the glazes are richer in colors and applications than this place is usually given credit for. Ht. 7½". James J. Rorimer Coll. Metropolitan Mus. of Art.

"Sgraffito decorated earthenware bowl, Italian (probably Ferrara) 1400 to 1450." The mottled glaze has a T'ang feeling. Dia. 5½". Ht. 1⅞". James J. Rorimer Coll. Metropolitan Mus. of Art.

ITALIAN MAJOLICA: 15TH CENTURY

PLATE 115

made, and at Padua and Pavia. In Padua a potter named Nicoleti signed a large round medallion showing the Madonna seated amongst saints. In Pavia the Cuzio family signed a number of pieces in brown or green glaze.

"Orvieto Ware" of the 14th Century

The general name "Orvieto Ware" means little for very similar wares were found at Siena (the best ones), Cortona, Rome, Perugia and Faenza as well

FIG. 528. Majolica 15th cent. bowl very probably from Orvieto with light buff ground inside and yellow outside, the design being in pale green and aubergine. Dia. 12″. Metropolitan Mus. of Art.

FIG. 529. Italian 14th to 15th cent. jug probably from Orvieto with a shield with fleur de lis in relief and leaf also in studded relief. Ht. 11″. Metropolitan Mus. of Art.

FIG. 530. Todi jug (Boccali) of Italian majolica of about 1400 decorated in black on a white slip ground. The ware is red at the bottom where exposed and the inside shows red glaze effect. Ht. 10⅞″. Metropolitan Mus. of Art.

as in Orvieto. The earliest of these wares were dipped in tin enamel to cover only about two thirds to four fifths of their heights and the bottoms were covered with lead glaze. Later the tin covers to the bottom and to the edges of plates but even then the backs are in lead glaze. The ware is crude and reddish, rudely wheel thrown and without sheen. The colors are copper-green, light blue of copper or cobalt, manganese-purple and yellow-ochre, the light blue and yellow being rarer. Some crudely modeled relief heads or fruit were used. The painted designs are degenerated Near Eastern, Gothic and some have Coptic crosses. Animals, fish, birds and monsters are frequent as are also cross hatched backgrounds, which were used to replace flat washes with which the potters seemed to have trouble. Fakes have been cleverly made but the glazes are usually smoother and it is difficult to reproduce primitive drawing simple as it seems. During the 15th century a deeper cobalt blue, a brown and a clearer ochre-yellow were added. The wares also became less pictorial. Many were made for hospitals after the plague of the 14th century in which a quarter of the people of Europe died. Show pieces also occur in the 15th century and the factories and painters began to sign their wares.

"Green Florentine Ware"

"Green Florentine ware" is in the transition between the Middle Ages and the start of the Renaissance. It is finer with thicker glaze, it often has a soft grey tone, the colors are richer, the outlines are of manganese-purple (prob-

Florentine 15th cent. Nativity; five figures forming a persepio of painted terracotta. Ht. of Virgin 34⅞". Metropolitan Mus. of Art.

FLORENTINE 15TH CENTURY NATIVITY IN POTTERY

PLATE 116

FIG. 531. Majolica jug (Boccali). Outside covered with a creamy glaze and the inside ochre-yellow. c. 1400. Ht. 11″. Metropolitan Mus. of Art.

FIG. 532. Florentine albarello of majolica decorated in blue, manganese and yellow on light ground. c. 1450–1475. Ht. 9″. Metropolitan Mus. of Art.

FIG. 533. Albarello from Florence of 1425–1450 decorated in blue and manganese on white slip ground with arms of the Hospital of Santa Maria della Scala, at Siena. Ht. 12¾″. Metropolitan Mus. of Art.

FIG. 531a. Florentine? plate of brown clay with pinkish tin glaze, incised decoration and glazes of blue and yellow. Note Arabic inscriptions in roots of tree. Probably early 15th cent. Bequest of Mrs. Edward Wheelwright. Mus. of Fine Arts, Boston.

FIG. 533a. Italian 16th cent. carved slipware plate made in very much the same technique as the Gabri and Samarra types. Dia. 15⅛″. James J. Rorimer Coll.

ably learned from the cuerda seca of Spain) and the predominant color is a strong bluish green. The decoration is of animals, human figures and heads of portrait character. Two new shapes are the large dishes with broad horizontal rims and squat jars with two flat handles on the shoulder.

"Impasto Blue Florentine Ware"

"Impasto Blue Florentine ware" was undoubtedly inspired first by Chinese importations to the Near East. Also the Egypto-Syrian vases which had underglaze blue and black decoration and are of the 13th century may have built tradition. There are only a few pieces showing the transition from the

Fig. 534. "Green Floren-
tine" 15th cent. jar with
the twisted rope handles seen
on some Greek wares and a
design showing Western
Asian influences. It is of
brown pottery with tin glaze
and green and manganese
decoration. Ht. 14⅛". Metropolitan Mus. of Art. Gift
of V. Everit Macy.

Fig. 535. Florentine
drug-jar c. 1425–1450, decorated with thick enamel-like
impasto blue. Note also the
Near Eastern tendency to
break up the heavy mass of
the animal with circular designs. Ht. 8". Mortimer
Schiff Coll. Metropolitan
Mus. of Art.

Fig. 536. Early 15th cent.
Italian majolica jug with lion
head and studded leaves in
relief and decoration in yellow, green and manganese of
dull and impure quality. Ht.
9¼". Metropolitan Mus. of
Art.

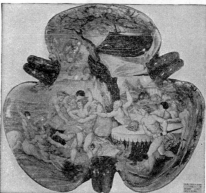

Pair of majolica albarelli of the 16th cent. decorated with medal-
lons in green wreaths of St. John and of a courtesan against grounds
of canary yellow and a general background of cobalt blue having
orange yellow floral ornaments. Ht. 12½". Ex E. H. Gary Coll. and
W. R. Hearst Coll. International Studio, Inc.

Trilobate *Vasque* of Urbino ware of the 16th
cent. decorated with grotesque figures and satyrs
in low relief on the outside and "The Abduction
of Hippodania" on the inside. Dia. 15". From
the W. R. Hearst Coll. International Studio,
Inc.

ITALIAN 16TH CENTURY MAJOLICA

PLATE 117

green style to the blue, one a dish showing Adam and Eve in the Musée Céramique, Rouen, which is strongly Near Eastern in style, has a slightly pinkish ground and various animals, dogs, etc., about the rim. Fern-like spots in deep blue are about the rise of this plate. Another has an Italian coat of arms and seven small animals with human faces again of Near Eastern type and this has both colors. It is in the Musée Céramique, Sèvres.

The blue technique drove out the green almost at once and was in turn supplanted by the Hispano-Moresque because of the rise of Spanish power. The animals, fish and birds are now similar to those seen on Saracenic silks and all of the space is crowded with design. This was a growing urge as can also be seen in the Kutaian wares of the 16th and 17th centuries. Mixed with these influences the Italian coats of arms and Gothic leaves are entwined. Very large vases were made and signed with factory marks below their handles. Many are from the pharmacy of Santa Maria Nuova and bear the hospital emblem, a crutch, while others from Santa Maria della Scala are marked with a ladder or bier.

The Florentines did not understand the technique of lustre but made similar designs in what is called "Hispano-Moresque-Italian ware" in blue or blue, manganese and yellow, with Gothic trefoils and six-petaled flowers, palmette leaves and twisted stems, tendrils and dots. The blue was no longer in thick lumps but light, transparent and greyish more like that seen on lustre ware.

FIG. 537. Albarello of the Hispano-Moresque style but decorated in heavy blue. It is probably Florentine. Italian 15th cent. Ht. 12". Mortimer Schiff Coll. Metropolitan Mus. of Art.

Polychrome effects with direct Western Asian, and not Hispano-Moresque, motives came into being by 1470. The "peacock-eye," "pomegranate" from Turkish sources were combined with the "scroll leaf" which now started all over Italy. Alberelli and large jars with two handles and a wide mouth were usual forms. Also tiles were made with the scrolls as can be seen in those from the Caracciolo chapel in the church of San Giovanni a Carbonara at Naples dating about 1440, those from San Petronio c. 1487 and those of the Bologna chapel at Bentivoglio in San Gaicomo of about 1490.

FAENZA AND "FAÏENCE"

FIG. 538.

While these various things were happening in Florence and spreading out over Italy, Faenza the great center for the Italian Renaissance style in pottery was growing. It was here that the art of Venice, Siena, Caffaggiolo, Ferrara and elsewhere had its origin. So important was this center that the name "faïence" became a universal term meaning tin enameled earthenware. The term was

Castel Durante dish of the 16th cent. painted by Giovanni Harin, 1508 with the arms of Pope Julius II surrounded by swags of fruit, figures of satyrs, dolphins, birds, etc., on a dark blue ground. Dia. 12¾". Ex Col. Duke of Newcastle. W. R. Hearst Coll. International Studio, Inc.

16th cent. Urbino dish showing Venus combing her hair and Vulcan heating a piece of metal over a fire. Dia. 10¾". Ex Baron Adolphe de Rothschild Coll. and W. R. Hearst Coll. International Studio, Inc.

Deruta 16th cent. dish with lustred design in relief. The center shows Judith with the head of Holofernes. Dia. 15½". Ex J. P. Morgan Coll. W. R. Hearst Coll. International Studio, Inc.

ITALIAN 16TH CENTURY MAJOLICA PLATES

PLATE 118

accepted in France in 1574 when a factory was started at Lyons. It is synonymous with "majolica" generally speaking and also technically with delft but is misapplied and wrongly used to designate porcelain.

The great contemporary authority on the beginning of majolica or faïence was Cipriano Piccolpaso who was a master potter himself and who detailed for us every step of the progress. I take the following from his notes:

1.—At Urbino and Castle Durante the clay was taken from the bed of the river in summer when the water was low.

2.—It was either dried or buried in deep pits in the ground.

3.—He notes that clay was traded; that for Venice from Ravenna and Rimini, Battaglia (near Padua) and Pesaro.

4.—After throwing on the wheel or modeling, the object was given a slight firing just to harden it enough to handle. This was called "a bistugio."

5.—It was then dipped in the enamel or the latter was poured over it.

6.—The "enamel" was prepared with greatest of care being crushed, pounded, sieved and mixed with water.

7.—After the "enamel" had dried the decoration was painted on with decision and certainty for the surface was porous and very absorbent so that the color took immediately into it and any hesitation meant a blotch.

8.—Sometimes the lees of wine with sand were burned forming an alkali which when blended with the colors formed a sort of extra glaze strengthening the colors and giving them brilliance. (Note:—This may have also been done with the Turkish and Damascus wares but I am not certain.)

9.—Another transparent glaze was then applied over the enamel decoration which gave a certain depth, whereas French and German wares lacked this overglaze as did also the Chinese enameled designs, borrowing their brightness from the enamel undercoat with which they united in firing. (Note:— Each man's own way is the best in his mind. The Chinese enamels had a glaze texture all their own and none of the underglaze came up over them. They were also so high fired a porcelain that the enamels had to be fired at a second and lower temperature.)

10.—The pigments were:

   1.—"Bianchetto" oxide of tin making opaque white.

   2.—"Verde" green from copper oxide with the addition of oxide of antimony or lead.

   3.—"Zallo" yellow from lead oxide, antimony and iron rust.

   4.—"Zallolino" light yellow from lead oxide, antimony and a little cooking salt and potash.

   5.—"Zaffara" cobalt blue was imported from the Near East through Venice.

   6.—Brownish purple was the manganese ore from several places in Italy.

He says that the red was not understood in his country. Odd examples he had seen but the color was uncertain and not to be depended upon. (We may say that this was probably copper red.) He says it was mixed from "Armenian bole" with lees of wine and painting the solution on a ground of "zallolino,"—which sounds a bit odd. However, the "Armenian bole" may have been earth containing iron and copper or may have actually been the prepared red the Turks were now using. It must not be confused with ruby lustre which was prepared, according to Piccolpasso, only by Maestro Cencio at "Ugobio" now called Gubbio. Hannover suggests that he refers to one Maestro Vincencio, son of Giorgio Andreoli who was celebrated for his ruby lustre.

11.—Brushes or "panelli" were made from donkey or goat hair while the finest were made from the whiskers of a mouse. (Whether this was simply legend brought from China I do not know but the Chinese do make fine brushes from mouse and other animals' whiskers.)

12.—A clean brush must be used for each color he says and this is an excellent rule for any painter to adhere to.

13.—The designs were traced on the ware by means of a pricked outline on a paper over which a sponge filled with black or red color was passed.

14.—The outlines were drawn in purple or blue.

15.—When painting the vessel was usually held by the artist on his left knee and supported with his left hand. (Amongst the earliest pieces bearing the Caffaggiolo mark there is a plate painted about 1511 showing an artist working just so. It is in the Victoria & Albert Museum.)

16.—With very fine work a table was sometimes used.

17.—The formulas for each part of the painting had been worked out as follows:

    a.—The morning sky and brightly lighted paths were painted in zallolino and bianchetto.

    b.—Woodwork and details of streets were in zallo and bianchetto.

    c.—Sky and sea were in zaffara and bianchetto.

    d.—Plowed land, ordinary roads, ancient ruins, etc., were in zaffara, manganese and bianchetto.

    e.—Green meadows and trees had zallolino with "ramina" (copper ashes).

    f.—Flesh tints were made without red by using zallo, zallolino and highlights of bianchetto. They all look yellow, therefore.

18.—Each color was mixed light "mista chiara," and dark "mista scura."

19.—After the decoration was completed the vessels received their coat of "marzacotto" and were fired in "cassette" or saggers, which were made with three small cones at the bottom called "pironi." (As the pieces were fired upside down there are always three small scars left in the glaze on authentic examples.)

20.—Firing was not done during the wane of the moon for the pieces would then lack brightness. This again is from the Chinese, and reminds us of the constant mystery which surrounded the making of pottery.

21.—The kiln was heated slowly and cooled even more slowly.

22.—Sometimes a second coat was given of lead oxide which would fuse at the low temperature of the muffle-kiln and add another layer of brilliant glaze. This was called "coperta."

So much for the process. About 1500 *pictorialization* and *show pieces* began. Either of these principles would be fatal sooner or later and both together made ruin certain. The plates were made with holes in the foot-rims for suspension and called "istorati" and "piatti da pompa" (state dishes) or again "bacili amatori" (lover's gifts) and have legends "bella" (beautiful), "diva" (divine), or "paragon di tutte" (the paragon of all) beneath portraits of women and sometimes an added pierced heart, flaming heart or clasped

FIG. 539. Urbino ewer of the 16th cent. with blue dragon spout, blue scrolls around handle and blue and yellow foliage. The inscription reads, "Sy Urbino II" around base. Barber called it Caffagiolo. Mus. of Fine Arts, Boston.

FIG. 540. Large majolica bottle from Faenza late 15th cent. showing a woman with the inscription "Fumisterre." Ht. 16". Ex Lord Tabley Coll. and W. R. Hearst Coll. International Studio, Inc.

FIG. 541. Faenza 16th cent. ewer of tin enameled earthenware. This shows some of the characteristics of German stonewares in design.

hands for good measure. An amusing example in the Louvre is in blue and yellow lustre such as was made in Deruta or Pesaro and has the portrait of a girl and the legend, "Who steers well his ship will enter the harbor." Still others are called "tondino" and have deep centers to be filled with sweets and are ornamented with cupids, portraits and love emblems.

Pharmacies of the times were places of grandeur combining meeting houses, confessionals and gossip centers. As our present day display of sanitation and scientific atmosphere was not known the customers were impressed by grandeur and elegance. Part of the show was made by the many jars upon each of which was a flowery abbreviation indicating the mysterious contents and set off with scrolls and foliage. Dishes and ewers for rose water showed Venus rising from the sea attended by sea-gods and bathing nymphs. "Vasi gamelii" were made for wedding presents and had scenes from the story of Cupid and Psyche or from the metamorphoses of Jupiter. "Nuzziali" were similar. Princely persons could buy vessels with scenes from the lives of Caesar or Alexander and sacred vessels had subjects from the life of Moses, St. Paul or Aaron.

Of course Raphael had nothing to do with the so-called "Raffaelle ware," nor did other artists of prominence paint these terrible potteries. Actually the potters helped themselves to anything they could get their hands on in the way of a design and made up tales to bolster the sale of their wares. When a drawing was made from a painting the signature was not forgotten. Thus there are pots signed by Raphael, Giulio Romano, Mantegna, Campagnola and the German painters, Durer, Cranach and Schongauer. Scenes from Ovid and Virgil were popular while biblical subjects were taken from the Old Testament as being richer in possibilities for luscious nudes. We are told that landscapes appear alone as decorations from about 1550 but were not general until the "decline" of the next century.

Certain subjects were well known and copied round about such as the:

"Trofei"—from the duchy of Urbino—weapons, armor and musical instruments "pleasantly" arranged in a reserve on colored ground.

"Rabeschi"—from Venice—interlaced lines and foliage in the manner of arabesques of damascened work.

"Cerquate"—principally from Urbino—oak leaves because of the connection with the della Rovere family (Rovere means oak-tree).

"Groteschi"—were ornaments ending in human figures or heads not to be confused with those of Rafaello del Colle, Giovanni da Udine and Battista Franco later at Urbino.

"Foglie"—leaves—at Venice and Genoa sometimes reserved on a colored ground or elsewhere on a white ground.

And so there are listed also "fiori" (flowers), "paesi" (landscapes) which came chiefly from Castel Durante, Genoa and Venice, "alla porcellana" (in the manner of porcelain) something like arabesques but with more lumpy spots of foliage, "tirate" (interlacements), "bianco sopra bianco" (white upon white) which was made chiefly at Urbino and Faenza and which has a cool white color on a warm white glaze, "quartieri" (compartments) and "candalieri" (literally candlesticks) which are said to resemble groteschi but are of greater symmetry of drawing. There are many more but these are the best known in the patter of collectors. Actually tons of majolica were turned out. There were

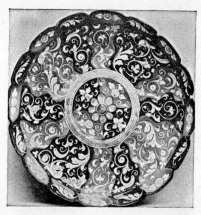

FIG. 542. Dish showing the "Foglie" type of pattern on a two colored background, made at Faenza about 1535–40. Metropolitan Mus. of Art.

fifty towns making it in the 16th century and twice as many in the 17th and 18th centuries. Thus by mass alone they accomplish as much as some other potters have by excellence.

From about 1540 onwards there are signatures usually in the form of monograms and often dates. In services usually only the largest pieces were marked or the largest piece (the "cappo mazzo"). Painters wandered from shop to shop so their signatures do not tell us much. The following chart may help to locate some of the wares:

Left: Caffagiolo plate dated 1522 with the coats of arms of Siena and of the Della Rovere Family. *"Bianco sopra bianco"* border. This plate is one of seven known showing the Seven Virtues in Italian Museums. They were made for the Papal Conclave of 1522. Dia. 10¾". From the W. R. Hearst Coll. International Studio, Inc.
Center: Siena plate of the 17th to 18th cent. Metropolitan Mus. of Art.
Right: Castel Durante dish with portrait and masks, dated 1546. Metropolitan Mus. of Art.

Left: 16th cent. Castel Durante dish with typical grotesques. Dia. 16½". Ex J. P. Morgan Coll. W. R. Hearst Coll. International Studio, Inc.
Center: 16th cent. Gubbio deep dish both painted and lustred. Dia. 10⅝". Ex J. P. Morgan Coll. W. R. Hearst Coll. International Studio Coll.
Right: Gubbio dish signed M. Giorgio in Ugubio and dated 1527. Painting shows St. Margaret and the Dragon. Dia. 9⅞". Ex J. P. Morgan Coll. W. R. Hearst Coll. International Studio, Inc.

Gubbio writing case of the 17th cent. showing the ornate baroque style. Metropolitan Mus. of Art.

Left: Castel Durante albarello of the 16th cent. showing a portrait of a Moor with large turban. Metropolitan Mus. of Art.
Right: Siena albarello with polychrome decoration, made about 1515. Metropolitan Mus. of Art.

ITALIAN WARES 16TH TO 18TH CENTURIES

PLATE 119

CHART OF ITALIAN FAÏENCE

Mark	Date	Location	Subject	Technique
Casa Betini 1487	1487	Church of San Petronio at Bologna / At present same	1200 tiles for pavement / Scrolled leaves	In blue outline, and blue, manganese purple, turquoise blue, yellow
One bears mark "Faenza" another date 1500	1500	Faenza Musée de Cluny	Alberello with grotesques	Yellow ground
1507 Faventine	1507	Now in the Bargello Florence	Dish with David and fallen Goliath	Polychrome

By this piece we attr. to the same hand: 1.—A plate in the Schlossmuseum, Berlin, with reproduction of Dürer's Prodigal Son, 2.—Another with ruins and "putti" cupids after Dürer, 3.—At Brunswick another with the death of Marcus Curtius, 4.—British Museum another with death of Virgin.

Mark	Date	Location	Subject	Technique
T.B. style of Melozzo da Forli	1510 about	1.—Now in the Bargello 2.—Now in Victoria and Albert Mus.	Parel with Martyrdom of St. Sebastian / Panel with the Resurrection	
F.R. Signed on front	About 1510	1.—Schlossmuseum Berlin 2.—V.& A. Mus. 3.—Salting Collection	Plate with legend of the Vestal Tuccia / Panel with Road to Golgotha after Lo Spasimo di Sicilia by Raphael / Dish with Dido and Aeneas	

(Faenza)

Mark	Date	Location	Subject	Technique
Signed:— Fata in Fae(nza)— Josef I(n) Ca(sa) Pirota 1525	1525	From Faenza earliest dated piece. Now in Gustave de Rothschild Collection	Dish with Joseph finding the cup in the sack of Benjamin	
Fato in Faenza in Casa Pirota	About 1525 When the Coronation took place	Faenza probably Now in the Museo Archeologico at Bologna	Dish with coronation of Emperor Charles V in church of San Petronio	
Crossed circle with dot or small circle in one quadrant P.F.B.F. around 1525	All about 1525	1.—Schlossmuseum 2.—British Mus. two panels without date	Plate with Adoration of Magi Madonna and Child Adoration of Magi	Green with all yellow and lavish use of blue, strong highlights

May be by the same hand as above examples then circle would be factory mark.

Note: In Faenza it seems that blue was used not only for the outlines but also for the ground. Also the backs have concentric rings of blue and purple. Casa Pirota the backs are with blue stems "alla porcellana," of the embossed dishes with blue and yellow coils. Faenza, in the case of enclosed compositions blue "alla porcellana" stems occur also on front decorations. Faenza at first but later in other sections, "a berettino" or "sopra azzurro" technique where the body is covered with a light blue enamel instead of the white. Sometimes combined with "bianco sopra bianco," on rise of plate.

Faenza as Hannover says, "A long full faced satyr's mask with tufted crest and foliated beard is of such frequent occurrence that it may often play the part of a missing signature in cases where the piece does not present other special characteristics unfavorable to its attribution to Faenza." Faenza and Casa Pirota produced the "scannellati" or pressed spiral dishes in relief with small centers containing one figure against yellow ground as a rule.

Mark	Date	Location	Subject	Technique
B.M. or Manara 1528 to 1536	About as dated probably 1535	(From Urbino) 1.—Earliest lost sight of 2.—Unknown 3.—Berlin Museum	Resurrection Adoration of Magi	Drawing in purple painting in more naturalistic colors with too strong orange
MF or ML and *Giano Brame dj pallermo 1546 in Faenza*	1546	(Faenza) From Faenza now in the Museum at Sigmaringen	Descent from the Cross after Marcantonio	Same style as above but "brilliant" technique
V R *in Faencia*	? Same time	Faenza Now in the Schlossmuseum Berlin	Death of Marcus Curtius	Same style
Faenza 1562	1562	Faenza Berlin	The head of Hasdrubal being thrown into the camp of Hannibal	Same style Raphaelesque but showing decline of technique
Cafaggiolo or *Chafagguolo* or *SPR* or a trident The SPR probably being "Semper" a motto of the Medici. Also *si volg* meaning "Glovis." Also *S.P.Q.F.* or *S.P.Q.R.* meaning: "Senatus populusque Florentinus or Romarus"	About 1511 to 1570	(Caffagiolo) 1.—Caffagiolo Now in the V. & A. Mus. 1511 2.—V. & A. Mus. has a late example with "Semper" mark in lustre	Majolica painter at work Among earliest pieces marked from Caffagiolo	Backgrounds for figures of deep lapis-lazuli blue in rough brush strokes. Use of stick to scratch designs in the ground

And many of the best ones have no mark at all perhaps because they were forbidden side by side with the "Semper" mark of the royal family.

fata i Siena da m° Benedetto plate in V. & A. Mus. thought to date around 1510 to 1520 or a little later. Also *B°* or *M°B* but they are various in quality.

Mark	Date	Location	Subject	Technique
Bartolomeo Terchi Romano 1727 Siena	1727	(Siena) Now in Berlin Museum	Oval picture panel with Triumph of Galatea	Pale tones after Marcantonio Raimondi and Agostino Caracci
Ferdinando Maria Campani	1733 1733	1.—Berlin Museum 2.—British Museum	Dish with the story of Moses after Raphael Dish with the Creation of the Stars, after Raphael	Same as above

362

363

Date	Inscription / Artist	Location	Subject	Description
1747	The latest known piece from Siena.	V. & A. Mus.	Dish with a pastoral or vintage subject by Campani in the Castelli Manner	
		(Castel Durante)		
1508	1508 a di 12 de Seteb. facta fu i Castel Durat. Zona Maria Vro	Castel Durante Now in Hearst Collection	Basin with the arms of Pope Julius II of the della Rovere Family	Arms on blue ground with yellow palmettes and trophies. reserved in white on blue
1508 or a little later	Pietro dal Castelo fecit on a scroll	Castel Durante Now in Bologna	Basin with Arms of Farnese family on blue, with palmettes, trophies, candakieri and putti	Palmettes in yellow, rest white on blue and blue on yellow
1510	Bastiane 1510 meaning Sebastiano	Castel Durante Oppenheim Coll. Now in Cologne	Plate with woman hung by feet for being unfaithful	Trophy border in yellow, ochre-brown and light green on blue
1519	Same as above Bastiane 1519	1.—Castel Durante Now in British Mus. 2.—Also a companion in V. & A. Mus.	Alberello with weapons and grotesques	Yellowish tones on dark blue and green ground
Same	1524–1526 in Castel Durante	1.—Now in Louvre 2.—Louvre	1.—Bowl with the Rape of Ganymede 2.—Bowl with Apollo and Marsyas	Raphaelesque but devoid of character, pale insipid
		These are similar to the following from Urbino		
		(Urbino)		
1521	1521 with a monogram composed of all the letters of his first name	Urbino or Castel Durante Now in the Basilewsky Coll. in Leningrad	Dish with enthroned king	Similar to above
?	Nicola da U. Same as above artist	Urbino British Mus.	Dish with a sacrifice to Diana	Similar
?	Nicola da Urbino	Louvre	Dish with Parnassus after Raphael	Similar

Mark	Date	Location	Subject	Technique
Nicola da Urbino fata in botega de guido da castello durante in Urbino 1528 Monogram made up of all the letters of his name Orazio Fontana to which is added:	1528	Bargello at Florence Berlin Mus.	Large dish with thirty-four figures representing the martyrdom of St. Cecilia Contest between the Musea and the daughters of Theseus	Similar
questo fu fatto nella botega de M° Guido vasaro da castello duranto in Urbino . . . 1542 The Guido is a son of Nicolo whom he seemed to have joined from about 1526 to 1540.				

(Castel Durante)

Mark	Date	Location	Subject	Technique
P. Mastro Simone in Castel Durante 1562	Same	Was in the Cajani Coll. Rome	Large covered jar. with inverted pear shaped body on slender pedestal with a shield and grotesques	Similar.
Hippolito Rombaldotti Pinse (pinxi) in Urbania	after 1635 1678 added	1.—Now in Louvre 2.—Milan in private possession	Bowl with Triumph of Flora Large vase with snake handles and a design with allegorical figures	More like a slightly tinted pen-drawing Similar to above
Giovanni Rocco de Castelli 1732	Same dave 1732	Now in the Berlin Museum	Panel with the Baptism	

It was painted at Urbania, formerly Castel Durante, but in pure Castelli style.

(Deruta)

Mark	Date	Location	Subject	Technique
I Deruta 1503	1503	From Deruta was in Castellani Collection. Now?	Votive-tablet with two women seated on a bed in presence of four kneeling figures	
1521	Same	Arezzo Mus.	Bowl with gold lustre with (in relief) Adoration of the Shepherds	
el frate in Deruta (on a few pieces from 1541 to 1554)	1550	Present location not known	Large dish with the Marriage of Alexander and Roxana	Blue outline and painted in blue and lustre like old pieces
1545 in Deruta frate fecit	1545	Louvre	Bowl with a scene from the Orlando Furioso of Ariosto	Drawing and shading in bistre, draperies blue and white with yellow highlights, green sward and dress of female in green

Note: Also lustre usually poor by this maker.

(Pesaro)

Inscription	Date	Location	Description	Notes
1540 fatto in Pesaro	1540	Ashmolean Museum Oxford	Dish with Creation of the Beasts	Commercial and poor quality of Urbino style
Girolamo da le Gabice in Pesaro	?	Now in British Museum	Bowl with Cicero expounding the law to Julius Caesar	Markedly superior though by same hand

Note: Many of these wares if not marked *fatto in Pesaro* (with the usual 16th century dates) would be mistaken for Urbino.

(Rimini)

Inscription	Date	Location	Description	Notes
in Arimini, in Rimino or in Ariminensis or 153 Julio da urbino in botega de mastro Alisandro in arimino			Found only on a few fragments at Rimini much like Urbino ware with brown tree trunks instead of black.	

(Ferrara ?)

Inscription	Date	Location	Description	Notes
Thomas Masselli Ferrarien Fec	18th	V. & A. Mus.	Dish with Bacchanalian rout	In manganese purple

Not necessarily from Ferrara and there are no other marked pieces.

(Verona)

Inscription	Date	Location	Description	Notes
1547 . . . in Verona	1547	Kunstindustrimuseum at Copenhagen	Bowl with arrival of Aeneas in Italy	Beautiful Urbino style, fine in composition and technique
1563 a di 15 genaro Guiseppe Giovanni Battista da Faensa— in Verona—M. Also the scrolls as stems on the back are not known at Urbino		Bacon Hall Norfolk	Dish with Alexander the Great with the family of Darius	Same style and by same artist

(Venice)

Inscription	Date	Location	Description	Notes
1540. Adi. 16. del. Mexe. de. Oturbe	1540	Ashmolean Museum Oxford	Dish with mermaid with wide border of arabesques with fruits, flowers and birds	Painted in blue on grey enamel
In Venetia in Co(n)trada dj Sta Polo in botega di Mo Lodovico		V. & A. Mus.	Dish entirely covered with arabesques	Style like above

Mark	Date	Location	Subject	Technique
Jacomo da Pesaro a Sta Barnaba in Venetia	1542	Sigmaringen Museum	Large "smaltino" Dish with Venus with Vulcan and Cupid	Painted in blue
1568 Zener Domenigo da Veneccia feci in la botega al ponte sito del Andar a San Paolo		Museum at Brunswick		Center picture with rim divided into panels with single figures
		(Gubbio)		
Maestro Giorgio (FIRST SIGNED WORKS) As a rule signed *M.G.* or *M.G. da Ugubio* or on important works *Mo Giorgio 1520 a di 2 de O'tobre in Ugubio*	1517–18	V. & A. Museum British and Berlin Museums	Service with housemark of owner (a pointing hand) surrounded by arabesques	Berlin dish is embossed and shows Oriental and Deruta influence. Others more freely curved grotesques like those from 1519 on. Golden Lustre has reddish tone. Also has ruby lustre.
		(Rome)		
Alfonso Patanazzi fecit. Urbini. 1606		V. & A. Mus.	Romulus and the Sabine Women on a large basin	Style like that of second type Urbino
		(Urbino)		
Fabrica di Maiolica fina di monsieur Rolet in Urbino, A 28 abrile 1773		V. & A. Mus.	Tall Roman oil lamp with four nozzles with dec. of clusters of berries	Red, blue and purple on white ground
		(Castelli)		
L.G.P. or *Liborio Grue* as he signed	(1701–1776)	V. & A. Mus.	Tureen with naked figures after Annibale Carracci	General type
Also Carmine Gentili who signed *C.G.P.* cr *Cne Gti P.*				
		(Savona)		
Six pointed star with letter S (Girolamo Salomini)		Sèvres Museum		Coarse and crude scalloped large dishes, etc.

Note: Star and S also appear enclosed in: *L'anno 1721 Agostino Ratti Fece in Sauona.*

A few added notes follow:

Faenza about 1560 produced a fine white enamel by Don Pino and Vergiliotto on bowls with perforated rims and dishes with radial embossments decorated in manganese outlines filled with light blue and touches of yellow. The subjects were "putti" (cupids) and such.

Caffaggiolo was a "castello" on the road between Florence and Bologna built by Cosimo de' Medici. Famous pieces from this kiln are the plate with a figure of Fame in Berlin, Diana and Endymion in the style of Botticelli in the Basilewski Collection and the one with St. George in the V. & A. Museum.

Siena is said to have had so many kilns in 1262 that they became a danger and were called to the attention of the authorities. The oldest product of Siena known today is the tile pavement in the oratory of Santa Caterina at Fontebranda which has much rich Renaissance design. Such tiles are distinguished by orange and "terra di Siena" red and it is these two colors that make it possible to associate certain dishes and alberelli with the place. The backs are distinctive and are drawn in blue and orange. Another stunt was the use of a blue shadow behind the profile on a plate. This was also done at Deruta but not in the same way. The oldest ware shows a diapered design made by the repetition of thin blue stems and yellow flowers recalling the Hispano-Moresque style of Florence but different. Some plates have numerous concentric borders, at times only lines and sometimes with scale or leaf ornament. Some are also made with "bianco sopra bianco" decoration combined with "alla porcellana" ornament in blue but most are polychrome, which included red, orange, orange yellow, copper green, deep blue, etc. but with warm colors dominating.

Castel Durante and "Urbino" called "Urbania" after 1635 is the general ground of much contention. It is where our friend Piccolpasso lived. A certain Nicola da Urbino was thought to have been the artist who painted the "Correr service" so called because it is now in the Correr Museum in Venice, but we do not agree for the service is classed very high among the "istorati" and has a delicate yellow in the flesh tints with also a pale pink from manganese; it is drawn by a man who knew anatomy and the general effect is soft. It is now agreed that it dates about 1515 (instead of 1482) and at this time we know that Nicola did some very insecure anatomy with hard outlines on the Gonzaga service and on a plate showing Solomon worshipping an idol. The artist who did the Correr service in 1515 thought in masses while the one who did the Gonzaga service in 1520 thought in outlines only. One real peculiarity of Nicola is that he coils and indents his clouds very much as the Chinese did. These clouds appear typically in the Gonzaga service, a point which may or may not be taken as vital evidence.

If the artists of other places wandered, those from Castel Durante did to a greater degree. Francesco Durante went to Urbino and then to "Monte Bagnolo near Perugia" though we cannot find that place. Guido di Savino went about 1535 to Antwerp. The Gatti family went to Venice as did also Francesco del Vasaro in 1545. But Urbino profited by this drifting.

Castel Durante did various wares but the best known are of the "trofei" type painted en grisaille. They also had the following properties: pale greyish yellow clay, dishes and plates only exceptionally showing black decoration; those with figures are bordered with a yellow line, while those with ornamental designs have a light grey instead of the yellow in most specimens and the designs are in a light greyish olive-green which is peculiar to them. Outlines are in blue or grey. At times a clear reddish-brown is used in the trophies instead of grey.

Fig. 543. Plate still showing strong Spanish feeling. Said to date c. 1500. Phoenix holding shield charged with arms of Raniere Family, Perugia. Lustred brown and blue. Dia. 16″. Metropolitan Mus. of Art.

Fig. 544. Deruta majolica plate with lustre decoration similar to one in Louvre attr. to c. 1520–1530. Tan, ivory and blue. Hercules and the lion. Dia. 15¾″. From Prince Kudacheff Coll., Florence, the W. R. Hearst Coll. International Studio, Inc.

Fig. 545. Majolica dish from Deruta. 16th cent. painted and also lustred probably about 1550 when painted technique replaced much of lustre. Dia. 16¼″. Ex J. P. Morgan Coll. W. R. Hearst Coll. International Studio, Inc.

Now returning to lustre ware which we left off with in Spain we come to the making of it in Italy which was a very different matter as one might guess after having looked over the other wares. At Deruta on the Tiber not far from Perugia and on the road between Todi and Orvieto they first made wares similar to those of Siena but these are difficult to distinguish and the place is known chiefly for its lustred pottery. Why or how this was the place to receive the seed from Spain is impossible to tell but about 1497 it came into being. One example, a votive tablet with two women sitting on a bed, is dated 1503 and marked "I Deruta." Also a relief of St. Sebastian in the V. & A. Museum bears the date 1501. The tin enamel had been known in this place at least as early as 1475.

Fig. 546. Deruta lustred dish of about 1530 with decoration only. The outlines are blue. Metropolitan Mus. of Art.

The forms are of jars in the shape of pine cones, two-handled vases, goblets, and heavy wide-rimmed dishes often painted with a woman's bust and such adages as the one about steering well one's ship, previously mentioned. The ware is of red or yellow clay and the backs have a simple transparent glaze much as did the Spanish ones. In fact it is said by no lesser authorities than Mr. R. L. Hobson and Mr. William Burton that "The earlier examples are hardly distinguishable from Spanish ware, and to the last the ware remained technically like earlier ware, though with perfectly Italian decorative treatment." The front is covered with tin enamel and fired and the painting is done with a peculiar light blue used as outline and shaded only slightly up from that without any attempt to do any real modeling. Finally this painting was covered and a third and lower firing given to the lustre. This has a thin, transparent glaze which in direct light has a delicate yellowish-olive or perhaps olivish-yellow tone, but when the light reflects obliquely it has a glow like gold or redder than gold, or sky-blue or iridescent like mother of pearl from which it gets its name "madre-perla" as it is called in Italy. Many of these wares have the clever device of low relief designs which make an uneven surface from which the light reflects with more variance.

The designs alone are rather stupid and flabby. Figures are often set on tile floors either flat or in perspective. The wide rims are usually divided "a quartieri" in scrolls or at other times in thirds with a sort of alternating plan but which is crude and non-rhythmical. The best period is between 1520 and 1540.

Unlustred Deruta wares are similar in style to Deruta lustre but are painted in intense shades of yellow and deep blue, ochre, and green. Strangely enough they show many three-quarter faces rather than the profiles used in lustre ware. These also have better borders. Piccolpasso's statement that as a rule out of a hundred pieces of lustre only six come out good may explain this. For we can hardly blame the workmen for slighting painting on wares which were likely to be destroyed anyhow. Here lies the reason for the decline and final obliteration of lustre. The Italians had an unconquerable desire to draw and paint pictures and lustre was just not the medium for them.

At the little city of Gubbio, on the eastern slope of the Apennines, pottery had been made through the middle ages, but in 1498 there came a potter exiled from Pavia and he called himself "Maestro Giorgio" being also a sculptor by profession. The place was owned by the Dukes of Urbino and they did not mind having him. He started to carry out some of his figures in glazed terracotta like that of the della Robbias and now we know of pieces in the church of San Domenico, in the Louvre, the Städelschs Institute at Frankfort and elsewhere. But none of his figures ever bore any lustre.

It is not known whether or not he brought the gold lustre with him but the red "ruby lustre" was certainly not made before his time nor afterwards to such perfection. His lustre colors were known as, "cangiante, madre-perla, reverbero and rubino," and became so famous that they were applied not only to wares made in his factory but others sent for the purpose. He created no new designs but his quality was high.

At first he followed Deruta designs but by 1518 he branched out and included grotesques and trophies after Castel Durante. When this change took place his dishes became light and more graceful. His first signed piece is a service made between 1517 and 1519 and shows the transition from embossed plates showing Oriental influence to large and freely curved grotesques. Most of the larger museums have examples of his work.

Little is known of the small towns of Pesaro and Rimini except that they did make similar wares. We illustrate two plates which are very much like the Deruta wares. Ferrara was under the protection of the Duke of Ferrara, Alfonso I. The ware was famous for its brilliant glaze of white. The potters came from Faenza and a large industry was carried on through

Fig. 547. Two polychromed plates from Pesaro showing similar border treatments to those typical of Deruta. Dias. 16¼″ and 16″. Ex Peyta Coll. and W. R. Hearst Coll. International Studio, Inc.

the first half of the 16th century, but there are no dated pieces and it is exceedingly difficult to make attributions. The dish with bacchanalian rout in the V. & A. Museum may have come from there for the artist called himself a "Ferrarian." Verona we only know through two pieces listed in our chart.

Venice passed laws prohibiting the importation of pottery in 1426, 1437 and 1455, yet we have little to go on until 1520 when it came under the influence of Faenza until 1550. Later they resemble the wares of Urbino but the wares from Venice are poor in tin and, therefore, have a comparatively transparent glaze. To try to counteract this the glaze was applied thickly and it is bluish or greyish in tone and seldom white. The name it is called by the Italians is "smaltino." The drawing is done in blue and shaded in blue while the highlights are painted in in white. The backs are decorated with a simplified "alla porcellana" scroll and at times radially fluted or striped with alternate thick and thin lines. The design, generally a shield, is enclosed in a circle considerably smaller than the bottom and the wide rim is filled with design in Persian or Chinese characters and we must remember that there was much communication with the East from this port. One of the earliest works is a service of which several pieces are known in the Knustgewerbe-museum, Berlin, bearing the arms of two Nuremberg families, Imhof and Schlaudersbach, impaled, and it is dated about 1520. For other pieces see chart.

The name Maestro Ludovico appears on pieces from about 1530 to 1550 which are strongly of Eastern influence and painted in blue on an enamel ground stained greyish-blue. Here is a distinct link in the entrance of "blue and white" wares to Europe. Another specialty of Venice was "foglie da duzena" (dozen foliage ware), which is also "smaltino" and painted in large curving leaves with round fruit in blue with touches of white for high-lights. They were probably a common ware in their day and Piccolpasso says they could be bought for about forty lire for a hundred pieces but it is interesting to note how a slight touch of Chinese influence called the attention even of the Venetians to the beauty of decoration as such.

Venice also made globular jars and alberelli with strong yellow, green and blue decorations in acanthus scrolls, flowers, rosettes and fruits around medallions of women's busts and warriors, old men, etc. These were painted on a white ground with a blue background also painted in with scratched spirals and scrolls. This mode reflected the Venetian school of oil painting and did produce some decorative effects but soon deteriorated.

Some ware was made with architectural drawings poorly drawn and having blue mountains and yellow clouds in the background. The drawing was done in indigo or manganese.

Guido da Marlingo seems to have come to Venice about 1542 from Urbino and Domenigo da Venezia also copied the Urbino style. The white ground vases are particularly close to the style, but can be distinguished by the spottiness of their colors and usually also have four or five concentric rings on the back.

Black glazed ware painted in gold and lacquer colors similar to those used on Venetian glass date from about 1600. In the 18th century a high fired and resonant ware with decoration of landscapes in blue and brown with sparing touches of gold on a pale blue or greyish white ground became the vogue. The molded technique was also used and passed on to Germany and eventually England.

Venice influenced other towns:—Padua made the sgraffito work and smaltino glaze was applied over relief flowers. Verona, Candiana and Treviso copied the Venetian "Turkish wares."

Urbino was the birthplace of Raphael (1483–1520) and also an ancient pottery center but we hear nothing until in 1477 Nicolo Pellipario who called himself Nicolo da Urbino made the Gonzaga service. His followers were Guido da Castello Durante, Maestro Guido Fontana Vasaro and Guido Durnatino in Urbino. He had three descendants, Orazio, Camillo and Nicolo the last two of whom are not known as potters. But Orazio Fontana, the grandson of Nicolo da Urbino was a great competitor of Xanto Avelli.

This Xanto Avelli was born at Rovigo and became a free lance painter in Urbino. He signed his work and ocasionally put the factory name on it. He never called himself "Maestro." He worked between 1528 and 1542 following the style of Nicolo the master of narrative "istorato" painting. He also took motives from engravings, woodcuts, Ovid's "Metamorphoses" (Venice 1497), Raphael's paintings, the Bible, Virgil, Livy and Ariosto. He was not so good a draughtsman or colorist as Nicolo and aside from the fact that he used a certain bluish green in clothing and drapery his work is not distinctive. Perhaps his best known piece is the dish in the Louvre with the Rape of Helen on it after Raphael.

Orazio Fontana signed his work, as did his grandfather, with a monogram

FIG. 548. Urbino bowl of first half of 16th cent. Metropolitan Mus. of Art.
FIG. 549. Pilgrim bottle in style of Orazio Fantana of 16th cent. showing "Bacchanalian Triumph." Metropolitan Mus. of Art.
FIG. 550. Urbino plate with figure of Justice and grotesques of type supposedly influenced by Raphael and dating c. 1565 or later. Dia. 19". Metropolitan Mus. of Art.

of all the letters of his name. He started about 1542 and became the favorite of all the dukes of Urbino. He made a great service which was presented by Guidobaldo II to Philip II of Spain, and also the equipment of the pharmacy of the ducal castle after designs of Battista Franco and Raffaelle del Colle. The story goes that Louis XV wanted to trade these pieces for statues in gold and Queen Christina of Sweden offered the weight of the service in gold. It consists of about 380 pieces and much of it is in the Sanat Casa at Loreto. Between 1565 and 1571 Orazio found a new style in Raphael after the Loggia in the Vatican. This was a contrast to all that had gone before. It was a frame, and concocted of baldacchinos, genii, chimaeras, masks and various terminal figures lightly drawn but in rich colors around small medallions placed symmetrically and simulating gems with figures in blue camaïeu or grisaille. Large snake-handled vases, great jugs, salt-cellars, etc., typical of the High Renaissance started about this time, and lasted to the 17th century and were widely copied afterwards. This kind of thing was made by the Patanazzi family; but the decline soon set in and the only revival was made by a Frenchman named Rolet who started a kiln in 1770 to fake Roman oil lamps.

Castelli was a town near Naples and there they used only blue, yellow, green and purple. It built up to between 30 and 40 factories about 1743 and used gold instead of lustre. The usual Bible and historical subjects were added to by genre in the style of Berghem and also landscapes with and without ruins. The work was technically fine and plates have rims and centers treated separately. Many were made to hang on the wall. Perhaps the best painters were the Grue family from Francesco Grue whose first signed piece was in 1647 to Saverio Grue who died in 1806. There was Carlo Antonio (1655–1723) who signed C.A.G., and Liborio (1701–1776) who signed L.G.P. Finally Saverio who was later the director of the Capo di Monte factory. Also notable was the Gentili family: Bernardo, Carmine who signed C.G.P., Giacomo and Bernardo the younger.

With the beginning of the 18th century Chinese porcelain had such an

FIG. 551. Urbino plate by Francesco Xanto (1534) showing Alexander presenting crown to Roxana, dated on back and inscribed including signature Xanto ·A·. Metropolitan Mus. of Art.

FIG. 552. Small faïence vase from Italy and dated 1777 which shows that this primitive sort of treatment and simple acanthus decoration carried later than might otherwise be supposed. Ht. 5¾". Plummer, Ltd.

influence that places like Delft copied it. At this time the wares of North Italy become more important and we can come to those later.

Meanwhile let us briefly review our findings:

1.—Lustre reached its greatest artistic perfection in Europe in Spain. The Italians brought it to greater technical perfection but almost from the beginning misapplied it trying to paint pictures with it.

2.—As an aid to the variations of color of lustre we find molding and modeling of surfaces in Spain and then much more in Italy.

3.—Color of all things in art seemed to appeal to the Italians most of all and it was heaped on to all ware as much as was possible and more than was good taste.

4.—The pictorial and narrative element which was entirely out of place on pottery became dominant and most destructive to the art. The Italians never seemed to grasp the beauty of an object in itself but always had a yen to wrap it with stories, sentiments and emotions.

Thus these wares were like horrible nightmare fantasies or potteries out of a dream. They had gnomes and giants, rapes, murders and all manner of unholy things, all daubed on them with glowing but often displeasing colors. They offended all but the cruel, the gluttonous and the depraved; they, better than all the tales of the Renaissance of sudden death and treachery, of hate and love unnatural, tell what the Renaissance was really like, and in them, so strange to the soul of man, we find a beauty of horror and fascination; we look at them as a city crowd will look at an accident and stand and shiver at the blood. They constituted an honest outpouring in the main but God preserve us from the sort of people who made them!

CHAPTER XVI

FRENCH, GERMAN AND NETHERLANDS TIN-GLAZED WARES

FAÏENCE OR DELFT

FRENCH FAÏENCE

THE art of lustre died because of the Italian desire to paint pictures for which it was too difficult a medium. The old art of modeling inherited from the Romans, Greeks and from the Near East, had been kept alive by the added beauty that uneven surfaces give to lustre. However, we shall drop it for this chapter and continue with the development of tin slip, tin enamel or tin glaze and the opportunities this metal made possible for decoration.

EARLIEST FRENCH FAÏENCE AND LYONS

The Italian potters taught the French the art of faïence and up to the 17th century it was sporadic. The earliest examples are from Provence, Agen and the church at Brioude where tiles were found decorated with manganese-purple and green and thought to date from the late 14th century. Benedicto Angelo de Laurent, the Italian potter, started work at Lyons in 1512 and continued until 1536. In 1556 Sebastiano Griffo from Genoa and Domenico Tardessir from Faenza made Urbino style wares, and in 1575 Giulio Gambino and Gian Francesco da Pesaro opened another kiln. Generally speaking the characteristics of the wares are these:
1.—Three conical mountains in the background of the landscapes. 2.—Waves arranged in regular rows in seascapes. 3.—Flesh tones which are reddish-yellow or orange. 4.—A distinctive light blue for sky and sea and the inscriptions refer to the compositions on the front of the plates just as they did in Italy. None are dated.

ROUEN

From 1540 to 1560 Masseot Abaquesne made tiles at Rouen with French Renaissance designs and the first dated example comes from there. There are two paving tiles from the Château d'Écouen, one at Chantilly and one still at Rouen all inscribed "à Rouen 1542." In the Musée de Cluny there is an altar step from the chapel of the Château de La Bâtie d'Urfé decorated with canopies, flaming urns, winged female figures and angels playing musical instruments in pale blue, yellow, light green and manganese on a white ground. A cartouche in the center dates these 1551.

Nothing more is known until in 1644 Nicolas Poirel started a kiln followed by Edme Poterat and his son and we are told that during the reign of Louis XIV their wares were noted for large sizes and were decorated in blue, or in blue combined with red or yellow-ochre. The designs were of palmettes, scrolls and festoons in radial arrangements on the wide borders and Chinese elements were combined with "classical baroque."

Fig. 553. Panel of faïence tiles from Rouen. 17th cent. Length 19¾". Metropolitan Mus. of Art. Note: These tiles are not correctly assembled.

Fig. 554. Rouen 16th cent. panel of tiles, Masseot Abaquesne. Length 38". Metropolitan Mus. of Art.

Fig. 555. 16th cent. Rouen faïence dish. Interesting glaze of mottled type which we have seen from Crete, through Near East and Far East, and finally which was Rockingham and Benton ware of later times. Dia. 18⅛". Metropolitan Mus. of Art.

Fig. 556. Faïence albarello from Laurent Abaquesne, Rouen. 16th cent. showing strong Italian influence. Metropolitan Mus. of Art.

MOUSTIERS

The Clérissy family made pottery at Moustiers before 1700 and these wares were also large and were decorated with hunting scenes from the engravings of Tempesta. They also made large rectangular trays with light baroque decorations after Bérain, first in blue on white and then polychrome. About 1677 one of the Clérissy family went to Marseilles in St. Jean-du-Désert where he made potteries like the Moustiers ones.

NANTES, NÎMES AND NEVERS

Gian Ferro established himself in Nantes in 1588. In Nîmes the potter Sigalon signed a pilgrim bottle of Italian style in 1581. In Nevers the three brothers named Conrade, kinsmen of Giulio Gambino of Lyons and Faenza, started in 1578 but there is also evidence that Scipio Gambini had been there before that. Lastly by rumor there was supposed to have been a potter named Oratio Borniola at Le Croisic to whom is attributed the ribbed dishes with fine scrolls in blue and orange-yellow dating around 1630, but similar things were also made at Antwerp and other northern cities.

The wares at Nevers followed Urbino and Faenza in both blue and white and polychrome but great baroque jugs with dragon handles were distinctive and had hunting scenes on them. Large oval basins such as the one in Cluny with the Triumph of Amphitrite were made, the outlines being in manganese, nude figures in two shades of yellow or also in manganese and a typical use of the same color, in draperies, tree trunks and other details, which never occurs in Urbino. The rims of these are also treated separately from the centers as is not the case in Urbino ware.

FIG. 557. Polychrome dish of Nevers ware showing Italian influence particularly in grotesqueri of border. Dia. 9¾". 1644. Metropolitan Mus. of Art.

FIG. 558. Nevers, so-called "Persian style" (A.D. 1640-1700) faience plate. Dia. 9¾". Metropolitan Mus. of Art.

The Conrade family copied the della Robbia sculptured ware. The third brother, Augustin, founded a school of potters and Pierre Custode made the "Bleu Persan" ware typical of the second period of Nevers. It has charm but little to do with Persian design. There are three types: 1.—blue glazed ground with white decoration and at times gilding, 2.—yellow glazed ground painted with white and on top of it blue so that the blue does not turn green over the yellow, 3.—white tin enameled ground with polychrome, blue alone or less frequently, green decoration. The first is common, the second rare and the third almost nonexistent. There are Chinese figures in green on white, blue on white and also manganese on white, the latter showing distinct Delft influence. There were also "marbled" wares splashed with white on blue as in the wine cooler from Vestlandske Museum, Bergen. Note how again the old Egyptian technique crops up as we have seen it in Crete, Italy, T'ang China, Persia and elsewhere.

Nevers, being a large pottery center a little later than Rouen and Moustiers, copied both wares. It was a strongly Catholic city and the potters made sacred figures and holy-water stoups to set in niches at street corners. It is here also that "Faïence Patriotiques" were plentiful; jugs, cisterns, barrels and plates painted with childish crudity with such subjects as the Bastille,

FIG. 559. Nevers pilgrim bottle dating between 1640–1700. Ht. 9¾". Metropolitan Mus. of Art.

FIG. 560. Nevers ewer of faïence (1640–1700). Ht. 12¾". Metropolitan Mus. of Art.

tree of liberty, etc., and inscribed with "La Liberté ou la Mort," or "Ca Ira Vive la Nation," etc. These are of course late and of little value but many have been sold in America since the late craze for French provincial antiques, just as also hundreds of "Empire" vases which are not even made in France have been sold. The Nevers ware is of whitish-buff clay, can easily be scratched, and the blue glaze is warm, soft, very smooth and apparently even but when seen with the magnifying glass is full of tiny sunken holes or specks. The white pigment is chalky and in the same detail may vary from an enamel-like thickness to transparent thinness. The brush strokes are apparent and the handling is pretty rough. Lastly the weight of the ware is surprisingly light for the thickness of the walls.

The course that these wares went through is much like that so often seen in Europe: First Italian feeling, second in the 17th century Chinese influences, third the polychrome gave way to the blue and white with manganese outlines probably because it was easier to make, fourth classical themes again giving way to late Ming and a reversion to polychrome; and at the end of the 18th century the growing effects of Napoleon's conquests and the Revolution.

GERMAN FAÏENCE

The faïence of Spain, Italy and France had little to do with that of Germany. There is as much difference as there is between Latin country music and German music. The north country liked stoneware and the craving for color is replaced by a demand for modeling. The earliest example we know is a plate dated 1526 in Nuremberg. It purports to show Samson and Delilah but it is in the style of Burgkmair and they are all dolled up with puffed sleeves and other details of the costumes of the period. The colors are in the Italian manner, manganese, blue, yellow and light green. Another dated 1530 is in blue only, similar to the Venetian wares of even date and shows the Madonna and Child on a crescent while still another dated 1531 is of similar treatment and shows a half figure of a woman in German costume.

FIG. 561. Lower Rhine earthenware plate decorated in brown, green and yellow with border dated 1783. Dia. 8¾". Metropolitan Mus. of Art.

A fluted bowl in the museum at Sigmaringen recalls the embossed dishes of Faenza and Castel Durante and here also is a ring shaped bottle of 1544. This shape originates with the metal work of the Near East and was also made in pottery there, later coming to Italy and thence throughout Europe; but it became especially dear to the hearts of the Germans. It is an impractical form holding little and unfitted to the hand of man, but it offered the potters a chance to show off their technical skill. At Ulm there is an alberello with a portrait of a woman on it and a dish in the style of Deruta is in the Hamburg Museum. I know of nothing much more of this type.

One note that Hannover makes which is of interest is that some of these plates have been called Swiss but are proven to be of German origin because the Swiss plates have a small loop set on the back perpendicular to the rim and radially, for the purpose of hanging them on the wall. How infallible this is I do not know.

Owl jars or "Eulenkrugen" were not only made in stoneware but also in the imported tin glaze on pottery and there is one believed to have been made by Augustin Hirsvogel of Nuremberg which has underglaze blue and shields on its breast modeled in relief and is seemingly painted with oil colors and gilded. Between the legs is the date 1540. The heads on these jars are removable from the neck. They were supposed also to be Swiss but are now allocated to South Germany. Many fakes are made by Fleischmann of Nuremberg and others. A double eagle is spoken of by Robert Schmidt (*Der Cicerone,* II, p. 667 f.) also treated with underglaze blue and with shield painted with oil color. It is now in Coburg. The owl jars remind us of the Shang period (1766–1122 B.C.) bronze ones of China. These could never have been seen by the German potters and one wonders what the origin of their jars could have been. Perhaps the owl is just a good solid form which is sufficiently jar shaped to suggest itself. There is one theory for the design which we shall quote under the stoneware section but it does not seem fundamental.

From about Kreussen came cylindrical jars (one of which is dated 1618) which are painted in blue on white. Hamburg produced similar ones the earliest of which is dated 1624 and from Hanau again similar ones reach from 1661. They might be called alberello forms but with convex rather than concave sides. They have escaped the blight of Italian pictorial ideas and are decorated with symmetrical flowers of Indian origin which came in via Holland. However the constant use of the spiral with them seems indigenous when we remember the Halstadt Culture, but how the motives of that very ancient culture could have been brought to the 17th century is a question. Toward the end of the century the quality of these wares deteriorated, the blue getting darker and heavier, the glaze coarse and glistening and the brushwork less deft.

Faïence of Hamburg

Another early ware which reached its height about 1640 to 1650 has been found around Hamburg and the arms of Hamburg and of Hamburgers are commonly painted on it. The last dated piece is 1656. Some have letter signatures which have not been identified. There are a few dishes but not in quite the same direct spirit as the jugs which are more numerous. These latter are well formed with flaring foot and narrow cylindrical neck from which springs a strong handle down to the body. The ground color is warm due to the body toning through the tin enamel. The blue is strong and bright and touches of yellow are used. Most of them have a front medallion of a merchant's mark, an emblem, a shield of arms or something of the sort. Only one is known with flowers and it is probably of a different source.

Other German Faïence

With the opening of the factory at Hanau in 1661 by two Dutch potters and another in Frankfort-on-the-Main in 1666 Far Eastern influences are felt as translated by the Dutch, and the latter factory is renowned for its large blue and white jars and plates in a sort of remote late Ming style. Erfurt, in Thuringia, Potsdam (where powder blue was tried), Berlin, Dresden, Ansbach, Nuremberg and Bayreuth also made poor copies of Chinese blue and white and polychrome wares. French painting of naturalistic flowers was done by the glass painters such as Johann Schaper and Abraham Helmhack of Nuremberg who did landscapes and figures in black and called "schwarzlot," or in polychrome. This influence came through Strasbourg and Marseilles and was carried on to rococo forms by Johann Tännich, Ludwig Ehrenreigh and Johann Eberhardt among others who followed in factories at Kiel and Mosbach.

But it is obvious that faïence was a poor thing in Germany and the preference was all for the stoneware which we shall take up shortly.

"DELFT" OR THE FAÏENCE OF THE NETHERLANDS

In the Low Countries things were different for "Delfsche porselyn" was a great influence in Europe in the 17th and 18th centuries. It was Italy again that was the first source. In 1548 Guido di Savino set up shop in Antwerp where his sons had already been struggling and this started the work. A tile memorial to them and dated 1547, now in the Vleeschhuis Museum, Antwerp, is considered the oldest work of faïence made on Netherlandish soil. It is definitely Italian in all respects.

There are also many small alberelli from the hospital at Middleburg which was destroyed in 1570. Some tiles are found so frequently in certain places that they would seem to have been made in the Netherlands rather than in Italy, though they show very close similarity to pieces from Florence. Bernard Rackham says in the 14th edition Encyclopaedia Britannica, "About 1560–70 maiolica potters from Antwerp carried their art as Protestant refugees to the northern provinces which were to be Holland (by 1579) and England." Rotterdam and Haarlem became centers of production of earthenwares and wall-tiles with animal, flower and fruit motives in strong coloring, and large tile work pictures with figure subjects. Toward 1650 Delft came to the fore and for more than a century continued with its numerous potteries, known by their signs (the Peacock, the Star etc.) as a thriving center of industry exporting its wares all over the civilized world. It is difficult to prove any piece actually of this period but it is agreed that several dishes with overloaded design in blue may possibly be.

Strangely, it was the failure of the beer business that helped Delft ware. Strong competition had made the breweries fail and someone had the idea that the new industry of potting might be housed in them. Men were out of work, thus capital, a roof and willing hands were all ready. The Guild

of St. Luke founded in 1611 had only ten members up to 1640. Now between 1651 and 1660 there were 20 and between 1662 and 1663, 12 more were admitted. The "plateelbakkers" became so important that they took family names. Up to that time they had passed the baptismal name in the genitive form to their children. This great success was in spite of the fact that the clay had largely to be imported from Tournai and Mülheim.

FIG. 562. Dutch cup of red earthenware ornamented with a cock inside and borders outside in green and yellow slip under transparent glaze. Italian in feeling. 15th–16th cent. Dia. 5″. Metropolitan Mus. of Art.

As this was a purely commercial influence let us digress for a moment and consider this new

Right: Large deep dish with brown body and tin white glaze decorated in blue underglaze. Text is the Ten Commandments, etc. 17th or 18th cent. Dia. 15¾". International Studio Art Corp.

Left: Plate, 17th cent., probably of Ster factory. Dia. 12". Metropolitan Mus. of Art.

Right: Ewer made at "Rose factory," marked *Roos* in blue, having typical famille rose design but shape showing Near Eastern influence. c. 1700. Ht. c. 12". Metropolitan Mus. of Art.

Left: Dish with grotesques in Urbino, Italian style. c. 1600. Decoration in yellows, browns and blue on white ground. Back also white. Dia. 5½". Metropolitan Mus. of Art.

Center: Plate with mark of Miss Amerensie van Kessel, proprietress in 1675 of factory "De Dubbele Schenkkan." Kakiemon style with light colors of red, blue, green and gold with turquoise. Dia. 12¼". International Studio Art Corp.

Polychrome plate with mark of A. Pynacker. The border in three shades of blue and center with "carnival figure" in blue, red, green and yellow. Dia. 15¾". 17th cent. International Studio Art Corp.

DELFT OF VARIOUS STYLES

PLATE 120

Set of 12 Delft plates from the Porceleijne Bijl (Porcelain Axe) under Huibrecht Brouwer and dating late 17th to early 18th cent., representing the months of the year. Dias. 9 1/16".

DELFT PLATES FROM "PORCELAIN AXE" FACTORY

PLATE 121

Set of "month of year" plates continued.

DELFT PLATES FROM "PORCELAIN AXE" FACTORY

PLATE 122

force: I have spoken about religion as a weapon and its effect in bringing lustre to Spain, nay the East to Europe. We have noted how art was, as it were, turned off and on by the ancient conquests of arms. Here we meet a new and powerful force *which may be devastating to all art for centuries*.

Briefly it seems to follow in about this way: First there were chieftains of brawn and brains who led tribes or nations as naturally as a stag leads his herd. When they conquered they looted, and artists were employed to make glorified statues of them or to please their tastes. Secondly there stood in the market place an unarmed man who spoke about a Heaven to come after death and put ideas of good and evil in the heads of the masses so that they would rise up and overthrow the chieftains. When these men conquered there was not much for artists to do, but soon the various churches again put the artists to work glorifying Heaven and helping to keep the masses impressed. Thirdly came the invention of the real use of money as a weapon and it was found that with wealth the churches could be bought, arms could be hired and one could sit on top of the world. Men said, we shall skip the trouble of fighting for an earthly heaven, we shall skip all ephemeral promises of some heaven to come after death, we can see clearly that we can buy our own heaven with money. Of course artists were needed to decorate this heaven. But certain troubles arose which are not yet solved.

The invention of the new weapon *money* did not stop the efficiency of the old ones and when one man got all the chips at times those who wielded *religion* would talk of the evils of wealth and the masses would rise up and take away the money from the rich man, or some gentleman who believed in the more direct weapon of *force* would simply pull a gun and take what he liked. Each time the power becomes too great in one of these forces the other two upset it. We have recently seen great stacks of wealth in the world and we are seeing them melt away under the rising of the masses on the "religious principles" of the trade unions, revolutions, strikes and such, but these mass movements even in Russia have finally given way to the old original primitive power of a leader and the use of force. I predict that the chieftains will fight it out, then there will be a revival of the talkers with new principles and then again will come the laxity which permits accumulation of personal wealth. Only to go through the cycle again. As we later trace the results of money-getting on the arts of the 18th century it will be seen exactly how the blight works. Now in the 17th century the mass movements of the churches both Christian and Muslim as well as Buddhistic had had their day; we enter upon the day of the merchant and we shall see what his effect is upon the 18th and 19th centuries so far as ceramic art is concerned.

The Dutch continued the Italian habit of taking designs from the painters of the period. Biblical and genre subjects surrounded with baroque ornament prevailed. Lastly great interest had centered in China and Japan because of the rising power of the Dutch East India Company.

This company had been chartered in 1602 for the purpose of regulating trade in the Indian Ocean and to help in prosecuting the long war for independence against Spain and Portugal. It was a long and arduous route necessitated by the war with these countries, around the Cape of Good Hope, but it seemed to pay and many companies were formed in competition pursuing it and fighting among themselves. The formation of one company was accomplished to do away with the contention and it had the rights to maintain sea forces, plant colonies, erect forts, make peace or war, coin money and maintain full administrative, judicial and legislative authority from the Straits of Magellan westward to the Cape of Good Hope. The headquarters were in Batavia, Java. In 1638 to 1658 it expelled the Portuguese from Ceylon and Malacca. It grew throughout the century and in 1669 it had 150 ships for trading, 40 war ships, 10,000 soldiers—and it paid a dividend of 40%. It had eight governments:—Amboyna, Banda, Ternate, Macassar, Malacca, Ceylon, Cape of Good Hope and Java, while trading posts were placed in Bengal on the Coromandel Coast, at Surat, Gambroon (or Bunder Abbas) in the Persian Gulf and in Siam. Thus we see that it had *no direct contact with China* and although many porcelains and other works of art were brought to Holland by trade, they were little understood. *This accounts for the whole spirit of 18th century appreciation of Chinese art, or lack of it.* It was thought exotic and strange and was never taken seriously. Few, if any, could tell Japanese design from Chinese and who cared? Both were frequently mixed with Renaissance design and baroque scrolls surround Chinese figures or what were thought to be Chinese figures. But some craftsmen did make remarkable copies of Chinese vases even if they knew nothing about their reason for being, and this is the second great wave of Chinese influence. The first came across the top of the world on the Northern Caravan Route to Turkey, Damascus and on to the shores of the Mediterranean. This second came the long way around to the coast of Holland. It was borne solely by commercialism and probably no other cargo was so precious even from the long range dollars and cents basis.

DELFT PAINTERS

Frederick van Frijtom was a great landscape painter from 1658. The only fully signed panel by him is in Amsterdam and was done about 1660 in blue on white and has most interesting trees and rock formations, figures, and

FIG. 564. Shaving basin with buff body, tin glaze and underglaze blue with iron red and gilding added. Late 17th cent. Delft ware. Length 12". International Studio Art Corp.

FIG. 563. Late 17th cent. blue and white plate with Chinese design. Dia. 10". Metropolitan Mus. of Art.

a bridge. It has a fine feeling of depth. Also attributed to Van Frijtom are a number of plates with centers painted and wide rims left plain.

Abraham de Cooge was also a well known painter in oils who came from Haarlem but as he only dated and did not sign his pieces they are difficult to identify.

FIG. 565. Set of twelve plates showing "The Passion of Christ" with a four line inscription on the back and the monogram of W. Kleffius the maker who worked in the style of Lambertus van Eenhoorn and started his factory 1663. Dias. 10¼". From the W. R. Hearst Coll.

Aelbrecht Cornelis de Keizer did sign his work AK in monogram and in the Louvre there is a beautiful bottle by him which has a fanciful Chinese bird surrounded by feathery flowers and foliage. There is also a well established small square tea caddy with a "happy boy" in medallion on a ground of conventional flowers very like the Chinese. But his style was soon copied even to the monogram. Mr. Hannover says he translated the Japanese and Chinese porcelain pictures with "dauntless fantasy" but I think him a bit too dauntless myself. He was followed by his two sons-in-law, Jacobus and Adriaen Pijnacker. All worked in polychrome as well as blue on white. Adriaen signed his work APK usually in red and many forgers also copied him. He later made blue, red and gold ware after Imari with figures and less formal than the originals.

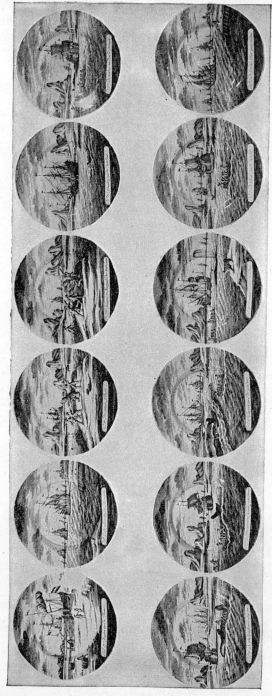

FIG. 566. Set of twelve plates possibly by Justus Brouwer or at least very much in his style and of about 1700. Dia. 10". From the W. R. Hearst Coll.

387

Among other great painters were the family of Wouters van Eenhoorn, his sons Lambertus and Samuel, and their rival Louwijs Fictoor whose signature LF is hardly distinguishable from their LVE. They all made blue

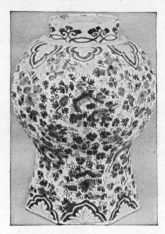

FIG. 567. Pair of vases decorated in Chinese manner, Delft, late 17th or early 18th cent. Ht. 5½". Metropolitan Mus. of Art.

FIG. 568. Blue and white Delft jar of strong Chinese influence, dating late 17th or early 18th cent. Ht. 10". Metropolitan Mus. of Art.

FIG. 569. Delft 17th cent. candlestick with blue decoration on white, probably copy of Ming Chinese example. Samuel van Eenhoorn, 1674. Mark SE VIII in blue. Gift of Seth K. Sweetsor. Mus. of Fine Arts, Boston.

FIG. 570. Cruet and stand marked AP in red and attr to Adriaen Pijnacker c. 1680. "Old Imari" style in red, blu and gold. Ht. 6¾". Metropolitan Mus. of Art.

and white and liver colored styles making a specialty of the "cachemire" style which was supposed to have originated with Lambertus van Eenhoorn. Others were Ghicbrecht Lambrechts Kruyk who did blue and white on a bluish glaze, Samuel Pererius van Berenvelt, Claas Jansz Messchert, Jores Mesch specializing in blue and white, Jacob Wemmersz and his son Rochus Hoppestyn, Cornelis Cornelisz van der Hoeve, Augustijn Reijgens and many others including Lambartus Kleffius who claimed to have invented a red stoneware, on down to David Kam who purchased the old factory of Claas Messchert and made pieces with colored glaze over slip.

Toward the end of the 17th century the factories came into the hands of merchants who ran them simply for profit and deterioration set in with only a few of the older potters standing out a while for quality in work.

POTTING METHODS

These potters worked in two ways. In one process the colors, which were green (a mixture of cobalt and antimony), red (made from the finest sifted bole) and less extensively yellow (of antimony) and violet (from oxide of manganese) were painted, having been mixed with water, within an outline made of cobalt and iron oxide or merely an impure blue called "trek" upon the dry and dusty tin-enamel in which the piece had been dipped after a preliminary light firing. The tin enamel had not yet been fired, of course, and was very absorbent and unpleasant to work on. When the painting was finished it was powdered by the so-called "vloerwercker" with a "kwaart" which was a fine dust of colorless lead glaze. Then the piece was fired at a

high temperature and at a single operation the tin glaze, the metallic oxide colors and the lead glaze were fused into one. The "kwaart" acted like the Italian "marzacotto" and gave more brilliance to the colors just as varnish does to a painting. The undecorated side did not receive this treatment and is therefore more rough, while the face of the piece has typically tiny specks as though pricked with a needle. With the blue and other colors, of course, there was no possibility of really imitating Chinese wares in anything but the drawing, which we have already criticised.

FIG. 571. "Hoti" or god of wealth and happiness, made and signed by Lambertus van Eenhoorn. Decoration blue on white. Ht. 8½". From W. R. Hearst Coll.

The other method was the same with the addition of another (or third) firing for iron red which was painted on the fused glaze, and a fourth for the gilding. Each of these colors takes successively lower heats to set them and will not stand the higher temperatures. This is the way the Japanese wares were copied. Similarly in attempting to reproduce some of the Chinese wares the blue was painted on the tin enamel surface and fired while the other colors were added later, these usually being an enamel-like green and iron-red. In all these methods requiring a third firing the "kwaart" was omitted. Up to about 1650 they stuck to the blue and white technique and then with great suddenness developed a full palette adding to the above colors black, and by the 18th century a rose similar to the famille rose of the Chinese.

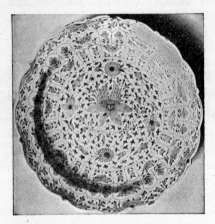

FIG. 572. Blue and white Delft plate with Chinese design. 18th cent. Dia. 12⅛″. Metropolitan Mus. of Art.

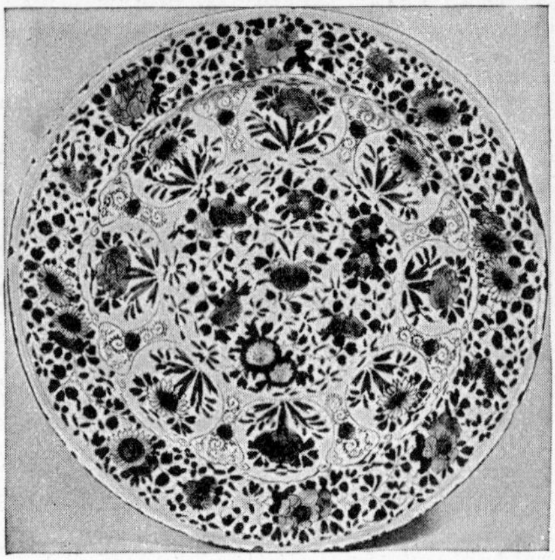

FIG. 573. Late 17th or early 18th cent. Dutch plate with Chinese design in blue on white ground. Dia. 10¼″. Metropolitan Mus. of Art.

The Hollanders did not add much, if anything, to the art of ceramics but they did act as a means of distribution of ideas and particularly those of Far Eastern art. It is true that they became sidetracked in the painting of pictures on ceramics but this was probably due to the Italian influence and their quaint genre subjects were their own and have some appeal. Among their own quaint ideas are the musical plates which had on them scores with

FIG. 574. Three 17th cent. tin enameled tiles. 5″ square. Metropolitan Mus. of Art.

verses written in open book medallions accompanied by various designs of musical instruments and other decorations. These were used after dinner in general singing. The Dutch were great singers and everyone carried a song book in his pocket so one can imagine the popularity of these plates.

It was in the 18th century which we shall come to later that the tasteless oddities were made.

CHAPTER XVII

EUROPEAN MODELED AND MOLDED WARES TO THE 18TH CENTURY

THERE has always been a tendency to imitate metal in the making of pottery and although this led in many instances to the worst faults in design and technique it also led to unforeseen benefits such as the discovery of lustre and the development of modeled wares. The spontaneous scratching of the surface and pinching up of the clay to decorate primitive potteries shows us that sculpture is so much a part of potting that it is difficult to separate the two. The work of the della Robbia family may be considered pottery by some and sculpture by others though, of course, it is both. The imitation of metal vessels developed this sculptural tendency and led to the wares of Kertch, Apulia, Campania and finally and worst of all Canosa but somewhere along the line this imitation had changed to sculpture. At the worst we can blame the metal copying for relief in imitation of repoussé and for a too slender structure such as fragile handles and spouts practical in metal but not in fired clay. At best it led to all the beautiful modeled work of the ages. While sculpture as such must be judged independently.

ARRETINE WARE OR TERRA SIGILLATA

During Roman times along with the wares of bad taste good sensible use was made of metal forms thoughtfully adapted to pottery as a medium, as we can see in the examples from Arezzo or Arretium in Etruria and which are variously called, "Arretine ware," "Samian ware," or "terra sigillata." The second name is a misnomer and is not used today. The last has become the name for the whole group of wares, usually of red body but sometimes of black in the earlier examples from Arezzo, and found in Italy, Spain (though not made there) and the Near East where they had been traded, as well as in France. A similar ware was made by the Gaulish provinces of Rome such as Graufesenque, Lezoux, etc. The molded reliefs or "sigilla" were separate stamps applied to a model vessel which was then cast in a mold used to make others complete. The forms are simple and usually without handles, consisting of bowls, cups and saucers of cylindrical or globular forms. Dr. Dragendorff's chart gives an excellent idea of the development. The first decoration was copied direct from embossed silver ware from Alexandria and Antioch and the bodies are covered with foliate and floral designs, masks and various decorative details, human and animal figures, shown in processions, sacrifices, hunts, battles, dances, feasts and various rituals and episodes of the life of the times. The lustrous effect of these wares was produced by an alkaline glaze which also imparts a deep richness to the color. Potter's signatures were made in the mold and appear on the rims, bases or in the designs inside or outside of the vessels usually enclosed in a rectangle, foot-print or other fancifully formed tablet, either sunk or in relief. Some of the wares were plain and were signed inside the base. Full names or abbreviations were used as for instance the potter Marcus Perennius signed M.Pe, M.Per, M.Pere, M.Peren and also M.Perenni. Various slaves' names also appear on his vessels sometimes alone or at times with his signature. Some names represent factories. All the available material from these vessels has been tabulated and has been a great aid in establishing dates of other Roman objects, archaeological sites and other data. The ware dates from about 200 B.C. to A.D. 100 in Italy but continues in Gaul to about the middle of the 3d century.

GAULISH TERRA SIGILLATA

The French product is much like the Italian except that the ware is harder, the color darker and brighter and the decoration in lower relief and with smaller figures. In other words it is a technically better product but artistically deteriorated. The names are Gaulish and even Roman names are spelt in Gaulish fashion. The early bowls are cylindrical and then become hemispherical.

GERMAN TERRA SIGILLATA

In the Rhenish pottery which was first grey or black and later red an invention was made called "barbotine" which was simple slip applied by piping much as a caterer decorates a cake with frosting. It was first used to make small flowers on the rims of flat dishes but by the 3d century began to replace the molded design on standard Roman shaped vessels. This is a completely new technique for Europe and was much used not only in Germany but elsewhere such as at Lezoux. Another "invention" caused by the desire for complicated shapes which could not be cast with their designs in molds, was the application of plaques or medallions bearing designs pressed in them. Of course, this was only a revival of a very ancient stunt but now it became very popular and we see portraits of emperors, theatrical scenes, gladiatorial contests, etc. with explanatory inscriptions. It is interesting to see that the North Countries which had not been at all interested in painted wares now became enthusiastic enough in modeled wares to add technical processes. However, when the Roman power withdrew, the people of all Europe sank again to the making of crude primitive pottery unglazed but nevertheless showing strength of design.

MEDIEVAL POTTERIES OF EUROPE

FRANCE

It will be remembered that from 330 Constantinople was gaining power while Rome was losing. In 486 Gaul was lost and by the 7th century the

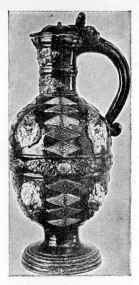

French 16th cent. Avignon ewer much like some found in Germany in general form. Ht. 14¼". Metropolitan Mus. of Art.

Faïence pitcher attr. to 15th cent. of type known as *poteries de Savignies* but probably from *Beauvais* or *Avignon*. Simple and well worked out design of good proportions. Ht. 6⅜". Metropolitan Mus. of Art.

French 16th cent. Normandy vase of faïence labeled *"Pré d'Auge."* A bit top heavy and weak at base. Ht. 10⅜". LeBreton Coll. Metropolitan Mus. of Art.

French 17th cent. pilgrim bottle after metal repoussé one, possibly. Ht. 9½". LeBreton Coll. Metropolitan Mus. of Art.

MEDIEVAL POTTERIES OF FRANCE

PLATE 123

Roman Empire was at a low ebb. In 406 the Barbarians crossed the Rhine and invaded even into Spain while in 718 to 732 the Muhammedan invasion was beyond the Pyrenees. Invasion, famine, plague and pestilence did not make a very fertile soil for the growth of the art of pottery and even under Pippin and Charlemagne in the 9th century there was more interest in conquest than in the arts. The wares were at first crude and unglazed but later were covered with a soft galena or lead sulfide glaze stained brown with iron or green with copper. The old methods of decoration were used combined with scratching, impressing, and application of strips of clay. Slip was used and where the glaze would often be yellowish or brown on the clay proper it was green over a white slip or greyish blue toward the end of the 15th century. Rarely painting was done with white, brown or red clay but more frequently various colors were combined in relief decoration, and some of the vessels were in human or animal forms taken from those of metal aquamaniles (vessels for pouring water on the hands before and after eating with one's fingers or for church ceremony). Many of the forms were typically French Gothic and those from Avignon, Beauvais and Savigny are alike in that they are good craftsmanship.

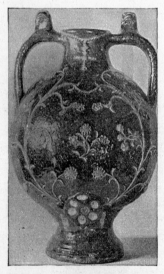

Fig. 575. French cistern with red body and brown slip and glaze of transparent lead type, under which is white appliqué of flowers. (c. 1770). Ht. 17". Plummer, Ltd.

Fig. 576. Ewer with brownish lead glaze and touches of yellow and green, probably from Avignon. Late 16th or early 17th cent. Ht. 11⅛". Metropolitan Mus. of Art.

There were many instances recorded of the bringing in of Italian and Spanish workmen by certain nobles. The Duke of Burgundy brought Jehan de Moustiers and Jehan-le-Voleur in 1391 to paint tiles for his palaces at Arras and Hesdin. At Poitiers, Duke Jean de Berry had John of Valencia, the "Saracen," do tiles in the Spanish manner in 1384. But these seemed to have no effect on the pottery of the country and even later when Francis I

(1494–1547) brought Girolamo della Robbia from Italy to decorate his "Petit Château de Madrid" in 1529 and when Masseot Abaquesne came to manufacture at Rouen about 1542, there seemed to be no effect on other potters.

It was in the 13th century that glaze was revived by the Savignies near Beauvais and in the 14th century La-Chapelle-des-Pots near Saintes became another important center. A little Italian influence was found in the use of the "sgraffito" method of decoration in slip, and either Spanish or Italian influence in the adoption of the alberello form about 1500. In Normandy there was also an industry for the making of gable finials of pottery with polychrome glazes.

GERMAN POTTERY

In Germany conditions were the same but in the 14th century the first stoneware was made. It was a high fired, semi-vitrified ware. Before this the pottery was brown and with ornate Gothic cut, stamped and applied decoration. The best known example of this ware is to be seen in the reddish-brown earthenware cup from Dreihausen, near Marburg in Hesse, which dates about 1400 and is now in the Kunsindustrimuseum, Copenhagen. This is not a cup one would drink from comfortably and we need not go into an aesthetic criticism of it.

Floor-tiles were unglazed in Germany with stamped or molded designs, while those in France and England were often two colored inlayed and glazed wares. Tiles were also used in Germany for stoves and were unglazed at first. Others were designed for architectural use.

ITALY

The obsession for painting which gripped Italian potters due to the wonderful new discovery of tin-enamel and the possibilities of colors of all sorts, blinded them to the possibilities of sculptured form but it is natural that in Italy sculpture should also occur and, if the potters in general were found lacking, it was the sculptors who took up the art.

LUCA DELLA ROBBIA (1399–1482)

There are no real prototypes for the works of the della Robbias. Technique had just come to a point where tin-enamel could be made to cover flaws in material and still be made so thin as not to clog up the details of fine sculpture. Luca was the son of a Florentine named Simone di Marco della Robbia who apprenticed him to Ghiberti. No sculpture of the 15th century surpasses his singing gallery in the cathedral at Florence, now in the Museo del Duomo, but his most important work is the tomb of Benozzo Federighi, bishop of Fiesole, which is now in the church of SS. Trinita in Florence. An effigy of the bishop lies on a sarcophagus sculptured with reliefs of angels holding a wreath which contains the inscription while above are the three-quarter figures of Christ and St. John and the Virgin. The whole is surrounded by a rectangular frame of tiles of exquisite beauty, painted in realistic colors with designs of flowers and fruit. From 1442 to 1446 he worked upon the

"Madonna and Child" by Luca della Robbia showing the superb sensitiveness of facial expression, sure knowledge of anatomy and fine modeling of the hands which mark this great genius. Ht. 31½". Metropolitan Mus. of Art.

"MADONNA AND CHILD" BY LUCA DELLA ROBBIA

PLATE 124

"Ascension and Resurrection" and reliefs of the "Madonna between two Angels" in the Via dell'Agnolo.

It is not necessary to list all of his great works. They are all known and mostly in museums. Many of those attributed to him are by younger members of his family or students, if not by actual forgers. We must, however, state that it is untrue that his earlier works were white or blue and white; actually among the earliest are medallions of the four Evangelists in the vault of the Brunelleschi's Pazzi chapel at St. Croce which are colored in various shades of blue, black, purple, yellow and green. His chief pupils were Andrea, his nephew, and Agostino di Duccio.

FIG. 577. Plaque representing "Prudence" by Luca della Robbia (1399–1482) made in Florence of tin enameled terracotta with some ordinary lead enamel also. Dia. 69". Metropolitan Mus. of Art.

ANDREA DELLA ROBBIA
(1435–1525)

Andrea's works are not less beautiful than Luca's and he extended them to various architectural elements such as friezes, lavabos, fountains and large retables. There is only one sculpture in marble by him and that is an altar in S. Maria delle Grazie near Arezzo.

The characteristics of his work are a great sweetness and grace of pose. Although he did many reliefs of the Madonna and Child, they are all different and all beautiful. Sometimes he omitted the glaze from the bare parts such as the faces, hands and feet of his figures particularly when well modeled in the realistic manner. This was, of course, an old custom of the T'ang and Ming sculptors of China. The treatment is to be seen in his tympanum relief of St. Dominic and St. Francis in the loggia of the Florentine hospital of S. Paolo which is a design suggested but not slavishly following a fresco by Fra Angelico in the cloister of St. Marks. One of Andrea's most remarkable achievements is the series of infants in white on blue ground executed for, and set in front of, the foundling hospital in Florence. Around many of his medallions he used decorative but realistic fruits and flowers in colored enamels while the main relief is left white. Again it is not necessary to give a comprehensive list of his works, most of which are well known, but only to warn against forgeries mysteriously occurring in dealer's hands.

THE SONS OF ANDREA DELLA ROBBIA

Andrea lived to a ripe old age and had seven sons, five of whom worked with the father and carried on the studio. Of the work of Luca II we know

The "Adoration" by Andrea della Robbia (1435–1525) in glazed terracotta showing less stiffness than the work of Luca and a sensitive beauty of both features and hands, of composition and of movement which ranks it high amidst the great art of the world. Ht. 36". 15th cent. Florence. Metropolitan Mus. of Art.

"ADORATION" BY ANDREA DELLA ROBBIA

PLATE 125

chiefly the very beautiful tile pavement in the upper story of Raphael's loggia at the Vatican made under the supervision and at the request of the painter in 1518.

Giovanni's (1469–1529) work is not distinguishable from that of his father in many cases in his early days but soon deteriorated. In the tympanum of the arch of a lavabo in the sacristy of S. Maria Novella at Florence, made in 1497, is a relief of the Madonna between two adoring angels which is of his enameled ware while the basin is of marble. Probably his most important work is the frieze on the outside of the Del Cappo hospital at Pistola. It is polychrome and represents the "Seven Works of Mercy." Six are by Giovanni and the seventh was made by Filippo Paladini of Pistola in 1585. Giovanni's chief pupil was Santi Buglioni (b.1494) who entered the shops in 1521.

Girolamo (1488–1566) was an architect and sculptor in bronze as well as in "della Robbia ware." He went to France and spent some forty years in

FIG. 578. Madonna and Child of the 15th cent. Tuscan school. Ht. 51″. Metropolitan Mus. of Art.

FIG. 579. The "Boy St. John" by Giovanni della Robbia, Florentine 15th–16th cent. of terracotta enameled and painted. Ht. 15″. Metropolitan Mus. of Art.

FIG. 580. This kneeling madonna by Giovanni della Robbia is of terracotta partly glazed, poly-chromed and gilded. 15th cent. Florentine School. Ht. 16⅝″. Metropolitan Mus. of Art.

the service of the royal family. Francis I employed him to work on a palace in the Bois de Boulogne called the Château de Madrid, and which was decorated richly with enameled ware in tiles, friezes, medallions, etc. largely baked at Suresnes.

Examples of della Robbia pottery may be seen in most important museums though the finest examples are, of course, still in the buildings of Italy loved and respected by the people of all classes.

OTHER SCULPTURED WARES OF ITALY

Aside from this truly great dynasty of sculptor-potters which terminated toward the end of the 16th century there was little of note. Maestro Giorgio

Andreoli is supposed to have done a lustred relief of St. Sebastian now in the V. & A. Museum but this is highly questionable and nothing to be proud of. Orazio Fontana, Antonio Patanazzi and others made vases with more or less ornate handles and that is about all.

FIG. 581. Florentine 16th cent. altarpiece "The Assumption of the Virgin" in enameled terracotta of the della Robbia school. Ht. 118½". Metropolitan Mus. of Art.

FIG. 582. This is a fine large terracotta of Hercules and Antaeus done in the style of Giovanni Bologna, 16th cent. Florentine school. Ht. 35½". Metropolitan Mus. of Art.

FRENCH MODELED WARES

St. Porchaire—Orion—or Henry II Ware

The honorable William Burton has stated that Henry II ware is worth more than its weight in gold and, alas, it is, therefore, our duty to describe it. The body is of white clay with a cream colored glaze. The designs are impressed, while the clay is still soft, with metal stamps like those used by book-binders, and different colored slips are rubbed into the impressions. The ware is then turned down smooth. Ochre-yellow, brown, green, violet, black and blue with very rarely red are the colors used more or less in the order of their rarity. Finally, after the assembling of much architectural detail in miniature, such as applied reliefs, statuettes, inlays imitating pavements, scrolls, pillars, etc. all more or less inlayed as described above, the lead glaze is applied and it is fired in the "grand feu" (high fire).

The ware so made was designed to serve the humble uses of cups, ewers, salt cellars, candlesticks, bowls with covers and such. It usually bore the

MING: DOUBLE-GOURD VASE.

Cloisonné outlines of designs. On upper bulb are Shou Lao, God of Longevity, and Hsi Wang Mu, Queen Mother of the West; on lower bulb are the Eight Taoist Immortals.

Ht. 18¾ inches   C. 1500   Eumorfopoulos Collection

St. Porchaire or "Henri II" ware of the earlier and less ornate type so far as modeling goes. (1524–1563 A.D.). Ht. 5″. Metropolitan Mus. of Art.

Salt cellar of the worst possible involved taste such as is seen in late St. Porchaire wares. Made about 1550. Ht. 6⅞″. Metropolitan Mus. of Art.

Tazza without cover of the St. Porchaire ware, with heads applied around the stem irregularly and with the wide border designs around the cup and the base irregularly brought together. Ht. 5″. Metropolitan Mus. of Art.

St. Porchaire, Henry II ware, known also as Orion ware. It was thought incorrectly to have come from there. Ht. 5¾″. Metropolitan Mus. of Art.

ST. PORCHAIRE "HENRY II" WARE, FRANCE, 16TH CENTURY

PLATE 126

devices of Francis I, Henry II or the crescents of Diane de Poitiers. For many years its source was unknown and much mystery enshrouded it. It was said to have been made by pupils of Benvenuto Cellini, God forbid!— or by Pagolo or Ascanio or even by poor, worthy Girolamo della Robbia (Would his father not have turned over in his grave?) or by the printer Geoffroy Tory. Later it was "proven" to have come from Orion, near Thouars, but now we know that it did originate at St. Porchaire in Poitou between c.1525 and c.1560 or 1565. Hannover divides it into three groups:

1.—Earliest—The least ornate, of Italo-French Renaissance style, only in black and brown.

2.—Middle—Ornate decoration and in varied coloring.

3.—Late—Oriental enlacements or arabesques, baroque and grotesque shapes, certain liquid jasper tones and the giving up of the inlay technique for painted slip.

There is nothing to recommend this ware either from an artistic or technical viewpoint yet in 1859 a salt cellar brought 12,500 francs and in 1884 a candlestick fetched 92,000 francs. I have not had the curiosity nor heart to search further but needless to say such prices have also set the forgers on the trail.

Let us pause in passing to note that this same technique and the very similar one of hand incising and inlaying was employed in the Korai period, Korea, with some of the most beautiful and tasteful of results. It is not the technique which makes for beauty but the feeling and intelligence with which it is used.

FIG. 583. French 16th cent. tankard attributed to Bernard Palissy (about 1510 to 1590) of simple form and better proportions than most things he did. Ht. 6¾". Metropolitan Mus. of Art.

BERNARD PALISSY (1510–1590)

Before we can come to the German beer drinkers and their wares we must pause to contemplate Bernard Palissy whom France includes among her "plus pures et plus belles gloires," though in Germany he is known as "eine gefallene Grösse." One may take his choice.

Our records from Palissy's own autobiography tell us that he was born about 1510 (though he does not remember the date himself), either in Saintes or in Agen in southwest France. He says he was a dreamer yet paid little attention to religion not guessing what an important part it was to play in his life. He seems to have gained that typical Renaissance spirit of inquiry into natural science which we see reflected in the notebook of Leonardo da Vinci who died about the time the boy was eight or nine years old in Cloux, France, not so very far from his birthplace. Bernard became a glass painter and land-surveyor. He tells us that a "geometrician" became interested in his precocious intelligence and took him away for further training. Of course the naturalist is no more than a grown-up boy with an investigating mind and Bernard seemed to carry his interest in snakes, frogs, fish and the like beyond that of most boys.

He roamed through France working at his trade of glass painting for the windows of cathedrals, learned to blow glass, became something of a chemist and also a landscape-gardener and in about 1539 settled in the old town of Saintes and commenced to raise a family. This town had seen much history and interested him mightily. Also the cathedral of St. Peter was being erected so there was work to keep him busy. In 1544 the government gave him the task of investigating the salt swamps and he worked out a system of water supply for the town as well. He had become an honored citizen, a church goer and was respected by all.

These were troubled times, for the Reformation was under way and the thunder of the cannon of Boulogne-sur-mer which the English attacked a bit to the north, the tramping of troops and threats to peace might well have worried Bernard but they did not. It took a little white cup to wreck his life and make him famous! The Fates placed before him in the collection of a friend a small white porcelain undecorated cup without a handle, from China, and the dreadful whimsy was accomplished for in his own words, "like a man who gropes in the dark," *he set himself to make one like it*. Little did he know that the little cup was the result of generation on generation of clever work by thousands of careful Chinese. It looked so simple! "From that moment," he says, "without regard to the fact that I had not the least acquaintance with potter's clay, I gave myself up to searching after enamels."

He learned about the peasant ware about him and rushed home from work to plunge into experiments. He built himself a kiln, tore it down and built another. He hired men to bring him wood for firing and more and ever more wood. He spent money for expensive chemicals sent from afar. He lost his job for it was obvious that his mind was not on it. Poverty like a blank wall seemed to shut him from his simple conquest. He borrowed all he could and poured the proceeds into his furnace which now consumed the very food of his starving children. He was destitute and begged, yet some enamels would run while others would not melt at all, some changed color for no known reason and others chipped off. Never, never could he get it just right. Long since he had forgotten the subtle poison he had imbibed from the little cup which seemed to dance in a haze before his mad and staring eyes. He burnt the furniture in his house and ripped up the boards from the floor and finally developed—what? A porcelain like that of China? No. A soft porcelain? No. A stoneware? No. A ware which, we must admit before the chuckling fates, was less good than the simple contemporary ordinary wares of Spain and Italy; just a crude peasant pottery of another sort. But the mad man had something. That everyone had to admit.

We would like to be able to tell that he took this humble material and wrought great works of art that remained for ever after monuments to his tenacity and unconquerable spirit. We would like to show the moral of self-sacrifice and the sure reward of that inner fire which burns from the soul. But alas! Bernard was no more an artist than a potter. At least we can grant him that he did not go to copying the St. Porchaire ware, the works of Hirsvogel or of the Italian majolica makers. He had the first element of art; independence of spirit and he did turn to nature. But his mind was not imaginative, it was that of a scientist and an exact one. He saw reptiles and fishes as objects and took little notice of the *space* with which nature divides things and the conflict often brought about by their proximity. Thus upon a single platter he would make a stream about the bottom with the rim for shores and an island in the center and would fill the water with many fishes which might devour each other and the shores with lizards, snakes, insects, shells, foliage, etc. all in high relief. The wheel was unknown to him. His glazes were marbled and clouded in brown, blue and purple on the back. On the front things were carried out in their natural colors. French students have made careful zoological and botanical lists of his subjects which are all quite recognizable and we find for instance:—various snakes:—adder, necklace, etc. —fish such as mullet, eels, tench, roach, gudgeon, ray, etc.—lobsters, crabs, snails, crayfish, cockles, welks, water snails, limpets, turritellas, scallops, murex, etc.—among the plants are ferns, the strawberry, oak leaves, acorns, ivy, bramble, olive, mulberry, etc. —Palissy called these wares

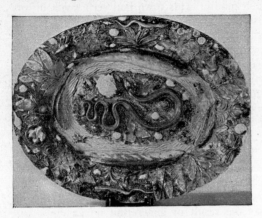

Fig. 584. Ornamental plaque-platter by Bernard Palissy. The back is covered with glazes of blue, chocolate, white and green. Length 21". c. 1560. Plummer, Ltd.

"figurines rustiques," and people admired them and put them on their sideboards, for no one could possibly eat off them.

Then came the Constable of France, Anne de Montmorency in 1548 from Saintonge, where he had been sent to suppress a revolution, and he gave Palissy a fine job, the making of a grotto in the park of the Château d'Ecouen. He built a shop for him and assigned the location of the grotto to an artificial crag to which water was brought from springs for a fountain. No part of this or his other grottos now remain, but the work brought him fame at the French Court and he was appointed *"Inventor of Rustic Pottery to the King and Queen-mother."* Meanwhile he had joined the Huguenots and was thrown into prison when the town of Saintes was taken by the Catholics, and later escaped to Paris under the patronage of Catherine de' Medici and her sons.

Catherine was just having the Tuileries built for her by Philbert de l'Orme and as a grotto was desired Palissy was set up in the garden of the Tuileries. Here he began to cast silver embossed dishes for his pottery forms and made strapwork and pierced borders, etc. He lived in Paris some 25 years in peace but in the palace Catherine was afraid of the influence of Admiral Coligny on Charles IX and the possibility of war with Spain. It was a good time for such an endeavor but Catherine thought it best to have the good admiral assassinated. This, however, failed and she bethought herself of another plan which was rather like burning down a house to kill a mouse; the simple idea of massacring all the Huguenots including the offending admiral who was of this faith. On St. Bartholomew's Day, August 24th, 1572 occurred one of the most bloody and terrible massacres known to history and it spread throughout Paris and thence throughout France. Poor Palissy was captured and thrown into the Bastille when he was nearly 80 and there he died in 1589 or 1590. Catherine licked her lips and went about the gentle pastime of encouraging her sons to partake of all manner of dissipation and licentiousness to keep their mental capacities such that they would not hamper her strange ambitions.

A few of Palissy's wares were copied probably by G. Dupré about 1600. There have also been casts from his worn-out molds, some imitations and forgeries as is understandable when we hear that a piece brought £1365 in 1911 in an English sale.

FIG. 586. 16th cent. dish. Style of Palissy but deeper in relief and more ornate. Dia. 10″. Metropolitan Mus. of Art.

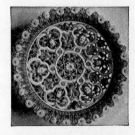

FIG. 585. Dish having figures symbolizing Temperance, the four elements the various arts, sciences, etc., which was cast by Palissy from the well known pewter dish by François Briot. French about 1570. Dia. 15¼″. Metropolitan Mus. of Art.

FIG. 587. Dish by Palissy probably modeled after or actually cast from a silver one after he went to Paris to work for Catherine de Medici about 1550. It lacks ceramic feeling but does show meticulous craftsmanship. Dia. about 10″. Metropolitan Mus. of Art.

I do not believe his things were taken very seriously even in his time but his success was due to a colossal belief in himself and his omnipotent intelligence along with his earnestness. People believed him because he was very sure.

The real Palissy ware is of white body with reddish-yellow tint. It effervesces when touched with acids. Black was not successful and red gave him difficulties. He never did obtain a real white body. His glaze is finely crackled and bright and glossy.

GERMAN MODELED WARES

Hafner Ware

Hafner ware consists of stove tiles or heavy jugs made about the middle of the 16th century. The earliest are green and less often yellow or brown. About 1500 combined colors began to be used and not until 1533 were copies made of tiles in the Swiss technique and actually painted such as the first with a picture of David and Bathsheba on it. In the castle of Hohensalzburg is a Gothic stove dated 1501 which has much plastic or pressed mold decoration. Most examples have none of the hand technique of modeling. At first the tiles are small but later they made up a whole side including cornice, plinth and pilasters. By this time the various colors were employed and to the green, yellow, purple and blue of lead glaze colors a white tin-enamel was added. Tin was also added in various proportions to the blue color. Faults in firing and glaze are often seen.

Nuremburg seemed to be a center but the industry spread over Germany and Austria and such places as Cologne, Danzig, Lübeck, Rostock, Stralsund and Villingen in the Black Forest. About 1550 there was a revival of the plain green stoves which showed up the modeling better. Some were supplemented with a brownish black and black graphite. By the 17th century they were made of tiles in low relief which showed the transition to the tin-enameled tiles of the 18th century but even then the South Germans retained their relief decoration. Gilding was applied and the subject matter was usually religious, showing the fervor of the times.

Hafner Ware Vessels

Hafner ware was first known as "Hirsvogel" because Augustin Hirzvogel was supposed to have originated it but this was found to be untrue. It dates after 1550, most of it, and aside from stove tiles, consists of mugs of torso-shape, melon or ovoid shape with flaring feet and either small or wide mouths heavily rimmed. Frequently a twisted handle springs from the shoulder to the neck. The decoration is accomplished by means of small ridges or cloissons applied to the surface and outlining the design. These were squeezed from a cone and to these are added small leaves, flowers and figures made in pressed molds. The colored glazes are of lead type and comprise blue, green, brown, manganese and yellow plus white tin-enamel and are kept separate by

FIG. 588. Three Hafnerkrug pieces from the workshop of Paulus Preuning, Nüremberg, the first two in Vienna and the third in Munchen. About 1550. From *Alte Deutsche Kunsttöpfereien.*

FIG. 589. Green glazed earthenware tile with coat of arms and date 1580, made in Germany. Metropolitan Mus. of Art.

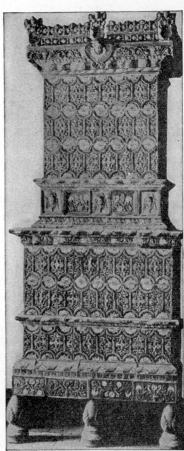

German green tile stove. 16th cent., exact kiln unknown. The reliefs are supposed to represent the "four parts of the world," and because America is prominent, it is known as "The America Stove." International Studio Art Corp.

Nuremberg Stove of the 16th cent. Composed of two parts with a partly open-work gallery at the top. It is in many colors. International Studio Art Corp.

GERMAN TILE STOVES 16TH CENTURY

PLATE 127

the ridges which frequently stand out in white. Some are divided into horizontal bands with scroll and two color treatment. Others have arches in which are figures representing Charles I, Ferdinand I, Anne his wife, Elector John Frederick of Saxony, the Reformers, etc. as well as biblical and mythological subjects like those on the stoves. It is interesting to note that identification of the ware as having been made by Paul and Kunz Preuning was brought about by documents of their arrest and conviction in Nuremberg in 1541 for having made a jug with a Crucifixion and at the same time musicians and peasant dancers on it.

FIG. 590. Hafner-krug, Sachsen, of 1570 made by Master Merten Koller in Anna-berg. Now in the Kunstgewerbe Mus., Dresden.

FIG. 591. Hafner-krug of 1569 by Master Merten Koller of Annaberg, now in Dresden. From *Alte Deutsche Kunsttöp-fereien.*

SILESIA HAFNER WARE

"Silesia Hafner Ware" comprises a group of dishes in which the designs are scratched with a sharp instrument and which have glazes containing tin. One in Berlin has the arms of Balthasar von Promnitz, bishop of Breslau and is probably the earliest known. The technique is perhaps more closely associated with painting than modeled wares but we have included them in this section because they are incised and are close to the above ware.

Both these wares are rather crude and sometimes over crowded but they are honest and we see in them something not very far distant from the famous "Three Color Ming" wares of China. The colors are rich and attractive, and they are in good keeping with the rich velvets and brocades of the times or equally appropriate for sturdy oak or walnut tables.

Here we see a meeting of two different spirits of the German people who love their good food and drink but are also religious and even hard. Perhaps it is the old nomadic self-discipline, in fighting in the field and then relaxing with roisterous drinking and stuffing of food. The German may be lean and hungry like a wolf or fat like a pig. They are not two different men but one and the same; the animal before and after the hunt, and the world would do well to keep it in mind. So these wares express the duality of the German personality perfectly.

"STEINZEUG" OR GERMAN STONEWARE

Typical of the German people is the stoneware reminding us of the rich burgher who loves good beer in generous measure and cool as spring water. The early jugs are large round-bellied affairs with cylindrical necks and rimmed mouths. The "bartmann" or "greybeard" jugs have an old man's head modeled on the neck with beard spread out on the shoulder much as the owners probably spread their beards over their own paunches. Other decorations on them tell us what seemed sacred and what comical. As Hannover says, "what men thought of Christ, of the Pope, the Emperor, the lansquenet, the peasant, women, the chase, trade, county fairs and much else between heaven and earth, whilst coats of arms and merchants' marks are a proof that these jugs and tankards were not show pieces, but household gear to which men felt themselves thoroughly and closely attached."

FIG. 592. A "Bartmannkrug" of brown and some blue earthenware dated 1603 and made in Germany for the Coronation of James I of England.

FIG. 593. Cologne-Frechen late 16th cent. *Bartmann* with one floral medallion on front. The glaze is mottled brown. Ht. 8⅛". Metropolitan Mus. of Art.

FIG. 594. Frechen jug with the *bartmann* less important and a coat of arms added. Dark brown glazed earthenware of the late 16th or early 17th cent. Ht. 7¼". Metropolitan Mus. of Art.

The stoneware itself is something in a way like the first porcelain of the Han Dynasty in China, being composed of ordinary clay which is, however, fired at so high a temperature that it became "fritted" or fused into a hard substance proof against scratching with a steel knife and impervious to liquids. The special clay containing flint could not be found everywhere and so manufacture was confined to districts about the Rhine from Cologne to Coblenz and in Flanders at Raeren. The chief places were in Höhr, Grenzhausen, Siegburg, Cologne, Frechen and Raeren. It was also later tried in France and the Netherlands but it was not of sufficient merit to interest us.

The method of making is this: The clay was beaten in water and washed thoroughly. The flint is burnt or calcined, ground fine and suspended in water and then mixed with the clay, after which the whole is dried in a kiln until doughlike when it is well kneaded, beaten, and tempered to be ready for molding. The glaze is usually produced by common salt which is thrown into the kiln at a certain time in the firing when the highest temperature

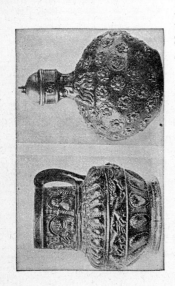

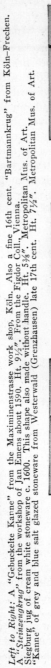

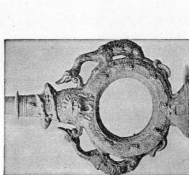

Left to Right: A "Gebuckelte Kanne" from the Maximinenstrasse work shop, Köln. Also a fine 16th cent. "Bartmannkrug" from Köln-Frechen. A "Steinzeugkrug" from the workshop of Jan Emens about 1590. Ht. 9½". From the Figdor Coll., Vienna. This shape also made without handle. Ht. 5⅜". Metropolitan Mus. of Art. Siegburg jug of cream white stoneware c. 1600. "Kanne" of grey and blue salt glazed stoneware from Westerwald (Grenzhausen) late 17th cent. Ht. 7½". Metropolitan Mus. of Art.

Left to Right: Jug from Raeren after Emens', dated 1598. Brown glaze, and with the arches which came into use in 1580. Ht. 10½". From W. R. Hearst Coll.
A "Ringkrug" from the "Töpferfamilie Knütgen" during the middle of the 16th cent. From *Kunst und Kunsthandwerk.*
Siegberg tankard with the usual white clay and transparent glaze and having low relief molded decoration rather unevenly applied. c. 1560. Ht. 9⅜". Metropolitan Mus. of Art.
Ewer from Raeren of the early brown ware dating during the 16th cent. The body is white. Ht. 12⅞". Metropolitan Mus. of Art.

GERMAN STONEWARE 16TH AND 17TH CENTURIES

PLATE 128

had been reached and no more smoke was given off. The heat volatilizes the salt so that the chlorin escapes, leaving the soda behind to combine with the silicic acid in the clay which forms a thin covering of soda glass on all exposed surfaces which is of great hardness and resists ordinary acids. The kiln used was the horizontal reverberatory type.

As the firing was done all at once and at high temperature few colors would not be destroyed. The Siegberg clay was white and a colorless glaze was used. Most of the other clays contained iron enough to turn them reddish which when covered with the salt glaze makes brown. A blue was obtained with cobalt and purple with manganese.

The Westerwald stoneware became grey in body and had floral patterns in the above colors. It was wheel-turned and yet shows traces of the in-heritance from metal. However, we can also see quite clearly that leather jugs were also prototypes as in the triangular ones and some of the pilgrim bottles. This recalls that the wares from Susa were influenced by leather prototypes and also that one of the Chinese jars found in the Philippines appears at first glance to have been actually made of leather.

When the pieces were thrown on the wheel a "stege" or templet of metal was used to true them and though this lost some of the feeling of the hand of the potter, these German wares were so worked over with design that a certain human touch was regained. The handles were freely hand fashioned and were often so pressed to the body while still damp that slight distortion of the body took place. The molded plaquettes were so applied with incising that they appeared more a part of the body than is usual with the employ-ment of this process.

Most of the designs were taken from contemporary engravings such as in Cologne, Heinrich Aldegraver, in Siegburg, Beham Solis, Virgil Solis, Jost Amman and Theodore de Bry, while in Raeren they were after Cornelis Bos, Balthrazar Sylvius, Adriaen Collaert, Abraham de Bruyn and Konrad Golt-zius. Also at Raeren many Siegburg designs were copied.

A little after 1632 when the Swedes sacked Siegburg the potters from there and from Raeren moved to the Westerwald district near Coblentz, where at Grenzhausen and in Höhr the industry continued until the 18th century.

DESCRIPTIONS OF VARIOUS STONEWARES

Cologne was the site of the earliest stoneware. Shapes of a brownish-red pottery made at the start of the 15th century were similar and some time between 1520 and 1540 stoneware was in real production. Other early sites were Siegburg and Frechen nearby. Sherds found in the Maximinenstrasse and Komoedienstrasse, Cologne or "Köln" have been arranged by Otto von Falke as follows:

KÖLN (COLOGNE)

MAXIMINENSTRASSE

1.—Globular jugs with wide cylindrical necks and decorated with oak branches and rose stems combined with figures at times and also with the "Tree of Jesse" showing the genealogy of Christ, in relief.

2.—"Greybeard" jugs called "Bartmänner" invented here and soon copied at Frechen, Siegburg and Raeren.

3.—The use of oviform bosses in single or double rows and small round medallions with busts in antique style.

4.—Figure ware with subjects from history, religion and mythology on the tall "Pinten" and "Schnellen" or tall truncated conical mugs usually decorated with three matrices each having a complete design in itself.

These are all between 1520 and 1540.

FIG. 595. Frechen "Bartmannkrug" dated 1593 and inscribed, "Who knows if it is so true?" Ht. 14¾". The cover and handle, of course, are of pewter. From the W. R. Hearst Coll.

FIG. 596. Three pieces of Cologne-Frechen ware from the shop of Eigelstein of about 1560–1570. All have brown speckled glaze. The triangular one suggests a leather prototype. From the Oppenheim Coll.

FIG. 597. Rare Köln-Frechen brown glazed "Kanne" with vine and bird pattern and dating about 1540. From *Alte Deutsche Kunsttöpfereien.*

KOMOEDIENSTRASSE

The factory here seems to have been in the latter part of the century and not so active.

1.—"Bartmann" jugs globular but with nearly rectangular greybeard on the neck, a narrow frieze about the body and acanthus leaves pointing up and down from it.

2.—Other wares not distinguishable.

FRECHEN

At Frechen we find:

1.—"Bartmann" jugs exactly like those described above but with the ornamental frieze replaced by a saying such as "Drink und est, got nit vergest" (drink and eat, forget not God).

2.—Another type more ovoid and covered with prunts arranged like bunches of grapes.

3.—From a little earlier than 1600 stylized, grimacing "Bartmann" on a narrower neck and with three large medallions of round or oval shape with shields of arms such as those of Cologne, Amsterdam or England or rosettes and roughly molded heads.

EIGELSTEIN

At Eigelstein they made:

1.—"Schnellen" with only slightly rounded panels having a medallion in the center of each with a head or allegorical half figure, joined edge to edge to form triangular vessels.

2.—Similar types with a spout.

3.—Others with female allegorical subjects on almost cylindrical bodies and designed after Peter Flötner, or with lovers near a fountain.

These are difficult to distinguish particularly as the factory was moved to Frechen at the end of the 16th century.

The common characteristics of these wares are: 1.—a body of grey, 2.—a few are grey or yellow toned but these were probably kiln failures, 3.—usually a chestnut brown or somewhat lighter, 4.—an elliptical string mark on the bottom where they were cut off the wheel not unlike those of Japanese potteries.

The shapes can be seen in the illustrations but it should be noted that the Cologne mugs generally contract more than the Siegburg ones which are more slender and graceful. Hannover says, "On the banks of the Rhine makers of jugs were called 'Euler, Eulner or Ulner' and they are assumed, on the strength of this appellation, to have made owls as a kind of emblem of their handicraft." Perhaps this is a surface reason for their making them but the owl is a very pot-like bird and too an ancient emblem of night.

SIEGBURG

At Siegburg the potters found pure white clay and it retained its whiteness even after firing. The glaze was made colorless though at times blue was used and rarely a yellowish-brown or reddish color to touch up parts of the design. Some of the oldest shapes are even without salt glaze and have

Fig. 599. *"Kanne," "Schnelle"* and *"Schnabelkrüge"* or *"Schnabelkanne"* of salt glazed stoneware from Siegberg. Hts. 9″, 15¼″ and 9½″. Metropolitan Mus. of Art.

Fig. 598. Siegburg pieces: 1.—*"Flasche"* of gourd shape from the workshop of Anno Knütgen. Late 16th cent. 2.—*"Trichterbecher"* of same period. 3.—*"Eulenkrug"* (owl jug) of the same period. 4.—*"Henkelkanne"* of about 1600. 5.—*"Ringelkrug,"* 15th cent. 6.—*"Kanne"* with Renaissance oramentation, c. 1570.

globular bodies, funnel neck and a wavy spreading foot shaped by pressing down with the fingers. 1.—The earliest were decorated with a holly-leaf incised in rude manner. Later ones had applied medallions in relief. Some were made with double walls, the outer one pierced with Gothic architectural tracery. The color of these was grey dappled with yellowish and brownish patches probably from contact with the flames of the kiln.

Other Siegburg wares were:

2.—Tall slender "Schnelle" with three panels. By the 16th century the potters had lost so much of the spirit of design that they often repeated one panel twice on the same pot.

3.—"Schnabelkrüge" (beak-pots) with globular bodies and long spouts rising from the side nearly to the height of the tall cylindrical neck and attached with a tubular link or "Dille." These usually date between 1560 and 1610 but are known as early as 1528 and as late as 1631.

4.—Pilgrim bottles are rare products of Anno Knütgen and his assistant the signer of F.T. about 1559 to 1568.

5.—"Leuchtervasen" (large jars with handles formed as sockets for candles).

6.—Goblets.

7.—"Birnkruge" (pear jugs).

8.—"Pullen" (footless globular bottles with short narrow necks).

All those from #4 on were supposed to have been made by artists in good old Gothic style.

A few of the artists' names are known; those of the Knütgen family, the Simons, Flach and Omian. Christian Knütgen was the chief representative of the Late Renaissance style at Siegburg. His oldest work is dated 1568, but it was 20 years later that he made his spouted jugs with a lion mask under the spout. Hans Hilgers pieces are found frequently but are not of top quality. They date between 1569 and 1595. Various other initials appear but cannot be traced such as LW, FT, etc.

In 1830 Peter Löwenich opened a kiln in Siegburg and made wares good enough to fool the museums and private collectors even in the Rhine valley. His clay is more bluish or yellowish grey than white and the style is lacking. At Höhr other 19th century copies were made but the rims are flat instead of rounded and they are more shiny. The old ware may shade off to a slightly brownish tone but it is quite different.

RAEREN

Raeren made a brown ware which later turned to grey in imitation of the Westerwald wares. On the grey, blue was occasionally used. A three handled jar is supposed to be original here. Out of a lot of copyists there rose unaccountably Jan Emens who signed between 1568 and 1594 with IE, IEM, IAN, YAN and EMENS. His first work was the copy of a large Schnelle of the shop of Anno Knütgen but made larger. It shows Judith, Esther and Lucretia. There is a fairly architectural quality in his work but I far from agree with the enthusiasts who say his proportions are perfect and that his works compare favorably with the best Greek vases, poor as many of them are. He often used a lion head with jaws curving together as though they

FIG. 600. Siegburg jug of the 17th cent. white stoneware. Ht. 9½". Metropolitan Mus. of Art.

FIG. 601. Siegburg "Bierbrug" dated 157? from the Museums für Kunst und Industri, Vienna.

FIG. 602. Two Raeren "Kanne" grey with blue glazes, the first dated 1605 and the other also of the first parts of the 17th cent. Hts. 20". From the W. R. Hearst Coll.

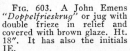

FIG. 604. A brown glazed krug with the coats of arms of Munzenburg and Amsterdam. Ht. 12¼". From the W. R. Hearst Coll. Dated 1599. Raeren.

FIG. 603. A John Emens "Doppelfrieskrug" or jug with double frieze in relief and covered with brown glaze. Ht. 18". It has also the initials IE.

had held a ring but there is no evidence of rings having been made. He made a broad band about the body of his pieces and filled it with any material that came to his hand from engravings, etc. Thus we have the "Peasant dance jugs," "Susanna jugs," "Paris jugs," etc. In 1580 he began the "Blauwerk" having light grey body with blue decoration but did not entirely give up the brown ware. At the same time came a changing of the frieze into arches and a more detailed treatment of both the architectural elements and the figures. It seems again that the artist starting out with inspirational fire has found it necessary to replace original thought with labored detail *hoping* to win applause by showing how much trouble he has gone to rather than *commanding* applause by some new vitality. I always feel that the artist who shows the sweat of detail dripping from his brow is like an untrained athlete and that he gets just about the same raspberry from the crowd. This may be heartless but after all does he not owe it to himself and to his audience to keep on his toes? Jan Emens had something, but his "Blauwerk" proves that he did not know he had.

Engel Kran was a pupil and imitator and his proportions were less good. He often tried hard to get more figures in his friezes than the master could.

Baldem Mennicken who signed work between about 1575 and 1584 was a better copyist and therefore more dangerous competitor. His work may be called softer. Merten Mennicken, his son, copied the copyists. One wonders why these men did not either learn more about their art of modeling or give it up. Possibly they looked at their wares with eyes half closed as some painters do at their pictures or just put on texture as an upholsterer might tack tapestry on a chair. The Mennicken family went to Grenzhausen and the wares there were then indistinguishable from those of Raeren. It is true that Anno Knütgen, quickly followed by the Mennickens, made "Ring-krug" or "ring-jug" designs and later "double ring jugs." We know of no triple ones but they will probably be tried someday, and will probably be thought three times better than single ones. By 1630 the Westerwald had taken the lead and Raeren declined. In 1880 a Hubert Schiffer made pretty good imitations but having been cast in plaster molds, they can readily be distinguished. He signed his wares HS but dealers found they could grind this off and sell, to those who were not informed, these 19th century imitations for old ones.

WESTERWALD

Westerwald or "Nassau" stoneware was made for about twenty miles around Grenzhausen including the towns of Grenzau and Höhr where there

FIG. 605. Westerwald jar with screw top. Salt glazed stoneware in grey and blue and comes from either Hohr or Grenzhausen. 18th cent. Ht. 10". Metropolitan Mus. of Art.

FIG. 606. Early 17th cent. gray and blue jar probably from Westerwald. Ht. 6¾". Metropolitan Mus. of Art.

FIG. 607. Westerwald possibly Grenzhausen "Kanne" of grey and blue salt glazed stoneware. 17th cent. Ht. about 10". Metropolitan Mus. of Art.

was a guild of their own and where about 1590 refugee potters from Siegburg and Raeren settled. We cannot distinguish between the ware of nearby towns for the clay was all the same and the families of potters spread out. "Blauwerk" is typical of the section and can be told from that of Siegburg only by the signatures. Manganese was occasionally used and also brown glazes like those of Cologne. Plastic decoration soon gave way to stamped or incised design. During the 16th and early 17th centuries there was some life and interest but soon the short fat mugs of "Pinte" type and colossal jugs were devised with baroque style and more and more lifeless designs. These latter are attributed to Johann Kalb.

With the baroque, however, the unholy touch of architecture was removed and portraits were made of such people as the rulers of England, France and the Netherlands. William III of Orange, Queen Mary and Louis XIV

FIG. 608. Westerwald, German figure (one of pair) in salt glazed stoneware of grayish white. 18th cent. Ht. 7½". Metropolitan Mus. of Art.

FIG. 609. Grenzhausen, Westerwald, "Kanne" or tankard of gray and blue salt glazed stoneware. 17th cent. Ht. 6½". Metropolitan Mus. of Art.

FIG. 610. Westerwald 18th cent., German sand container of gray salt-glazed stoneware. Ht. 6¼". Metropclitan Mus. of Art.

were favorites. Arms, heraldry and figures disappeared and designs of lozenges, rosettes, palmettes, bosses, bunches of grapes, lions' masks, cherubs' heads and stars took their places. Many of these wares now took the simple shapes of the pewter jugs of the period and the designs of pomegranates and flowers were made from Indian palampores which carry right through to the Pennsylvania German potters of the New World. Rococo was the style of the day but for some reason was not noticed by these potters. Hannover aptly says, "A bourgeois craft became a rustic craft; stoneware became a peasant art." How strange this is! Here just as we were giving up in despair, for some unknown reason a backwash occurs in a place to which the potters and their children fled and their art is fed again with the rich strong blood of peasant art, stripped of all pose and ostentation, throwing off all architectural props and becoming alive again. Thus the saltcellar which looks almost Romanesque is to quote von Falke, "countrified baroque." Oh, there were queer twists to the thing and we find hand warmers in the shape of prayer books so that one could gather admiration and credit for being pious while merely warming the hands. There were vessels in the forms of barrels, cannon, etc., but even in these there is an honest humor and lack of pretense.

Stonewares were made elsewhere also, particularly as copies of the Rhine types, such as at Bouffioulx, Châtelet, Namur, Bouvignies, Verviers and Dinant. In Bavaria at Kreussen and in Saxony wares which were made were their own. The Kreussen ware seems to have sprung from Hafner ware. It is of greyish-white which fires red because of its iron content and was coated with a brown glaze which was at first clear but becomes toward the end of the 17th century and into the 18th century more and more opaque. It falls into two groups as follows:

1.—The designs are looted on and are covered with brown as well as the backgrounds of the pots.

2.—The designs are painted with various enamel colors such as blue, red yellow, white and green often with gold added.

These two styles overlap but the painted ones start in general about fifty years after the plain ones had started, although the oldest known is dated 1614 (in the Germanischesmuseum, Nuremberg) and the oldest painted one is dated 1618. The Kreussen mugs are low and broad and always have pewter covers. Polygonal bottles have pewter screw tops. Jugs are decorated with a horseman, a stag or a shield of arms.

In Saxony jugs of the above sort are distinguished by parti-colored palmettes scattered over the body and lozenge or cross hatched line texture back of the relief figures. "Trauerkruge," mistakenly believed to have been used for the funeral repast, are decorated with horizontal rows of circles or segments of circles (usually three rows) in black and white or red. It is probable that these and the Kreussen wares were decorated by glass painters.

There was a period here in America when stoneware decorated all the grand dining rooms in oak and with stained glass windows. A Siegburg "Mars tankard" brought £201 in Copenhagen in the Frohne sale in 1910, an owl jug in the Oppenheim sale at about the same time brought 9,100 marks, another by Jan Emens with the Flight of the Centaurs brought 23,500 marks. However, now it is difficult even to find examples for illustration here. The Randolph Hearst collection is the last in which there were a great number and these have been more or less dispersed at low prices comparatively speaking.

And so we have traced the course of the lustre wares and their end, the ever growing course of the enamel wares and the developments of stoneware with its tendency to become less and less interesting and more and more decorated with various colors. In the 18th century we see the end of hand-made potteries and the loss of human appeals.

FIG. 611. Kreussen tankard with brown glaze, 17th cent. Ht. 5½″. Metropolitan Mus. of Art.
FIG. 612. Kreussen jar, 17th cent. Ht. 9″. Metropolitan Mus. of Art.
FIG. 613. Tankard of grey, blue, and violet salt glaze stoneware from Grenzhausen c. 1640–1700. Ht. about 10″. Metroplitan Mus. of Art.

FIG. 614. Kreussen krug dated 1665 showing saints. Ht. 6½″. From the W. R. Hearst Coll.
FIG. 615. Stoneware jar with screw top for cover. Salt glaze of dark brown painted with enamel colors. Ht. 6½″. Metropolitan Mus. of Art.
FIG. 616. Kreussen 17th cent. brown glazed tankard with polychrome enamel decoration. Ht. 5⅜″. Metropolitan Mus. of Art.

FIG. 617. Hexagonal screw top flask from Kreussen with enamel painting of biblical figures. Early 17th cent. Ht. 13″. From the W. R. Hearst Coll.
FIG. 618. Kreussen "Elector tankard" showing the Elector and his wife. The glaze is brown, 17th cent. Ht. 10″. From the W. R. Hearst Coll.
FIG. 619. Salt glazed jug, German 17th cent. possibly Ober-Hessen 18th cent. Ht. 8¼″. Metropolitan Mus. of Art.

CHAPTER XVIII

YÜAN PERIOD IN CHINA

(1280–1368)

THE last of the Sung emperors cast himself into the sea and China was conquered by the Mongols in 1280. The three grandsons of Jenghiz Khan were Mangu, the elder, Hulagu who was sent to take charge of Persia and Kublai who took charge of China. Mangu had died in 1260. The conquest had caused famine in the Western Asian areas but Kublai was an enlightened ruler and China prospered under the 35 years of his reign. He was the acknowledged sovereign of a greater territory and population than any ruler has ever known 'in this world. It is said that "The Chinese seals which Kublai conferred on his kinsmen reigning at Tabriz are stamped upon their letters to the kings of France, and survive in the archives of Paris," and further that "Adventurers from Turkestan, Persia, Armenia, Byzantium, even from Venice, served him as ministers, generals, governors, envoys, astronomers or physicians; soldiers from all Asia to the Caucasus fought his battles in the south of China." He encouraged culture, was tolerant as concerns religion, even trying to get European priests to aid in the education of his people and failing that obtained Tibetan Buddhistic priests, appointing a young lama, Mati Dhwaja, the head of the church and prince of Tibet, and above all he was a great builder. The accounts of Marco Polo tell us of the glories of his capital of Khanbaliq or Cambaluc situated about where Peking is now.

Kublai died in 1294 and the following Mongol rulers were of no special account. However, during this time some things took place which are of considerable interest to us. Trade routes with the Near East were made safe. Muslims in great numbers came to China and the Arabs conquered the western tip of Sumatra. The Franciscan Friar John of Montecorvino arrived the year of Kublai's death and within 30 years built a community of several thousand. Friar Odoric and the papal legate John of Marignolli helped. The merchants were not far behind the holy brethren.

As may be guessed the taste of the Mongol conquerors was not of the most sensitive. It was not unlike a bunch of cowboys, lumbermen or oil-drillers dictating the artistic works of today. Virility was not lacking but the ornate became desirable instead of the beautiful Sung economy. Drama was originated but the art of painting was chiefly carried on by copyists or by those who wished to make flamboyant show.

YÜAN CERAMICS

As rewards, the lieutenants of the Mongol army were apportioned territories and those whose land included pottery towns lost no time in taxing them to the limit so that they withered and died.

The old Sung kiln sites along the Yellow River had, as we have seen, in many cases been left by the workmen when the first part of the invasion took place. Probably most of them continued but under not very happy circumstances. It is certain that Ting, Tz'u Chou, Chün, Northern celadon, "Ying ching" and the various Tsung se or dark brown ware continued, many of them being probably hardly distinguishable from the Sung wares. A warning should certainly be sounded that every piece showing bad taste is not Yüan and every piece showing simple beauty is not necessarily Sung. It should also be pointed out that the Yüan period has become a sort of dumping ground into which all things neither distinctly Ming nor distinctly Sung have been shoved by those who were afraid to say simply that they did not know at what time certain things were made.

The drive south had acted as a temporary benefit to the southern kilns and of them all Ching-tê Chên grew the most. This place was located just east of the large Po Yang Lake in northern Kiangsi province not far south of the Yangtze River. It became the largest and most important pottery center in the whole world even up to the present time, due to having the necessary materials close at hand, being situated on the Ch'ang River which made export easy, and finally to having gained its strength at just the right time. The wares made there were known under different names such as: Chên yao, Ching-tê yao, Fou-liang yao, Jao Chou yao, Jao yao, Ch'ang-nan yao and Nan-ch'ang yao. The town is and probably has always been a market town or "chên" from which the name derives. Its first name was Ch'ang-nan Chên but this was changed by the Sung Emperor Chên Tsung who ordered the "nien hao" or name of the period to be used on the wares. This name was Ching-tê (1004–1007). The district town was Hsin-p'ing now Fou-liang in the prefecture of Jao chow and it is recorded that this was a center for the making of pottery from the Han period. We need not go into all the Chinese chronicles but it is interesting to note that during T'ang times in the 4th or 2nd year of Wu Tê (A.D. 621) or (A.D. 618) "porcelain jade" called also "false jade" was sent as tribute to the Emperor and from that time it had become the custom for the town to provide the court. We may also note that one potter, Ho Chung-ch'u became renowned but we do not know what his work was like. It was also written that some 300 kilns were at work in the town in the Sung dynasty.

Many of the kilns were in outlying small towns such as Nan Shan, south of the city, and Li-ts'un, Hu-tien, Hsiang-hu, Fu-tien-ts'un and Wang-ts'un, east of the city (see map by A. D. Brankston). Mr. Brankston in "Early Ming Wares of Ching-tê-chên," published by Henri Vetch, Peking, 1938, says, in speaking of the general wares found in the district of Fou-liang, in which the kilns worked, "Outside the town there are literally hundreds of kilns, large and small." And in touching upon Hu-tien says, "Blue decorated wares are found only at the western edge of the site and are mixed with scattered pieces of ying-ch'ing (shadow blue), and plain white porcelain. As one advances eastward the blue and white become scarcer, and finer pieces of ying-ch'ing more numerous, until, at the eastern edge there is a steep slope which contains nothing else except the finest ying-ch'ing with engraved designs. So it appears that the work progressed roughly westward." Later he says, "In addition to the above types there are stemcups and bowls of coarse grey ware with a chocolate coloured glaze. These are scarce, and appear to have been made of unrefined clay; they may have preceded the Sung ying-ch'ing wares or perhaps were a coarse variety of later date."

Again in speaking of the seggars found he says, "The first for firing ying-ching dishes of the Sung dynasty is of porcelain. The second, which comes from the western edge, is probably of the 14th century and is made of a coarse red earth. So it appears that during the Sung dynasty white clay was as plentiful as red earth and that by the 15th century it was necessary to look elsewhere for seggar material. This may mark the change over from natural fusible white clay to a mixture of kaolin and petuntse." He goes on to say that much the same conditions seemed to hold true of other sites in the vicinity and I think his deductions perfectly sound.

Nothing definite can be found out about Ching-tê-chên until we are able to sink shafts in various places.

We cannot definitely attribute Sung nor Yüan wares to this place yet but let us glance at the Chinese descriptions:

The *Memoirs of Chiang* (start of 14th century) state:

1.—They were pure white, 2.—without flaw, 3.—called "Jao Chou Jade," 4.—rivalled the red porcelain of Chêng-ting Fu and 5.—the green of Lung-ch'üan in beauty. (Of course this last does not tell us that they were anything like Lung-ch'üan wares, but simply that they were rated as highly.)

The *Ko Ku Yao Lun* (1387) says:

1.—They were thin in body, 2.—plain white with contracted waist, 3.—"hair mouthed things" which Bushell translates as meaning "with unglazed rims," and 4.—were lower in price than Ting yao.

The *Ching-tê Chêng T'ao lu* (1815) which brought together many otherwise unrecorded facts says:

1.—Chün yao was copied toward the end of the Sung dynasty and 2.—Chi chou ware was also copied with its crackle. This last tells us little because we have not yet identified Chi chou yao.

Some pieces have been reported found in the locality and Hobson describes them as follows: "The glaze is usually of a warm ivory tone, tending to cream color; it is hard and usually discontinued in the region of the base both underneath and on the side, and the exposed body is rather rough to the touch." (For further reference: *Chinese Pottery and Porcelain*, p. 157.) He further states that he sees no reason why they might not have copied Lung-ch'üan yao as did many other factory centers and we may add that our vase from "below the Suburban Altar site" and of Kuan yao confirms one more such site along with Chü-chou. In explanation of the reference to

Chün yao he cites a late 12th century passage quoted by the *T'ao lu* which says that in the Ta Kwan period (1107–1110) there were among the Ching-tê Chên wares "furnace transmutations" (yao lien) red as cinnabar and caused by the planet Mars approaching its greatest brightness when things happened magically and contrary to the usual order and that the disturbed potters broke these to pieces in their fear. This may be the same or a similar reference to that concerning the original Chün yao.

Hobson further quotes the *Po wu yao lan* (1621–1627): "Bk. ii., fol. 8 verso." "The body was thin and glossy (jun), the color white, the ornament blue or green (hua ch'ing), and compared with Ting ware it was little inferior." But he thinks that the reference may have been confused with the "ch'ing pai" or "blue-white" of early writers and says that the rest of the sentence seems based upon the *Ko ku yao lun* statement. One wonders whether perhaps he, in his fear of the meaning of the word ch'ing, may not be discrediting the author too severely, particularly now that we know of a number of blue and white examples which are certainly pre-Ming and very possibly Sung. (See the last of that section.) I am inclined again to believe that our Chinese writers spoke the truth quite clearly for those who wished to understand.

From the *Memoirs of Chiang* we learn that across the river another group of potters made a brownish yellow, or yellow-black ware "huang hei" at a place called Hu-t'ien and that the ware was called "huang liao" or "yellow stuff" and not much thought of. It could not be sold in the southern provinces, but only in Anhwei and Kiangsu. We are told that Chêkiang, Fukien, Kiangsi, Kwangtung and Kwangsi all preferred the "ch'ing pai" or greenish white ware. He also tells us that the finer wares were made from clay imported from Chinkêng while the local clay was used for the coarser wares and saggers. This imported stone was called "shih." The glaze was made of "glaze earth" from Ling-pei mixed with ashes of brushwood from the Yǔ-shan hills, which had been burnt with lime and persimmon wood. Mr. Hobson notes that this is essentially the same as the 18th century description.

The shapes of Yüan wares have been listed in the Bushell translations and although these are quoted with reserve by Hobson I know of no better ones. They are as follows:

1.—Bowls "wan" with high feet and with fish and water ornament.
2.—Platters "t'ieh" with "glazes shaded in different tones." The text reads literally "fa yün" meaning "emit mist" or perhaps "clouded," with "sea eyes" and "snow flowers."
3.—Dishes "p'an" of the horse hoof and betel-nut kinds, the latter suggesting a brownish red color.
4.—Large bowls "yü" with lotus ornament (or shaded like a lotus flower), or of a "square form with indented corners."
5.—Bowls and platters "wan t'ieh" with painted decoration "hsiu hua" literally "embroidered ornament" with silver designs "yin hsiu" literally "silver embroidery or painting" with fluted sides and with "encircling strings"

(lung hsien)—which means literally "play lute"—and which I cannot make anything out of in any way.

6.—Incense burners of many forms and modeled after bronzes and those shaped like fabulous beasts which "eat tigers and can go five hundred li at a bound," as well as those shaped like "ting" with three or four feet, "i" like cups in the ancestral temple, "li" like large iron cauldrons, or with "elephant's legs" or like incense caskets or barrels.

7.—Vase forms such as the "ku" goblet, "tan" gall bladder, "hu" wine pot with spout and handle, "ching" or Buddhist washing vessel, "chih tzŭ" gardenia, "ho yeh" lotus leaf, "hu lu" gourd, "lü kuan" musical pipes, "shou huan" with ring and mask handles and the "liu li" forms.

FIG. 620. Shu-fu yao bowl of rough, pinkish buff ware with a bismuth-white glaze. The decoration is of flying cranes, clouds, a scroll border and the two characters shu and fu in low relief. Dia. 8". Warren E. Cox–John Platt Coll.

Shu fu yao we learn from the *Ko ku yao lun* had a small foot and molded design "yin hua" and those having the characters shu fu meaning pivot palace are highly valued. It says that the contemporary wares (it was published in 1387) have a large foot and plain white glaze lacking in "jun" brilliancy. It tells us that there are also some of "ch'ing" color and that those with "wu sê" or "five colored" ornament are very common. This we may say is strange for we find none of them that can surely be given the attribution. There are also "ch'ing hei" or "dark green" wares with gilt ornament, chiefly wine pots and cups which are said to be very lovely.

In Hsiang's Album (*op. cit.*, Fig. 21) is shown a gourd-shaped bottle with engraved dragon and cloud design which we are told was copied from a specimen of Northern Ting and bears the mark shu fu under the foot.

From the John Platt collection I have a bowl which was attributed to the Yüan period by the late Mr. Bosch Reitz of the Metropolitan Museum of Art and I had a discussion of it with Mr. Theodore Y. Hobby and he sent me the following reference: "At Nan Shan, ying-ch'ing wares were also made, but apparently were of a coarser quality than those of Hu-t'ien. Also there were wares with pure white glaze, either undecorated or with very slight moulded petals, dimples or nipples. These types also occur at Hsiang-hu, but, apparently unique to Nan Shan, are the wares with pale blue opaque glaze over moulded designs which are generally accepted, on the evidence of the *Ko ku yao lun*, as Yüan Shu-fu or palace ware."

"There may have been other kilns in the town of Ching-tê Chêng which made the imperial wares so marked. Of this type there are large lotus-form bowls, dishes on small foot-rims and stem cups. The bases are unglazed and usually oxidized to a salmon-pink color, the glaze is thick, fatty and opaque, of a pale blue-green color. The decoration, moulded inside, is generally of flowers or phoenixes. The best pieces have the characters Shu-fu moulded among the flowers, one on each side of the dish. Some of the bowls have a little incised decoration outside and some are marked inside with good wish characters such as fu (happiness), lu (emolument), or shou (longevity)." This throws more light on the ware that was said to have been made by private factories about Ching-tê Chên and to have been the most important of the period. The bowl we have is of a salmon pinkish tinted buff body, rough and heavy. The glaze is a cold white, hardly bluish but surely not warm in tone. The characters appear in it though it is difficult to photograph them as they are in low relief, set between flying geese and clouds.

Other large pottery centers were Nang-fêng Hsien in the Chien-yang Fu also in Kiangsi where the *T'ao lu* tells us another ware was made of white or yellowish white with designs of blue, and a third factory was at Chien-yang in Fukien province which we have discussed under the Sung section as the source of the "hare's fur" and "partridge" tea bowls.

Taking the same sequence of wares as we adopted in the Sung section let us examine the other wares in order:

FIG. 621. Wine ewer of Ying Ch'ing type of Late Sung or Yüan (1127–1368). Eumorfopoulos Coll. #B14.

FIG. 622. Ying Ch'ing wine ewer of white porcelain burnt brown where exposed and having a bubbly glaze with faint bluish tinge. Sung or Yüan (1127–1368). Ht. 5¼". Eumorfopoulos Coll. #B22.

FIG. 623. #B16 of Eumorfopoulos Coll. a wine ewer which also should be called Late Sung or Yüan (1127–1368) of Ying Ch'ing type and thin enough to be possibly Ju yao. Dia. of saucer 5¾".

"Ying ch'ing" wares certainly carried into Yüan and Ming and later times. I quite agree with Mr. Hobson's attribution in the Eumorfopoulos Collection of #B22 as "Sung or Yüan" but feel he should also certainly include #B16 which he calls "Sung" for they well may have been made by the same potter and are both more likely to be Yüan than Sung because of their strong western feeling and obvious derivation from thin handled metal forms. In the same category should fall #B13 and #B14. (See illustrations.)

Even later should be #B34 and #B35 which are exceedingly heavy and of a shape already tending toward Ming. I show a Chu chou celadon example of my own for general comparison. The ornate design, exceedingly heavy potting and form of them would in my opinion have to be outweighed by strong evidence to disprove them Yüan or Ming.

FIG. 624. Ying Ch'ing type vase which I do not believe could possibly be of "Ju type." The heavy potting, shape and ornate relief design would indicate Late Sung into Early Ming period. Ht. 9¼". # B34 Eumorfopoulos Coll.

FIG. 625. Heavily potted jar of white porcelain burnt red where exposed and with Ying Ch'ing bubbly palest blue glaze, not possibly Ju yao and of the Late Sung to Early Ming period. Compare with Chu Chou celadon in form and decoration. Ht. 16¼". # B35 Eumorfopoulos Coll.

FIG. 626. Typical Chu Chou celadon jar heavily potted and with relief decoration not unlike that of the two Ying Ch'ing examples shown. Ht. 12". Warren E. Cox Coll.

FIG. 627. Vase of bronze form (hu) of white porcelain slightly browned where exposed at the foot-rim, and a bubbly pale blue glaze. Ht. 5¾". # B1 Eumo. Coll.

FIG. 628. Lung-ch'üan vase (fêng wei p'ing) of grey porcelain burnt red-brown where exposed and with a sea-green glaze over applique design. Dated 1327 A.D. Ht. 28". Sir Percival David Coll.

Neither of the Kuan yao factories so far as we know survived the Mongolian conquest.

Ko yao undoubtedly persisted as a general type but the Chinese tell us nothing of the original source during this time.

Lung-ch'üan we have been given to believe stopped all work when the men moved to Ch'u-chou, the capital of Chekiang province, but this was not the case for in the Sir Percival David Collection there are several examples of typical Lung Ch'üan ware with Ming dates on them. Some workmen undoubtedly left while others remained and continued to work the kilns. It is difficult enough to distinguish the Ming from the Sung wares and in this we are uncertain but, lacking dated pieces, we certainly cannot as yet split them down to Yüan in period, although we know they were made.

The Yang Chiang factories in Kwangtung were not much harmed by the invasion and certainly continued without any definite break with the reddish brown body and glassy sort of glazes. It may also likely be that Yüeh factories continued. The bowls dug up at Showchow in Anhwei are called by Hobson, "probably Yüan" and they may be although other authorities place them in Sung times.

The Chün yao turned out at Yü chou we are told was coarser and the

Chün yao incense burner called Sung ? at the museum but more likely of the Yüan or even Ming period. It is of gray stoneware covered with a rather opaque light blue glaze. Ht. about 6". Metropolitan Mus of Art.

Center: Late Sung, Yüan "incense jar" of grey porcelaneous stoneware burnt red where exposed and covered on the outside only and down nearly to the feet with a transparent olive green glaze finely crackled and full of bubbles. Made at Chün chou. Ht. 10". Warren E. Cox Coll.

Right: Chün type vase of the Yüan or Ming period. This type largely of the light blue color with olive brown edges. Similar examples have been sold for Sung pieces but the difference in body and glaze and the so involved form would certainly indicate a later period. Ht. about 8¾". Freer Gallery of Art, Washington.

Yüan Chün type vase on stand of buff stoneware covered with an even but somewhat opaque greenish pale blue mat glaze. Ht. about 7½". Metropolitan Mus. of Art.

Right: Four incense burners or flower-pots of buff ware or grey ware burnt red and with various glazes of blue, lavender, and greyish tones. Hts. 7", 5", 7½" and 13¾". Yüan period Chün yao made at Yu Chou in Northern Honan. Eumorfopoulos Coll. # C89, C90, C91 and C92. Note: Some of the less ornate and sturdier ones are undoubtedly Yüan but the two lower ones are, in my opinion, Ming and show close resemblance in form to many that we find glazed in green and yellow-brown.

YÜAN CHÜN WARES

PLATE 129

glaze ran in a thick welt ending some distance from the base which was entirely unglazed. This change may have taken place in the Yüan dynasty or possibly have started in late Sung times and no authority states anything to the contrary on the fact that it may have continued well into the Ming and perhaps even later times. The present day placing of all cruder pieces of Chün into the Yüan times is ridiculous. However, certain radical changes take place in the design of Chün wares as can be seen by the vessels illustrated and these certainly show no simple Sung taste. I think it quite correct to place all of these wares later and am glad to say that the Freer Gallery, Washington, has called theirs Yüan or Ming. Even so I incline toward the latter attribution for, if these wares were in ordinary green or mustard yellow glaze they would unhesitatingly be so placed because of their shapes. The example from my own collection has an olive green glaze exactly like a Sung example shown in that section. The blue glazes are little different except perhaps slightly more opaque.

I have already spoken in the Sung section of the Tsung Sê (dark brown colored) wares and the fact that many of these are later. In general the more ornate designs and more glossy or treacly glazes on the globular examples show them to be Yüan or Ming. In the Eumorfopoulos Collection #C418 there is an example with the design of a "happy boy" amongst foliage, with an incised leaf band above which is a plain band with incised inscription "ta te pa nien ch'i yüeh — jih" or "eighth year of Ta Tê, seventh month ? day" i.e., A.D. 1305. An abbreviated form of the character tê is used in the inscription. This vase Mr. Hobson also calls a Tz'u Chou type. His decription reads: "Vase of gallipot shape, with globular body and small neck with projecting ridge." (This is the usual Sung everted lip.) "Buff grey stoneware with thick black glaze, the ornament formed by cutting away the ground and exposing the body, namely a broad belt with boys holding lily scrolls: a band of angular fret on the shoulder. The base is glazed. Incised leaf patterns above the base and a plain black band with the inscription." This does not relegate all similar pieces to the same period but simply gives us a milestone to judge by.

To show us that we cannot go entirely by the style of design, I am illustrating #C413 of the Eumorfopoulos Collection, a most disconcerting jar to pedants. Here we see an example with "Ming style" design on one side and "Sung style" on the other just as though the potter said to himself, "If they want an ancient design, let them look at this side. If they want a contemporary design, they may turn it around." Hobson calls this jar "Sung or Yüan" but, of course, no Sung artist could have *foreseen* the decadence in taste that was going to take place and I should say that it is definitely Ming. The ornate side shows typical Ming taste and the very idea of making the combination in one jar is a Ming stunt. It is even more amusing to see that on the simple side the potter has made his glaze more mat in effect. He was a knowing fellow!

If the Chien yao bowls continued, perhaps not so much to fill the desires of the conquerors as the demand in Japan, so also did the wares of that general section. Hobson has designated that territory as the source of what

FIG. 629. Jar of buff-grey stoneware with thick black glaze. This is a Sung form carried over. Ht. 10". Probably made at Tz'u Chou. Eumorfopoulos Coll. # C418.

FIG. 631. Top is jar # C413 Eumorfopoulos Coll. which shows what might be called Ming style on one side and Sung on the other. The pieces below are both more likely Yüan or Ming. Hts. 14" and 15".

FIG. 630. Rougher body and somewhat thicker glaze incline me to judge this piece as Yüan. It must be remembered that after about 1100 A.D. the northern sections of China were under Mongolian rule. Ht. 13". Warren E. Cox Coll.

he labels "Kian temmoku" though we must remember the legend that when Wên, the Sung minister, passed by all of the wares turned to jade and the potters ran away to Ching-tê Chên. Despite my aforementioned theory that

FIG. 632. Yüan jar. The base is glazed and finished with a spiral. Collectors must not conclude that this is an indication of Japanese manufacture. Ht. 14½". Eumorfopoulos Coll. # C411.

FIG. 633. The crude potting and ornate though poorly incised design lead us to place this jar as of the Yüan or Early Ming period. Ht. 14".

FIG. 634. Jar with grey body and rather glossy though thinly applied dark brown glaze. The background is filled in with white. Yüan or Ming. Ht. 14". Ex Edward Wells Coll. Judge Edgar Bromberger Coll. Brooklyn Mus.

this reference is to a *name* "jade ware" given or taken away by Wên and to the evidence of the jar and cover with the character for "jade" or the similar character numeral "five," incised on the bottom—I may have had one of these pottery bowls turned to jade in my hands once.

I met a very old Chinese gentleman who claimed that his brother had a cousin whose uncle lived at Yung-ho Chên, which is in Chi Chou district in the department of Kian or as we now know it, Chi-an Fu, in central Kiangsi near an old kiln-site, and that he, on a windy night but when the moonlight was strong, heard a high-pitched ringing like distant musical bells and, being impelled to follow the sound, came suddenly upon a bowl resting between the roots of a tree where a mole had no doubt turned it up from the earth. It had no color for it seemed part of the moonlight rather than simply to reflect it as would a common bowl, and, said my old friend, "He who says that moonlight is green will be contradicted by one who says that it is blue or one who claims that it is white." Perhaps we had better call the color ch'ing. "And white is a color," continued my friend, "for if white was absence of color, as Europeans describe it, it could not be seen when held up in the air while actually white can be most clearly seen of all." Well, to get back to the sound, it had been caused by the wind striking the so-very-thin bowl in just such a way and this seemed a remarkable and portentous thing to this man who picked up the bowl forthwith and sent it to his nephew who sent it to my friend with the express purpose of selling it to me.

We talked a little of what the price of such an object should be and drank rice wine while we talked. Soon I was so intrigued that I asked to see the bowl, thus showing my impatience and at the same time losing a certain amount of respect from my friend and doubling the price he had in mind. I was told that it would be too much of a shock for me to receive the impression of such an object upon more than one of my senses at once and after the lights were lowered the bowl was placed in my hands. It felt very beautiful, plain, thin as a breath and cold, cold as death. Then the lights were put on and it was no longer in my hands though the touch of it remained as does a kiss on a lover's lips. Perhaps I had not said the right words in praise. Perhaps my price had been too low. But in any event it was gone. Was it porcelain? Was it jade? Or was it the tissue of dreams?

"PHILIPPINE" POTTERIES

Brown Wares and Others

Though some are Sung and others are Ming, I decided that this would be a good place to discuss the potteries found in the Philippines, the East Indies and Malaysia. These were not made in such places but were probably produced in Fukien. Malcom Farley said he had found many sherds in that province which unmistakably corresponded. There are a number of different wares and Dr. Berthold Laufer properly allocated some of them with thick, opaque and oily glazes in a peculiar light blue, grass-green, dark green, olive green and lilac as "Kuang yao" made in Kuangtung province at either Yang-ch'un or Yang-kiang. This latter type is not found in graves and is probably all of Ming or later times. However, the "dragon jars," he says are of the Ming period, if in modern use, or of Sung period if found in burial caves. This, of course, is not a hard and fast rule but largely correct. He further shows the understanding of the natives (that is "the Dayak" to

Two renowned jars from the Sub-province of Abra, N. Luzon. The jar on the left is Magsawi, the famous talking jar. Photograph courtesy of Field Mus. of Natural History.

Jar made in Fukien province according to Malcomb Farley, but found in the Philippines and identical ware to the famous "talking jar." Loops repaired. Ht. about 9". Warren E. Cox Coll.

Chung Tze (brown pottery) vase found in the Philippines but made in Fukien province. The modeling and glaze are made to emulate leather sewn on as a covering. The upper part of the vase only is finished which would indicate that it probably stood in a rack of wood. Sung period. Ht. 24". Warren E. Cox Coll.

PHILIPPINE BROWN POTTERY (CHUNG TZE) JARS

PLATE 130

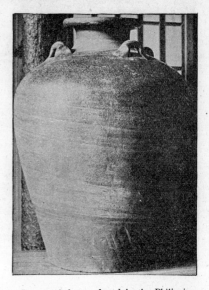

Sung period vase found in the Philippines
and made of brown stoneware with a grey-
brown glaze washed on helically about the
body. Ht. 23″. Warren E. Cox Coll.

Large jar of almost black stoneware potted
very thinly but of great weight. The glaze
is also thin and of a red-brown color. The incising about the shoulder recalls the decoration of Han bronze drums. It is probably
of the Six Dynasty period. Ht. 20″. Warren
E. Cox Coll.

Right: Chinese jar undoubtedly from Kwangtung but found in Abra Sub-province, N. Luzon.
These jars are a part of the price paid for a bride. They are sometimes used as liquor receptacles.
Ht. 8¾″. Glaze blue and green mottled and crackled. Field Mus. of Natural History.

EARLY CHINESE JARS FOUND IN THE PHILIPPINES

PLATE 131

to olive color. It is wheel-made and has a flat bottom unmarked. This is a
fine, powerful piece of potting not lacking in high technical skill so high fired
that it rings with a clearer and higher note than does the first porcelain made
in China of about the same period. The concentric ring decoration recalls
that found on bronze drums made in China during the Han period.

2.—A heavier type of red-brown body and with thin olive brown glaze applied only half way up the neck and two thirds of the way down the body in thin wash streaked around the jar as though done on the wheel is early Sung or earlier. The glaze is similar to that applied to the late Han porcelain jars and the method of application on the upper part only is the same. These jars have flat bottoms and the larger ones have loops on the shoulders for tying down a covering. There is never any ornamentation and the shapes are simple and well proportioned.

3.—Perhaps a little later in the Sung period comes the very large jar of simple form and covered with an olive green glaze. The body of this is a buff stoneware also hard enough to give a note when struck.

FIG. 640. Brown pottery jar with transparent green glaze which produces greenish-brown effect. Ht. 14".

FIG. 639. Brownish black jar found with a bowl inverted over the mouth. The decoration and treatment of glaze would seem also to indicate that this piece was made in Fukien Province. Ht. 10½". Ann Arbor from Dr. Guthe.

FIG. 638. One of a pair of large jars of grey-brown pottery with a light brown glaze over relief dragons the details of which are incised. Ht. 24". Warren E. Cox Coll. This is the type that Laufer established as of Ming dynasty.

FIG. 641. Greenish brown jar of the 18th cent. made in Fukien province and sent to the Philippines. Ht. 20". Ann Arbor from Dr. Guthe.

4.—Of late Sung or Yüan period are probably three distinctive types of Tsung Sê t'zŭ (dark brown colored pottery).

a.—The first type is surely Sung in all characteristics. The ware is reddish-buff and it has applied ridges and dots representing stitched leather over the upper half and shoulder. There are four flat leather-like loops on the shoulder and the glaze is of a dark porous brown carrying out the illusion. The shapes are not unlike the ones described under section three. The lower parts are simply daubed with the remaining glaze on the brush and I believe these jars were intended to fit into racks of wood on a ship deck for the upper parts are beautifully finished, and the daubing is far from attractive.

b.—The famous talking jar described above and one in our collection is of high fired buff stoneware, wheel-turned as are all of these and decorated with appliqués (bosses in the case of the talking jar and dragons, tao-teh monster heads and flames on clouds on ours) and covered with a dark brown glaze which goes light brown and reddish in places where it is thin. The character of the design on our piece makes me believe it is possibly Indonesian and likely from Sukotai-Sawankalock though excavations there have so far turned up nothing just like it. The technique would point to 13th or 14th century without much doubt.

c.—Of the height of the Sung period again is the beautiful buff-grey bodied ware of nearly globular body with slightly angular shoulder and truncated conical neck having a rounded lip-rim. The foot is concave without foot-rim. On the shoulders are four well made loops either plain or like rope and the body may be plain or slightly incised. The glaze is a beautiful soft, waxy, porous deep brown showing light where thin. Few of the northern Tsung Sê wares can rival this in fineness of potting and beauty of form.

A later continuation of the same ware is shown in the half spherical heavier jar found with bowl over the top. This is probably Ming.

5.—Undoubtedly of early Ming period are the squatty and, a little later, the tall forms of "dragon jars" made of brown pottery nowhere nearly so hard as the former wares and covered with a transparent blown glaze of various shades but never deep in color. These are decorated with incised and appliqué designs of clouds, dragons and occasionally flowers.

6.—Of late Ming and later come the plain jars of similar shape and covered with deep blue, green or white splashed with blue glazes and also the squat brown pottery jars having a dull olive brown glaze and found in various places in Kwangtung province.

7.—The crude blue and white and other pottery and porcelain dishes are all of typical Kwangtung, Ching period make or even later.

8.—Just recently through the kind introduction by Miss Josephine Hadley of the Metropolitan Museum of Art, I met Mrs. Kamer Aga-Oglu who had brought a box of sherds from the University of Michigan, Ann Arbor, which had been found in the Philippines. They included a number of "celadon" types including Sung, Ming and possibly later Lung-ch'üan pieces typical in all respects, some Ch'u-chou examples which showed the effects of burial and may have been Sung in period, others of typical Ming aspects, one unmistakable Southern Kuan piece showing narrow and well made foot-rim and brownish olive transparent, crackled glaze, a few of the dull white glazed pieces with buff-gray, coarse body and indications of unglazed rims inside showing that they had been stacked one upon another in firing without much care, and finally a number of odd pieces which I could not identify. These astute young ladies had shown the pieces to a number of able authorities and Mrs. Aga-Oglu is going to make a special study of them, reports of which I shall look forward to with interest.

YÜAN TING YAO

When the Sung capital was moved from Kai-feng Fu in 1127 the potters from Ting Chou are said to have gone along and it is said that a test of a collector's skill in China is that of distinguishing between the north and south Ting wares. Certainly we cannot make this distinction.

Many other factories also tried to pro-duce this ware and one of the best known is Hsüan Chou in Anhwei province. Others were Su Chou and Ssŭ Chou in the same province. In Shansi in Ho Chou a famous potter by the name of P'êng Chün-pao made fine copies of Ting yao in the Yüan dynasty. Another place in this province was P'ing yang Fu where Dr. Rücker Embden dug up a ware with fairly coarse yellowish body, slip and yel-lowish crackle transparent glaze. This, having a slip, we should class among the Tz'u Chou type wares but it was an at-tempted copy of Ting. The same gentle-man found a light grey bodied ware with thick, translucent yellowish glaze usually crackled near Yao Chou, Shensi province. These were Sung kilns which continued through the Yüan and into the Ming dynasties, though their output was not very important.

FIG. 642. Dish of the Yŭan period made at Ching-tê Chên to imitate Ting yao and probably actually after a Ting specimen judging by its design. The ware is white and the glaze whiter than the whitest Ting. The foot-rim is glazed and the edge is left unglazed although the ware is such that it would probably fire per-fectly true. Dia. 6⅛". John Platt–Warren E. Cox Coll.

In the southern part in Kiangsi province at Nan-fêng Hsien and at Yung-ho Chên were made Tu Ting yao and the other wares including a purple or brown (T'zu) type, but nowhere could any kiln compete with the Ching-tê Chên makers of "nan Ting."

Data is lacking for the allocation of many of these Ting wares. The factories were not continuous and some of the provincial wares were very good. In all of them there was an increased tendency to crowd the design and in some a reversion took place toward the more ornate T'ang period shapes. Molded decoration almost entirely supplants incised and one may say in general that the glazes were more likely to be glossy or even glassy.

Tz'u Chou Type Yüan Wares

It will be remembered that the *Ko ku yao lun* (1387) stated flatly that Tz'u Chou wares of the contemporary times were not worth collecting. Its date brings us into Ming times but we would suppose the same applied to the slightly earlier wares. We do not quite agree with this statement but we must admit that the more ornate design on the globular Tz'u Chou jars with the addition of dark red, green and sometimes yellow, began to lose charm and become something like Ming paintings; dull and over ornate copies. Shapes too become more baroque. That tightness of line between bottom and top that lends to the Sung wares simplicity has relaxed into crooked S curves as may be seen in the dark glazed incised specimen illustrated.

FIG. 643. The dark brown body, angular shoulders often seen in Tz'u Chou vases of the Yüan period, and "mishima" inlay of this piece indicates to me that it is of late Sung or Yüan period. Ht. 16¼″. The Cleveland Mus. of Art. Dikran G. Kelekian Coll.

One type found in northern China and quite possibly made at Tz'u Chou itself reverts to a more or less T'ang shape somewhat exaggerated. I illustrate the well known one from the Freer Gallery of Art, Washington, and submit with all due respect that I think the neck too slender and small for the heavy body and the incised floral decoration distinctly decadent. It was at first thought that these vases were of early Sung date, "near to T'ang," but we have already noted that the Mongolian invasion brought with it this flamboyant and somewhat Near Eastern feeling and I should allocate these specimens in the Yüan period on the grounds that the potting of the bases is rough and sloppy with wide and deep footrims, the taste decadent and the technique late rather than early. In the Samuel T. Peters Collection at the Metropolitan Museum of Art is a better proportioned and plain white glazed example which is a prototype.

In the past several great collectors paid high prices for these vases, thinking, I suppose, that they were the super super of carved wares and forgetting the real beauty of the fine and spontaneous line incising of the Sung period. The designs on every one are stiff, labored and wooden. If the old Chinese saying is true, that a leaf dies, if it is touched twice with the brush, how much more true it is when the leaf is whittled all around with the knife. In any event the prices were nearly top for Sung wares until recently in the Mrs. Christian R. Holmes sale immediately after a Chi-lü Hsien vase brought $1,350. An excellent specimen of this carved Tz'u Chou ware some 17 inches high brought only $500, and was, I believe, bought in at that. Formerly $5,000 would have been thought low.

The tendency shown in these vases toward sharper reversed curves can be seen in the simple black painted Tz'u Chou type wares in which the body is more gritty due to less care in refining it and lower fire temperature. The glazes are often not crackled (though this is not always a rule to be depended upon), the black is often blacker and the design more crowded. However, all style was not lost as can be seen in the incised jar with the somewhat wobbly but nevertheless expressive drawing of wilting long leaves and small flowers. This has a yellowish glaze with good imitation "tear stains" like those of Ting ware on it. Also a certain type of ware which I have not been able to allocate and two specimens of which are shown herewith, are well made of grey stoneware and covered with a brown or pinkish buff crackled glaze and painted with brown in sparse, well designed flowers. The cylindrical

FIG. 644. Tz'u Chou type vase like # C410 and # C416 of the Eumorfopoulos Coll. which are designated Yüan. Ht. 10½". Warren E. Cox Co.l.

FIG. 645. Vase. Late Sung or Yüan. Ht. 15½". Freer Gallery of Art, Wash.

FIG. 646. Tz'u Chou of the type called Yüan by many authorities but very likely of the Ming period. Ht. about 13". Gift of Mrs. Samuel T. Peters. Metropolitan Mus. of Art.

FIG. 647. Two jars with a flower pot, the one is Sung, the other jar and flower pot are Yüan. Hts. about 6". Warren E. Cox Coll.

FIG. 648. Wei Hsiang gallipot of the Yüan period. Ht. 9½". Warren E. Cox Coll.

FIG. 649. Tz'u Chou type jar of Yüan or Ming period. Ht. 13". Metropolitan Mus. of Art.

FIG. 650. Tz'u Chou of Yüan or Ming period. Metropolitan Mus. of Art.

FIG. 651. White porcelain vase of the typical Yüan shape. Ht. 8½". Warren E. Cox Coll.

Tz'u Chou type jar of brown stoneware with slip and glaze giving a deep cafe-au-lait tone. The masterful painting of bird and flowers in black speaks of the great artistry sometimes found in paintings of the period. About the neck is a peculiar orange toned iron red overglaze band. Ht. 10″. Warren E. Cox Coll.

Jar of buff-grey stoneware with white slip and warm white glaze closely crackled and clouded with pinkish grey and buff stains, painted with a spirited horse design in black and brown slips. Yüan period. Ht. 10″. Eumorfopoulos Coll. # C359.

Left: Yüan incense burner (ting) of Tz'u Chou ware with brown glaze at bottom, a white slip and transparent glaze on upper part and swift, sure paintings of birds and plants. About the neck is a band of orange-red overglaze color. Many Yüan examples show as great a mastery of painting as the Sung ones. Ht. 6¼″. Warren E. Cox Coll.

Center: Yüan Tz'u Chou of grey stone ware with pinkish glaze and decoration in brown. Ht. 8½″. Ex Warren E. Cox Coll.

Right: Jar of grey stoneware which burns red where exposed in the cracks on the shoulder. In this case the incising was done before the slip was applied and the cream glaze runs with "tear drops" like the Ting yao glaze but more ivory in color. Yüan or Ming. Ht. 9″. Warren E. Cox Coll.

YÜAN DYNASTY TZ'U CHOU TYPE POTTERIES

PLATE 132

vase has also a band of dark reddish-brown around the neck. These are Yüan or Ming, probably the latter, and often have molded marks on the bottom probably indicating the maker.

BLUE AND WHITE YÜAN WARES

We have already made note that the *Po wu yao lan* refers to Ching-tê Chên wares which may be construed to mean blue decorated white wares, and which were said to have been made during the Yüan period. Much evidence seems even to point to a late Sung origin for blue and white ware as we have said, but the making of these things was in a highly experimental stage, the blue was dull and it is evident that the Chinese did not know how to handle it. Note as an instance the way the glaze cracked and broke open on the little bowl belonging to Mr. d'Ancona, particularly where it goes over the blue design. (See last part of Sung section.) Note also that the Chinese blue was uneven and lumpy to apply.

FIG. 652. Yüan or Early Ming period blue and white jar and cover. The decoration is in dark mottled blue and the glaze slightly bluish white. Ht. 15″. Mus. of Fine Arts, Boston.

FIG. 653. Yüan or Early Ming period vase with grayed and reddish under-glaze blue and a thick translucent glaze of cream tone. Ht. 7½″. Metropolitan Mus. of Art.

FIG. 654. Blue and white jar called Yüan but which may possibly be a little earlier. The ground is slightly toward a buff tone and the blue somewhat grayed. Ht. 16½″. Metropolitan Mus. of Art..

One group of heavy porcelains seem to contain iron for they burn red in some places where exposed. The shapes seem more Mongolian than Chinese and yet the blue is no better developed than on the thinner Sung types. These we place in the Yüan period.

Another and finer type are the large jars with covers of Near Eastern feeling in form and quite full in their decoration. On these the blue seems to have been better mastered, the potting is thinner and the glaze no longer gives trouble. They are probably Yüan or Early Ming.

CHAPTER XIX

THE GREAT MING PERIOD

(1368–1644)

THE odd conception that artists are born and not made is ridiculous for artists take a lot of making after having been born, but some people do seem to have an inherent longing for the beautiful. Just as the Negro cannot resist bursting into song though he be doing the mostly lowly and rough work so the Chinese must pause to contemplate the beautiful though his world may be falling about his ears. Mere conquests and the killing of thousands of his brethren cannot stop him any more than can the crowding of life which our various western "civilizations" have impressed upon him. Thus the Mongolian conquest was turned to use, digested and brought about not disaster but simply new ideas.

The pure and simple taste of the Sung period had reached the pinnacle of perfection in China and perhaps in the whole world. I believe, and others agree with me, that the finest vases and bowls ever made in the world were made then. But Ming taste is also most appealing. It may be said to divide itself into two fields each of which became more and more exaggerated. The one is that of reaching utter perfection in technique, an almost inhuman perfection, while the other is in developing the greatest of boldness and flamboyant color. Porcelain was the real medium for both though some of the Ming potteries and stonewares are superb.

The Chinese did not "invent" porcelain. We have seen that around A.D. 200 a ware was made which contained the necessary ingredient, "Kaolin" or "kao-lin" which is said to mean "high ridge" or possibly a certain mountain named "Kao-ling" where the substance was found near Ching-tê Chên. More or less consciously all through the Six Dynasties, T'ang and Sung periods for some thousand and more years the substance had been used and harder wares were made. These wares also became whiter in body and more translucent but not all porcelain is necessarily distinguished by these characteristics. Kaolin is a non-fusible silicate of alumina which has the property of uniting at high temperatures with "petuntse" or "pe-tun-tse," which is a fusible bisilicate feldspar, to form porcelain. Dr. Hirth found embalmed in *Sung Pharmacopia* two early references to "pai o" which he proves to have been kaolinic earth and says it was not only used for medicine but also in painting pictures, so it would seem that it was recognized at least at this time.

With the kaolin and petuntse there was mixed some chalk, some silicic acid in the form of quartz or sand and a little magnesia, and then the materials were washed, ground, filtered and then kneaded with water into a mass suitable for handling. The potter then proceeded with molding, throwing on the wheel, modeling or hand shaping. Much stress was laid upon proper cleaning, for one speck of foreign matter might cause a flaw. How differently the Sung potters regarded such things. Though they did strive for perfect wares, they also had such faith in their various abilities to move the beholder that they had no fear of any such minor distraction; they thought of imperfection as a part of nature just as they would paint a worm-eaten leaf to make it look *more natural and true* than a perfect one.

When the potter had finished with the body he would dip it into a glaze composed of feldspar and lime and then the piece was fired at what the French call the "grand feu" or high fire of about 1350 to 1450 degrees Centigrade, or 2430 to 2610 degrees Fahrenheit. This brings about a chemical change making a hard, white, translucent and so vitrified material that it will ring like a bell when struck lightly. This substance we in the West have come to call "porcelain" though the original makers of it termed it "tz'u" (kiln) or "t'ao" (products of the kiln) or "yao" (ware), and drew no hard and fast differentiation. None of the early chronicles in China seem to speak definitely of translucency yet pieces found at Samarra were translucent. We have already explained in the section on Kuan yao, Sung period, that the phrase, "see right through" may well have meant see right into the glaze, and not necessarily through the body.

Due to various attempts to achieve this true porcelain or "hard porcelain" which is so hard that steel will not scratch it, impermeable to liquids and unaffected by all acids other than hydrofluoric, we find some confusion in terminology. Thus "Medici porcelain" made in Italy in the 16th century and the 17th century French wares of St. Cloud, etc. were nothing but white clay mixed with a "frit" or ground glass and covered with a lead glaze. It was fired at 1100° C. and again at 1000° C. for the glaze, and this was called "Soft Porcelain," though of course, it was not porcelain at all. Meanwhile the Chinese, hearing of it, made what is loosely called, "Soft Paste," in the late Ming and later periods. This is at times changed in body but usually in glaze only. The substance used was thought to be soapstone or steatite but has later been determined to be pegmatite. It may not be quite so high fired as hard porcelain but is still much higher than the so-called "soft porcelain" of Europe. Much of it is of the Yung Chêng or late K'ang Hsi period and decorated in blue on white but some is Ming of undetermined but probably late reign and a soft yellowish-white. Aside from this one type it is the practice in China to fire body, underglaze decoration and glaze all at one time. Only when surface decoration in enamel and gold is used did they fire a second and third time, each, of course, at a lower temperature.

The glaze of feldspar, limestone and plant ash was said to have been made in early times with the burnt leaves of bamboo, peach or later with ferns laid between layers of the limestone and burnt then mixed with water. It is said that the brilliance and clarity of the finest porcelain was obtained because of the exact quality of this ash. According to Hobson and quoting Bushell's translations, the porcelain clay came from Hsin-chêng-tu in the Ma-ts'ang hills in four places named "The Gully of a Thousand Families," and "the Dragon Gully," etc. The stone was obtained from the Hu-t'ien district. Good earth for the glaze came from Hsin-chêng-tu also but the best was brought from Ch'ang-ling and I-kêng. The "ch'ing" color came from Ch'ang-ling as did the yellow, but the white was from I-kêng. All of these places were near Ching-tê Chên.—Later in the Wan Li reign (1573–1619) the last important one of the dynasty the pits at the Ma-ts'ang hills were worked out and those at Wu-mên-t'o were not so good. Also the special mixtures of earth for the very heavy vessels came from Yü-kan and Wu-yüan and were mixed with stone from the Hu-t'ien district.

WHITE WARE OR "BLANC DE CHINE"

The pure white ware or "Blanc de Chine" as the French call it, is termed in China "pai tz'u" or "Chien yao" and the latter term must not be confused with the ware of which the little brown bowls are made in the same locality. This white ware comprised all manner of porcelain objects and was a dense creamy white almost pure white and as Hobson aptly calls it, "like milk jelly or blancmange," and the glaze is so united with the body that one can hardly tell where one stops and the other begins. The glazes of all the later periods appear glassy, or dead white in comparison with the Ming ware. At times it has the palest suggestion of a rosy tinge. A late Chinese book tells us, "When the glaze is white like jade, glossy and lustrous, rich and thick, with a reddish tinge, and the biscuit heavy, the ware is of first quality."

The ware was made at Tê-hua or Tehwa in the Ch'üan-chou district of Fukien province about 100 miles south of Chien-yang. By A.D. 1700 the wares were plentiful and no longer dear. Decorated pieces were also made as is proven by an example in the Eumorfopoulos Collection, a double bottomed hot water bowl with designs in green, yellow, red and typical Ming turquoise green. Those impressed with Ming marks are always of later date, but makers' marks do appear on some early ones. The finely modeled religious figures are undoubtedly the best of the output. Graceful Kuan-yin figures represent the idea of the "Mother of Mercy" of the Italians or of simple fecundity and hold inverted vases, "the source of water in which everything grows," or a child, as do our Madonnas. Others represent Darhuma and other Buddhistic or Taoist deities. One unique specimen seems actually to be a Christian Madonna perhaps inspired by one of the fathers of the Church in China.

Most of the early wares have fire cracks inside the bottom due to the weight of the body but this is not an invariable characteristic. The K'ang Hsi ones are usually purer white and more detailed in modeling while Yung Chêng and Ch'ien Lung ones are inclined to be ivory in tone and filled with little bubbles in the glaze, seemingly an attempt to get the Ming creaminess but an unsuccessful one. Modern wares are of white body, thinly potted and with glassy, white glaze, but even these are beautiful little works of art for the few dollars they cost. Ming examples can bring four or five thousand dollars and are well worth it. Besides the kilns at Tê-hua many smaller

Left to Right: Late Ming or possibly K'ang Hsi figure of Kuan-yin, shown holding a ju-i sceptre and walking in water or standing on a cray-fish. Ht. 13". Warren E. Cox Coll.
Tê-hua figure of Kwan Yin which shows typically the rich creamy glaze attributed surely to the Ming period. Ht. 7½". C. T. Loo & Co.
Fukien figure of a dignitary with a four clawed dragon in relief on his robe. Note the slots left for the insertion of human hair. Attributed to Ming dynasty. Fuller Coll. Seattle Art Mus.
Fine Tê-hua figure of Darhuma in thoughtful attitude. Ming dynasty. Ht. about 6½". Ex Warren E. Cox Coll.

TÊ-HUA WHITE PORCELAIN FIGURES OF MING DYNASTY

PLATE 133

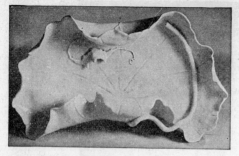 

Left: Late Ming writer's water-dish of white porcelain with a glossy pinkish and ivory toned crackled glaze. It was fired on 28 small spurs with bottom glazed. Dia. 10″. Warren E. Cox Coll.

Right: Typical Tê-hua "birthday cup" with swallows on one side for happiness and stags and pine trees on the other for long life. Dia. 5¾″. Warren E. Cox Coll.

Left: Fukien Tê-hua porcelain of the Ming period with white body finely potted covered with a creamy glaze of pure white. Ht. about 8″. Metropolitan Mus. of Art.

Center: Ming period vase of white porcelain carved in relief with archaic dragons and having a transparent glaze slightly crackled. Ht. 4¼″. Ex D. Abbes Collection.

Right: Tê-hua, Fukien vase of fine quality and beautiful proportions. "Wheel marks" remain. Glaze is somewhat pitted but of pure, creamy white. Ht. 17¼″. Warren E. Cox Coll.

Left: Ming "soft paste" shallow dish in the form of a flower probably to be used for water on a scholar's table. Dia. 2½″. Fuller Coll. Seattle Art Mus.

Right: Ming period Fukien bowl probably from Tê-hua. Inscription reads, "If there are not three persons present to carry out the traditional drinking rule, drink three times yourself to match the rule. This is a cup to drink from." Dia. 5½″. Warren E. Cox Coll.

MING BLANC DE CHINE WARES
FROM TE-HUA AND OTHER KILNS

PLATE 134

factories copied the ware and some of the big ones such as Ting Chou, Ping-
liang Fu in Shensi, and Ping-ting Chou and T'ai-yüan of the same province,
Yü Chou and K'ai-fêng Fu in Honan, Wu-yüan Hsien and Ch'i-mên Hsien
in Anhwei, etc., etc. But until more work is done in excavating we cannot
allocate any given piece, and indeed it is difficult to place them in their
proper periods. However, some of the greatest sculptors the world has known
and worthy to be ranked with the della Robbias and others of great fame
lived and died nameless leaving behind them a few of these beautiful and
vigorous works of art. It is a field which should surely fascinate the collector.

MING COLORED GLAZES

Colored glazes were made just as was the white with the addition of
antimony for yellow, manganese for violet, aubergine (eggplant which the
Chinese call "kai-pi-pe") or brown, copper for turquoise, green and several
reds including the famous "sang de boeuf" or "Lang-yao" of sacrificial ox
blood (not that the vases had anything to do with sacrifices except the
giving up of considerable money for them) and iron for nasturtium or dead
leaf brown and the highly prized green celadon colors. Varying temperatures
account for the production of different colors with the same ingredients and
transmutations produced Chün-like effects and also the "flambé" streaks
of pale blue or lavender in red. These latter were only begun in the Ming
period but later in the 18th century were well governed.

Crackle was perfected as an art in the Ming period and
the potters not only could make any shape and size they
wanted but graduate from large to small crackle, etc. The
turquoise and yellow glazes as well as the copper reds or sang
de boeuf are always crackled, the former rather finely and
called "trout scales" or "fish scale" and the latter "crab's
claw" as before. There are bottles on which the crackle takes
a helical twist and a figure of blanc de chine in the Eumorfopoulos Collection #D288 has the robe and hood crackled
while the face is unblemished.

Underglaze colors are painted on the biscuit, will stand the
high temperature of the "grand feu" and have the glaze over
them. Only two were successful, blue and red. The blue was
an oxide of cobalt and we do not know when or where it was
first used, but it was surely used *as a glaze* on T'ang pieces
and a colorless glaze may have been applied over the blue
in some T'ang wares. We also know of early pieces from
Persia and Syria but probably none go back much before the
6th or 7th century A.D. in China. The *Tao lu* (Julien, *op. cit.*,
p. 76) speaks of the crackled wares made at Yung-ho Chên in
the Sung period and says, "There were besides pieces with
plain crackled ground, to which they add blue decoration." Again it is said that
at Nan-fêng Hsien, in Kiangsi, in the Yüan dynasty, porcelain was made "of
refined clay but somewhat thick, and decorated as a rule with blue designs,
'ch'ing hua'." In the Eumorfopoulos Collection Catalogue, Mr. Hobson some-

FIG. 655. Tê-
hua porcelain fig-
ure with crackle all
over except on face
and fingers. Ht.
30". Eumorfopou-
los Coll. # D288.

FIG. 656. Early Ming or possibly Yüan blue and white vase of heavy potting, dull gray-blue and a creamy glaze. Ht. about 12″. Metropolitan Mus. of Art.

what hesitatingly designates #D1 as Sung, explaining that although some of these vases have designs which we are used to seeing on Ming porcelains, we are told by the Chinese that they are of Sung origin. This vase is not unlike the specimen I illustrate from the Metropolitan Museum of Art and which is called Ming or possibly Yüan. I show another under the Yüan section. The design is far less disturbing to me than the involved and poorly proportioned shape, with clumsy ring or loop handles, and the weight of the potting all of which would place them in the Ming times.

Far more Sung in shape and in decoration is a large jar from my own collection and a similar one #D14 in the Eumorfopoulos Collection which Hobson calls 15th century. The wonderful spirit and style of the "dragon horses" and the dashing wave borders, to say nothing of the beautifully done little rocks and flower passages make this seem surely an original work of art by some great master. The blue is dull and somewhat lumpy. The glaze is of soft ivory tone and crackled. The foot is slightly indented to give just a suggestion of a foot-rim. If it is of the Hsüan Tê reign (1426–1435) or the Chêng Hua (1465–1487) I know of nothing to equal it in those times. It is far more likely I believe that we will be able to push back many of these pieces as we learn more about kiln sites.

The underglaze red was made with the tiniest suggestion of copper oxide and fired in a reducing kiln. Again we do not know the source or time of beginning but tradition assigns it to the Hsüan Tê (1426–1435) reign in the Ming period when we do at least know that several kinds were developed. "Chi hung" was the color of the ritual cups used in the worship of the sun and it was divided into 1. "hsien hung" fresh or glossy red and 2. "pao shih hung" or precious stone red. The Po wu yao lan says, "For these they used a powder made of precious red stones from the West to paint the fish forms,

FIG. 657. An excellent example of the celadon made at Ch'u-chou but which has a design of Near Eastern feeling in underglaze red which appears reddish-brown and lustrous where it penetrates the green glaze. It is likely that the kilns in this district made the ware and the Ching-tê Chên took it up later using a lighter green glaze and white body. Dia. 11¾″. Warren E. Cox Coll. Ex Samuel T. Peters Coll.

and from the body of the porcelain there rose up in relief in the firing the precious brilliance of the fresh red ravishing the eye." This is, of course, a reference to the white cups with three fish or fruit on them. I show one from the Eumorfopoulos Collection which bears the Hsüan Tê mark. It is further stated that later in such periods as the Chêng Tê the red is relatively dull and weak and in the Chia Ching the earth required ran out so that the potters had to use overglaze red enamel "fan hung" instead. At times the red was also used under a light celadon glaze but was, of course, rather dull. The beautiful dish illustrated is the best example I know.

The art of overglaze coloring was the chief achievement of the Ming potters. These overglaze colors are simply oxides of various metals ground up in glass which melts at a fairly low temperature in the kiln and makes them adhere to the glass-glaze. Iron red is the "driest" of these colors and appears almost mat but even it had a small amount of flux of glass for filling in areas, though it was used drier for outlines. Violet blue did not come into use until the K'ang Hsi period. Ming yellow is usually rather muddy though some odd bright yellow specimens exist. Gilding was rarely used and was either fired or leaf applied cold. Manganese produced a dry brown and black and this black was washed over with transparent green enamel to produce the lustrous blacks used in large areas. All colors except the red and black were transparent and usually applied thickly.

It is difficult to generalize about the Ming period yet collectors can say that a piece has a Ming look or is "Mingish" as old Voron used to say. First we must realize that the length of this period of 1368 to 1644 is some 276 years and that subtracting these years from our present we would find ourselves back when the British conquered New Netherlands and about the time that Marquette and Joliet discovered the Mississippi River. Quite a lot has taken place since then and, if potters had been making pots at that time in America, they would probably be making different ones now. Do not let anyone ever tell you that China is a country in which nothing much ever happened and no changes were made. Her present history shows a bit of what she has been through many times. There were huge migrations, many conflicts and one major change due to the new weapon of religion for in the Chia Ching (1522–1566) reign the Emperor adopted Taoism. We also see the even newer weapon of commercialism taking art in its deadly clutch toward the end of the dynasty. Therefore when we say Ming we mean a multitude of things.

Since 1923 our conception has become more clear so that the admonitions given by Mr. R. L. Hobson in his book "The Wares of the Ming Dynasty" are not so necessary. However, a few points are worth making: First, we must realize that most of the Ming porcelain and pottery which we see was expressly made for export and is not representative of Chinese taste or the best of Chinese craftsmanship. It had to be made heavy to travel well. It was naturally designed to please our Western taste. Actually some of the most delicate and thinly potted wares the world has ever seen are Ming. Secondly, Ming is not a dumping ground for stray pots, nor, to quote him, "is it a locus penetentiae into which anything wrongfully posing as Sung or Yüan should be degraded when found out." This we see often in Tz'u Chou, Tu Ting and "crackle" wares which dealers call Sung and when pressed retreat by allocating in the Ming dynasty when actually some of them are not as old as our grandmothers. Particularly so treated are the wares of grey, buff, green or yellow having a coarse crackle and made for export to the East Indies. These have been stock in trade for many years and are made even today, if any kilns are working in South China at all. Again an almost universal acceptance of roof tiles or finials as Ming is evident in America and ladies like to have them made into lamps, even though the modeling may be very bad, "because they are Ming." Chinese houses and temples are built up to the present with just these wares. Another group which Hobson says is dangerous is the "three color" enameled wares about which we shall have more to say later. These are expensive and as he says, "Worse still, they have been published as Ming in large and expensive books. This is particularly true of those fine porcelains which have grounds of the precious green-black, green or yellow enamels." He is probably referring to such publications as "Chinese Porcelain & Hard Stones" by Edgar Gorer and J. F. Blacker which was quoted as an authority to me by an eminent German professor recently, though many K'ang Hsi pieces in it are called Ming.

Mr. Hobson goes on to say that it has taken years to smother the "Lowestoft myth" and I may add that even now I run across some old lady now and then who still believes it. Another type is the Kwangtung ware which varies and has been made up to modern times. But the most often seen late pieces called Ming are the Taoist deities, lions, birds, etc., "with iron-red biscuit" (or brown we may add) "freely exposed in places and the rest of the surface coated with the thick Canton glaze of mottled blue-grey, flambé red or celadon green which are almost invariably labelled Ming, and they are almost invariably of 19th century make." Another amusing reference is to ginger jars; he says, "Extract the ginger and place the pots on the shelf. They become Ming in the twinkling of an eye."

I further quote, "And so for the benefit of the beginner a warning note is needed; but it must not be taken as a general tirade against the dealers in antiques. There are dealers and dealers. Those who take the trouble to study the things they handle—and most of them do that—are the best friends to the searcher after truth in this particular field. But there are still people who will pass off anything Chinese as Ming, partly out of ignorance, but mainly because the name Ming is something to conjure with. *A convenient philosophy tells them that there are many doubtful specimens, and that they are at liberty to give themselves the benefit of the doubt, and further, that the less they know of the subject the more doubt there is to benefit from.*" (The italics are my own.) "These sophists are a nuisance and should be exposed on every occasion, if only for the good time that is wasted by the conscientious members of the trade in correcting the errors which they disseminate."

The above attitude has been very well developed by many small dealers who supply the decorative trade with lamp bases for they can gamble on the fact that once a sale is made for this purpose the customer will never raise the question of authenticity. Also the convenient covering of the bottom in mounting makes it difficult to examine such pieces. But the sophists are not all small firms. One of the largest in the country recently sold a man who hired me for appraisal a dozen pieces which were misrepresented and sold for many times their value. The amusing thing is that they willingly and without demur refund the money when caught, but go merrily on in their practices because the average pays. The only way to put a stop to this sort of thing is to persuade all collectors and people who buy even solely for decorative reasons to take the trouble to find out and then to press the matter.

The Ming body is fine and unctuous, white and smooth as is the fine Sung stoneware, the difference being only in color. When the fingernail is scratched on it there is no unpleasantness. The New York collector Mr. Robert West calls it a "macaroni foot" and the feeling is not far different from that of uncooked macaroni. Sometimes there are little pits and again there may be small traces of iron which give a rusty red or brown look where exposed.

The Chinese described the glaze as being like "massed lard" and it is valued for its thickness and flawlessness. Even if there was the slightest flaw in the early times of Hung Wu the piece was ground smooth and reglazed. But this glaze is always slightly undulating. It has been likened to an orange peel but this is exaggeration unless a very smooth orange is considered. There are also slight tubercles like grains of millet and depressions which have been named "palm eyes"—"tsung yen." Mr. Nai-Chi Chang has recently explained to me that this is not the correct translation for the word is actually t'ze tsung making the meaning "bristle holes" or we might say, "pig's bristle holes." The word t'ze is often omitted in writing though perfectly understood by the Chinese although it was not by the English translators. The Chinese also call it "chicken skin" which does imply the thousands of hardly perceptible pores that take away any glassy look from it.

Many Ming vases are slightly distorted both because of careless turning and through firing. Perhaps the potters felt this gave them a life which a dead symmetrical form might not have, but I believe it was not calculated in this dynasty. In any event it is never very great. When a vase had to be made in a top and bottom section the Ming potters did not try very hard to obliterate the joint but left it so that, even if it could not be seen clearly, it could be easily felt by running one's hand over the surface.

None of these considerations are to be found in *all* Ming porcelain. For instance, the *Shih ch'ing jih cha* tells us that the important way to judge porcelain is by the foot, and continues by saying that the Yung Lo (1403–1424) bowls have a glazed bottom and sandy foot. (You will note that at once we depart from our general description.) He goes on to say that Hsüan Tê (1426–1435) altar cups have a "cauldron bottom" probably meaning convex, and thin, wire-like foot, and that Chia Ching (1522–1566) pieces have a "loaf center," probably meaning convex inside, and rounded foot. It should be added that one should not condemn a Ming piece because the foot-rim is perfectly made because some are. It can only be said generally that the K'ang Hsi rim is usually better potted and a little more likely to have a groove to fit a stand. We find the following foot types:

1.—Grooved and well potted foot-rims accompanied with glaze in the bottom which may differ from that on the outside or may be of different color due to the covering of it in firing.

2.—Rounded and finely potted with glaze applied underneath. This is the spaghetti or macaroni foot of Mr. West's.

3.—Sharp edged like the thin Ying Ching wares of the Sung period, but usually more even.

4.—Crudely rimmed and unglazed beneath.

5.—Flat bottomed and with no glaze or just a thin patch dabbed on.

Numbers four and five disappear by K'ang Hsi times.

I need not say more about Ming forms for the illustrations will show them well enough. However, they are seemingly all somewhat extreme as related to Sung ones and it is interesting to make comparisons.

It is the habit of writers to dwell upon the glorious Ming color and it is true that designs of brocades and cloisonné were employed as well as parts from paintings and some studies from nature itself. But at the same time we must realize that the factories had set up the division of labor system. Later in the K'ang Hsi period we are told that a vase passed through *seventy hands* before it was finished. It was not so bad in Ming times but bad enough for anyone would admit that such a system would lose all of the personal character and feeling of an artist. We are also told that there was stealing of the precious blue and that, therefore, an artist was selected to do a large piece and another to do a small one and the average of the amount of blue they used was carefully calculated and dealt out to the painters. Can one imagine a real artist working under such circumstances?

There are several classifications of the types of wares:

1.—"Three color type" or "san ts'ai."

2.—"Five color type" or "wu ts'ai."

3.—"Mixed color type" or "ts'a ts'ai."

But these do not hold true entirely for the first may be porcelain or pottery having three or four colors such as green, aubergine, yellow, turquoise, dark blue, etc., while "wu ts'ai" has come to mean porcelain with the enamel decoration on a glaze, usually white, and "ts'a ts'ai" may be applied to both.

THREE COLOR WARES

The enamels were inclined to run in firing and the "three colored wares" often show a method of confining them by reticulation, incising the surface or laying small ridges of clay or cloisons on it. But the old myth that these wares were "copied from cloisonné" has no basis in fact. Actually the fictile wares came first. These enamels were fired in the "demigrand feu" or lower heat and are alkali-lead silicates. The objects so decorated were "gallipots" or "mei p'ing" meaning vase for prunus bough, barrel shaped garden seats, large temple jars with covers, flower pots, incense burners and some beaker shaped vases of tall and graceful shape. The first of them may quite possibly have been developed from the Tz'u Chou type with the added red, green and

Late Ming "san ts'ai" or three color porcelain figure of Kuan Yin. Ht. 13". Altman Coll. Metropolitan Mus. of Art.

Gallipot with pierced and modeled walls, cobalt ground, turquoise, straw and orange yellow. Ht. 10". Early Ming. Bequest of Isaac D. Fletcher. Metropolitan Mus. of Art.

Left: Late Ming enamel on biscuit bowl with dark green ground, aubergine, yellow and a glossy white outlined in dull black. Dia. 7". Bequest of Mary Clark Thompson. Metropolitan Mus. of Art.

Right: Ming incense burner (Ting) before Hsüan Tê 1426. Buff pottery with the neck and body pale aubergine, the legs and handles yellow green and the lip orange yellow. Glazes show iridescence from burial. Ht. 5½". Ex Warren E. Cox Coll. Mrs. Ogden K. Shannon, Jr.

THREE COLOR (SAN TS'AI) MING POTTERIES

PLATE 135

Fig. 658. Two pairs of small Ming "three color" vases, the larger ones with scratched design and green and yellow glaze, the smaller with ridges and glazes of yellow, green and aubergine. Hts. 8¼" and 6½". Warren E. Cox Coll.
Fig. 659. One of pair of vases of light buff pottery glazed with pale green, aubergine, and greenish yellow and showing iridescence from burial. Ht. 7". Metropolitan Mus. of Art. Gift of Joseph Koshland.

yellow glazes to which turquoise and the other colors were again added. Some are of coarse pottery body while others are of white porcelain but all are thick and sturdy in potting. Many are glazed inside and on the bottom with green thinly applied. The turquoise varies from a hard glaze looking like

a high fired one to a soft crackled type which seems to be more popular in the later reigns and continues into the K'ang Hsi and Chien Lung periods. The violet or purple blue also varies from fairly clear to almost black. The vases with leaf green or aubergine ground are supposed to be more rare and therefore more valuable. The European and American collectors have always valued this ware highly and only a few years back the firm of Parish-Watson bought the piece illustrated in "The Wares of the Ming Dynasty" (Pl. 52, Fig. 1) in London for 945 pounds sterling. This piece was from the Benson Collection and was a good but fairly late piece. Others have brought up to $15,000 but the general price of $5,000 would take most and later during the depression things changed considerably.

Naturally such prices attracted the copyists and some undiscriminating collectors have been taken in. A piece was sold in one of the important auction galleries in New York in 1938 which had been made in Japan and was put up by the anonymous "Famous Long Island Collector" and it brought over $800 though it was exactly of the type that we handled for lamp bases at $35 to $50. Of course, a collector is foolish to believe he can buy properly from one

Fig. 660. Late Ming "three color" porcelain figure of Kuan Yin having the thinner and more transparent enamels not found in earlier times. Ht. 23". Altman Coll, Metropolitan Mus, of Art,

who is afraid to give his name and also it is not likely that so well known and popular a ware would go for a fifth of its value. Bargain hunting does not pay in collecting.

Three color wares are usually decorated with stock designs such as Shou Lao, the god of longevity, some or all of the Eight Immortals, the Eight Immortals of the Wine Cup, Wang Chih watching the game of chess, and dragons, lions, peonies, flowers, peacocks, the flowers of the four seasons, and also with ju-i shaped lappets or pendant jewelry, gadroons and borders.

Monochromes of this classification are rare but not unknown and figures, such as the one shown from the Altman Collection, are sometimes very fine.

FIVE COLOR WARES

The "five color wares" naturally show a great deal of painting and it may be useful here to give a list of the subjects used, though this cannot be entirely complete, of course.

CONFUCIAN SUBJECTS

CONFUCIUS himself

KUAN YÜ, the warrior who was turned in the 16th century to

KUAN TI, the God of War seen in armor seated with uplifted hand or sometimes striding forward.

K'UEI HSING, the God of Literature who is usually seen as a demon with brush and writing equipment, and standing on a dragon-fish.

TAOIST SUBJECTS

SAN CHING, the spiritual trinity

SAN KUAN, the active trinity consisting of:

a.—Shang Ti who rules over the heavens

b.—Shou Lao who is the god of the southern star and long life and who is a transformation of Lao Tzŭ, the founder of the religion, and is an old man with a long beard and bald head with a large protuberance on it, said to have been caused by deep thought, and clothed in flowing robes on which the character "shou" or "longevity" is shown. At times he is seated and at times on the back of some animal such as an ox or water buffalo.

PA HSIEN, which are saints, demigods or genii which are about him and are known as:

a.—Chung-li Ch'üan, a bearded old man with a peach in one hand and fan in the other with which he wakes the spirits of the dead to life.

b.—Lü Tung-pin, who carries a sword and protects the world against monsters and plagues.

c.—Li T'ieh-kuai, the good spirit of magicians and astrologers and is shown as a beggar with pilgrim bottle and crutch.

d.—Ts'ao Kuo-chiu, the god of actors who carries castanets in his hands.

e.—Lan Ts'ai-ho, who may be a man or woman but always carries a basket of flowers and is the god of gardeners.

f.—Chang Kuo Lao, who is the god of writers and artists and always carries a twig and bamboo cane.

g.—Han Hsaing Tzŭ carries a flute and is the god of musicians.

h.—Ho Hsien Ku is the goddess of housewives but carries a lotus, why we do not know.

i.—Wên Ch'ang is another god of literature which is as a matter of fact watched over by five in all.

KUAN TI was borrowed by the Taoists from the Confucianists and is shown with a dragon on his robe and with a three-legged frog at his feet.

HSI WANG MU is the goddess of long life and is shown as a graceful, slender girl with a flowerbasket at times carried on a cane over her shoulder and is often shown under a flowering peach tree.

BUDDHIST SUBJECTS

BUDDHA, the founder who was supposed to have come into this world a rich and carefully protected boy but who was so shocked when he saw its unhappiness that he devoted his life to helping mankind, is shown standing on a lotus flower with one hand upraised or with a book.

KUAN-YIN is a perfect being who with only one more incarnation will attain Nirvana, and is also the goddess of mercy, the mother spirit and is frequently shown with a child in her arms or about her skirts, but is also seen with an inverted vase, the source of water in which things grow, representing the idea of fecundity.

SHAN-TS'AI is the name of the child who after several trials was permitted to help Kuan-yin in her deeds of mercy.

LOHAN, or in India, Arhat, or in Japan, Rakan are saints of which there are 16 in India and 18 in China, one of which is the popular:

PU-TAI HO-SHANG (or "Hotei" in Japan) the god of children and of earthly joys who is usually shown with his fat and naked belly and smiling face as he reclines against money bags.

ANIMAL SUBJECTS

Dog of Fo seen singly or in pairs as incense stick holders at Buddhistic altars and is like a lion showing his teeth and frequently has a collar of bells and is playing with a ball or cub. Pekinese dogs were bred to look like these.

Ch'i-lin (or kylin) is a strange animal which represents happiness and perfection and has a head half dragon's and half unicorn's, the hoofs of a horse, the tail of an ox and a scaly body but shaped like a deer. Two of these may be seen on the large blue and white jar.

Fêng-huang is the bird like a peacock or pheasant. It is supposed to live in the highest heavens and is a symbol of beauty and perfection. (Mr. Jean Delacour Bulletin of New York Zoological Society, Vol. XLIV, No. 6, Nov.–Dec. 1941 offers an interesting theory that it was Rheinart's Ocellated Argus pheasant.)

Lung is the dragon and appears in many forms as the symbol of Spring, the emblem of the Emperor and also a herald of storms and rains. It is said to have the head of a camel with horns like a deer, eyes like a rabbit, ears like a cow, a neck like a snake, the belly of a frog, scales like a carp, the claws of a hawk and the soles of the feet of a tiger. It also has long whiskers.

> Five claws indicate the rank of the Emperor and also princes of the first and second rank.
>
> Four claws show the ranks of princes of the third and fourth ranks.

Hsiang, the elephant is a symbol of power and strength as was also the leopard, tiger and lion.

Lu is the deer and represents long life.

T'u is the hare which is seen in the moon where it is preparing the elixir of life.

Fu is the bat which expresses happiness and good fortune.

Ho, the crane, the heron or the stork is supposed to live to a wonderful age and represents longevity.

BOTANICAL SUBJECTS

Sung, the fir tree, has many meanings including longevity and steadfastness.

Chu is the bamboo, strong because it bends before the wind.

The four season flowers are the
1.—Spring—peony
2.—Summer—lotus
3.—Autumn—chrysanthemum
4.—Winter—plum blossom
Note:—The latter is miscalled "hawthorn."

BUDDHISTIC EMBLEMS (Fig. 661)

Pa chi Hsiang are the 8 Buddhistic emblems
1.—The wheel in flames, "Lun."
2.—The conch shell expressing the wish for a lucky journey, "Lo."
3.—The umbrella of state presented to a mandarin on leaving his district to testify to his faithful services, "San."
4.—The tasseled throne canopy, "Kai."
5.—The lotus flower, "Hua."
6.—The urn with Buddhistic relics, "P'ing."
7.—The pair of fishes, symbolic of conjugal felicity and fertility, "Yü."
8.—The never ending knot or "entrails" another symbol of long life and the 8 Buddhistic commandments, "Chang."

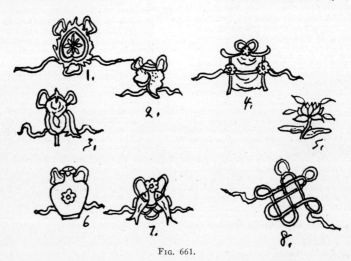

Fig. 661.

Pa Pao are the eight precious things (not to be confused with the above).
1.—The pearl of purity with a ribbon, "Chu."

2.—The picture, "Hua."
3.—The sonorous jade stone, the character for which has the same pronunciation as the one for good luck, "Ch'ing."

4.—Crossed rhinocerous horns, "Chüeh."
5.—A coin, the symbol of wealth, "Ch'ien."
6.—An open lozenge shape, symbol for victory, "Fang-Shêng."
7.—Two books as a warning against evil, "Shu."
8.—A leaf, probably artemisia, a symbol of prophecy, "Ai-yeh."

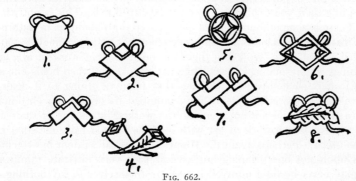

FIG. 662.

The 4 emblems of accomplishment are
1.—The chessboard
2.—The pair of books
3.—The lute
4.—Pair of scroll paintings.

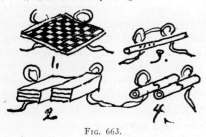

FIG. 663.

WAN-TZÜ is the swastika enclosed in a rhomboid sometimes with embellishments at the cor-ners or ribbons and represents ten thousand things or the whole of creation. The swastika is also representative of the heart of Buddha and it turns opposite to the Nazi one.

YANG-YIN is a circle with an S line drawn through the center. It expresses the duality of the universe such as male and female, perpendicular and horizontal (in landscape painting), night and day, etc. It also relates in some way to moon worship. (See its use also in the pottery of the Black Earth Region in Europe.)

PA-KUA is the octagonal arrangement of the eight traigrams which mean the elements Heaven, Vapour, Fire, Thunder, Wind, Water, Mountain and Earth. They are formed of three broken and solid lines.

PA AN HSIEN are the emblems of the 8 Taoist saints which we have described above but which are also often shown alone.

SHOU is the character meaning long life and it is often composed into a sort of design. There are many variations.

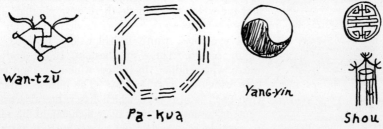

FIG. 664.

There are many more such symbols and these can be found in the "Chinese Reader's Manual" by W. F. Mayers (Shanghai 1874) and Giles' "Chinese Biographical Dictionary," among other well known books.

Thus Ming decoration comes into the story telling field. It may be said that it is a rule that *the more story a work of art has to tell in a literal sense, the less its appeal to the emotions.* This is perhaps because the immediate meaning ties down too definitely the imagination to permit *the emotional expansion which gives us the experience of aesthetic thrill.* Here again we have come across one of our technical appeals. Many artists today believe that the less meaning their work contains the more beautiful it is. This is not what we mean. There is a superabundance of such material all about us in nature such as, for instance, the clouds forming everchanging and meaningless patterns save what we ourselves read into them. Is not the great work of art, among other things, surely one which challenges us at once and then holds our attention and offers such depth of meaning that upon returning to it again and again we find that we have never fully plumbed its depths nor encompassed its entire meaning? Has it not *many stories* worked into it rather than simply one? Is it not that a work of art with *a story* has too little meaning rather than too much? Perhaps again the Chinese show real wisdom in attaching to their symbols not one meaning but several with very intricate ramifications which may never be fully unravelled even by themselves to say nothing of its being done by an imperceptive and blunt western mind.

Hung Wu or Chu Yüan Chang (1368–1398)

The overthrow of Yissun Timur, the last of the Yüan period Mongols, was accomplished by an ex-Buddhistic monk who, seeing conditions, threw off his

vestments and joined the rebel army in Central China. His name was Yüan Chang but he adopted the title name of T'ai Tsu and is better known by the reign title of Hung Wu. His capitals were in Nanking and at K'ai feng Fu. Nanking had been captured from the Mongols in 1355. It was Peking which fell in 1368 and not until 1381 did Yunan province return to the Chinese.

Ching-tê Chên had been closed from time to time during the Yüan dynasty and it was not open when Hung Wu took Nanking. But soon it was opened and the white wares made there were popular. The *Ko ku yao lun* says, "Among modern 'Jao yao' the good examples, white in color and lustrous, are highly prized. There are besides, ch'ing and tzu wares with gilding, including wine pots and wine cups which are very lovely." The phrase "ch'uang chin chê" is also used which has a literal sense of "cut or wound with metal" which might be taken to mean incised, as Hobson says. On the other hand Julien (*op. cit.*, p. 89) translates the phrase "noir-bleus et rehausses d'or" or, "dark blue wares with gilt ornament," and Bushell renders the passage as "porcelain of greenish black color pencilled with design of gold." This is typical of our difficulties in Chinese translations. Was the ware wound with metal or was metal laid on it?

Unfortunately we have no examples in America, which can be illustrated,

Fig. 665. White porcelain vase of almost Han form of *san ts'ai* (three-color) ware. Slightly mottled turquoise ground is hard and uncrackled, possibly felspathic, like bowl found at Chün Chou and is probably of Hung Wu period. Other colors yellow, green, aubergine. Ht. 22″. O. C. Raphael Coll.

of the wares of this period. Hobson lists a small number including a small bottle with relief decoration and of white porcelain mounted with silver which bears the arms of Louis the Great, King of Hungary (1326–1382), a pair of doubtful bowls in the Ezekial Collection of white with blue decoration of boys at play and having fire cracks where the foot-rim joins the body, a thin rounded foot and glaze under the base with a single ring for mark. These probably are later, two pieces in the British Museum one of which is Japanese and the other a bowl with landscape in bright blue and a border in reserved blue. Finally there is a large vase of the "three color type," which we illustrate and which he shows in color in the "Wares of the Ming Dynasty" (Pl. 2) and which the Chinese who owned it has incised under the foot with "Hung Wu nein nei yung chih ch'i" or "vessel made for use in the interior (or in the palace) in the Hung Wu period." The turquoise ground of this piece Mr. Hobson says appears hard and not like the later Ming and K'ang Hsi pieces. It may or may not be of the period.

Chien Wên or Yun Wên (1399–1402)

Chien Wên whose dynastic title was Hui Ti was young, had bad advisors and was led into a long conflict with his powerful uncle, Prince of Yen. The results were the horrible massacres of Nanking and the taking of the throne in 1403.

Yung Lo or Ti (1403–1424)

The throne was taken through a sea of blood and the capital moved to Peking in 1421, but the Prince of Yen was a good builder as well as conqueror. Most of the palaces of Peking may be attributed to him. He it was who built the "Porcelain Pagoda" at Nanking, though we must add that it is largely stoneware. It was during this time that the famous eunuch Chêng Ho went on an expedition into the Indian Ocean and visited Ceylon and Sumatra. In 1408 in revenge for an insult offered an envoy from China, the Chinese army invaded Ceylon and carried off King Vijaya Bahu IV and for 30 years tribute was paid to China. Thus we see another connection with the Near East for the island had previously been visited by the Arabs.

The kilns at Ching-tê Chên were continuously operated and the *T'ao-lu* tells us that a thick and heavy ware was made as well as the very thin ware known as "t'o t'ai" or bodiless and with embossed "kung yang" decoration and also red decoration "hsien hung." The *Po wu yao lan* says that cups were made with broad mouth and contracted waist to fit the hand, with "sandy foot and smooth bottom." The best were supposed to have two lions rolling balls drawn inside and also a six character mark of the period. Some had a four character mark reading, "as fine as rice," while others had mandarin ducks or flowers. There were also cups decorated on the outside with deep blue. It also says that the wares were costly even in Ming times and that coarse copies were made toward the end of the dynasty.

Hobson speaks of a bowl in the Franks Collection, British Museum similar in shape to the one I illustrate from the Metropolitan Museum but with five clawed dragons and clouds in slip and an incised mark of Yung Lo in archaic

FIG. 666. One of rare Yung Lo period (1403–1424) Ming bowls of white porcelain in shape and size exactly like that of a Ting yao of Sung period, having the same six radial indented lines and notches at rim. Dia. 8¾". Altman Coll. Metropolitan Mus. of Art.

FIG. 667. Fine white porcelain vase having Yung Lo mark in underglaze blue under foot and possibly of that period. Ht. 6". Ex D. Abbes Coll.

FIG. 668. White porcelain dish found in Korean tomb. Pure white though stained at unglazed rim. Glaze pure white, usually not crazed. Note radial lines on bottom and "loaf shaped" rise in center also relief flowers inside. Dia. 5¾". John Platt—Warren E. Cox Coll.

characters on the bottom inside. The example which I show from the Abbes Collection was sold for Yung Lo by Bluett & Sons, Ltd., London who are very careful dealers. I have not seen it but Mr. Abbes tells me it was very thin and fine. Note that the glaze is crackled. Hannover says that in the Hamburg Museum is a wine goblet (probably a "stem cup") decorated with dragons and clouds in the same technique as the one cited by Hobson and with a *Ch'ien Lung mark* (1736–1796). Other copies were, of course, made in Yung Chêng times (1722–1736), and there are modern copies from both China and Japan.

The similarity in shape of these bowls to the early and finer Korai ones may have been developed through those from Ting Chou or may have been a direct influence for there was considerable intercourse between Korea and China. In any event one need only look at the Ting bowl and the Korai one to see how very much alike they are in form.

Another type found in Korean tombs are only about 4 to 5 inches in diameter, have steep slanting sides, a flat bottom and a small rather deep foot-rim in some cases and in some no foot-rim. When the foot-rim is omitted the bottoms are concave making what might be the "loaf shape" inside or a somewhat convex bottom. The body is white and high fired and the glaze is pure white. Faintly suggested relief flowers are in the center of the bottom and the rims and a patch under the base are left unglazed. These may or may not be Korean wares, seem later than Sung and just possibly might be one of these early period Ming wares, and possibly of this period.

In the blue and white wares Mr. Hobson cites another bowl in the Ezekial Collection which is soft looking, has a sandy paste resembling "soft paste" and is painted outside with a landscape, much as are several fakes, and with a close diaper of spirals inside and the Yung Lo mark in greyish blue. The *Shih wu kan chu* mentions the color having been used in the period and calls it "Su-ma-ni" blue. It mentions also that Sumatra was a place from which the blue was transhipped in the next reign and it is possible that some might have come in the spoils which Chêng Ho brought back with him. Hannover speaks of a bowl at Dresden which is decorated in blue with a poem and landscape illustrating it. This is a thick and rather impure porcelain. It also has the mark.

Other bowls are painted in blue with a boy at play on the inside while the outside is coated with coral-red (iron red) glaze over which is pencilled delicate scroll and floral forms in gold. But the *Po wu yao lan* speaks of "hsien hung" wares which we take to mean underglaze red. In the British Museum is an underglaze red bowl in a 16th century leather case made in Venice showing that it is at least earlier than that. It has the mark "tan kuei" meaning literary success. Mr. Hobson makes this general observation, "The base of early" (He refers to the Ming period.) "bowls was often conical or convex underneath in contrast to those of the Chia Ching period which were convex inside; and this conical base is sometimes observable on red bowls, as in the case of one specimen in the British Museum which, in point of fact, bears the Yung Lo mark."

The "Porcelain Pagoda" had some tiles in the lower part and the ware is white and compact but granular when fractured. The glaze is pure and white while the body where exposed is pinkish. As a matter of fact these are also the characteristics of the bowls already mentioned and found in Korean tombs. Rücker-Embden reports in his notes to Ernst Zimmermann's "Chinesisches Porzellän," Munich 1915, p. 22, that he saw in Peking a fragment of tile reported to have come from this building and which had a translucent underglaze blue, and he says it was undoubtedly a porcelain and not stoneware.

We have no example in America and it makes us wish that some sort of exchange might be set up so that museums could swap duplicates.

HUNG HSI OR KAO CHIH (1425)

Nothing much that interests us happened in the reign of Kao Chih who took the dynastic title of Jen Tsung, except that Chêng Ho is reported to have gone on to Arabia and landed at Jiddah about 50 miles from Mecca.

HSÜAN TÊ OR CHAN CHI (1426–1435)

Chan Chi had the title of Hsüan Tsung and his was the most enlightened reign of the entire dynasty. He would have been an eminent scholar and statesman even had he not been Emperor. The bronzes and lacquer were of fine quality as well as the porcelains. If it had not been for the great Sung dynasty we might here point to the highest pinnacle of Chinese culture but, alas, the Sung period was never again to be equalled.

Ching-tê Chên was highly active and orders were also given to some 58 separate kilns, most of which were outside the jurisdiction of the "Ying-tsao-so-ch'êng" who was placed in charge of the Imperial factory itself. It is possible now to assign pieces to this reign with some assurance, and more material is available though it is costly and rare, and many fakes exist.

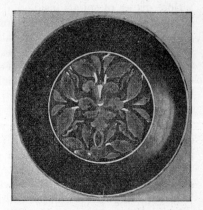

FIG. 669. Ming, Hsüan Tê (A.D. 1426–1435) bowl with greenish white glaze and underglaze blue and copper red. Inside is medallion at bottom with fish leaping from water, surrounded by border of fish, crayfish, crab and marine vegetation. Dia. 7". Metropolitan Mus. of Art.

FIG. 670. One of pair of Ming, Hsüan Tê dishes with deep and vivid underglaze blue flowers and foliage surrounded by iron red overglaze ground which allows small spots of greenish white glaze to be seen here and there. Dia. 7". Metropolitan Mus. of Art.

The *Po wu yao lan* states that the reign was famous for the underglaze red and also for Mohammedan blue. Also the greatest development of the "san ts'ai" or "three color" ware was made. The first place and highest rating was given to the porcelain stem cups of pure white and decorated with three fish in underglaze red, but there were also large bowls and small "cinnibar pots" which were "red as the sun." Added to these forms were pickle pots, small pots with basket covers and handles in the form of bamboo joints, and it is stated that all of these were unknown in more ancient times. In the "wu ts'ai" or five color ware there were flat sided jars with basket covers, round pots with flanged mouth for preserving honey, incense trays, vases and dishes. The white cups having the character "t'an" meaning "altar" engraved inside are known as "altar cups" though whether they were used for this purpose we do not know for sure. The material for these is refined and the ware thick and the form "beautiful enough to be used as elegant vases in the scholar's room." There were also, we learn, white cups for tea "with rounded body and convex base with thread-like foot, bright and lustrous like jade, and with finely engraved dragon and phoenix designs, which are scarcely inferior to the altar cups." At the bottom are the characters "ta Ming Hsüan Tê nien chih" meaning "made in the Hsüan Tê reign of the great Ming Dynasty." It also tells us that the glaze is uneven like orange peel "chü p'i." Further reference is made to the "chicken skin" and "palm eye" spots.

Three terms were applied to the red: "chi hung" seeming inclusive and "hsien hung" or "bright red" and "pao shih hung" or "precious stone red" the two divisions. None of these refers to overglaze red of the iron type and I do not agree with Hobson that the Chinese used "pao shih hung" to designate the red used in "painted design" or that "chi hung" designated the red "covering large areas." This is an entirely arbitrary meaning affixed entirely by himself. The *Po wu yao lan* states, "For these" (referring to pao shih hung) "they used a powder made of red precious stones 'pao shih' from the West to paint the fish forms, and from the body 'ku' there rose up in relief in the firing the precious brilliance of the fresh red ravishing the eye." In this connection Mr. Hobson states in "The Wares of the Ming Dynasty" (p. 29)— "The red precious stones from the west, rubies or cornelians, added in the form of powder, were traditionally supposed to have served this purpose, though of course *the color of the resultant red had nothing to do with the red of the*

Fig. 672. Hsüan Tê Ming dish with decoration in underglaze blue and copper-red on white ground. Dia. 10½". Metropolitan Mus. of Art.

Fig. 671. Hsüan Tê bottle decorated in underglaze copper red. Ht. 5⅛". Metropolitan Mus. of Art.

Fig. 673. Vase with Hsüan Tê mark with incised design, white glaze which shows on inside, and yellow enamel all over. Probably Ming, though there are many imitations of this sort. Ht. 14". Metropolitan Mus. of Art.

stones." The underlining is mine. In the "Later Ceramic Wares of China" he says (p. 52) "The Chinese accounts of the Ming underglaze red all allude to the 'red precious stones' as an ingredient of the glaze. Probably it was cornaline (ma nao)" (The *Century Dictionary* says, "Cornaline is an obsolete form of the word carnelian or cornelian.") and he continues "and, *though it can have had no possible effect on the red colour which is solely due to reduced copper oxide, it may well have added brilliance to the glaze.*" But again in "The Wares of the Ming Dynasty" (p. 62) he says ". . . certain hard stones (cornelian among them) were pulverized and mixed with the glaze. *Though not in any sense a colouring agent, it is not impossible that such powder might in some way have helped the development of the copper red colour.*"

One naturally wonders exactly what he does mean. One thinks of garnets as also possibly the stones used. And one comes to the conclusion that he was guessing and not frank enough to say so.

Concerning the use of garnets we may say, that alamandine, the precious garnet, is an iron-aluminium stone which breaks up "incongruently" or into other compounds when melted, including iron oxides some of which we know tend to produce a red color. Early experiments in producing the synthetic ruby were interesting to us for it is recorded that Fremy and Hautefeuille fused oxides of lead, aluminum and chromium in a large crucible for about seven to eight days in "a furnace used for glass making" and masses of imperfect and very thin rubies resulted. Certainly there might be a possibility that either ruby or garnet might influence the color of the red glaze.

Mr. A. L. Hetherington did the proper thing and consulted a chemist, Sir Herbert Jackson, who is also quoted by Hobson, and who says, "It is difficult to reconcile this well-established tradition with the actual scientific reactions which take place in the formation of a copper-red glaze. The colour is produced by the aggregation of minute particles of copper under suitable conditions which it is not necessary to elaborate. Suffice it to say that the best colour will not be produced if the amount of copper present exceeds a certain quantity, viz. about 5% or less. An excess of copper will produce a red or brown sealingwax effect instead of a brilliant clear red. In actual practice the copper is introduced into the glaze in the form of its oxide, and under the reducing atmosphere of the kiln the oxide is robbed of its oxygen and reduced to the metal itself in a very finely divided state. This process of 'reduction' would no doubt be assisted by the presence of a reducing agent such as ferrous oxide, and conceivably a ferruginous earth might act in this way. But the tradition of introducing powdered rubies or cornelian could not be explained on these grounds. These stones consist largely of alumina and silica respectively. The presence of these substances in excess in a copper glaze will tend to retard or even to prevent the copper coming out, or 'striking' as it is technically called. Alumina, therefore, in some excess, and to some extent this is true of silica also, would counteract a superabundant quantity of copper which otherwise might have produced the undesirable opaque effect. Some such explanation as this is the only one which provides a scientific foundation for this oft-quoted tradition." Here we perhaps approach the truth and by all means we should accept the Chinese statement.

The speaking of "minute particles" of copper reminds me of a physical and not chemical effect which may have a bearing. Some years ago I studied with the famous still-life painter Emil Carlsen and he showed me that no mixing of color would produce a deep and luminous red. The method of obtaining it was to lay over a pure white ground layer upon layer thinly applied of transparent rose madder. The depth depends upon the number of glazes given and they strangely produce an effect almost like the sang de boeuf porcelain. He explained that the light penetrates such a glazed surface and is reflected back by the white ground. One may think of white light going through the glaze and reaching the white ground already changed to a red color and on reflecting back becoming even redder.

Ming, Hsüan Tê stem cup called by museum "sacrificial cup" though I do not know why. Slightly concave unglazed foot, greenish glaze and dark red fish. Edge of glaze at foot shows yellowish color. Potting slightly irregular. Ht. 4". Metropolitan Mus. of Art.

Stem-cup with three fish in deep red. Base unglazed and bears Hsüan Tê mark inside. Ht. 3". Eumorfopoulos Coll.

Stem cup with Wan Li mark, aubergine fruits and dragons lightly incised in the body inside. Mark is incised as well as painted in blue. Glaze shows yellowish brown where it meets body clay at foot. Gives every evidence of being actually Wan Li and is rare example for I know of no other of period. Ht. 4". Warren E. Cox Coll.

HSÜAN TÊ AND WAN LI STEM-CUPS

PLATE 136

Hsiang in his album shows 12 examples of the red. Some are covered all over, some incised with designs and some painted either with lumpy designs or finely lined ones. One odd example shows the red used with blue and white and etched design. Another shows it combined with brown and green enamels.

Most of the stem cups in modern collections are actually of the Yung Chêng period (1722–1736) when many Ming pieces were copied by Imperial order, but Mr. Hobson feels that the three in the Eumorfopoulos, the Vernon Wethered and the Percival David collections are correct. The glaze is as the Chinese say, "like congealed fat," or like, "new fallen snow," which is especially descriptive as it has also slight undulations. The shape is said to have been derived from a Han form in carved jade but it might just as well have come from a bronze form similar to the one I show. I also illustrate one from my own collection which has a Wan Li (1573–1619) mark and which well may be later, for a comparison of the shape. This piece of mine has two dragons lightly incised in the biscuit before glazing and the fruits are of an aubergine tone rather than red, showing difficulties with the tricky copper red glaze. The Ming ones of our present period also had three fruits instead of the three fish, at times. In each case the color is so heaped up that it stands in definite relief. The only difference between the Eumorfopoulos piece and that de-

FIG. 674. Ming bowl with Hsüan Tê mark and of the period, with greenish white pure ground and deep red fish. Dia. 6″. Metropolitan Mus. of Art.

FIG. 675. Han bronze stem-cup. May have suggested porcelain ones. Ht. 5″. Warren E. Cox Coll.

FIG. 676. Lung ch'üan bowl of gray porcelain, burnt red at foot, with green glaze and copper red (appearing brown) decoration of two fishes. Dia. 6⅛″. Metropolitan Mus. of Art.

FIG. 677. Hsüan Tê, Ming stem-cup. Dragon horses, dashing waves, rocks in underglaze blue. Ht. 2¾″. Dia. 2¾″. Metropolitan Mus. of Art.

scribed by Hsiang is that in the former the mark is painted in blue on the inside and in the latter the mark is incised under the flat base of the foot. The other two mentioned agree with the Eumorfopoulos one except that the last one is only partly covered in on the bottom showing the hollow of the stem. The stem of mine is left entirely open at the bottom. It will also be noticed on comparison that Hsiang's is a little more chunky and less graceful in form, but whether this would constitute any definite difference I am not prepared to say. In point of fact there are two other examples in the Eumorfopoulos Collection #D4 and #D5 decorated in blue on white and in blue and white with red added, both of which carry the Hsüan Tê mark and both of which are much like Hsiang's form, the first not even having a flare to the lip. The later ones tend to become larger and heavier but are not so chunky as these.

The only example of single color red which satisfies Mr. Hobson is a small water pot for the writer's table and is in the Oppenheim Collection. It is a flattened oblate form with no base and no lip. The glaze is said to have a faintly bluish tint. It is also soft and rather dull and there are small spaces where the glaze has failed to fill in, and also "palm-eye" spots inside which are said to be signs of authenticity, but then my later bowl also has these. The mark in four characters in a square frame is faintly incised in the paste beneath the glaze of the bottom.

ENAMEL ON GLAZE WARES

Yellow and green enamel was used with iron red on the glaze in Sung wares of Tz'u Chou type. Hsiang shows a pagoda model with green roofs, yellow doors and red railings which he calls "wu ts'ai fu sê" or "applied colors." All of our authorities seem to compare the thick enamels of the Hsüan Tê period with the thin and more perfected ones capable of being used for very delicate painting in the Ch'êng Hua period (1465–1487). Mr. Hobson mentions a cut down vase in the B.M. which is square and decorated with a design of cranes and lotuses in "strong enamel colours and underglaze blue and has the Hsüan Tê mark in a fine Mohammedan blue." He also mentions the Winkworth one with well carried out design in red, green, brownish yellow and typical Ming turquoise blue, and says the enamels stand out thickly from the glaze while under the base is the Hsüan Tê mark together with the cyclical date corresponding with 1433 of our era.

I now submit an interesting piece from my own collection. The body is of fine, smooth texture and white. It has all the qualities of a true Ming body. The glaze is of copper red rather light in tone and more nearly a deep "peach bloom" color showing considerable of the mottling seen in that glaze. On one side the glaze was thinner and therefore lighter whether by accident or purpose we cannot tell but over this area is a beautiful painting of three immortals descending on clouds to a palace floating on a choppy sea. The technique of the painting of the waves is similar to that of the blue and white stem cups except that it is better and it has much the treatment that was copied from such paintings by

FIG. 678. Late Ming vase with Hsüan Tê mark and red glaze like that of fish on white bowls or "peach bloom" rather than of sang-de-boeuf type. Decoration in translucent enamels of green, yellow, white. Mark, though dull blue and generally Ming in character, does not correspond with handwriting of Hsüan Tê period. Ht. 20½". Warren E. Cox Coll.

Kōétsu, Sotatsu and Kōrin in later times in Japan. Under the foot is a strong Hsüan Tê mark in deep blue. The glaze inside and on the bottom is pitted with the "palm eye" spots and is of a greenish white. The potting is generally heavier than any K'ang Hsi vases of similar size.

It is likely that all the colored glazes we know as belonging to the Ming period were employed either as single colors or under enamel decoration during this reign. A dish in the Eumorfopoulos Collection #D214 is described as having dragons faintly traced in white slip on the inside and covered on the outside with a deep but brilliant blue glaze. It has the six character and double ring mark and was sent from China as an example of the listed "chi ch'ing" or "sky clearing blue." Another in the same collection is a celadon bowl with three feet #D215 and it has a four character mark in double ring. Also #D61 has pale underglaze blue and some green. I know of no examples in America.

MOHAMMEDAN BLUE

Used with enamel colors or for the marks when they were not incised, or for a general covering color rarely, was the deep blue. The *T'ao lu* tells us that "su-ni-p'o" blue was used for painting up to the reign of Ch'êng Hua (1465) when the supply ran out and only the common blues were available. It further tells us that the blue and white of the Hsüan Tê ranked first. Variously called "su-ni-p'o," "su-p'o-ni," and "su-ma-ni" probably with reference to the place it was thought to come from, or "hui hui ch'ing" meaning Mohammedan blue, or again as "wu-ming-i" in the Sung period, this color is supposed on good authority to have come from Western Asia in early times of the T'ang dynasty, and to have been increasingly imported since then. The Ming Annals tell us that in 1426, 1430, 1433 and 1434 "hui ch'ing" was brought as tribute from Sumatra. However, it must not be supposed that this blue was used on all wares of the period and, in truth, there is some little confusion concerning it, for some said it was pale as contrasted with the Chia Ching (1522–1566) blue while others say it was "deep and thickly piled and very lovely." The answer is probably that it was used both ways. We also learn that it was difficult to handle because it would run in firing and, therefore, it was mixed with the regular Chinese blue, which was dull and lifeless.

In *Hsiang's Album* are seven examples. Five show the blue confined to pencilled borders while the other two show dragons in clouds and "dragon pines." The stem cup in the Metropolitan Museum and others in England are all rather delicate and in contrast with them is the pilgrim bottle in the Franks Col., B.M., which is decorated with a heavy branch of peaches and foliage painted heavily in a blackish cobalt blue which shows inclination to run. This vase bears no mark but has a box bearing the seal of no less a person than Mr. Hsiang himself! This is not very conclusive evidence and, in fact pieces in such boxes are always suspect, but in this case the box is taken seriously in England at least. There are also the often shown "Swaythling" and "Trenchard" bowls mounted in silver rims and handles in the 16th century in England. These are painted in dark outlines and filled in with dark blue.

Wine ewers were made for the Mohammedan market, and on these the glaze is rather thick and bubbly, of greenish cast and inclined to run while the blue is mottled light and dark. Finally at Old Fostat in Egypt was found the bottom of a bowl now in the B.M. and it has the mark in four characters and a medallion of kylin playing painted in a greyish blue.

During the Chia Ching period a certain Mr. Ts'ui made wares, we are told, which some thought superior even to those of Hsüan Tê and Ch'eng Hua periods and could be distinguished only because they were larger than the originals. There is a deep bowl in the Salting Col. (Pl. 16, *Wares of the Ming Dynasty*) which may be by his hand. Mr. Ts'ui started a long line of imitators beginning just 100 years after the originals were made and extending down to the present. During the Yung Chêng and Ch'ien Lung times a type was made usually painted with lotus scrolls and these were given a flat wash first and then darker blue was heaped up over it. The same technique occurs on what appear to be originals and those of the Chêng Tê period (1506–1521). Of course Japan and other countries also took a bit of trouble in trying to make copies, but once a few of the real pieces are handled the immediate difference can always be seen.

Fig. 679. Hsüan Tê Ming dynasty jar with strong underglaze blue of Mohammedan type. Metropolitan Mus. of Art.

Fig. 680. Double walled "Three color" jar with outer wall pierced and modeled. Cobalt, turquoise, yellow, straw, green and aubergine. The inside yellow green. Early Ming, probably Hsüan Tê. Ht. 11½". Bequest of Edmund C. Converse. Metropolitan Mus. of Art.

The "san ts'ai" or three color porcelains of this reign are numerous but the rich westerner's demand for color makes them fairly expensive. The *Po wu yao lan* says, "Again there are the beautiful barrel shaped seats, some with openwork ground, the designs filled in with colors, gorgeous as cloud brocades: others with solid ground filled with colors and engraved floral designs so beautiful and brilliant as to dazzle the eye: both sorts have deep green background." Others have a blue ground, filled in with designs in colors, like ornaments carved in lapis lazuli "shih ch'ing," according to Bushell's translation. Generally our present authorities are contented in dividing these wares into Early Ming, Middle and Late. However, this reign undoubtedly produced many of them.

Other Hsüan Tê types are as follows:

1.—Gilt on white as seen on a dish in the B.M. with thick, lustrous greenish glaze and gilt decoration of lotus scrolls similar to those seen on the red bowls. This has the mark in blue.

2.—Wares with, "crackled grounds like ice," and supposed to rival Kuan and Ju yao. This may include celadon, Ko or even Ying Ching types.

3.—The *Chiang hsi t'ung chih* according to Bushell's translation tells of a porcelain with yellow ground which Mr. Hobson assumes to be blue and white with yellow painted in the background.

4.—Again the same source tells of pots made for fighting crickets, which were painted gold and these are spoken of in the collected works of Wu Mei-ts'un.

CH'ÊNG HUA OR CHIEN SHEN (1465–1487)

The intervening 30 years between the end of the Hsüan Tê and the beginning of the Ch'êng Hua reign was somewhat of a mix up, for Ying Tsung, if we call him by his title name, was a weak individual and succeeded in being defeated and shamefully captured by the Mongols. His brother Tai Tsung ruled for 6 years and then the less popular brother was returned to the throne. The periods are known as Chêng T'ung (1436–1449), Ching T'ai (1450–1456) (known chiefly for fine cloisonné) and T'ien Shun (1465–1487). Then the son took the title of Hsien Tsung and at once fell under the influence of his chief concubine, Wang Kuei-fei, and an ambitious eunuch, Wang Chih, but at least the Great Wall was repaired, the Grand Canal deepened and porcelain and literature were again encouraged.

The free use of the mark by imitators shows us that they had heard of the importance of this period, and the *Po wu yao lan* says, "In the highest class of Ch'êng ware it is impossible to surpass the stem cups with spreading mouth and flattened sides decorated in colors with grape vine pattern. They excel the Hsüan Tê cups in workmanship. Next to these come the wedding cups 'ch'uan pei' decorated with plants and grass insects, which are delightful; the tub-shaped cups with hen and chickens; the wine cups with figure subjects and lotuses (or the translation may mean wine cups shaped like lotuses with figure subjects for decoration); shallow cups with the five sacrificial vessels 'wu kung'; small cups with plant designs and insects; blue-painted cups thin as paper; small flat dishes for chopsticks, painted-in colors; incense boxes and all manner of small jars, all extremely fine and pleasing. In my judgment the Ch'êng yao blue and white does not equal that of the Hsüan yao; but the colored ware of the Hsüan court is inferior to that of the Hsien court." (It will be remembered that Hsien Tsung was the posthumous title of Ch'êng Hua.) It continues, "The reasons are that the blue of Hsüan ware is su-ni-p'o blue and this was exhausted after that reign, so that in the Ch'êng Hua period only the ordinary class blue was used, and that the colors of the Hsüan ware

are deep and thick and piled on and consequently not very beautiful, while those of the Ch'êng Hua are rather thin and subdued in color and produce a pictorial effect. This I consider a well grounded opinion." (Translation by Bushell.)

Although it is related that the last of the envoys came from Sumatra in 1486, nevertheless there is no evidence that they brought the blue on every call and there seems sufficient evidence to the point that Mohammedan blue was not being used. We know of no pieces with it of the period although certainly a number of things *seem* to be of this period and still have it, though the majority do not.

Among known examples of the period are: the cup in the B.M. decorated with imaginary animals on a dashing wave ground and similar to the one in the Metropolitan Museum, the first having a Ch'êng Hua and the second a Hsüan Tê mark. Another example in the same London museum was presented by Li Van Ch'ing of which Hobson wrote, "as its attribution is supported by one who is reputed the best judge in China, we feel safe in regarding it as an extremely likely specimen." It is of fine white paste with thick glaze of greenish tinge and is decorated in pure silvery blue with five figures, and bears the Ch'êng Hua mark. The "palm eye" spots are present and it seems that the glaze is full of microscopic bubbles. Mr. Hobson says the texture is like that of much handled marble as is that also of the Eumorfopoulos Col. #D8. The blue is said to be indigo in the latter. The base is convex beneath and marked with the six character mark.

Hsiang shows a number of colored wares which are yellow, green and aubergine applied apparently both over a glaze and direct on the biscuit. He also shows a cup much like the "chicken cups" but with geese in flight over water dotted with sprays of ling ching fungus. The "chicken cups" are described by the *Po wu yao lan* as "thin and diaphanous as a cicada's wing, so that the finger nail shows clearly through them," and also, "The design is of cock and hen instinct with life and motion, reminding one in every detail of a water color picture by one of the court artists of the Sung Dynasty. The flower is in the style of Huang Ch'üan." Hannover comments, though I do not know from what source, "Even towards the end of the Ming period a 'chicken cup' or 'chi kang' was regarded in China as a treasure, for which a price of $100,000 cash was not too high." Unfortunately we have no examples in Europe or America that I know of.

Examples of the heavier ware are to be found in the Hainhofer Cabinet at Upsala—and an egg-shaped box mentioned by Hobson as in the Oppenheim Collection which is still thin and is decorated with rocks and grapes in green, yellow and red.

Still heavier are the baluster shaped vases of the type of one in the B.M. with greyish crackle glaze and bold lotus scroll in leaf green, yellow, bluish green and manganese added to a little underglaze blue. The potting of this piece is obviously thick and the base is flat and unglazed except for a sunk panel in which is the mark of the period in blue. This cannot be anything but an Early Ming piece and therefore of this period, for it could not very well be earlier. Mr. Hannover does not agree; he says, "To

Left: Vase similar to Eumo. Coll. # D64 and also marked Ch'êng Hua. Greyish white crackled glaze with floral design in underglaze blue and enamels. Ht. 18½". H. B. Harris Coll.

Center: Vase with turquoise ground and design in green and yellow with brown outlines, probably Chêng Tê or later judging by more advanced technique and more naturalistic style. Ht. 17½". Grandidier Coll. (Louvre)

Right: San ts'ai or "three color" vase formerly from Parrish-Watson and now belonging to Bernard Gimbel. A preponderance of unevenly applied turquoise glaze, probably of Wan Li period.

Left: Late Ming "three color" vase with rough foot rim but grooved to fit stand contrary to R. L. Hobson's suggestion that this occurs only in K'ang Hsi specimens. Ground, aubergine; flowers, straw and turquoise. Ht. 19". Metropolitan Mus. of Art.

Center: Late Ming porcelain vase of "three color" type but design only in turquoise, white and black. Ht. 15". Metropolitan Mus. of Art.

Right: Late Ming "three color" vase with turquoise ground and aubergine and straw colored flowers. Ht. 19". Metropolitan Mus. of Art.

SEQUENCE OF VASES FROM CH'ÊNG HUA REIGN

PLATE 137

attach definitive weight to such loose identifications is, however, doubtless to overestimate our present-day knowledge as to the earliest true porcelain. As a rule, we should doubtless content ourselves with the definition 'Early Ming' for such articles as those here in question." He is referring to those cited by

FIG. 681. Ming, Ch'êng Hua (1465–1487) jar with white ground, two pale green enamels, yellow, pale uneven iron red and aubergine. Ht. 4½″. Metropolitan Mus. of Art.

FIG. 682. Ch'êng Hua blue and white jar. Ht. 4¼″. Metropolitan Mus. of Art.

both Zimmerman and Hobson with whom I am inclined to agree definitely because of the following course of reasoning:

1.—It is reasonable to assume that when one period copied the mark of another period it did not occur, as a rule, at least until that period had acquired

FIG. 683. Ming, Ch'êng Hua beaker or *ku*, after bronze form, with white ground, opaque yellow-green, clear yellow, palest aubergine and dull iron red decoration. Ht. 8½″. Metropolitan Mus. of Art.

FIG. 684. Ch'êng Hua blue and white vase having charming quality of delicate drawing typical of this period. Metropolitan Mus. of Art.

sufficient antiquity to become interesting. Usually a few hundred years had to go past before a mark would become interesting. And even Mr. Ts'ui made his copies of Hsüan Tê and Ch'êng Hua ware in the Chia Ching period some 35 to 75 years later.

2.—Thus these vases *and marks particularly* would probably not have been copied much before 1525 which would make them no longer "Early Ming."

3.—The marks could not very well have been used earlier than the period designated unless the potters were clairvoyant.

Therefore, I see no reason for not stating that they are of the period and I think Hannover is being a little too cautious. We must remember that it is the truth we are after and from that viewpoint *it is quite as bad to make a late attribution as it is to make a too early one.* All too often an example is given

FIG. 685. Numbers D63, D64 and D65 of Eumorfopoulos Coll. D64, crackled vase on left, bears a Ch'êng Hua mark in square frame in the underglaze blue. The other two are probably Chêng Tê (1506–1521) or later. Hts. 12¼″, 14¼″, 15½″.

the general label of Ming when it obviously cannot belong at all in any of the reigns of the dynasty each of which had certain more or less definite characteristics and some of which are fairly exactly defined. If a piece does not fit into these characteristics it should be suspect at once; if it cannot be placed in a reign, it *may* be a later Ming copy but is 90% more likely to be a Yung Chêng copy, a Jap copy or a perfectly modern commercial copy. Oddities do occur but, if none of the standard books seem to describe them, the collector had better be very, very careful and quite prepared to gamble on a 100 to 1 shot.

The B.M. vase of the sort we are discussing is very similar to another which also bears the mark and belongs to H. B. Harris (See Pl. 17, *The Wares of the Ming Dynasty*.) while the Benson one has a Hsüan Tê mark probably indicating that it was a type that carried through Early Ming times. The Eumorfopoulos Collection has one #D63 without mark, another #D64 that has the Ch'êng Hua mark and finally #D65 without mark. A perfect one (Pl. 18, *The Wares of the Ming Dynasty*) from the Grandidier Collection has again no mark and is decorated with a lotus on turquoise ground. It seems obvious that these vases started in the Hsüan Tê period with a crackle ground and continued so into our present Ch'êng Hua period toward the end of which or shortly afterwards the style changed to include a completely enameled ground like the other "three color" wares. The shape, somewhat elongated as to neck and then with the addition of handles which tend to become more and more ornate, was continued in Late Ming days and quite possibly into K'ang Hsi times with a similar enamel treatment. With more study this may form a series valuable for comparisons. For the present I should not place the enameled ground ones any earlier than the Chêng Tê reign (1506–1521).

It is interesting to note in passing that few of these vases have escaped the break at the flaring and unstructural lip-rim.

Red ornamented wares are mentioned by the poet Kao Tan-jên who says in one passage, "ruby red bowls and cinnabar dishes were cleverly made and fine and more costly than Sung ware." The larger stem cup of the Eumorfopoulos Collection has been suggested as of this reign and it has a hollow foot, is unmarked and the bowl is more expanding. This is borne out by #55 in *Hsiang's Album* which also has a rim "more expanded." This would also agree with the vase forms the lips of which are of wider flare.

The *T'ao-shuo* speaks of "wine cups with high-flaming silver candle lighting up red beauty; brocade-design cups; cups decorated with swings, Dragon-boat Procession, famous scholars and playing children; cups with trellis-frame of grapes, with fragrant plants, fish and water weeds, gourds and aubergine fruit, the 8 Buddhist Emblems, 'yu-po-lo' flowers (a dark colored lotus) and Indian lotus scrolls." Some of these are explained by Kao Tan-jên's verses:

FIG. 686. Double gourd bottle of "three color" Ming ware with deep blue ground and decoration in yellow, aubergine and turquoise outlined in white. Ht. 19⅛". Ex Warren E. Cox Coll. Jacob Rupert Bequest. Metropolitan Mus. of Art.

1.—The "high flaming silver candle" is a picture of a girl looking at "hai-t'ang" (cydonia) blossoms by candle light.

2.—The swing design shows boys and girls in swings.

3.—The "Famous scholars" are usually Chou Mao-shu with his beloved lotus, and T'ao Yüan-ming with his chrysanthemum.

4.—The five children are usually under a pine tree in the "Playing children" design although not always and this is undoubtedly the basis of the "Prince of Hirado" design of Japan.

It is interesting that with the breaking away from the old traditional bronze forms and the inclination toward more flamboyancy, naturalism as seen in gourd and melon shapes became more marked. Of course these are not new forms, but so naturally are they done now that it seems that the potters went

back and took another look at nature. If we are to credit *Hsiang's Album* the
results are pretty terrible.

HUNG CHIH OR YU T'ANG (1488–1505)

Yu T'ang's unnotable career was under the title of Hsiao Tsung. The
appointment of the director at Ching-tê Chên was abolished in 1486 and discontinued until 1505, but some work was done and the reign is known for its
yellow wares. Also it continued the enamel decorated ones. Hsiang shows:
1.—an incense burner of archaic form in a yellow like that of a steamed
chestnut "cheng li," 2.—a wine cup shaped like a sunflower "k'uei hua" and

FIG. 687. Ming, Hung Chih (A.D. 1488–
1505) jar and cover of heavily potted porcelain with pale greenish, faintly crackled,
glassy ground decorated with dark muddy
red, dirty yellow and speckled green. Obviously not made under imperial supervision.
Ht. 6½". Metropolitan Mus. of Art.

FIG. 688. Pair of Hung Chih blue and
white vases given as definite attribution by
museum, but recalls certain Sung Tz'u Chou
wares. Shape a little more accentuated at
waist and drawing a little more crude. Hts.
c. 9¾". Metropolitan Mus. of Art.

yellow outside with white inside, 3.—a spirit jar of the bronze "yu" form also
yellow, and 4.—a wine pot of gourd form with yellow body of pale tint "chiao
hung" with the stalk and leaves which form the handle and spout in brown
and green respectively.

We have had a yellow glaze since T'ang times of course and the Ming glaze
though somewhat harder was not much clearer as a rule. The yellow enamel
was also dirty and so transparent as to partake of whatever color was under
it. Only occasionally do we find a piece which seems correct in all respects
and is yet clear and bright. Mr. Hobson cites a dish with the mark which has
a ground of "soft yellow" the glaze looking as though particles of yellow were
suspended in it and as though it would otherwise be transparent. He says,
"These particles are naturally thinner on the higher edges of the piece and
more thickly accumulated where the glaze has been pooled in the hollow parts,
so that we get a graded rather than uniform coat of color."

The two plates shown are similar to another in the V. & A. Mus. which has
the mark of the period. They have fairly strong underglaze blue decoration
with the ground of yellow painted in afterwards and given a second firing.

The glaze has the same light "chicken skin" texture as seen on the Hsüan Tê cups.

This same sort of rich, pure glaze is found on beautifully potted pieces of clear white, slightly browned at the edge inside the foot-rim and of very slightly greenish tint. There is an example in the Franks Collection which is

FIG. 689. Plates called 16th cent. but probably actually of the Hung Chih period as right one is identical in design to one bearing that mark in V. & A. Mus. Underglaze design and overglaze lemon yellow enamel. Dia. 8½" and 9½". Metropolitan Mus. of Art.

similar to the yellow ones mentioned above in technique. The fine glaze is used on the outside but the mark underneath is covered with an ordinary glaze.

This period also produced the beautiful "three color" figure of Kuan Yin in the Morgan Collection with yellow, green and aubergine glazes, which is dated to correspond with our year 1502. I tried to get a picture of this piece but Mr. Morgan would not allow its publication.

The writers of the times do not mention blue and white ware or red wares but they doubtless continued.

CHÊNG TÊ OR HOU CHAO (1506–1521)

Chêng Tê was only a child encouraged to a life of self-indulgence and vice by ambitious eunuchs so that he would give them no trouble in the management of affairs to suit themselves. He was finally persuaded to proclaim himself the Living Buddha.

In 1505 the Portuguese led by Francisco de Almeida landed in Ceylon and in 1509 a trading post was planted in Sumatra while in 1517 a fort was erected at Colombo. It is also to be remembered that Magellan started in 1519 on that memorable voyage around the world. He was killed by natives in 1521 but the little *Vittoria* finally reached Seville with 31 men. The earth was getting smaller.

A fresh supply of the "Mohammedan blue" was obtained. The factories at Ching-tê Chên were reorganized and rebuilt. "Mohammedan scrolls" and the use of Arabic inscriptions came into style. These were not entirely for export purposes but for the large Mohammedan population in China. Some of the

Ming period, probably Chêng Tê reign, pottery Buddhistic figure with the head and neck left unglazed and yellow and green glaze covering the remainder. Ht. 52". Fuller Coll. Seattle Art Mus.

LARGE MING "THREE COLOR" BUDDHISTIC FIGURE

PLATE 138

objects such as brush rests and ink slabs are of typically Chinese taste. Many of the blue and white wares were mounted in silver in Europe and England. The "Mohammedan scrolls" or "hui hui wên," as the Chinese call them, are flowers of round silhouette connected by S formed stems with rather evenly distributed scroll shaped leaves. It was probably first a textile design. We have seen it before on the baluster shaped vases with crackle ground and enamel decoration and the large one with dragon handles and enameled ground shown is probably of this period.

The Arabic inscriptions are sometimes badly written so as to be hardly readable but make artistic decorations. They usually consist of quotations from the *Koran* or sayings such as those on the brush rest shown herewith.

The best color of the Mohammedan blue was supposed to have been mixed with one part only of the native cobalt while the poorer class was proportioned about six to four. The stealing of the blue, one would suppose, probably meant

FIG. 690. Chêng Tê brush rest for Mohammedan scholar's desk. White porcelain with bubbly greenish white thick glaze and underglaze blue decoration including two square medallions containing hardly legible arabic script. Length 8¾". Metropolitan Mus. of Art.

FIG. 691. Chêng Tê bowl of greenish white porcelain with light and greyish underglaze b'ue decoration. Dia. 6". Metropolitan Mus. of Art.

that all pieces on which it was used were not made in the Imperial kilns. It was this type of blue and white ware which served as the prototype of the "Medici porcelain" and some of the Turkish wares. The color is indigo rather than the cobalt tone we would expect and often it is dirty and spotted looking in the large areas. It was so difficult to handle on a slender brush that the artists were more successful in laying washes than in making outlines. A technique was devised of incising the outline and filling it in with color and it is seen on dragon dishes and jars.

There are several pieces of this sort in the Eumorfopoulos Col. and also one in the Grandidier Col., in the Louvre. The French one is slightly more mottled than the British one but both have flat bases. Both are also rather ornate.

In the Winkworth Col. is a globular jar painted with mottled ju-i pendants about the shoulder, scrolls setting off four incised panels and conventionalized lotus petals around the bottom. Mr. Hobson states that this has a fine grained body and is burnt brown on the unglazed base. The openwork and ogee medallions are painted in underglaze blue and red. The incised work is rather poorly designed and to add to the technical stunts, the medallions are set off by appliquéd ridges of beading. A cup that belongs to Mr. Vernon Wethered has a similar incised and beaded treatment (see *The Wares of the Ming Dynasty*, Pl. 27).

FIG. 692. Ming, Chêng Tê dish with incised design of dragon in yellow green,
showing some iridescence. Greenish white
ground. Dia. 8″. Metropolitan Mus. of
Art.

FIG. 693. Chêng Tê vase with
four ogival medallions reticulated
and colored with underglaze blue and
red while rest of decoration is in
blue only. Ht. 13½″. S. D. Winkworth Coll.

There is a square bowl in the B.M. with mark of the period and underglaze
Mohammedan blue decoration set off with clear yellow ground somewhat better
than the average of the preceding period, and Hsiang shows a complicated
lamp and also a helmet shaped cup with the same treatment and the yellow
described as like "steamed chestnuts."

The V. & A. Mus. has 2 saucer dishes with Chêng Tê marks and they have
incised dragon and cloud designs. The claws of the dragons are in emerald
green "ts'ui lü" over a white glaze of the same color as was used on the Chia
Ching bowls with green and gold decoration. Mr. Hobson says that this green
is "iridescent with age." All green enamels so thinly applied are naturally
iridescent when they are transparent due to the uneven breaking up of the
light rays which penetrate them and are reflected back from the white glaze
beneath. Such iridescence is characteristic of the so-called "apple greens" of
the K'ang Hsi period. The corroded surface iridescence due to age is quite
a different thing and does not appear on these wares so far as I have observed
them.

The "three colored wares" are represented by one in the Oppenheim Collection with the Chêng Tê mark on the neck, and several others. The technique
was simply carried on in traditional manner. In the M. Leon Fould Collection
is a brush washer of which Mr. Hobson says, "In this class of ware, which
would seem to have been a specialty of the Chêng Tê potters, we see the Ming,
'three-colour' scheme at its best." Here then we agree with him and point out
that another ware had reached its apex and was to decline thereafter.

Many wares of the period in the blue and white and celadon types are those
found in Egypt and the Near East, for this was an active time of trade.

CHIA CHING OR HOU TSUNG (1522–1566)

Hou Tsung took the title of Shih Tsung and contrary to all our former
emperors who were Buddhistic, he became a Taoist full of religious zeal. He

wielded his religious weapon with very unpleasant results for his Buddhistic rivals. Taoism had now degenerated into a mystic group of superstitions surrounding the ideas of immortality. Odd it is that this time was almost contemporary with the search for the fountain of youth by Ponce de León (1460–1521) in Florida.

Hou Tsung in 1536 had the Buddhistic temples burned down and destroyed while the gold and silver in them was melted up and then, on his death bed, when he was sure that the promises of immortality of the Taoist priests were not going to be kept, he reversed his orders and had their altars destroyed. But what particularly interests us is that *during this reign no Buddhistic art is likely to have been made, at the Imperial kilns in any event.* Also while the Emperor was busy worrying about his life-span the Mongols were raiding the north and the Japanese pirates visited the coast in many expeditions.

The Taoist designs of Eight Immortals, the "ling chih" fungus, the crane, deer and pine tree all of which represent long life, Hsi Wang Mu and the peaches of immortality came into favor. The authorities give much data about the new designs and we have not the room for all of it here, but a few follow:

Dragon—The dragon is shown with flames, clouds, fungus water chestnuts, lotus scrolls or holding the 8 triagrams. Two dragons have between them the "kan chu" or pearl of purity. Other dragons are with the characters

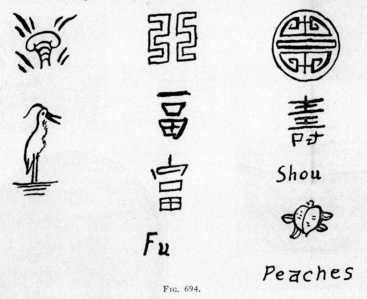

Fu

Shou

Peaches

Fig. 694.

"fu" happiness or "shou" longevity or with lions or "fêng huang" birds. These dragons are not like the early ones which look more like lizards and have divided tails.

Phoenix—The phoenix or "feng" or "Feng-Huang" (or "Ho-ho" bird of the Japanese) was an emblem of the Empress and we have described it in our earlier list. It is sometimes seen with other birds in pairs paying court to it. Actually it is incorrect to call it a "phoenix" for the meaning is quite different.

Lion Dog—The "shih tzŭ kou" appears in many ways.

Flying Lion—"Fei shih" or flying lion was popular.

Three Rams—These symbolized the return of Spring.

Peacocks were shown among the "Feng-Huang" but should not be confused with them.

Fish—The carp "li" or "p'o," the perch "kuei" and mackerel "ch'ing" were all used.

Also the seasonal flowers, mountains, landscapes and particularly water falls were popular, while the curling waves and rocks which Hobson calls the

Right: "Five color" jar. White porcelain with slightly greenish white glaze, dark underglaze blue ("Mohammedan blue"), dark red, green, yellow. Design of carp. Ht. 9½". Metropolitan Mus. of Art.

Left: Stem cup signed by maker, Lin Shaw T'ien. Glaze inside slightly greenish-white with crackles hardly perceptible. Ground deep yellow. Design bright green, dark aubergine. Dia. 6½". Warren E. Cox Coll.

Right: Box and cover in enamels of red and green with turquoise added. Under bottom is legend in blue, "seal box for use as required." Length 5½". Eumorfopoulos Coll. # D94.

Bowl with bold and spirited underglaze blue painting. Heavily potted. Dia. 7½". Metropolitan Mus. of Art.

Right: Blue and white dish having inscription behind seated figure. Dia. 6½". Metropolitan Mus. of Art.

CHIA CHING PORCELAINS

PLATE 139

"rock of ages pattern" referred to the heavenly land, a Taoist island off to the east. And added to these are all the Taoist emblems, children at play and the other immortals.

Our old friend Hsiang Yüan-p'ien whose album we have often quoted was probably still alive but he does not illustrate anything of this period. Other books such as the *Shih wu kan chu* published in 1591 and the *T'ao shuo,* as well as the *Annals of Fou-liang,* translated by Bushell give us information.

Officials at the factories were rotated bringing about healthy competition for the job. The Jao Chou earth and that from Ma-ts'ang are supposed to have been used up so that the bodies were not so good. The *Shih wu kan chu* tells us also that the "hsien hung" red was gone and the potters had to use iron-red overglaze color instead. However, to make up for these losses the Mohammedan blue was plentiful and it was used to make a fine dark blue, which is likened to violet ink but I think this reference is to the *density* or *consistency* of the color and does not mean that the blue itself was actually violet in shade, for it is not on existing specimens. It was also mastered so that it neither ran nor turned black. Yet the technique was not shaded but consisted still of outlines filled in with flat washes. What may be called the first "Hawthorn jar" is in the Kunsindustrimuseum, Copenhagen, though the pattern is a T'ang one as we know. The background of this jar does not show the "cracked ice" treatment but the blossoms of the prunus are well drawn. A fine Imperial Dragon jar is in the V. & A. Mus. and has borders of lotus scrolls. Some of the fish bowls are enormous and unbelievably well made. On the other hand it was said that the tiny boxes painted with blue designs were so good that even the Imperial factories in later times could not better them.

The *Po wu yao lan* tells us of small white cups already mentioned as "altar cups" and used in some way for rituals by the Emperor. It says these are not quite so fine as those of the Hsüan Tê period but beautiful in form and inscribed inside with characters "ch'a" tea, "chiu" wine, "ts'ao t'ang" decoction of dates or "chiang t'ang" decoction of ginger. The *T'ao shuo* says these cups are "white as jade," but some are said to be bluish or yellowish and these "are not worth collecting." In truth the Chinese collectors think less of the wares of this reign than any other of Ming times due to the poorer body clay. Hannover also says that forgeries of the mark are not so numerous, though the Japs made use of it at times.

The "five color" wares were about perfected and wares with polychrome decoration on monochrome grounds were outstanding, particularly those with gold decoration on red or green ground. Sometimes this latter was combined with blue and white as in the V. & A. Mus. example with slightly convex center, concave underneath, no foot-rim and inside a band of emerald green enamel with lotus designs in gold while in the center is a stork and cloud design in dark blue. Outside are two peach boughs and birds in blue. The mark reads, "ch'ang ming fu kuei" or "long life, riches and honors," which occurs on many pieces of this period. The green enamel is likely to be the "ts'ui lü" mentioned in the *T'ao shuo's* list. The overglaze reds vary from a dark opaque brick-red to a translucent tomato-red, which, having more flux, is more translucent, but all of them show brush marks. It may be interesting to note here for comparison that the red of the K'ang Hsi period (1662–1722) was thinner and dryer and more of a light coral color. A somewhat less rich color was also obtained by the Kioto potter Eiraku and others who copied it got a sometimes darker and more muddy color and sometimes a lighter color but never a redder red. The color was also applied to stem cups as in the Oppenheim one which is formed by a section of a sphere set stiffly on a slightly flaring stem.

Here we have the chief copyist reign but a reign that was itself not so honored. Some new colors were supposed to have been invented such as "dead-leaf brown." Some new shapes were invented; tobacco became known in 1530 and some of the forms made for bases of narghilis date shortly afterwards.

From the lists of the palace supply we find there were also octagonal jars, libation cups of helmet shape and ancient bronze forms including the "hsi" or rhinocerous carrying a vase on its back. One may wonder why it is that I say that due to the change of religion we are to look for recognizable changes in the art and then call it a "copyist reign," and tell of the imitating of these old forms, but it must be remembered that there were Taoists long years before the Chia Ching reign and that the very nature of the religion created interest in things long past. Also we are now witnessing the decline which led to a leaning on the past. There was nothing new in Taoism; the newness came only in the absolute adoption of it.

It was not easy to supply the Imperial Household. We read that in the year 1554 among other requirements there were demanded 26,350 bowls with dragons in blue, 30,500 plates, 6,900 wine cups, 680 large fish bowls, 9,000 tea cups, 10,200 bowls and 19,800 tea cups of another pattern, 600 libation cups and some 6,000 ewers or wine pots. Matched table sets came into use and in 1544 we hear of an order for 1,340 of these sets or "cho ch'i" comprising 27 pieces: 5 fruit dishes, 5 food dishes, 5 bowls, 5 vegetable dishes, 3 tea cups, 1 wine cup, 1 wine saucer, 1 slop bowl, 1 vinegar cruet.

Of the "three color," nothing is said but they no doubt persisted and in fact there is strong evidence that the technique changed about at this time. One sort had low fired enamel designs used over outlines in brown, probably manganese, and this would be a technique not unlike the cuerda seca of the Spanish. These are frequently bowls of yellow, green or aubergine grounds on which designs filled in with complementary colors are aided with greenish white. They are much like the enamel on biscuit K'ang Hsi ones except that in the Chia Ching ones there is often a white glaze which emerges under the base. A fine example is in the Grandidier Col. And others are in the Percival David Col., the B.M., etc.

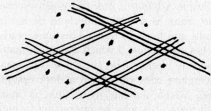

Fig. 695.

These wares were reproduced in the Yung Chêng and other periods.

Other "mixed colored wares" of the "red and green" family occur with white ground. These colors are also added to by use of an impure yellow and a turquoise green which we are told takes the place of the later blue enamel. Mr. Hobson shows an example from the R. F. W. Brandt Col. which has a "trellis" border of triple lines crossing each other to form diamonds in which are four dots, and he says that this is a typical design of the period.

The "five color" type with strong underglaze blue enhanced by numerous enamels was well done and prepared for its full use in the Wan Li reign to follow. Of course all of these colors were also used as monochromes.

There were not many individual potters known, as the factory methods did away with personal signing of pieces, but a few names emerge and they are of famous copyists. Chou T'an-ch'üan made fine copies of Ting yao and we have already spoken of Mr. Ts'ui who specialized in making Hsüan Tê and Chêng Hua copies. An amusing story is told about the former gentleman: Wên Wang vessels in the form of Shang bronzes were his specialty. These were said to have been made in a ware which after a bit of wear or artificial rubbing could not be distinguished from Ting yao. It seems he was permitted to examine a famous tripod censer or "li" belonging to the Great President of the Sacrifices, Mr. T'ang, and risking severe punishment, took measurements of the vessel with his hands and a record of the design on a piece of paper concealed in his sleeve. After some six months' time he procured another audience and astonished Mr. T'ang by producing the copy, perfect in every detail in replica of the older object. So delighted was Mr. T'ang by this seeming magic that he bought the reproduction for forty ounces of silver and placed it by his original. Some years later another collector became infatuated with the two beautiful Ting censers and after dickering a bit bought T'an-ch'üan's copy for 1,000 ounces of silver and went away happy.

But the real story comes to me from the same old gentleman who permitted me to hold the invisible jade bowl from the Kian factory and this is his version: It seems that another cousin of still another brother in going through some ancient family papers came to one which bore a seal dated as of the Chia Ching reign in the year of 1537, the year after the Buddhist temples were destroyed, and this paper was a confession of one of his ancient ancestors who was a good Buddhist and yet a servant of the famous Mr. T'ang who had changed his religion as it was necessary to do in order to hold an important office. The ancestor, whom we must for reasons of delicacy allow to remain nameless, confessed that, feeling that Mr. T'ang knew not the difference between the true and false religion or anything else, tested his theory by one day switching the positions of the Ting yao and the Chou Tan-ch'üan incense burners. There was no commotion in the house and the ancestor then began to feel that he should profit by his insight into human nature. He, therefore, went to the honorable Mr. Chou Tan-ch'üan and bet him that unaided he could not make still another perfect incense burner, saying that, if he did so, he, the servant of Mr. T'ang would pay another forty ounces of silver for it, while, if he failed Chou Tan-ch'üan must pay him ten ounces of silver. The challenge was taken up and the poor ancestor had to pay and take the incense burner for forty ounces, for the second copy was as good as the first. He then replaced the original with the second copy, remembering it to be the one now on the left, and added what he was sure was the original to his own private collection, which he kept very private indeed. His certainty, however, was

Left: Vases, aubergine (dark) ground with green blotches and orange-yellow heads, enamel on biscuit. Ht. 11″. Metropolitan Mus. of Art.

Right: Blue and white square beaker. Design shows scholars and immortals. Ht. 11″. Warren E. Cox Coll.

Bowl with enamel decoration. Outside predominantly iron red, blue inside. 16th cent. Dia. 4″. R. W. Brandt Coll.

Right: Perfume sprinkler having clear greenish white glaze with slightly lavender tinted blue decoration. Has had foot cut and top rim cut down. Cup fitted with platform half way up, perforated with seven holes. Ht. 7″. Warren E. Cox Coll.

Circular box and cover decorated in blue with children and flying cranes amid clouds which are Taoist motive. Dia. 15¼″. Metropolitan Mus. of Art.

Cup with eight immortals painted on octagonal form. Dia. 4″. Metropolitan Mus. of Art.

CHIA CHING PORCELAINS

PLATE 140

shaken when after all this, Mr. T'ang sold the collector the one piece and kept the supposed original for himself, gloating over the fine points of the one he kept. Being a poor man the ancestor could never sell his, whether it was the original, as he first thought, or the copy, as he was beginning to believe, so when he died he passed it to his heir and so it came down from hand to hand through all the years to the present day. My Chinese friend then produced what appeared to be a fine example of Ting yao but asked so high a price that I could not reach it, although I might have tried harder had I known it was by Mr. Chou Tan-ch'üan. Do you suppose the canny Mr. T'ang, noticing a slight rearrangement of the pieces and having a sharp eye, simply put them back in their former places? Could the second collector have known what he was doing after all and did he get the real Ting yao? Who will ever know?

Mr. Tz'ui's ware was known as "ts'ui kung yao tz'u" or "Mr. Tz'ui's porcelain," and was eagerly sought even during his lifetime. The colors of his monochrome and blue wares were perfect but, whether purposely as a matter of distinction, or simply carelessly, his cups were all of different size from the originals. Of course, if he had cast his pieces from the old pieces, a shrinkage would have taken place which in our present wares is about 1/10th to 1/12th but the *T'ao lu* and other authorities do not tell us whether they were larger or smaller, which is unfortunate.

Some works say that his wares brought higher prices than the originals while others say they were fit to be "used to put fruit stones in." Of course we of today would gladly pay a full Chêng Hua price for a piece, if we could be sure he made it.

Wan Li or Yi Chün (1573–1619)

The five year intermediate reign of Lung Ch'ing or Tsai Hou was interesting to us only because the Mongols were put back into their places and many years of peace followed.

The son of Tsai Hou took the title of Shên Tsung and became Emperor at 10 years of age. He was a fine young boy, but the eunuchs soon saw to it that he became known as bad tempered and licentious. The Japs invaded Korea under Taiko Hideyoshi and the Tartar chieftain Noorhachu was a threat which soon developed into conflict and loss for the Chinese, for it was he who was destined to be founder of the Manchu Dynasty.

Meanwhile the Dutch Admiral Spilberg landed on Ceylon and was asked to help oust the Portuguese which he did for his own good reasons, and in 1602 Sir John Lancaster was well received on the island and 11 years later a factory was opened for trade.

A few new designs were added during Lung Ch'ing times as follows:
1.—Clusters of chrysanthemums "to to," 2.—tuberose or iris "yü tsan hua," 3.—jasmine "ch'ang ch'un hua," 4.—all the flowers "k'uei hua," 5.—flowers of the four seasons supporting four characters heaven, earth, fair and fruitful "ch'ien k'un ch'ing t'ai," 6.—interlacing scrolls of mutan peony, 7.—the Tartar pheasant "chai chih," 8.—flying fishes, 9.—monsters in sea waves, 10.—faint wave patterns "tan shui," 11.—curled waves and plum blossoms, 12.—genre subjects "jên wu," 13.—historic figure subjects "ku shih," 14.—children hold-

Left to Right: Beaker shaped vase with neck truncated. Ware smooth and white. Glaze greenish. Underglaze blue deep, vivid and inclined to run. Ht. 9″. Warren E. Cox Coll.

Wan Li bottle of grace and strength. Ht. about 23″. Thompson Coll. Metropolitan Mus. of Art.

Blue and white vase, blue of vivid brilliant quality. Diameter of mouth and foot and height of neck all alike. Height of body 3½″ times this dimension. Ht. c. 24″. Altman Coll. Metropolitan Mus. of Art.

Superb gallipot with ju-i design about shoulder, eight precious objects and nien hao of Wan Li. The painting shows all the strong, dynamic power of best of the reign. Ht. 20¼″. Warren E. Cox Coll.

Jar with spirited painting of a horse dashing over waves amid clouds. Ht. 5½″. Warren E. Cox Coll.

Blue and white vase with delicate painting but somewhat spiritless. Metropolitan Mus. of Art.

Deep bowl and cover, Wan Li or slightly later, painted with simple charm though in poor, uneven quality of blue. Ht. 9″. Metropolitan Mus. of Art.

VARIOUS STYLES OF DRAWING ON WAN LI BLUE AND WHITE WARES

PLATE 141

ing branches and finally a design called a "joyous meeting" which Mr. Bushell describes as a pair of magpies and Mr. Hobson says was of two sages. We are also told that they incised dragons under the glazes and made jars with peonies and peacocks in gold and covers with lions on them.

There are two pieces in the B.M. while other collections include a few more but they might be of either the preceding or following reign so far as technique goes.

At the beginning of the Wan Li reign the factories at Ching-tê Chên were humming with activity, and the workmen were so pressed that they went daily to the temple of the God Chao, a potter of the Chin dynasty who had been deified. But a new God Chao took his place and this is how it happened: An order was given for the large fish bowls which for some reason would always come out warped or cracked. The Imperial Officer was wrathful and threatened dire punishment to all the potters. Again the fire was made and all prayed that the labor of many months would turn out all right, but the divine T'ung threw himself into it and was consumed whereupon the bowls came out beautifully. He was then deified.

The clay now came from Wu-mên-t'o but there were difficulties in transportation and so, quite often an inferior type was used. The Mohammedan blue had completely ceased probably due to Dutch intervention and coastal difficulties with Japan. The underglaze red was revived but was not so good as the fine color of the 15th century. Trade was extensive overland and many heavy pieces were made for export. The Chinese themselves have chiefly disparaging things to say about Late Ming wares and Wan Li in particular.

The T'ao shuo gives us these new shapes: trays for wine cups "pei p'an," flower vases "hua p'ing," flat backed wall vases in the form of a gourd, screens "p'ing," hanging oil lamps "ching t'ai," pricket candlesticks "chu t'ai," jars for candle snuff "chien chu kuan," chess boards "ch'i p'an," furniture for the writing table, brush handles "pi kuan," brush pots "pi ch'ung," brush rests "pia chia," pallette water droppers "yen shu ti" and various boxes for perfume, betel nuts, hats, handkerchiefs and fans. Here we can see the foreign influences at work and many things are made which are inappropriate for the material. The censor Wang Ching-min protested that many items were only extravagances, and particularly mentions candlesticks, chess boards and jars for holding the men, as well as handles for brushes, which would break easily. We are told that about half the obnoxious articles were cut off the lists at his protest, and that they numbered 96,000.

New decorations are said to be: full-faced dragons "chêng mein lung," squatting dragons "tun lung," ascending and descending dragons, winged and threadlike dragons, the "Hundred dragons," fabulous monsters paying court to the celestial dragon and to the archaic dragons, sea horses "hai ma," and many birds, animals, etc. The "ch'i-lin" appears often, and was said to portend the coming of a virtuous ruler and they certainly needed one but the two that followed were not so fine as might be.

Most of the above were rendered in blue and white but we read also of the following: 1.—blue and white bowls with five colored phoenixes flying through seasonal flowers; 2.—blue and white dishes with dragons or lotus

Ming bowl decorated in grey-blue under glaze.
Dia. 5¾″. Metropolitan Mus. of Art.

Ming blue and white vase which
probably dates in Wan Li period.
Ht. 15¼″. Metropolitan Mus. of
Art.

Box and cover with dragon and floral design in
strong blue. Length c. 9″. Metropolitan Mus. of
Art.

Blue and white Late Ming jar possibly from
South China. Such little pieces found in Philippines and Malaysia. c. 1600. Ht. 3″. Metropolitan Mus. of Art.

Ting form incense burner. Feet in form of
archaic dragons, tails winding about body in
relief and forming handles. Underglaze blue
and yellow enamel. Mark of Wan Li in double
ring. Ht. 6¼″. Eumorfopoulos Coll.

Left: Plate with light blue decoration. Late Ming. Dia. 15″. Metropolitan Mus. of Art.
Right: Jar of heavy type with vigorous painting. Ht. 5″. Metropolitan Mus. of Art.

WAN LI WARES

PLATE 142

Stylization easily seen in pieces of Wan Li period, last great epoch of Ming dynasty (1573–1619). It may be designated as an elongated, tall stretching almost to the grotesque and at times a top heavy look due to mouth being so much wider than base. Blue and white of strong color. Metropolitan Mus. of Art.

Beakers of "wheat sheaf form" taken from bronze models, with flanges or suture marks maintained about middle and lower parts. Heavy white porcelain with strong underglaze decoration in blue and overglaze iron red and green enamel. Period mark on flaring mouths. Ht. 34". Metropolitan Mus. of Art.

Left: Beaker with design outlined in black and washed with aubergine in ground of full yellow glaze. Base has white glaze and mark of Wan Li in blue in a double ring. Ht. 9½". Eumorfopoulos Coll. # D115.

Right: Wan Li beaker in brilliant enamel "five color" decoration, having six character mark at lip, reading "Great Ming dynasty, reign of Wan Li made in." Ht. 12". Boston Mus. of Fine Arts.

WAN LI BEAKERS OF "THREE COLOR" AND "FIVE COLOR" TYPE

PLATE 143

scrolls engraved; 3.—cups with nine dragons painted in red among blue and white sea waves; 4.—cups with nine blue monsters in red sea waves; 5.—cups with red sea waves with white crests; 6.—cups with yellow hibiscus flowers or enameled chrysanthemum flowers inside; 7.—incense burners with clouds and dragons worked in relief; and 8.—incense burners with designs carved in open work.

Special color arrangements were as follows: 1.—white inside and designs reserved in blue on the outside; 2.—blue ground with white designs all over; 3.—garden seats with aubergine lotus flowers on yellow ground; 4.—golden brown tea cups with engraved dragons and lotus scrolls; 5.—incense burners with enameled decoration on a yellow ground; 6.—vases of white porcelain with phoenixes and flowers engraved under the glaze; 7.—banquet dishes "shan p'an" white inside and with dragons in clouds outside painted in red, green, yellow and aubergine.

In this one reign we find more different qualities of material and technique than in a great many others put together. Tall, crude vases very heavily potted stand a yard in height and have the nien hao of Wan Li in six characters on the lip. Their glaze is heavy, greyish and bubbly. Then there are small, fine pieces with soft glaze easily scratched and crisp, thin porcelain with glossy glaze. The blue itself may be good Mohammedan quality, or dark like the Chia Ching, or pale and silvery, but usually it is simply dull and not very colorful. This was due to the first real improvements of the Chinese native blue which was to become so very bright and beautiful in the K'ang Hsi period. And the painting was direct and vigorous, weak and sloppy, careful and

FIG. 697. Wan Li blue and white cup with silver gilt mounts. Ht. 8½". Dia. 14". J. P. Morgan Coll. Metropolitan Mus. of Art.

FIG. 696. Small Wan Li bowl of blue and white mounted in silver gilt foot, rim and handles probably of late 16th cent. Dia. about 7". Metropolitan Mus. of Art.

painstaking or just plain poor. Variety was certainly the spice of Wan Li life.

A number of cups and ewers were mounted in Europe with silver or silver-gilt mounts that have assisted us in dating them. A number of these are cited by Hobson and I show a few from the Morgan Collection. A very fine example which belonged to Messrs. S. J. Philips has a nipple on the side which is an indication that it was probably originally designed as the base of a hubble pipe for Near Eastern use. I show an unmounted one of the same shape from the Metropolitan Museum of Art. In the Rosenborg Palace, Copenhagen, is a hexagonal box with handles and cover painted with figures crudely drawn in a dull blue and having the typical muslin-like texture of the glaze of this period. It was brought to Denmark in 1622 by Admiral Ove Gedde, who commanded the first Danish expedition to the East Indies, and given as a present to Princess Sophie Hedvig in 1723, some hundred years afterwards.

Thin porcelain types are frequently dishes with moulded borders. The ware is white, resonant and thinly potted while the glaze is clear and lustrous. There is often sand adhering to the foot-rim and pin holes in the glaze. Radiating wheel marks under the base, not to be confused with spiral marks, are signs of summary execution common on the ware. However, the work is fairly skillful and the brush was handled with speed and ease. The blue on these is usually pale and silvery.

Mr. Hannover says that these pieces are of rare occurrence and describes the white as being just slightly greenish. He goes on to say that the blue

FIG. 699. Ming blue and white bottom part to narghili or water-pipe dating c. 1600. Metropolitan Mus. of Art.

FIG. 698. Fine ewer of blue and white Wan Li porcelain mounted with silver gilt base, cage, handle and top. Ht. 13⅝". J. P. Morgan Coll. Metropolitan Mus. of Art.

has two tendencies, one to go toward black or indigo in tone and the other to go toward violet, but in almost all shades it has the tendency to run. He also says, "The bottom of a Ming piece often shows, under the glaze, faint radial lines in the paste, and where the foot-ring occurs it is often slightly brown." He further states that the paste has a "greasy" feel but I think that that is a bit exaggerated while Mr. Robert West's comparison to a piece of uncooked spaghetti is more like it.

"Porcelain House" is a good instance of the interest that the Near East took in these wares. It was called "Chini hane" and is in the Ardebil Mosque which was published by Dr. Sarre in "Denkmäler persischer Baukunst" in which is a picture showing some 500 bowls and jars. This mosque was built by Shah Abbas whose reign very nearly coincides with the Wan Li. It was 1586–1628 while Wan Li was 1573–1619. Most of the pieces collected were blue and white although there are some celadons and a few colored pieces. Hannover points out an interesting point and that is that none of the five piece sets called "garniture sets" are included and he deduces that these were first made in the 17th century to order for the Dutch market. Hobson says, "Another kind of vase, dimly seen in the back rows of Shah Abbas' Collection, is the large ovoid jar with loop handles on the shoulders. These, one imagines, were used as water jars on board ship and were traded widely in the East Indies and on the mainland. Sometimes they were protected by wickerwork or rope bands, as in the case of the Tradescant jar in the Ashmolean Museum, Oxford." This is the type we have described under the Philippine section.

"Kuei kung" or "devil's work" was made in some of the earlier reigns but now a further development of these incised and delicately modeled pieces took place. The modeling was often left unglazed, though some were covered with red with gold over that and some had blue and white decoration added as does the Metropolitan Museum one shown. Others had blue, yellow, green or aubergine washes to vignette the ornamentation. Another trick was to build up the ornament with slip and others had pierced work or "ling lung." It is doubtful if the K'ang Hsi workers ever reached the all round proficiency in this sort of lace work that the Late Ming potters accomplished.

Another type which seems to try to give the effect of "ling lung" work with a cheating on the labor is carved in the same way but in very low relief. These in turn were copied more and more crudely to the present day.

The "san ts'ai" or "three color" work went right on and into later times.

Fig. 700. Bowl and cover of *"kuei kung"* or "devil's work" with pierced fretwork and medallions in high relief showing traces of color and gilding. Ht. 6". Metropolitan Mus. of Art.

Fig. 701. Bowl and cover with blue and white design and high relief figures in medallions. Of the late Wan Li Period. Ht. 6½". Metropolitan Mus. of Art.

Hobson makes three divisions in it which may be helpful: He says that all of these glazes contained *soda, lime, lead* and *silica*. The early ones contained more silica and lime, were less fusible and less durable as well as being more opaque such as can be especially seen in the opaque violet. . . . The Chêng Tê type contained more lead making them more fusible, durable and transparent. . . . The Late Ming ones are fired in the muffle kiln and are softer yet, containing a higher proportion of lead and are fired at lower temperatures. These enamels were used in both the "san ts'ai" or three color type and the "wu ts'ai" or five color type and these were more easily controlled so that the designs could be outlined with dry pigment instead of resorting to incised or raised outlines. This seems a very sound analysis and much to be depended upon but I believe by careful comparisons most of these wares can be properly allocated within their proper reigns.

The molded wares came into vogue more extensively in the 18th century after the Wan Li period and continued through that century as is testified to by Père d'Entrecolles. This is also proven by the often published crayfish in the Hainhofer Cabinet at Upsala, which is yellow and has signs of gilt while the waves are thin and lustrous green with white crests.

The "sur biscuit" technique was certainly used a century before Wan Li but the Chinese writings are not very clear on the subject. However, the jars called "wave and plum blossom" jars are identified without any doubt and we have many examples of this type with rounded shoulders, wide cylindrical mouth and covers, which are certainly Wan Li or earlier, and are treated in this technique. Some have green and some aubergine grounds. Odd specimens of the sort are also treated over the glaze.

The "wu ts'ai" or five color ware had come to mean polychrome decoration including more than five colors and is so typical of the Wan Li period that it is often referred to as "Wan Li wu ts'ai yao." It now includes besides the underglaze blue: 1.—light green, 2.—dark green, 3.—aubergine, 4.—yellow, 5.—Ming iron red "fan hung" which is a rather glossy deep red of tomato color and iridescent at times, 6.—manganese brown, 7.—turquoise green. Deep blue was not being

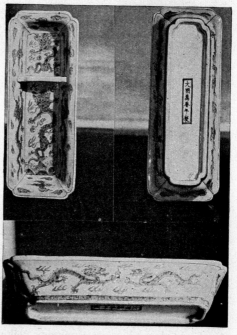

Fig. 702. Exceedingly rare but absolutely authentic Wan Li period brush tray with rest (which has been restored by Samson). The ground is of a soft but clear yellow and the dragons are of green and pale aubergine. All enamels are on a white glazed ground. The Wan Li mark is in deep underglaze blue. Ex Warren Cox Coll. Walter Blumenthal.

Left: Early Ming "Three color" gallipot with the more opaque type of enamels. The ground is cobalt blue and the design is in clear bright turquoise, yellow and creamy white. Under the foot and inside the neck is a thin wash of yellow green not used elsewhere. Ht. 12". Courtesy of Walter Blumenthal.

Right: "Three color" type jar and cover of dense almost white porcelaneous ware covered with various enamels held in place partially by low cloisonns. The ground is a soft but bright turquoise and the other colors are dark blue, aubergine, pale gray and white. Late Ming. Ht. about 15". Metropolitan Mus. of Art.

Left: Late Ming vase with enamel on biscuit, aubergine ground, green rocks and waves in three tones and yellow. Ht. 13". Bequest of Mary Clark Thompson. Metropolitan Mus. of Art.

Right: Fine Wan Li candlestick in colored enamels on a yellow ground, one of pair from the set in the British Mus. Ht. 28". C. T. Loo & Co.

SAN TS'AI (THREE COLOR) MING POTTERIES AND PORCELAINS

PLATE 144

used in enamel very often because the underglaze blue took its place.

The general styles that prevailed were:

1.—Underglaze blue, green, muddy yellow and red.

2.—Underglaze blue, green, yellow, aubergine, iron red and green-black (made by putting the transparent green over the manganese). This type usually has figure designs. This was copied in K'ang Hsi times but the red was lighter and less deep.

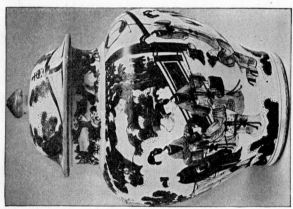

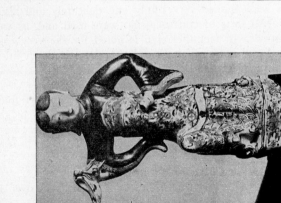

(a)

(b)

(c)

(a) Wan Li ewer in the form of a dancing girl whose one arm acts as a handle and the other as a spout. The decoration is of rich "five color" type with strong underglaze blue and the jacket is of deep, fine iron red. Herbert Devine.

(b) Ming 17th cent. "five color" jar and cover with greenish white ground, deep underglaze blue, clear yellow, three greens, a pale and clear iron red, deep aubergine and strong black. Ht. 18″. Metropolitan Mus. of Art.

(c) Two similar "five color" vases, the one with the fan being Ming and the other with the crane K'ang Hsi, showing almost identical technique of drawing and similar shapes. Hts. 7½″ and 7¾″. Metropolitan Mus. of Art.

FIVE COLOR (WU TS'AI) MING PORCELAINS

WITH COMPARATIVE K'ANG HSI EXAMPLE

PLATE 145

3.—All the enamels used but dominated with the red and green as a development of the Chia Ching style. Often the background is of diapered lightly painted lines. The blue is omitted.

Mr. Hobson gives us an amusing note to the effect that this type was copied "with disconcerting fidelity" probably by a factory in the 19th century which signed its wares with the mark "shên tê t'ang." In one interesting specimen he says the words "po ku" were added proclaiming the dish to be an "antique made at the Shên Tê Hall."

4.—Garden seats were supposed to have been made with brown dragons and lotus flowers on yellow ground, but we have none.

5.—Incense burners were supposed to have been made with the five colors on a yellow ground. They are probably like the K'ang Hsi famille jaune wares. One interesting piece is a bronze beaker form in the Eumorfopoulos Col. #D115 with brownish yellow glaze and a design outlined in brown and washed in with aubergine. This was bought by Frank Partridge at Southby & Co., May 30th, 1940, catalogue #264. One should not be surprised to find other odd combinations from time to time.

Hannover points out an odd specimen in the Salting Collection, V. & A. Mus. It bears the mark of Chêng Tê and may be of the period or might possibly be later Ming, but it is a bowl having large fishes in underglaze red while others are in the five color enamels and these are also employed in the polychrome border. He goes on to argue that, "Here we have evidently a specimen anterior to the time when the formula for five color painting was finally determined, and this seems, as far as can be judged, to have happened as early as the reign Wan Li. For when the Chinese speak of 'Wan Li wu ts'ai,' this undoubtedly implies that the five color painting, which otherwise in its final form belongs chiefly to the time of K'ang Hsi, has already in the latest period of the Ming dynasty to a certain extent assumed its later typical form." This logic does not hold any more than the argument that whenever we speak of a "Chippendale chair" or a "Renaissance scroll" we mean a chair actually made by Chippendale or a scroll actually made in the Renaissance. It is safe to say that in the Wan Li period the style was forming but not that it was formed or "finally determined."

Sometimes the enamels were applied very thinly and delicately and also very crudely and heavily. All sorts of craftsmanship were used and, as we have seen, many combinations. In fact the reign is noted for the very extremes to which it reached and not until later did things settle down into definite ruts of mechanical procedure and commercial practice.

Among the monochromes we find the following listed:

1.—White bowls of Yung Lo were imitated as were many of the other fine wares and the bodies and glazes are so nearly alike that we have to judge by style alone in making attributions which are always uncertain.

2.—Yellow of the "hung chih" type was also made along with golden brown and dead leaf brown.

3.—Aubergine was copied after the Chia Ching wares.

4.—Green of a fine leaf color was applied both direct on the body or over a grey or white crackled glaze.

5.—"Apple green" was also said to have been made.

6.—Celadon was made at Ch'u Chou and at Ching-tê Chêng among other places. In the V. & A. Mus. is a bowl with blue inside and pale celadon outside and French metal mounts that seem to indicate it is of about this period. In the Eumorfopoulos Col. is a low bowl with pale clair de lune celadon glaze and marked, "To be treasured in the Ju-ch'eng family in the 'hsin mao' year of Wan Li." (*i.e.* 1591) But we shall say more about celadon shortly.

7.—Hobson says there is a bottle of the flambé type in the B.M. but it must have been an accidental piece, I believe.

8.—Black, not unlike the "hare's fur" of the Sung Chien yao but blacker, was made.

FIG. 703. Ming dynasty gallipot of porcelain covered with a blue glaze. Ht. 13". Metropolitan Mus. of Art.

FIG. 704. Wan Li vase with brilliant black glaze turning to brown at edges. Ht. 15". M. Calmann Coll. (Paris).

FIG. 705. Ming, Wan Li pale "celadon" large dish probably made in South China for the Indian market. The design is of white slip applied through a tube. The glaze is poor and considerably pitted. Dia. 15". Metropolitan Mus. of Art.

9.—Black of the mirror quality is said to have been invented during the K'ang Hsi times by Père d'Entrecolles but Hobson says it was made in Wan Li times, backing his statement with a vase from the Calmann Col. (Pl. 42, *The Wares of the Ming Dynasty*), which has been frequently illustrated and which has every appearance of being Ming. He says of it, "The brown emerges prominently where the glaze has run thin on the raised parts, and conversely the black is more intense where the glaze has run thickly.

Marbled wares of the old T'ang type with mixed clays were again made and others had mixed slips or glazes as the case might be. One in the Eumorfopoulos Col. has the mixed slips and the mark "Modeled by Ch'ên Wên-ching in Ting yu year of Wan Li."

A steatitic slip of paint-like, opaque quality was used from K'ang Hsi onwards, but the Ming slip is liquid looking and translucent, probably of very thin porcelain clay. It was applied with a brush much as we see later in Minton and Sèvres wares but, of course, with more simple and tasteful designs. The ground used under this work was brown, deep blue or celadon. Flowers and rarely birds were painted. The shapes were bottle vases, flower pots, narghili bowls, ewers, jars and some large plates made evidently chiefly for trade in Indian and Persian markets for much of this ware is found in these countries. It is probably all the output of one factory which lasted well beyond Ming times but specimens have been found with Wan Li marks and some may be even earlier. Sometimes the slip is left dry and sometimes it is glazed over.

Another group of export wares is heavily built of a strong but coarse body which burns reddish brown and usually has sand or grit adhering to the foot-rim. The color varies being: slaty blue, celadon, light coffee brown or dark brown and the decoration is of crudely applied slip. An associated ware is also coarse and greyish blue and white and is decorated with Ming turquoise green or leaf green and red and white over incised designs. It has been suggested that some of this ware may have been made in Korea but there is no evidence to support the guess. However, we know of no place in Fukien province either for that matter. Wherever the factory was it continued long after Ming times.

As early as Wan Li the exceedingly tasteless association of porcelain and lacquer was made as is proven by a vase in the B.M. Lacquer is a more or less transparent varnish made from the sap of certain trees or from certain insects which suck this sap in China and Japan. It is applied cold having been dissolved in solvents. The vase mentioned is a beaker of typical Wan Li shape, square in plan and with the usual decorations of Imperial dragons and rock and wave borders rendered in green and red lacquer on a brown ground with details incised and lined with gold. There is a Wan Li mark in the usual place on the lip and it and the lion handles are in underglaze blue while the rest of the surface is left without glaze to receive the lacquer. To quote Hannover, "When this" (lacquer on porcelain) "is inlayed with mother of pearl, we have the *laque burgauté* of the French, which in its time seems to have enjoyed a somewhat undeserved popularity."

T'AI CH'ANG OR CH'ANG LO (1620–   )
T'IEN CH'I OR YU CHIAO (1621–1627)
CH'UNG CHENG OR YU CHIEN (1628–1644)

The last three reigns of the Ming Dynasty amounted to very little. The first lasted only a few months. The next emperor Yu Chiao took the name of Hsi Tsung and proceeded to devote himself to carpentry while a nurse and eunuch ruled. One is reminded of the French king and his clocks. Finally Yu Chien took the name of Chuang Lieh Ti and, through the irony of fate, was a good man and earnest ruler but through treachery the gates of Peking were opened to a rebel force and he retreated to the "Mei Shan" or "Coal Hill" and there in sight of the city hanged himself with his girdle. After futile attempts to re-establish the survivors of the royal family against the Manchus a final stand was taken in Kwangtung by Kuei Wang but he had to retreat to Burma and also committed suicide in 1662.

Nothing is recorded of Ching-tê Chêng and the wares of the times are very much on the decline showing only poorer and poorer workmanship. Shortly after the end of Wan Li the Dutch in 1624 obtained a foothold in Formosa and there was evidently a great trade in blue and white wares with European modifications of shape.

Polychrome wares continued, of course, and they had the Wan Li color schemes. One variation was a blue and white ware with a wash of transparent green over it, as may be seen by a vase in the Grandidier Col., Louvre, Paris.

CONTINUOUS WARES

I have tried to give a brief suggestion as to the characteristics of the wares of the various reigns of the dynasty. I think it has been clear that technique replaced good taste to a considerable extent. Modeling became "devil's work," glazes became almost too refined, many colors led to less well

FIG. 706. Ming, T'ien Ch'i period (1621–1627 A.D.) dish of greenish white ground decorated with underglaze blue, light and dark iron red, yellow green, brown black and yellow enamels. Dia. 6". Metropolitan Mus. of Art.

FIG. 707. Ming, T'ien Ch'i (1621–1627 A.D.) dish with same colors as other specimen. The writing on it is a quotation. Dia. 6". Metropolitan Mus. of Art.

FIG. 708. "Ko yao" cup attributed to the Ming period. It has a sandy buff body and gray crackled glaze not so strong as the photo would suggest. Ht. 4". Metropolitan Mus. of Art.

considered painting, relying for its effect on the splash of the whole bouquet of colors. In other words there were many mediums of expression but not a great deal to express. . . . Or perhaps there was too much to express in the way of undigested emotions. It is really impossible ever to tell what is the matter with an art; it either springs from the earth in all perfection as does a beautiful flower to move one, or it does not. One cannot say, "I would have been moved by such a singer had her register been an octave lower, her overtones richer, her diction less pronounced." One might eventually improve a voice by such criticisms but then one would not be moved by it unless the voice suddenly blossomed out beyond all such rules of criticism. What could be more ridiculous than a lover making love to rules? Nothing unless it be an artist working to rules. . . . No, if art is successful, we can find a thousand reasons why we liked it and were moved while, if art does not move us, all we can say is that we were not moved. So with the pageant of Ming art and achievement we must admit that the show was well set but our hearts neither felt the weight of sadness, the lift of great joy nor any other emotion.

Some wares, however, carried through from the days of T'ang and Sung and did not die completely during Ming times. We have already spoken of the Tz'u Chou types of Yüan and Early Ming, of the Tsung Sê t'zŭ or dark brown types including those found in the Philippines, of the Chün yao and of blue and white wares, but others too were carried on.

Ko yao, as may be seen by the small cup shown from the Metropolitan Museum was imitated in a shape which shortly later was turned into an "apple green" by the addition of a transparent green enamel over the crackled glaze. We have also seen a crackle developed on the baluster shaped vases mentioned under the Chêng Hua reign and have noted how they gave way to enameled backgrounds. Again a crackled ware will be taken up shortly under what Mr. Hobson calls "Kiagnan Ting" wares. But often one sees a Ko yao example very much like the Sung ware except that it had a more porcelaneous body of the type of paste we expect from Ching-tê Chêng or a shape which could only be Ming.

Fig. 709. Lung Ch'üan yao dish of early Ming type with foliated edge, incised design of rather ornate character but covered with a creamy grey green glaze, which is un-crackled and pitted as may be seen inside the foot rim on the back. Dia. 12½". Warren E. Cox Coll.

Fig. 711. Celadon made at Wen Chou in late Ming times according to Sir Percival David. Exceedingly heavy, having walls about ¾" thick at the foot. The ware is white burnt red-brown at foot and the glaze is light yellowish green and more opaque than that of Ch'u-chou. Finely crackled. Ht. 12¾". Lem S. Tsang–Warren E. Cox Coll.

Fig. 710. A "Sêng-mao-hu" or monk's-cap jug of celadon glaze having the characteristics of Lung-ch'üan, and a blue underglaze mark of Hsüan-tê. Handle and cover new. Ht. 7¾". Note: These also occur in Hsüan-tê red and in Yung-lo white with incised design of eight Buddhistic emblems supported on lotus flowers, indicating a ceremonial use.

Celadons continued to be made right through the period in various places. Of course, one thinks of Ch'u Chou as the site for the largest output of Ming celadon and that is undoubtedly the case but it must be clearly borne in mind that Ch'u Chou had kilns and made pieces in Sung times and also that very similar wares were made well into K'ang Hsi times and probably even later. So similar are these that experts cannot distinguish them from Ming wares. It has, I believe, also been made clear that the kilns at Lung-Ch'üan did not cease work but proceeded to make excellent examples at least into Ming times. And again we know that Ching-tê Chêng was striving all along to copy these popular wares, while factories in Kwangtung and elsewhere were also working with the same thing in mind. Sir Percival David told me that the very heavy vase with frosty glaze shown herewith is from Wen Chou and is of late Ming period. From Yang Chiang in Kwangtung come some of the slip decorated pieces described above and other recognizable lower fired southern celadons, while another large source was from Show Chou in Anhwei.

The Lung Ch'üan wares did not change in quality or technique from those of the Sung period and would be indistinguishable save for the fact that some of them are dated such as those in the collection of Sir Percival David.

An example very likely to be from the Ching-tê Chêng factories is the ewer or jug "hu" of pure white ware showing only the slightest trace of brown near the edge of the glaze where the foot is exposed and covered with a light celadon glaze much like a lighter type of Lung Ch'üan. This piece has an underglaze Hsüan Tê four character mark and it is interesting to note that another of the same form was lent by the Chinese Government to the London, International Exhibition of Chinese Art 1935–6 and is described as having a "ruby-red glaze and mouth in the form of a priest's hat." This red one is of the same height and has the same mark—proving rather conclusively that they were both made at Ching-tê Chêng where the red glaze was developed. Brankston shows a white one (Pl. 2, *Early Ming Wares of Ching-te-Chên*) with incised design of probable Yung-Lo period.

The large oval vase with a Chia Ching mark which is so over fired as to

FIG. 712. Ming Chêng Tê vase and lamp for floating wick made at Ch'u-chou for Mohammedan trade. The vase has the character *shou* (longevity) on one side and *fu* (happiness) on the other. The ware has burnt red where exposed and the glaze is faintly crackled and frosty from burial. Hts. 7″ and 8″. Lem Sec Tsang Coll.–Warren E. Cox Coll.

FIG. 713. Show Chou, Anhwei, dish of grey porcelain burnt brown where exposed and having a glassy crackled glaze of olive-green. Dia. 12″. John Platt–Warren E. Cox Coll.

504 POTTERY AND PORCELAIN

appear more like a crackled "Ting type" but which shows the clear pale green crackled glaze inside is more likely from Kiangsu or Anhwei, for the buff body is much like that of the so-called "Kiagnan Ting" wares.

Quite possible it is that the dish with unglazed bottom, rounded foot-rim glazed over and rich, crackled glaze is from Show Chou in Anhwei for it has many characteristics similar to the deep bowls which we described at the end of the Sung section.

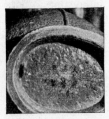

Fig. 714. Chia Ching (1522–1566 A.D.) vase with underglaze blue mark of the period, of brown stoneware with uneven glaze of the "orange peel" type café au lait in color on the outside and under the foot, while inside it is a pale "celadon" green. The shape is after a bronze form with naturalistic animal handles. Ht. 16¾". Warren E. Cox Coll.

The strong influence of Mohammedan design is to be seen on the two small vases with loop handles and the lamp in the form of a sanctuary and these seem to be Ch'u Chou ware of refined but typical sort, probably dating from the Chêng Tê period when that influence was strongest as is proven by the many blue and white wares with Arabic writing. Other refined examples from the same factory are the hat rest and the small toilet water holder in the "duck shape" in which urinals were often made but too small for such a purpose and having a lip for pouring. The large dish will serve to show how the design became more ornate and less well organized.

The striving for greater and greater weight to stand shipment resulted often in fire cracks which opened up during the firing in the kiln. This may be seen in the hot water bowl designed to keep rice hot while eating and also in the very large jar which has a globule of the glaze showing where it oozed through the crack. Often at Ch'u Chou the glaze was so thickly applied that it ran down in large drops at the bottom so that they had to be ground off or stands had to be made to fit their irregularities so that the vase would stand straight. Such large drips can be seen on the foot-rim of the jar and about the bottom of the amphora vase as well as on the side of the small mouthed "gallipot." These last two are of the deepest and richest green I have seen from this kiln site.

One of a pair of vases in the V. & A. Mus. is shown by Hobson in *The Wares of the Ming Dynasty*, Pl. 46, Fig. 2 and is of a pale watery green thin glaze rather greyish in color and is incised with flowers and an inscription dating it 1547 or the Chia Ching reign. This is interesting for wares of the type have been offered for sale as "Early Sung."

Glancing at a few of Sir Percival David's we find the following:

1.—LVIII Ch'u Chou vase, Hsüan Tê (A.D. 1432).

2.—LIX Vase from same kiln and similar, in shape, to the Ching T'ai period (1454).

3.—LX Flower pot of the Chêng Tê period (1517) and also from Ch'u Chou.

Finally I show another vase from the Lem Sec Tsang Collection which is inscribed according to the translation of Mr. Han of the Metropolitan

FIG. 715. Ch'u-chou vase of beautiful proportions and fine rich glaze running to heavy drops at the bottom. Ht. 23¾". Warren E. Cox Coll.

FIG. 716. Fine Ch'u-chou bottle of the Ming period which was some years ago exhibited at the Metropolitan Mus. of Art and catalogued at the Mrs. Samuel T. Peters sale as, "Lung Ch'üan Sung period." Ht. 18½". Warren E. Cox Coll.

FIG. 717. Ch'u-chou vase of the Ming period with exceedingly thick, rich green glaze. Ht. 12¼". Lem S. Tsang–Warren E. Cox Coll.

FIG. 718. Small Ming period vase made at Ch'u-chou. Vigorously incised and has soft pea-green crackled glaze. Ht. 6½". Mrs. Warren E. Cox.

FIG. 719. Early Ming Ch'u-chou vase of greyish porcelain burnt brown where exposed and covered with a rich, transparent grey-green glaze over an incised design. Ht. 9". Warren E. Cox Coll.

FIG. 720. Reticulated hat rest of Ch'u-chou ware of the Ming dynasty. Warren E. Cox Coll.

FIG. 721. Lung Ch'uan yao "celadon" dish of white porcelain with incised lotus design covered with a greyish olive-green glaze rather thinly applied. Dia. 18". Warren E. Cox Coll.

Museum of Art, "The faithful person, Chou K'un-hsi a native of Hsi-yü, respectfully offers a pair of precious vases before Mme. Ma Ch'i seated to the rear of the hall. In donating this present he asks that she will protect the

FIG. 722. Ch'u-chou toilet water bottle with incising to indicate the plumage of a duck. Length 7". John Platt–Warren E. Cox Coll.

FIG. 724. Ch'u-chou large jar showing glassy crackled glaze and typical large drips around base, also a rather not unusual fire-crack through which a large drop of the glaze has come. Ht. 19". Warren E. Cox Coll.

FIG. 723. Ch'u-chou yao hot water bowl made with shallow concavity at top and a hole in the bottom so that it can be filled with hot water to keep rice or other food warm. Dia. 6⅝". Warren E. Cox Coll.

FIG. 726. Ming Ch'u-chou ware temple vase dated with the year equivalent to 1625. It has a rich green glaze of olive tone. Ht. 18". Lem Sec Tsang Coll.– Warren E. Cox.

FIG. 725. Ch'u-chou vase (fêng wei p'ing) of greyish porcelain burnt red brown where exposed and with pale green glaze over an incised design. The inscription reads: "Made on a lucky day in the seventh month of the seventh year of the Hsüan Tê period (1432 A.D.) for use in the palace (fu) of the T'ien-shih (Taoist pope)." Ht. 17.3". Sir Percival David Coll.

FIG. 727. Ch'u-chou vase (fêng wei p'ing) of greyish porcelain with light pea-green glaze over incised ornament and writing: "In the fifth year of the Ching T'ai period (A.D. 1454), the believer Yang Tsung-hsin of the hamlet of Chên-an in Fu li, etc." Hobson says that the Ching T'ai mark seldom appears on porcelain though it does most often on Ming cloisonné. Ht. 26.8". Sir Percival David Coll.

506

peace and luck of his daughter," and it is dated, "on the day of the eighth month of the fifth year of T'ien Ch'i" or 1625.

Later in the K'ang Hsi section I shall show a specimen unique so far as I know and which many experts have called Ming but which is dated as of that later reign. Thus we have some stepping stones but they are rather far apart and seem to teach us only that we must not be too pedantic so far as dating celadons goes and that to try to judge by style, as Mr. Hobson would have us do, is, to say the least, difficult.

FIG. 728. Ch'u-chou flower-pot (p'ên) of greyish porcelain with grey-green glaze having some crackle near the bottom. On it is incised under the glaze, "The believer Ch'ên O of the eastern Suburb of Li-shui Hsien in the prefecture of Ch'u-chou has resolved to offer joyfully ten pieces to the Liu Ho Ssŭ (Buddhist Temple), that they may be placed before the Kuan-yin with the prayer that his mother may live a very long life, that he and his wife may grow old together, that every member of his family may be lucky, that he may have many prosperous sons and grandsons, that he may be able to perform meritorious deeds (in the service of Buddha) and that they may all enjoy happiness. Made in the middle ten days of the eighth month of the cyclical year Ting ch'ou of the Chêng Tê period." (A.D. 1517) Dia. 8.8″. Sir Percival David. Coll.

FIG. 729. Vase on left has mark of Ch'ên Chên-shan and a crackled watery celadon glaze. Ht. 10½″. S. D. Winkworth Col. Vase with handles has an inscription with date equal to 1547, and a pale celadon somewhat crackled glaze thinly applied. Ht. 12″. G. Hart Coll. Victoria & Albert Mus.

"KIANGNAN TING" AND OTHER CREAM GLAZED WARES

What we have said about the wide distribution of celadon wares is almost as true of the cream glazed wares. We have spoken of the Yung Lo and other rather close imitations of thin, white Ting yao. We have also indicated the continuance of slip covered and painted or incised decorated Tz'u Chou types. Now, during the Ming period, there developed wares which were perhaps influenced by both of these. They cannot truly be called Tz'u Chou types because they are not treated with slip, the bodies being sufficiently light where covered with the glaze to allow a cream color or to only slightly stain the crackle in it. They have loosely been put under the general name of Ting yao and as the provinces of Kiangsu and Anhwei were formerly united and called Kiangnan, and we are given to understand that most of the ware was made in these places, Mr. Hobson has given the general name of "Kiangnan Ting" to the wares. Obviously this is a rather ambiguous and not very well defined classification and it covers some very different looking wares but until we get further actual information we shall

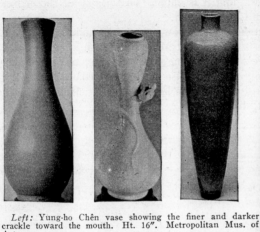

Left: Yung-ho Chên vase showing the finer and darker crackle toward the mouth. Ht. 16″. Metropolitan Mus. of Art.

Center: Ming pottery vase of the type called "Kiangnan Ting." Buff body, white slip, crackled creamy glaze. Ht. 4½″. T. C. Lee–Warren E. Cox Coll.

Right: The finest example I know of the Yung-ho Chên type. Ming. Ht. 7″. Metropolitan Mus. of Art.

Ting type vase. Grey stoneware, cream glaze. Ht. 12¾″. Warren E. Cox Coll.

Yung-ho Chên Ming vase. Ht. 19¾″. Warren E. Cox Coll.

Yung-ho Chên vase of the type called "Kiangnan Ting" by Hobson but having a rich camellia-green crackled glaze. Ming Dynasty. Fukien province. Ht. 13¾″. Warren E. Cox Coll.

Kiangnan Ting vase of the usual light buff body heavily potted, covered with a thinly applied very finely crackled cream white glaze. Similar in form to some of the "three color" examples, but more beautiful in proportions and details of potting. Ht. 14″. Ex Samuel T. Peters Coll. Warren E. Cox Coll.

"KIANGNAN TING" AND RELATED WARES OF THE MING DYNASTY

PLATE 146

have to be contented with it. In the Sung section we have mentioned a few of the sites such as Hsiang-shan, Ssŭ Chou, Su Chou, Hsüan Chou and it is likely that these all continued more or less active, but particularly in what is now Kiangsu the *T'ao lu* tells of a place called Pai-t'u Chên where potteries were reported to have been made since Sung times constructed of the local clay and "very thin, white and lustrous, beautiful in form and workmanship." There were several hundred potters and the kilns were chiefly owned by a family of potters named Tsou. I know of no actual excavations at this site, but undoubtedly some of the wares we have originated there.

In Shansi there were four sites: 1.—P'ing-yang Fu, 2.—Ho Chou, 3.—

P'êng Chün-pao and 4.—Yu-tzŭ Hsien. The first ware, we are told by the
T'ao lu, was white but had a discolored glaze and this is borne out by excavations there which disclosed a heavy painted and carved ware like a
crude Tz'u Chou with rather close all-over design in the painted ones and
high relief but crude work in the carved or molded ones, which are often
after bronze forms. At Ho Chou the potteries existed from T'ang times
and made at all times a refined and well potted ware though inclined to be
yellowish in tone. At P'ang Chün-pao in the Yüan dynasty a goldsmith from
Ho Chou made wares that the *Ko ku yao lan*, an almost contemporary work,
said were exactly like Ting but "short" and "brittle" and not worth much,
"But dealers in curiosities give them the name of 'Hsin ting' or 'New Ting,'
and amateurs collect them at great cost, which is most ridiculous." At Yu-
tzŭ Hsien in the north again a crude pottery was made.

Yao Chou in Shensi was a source of flat-bottomed bowls called "little
seagulls." But going south we must not forget the kilns at Chi Chou and

FIG. 730. Kiangnan Ting vases of the late Ming period.
Hts. 13″ to 10″. Warren E. Cox Coll.

FIG. 731. Bowl and
cover found at Swankalok
and dating late Sung to
early Ming. The decora-
tion is in dull, blackish
blue and the ware is red-
dish-buff. Ht. 4½″. N. M.
Heeramaneck Coll.

those at Nan-fêng Hsien both in Kiangsi province. The latter made a heavy
"t'u ting yao" in the Yüan dynasty and undoubtedly later. The Chi Chou
kilns were situated at Yung-ho Chên where there were five factories according to the *Ko ku yao lan*. This will be remembered as the locality of the
potteries that turned to jade. The *T'ao lu* tells us that crackle was a specialty
and to quote, "These are the wares made in the Southern Sung period. Originally they were a special class of ware made at Yung-ho Chên. . . . The
clay was coarse but strong, the body thick and the material heavy. Moreover, there were 'millet coloured' (mi sê) and pale green (fên ch'ing) kinds.
The potters used *hua shih* (steatite) in the glaze, and the crackle was in
running lines like a broken thing. They smeared and blackened the ware
with coarse ink or ocherous earth; then they finished it. Afterwards they
rubbed it clean, and it was found to have hidden lines and stains of red or
black, like cracked ice, beautiful to look at. There were besides pieces with
plain crackled ground, to which they added blue decoration." (Hobson's
translation probably from Bushell.) This was of the Sung dynasty but
leads us to believe that some of the heavy crackled wares and some of the

Fig. 733. Early Ming or Yüan blue and white bowl of buff ware. The blue is dull and grey where covered by the thick glaze and black where exposed. Dia. 7". Warren E. Cox Coll. T. C. Lee Coll.

Fig. 732. Kiangnan Ting vase of another typical form sometimes having cloud scroll handles. These were usually made in a two piece mould and the handles applied afterwards. Ht. about 11". Warren E. Cox Coll.

Fig. 734. Two fine vases of Kiangnan Ting ware the large one having loose suspended rings evidently fired in one piece and cut away from the post supports which were in the loops. Ralph M. Dudley Coll. The other is one of a perfectly matched pair in the L. G. Sheafer Coll.

dull blue on crackled ground wares found in Malaysia and Borneo may be the ones described, and these both continued to Ming and even later times.

In actual wares I think that it is obvious that they divide themselves into two main classes: First, the glossy and white or nearly white ones with hardly perceptible crackle or no crackle at all. These have bodies ranging

from buff to white or nearly so and which are not hard but typical pottery very easily cut. They are largely molded and often have relief ornamentation or handles of cloud scrolls, lions, t'ao teh heads, etc. I do not contend for a minute that these are all alike or made in one place for, as one can readily see in the illustrations, the very weight of the potting varies considerably, but they are similar in technique and general appearance. . . . Second, the group which I think likely to be

Fig. 735. Yung-ho Chên bulb-bowl with pressed and incised design. Usually these pieces have no decoration. Ming Dynasty. Dia. 9¼". Warren E. Cox Coll.

those described as from Yung-ho Chên which are generally wheel-turned to buff to brown ware and with a crackled glaze often stained deeper toward the lip-rim and only seldom decorated with relief appliqués, hand modeling or stamped and incised design as in the bowl illustrated. These too are pottery and neither porcelain nor stoneware. The foot-rim may be flat or often slightly bevelled on the inside and outside edge. My impression after long discussions of the subject with the late Malcolm Farley is that the first class of ware is found in the Kiangnan section while the second was found extensively by him in Kiangsi and Fukien provinces further south. It is unfortunate that he never was able to bring over his sherds from China to prove his points conclusively.

Both these wares and similar wares were continued into modern times. I show a most interesting specimen which I recently acquired. In shape it is less strong but much more refined than the Ming ones. The potting is thinner and the ware harder, being porcelaneous. It is incised under the bottom with a freely drawn K'ang Hsi nien hao mark and on it is incised two ch'i-lins or kylins on either side with their prancing feet on 4.—a *chüeh* or rhinocerous horn, 5.—a *ch'in* or stringed instrument partly covered with its

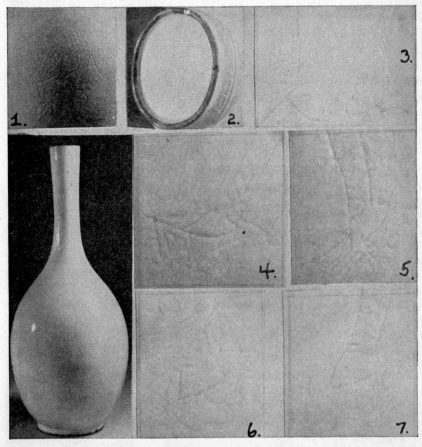

FIG. 736. K'ang Hsi "kiangnan ting" bottle refined form. 1.—Kylin decoration incised on either side. 2.—Note the thinner and deeper foot-rim which is slightly beveled and burnt brown where exposed. 3.—The mark is freely and swiftly incised and reads K'ang Hsi nien chih. 4.—The *chüeh* or rhinoceros horn under the right front foot of the kylin. 5.—The *ch'in* or stringed musical instrument with its bag cover half drawn over it which is under the left front foot. 6.—The *ai-yeh* or artemisia leaf which is under the right hind foot. 7.—The *p'ing* or vase which is under the left hind foot. Ht. 14¾". Warren E. Cox Coll.

covering bag, 6.—an *ai-yeh* or artemisia leaf and 7.—a *p'ing* or gourd shaped bottle, a strange mixture of Buddhist and other objects. This links the type with K'ang Hsi at least and the hard biscuit would seem to indicate a kiln site in or near Ching-tê Chêng, which is also in Kiangsi province, of course.

Finally I show what is, so far as I know, an entirely unique specimen of the second group, like in body clay, like in potting and identical in shape to the cream crackled ones but covered with a deep, rich leaf-green glaze having just about the same crackle as the cream ones. The glaze is entirely different from any of the more or less transparent ones used on the "three color" wares or on the porcelains and it has a typical "orange skin" undulating surface. Perhaps this piece is the prototype of the K'ang Hsi and Chien Lung crackled greens of well known fame and known as "camellia green," etc. In any event it is unique as a Ming specimen.

Tz'u Chou Type Wares

Though Ching-tê Chêng is the largest and most important group of kilns the world has ever known those at Tz'u Chou are undoubtedly the most continuous having lasted from the 6th century or earlier right up to the present. Moreover many of the other kilns that made this ware continued also and I am told that nowadays one can buy bowls, figures and various vessels very nearly like the early ones for household use.

In the Sung and Yüan sections I have mentioned the tendency just before Ming times to elaborate Tz'u Chou type wares by the addition of iron red and enamel colors. In fact it was very likely this type of ware that became the prototype of the "three colored" wares of Ming fame. However, tradition is strong in China and many monochrome paintings were done all during the Ming times distinguishable only by the style of the decoration and the form and consistency of the pot itself. One thing the artists could not get away from was the laxity of the side line of the vases into strongly curved S tendencies. They undoubtedly actually thought these new forms better and had no idea of giving them up. I show a vase of typical character decorated with a lotus loosely drawn, a happy boy and a bird along with characters. Another example is the blue ewer from the Metropolitan Museum less well potted than Six Dynasties examples and with crude decoration. All

FIG. 738. Fish-bowl of Early Ming times of stoneware with figures in relief representing the Eight Immortals. Probably of the Chia Ching reign. Dia. 23″. John Sparks, Ltd.

FIG. 737. Wine ewer of gourd shape with tiger spout and handle, of buff-gray stoneware covered with glossy slip and glaze and painted in brown. Note the scratching out of the veins of the leaves. Ht. 11¼″. John Platt—Warren E. Cox Coll.

FIG. 739. Tz'u Chou type jar from northern Honan and of the Ming period. The decoration is in black swiftly painted and scratched out for details. Nasli Heeramaneck Coll.

Ming T'zu Chou figure of Lao Tzŭ in buff pottery with cream slip and glaze, and brown details. Ht. 7". Ex Warren E. Cox Coll. Mr. George Gillett.

Ming period Tz'u Chou showing a man of means, probably an official, together with his wife, holding the sceptre, his concubine and his horse. The artistry and gentle humor of this work shows to what heights some of the Ming artists could rise. Ex Warren E. Cox Coll. Mrs. Charles Porter Wilson.

Ming Tz'u Chou vase of good form but somewhat less dynamic design than is seen on the Sung examples. The other side shows a "happy boy" and there are several characters. Warren E. Cox Coll.

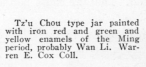

Tz'u Chou type jar painted with iron red and green and yellow enamels of the Ming period, probably Wan Li. Warren E. Cox Coll.

TZ'U CHOU TYPE WARES OF THE MING DYNASTY

PLATE 147

the painting was not of this character as we found in the two brownish examples which I show in the Yüan section as they may possibly be of that period. These are decorated simply and well, as is also the pillow from the Heeramaneck Collection.

That modeling became important we can see in the fine large fish bowl in the John Sparks Collection, London in which the Taoist figures are in fairly high relief. This is called "Early Ming" by them but I should be inclined to place it in the Chia Ching (1522–1566) or strongly Taoist times. I should also see no reason for not so placing the fine figure of Shou Lao, god of the southern star and of long life, and one form of Lao Tzŭ himself seated with an adoring child holding a plum beside him and loving animals: the stork, the tortoise and the deer, all representing long life, about him. This is decorated in two shades of brown or in brown and black. (Another Ming custom.)

FIG. 740. Buff stoneware vase, showing the more flamboyant line of the Yuan and Early Ming potteries. Ht. 13″. Warren E. Cox Coll.

FIG. 741. Tz'u Chou type pillow of buff grey ware with white slip and transparent glaze. The fine painting is in black. On the bottom is a three character inscription stating it was made by the Chang family. It is agreed that such marks came into use only in Ming times. Length about 12″. N. M. Heeramaneck Coll.

FIG. 742. Ming pottery of Tz'u Chou type of reddish color with white slip, darkest aubergine or black slip decoration and blue glaze. The aubergine is used inside. Ht. 8″. Gift of Robert E. Tod. Metropolitan Mus. of Art.

Another fine figure group shows a dignitary of importance with his wife on his right, a lovely concubine or second wife on his left and his horse behind him saddled and ready to carry the master. The human charm of this group speaks for itself. Thus we must not look with lack of interest upon Tz'u Chou works of later times.

FIG. 743. Tz'u Chou jar. Ht. 9¾″. Eumo. Coll. # C295.

FIG. 744. Tz'u Chou type jar. Ht. 9½″. Eumo. Coll. # C308.

Dating is difficult but we have a few milestones as follows:
1.—In the Eumorfopoulos Col. #C295 is a jar dated to correspond with 1446 which is in the brief and unimportant period of Chêng T'ung (1436-1449). I have not seen this piece and cannot describe the ware but the design might well be a Sung one and Hobson says it is of a grey

stoneware with white slip and cream glaze, painted in brown and with a brown glaze inside. We assume the foot-rim to be about as expected as nothing is said of it.

2.—Another #C308 in the same collection is of "grey porcelaneous ware with white slip and painted in black under a creamy glaze." It has also a black glaze inside and at the lip. This piece has the Wan Li (1573–1619) six character mark on the shoulder. The large fish is characteristic and I should assign all of the bowls on which these appear, if not to Wan Li, at least to the Ming period judging not only by their style but also by the body and glaze. These are sometimes called timorously "Yüan."

3.—There are a number of specimens with enamels combined with slip painting which also bear Wan Li marks showing us that this type reached at least into late Ming times. They probably continued later.

One more note must be added. A whole group which we have classed as Ming to date must now be assigned to Southern Sung and very likely to our central Kiangsi kilns on the evidence of the small dated example of A.D. 1203 now in the Metropolitan Museum of Art. This ware is of a rather rough and sandy buff body with white slip and a yellowish cream glaze sometimes crackled and sometimes not. The painting is rather greyish black and though spirited is often of an all-over pattern less pictorial and less naturalistic than the Tz'u Chou ware itself. The incorrect idea that the glaze should always be crackled in old pieces is pure nonsense for at this time very few kilns could control crackle and the various factors both chemical and physical of this particular ware seemed fairly well balanced so that it fell on one side or the other as chance dictated.

TSUNG SÊ T'ZŬ (DARK BROWN COLORED POTTERY)

The little tea-bowls made at Chien-an or Chien-yang were certainly continued in Ming times, if not so much for the Chinese, at least as an item of trade with the Japanese who so appreciated them. It is my firm belief also that the "Kian Temmoku" bowls, despite the jade legend, continued and I may insert as helpful evidence that one can buy just such bowls of quite modern appearance in and about Chi-an, Kiangsi province up to modern times.

A small pot in the B.M. has a buff stoneware body and translucent brown glaze. This was found in a tomb in the Chien-ning district which has been dated as of 1560 or Chia Ching (1522–1566) period. Many of the so-called "Honan Temmokus" have all the characteristics of Ming potting. I think they were actually made in Honan and the rounded, bevelled or very heavy foot-rims, the glossy blue-black glaze, the generally poor potting and the angular or involved and exaggerated shapes all indicate a Ming and probably late Ming date for their manufacture. The ware is more like oatmeal than the rough and sandy buff ware of Chi-an. It usually has small black specks in it which are probably frit and had something to do with the wobbly shapes because it was hard to work with and inclined to wilt in firing. This body runs from buff to brown and reddish brown. Where the

FIG. 748. Vase of buff-white ware burnt reddish-brown where exposed. Glaze is blue-black and light brown. Probably from Honan and the exaggerated form suggests Mongolian influence, late Sung or Ming. Ht. 9½". Eumorfopoulos Coll. # B258.

FIG. 749. Probably worst specimen of four known is this vase with long, wobbly neck and splash of glaze running off bottom. Without doubt a kiln waster. Ht. 10½". Metropolitan Mus. of Art.

FIGS. 746, 747. Tsung Se vase of light grey porcelaneous ware with even blue-black glaze shading to tan at lip and running down to an uneven edge near bottom. Note below the even edge of blue-black glaze and wide, bevelled foot-rim and glazed bottom, more like Ming than Sung. Ht. 10". Warren E. Cox Coll.

glaze is thin it takes a light tan color.

Potters at times made flecked effects or again large splashes and drips of so tricky a method as to be almost Japanese in character. This whole type of amphora is interesting. There are four known; one in the Oppenheim Collection besides the three shown. One has a gray-white body, two buff or buff gray and mine, the most perfect in form and in potting is of gray stoneware. The foot-rims are all bevelled and I believe that this together with the exaggerated S shapes place them as very late Sung into Early Ming. The glaze is that expected from Honan as is also the wobbly potting which shows

ware. The foot-rims are all bevelled and I believe that this together with the exaggerated S shapes place them as very late Sung into Early Ming. The glaze is that expected from Honan as is also the wabbly potting which shows particularly in the neck of the one owned by the Metropolitan Museum of Art.

Finally there are the so-called "Tz'u Chou Temmokus" or globular large jars with incised glazes which we have seen from Sung times. Hobson placed all of these into the "Sung or Yüan" period but just as there are some that agree perfectly with Sung technique so there are also Yüan examples and also Ming ones, the latter distinguished by the glossy and treacly glaze, the thinner potting, though still rather heavy, and the ornate floral decoration. That some of this style are even later than Ming is fairly certain.

FIG. 750. Ming or even later example of what Hobson called, "Yuan temmoku" but which we term Tsung Se (brown pottery) and which dates from Early Sung to the 18th cent. Ht. 12¾". Warren E. Cox Coll.
FIG. 751. Brush holder with reserve design perhaps made with an actual leaf. The body is brown stoneware and the glaze brown with a suggestion of oil spots. Ht. 10¾". Warren E. Cox Coll.
FIG. 752. Tsung Sê jar of reddish-brown stoneware with light brown shaded to blue-black glaze. Note uneven and poorly made lip-rim. Ht. 7¼". Warren E. Cox Coll.
FIG. 753. Light buff stoneware jar, body burnt brown where exposed and covered with a blue-black glaze showing streaks of light brown. Honan of the Ming Dynasty or later. Note again uneven potting of lip-rim. Ht. 8¼". Warren E. Cox Coll.

CHÜN YAO

The contemporary Chinese books evidently feel that Chün yao of later than Sung times is not worth mention. The only reference given by Hobson is from the K'ang Hsi Encyclopaedia, the *Ch'in ting ku chin t'u shu chi ch'êng* which contains two references to large supplies of vases and wine jars "p'ing" and "t'an" being sent to Imperial order during the Hsüan Tê and Chia Ching periods from Tz'u Chou and "Chün Chou" now Yü Chou. Then there is also the reference that in 1563 both the subsidy and the tax on "Chün Chou" wares were abolished. Hobson says he does not know if the modern Yü Chou wares are just a revival or a continuation. I am inclined to the latter belief and to the opinion that many of the so-called "Yüan Chüns" are Ming and later. The modern wares as sold in Peking are of buff ware often washed over with a brown where exposed and the glaze is often thinner than the old and more greyish. However, other specimens that come on the market are of porcelaneous ware greyish in tone and with a dull red glaze. These probably were made at Ching-tê Chêng.

Later in the Eumorfopoulos Catalogue Mr. Hobson makes the interesting suggestion that the "Chün Chou" potters may have adopted the san ts'ai or three color enamels and to support this theory he shows a bowl #C96 which has a grey stoneware body quite like that of Chün yao but a bright peacock glaze with a splash of almost black aubergine on it very much like the three color glazes. He, however, does not go so far as to say that *all* the potteries were so made and wonders where the Ming and later examples are. . . . He then goes on in "Chinese Pottery & Porcelain" to say, "At any rate, the taste for the old Chün glazes was far from dead, for Hsiang Yüan p'ien included a number of them in his selected series formed in the 16th century and a celebrated potter, named Ou, at Yi-hsing in the late Ming period, made a reputation by his clever copies of them."

Now as to the actual wares let us say to begin with that many of the ornate incense burners now allocated in the Yüan period are undoubtedly Ming in taste. Secondly there is no reason to include all of the so-called "Yüan tz'ŭ" or "wares of the Yüan dynasty" with their thick and crackled glazes in that period. The Chinese books do not back this up and it is a purely arbitrary allocation. I think it happened this way. Many high prices were paid by rich men for Chün specimens. The collectors of these things did not always have the best of taste and they were readily appealed to by the large and involved specimens which seemed to them important and valuable. In time these were proven definitely not to be Sung taste and therefore our authorities pushed them gently into the Yüan catch box which was not so bad as calling them Ming to one of the old time collectors of Sung wares. Why not face the issue squarely? The shapes and the potting of these pieces, if they were covered with green or yellow transparent lead glazes would tell us that they were Ming at once. There is nothing contrary to this decision in Chinese books. Let us call them Ming, and at that they are a lot better potting than the large "Honan Temmokus" just described and which are confidently given the Sung attribution.

The "Yüan tz'ŭ" bowls of heavily crackled glazed ware are also earlier than the Yüan period as was proven by the finding of them at Turfan by Sir Aurel Stein. In other words these thick, transparent, crackled glazes continued over a long period of time and I believe up to the present. The various Chün wares indicate that they were made contemporaneously and that would surely show that several kilns were at work with them. During the Ming times still others made imitations.

We have examples of the Yi-hsing wares and shall describe them more fully in the later sections of the book. The bodies are brown or at times yellowish and the glazes streaky and of lavender color but opaque. The ones with light body are made to imitate "Ma Chün" or "soft Chün," but are not so good being harder, with a glaze of crystalline texture and having "rather thin and feeble patches of dull crimson," to quote Hobson.

The class of "sha t'ai" ware or "sandy body ware" has been given the name of "soft Chün" by Hobson and it seems a fitting one. Mr. Bahr has said it is known as "Ma Chün" by the Chinese and is widely known as of the Ming period, but again to quote Hobson, "No reason is assigned for either the name or the date and both seem to be based on trader's gossip to which no special importance need be attached." (*Chinese Pottery and Porcelain*, p. 127.) However, later in the Eumorfopoulos Collection, Mr. Hobson says, "Then there is the so-called 'Soft Chün'—the Chinese call it Ma-chün, deriving the name from a potter called Ma—a beautiful ware with buff (It sometimes burns red at the edges.), earthy looking body and a thick opaque glaze finely crazed and rather crystalline in texture but with a surface more waxen than that of typical Chün glaze. Its color is usually pale lavender blue, sometimes peacock blue, and it is usually broken by a splash or two of crimson red. The forms of the 'Soft Chün' wares are sometimes Sung or Yüan, but often typically Ming." Evidently Mr. Hobson became further convinced of the "trader's gossip" as time went on, but whether Mr. Ma made them or not and wherever they were made let us add that the potting is exceedingly heavy and crude and is far more likely to come from some other kiln than from that of the ancient Chün tradition.

KWANGTUNG YAO OR "KWANG YAO"

In the southernmost province of China, Kwangtung, there are many kilns and some are reputed to be of ancient date reaching back as far as T'ang but less excavation has been done here and we skip from the Han potteries found by Prof. Jansie in the Southwest and Anam to those of Ming and later times for this general southern section. We must not forget that Dr. Laufer assigned a number of the wares found in the Philippines and East Indies to Fukien and Kwangtung provinces.

Perhaps the best known kilns are those of Shekwan West, close to Fatshan, and often the wares are called by either name. It was here that an imitation Chün yao was made and probably two other wares which are well known.

The first of these is a sort of flambé on a dark brown body of reddish tone. The glaze may be olive brown, blue black or green and on it are streaks and flecks of white, light buff, grey and grey-green with often bright

FIG. 756. Kwangtung pitcher with dark brown body and brown glaze flecked with pale blue except at rim. Called "Sung" by Metropolitan Mus. of Art but is actually Ming. Most of these wares are even later. Ht. c. 3". Metropolitan Mus. of Art.

FIG. 754. Kwangtung jar of dark buff stoneware with incised design under yellowish brown glaze. Ht. 5". Warren E. Cox Coll.

FIG. 755. Kwangtung early Ming pottery jar with buff body heavily potted, rounded, crude foot-rim, bottom daubed with glaze. Glaze opaque, pasty greenish white, thickly applied over lightly incised floral design. Ht. 10". Metropolitan Mus. of Art.

blue breaking through. Mr. Hetherington says quite truly that the Chinese insist that this ware originated in Sung times and that their opinions are to be respected. However, he and Hobson and all western authorities seem to agree that most of these wares are 18th century or later and that only a few, if any, are Ming. I see no reason for not including the gallipots with wide shallow foot-rims and rich glazes in the Ming category.

Gallipot of usual heavily potted but light weight brown ware covered with light blue glaze shading to lavender over relief appliqué design. Ht. 12½". Ming. Ex Samuel T. Peters Coll. Warren E. Cox Coll.

Left: Symbol of Earth in Shekwan "Fatshan" ware with buff body and dull creamy glaze having crackle stained blue-grey on corners. Alternating center panels contain flowers and inscription in archaic characters reading: "As long a life as Kwan Chen T'ze who lived at Kong Tung for 1200 years." (Translation by Mr. Nai Chi Chang.) Ht. 12". Warren E. Cox Coll.
Right: Early Ming jar of grayish white ware with foot-rim and bottom dressed with brown. Glaze greenish white with brown crackle. Decoration carved in surface. Ht. 18". Ex Samuel T. Peters Coll. Warren E. Cox Coll.

"Canton ware" Ming vase of dense grey pottery which burns reddish brown where exposed, covered with finely crackled deep green glaze shading through aubergine and pale blue to lighter blue-green. Ht. 11¼". Warren E. Cox Coll.

"KWANGTUNG" WARES MADE NEAR CANTON IN MING DYNASTY
PLATE 148

Figures of this ware with the hands and faces left unglazed and covered with the flecked glaze, a dull red glaze, a green glaze and also a celadon type glaze are seldom, if ever, Ming but are always so called by dealers of the smaller shops.

These glazes contain lead and large amounts of phosphates. The mottled effects are due to iron and not copper according to William Burton but some little copper may be present.

Hobson reminds us that the names of the famous potters Ko Ming-hsiang

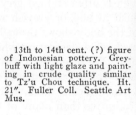

Indonesian architectural ornament said to have been found at Sukotai-Sawankalock, twin cities which were capital of Siam in 14th cent. during strong influence of Mongols. It appears to have been made by some wandering Chinese potter. The glaze is grey-white. Ht. 22″. Fuller Coll. Seattle Art Mus.

13th to 14th cent. (?) figure of Indonesian pottery. Grey-buff with light glaze and painting in crude quality similar to Tz'u Chou technique. Ht. 21″. Fuller Coll. Seattle Art Mus.

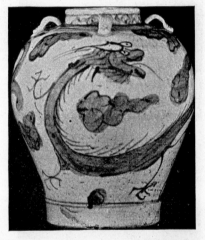

Indo-Chinese jar of crude manufacture similar to late Korean ones. Decoration in blue. Ht. 10¾″. Freer Gallery of Art, Wash.

Jar claimed to be Sung but more likely Ming or later from Indo-China, but possibly made in China. Brooklyn Mus.

INDO-CHINESE WARES INFLUENCED OR MADE BY MING POTTERS

PLATE 149

and Ko Yüan-hsing have nothing to do with the Ming or Yüan dynasties. He also speaks of other potters but they do not particularly interest us for they were not great artists in any sense.

On the evidence of Captain Brinkley (see F. Brinkley, "Japan & China" vol. ix., p. 261) we attribute the other well known ware to Kwangtung potters though as to whether it was made at Shekwan near Fatshan we are not certain. This has a buff body which at times in later specimens has been washed over with a dark brown clay. The glaze is thick, opaque and paint-like but filled with crackle which is often stained grey or blue. The color of the glaze may vary from pinkish to buff or greyish white or light blue and where it runs thin a light tan of the body shows through. This occurs often on the high ridges of the often used relief decoration which may be molded by hand, applied or cast in the form. We often see a sort of broad gallipot with relief band of flowers about the body but other shapes such as the fine symbol of earth illustrated also occur. Hobson calls these "imitative wares" but I fail to see how they are any more imitative than many of the others and in truth they have a soft quality and charm all their own.

Fig. 757. Kwangtung yao jars, the larger showing a greenish brown glaze of "celadon" type and the smaller being of light gray blue with deep maroon patches. May be late Ming. Hts. 8" and 6½". Warren E. Cox Coll.

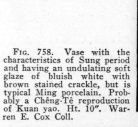

Fig. 758. Vase with the characteristics of Sung period and having an undulating soft glaze of bluish white with brown stained crackle, but is typical Ming porcelain. Probably a Chêng-Tê reproduction of Kuan yao. Ht. 10". Warren E. Cox Coll.

Still other types are also attributed to the province such as the greenish-white jar shown from the Metropolitan Museum and the two heavy jars from my own collection. These last seem to have been made in a variety of glazes and yet all to have been potted with the same technique and great weight. These are declared to be Sung but are more likely of the Ming period. Still other types which are probably of the 18th century or even later, though some may have originated during Ming times are the rough, brown bodied wares with similar pasty blue glazes having red blotches in imitation of Chün yao. These are certainly from Kwangtung but where we do not know.

I submit one more vase which may be from Kiangsi or Kwangtung. It has a white porcelain body with rough and gritty foot-rim but the glaze is of rich bluish white, unctuous and thick and has a buff crackle. The potting is purposely irregular though it is wheel-made. Possibly this piece was made in Ching-tê Chêng but the potting seems more primitive than we would expect there. The glaze is of "Kuan" (or Imperial Sung) type.

Yi-hsing Yao

The city of Yi-hsing is on the west of the great lake in southern Kiangsu and south of the Yangtse River. It is about 200 miles west of Shanghai and the clays found there were found after firing to be cinnabar red, dark brown, "pear-skin green" and light red in color while other colors could be produced by mixing these. A priest was the first to make, "choice utensils for tea-drinking purposes," of these clays but his secret was stolen by Kung Ch'un in the Chêng Tê period (1506–1521) and his famous wares are described as, "hand made, with thumbmarks faintly visible in most of them," and "of the subdued lustre of oxidized gold," and of great accuracy and simplicity of shape. Hsiang published two said to have been sold for five hundred taels, and they are hexagonal grey-brown and ewer-shaped vermilion red. Our friend Mr. Hsiang writes of them that they turned to jade green when tea was made in them but adds that he had not seen the phenomenon personally. This is probably a misunderstanding of a reference similar to that made during Sung days to the effect that white cups were good for red tea and brown cups for green tea as they "brought out the color."

There are a number of potters of Ming times who were known for the ware: Shih Ta-pin, Li Chung-fang, Hsü Yu-ch'üan, Ch'ên Chung-mei and Ch'ên Chün-ch'ing were all famous along with Tung Han who in the Wan Li period made the first with "elaborate reliefs" on the surface. Hobson tells us moreover that Ch'ên Chung-mei made incense boxes, vases and weights for scrolls with fine carving and that he even made figures such as Kwan Yin. The Japanese are said particularly to like the work of Hui Meng-ch'ên who was also a Ming potter.

It must be explained that these wares vary not only in color but in hardness and finish. Some are as soft as lowest fired pottery while others are of real

FIG. 760. Yi-hsing teapot of red terracotta. Probably as late as the 18th cent. Length 6". Freer Gallery of Art, Washington.

FIG. 759. Yi-hsing pottery tea-pot of late Ming, probably Wan Li. Has seal of Ming Tsao and signature of Ming Yuan. Usual reddish ware with dull white blossoms. Ht. 5¼". Fuller Coll. Seattle Art Mus.

stoneware. Accuracy was considered a vital point and the spouts had to be straight while the covers fitted with a convex curve inside probably because such covers would drip the moisture collected on them back into the center of the liquid. Rarely glazes very like the "soft Chün" types were employed to imitaté Chün yao, and others were similar to Kwangtung types of glaze. Ou, the famous imitator, also made Kuan and Ko types of glaze, and some of his work was considered good enough to be copied in the Yung Chêng period.

I was recently sent an example from China which is of red ware with a turquoise glaze etched to give an uneven surface much like that of corroded bronze.

Though the wares began as simple and well designed works of art the usual tendency for modeling to become ornate took hold and soon we have all sorts of involved and tricky stunts employed.

MORTUARY AND ARCHITECTURAL POTTERY

While our interest has properly centered upon the great producers of ceramic wares we must not lose sight of the fact that nearly every town in China had a kiln to supply daily needs and mortuary wares. We find during Sung times less and less pottery used for the tombs but some exceedingly fine wares were so employed. In Ming days De Groot tells us in *The Religious System of China* (Vol. ii, p. 809) the tomb of an important man contained: "a furnace kettle and a furnace both of wood, saucer with stand, pot or vase, an earthen wine-pot, a spittoon, a water basin, an incense box, a tea cup,

FIG. 761. Ming pottery incense burner, probably part of a temple set of five pieces including two vases and two candlesticks. The teak cover has, of course, been added later. The glazes are of green and mustard yellow. Ht. 23½". Metropolitan Mus. of Art. Altman Coll.

FIG. 762. Double tubular vase of the form called "Ying-hsuing," which words taken individually mean "eagle" and "bear" figures of which usually appear on one side holding the cylinders together, but taken together mean "champion." Such vases were given as rewards for military prowess and were originally a bronze form of T'ang or earlier period. Ht. 14½". Warren E. Cox Coll.

a tea saucer, two chop sticks, etc. . . . two wooden bowls, twelve wooden platters, various articles of furniture including a bed, a screen, chest and a couch all of wood; 16 musicians, 24 armed lifeguards, 6 bearers, 10 female attendants; the spirits known as 'Azure Dragon,' the 'White Tiger,' the 'Red Bird,' and the 'Black Warrior'; the Spirits of the Door Way and ten warriors, . . . all made of wood and a foot high." Sometimes chiefly wood was used and again nearly everything might be made of pottery. Hobson says, "Even in the humblest tombs one might expect to find bowls and jars to contain the offerings of food with which the dead were always supplied."

The collection in the B.M. shows pieces from Szechwan province which are of reddish earthenware with opaque chocolate brown glaze sometimes having variegated milky grey splashes. Many of the jars have roughly modeled dragons on them. The Philippine finds which I have described are of better pottery. Another well known type is of hard, buff body unglazed on the bottom and covered with turquoise, brownish yellow and dark aubergine glazes inclined to chip off. The objects are generally molded and fairly thin. These should not be confused with the "three colored" wares described above. Many of these crude wares are not Ming at all but of much more recent date. Some large and ornate pieces such as incense burners have added to the colors mentioned above, green, violet, various blue and brown glazes all of the glassy type and all seeming to have a bad hold on the body much as did most T'ang glazes, and they are undoubtedly of a very similar consistency.

There is also the actual "Three color pottery" in contrast to the "Three color porcelain." This has a red or buff pottery body and much the same range of shapes and color treatments that are seen in the porcelain ones. They are not valued quite so highly on purely technical grounds.

The architectural pottery is much the same as the wares described above and occurs in the forms of tiles, vases for out-of-door use, finials, etc. The glazes of these are usually green, yellow, turquoise and aubergine or dark blue. A few dated specimens exist: In the Messel Collection one corresponds with 1529 and in the Louvre is one with a Wan Li mark. Mr. Hobson speaks of one in the Lindley Scott Collection, "It would almost certainly have been assigned to Ming date, were it not for the incised inscription, which gives the year of its manufacture as 1659." This is fifteen years after the end of the Ming period. The Ming designs were copied exactly right up to the end of the 18th century and later.

I recently discovered in the home of Harrison Cady, a fine figure about two feet high which has an inscription on the back of the seat which reads, "At Tien T'an mountain the Taoist temple 'Ho Shih T'ang' the Taoist believer Li Tao Ming spends his money freely in ordering one set of 'Three Officials' and one set of 'Kuan Chao.' " (The three officials are the Official of Heaven, the Official of Earth and the Official of Water, and are Taoist gods. The "Kuan Chao" are the three heroes of the Three Kingdom period, Liu Pei, Chang Fei and Chao Yün, under Kwan Yü who is also being called Kwan Ti, god of war.) "The followers of this temple are Ts'ui Tien and Ts'ui Yu. This dedication is on the 17th year of the Chêng Hua period (1465–1487) of the Great Ming Dynasty." (1482) "Offered by the usher stationed in

Chêng Hua figure dated the 17th year of the reign (1482) and made in Shan Si province to offer to the Taoist temple Ho Shih T'ang on Tien T'an mountain, Yang Chen hsien in Che Chow division. It is of the usual buff clay with green and amber glaze. Ht. 23½". Harrison Cady owner.

CHÊNG HUA MING FIGURE FROM SHANSI PROVINCE
PLATE 150

the city, Ch'iao Ping and his son Ch'iao Pin in the district of Yang Chen, division of Che Chow Shansi province." Thus we have in this remarkable example a monument which tells us not only the date but the probable location of its manufacture. (See Pl. 150)

The sculpture of the Ming dynasty is filled with action and design, though sometimes the fullness of the latter somewhat overshadows the former. But the very exuberance, the diversification of interests, the added pressure of life which caused the Ming potters to overdo their vases and expend efforts in useless virtuosity in a dozen different ways, has imbued their modeling of figures with an appeal that anyone can understand. The aim was for naturalism and proportions were as near those of life as possible. You may wonder at my enthusiasm for these modelers of figures when I have had to condemn most of the makers of vases but it should be understood that the art of modeling figures is really less difficult than that of making a fine vase. The

Pottery figure of Lohan glazed straw, green and amber colors. Ht. about 50″ with stand. Metropolitan Mus. of Art.

Ming pottery figures of Paranirvana (the "sleep" of Buddha) dated 1494. Remembering that these figures are only 10″ tall I think that their facial expression compare very favorably with those of the life sized Lohan ones. The ware is very light buff and the glazes are light mustard yellow, bright leaf-green, straw and black, and they adhere closely to the body. Ht. Lower group 15″. Ht. Standing figures 10″. Metropolitan Mus. of Art.

MING POTTERY FIGURES

PLATE 151

latter is a more sensitive expression just as might be a still life by Chardin which would be more difficult to copy than a caricature by Hogarth. These Ming works never have the *style* of T'ang examples, but they are alive and interesting.

Distinctions are difficult at times between Ming and modern figures of this sort simply because the modern artists working in some small Chinese town might still be following the Ming tradition and using the same materials. But strange as it may seem there is also great difficulty in distinguishing between Ming and T'ang figures in some instances when the simple green and brownish yellow transparent glazes were used. An excellent example of this difficulty is found in the six large seated Lohan statues which came on

Fig. 763. A roof tile finial of glazed pottery in yellow and green, of the Ming dynasty, one of a pair. Ht. 21½″. Fuller Coll. Seattle Art Mus.
Fig. 764. Ming pottery figure showing traces of polychrome on a reddish clay. Ht. 21″. Metropolitan Mus. of Art.
Fig. 765. Pottery figure of Lohan glazed in straw, green, and amber colors. Ht. about 50″ on stand. Metropolitan Mus. of Art.

Fig. 766. Pair of Ming roof tile figures of buff pottery glazed in green, straw and orange yellow. Ht. 11″. Metropolitan Mus. of Art.

Fig. 767. Ming roof tile of buff pottery with yellowish glassy white glaze, strongly crackled on the figure, yellow green, orange yellow, warm brown and black glazes. Ht. 17″. Metropolitan Mus. of Art.

the market some years ago and were sold to the British Museum, Pennsylvania University Museum and Metropolitan Museum of Art. All were unhesitatingly called T'ang. The origin of these figures is unknown because they were reported to have been cached in a cave temple, "almost inaccessible on a mountain top near Ichou in Chih-li," as it is described by F. Perzynski who went there after the figures were brought out and found a "few fragments" of the figures, "which had evidently been broken off in the attempt to remove them through the narrow aperture of the caves." In Hobson's words, "On the

Above — MING: HSÜAN TÊ PERIOD STEM CUP WITH THREE FISH IN BRILLIANT RED UNDER THE GLAZE.

Ht. about 3 inches   Sir Percival David Collection

Below — MING: HSÜAN TÊ PERIOD DISH WITH CHI LUNG OR SACRIFICIAL RED GLAZE.

British Museum

FIG. 768. Two Ming roof tiles, one in aubergine of dark color, bright green, yellow and straw, and the other in black brown and blue glazes. Ht. 13″. Metropolitan Mus. of Art.

FIG. 769. Ming pottery roof-tile with the usual green, yellow, etc., glazes. Ht. 15″. Metropolitan Mus. of Art.

altar of the shrine he found an incense burner of glazed ware, which he attributed to the Yüan dynasty, and there was a tablet recording the restoration of the altar in the Chêng Tê reign." Hobson adds that, "It is interesting to note that Mr. Perzynski assumed at once that these figures are of T'ang date." (See *Chinese Pottery and Porcelain,* p. 35, footnote.) Now let us weigh the evidence for there has been some controversy on the subject:

FOR T'ANG ATTRIBUTION

1.—The ware is near white and comparatively hard pottery.

2.—Hobson says, "The surface is covered with a brownish green glaze which is clearly a survival of the Han glaze." But he gives no chemical analysis or proof. We suppose he means that the glaze has the general aspect of a Han lead glaze.

3.—Referring to the design on the robe of the figure at the B.M. he says, "The same prunus design occurs on a typical T'ang bowl in the Eumorfopoulos Collection stencilled white in a green ground." Neither design was stencilled but the blossom design was used in T'ang times.

4.—He continues, "The colorless glaze on the fleshy parts has acquired a brown stain from the dripping of the cave moisture, and developed minute crackle, both of which features are observable on some of the glazed vases from the T'ang tombs; the pupils of the eyes are black." It is to be noted that he speaks of a stain which could occur in a short time but not of erosion or corrosion of the glaze. The crackle would have occurred in firing and it is only on the light "fleshy parts" as he says, though a very little here and there occurs elsewhere.

5.—He goes on to describe the glaze and concludes, "The technique, then, is that of the T'ang wares, but instead of being made in a mould like the grave statuettes, this monumental figure is modelled in the round by an artist worthy to rank with the masters of sculpture and painting who made the T'ang period famous."

NEUTRAL OBSERVATIONS

1.—The body could be *either* T'ang or Ming. It is actually harder than that of most figures so glazed of the T'ang period but in all fairness this might be because of the large size and special care in potting.

2.—The glazes are undeniably of the Han type, T'ang type and also Ming type being ordinary lead glazes. They are certainly more heavily applied than those on most of the yellow and green glazed figures but this again may be because of the large size.

3.—The designs are, of course, after the fabrics which they represent and might be either T'ang or Ming. The prunus blossoms were so far as I know used at all times after they were originated and we certainly see them in Sung and Ming times as well as on K'ang Hsi "prunus jars."

AGAINST THE T'ANG ATTRIBUTION

1.—The glazes adhere to the body far better than do any of those on other T'ang figures I have seen. Most of these figures have strongly crackled glazes that tend to come off in small chips here and there. In applying the glazes heavier this tendency would be increased, that is they would crackle more and set up a greater tension between body and glaze so that one would expect to see small places where they had come off, particularly on such large surfaces.

2.—Mr. Theodore Y. Hobby has told me that the green is much like that on Ming vases, with which he has made comparisons.

3.—The frosty iridescent sheen seen on T'ang glazes and seldom absent at some place however small on pieces of this period is not in evidence on these figures. This iridescence also occurs on Ming pieces though not invariably. It appears on temple pieces as well as interred grave pieces much as does the green of bronze patination and one would especially expect to see it on figures which had been many centuries in caves where moisture had dripped on them. There is in fact no sign of erosion or decay of the glazes at all that is apparent and this is amazing for T'ang examples.

4.—On the grounds of style we expect exaggerations in T'ang figures which are seldom correct anatomically and usually gain style and design thereby. The Indian influence is often met with and can be seen in the narrow waists and broad shoulders, or again the heads may be too large in scale or the legs elongated. This was done as consciously as it is done by our modern advertising artists for women's clothes today. Yet these figures are perfectly exact and correct in their proportions as are, in fact, many Ming figures. I believe this to be the strongest argument for a Ming attribution. Certainly the artist who made them was aiming for naturalism rather than style.

5.—Not as conclusive evidence but worth note is the fact that during T'ang times most figures were made with the pupils of the eyes prominent and bold while it is characteristic of Ming figures that they often have narrow, slit eyes sometimes upturned at the corners in a more Mongolian expression. I think this change took place after the Mongolian invasion of Yüan times, in common wares at least.

6.—The conventionalized rock bases which without a doubt belong to the figures are often seen under Ming examples and *I have never seen any of this ornate style on T'ang examples*. These clumsy conventionalized rocks would certainly be picked as typically Ming, if seen alone.

7.—Much of the impressiveness of the figures is brought about by the concentrated squint of the eyes which command one as would a pointing finger in an advertisement. If one looks at the figures alone, exclusive of the heads, they become stodgy, sagging and totally lacking in the spirit of T'ang figures. The hands are posed and without vitality or life though they are very correct anatomically.

A comparison of these figures with the Ming "Paranirvana" group also of the Metropolitan Museum, remembering, of course, that the latter are only 10 to 15 inches high, shows a great similarity in the facial treatments and perhaps a balance in favor of the latter which are naturally less detailed but certainly far more moving in emotional expression. The colors of the glazes of these Ming figures and the large ones are similar as are also the textures of the glazes.

Finally, of course, there is the evidence that the other objects found in the caves were of Yüan and even Ming times, though this I do not give much weight to for frankly I do not believe the figures were very long in the caves. There was no sign that they had been *made* for these caves at all.

The question, of course, simmers down to whether the characteristics of these figures are due to their unusual size or are due to their having been made in the later period and I must say that I favor the latter analysis. This, however, does not in any sense condemn them as works of art. Often we are too quick to condemn a whole period such as the Ming or that of Rome because of some atrociously bad things which were perpetrated in it while a greater study and resulting insight will help us to appreciate the fine things which also were done. The very difficulty in distinguishing at what time these large figures were made shows us that some exceedingly great qualities prevailed for hundreds of years.

I am gratified to see that, after having written the above and having told Mr. Alan Priest, curator of Far Eastern Art of the Metropolitan Museum of Art, that it was my intention to publish the figures of seated lohans as Ming, he in his recent book on Chinese Sculpture has said, "These figures were called T'ang when they first appeared, and most of the owners up to this moment have stuck to that dating. A careful comparison with T'ang and Ming glazes shows the glazes on the Museum lohans to be far closer to Ming, and as the sculpture itself seems closer to Ming we suggest the later date." I had not told Mr. Priest *how* or *why* I thought both the glazes and the modeling were, not closer to but actually, Ming.

CHAPTER XX

THE CH'ING DYNASTY

Nurhachu the Manchurian (1559–1627) had a great army which had threatened China for some years. His country is in the basin of the great river Amur and its tributaries, the Sungari and Ussuri. This was an agricultural land but cold, and the people always looked to the South as a land of warmth and fertility. The people were of those great nomadic tribes that wandered about the Siberian plain, across the Bering land bridge that is believed to have existed, to America and back to settle finally and fish and raise crops. The Khitan Tartars ruled in the 10th century along with their conquered lands in Mongolia and Northern China. The Nüchens, founders of the Kin Dynasty overthrew them and ruled in late Sung days until they were in turn overcome by the Mongols.

The Ming Dynasty ended in 1644 when a rebel set himself up in Peking and the Emperor committed suicide. The General Wu San-kuei joined forces with the Manchurians to oust the usurper and this ended in the placing of a Manchurian prince upon the throne of China. It was a remarkable happening for the Chinese were ten times stronger in numbers and much richer. Nurhachu had in 1618 beaten three Chinese armies larger than his own but died in 1626 or 1627 an old and worn out man, but his son, T'ai Tsung carried on and finished the conquest taking China but wisely following the Chinese religion, literature and culture. His reign was under the dynastic title of Ta Ch'ing and he died in 1643 leaving his son Shun Chih at the age of nine to rule, and it was he who ascended the throne in 1644, the last year of the Ming Dynasty.

As a sign of subjugation the Chinese were forced to wear pigtails. Various attempts were tried to regain the throne and it was not until 1662 that the last of the patriots were driven to the Burmese border.

K'ANG HSI (1662–1722)

K'ang Hsi was the son of Shun Chih and when he died in 1661 this son was only eight years old, but when he was only 14 he took command and began to prove himself. He was described by a contemporary European priest who said, "This prince was one of the most extraordinary men who ever lived and who are only met with once in the course of several centuries.

532

He placed no limit to his desire for knowledge, and of all of the princes of Asia there was none with so great a taste for the arts and sciences."

His reign was not all sweetness and light for in 1673 the San Fan Rebellion had to be put down and it took eight years until 1681 during which time the Emperor led his own troops.

Europe was exerting more and more pressure. Catholic missionaries, Dominicans and Augustans from the Philippines, Franciscans from Italy and members of the Société des Missions Étrangères from Paris came in great numbers and were put in charge of the Bureau of Astronomy (the Jesuits), of mapping the country and given other scientific work until by 1700 there were probably about 300,000 Catholics in China. But by 1800, because of controversies, the French Revolution and its repercussions, etc., the number was reduced to about 200,000. The Portuguese retained Macao and the French, Dutch, British and Americans were increasing their trade.

Here we pause, for clearer understanding of some of the after effects, to relate a most unsavory chapter in English history which does not make John Bull seem quite the benevolent white father to the heathen that our school books lead us to believe. The East India Company had the monopoly of trade in England and at first the Chinese teas, silks and cottons were paid for by specie, but soon, to quote the *Encyclopaedia Britannica* 14th Edition (Vol. 5 p. 536), "The importation of opium, chiefly from India and on British ships, brought a reversal of the balance of trade." The Chinese were aware of the results of this insidious poison and took steps to regurgitate it. The Chinese government destroyed the stocks of drugs and forced the merchants to give bond that they would not engage in the further importation of dope. The Opium War was started for the British thought this action too high-handed. But thank heavens we have the pleasant task of telling about the things which China gave to Europe rather than the exceedingly unpleasant one of relating what Europe gave to China, except wherein such gifts effected the ceramic arts.

The first obvious results upon the industry of pottery making were that almost all production ceased while wars and rebellions raged throughout the 18 provinces between 1640 and 1680. Ching-tê Chêng itself was invaded during the San Fan Rebellion but that it was working earlier we know because of two orders in 1654 and 1659 that were sent down from the Palace by Shun Chih for large "dragon bowls" 2½ feet high, 3½ feet in diameter and with walls 3 inches thick and 5 inches at the bottom—and for plaques 3 feet by 2½ feet and 3 inches thick—which could not be made. We also hear that the industry was under Viceroy Lang T'ing-tso.

In 1680, after the rebellion, K'ang Hsi made plans for the establishment of the various crafts in the Palace precincts in Peking but the plans were abandoned. Shortly after Ching-tê Chêng was rebuilt with Imperial funds. The *T'ao shuo* tells that the officials were carefully selected, that funds were ample and that several thousands were put to work. It says that the producers became rich, sparing no labor and not grudging expense so that the wares turned out were novel in design and improved daily. It says, "Even when compared with that of former dynasties, which used to be lauded as being as precious as gold or jade, there is some that excels, none that fails to come up to the old, and, if it be not now described, after generations will be unable to discuss it." Thus the duties of recorder were taken seriously.

The good Père d'Entrecolles was on the spot and wrote a description of the place in 1712 at the height of the reign. He says it was on the right bank of the Ch'ang River, encircled by hills, with its double and triple lines of junks in the port, the whirling flames blazing away at the sky from the kilns which made it seem like a city on fire or an inferno, the huge population estimated as a million, all interested in one way or another in the "three thousand kilns." He said that there was work for all even the halt, the lame and the blind who could at least grind color.

No less a person than T'ang Ying, the director of the Imperial Factory in the later reign of Ch'ien Lung tells us more of the same in his book "Twenty Illustrations of the Manufacture of Porcelain."

S. W. Bushell, C.M.G. who was keeper of the Far Eastern Art department of the Victoria & Albert Museum at South Kensington, London made a translation of the *T'ao shuo* to which all modern scholars admit indebtedness and though his opinions may not all be ours they are well worth looking into.

He thought that this period, the K'ang Hsi, was the "Culminating epoch by common consent of both eastern and western connoisseurs," but we cannot agree for we now have added perspective not possible for him in his day.

He also wrote that Lang T'ing-tso, viceroy of Kiangsi and Kiangnan, was distinguished by the famous ware known as Lang yao but Hobson says, "The idea may be dismissed as in the highest degree improbable." Hannover says, "This advance was connected with the names of two remarkably able men. One of them was Lang T'ing-tso who had been entrusted with the supervision, during the previous reign, of the imperial factory and is said to have invented the so-called Lang yao." And later he says, "Others maintain that it (the name) is derived from a whole family of potters of the name of Lang." Well one man's guess is as good as another's.

All authorities agree that the brilliant renaissance in ceramics was due to the work of Ts'ang Ying-hüsan who was secretary of the Metropolitan Board of Works, appointed in 1683 superintendent of the Imperial Factories at Ching-tê Chêng.

The Shun Chih and early K'ang Hsi wares are simply transitional and of no great importance. Hobson says the only dated one he knows belongs to Dr. Lindley Scott and is a figure with glazes "in three color Ming style." He also speaks of a bowl in the B.M. marked "Ta Ch'ing nein chih" (made in the great Ch'ing dynasty) and says "Such a mark would be appropriate in the first reign of the dynasty and no other." Such may be the case but I cannot see his line of reason for such marks were used throughout the Ming dynasty (referring to the dynasty only and not the reign) and could also have followed as a habit.

He also mentions a group of pieces which were brought up from ships including the Haarlem which were sunk in Table Bay in 1648 and describes them as being thin, crisp, lightly moulded with leaf-shaped panels and painted with slight floral designs, deer, birds, etc., and human figures such as "long Elizas" which the Dutch called "Lang Lijsen," in various blues including a pale silvery, dark indigo and sapphire. The marks on these are the apocryphal date mark of Ch'eng Hua and of K'ang Hsi besides a number of complimentary marks such as "yü" or "jade," and a few "hall marks."

It is among these thin wares with bright enamel decorations that we should look for examples of the early "famille verte" porcelains and not, he says, among the black hawthorn vases which are not likely to have been made before the reconstruction of 1680. The *T'ao lu* says they made "eel yellow," turquoise and "spotted yellow" wares which were the most beautiful. It also says, brown, purple, green soufflé red, soufflé blue and pale yellow which were also good.

BLANC DE CHINE OR WHITE WARES

The pure white wares were not popular and are seldom seen because there is a growing itch to decorate if not with design at least with rich color. Then too white was the color of mourning and such wares were demanded by the court and probably also by lesser households for such ceremonies. White was the color used in worship of the "Year-Star" and also at times for special scholar's desk furniture. Such wares were made both at Ching-tê Chêng in Kiangsi and at Tê-hua in Fukien province. The finest clay was put aside for them for by now they had to be flawless to sustain appeal. The finest are called "t'o t'ai" or "bodiless" ware and Père d'Entrecolles says some had to be put on cotton wool for fear of damage and the glaze had to be blown on it as it was not safe to hold and dip. But there were also heavier wares and the decoration ran from "an hua" or "secret decoration" incised and engraved or molded or made with delicate traceries of liquid white clay (slip) or

FIG. 770. K'ang Hsi figure made at *Tê-hua*, Fukien province, of *Pu-tai*. Glaze thinner and more glassy than that of Ming. Cream-white. Ht. 4¾". Mus. of Fine Arts, Boston.

FIG. 771. Brush pot, K'ang Hsi. Heavy foot rim about ¾" wide, unglazed. Tê-hua. Ht. 5½". Metropolitan Mus. of Art.

FIG. 772. "Blanc de Chine" figure of Kwan Yin walking on water. Tê-hua. Slightly greenish. ½" foot roughly glazed inside with fire crack. Ht. 15". Metropolitan Mus. of Art.

K'ang Hsi Tê-hua, Fukien, figure of Ma Ku with fawn of slightly
greenish white and having about half-inch foot with fire cracks and
glazed inside. Better than average example. Ht. 14½". Metropolitan
Mus. of Art.

K'ANG HSI "BLANC DE CHINE" FIGURE

PLATE 152

gypsum to boldly cut relief work and "a jour" piercing often of surprising delicacy descended from the "kuei kung" or "devil's work" of the Ming Dynasty. Occasionally a loose or free moving belt was made of free working rings, and chains, while low reliefs were built up on the ware with shavings of clay worked up with a wet brush, and reliefs were worked separately and luted onto the vessel with liquid clay.

Fig. 773. Bowl of *Kuei kung* (devil's work) reticulation on which are round medallions each containing two figures in high relief crudely modeled. Type originated in the Ming dynasty but this example is labeled K'ang Hsi. Dia. 3½". Ex Avery Coll. Metropolitan Mus. of Art.

Fig. 774. Reticulated K'ang Hsi "blanc de Chine" incense burner. Ht. 3½". Metropolitan Mus. of Art.

It is obvious from this description that more and more accent was being put upon lacy effects and delicate detail; upon perfection and not upon feeling. Meanwhile Tê-hua, which since 1550 or earlier had been turning out such beautiful figures continued making them but harder and whiter, more perfect and more detailed as may be seen by the examples illustrated. That old designs also were used is proven by the small octagonal box and cover from the Metropolitan Museum of Art which is very close to the form of a Sung period ying ching model.

BLUE AND WHITE WARES

The most numerous of the K'ang Hsi wares and probably the most important, if we judge by their effect on the rest of the world, are the blue and white wares. They were popular right up to the end of the period when the famille rose porcelains began to take their place. Hobson says of them, "When my lord of Bristol (*Diary of John Hervey, First Earl of Bristol*) in 1690 bought from 'Medina ye Jew' and 'Collemar ye Dutchman' tea-pots, large jars, china beakers, old china bottles, dishes, rice-pots, etc. 'for dear wife,' he had to pay substantial sums. But they are nothing to the price which the amateur will gladly give today." Bushell tells us that a first grade "Hawthorn" was bought from the Orrock Coll. for 230 pounds sterling but that one like it sold recently for 5,900 (Louis Huth Coll.). I must add that now the prices are at the lowest possible level because of the enthusiasm for earlier wares. Thus it is an excellent time for a collector to acquire these always beautiful wares.

Neither Europeans nor the Japanese have ever been able to make anything

Left: Fine prunus jar or "Hawthorn jar" with original cover and deep, vibrant blue ground. Ht. 10⅜". Altman Coll. Metropolitan Mus. of Art.

Right: K'ang Hsi gallipot painted vigorously in Ming style but somewhat more stiff. Form exaggerated in width of shoulder and smallness of neck. Ht. 6½". Altman Coll. Metropolitan Mus. of Art.

K'ang Hsi blue and white temple vase with beautiful landscape painting in deep vibrant color. Ht. 29". Metropolitan Mus. of Art.

One of pair of blue and white bottles with squirrel and grape design. Ht. 7". K'ang Hsi. Ex D. Abbes Coll.

K'ANG HSI BLUE AND WHITE PORCELAINS

PLATE 153

comparable with good K'ang Hsi examples. The body is clean and dense, close grained, pure white and of an unctuous smoothness. The potting is perfectly true. The glaze is clear and limpid, lustrous and with only the very faintest tinge of green. The blue may be either light or dark but it should always be clear and without any reddish tinge or grey impurity. This is of the greatest importance in valuing a specimen.

K'ANG HSI COMPARED WITH MING TECHNIQUE

In K'ang Hsi painting the outlines are reduced to the slenderest possible guides and graded washes for shading are employed while Ming washes are flat. The foot-rim is well potted, neat and true with clean, straight sides or a groove to fit a stand. This is not to say that occasional Ming pieces may not also have a groove for the same purpose. There is a glaze underneath the bottom which comes up to a little way from the edge of the foot-rim and the body where exposed at this point is often slightly browned in firing.

There is seldom any bad drawing. One might almost wish that there was just to prove that the work had been done by human beings. Hobson tries to be kind in this passage, "But this mechanical skill could never have won for K'ang Hsi blue and white its world-wide recognition, had it not been for the beauty of the blue. One feels that manufacturers realizing this allowed the design to become more and more the mere vehicle for the blue." (*Later Ceramic Wares of China*, p. 12) Well now, I think we can hardly

FIG. 776. Blue "Hawthorn jars" of fair quality. Note different treatment of background, one said to represent branches against ice; the other, blossoms floating on water. Ht. 9½". Ex Warren E. Cox Coll.

FIG. 775. K'ang Hsi "Hawthorn vase." Ht. about 12". Courtesy of Graham & Son.

agree that this could have been conscious control on their part; one can hardly imagine a Manchurian overseer saying, "Draw without spirit, with perfection but without feeling, for it is the blue we wish to show off and not your drawing," as a gem merchant might plan the design of a piece of jewelry. No, I think it reduces itself to the simple fact that there *was* no feeling and I shall make this more clear as we go into the 18th century.

Everyone is familiar with the "prunus jar," the "hawthorn jar," or the flower bedecked "ginger jar." We all know that the design represents early spring blossoms against ice and it is interesting to know that these jars were given, filled with tea or sweetmeats as New Years' presents to friends with the perfect understanding that the jar was to be returned later much as were the pie tins between farmers' wives in early American days. There are many of these jars and even pairs or near pairs to be had for a few hundred dollars but a small group in Dresden are said to have been purchased at the price of a regiment of soldiers by Augustus the Strong who built the collection between 1694 and 1705. Let us hope this was a mere figure of speech. The one I show from the Altman Collection is thought by Mr. Theodore Hobby to be of finest quality and I am only sorry that we cannot possibly reproduce its color of deep, vibrant blue. There is supposed to be a difference in the quality of drawing and perhaps some of these jars are a bit more free than others within the set brackets of K'ang Hsi limitations. It is said that in some instances the prunus design was degraded to a mere pattern of blossoms without stems and that this pattern is not suitable for large surfaces though effective in borders and on small areas. And guess who said this—the man who spoke of the design as a proof that the large Lohan seated figures were T'ang and not Ming and the man who lauded the pattern on T'ang plates. Neither Bushell nor Hannover agreed on this point of "degradation." The latter shows a fine little specimen rare because most of these jars run from about 9 inches to 11 inches and he states that in China these jars were never valued so highly as in Europe. He mentions one which sold in the Huth sale at Christie's for 6,195 pounds sterling or some $30,000. He also gives a warning against modern fakes.

Of course such prices were the result of competition between rich men and were based on the fact that only a limited number of these jars were available. I know collectors who carry around small sample sherds in their pockets so as to compare them with vases seen in the auction and sales rooms. Technically this is a good stunt, if you are interested in getting a piece a fraction deeper in color than the next fellow's but if one has to judge one's *emotional response* to a work of art in this manner, one might as well carry around a sample to test the softness of his lady's skin and another to compare the color of her eye. This is not art but a picayune and fussbudget way of collecting which can appeal only to small minds.

The wares were all factory made and the people who made them knew what they were worth. We seem little different from the Philippine natives who went frantic over the glazed pots brought to them by the Chinese and which they themselves could not make. The Chinese often smile at our love for ordinary objects and lack of appreciation of the finer things of art and life.

This factory work was organized so that there were specialists for every step of the making and decorating of a pot; for drawing the lines around them, for outlines of flowers, for outlines of birds, for those of human figures and for animals, for painting landscapes of one sort or another, for filling in the designs with shadings, for making backgrounds, for inscriptions, marks and seals.

Père d'Entrecolles' comments on the painters are not very complimentary. He classes them with ordinary workmen and compares their ability with that of a "European apprentice of four months' standing." But Hobson says his remarks are colored with foreign prejudice and that he did not understand the conventions of Chinese drawing. This seems a bit out of place in that Hobson spent very little time living in China and the good priest lived and studied there for many years. However, this is one sort of convention which I might call the Convention of Commercial Short Cuts. It is quite different, as you may imagine, from that sort of convention which originated in the economy of space necessary among nomads. The one is a living force struggling to speak within limits. The other is a short cut forced by boredom and repetition. The one has the simplicity of the beginning of life while the other is simple death. I do not accuse Mr. Hobson of anything, but I say that he may have been unconsciously influenced in his admiration for prunus jars by his knowledge of the prices they fetched in the auction rooms.

So much for prunus jars and they do not deserve the diatribe which I have given but what goes for them goes for the other famous K'ang Hsi wares such as the "sang de boeuf," the "peach bloom" and the "famille verte." But let us say that they are not entirely to be condemned simply because they have been grossly overrated. They would have been just as good and just as bad had they not been adopted by high society. They are often as decorative as a nice piece of chintz or hand blocked linen or wall paper but few are great works of art.

OTHER BLUE GROUND WARES

One reason that the line and wash ground representing ice was done was simply that it was easier than trying the almost impossible feat of obtaining a perfectly even ground of blue. Another means had to be adopted, for applying such a ground with a brush was impossible. Therefore wave textures were tried, but they too were hardly satisfactory. Some vases simply were treated with brush patches like scales overlapping, but they gave as mussy an effect. Most of these wares had medallions of rectangular, square or fan shape in reserve and containing design of some sort such as peony flowers, figures, etc. There was also an odd variation of short necked club shaped vase with what Hobson calls "rose and ticket" design, the tickets being small oval medallions on the shoulder sometimes left blank like ticket labels. He says of these that they were painted with the best blue but must have been export wares because they occur in garniture sets.

Entirely foreign to Chinese taste are these "garnitures de cheminée," as the French call them or "chimney sets" or "mantelpiece sets" as the English call them, consisting of three beakers and two large jars with covers. These are not at all to be confused with the Chinese sets of two candle sticks, two vases for holding flowers or incense sticks and a center burner for use in front of a shrine. They are in fact typical of the bad taste of the Europeans of the time; made in huge sizes, each trying to outdo the last in scale, in ornateness of decoration and variety of color. These sets were designed to

K'ang Hsi soft paste blue and white vase with brown crackle which may or may not have been intentional. Ht. 10". Metropolitan Mus. of Art.

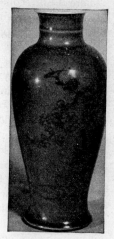

K'ang Hsi vase with four character Ch'eng Hua, Ming mark in blue under foot. Cornflower blue with underglaze blue design. Foot shows very smooth clay. Delicately potted. Ht. 8". Warren E. Cox Coll. Ex John Getts Coll.

Bottle with three brown-edged discs on neck. Suggests Near Eastern influence. Ht. about 10½". Avery Coll. Metropolitan Mus. of Art.

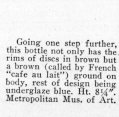

Going one step further, this bottle not only has the rims of discs in brown but a brown (called by French "cafe au lait") ground on body, rest of design being underglaze blue. Ht. 8¼". Metropolitan Mus. of Art.

SOFT PASTE, BLUE-GROUND AND CAFÉ-AU-LAIT UNDERGLAZE
BLUE DECORATED EXAMPLES

PLATE 154

place before the shrine of the great god I AM, the master whose portrait often hung above the mantelpiece commanding the European household.

Other wares of white on blue type are slender jars with contracted necks and decorated with archaic dragons and floral scrolls as well as the ewers and rose water sprinklers for the Western Asian market. Some of these have leaf shaped panels or mirror shaped ones filled with floral decoration. Ju-i borders

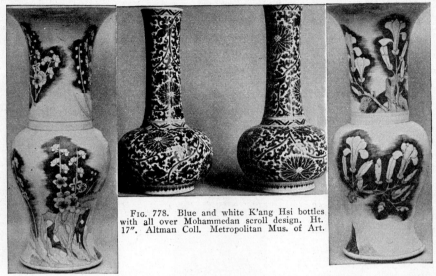

FIG. 778. Blue and white K'ang Hsi bottles with all over Mohammedan scroll design. Ht. 17". Altman Coll. Metropolitan Mus. of Art.

FIG. 777. Similar to common magnolia patterned vases is this with prunus blossoms which, however, are not in relief. Ht. 17". Havemeyer Coll. Metropolitan Mus. of Art.

FIG. 779. Magnolia blossoms on a "temple jar" shape set off by horizontal shading in blue on white ground thus eliminating heaviness of solid ground and using texture easier to obtain than a perfectly even ground. Design in low relief. Ht. about 17". Metropolitan Mus. of Art. H. O. Havemeyer bequest.

or "lambrequin" borders often finished the upper parts of the shoulders or about the neck just below the mouth. One of the rather pleasant ideas was to draw magnolias or blossoms and set them off by a series of horizontal brush strokes in blue but only filling part of the ground. Some of these have the flowers in low relief and are probably a bit later than the others.

BLUE ON WHITE WARES

In the blue on white wares we see all of the Ming devices with others added. Land and sea scapes are sometimes interestingly stylized and pheasant and

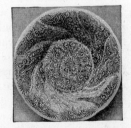

FIG. 780. K'ang Hsi plate with carved border and underglaze blue decoration. Dia. 14". Avery Coll. Metropolitan Mus. of Art.

FIG. 781. This plate shows a European trio, perhaps Austrian or Hungarian for lady seems to be playing a zimbol. K'ang Hsi. Dia. c. 12¼". Avery Coll. Metropolitan Mus. of Art.

FIG. 782. K'ang Hsi blue and white dish with wide rim in feeling of some Western Asian and Spanish wares of lustre type, but this may have originated in China. Dia. c. 18". Metropolitan Mus. of Art.

rock motives are often well done. Baskets of flowers are stiff but popular decorations for European taste. The old "Mohammedan flowers" of circular form joined by S shaped stems were made more ornate. The use of mirror shaped medallions was to suggest that they were actually mirrors in which you might see the landscape reflected from over your shoulder.

Not satisfied with making all possible varieties and combinations these artists naturally tried to make things more real by modeling them. This also made the work more costly and difficult to do. Père d'Entrecolles tells us how the Chinese were put to it to satisfy the European's taste for eccentric shapes and had to keep many moulds to make them. Some, like the winged

Fig. 783. Blue and white bowl with reticulated medallions. K'ang Hsi. Dia. 5⅛". Avery Coll. Metropolitan Mus. of Art.

Fig. 785. K'ang Hsi bowl with blue decoration about rim, also under reticulated sides. Note precision and delicacy. Dia. 6". Metropolitan Mus. of Art.

Fig. 784. Grotesque bottle with flamboyant handles in white porcelain with crudely drawn underglaze blue design. K'ang Hsi. Avery Coll. Metropolitan Mus. of Art.

handled bottles were copied from Venetian glass, others from various European wares and others came out of the heads of the merchants themselves. Most of these wares were painted in dull blue often with meaningless designs and the sharp and inappropriate rims of the plates and vases were inclined to chip and scale. Just a little later this was overcome by protecting the rims with a brown glaze that would stand the punishment of shipping and handling better.

In 1677 the district prefect ordered that no sacred writing and no reign-name of the Emperor could be put on porcelain as it might be broken and so the name would be desecrated. One suspects that he might have felt that the wares themselves were hardly complimentary, but, of course, he did not say that. The rule could not have been long obeyed but it may have started the custom of using various other names and symbols much to the resulting confusion of modern collectors. Even the reign-names of Hsüan Tê and Ch'êng Hua of the Ming Dynasty are more often seen than K'ang Hsi. Often simply the double ring is used. The character yü meaning jade is supposed to indicate authenticity and good quality but it was copied too. An odd mark like the letter G seems to occur on straight necked bottles which were probably made for some single firm in Holland. This mark occurs on both enameled wares and blue and white. Other symbols and marks can be seen in the tables of marks.

Excellent blue and white vases with bold and direct paintings. Hts. 17⅝″ and 13⅝″. Fuller Coll. Seattle Art Mus.

Beaker with landscapes set off by lambrequins of ju-i pattern and columns. Ht. c. 18″. Metropolitan Mus. of Art.

Temple jar of good proportions with vivid decoration in underglaze blue of court life. Ht. 18″. Metropolitan Mus. of Art.

Amphora of semi-eggshell porcelain with decoration in dark cobalt blue. Six character mark of reign under foot. Ht. 6¼″. C. T. Loo & Co.

Bottle of late K'ang Hsi. I give this attr. because of its elongated form, a mannerism which becomes quite popular in Yung Ch'eng period immediately following. Not very good porcelain and decorated with weak blue dragon design. Avery Coll. Metropolitan Mus. of Art.

K'ANG HSI BLUE AND WHITE WARES

PLATE 155

Chinese "Soft Paste"

We have described the so-called "Chinese soft paste" called "hua shih" by the Chinese and also termed "steatitic porcelain." In 1923 in the "Wares of the Ming Dynasty" the term "soft paste" is used both with and without quotation marks. In 1925 in the "Later Ceramic Wares of China" Mr. Hobson calls it an "American name, which like so many stereotyped terms in ceramic phraseology will not bear examination." Hannover goes a step fur-

Fig. 786. Sprinkler bottle such as those used extensively in Near East. We again see disc with brown edge. Avery Coll. Metropolitan Mus. of Art.

Fig. 787. Bottle of white porcelain of K'ang Hsi period having blue decoration and projecting edge of center disc in brown glaze. Metropolitan Mus. of Art.

Fig. 788. Soft paste or "steatitic" ware with *"peau d'orange"* surface and design of vases painted in underglaze blue. Note coarse crackle and irregular highlight. K'ang Hsi. Ht. 9". Ex D. Abbes Coll.

Fig. 789. Deep cup of blue and white soft paste of creamy texture and light crackle. Base has apocryphal six-character Cheng Hua mark but piece is of K'ang Hsi period. Ht. 4¼". Guy Mayer Coll.

ther and says in his book published in translation by Rackham that same year, "It is an imitation of the old fên ting,"—(This I must say is doubtful.)—"which is erroneously regarded by the Americans as a soft paste porcelain, and for which they therefore pay enormous prices." To go back to Hobson and to continue the quotation above, he says, "Soft paste to the European ear suggests the artificial porcelains of Sévres and Chelsea, of which the body or paste was indeed relatively soft, whereas that of the Chinese ware is intensely hard. The glaze, on the other hand, is softer than the ordinary felspathic glaze; it contains a softening element of lead and is often crackled." Neither Mr. Hannover nor Mr. Hobson come right out and say that they think the body of this ware is as hard as the high-fired white porcelain and in truth it is not. They are both so intent upon distinguishing the meaning "to European ears" that they lose sight of the actual distinction and I doubt very much if any American actually thought that Chinese soft paste was like Sévres or Chelsea soft paste which incidentally is not "porcelain" at all.

Vogt made an analysis of the Chinese ware and declared that it does not contain steatite or soap-stone at all but actually pegmatite without any trace of magnesium. He obtained his samples from San-pao-p'eng, the source for many years. I cannot resist giving one more quotation which perfectly shows the Englishman's point of view. Hobson says, "We have, however, preserved the term 'steatitic' to distinguish the special ware made with the hua shih." Has he indeed! An American is wrong because he uses a term which is correct but somewhat confusing to a European while an Englishman, knowing definitely that he is wrong preserves the usage of misinformation for future generations. I hope this clears up the matter of soft paste, both Chinese and European, once and for all. The Chinese soft paste is just that and the European will be explained in its place, but certainly is not "soft paste *porcelain*" in any sense, for it is not porcelain.

Père d'Entrecolles tells us that the body was made of the hua shih, an unctuous, soapy material in the proportions of eight parts to two of petuntse, taking the place of the kaolin used in the regular porcelain, and goes on to say that it "is rare and far more expensive than the other porcelain. It has an extremely fine grain; and for purposes of painting when compared with ordinary porcelain, it is almost as vellum to paper. Moreover, this ware is surprisingly light to anyone accustomed to handle other kinds; it is far more fragile than the ordinary, and there is difficulty in finding the exact temperature for its firing. Some of the potters do not use hua shih for the body of the ware, but content themselves with making a diluted slip into which they dip their porcelain when dry, so as to give it a coating of hua shih before it is painted and glazed. By this means it gains a certain degree of beauty." The Chinese have always treasured it and asked high prices for it and the best artists painted on it often in the style of the Early Ming artists. It was also made in later reigns.

POWDER BLUE WARES

The difficulties of laying an even underglaze blue ground can only be appreciated if one has tried it. A general idea of the troubles involved can be obtained if one tries to get an even effect with ink on blotting paper. The biscuit of porcelain is immediately absorbent and each stroke of the brush sinks into it with graded values depending upon the amount of color in each part of the brush at the beginning and end of the stroke. One cannot smooth it out or smooth it over for the color does not remain wet long enough. This difficulty led to a very beautiful ground technique.

In the Ming Dynasty the potters had sometimes blown powdered glazes onto their wares but this was only in odd instances. Our old authority Père d'Entrecolles says, "as for the soufflé blue called tsouri tsim (ch'ui ch'ing),

Left: Powder blue vase having deep, rich color. Ht. 17½″. Warren E. Cox Coll.
Center: Powder blue "club-shaped" vase over white porcelain and with gold decoration necessitating another firing. Ht. 17″. Metropolitan Mus. of Art.
Right: Powder blue jar and cover with reserved medallions painted in famille verte enamels. Ht. 18″. Metropolitan Mus. of Art.

Left: Small "club-shaped" vase of powder blue white porcelain with reserve medallions having well styled paintings. One shown seemingly of an immortal with scroll in hand, seated above a raging stream on grotesque dragon. No mark but ware is typical. Ht. 9″. Metropolitan Mus. of Art.
Center: Excellent quality white porcelain vase with gold ornamented powder blue ground and reserved medallions with famille verte flower paintings already showing ornate qualities of following periods. White is tinged with green and pitted here and there. Ht. 17″. Metropolitan Mus. of Art.
Right: Temple vase of rather rough powder blue with reserve medallions also painted in underglaze blue. Ht. 30″. Metropolitan Mus. of Art.

POWDER BLUE K'ANG HSI PORCELAIN

PLATE 156

the finest blue prepared in the manner which I have described, is used. That is blown on the vase, and when it is dry the ordinary glaze is applied either alone or mixed with tsouri yeou, if crackle is required." Hannover says, "As the French term indicates, it was not painted, but blown through a bamboo tube with gauze at the end, on the biscuit, and glazed after dry-

FIG. 790. Powder blue bowl with reserved medallions inside and out, edged with iron red and painted in famille verte enamels on rumpled white ground. Dia. 6½". Metropolitan Mus. of Art.

FIG. 791. Pale powder blue plate with rumpled glaze and smartly drawn design in dark blue and underglaze red. Dia. 8". Metropolitan Mus. of Art.

ing." Hobson says, "Another type of blue glaze is manufactured by a different method, the cobalt being sponged or painted onto the body of the ware or sprayed on it in a dry powder and the glaze added as in the case of the blue and white." Whom are we to believe? Was the blue blown on wet in solution as a spray or was it blown on dry as a powder? Logic would seem to indicate the former for a man who was on the spot speaks of its being allowed to dry before glazing. Also if a dry powder was blown onto a surface it would have to have some wet or sticky surface to hold. Otherwise the powder would drop off. I may add that I have never seen a piece which shows any suggestion of having been "sponged."

In any event the glaze was most delicately applied, probably by spraying again, so that it did not disturb the blue, and the result was a fairly even surface of brilliant but soft blue with only slightly uneven cloudiness and which on close examination is seen to be filled with small particles sometimes blurred with slight running and sometimes quite sharp and clear, but never leaving any white showing except where a mask has been applied. Some are, as it were, close in texture and some are more broadly speckled as may be seen in my vase and the plate and bowl from the Metropolitan Museum. This has no relationship to quality or period. Masking was done

FIG. 792. Fine K'ang Hsi powder blue club shaped vases with reserved medallions in famille verte colors. Ht. 17". Metropolitan Mus. of Art.

by the simple application of pieces of paper cut out in the forms desired and pasted on temporarily while the spraying was done. These were removed after the piece had dried and the decoration (either in blue or, after glazing and firing, in enamel) was painted in. This ground was also beautiful when gold or silver painting was done over the glaze in a low firing (see the club shaped vase illustrated, also the jar and cover), but often these metallic designs are rubbed off or have, in the case of silver, corroded to black. The making of garniture sets tells us that a number of these vases were made for export trade and on these the drawing is usually perfunctory but occasionally we see something with real character such as the small club shaped vase illustrated with its tall rectangular "mirror shaped" panel.

Odd examples exist on which there are powder blue medallions set among famille verte grounds and as time went on nearly every possible combination of all the techniques took place some being much like neapolitan ice cream in artistic effect. Bushell also mentions especially those with medallions decorated with fishes and other designs in red and gold.

<h2 style="text-align:center">"Mazarine Blue"</h2>

The term "mazarine blue" is foolish, for Cardinal Mazarine died in 1661 a year before K'ang Hsi came to the throne so it would have been difficult for him to admire this color invented in that reign. This is a very deep and

somewhat reddish blue of great brilliance even though dark. It is often a blue glaze applied over a white glaze but sometimes the white glaze was eliminated except for a light ring around the edge of the foot which causes the blue glaze to hang in a rich rounded rim at this point. (See description of this technique under sang de boeuf section.) The bottle from the Metropolitan Museum and my small gallipot are good in this respect while the gallipot from the museum is not, but this again is no definite proof of period, for it so happens that my piece bears a Ch'ien Lung mark.

Fig. 793. K'ang Hsi vase of dark blue called "Mazarin blue." White ware heavily potted and with pale green glaze inside more like Ch'ien Lung "celadon" than anything else. Ht. 13". Metropolitan Mus. of Art.

<h2 style="text-align:center">Blue Put in Press Ware</h2>

Père d'Entrecolles tells us of another blue and white ware which he says was a lost art even in 1712. In this ware the design is only visible when the vessel contains liquid. It was made very thin and a blue design was painted inside and then covered with a thin slip, we assume by dipping and wiping off the outside. Then glaze was applied over the inside slip. It was then put on the lathe and pared down without cutting into the color. Then the exterior was glazed and the whole baked. However, so far as I can find out, no western collector has ever seen a piece of this ware.

Still one more technique which is rare is that of incising the design and rubbing blue into it, then wiping off the ground and glazing over the whole.

FIG. 794. K'ang Hsi bowl with medium to pale underglaze blue and fish in light olive green showing tiny specks of red and really intended to be red of *"rouge de cuivre"* or underglaze type. Dia. 7½". Metropolitan Mus. of Art.

FIG. 796. K'ang Hsi dish with underglaze blue (not as strong as it appears in picture) and blossoms in underglaze red to green tones. Dia. 10". Metropolitan Mus. of Art.

FIG. 795. K'ang Hsi beaker with deep vivid blue, pale red (or peachbloom) and pale green decoration, first two being underglaze and latter a glaze applied over white ground. Ht. c. 17½". Mark is double circle enclosing lichen. Bequest of Mary Clark Thompson. Metropolitan Mus. of Art.

This inlay technique is like that of the Korean inlayed wares but usually is more delicate. (See example in Ch'ien Lung section.)

UNDERGLAZE RED

The underglaze red or "rouge de cuivre," as the French say, is the same copper color as was used in Hsüan Tê times and is employed alone or with the blue. During this reign there was not much improvement if any, but later it was mastered at least technically. The same two kinds of painting continued, one with slender lines like the blue decoration and one with heaped and lumpy design like the old fish cups of Ming. The color may vary from sang de boeuf to what we call "peach bloom." At times it is under a celadon glaze but these are not often K'ang Hsi and the red is not improved by a green wash over it.

SANG DE BOEUF

The Hsüan Tê reds of copper glazes were famous but the material ran out and the art was lost in the Chia Ch'ing reign of the 16th century. The revival of the art in the K'ang Hsi reign is entirely unexplained. Some have said it was done by the Lang family. Others maintain it had something to do with Lang T'ing-tso, the viceroy, or that he actually invented it. The *T'ao lu* mentions neither "Lang yao" nor Lang T'ing-tso which would seem strange. Therefore we must agree with Hobson that this is all nonsense and, for lack of a Chinese name of real meaning, turn to calling the ware by the French name of "Sang de Boeuf," meaning "ox blood." We already call many of the Ch'ing Dynasty wares by French names because they were so very much appreciated in that country.

Père d'Entrecolles, in a letter dated 1722, says this about the ware, "This red in the glaze, 'yu li hung,' is made with granulated red copper and the powder of a certain stone or pebble of reddish color. A Christian doctor told

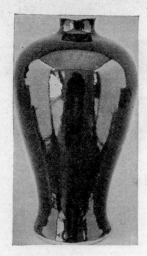  

Left: Type known as "crushed strawberry" red with mottling through it. Ht. 7". Metropolitan Mus. of Art.

Center: Vase of K'ang Hsi period showing slipping down of glaze from lip allowing crackled buff glaze to show and narrow white rim at bottom of glaze intended to hold ox-blood red from dripping over and causing it to form a thick welt. Shape typical. Ht. c. 18". Metropolitan Mus. of Art.

Right: Vase of unusual shape derived from that of Han pottery or bronze. Lip has been cut and mounted with metal rim. Note pores similar to those in human skin in glaze. Ht. 7". Metropolitan Mus. of Art. Altman Coll.

Left: Jar and cover with deep red color against small areas of greenish cream at lip and on cover. Ht. 16½". Metropolitan Mus. of Art.

Center: Deep cherry-red bottle of typical shape for sang de boeuf glazes. Note glaze on this has run over bottom edge and been broken away despite fact it is obviously of period. Ht. 16⅞". Metropolitan Mus. of Art.

Right: Vase with deep red glaze running unevenly down over body and thinning to buff at lip. Inside and under foot has slightly greenish cream glaze with buff crackle and uneven indentations where bubbles have burst and glaze flowed together again. Note definite white rim of glaze around foot-rim placed there to keep red from overrunning it. Ht. 17½". Ex Eumorfopoulos Coll.

TYPICAL K'ANG HSI SANG DE BOEUF VASE FORMS

PLATE 157

Left: K'ang Hsi peach bloom *"ring necked bottle,"* the third of the classic forms and one which appears more rarely than the "chrysanthemum" and "amphora" bottles. Ht. 7¾". Metropolitan Mus. of Art.

Left: "Amphora" which is probably finest and most beautiful proportioned of the three vase forms and which also occurs in clair de lune glaze. Ht. 6". Metropolitan Mus. of Art.

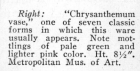

Right: "Chrysanthemum vase," one of seven classic forms in which this ware usually appears. Note mottlings of pale green and lighter pink color. Ht. 8½". Metropolitan Mus. of Art.

Box for vermilion paste for use on seals and not for the ladies' rouge, though such pieces are called "rouge boxes." So true are these to size that covers and bottoms of different boxes are often put together when other members are broken. Dia. 2¾". Metropolitan Mus. of Art.

Jar with small mouth also for water for scholar's table of typical shape. Ht. 3½". Dia. 5". Metropolitan Mus. of Art.

Plate said by museum to be "Late Ming" and perhaps of that time though same shape occurs in K'ang Hsi pieces of this ware, though plates are rare. Dia. 7". Metropolitan Mus. of Art.

Coupe for water for the scholar's table of typical shape. Dia. 4½". Metropolitan Mus. of Art.

TYPICAL K'ANG HSI "PEACH BLOOM" FORMS

PLATE 158

me that this stone was a kind of alum, used in medicine. The whole is pounded in a mortar and mixed with a youth's urine and the ordinary porcelain glaze; but I have not been able to ascertain the quantities of the ingredients, for those in possession of the secret take good care not to divulge it. This mixture is applied to the porcelain before it is fired and no other glaze is used; but care has to be taken that the red does not run to the bottom of the vase during firing. They tell me that when they intend to apply

FIG. 797. Cherry red bowl shading from light to deep color. K'ang Hsi mark. Dia. 4¼". Perry Moore–Warren E. Cox Coll.

FIG. 798. Rouge de fer or iron red K'ang Hsi vases with some enamel decoration also added. Ht. 19". Metropolitan Mus. of Art.

this red to a porcelain they do not use china stone 'petuntse,' but they use instead of it, mixed with the china clay 'kaolin,' a yellow clay prepared in the same manner as the petuntse. Probably it is a kind of clay specially suited to receive the color." (Hobson's translation.) We have discussed the matter of the red stones in the Hsüan Tê section. It should be added that Hobson has declared that K'ang Hsi examples may be distinguished from later ones and modern fakes because the glaze on those of this reign forms a welt at the bottom and does not run over so that it has to be ground off. This is largely so but not at all invariably for there are at least four fine examples in the Altman Collection at the Metropolitan Museum of Art which have the glaze running off. One of these, the cherry red bottle shown, is one of the finest in this large group. It has also been neglected by both Père d'Entrecolles and Hobson to point out *how* this glaze is so controlled. This was done by applying a narrow band of white non-running glaze about the bottom which would not melt quite so readily as the red glaze and acted as an adhesive rim for the red glaze to hang on and build up on. Mr. Theodore Y. Hobby, keeper of the Altman Collection, has gone over this matter with me and agrees entirely. The reader will be able to see the white rim on the jar with cover and the tall vases from this collection and the Eumorfopoulos Collection although one cannot always see the rim for it is often entirely covered by the red glaze.

The Sang de Boeuf glaze is glassy but full of bubbles not unlike that of a rich Chü-chou celadon type and on the surface are many little pores which vary in size and number but are always present. There is a faint but distinctive crackle hardly apparent but always present. The color seems to form in small spots or blotches actually like clotted blood and sometimes these are small and blended or again they may be large and, to my mind, rather unpleasant as in the "strawberry red" type. The foot is usually, but not always, well turned and perfect. It is, so far as can be seen, exactly like other K'ang Hsi porcelains, white or greyish white and having some pores and very smooth. There is glaze applied on the bottom. Hobson says, "There is no red under the base, but here the glaze is sometimes a faint

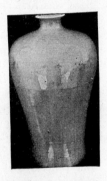

K'ang Hsi vase with canary yellow glaze of glossy, transparent type over incised design. Ht. 9⅝". Altman Coll. Metropolitan Mus. of Art.

"Celadon" vase of pale green in form called "chrysanthemum." Has little relationship with earlier celadon glazes and is valued about as high as other single colored K'ang Hsi wares for its perfection. Ht. 8¼". Altman Coll. Metropolitan Mus. of Art.

Canary yellow vase with transparent glossy glaze always associated with this color. Ht. 9½". Metropolitan Mus. of Art.

K'ang Hsi gallipot heavily potted and covered with brown crackled white glaze as in "apple-green" wares but in this case with pale grey-blue transparent enamel. Ht. 7½". Metropolitan Mus. of Art.

"Amphora" shaped vase of clear palest blue white called "Clair de lune" or moonlight color. One of rarest and most costly K'ang Hsi wares and shape which also occurs in peach bloom glaze is by some considered most beautiful ever devised in ceramics. Ht. 6". Altman Coll. Metropolitan Mus. of Art.

K'ang Hsi vase with cafe-au-lait crackled glaze. Ht. 8¼". Metropolitan Mus. of Art.

"Celadon" of light pea-green glaze over pure white porcelain. Handles modeled separately and attached, being left in biscuit and colored black. Double ring and lichen mark under foot in under-glaze blue. K'ang Hsi. Ht. 13¼". Warren E. Cox Coll.

K'ANG HSI SINGLE COLORED PORCELAINS

PLATE 159

greenish or buff crackle." Actually it is often olive green either plain or mottled and at times it breaks into pink or red in patches. Several of the Altman ones are like this. Of course, it would depend on how the piece was fired and how much heat was kept away from the protected glaze under the foot which is usually otherwise exactly like that applied on the body.

Again it is said that streaked ones are not of the period. This is so if one counts the prominent streaks such as we see in flambé wares, but many fine K'ang Hsi Sang de Boeufs have greyish streaks in the glaze. These may or may not be desirable depending upon the point of view.

The inside of most specimens is finished with a buff crackled glaze or greenish glaze having the same characteristic crackle and, in fact, specimens are found which are covered all over with this light glaze. Very often the red glaze slips down irregularly from the lip or over the shoulder leaving greenish white or buff areas. This, it would seem obvious to me, could only occur if a light colored glaze was first applied either all over the vessel or blending into the red glaze near the top, for certainly the color could not *slip in the glaze*. It may be answered that a broken sherd shows no light glaze under the red and I can only say that where the glaze is red I believe the red glaze and the light glaze have melted together to form one. In other words I believe that Père d'Entrecolles in this instance was describing the ware from hearsay, as he more or less admits, and that he missed entirely the method of manufacture. I think the vase was made, the light glaze applied, the red glaze either painted over it or blended into it, and that the white rim at the bottom was an entirely different glaze over which the red ran and collected. It is interesting to note that, if this is the case, the potters used much the same process that Emil Carlsen did in painting pictures of the ware in oils, that is, a translucent red over a white reflecting surface.

There are certain general shapes but also odd ones that crop up from time to time. They are all simple and without decoration even of the molded or modeled kind we see on celadon.

A further note should be added that Mr. Walter Howat has told me that the red color could only be brought out in the impurities existing in a muffle kiln. He states that he could turn the reddest piece blue or green by refiring in a kiln that would drive off the impurities united with the copper. I should very much like to go into a series of such experiments but we have not the sherds with which to work.

Occasionally Sang de Boeuf wares are considerably blended. One in the Altman Collection is grey, green, red and rose colored. Others may be "ashes of rose" color all over and are valued quite as highly as the red ones.

I have gone into this full description not only for technical reasons but because it should be understood that a sort of arbitrary, or what I call "stamp collectors," valuation has been placed on these wares of the K'ang Hsi period. A good Sang de Boeuf should bring from a few thousand dollars to ten times as much, if K'ang Hsi, while just as well made and colorful a piece of the later periods may bring two hundred and a modern example can be had for $15 or less. It behooves the collector to be wary!—and to know what he is doing when he buys a piece.

"PEACH BLOOM WARES"

We Americans seem to have invented the name "peach bloom" for the wares that the Chinese call "p'in kuo hung" or "apple red," "p'in kuo ch'ing" or "apple green" and "chiang tou hung" or "bean red," probably referring to the kidney beans which are mottled pink and green with brown spots. All of these terms have some of the qualities which the wares show for it varies from pink shading to liver color and red and contains splotches and irregular mottlings of light green, olive green and brown. This may sound like nothing very beautiful but in truth it is one of the softest and most harmonious color combinations imaginable. The glaze is usually thin and regular but at times occurs thick and fluid enough to run down the sides in ridges and drips. The color is said to be of copper as in the other red glazes but it can also be obtained by the use of chrome tin. The glaze is not crackled.

The small articles covered with this glaze are pearls of true perfection. The ware is white and perfectly pure. The potting is so perfect as to be entirely lifeless. The small and narrow foot-rims are perfectly made. The mark should be perfectly centered and beautifully written in blue under a palest greenish white glaze under the foot. This underglaze blue must be of clear color and not purplish or greyish in cast. No decoration was used save the lightest of incising, usually a dragon on the water pots, in round medallions.

The shapes can be seen in our illustrations and they comprise only a few though some doubtful odd shaped ones are claimed as of the period. The collector should be very careful indeed if offered anything other than the three vase forms, the "writer's coupe," the small round box, the small incurving bowl and the dish. Sizes also run fairly close together, although rarely the shape may have been made in a larger size for some very special gift from the court or for some special occasion.

Prices run very high depending on the quality of potting and the color. A few hundred dollars may be paid for a piece of the period but having ordinary color while $15,000 and even $20,000 have been paid for a single specimen. In the sale of Mrs. Christian R. Holmes' Collection, April 15th 1942 a pair of "ring necked vases" brought $9,200 though there was some roughness of the rings about the neck and the marks were far from the finest. Of course, these were depression days and it is rumored that Mrs. Holmes paid $60,000 for the pair. They were bought in by the dealer who sold them to her.

Many modern or later reproductions are exceedingly close to these wares. There is a typical example which was offered to me for a few thousand dollars recently. Of great importance is the quality of the mark and the close adherence to shape. But the collector must also know his glaze and the quality of the glaze under the foot which can only be learned by comparison with the best pieces. This latter must be not too glossy or regular, it has small pores and should not be too greenish, in fact nearly pure white. Beware of an irregularity in rim or lip. The reader may wonder why all this sudden stress upon perfection and I can answer simply that that is all these wares have to recommend them. Every last touch of the hand of man has been ironed out and obliterated. They are turned about as true as a piece of machinery.

In its way a peach bloom amphora is as difficult to make as a battle ship and with all our boasted ability we, here in America, or in the western hemisphere for that matter, have never been able to make one. But what of it? Is a line ruled by a perfect draughtsman as beautiful and alive as a line by Whistler, Li Lung-mien, by Rembrandt or by Chou Wên Chü? I think not. From the earliest days of childhood when with teeth set on tongue, eyes squinted and breath held the artist of perhaps six years tries to guide his crayon where he wants it to go, to the days of the mastery of brush or etching point, the artist is struggling for that control which will give him a free moving and undistracting medium with which to express himself. This is what tires artists as much as careful shooting tires the marksman. This is a sort of self-discipline that many artists simply cannot hold themselves to, and therefore, finally break down and go "modern" or resort to the ruler, the templet and other mechanical means. But the breakdown, even though expressed in so great a perfection as a peach bloom vase, is there, and is death undisguised to the eye of one who can see.

SANG DE PIGEON WARES

Still another red was obtained with copper oxide and that is the ware commonly known as liver-colored but which the French call "Sang de Pigeon," with perhaps too much complimentary poesy for although this ware can be rich and beautiful it certainly does not rival the pigeon blood of a ruby.

Most of these are Yung Chêng but they undoubtedly originate in late K'ang Hsi times. Hobson speaks of them in "The Later Ceramic Wares of China" (p. 55) but does not show an example. I do not know of one which could be proven to be K'ang Hsi.

We shall describe the glaze in more detail in the Yung Chêng section. Suffice it to say that it is perfectly even in color, not crackled, thinner in application than the Sang de Boeuf and yet can be deep and rich in color. The surface is pitted in the "chicken skin" effect or sometimes glossy.

"CORAL RED" OR IRON RED

Iron red, actually made from iron oxide, is not an underglaze color or a glaze color as are the above copper reds, but must be fired at a comparatively low temperature over a glaze. The Chinese call it "fan hung" and collectors have come into the habit of calling it "coral red" which it does closely approach if one thinks of the deepest possible coral color although a good eye will see that it is slightly more toward the yellow side and not quite so bluish. We are told that the oxide was applied to the glaze with "ox glue" and that it borrows its gloss from the silica of the underlying glaze but is often mat in surface. It had been used in the "five colored" wares of Ming and naturally continued with the famille verte wares. As a monochrome it is usually later than K'ang Hsi. The color is always lighter from K'ang Hsi times on due to greater refinement; the Ming color being more dull and dark, if applied heavily at all as in Wan Li times.